D0776994

PUBLICATIONS ON
ETHNICITY AND NATIONALITY OF THE
SCHOOL OF INTERNATIONAL STUDIES
UNIVERSITY OF WASHINGTON

Volume 3

This book is sponsored by
Comparative Studies in Ethnicity and Nationality
of the School of International Studies
of the University of Washington

ETHNICITY AND NATIONALITY

A BIBLIOGRAPHIC GUIDE

G. CARTER BENTLEY

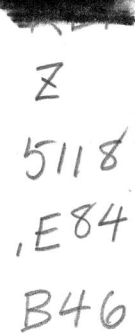

Z
5118
,E84
B46

UNIVERSITY OF WASHINGTON PRESS

SEATTLE AND LONDON

INDIANA
UNIVERSITY LIBRARY

APR 18 1983

NORTHWEST

Copyright © 1981 by the University of Washington Press
Printed in the United States of America

All rights reserved. No part of this publication may be reproduced or
transmitted in any form or by any means, electronic or mechanical,
including photocopy, recording, or any information storage or retrieval
system without permission in writing from the publisher.

Library of Congress Cataloging in Publication Data

Bentley, G. Carter.
    Ethnicity and nationality.

    (Publications on ethnicity and nationality of
the School of International Studies, University
of Washington ; v. 3)
    Includes indexes.
    1. Ethnicity—Bibliography.   2. Nationalism—
Bibliography. I. Title. II. Series.
Z5118.E84B46 [GN495.6]   016.3058 81-51280
ISBN 0-295-95853-7   AACR2

jwe 4-15-83

CONTENTS

FOREWORD

This bibliography is the third volume in an ongoing series of publications produced by faculty and graduate students associated with the program in Comparative Studies in Ethnicity and Nationality (CSEN) in the School of International Studies at the University of Washington. It has been six years in the making. Carter Bentley began work on the project in the summer of 1975 under the direction of Professor Charles Keyes, a member of the CSEN program faculty. Mr. Bentley was then a research assistant for the CSEN program, which received funds to support his work from the Graduate School of the University of Washington. It was apparent when Mr. Bentley began work on the project that although there were a number of specialized bibliographies available, particularly on ethnic groups in the United States, there was no general bibliographic guide to the major theoretical works or to the important monographs and articles written by social scientists and area specialists on ethnic groups in different parts of the world. Since, therefore, it seemed important to encourage Mr. Bentley to complete the project, additional funds were obtained from the Graduate School. The CSEN program, which was then operating under a grant from the Office of Education, U.S. Department of Health, Education, and Welfare, under Title VI of the National Defense Education Act (Section 601 [a]), also provided some funds to Mr. Bentley under the terms of that grant. At the end of the summer of 1977, Mr. Bentley had compiled over 1100 entries, over 300 of them annotated.

In 1977-79, Mr. Bentley went to the Philippines to carry out field research for his doctoral dissertation project. While he was in the field, the bibliography was typed in mimeographed form. As soon as it was finished and scholars in the field became aware of its existence, requests for copies began to come to us. It seemed clear that the bibliography filled a need among specialists in the field and that it should be published. Upon his return from the Philippines, Mr. Bentley agreed to postpone the writing of his dissertation to revise the bibliography for publication. Once again, the Graduate School provided funds for Mr. Bentley to do the revisions in the summer of 1979, which made it possible for him to update and double the number of entries and to make it more representative of the literature in fields less fully covered in the first draft.

A selective bibliography in a field that touches so many world areas and crosses several disciplines will surely be welcomed, but is bound also to make discriminations that will leave some scholars in some specialties unhappy. However, it seems to me that the bibliography has several features that are invaluable to all specialists in the field. One is that it provides scholars in one area or discipline with an instant guide to important literature outside their areas or disciplines that should make it easier for them to do comparative and interdisciplinary research and teaching. Second, it recognizes the close connection between the study of ethnicity and the study of ethnic-based nationalist movements and provides a resource for scholars working on either or both types of issues. Third, the bibliography contains a unique feature that will make it of great value as a teaching aid as well as a research tool, namely, the analytical content outline that provides teachers and students in the field a way of constructing a draft of a syllabus for a course or a bibliography for a term paper in a matter of minutes for eight social science disciplines and for numerous subdisciplinary specialties. The area index also makes the bibliography useful to area studies specialists for the same purposes.

In developing and preparing this bibliography, Mr. Bentley received throughout encouragement and cooperation from the faculty of CSEN. In addition to the funding from the Graduate School of the University of Washington and from the United States Office of Education, CSEN received support during the preparation and typing of the manuscript from the College of Arts and Sciences and the School of International Studies at the University of Washington. The CSEN program is grateful to the sponsoring agencies for their financial support. The opinions stated in the bibliographic essay and in the annotations are, of course, those of Mr. Bentley and do not necessarily reflect the views of the sponsoring agencies.

A bibliography is a gift to a profession. Mr. Bentley took time away from the completion of his academic training to finish this volume. So, we owe our gratitude most of all to him.

PAUL R. BRASS
Chairman,
Comparative Studies in
Ethnicity and Nationality

ACKNOWLEDGMENTS

This bibliography has been helped along by many persons at various points in its long gestation. Library personnel at the University of California, Berkeley, Stanford University, Western Washington University, and the University of Washington helped locate elusive source materials. The Interlibrary Loan office at the University of Washington Suzzallo Library worked especially hard to obtain books not in the University of Washington Collections. Professors Charles Keyes and Jonathan Pool pointed out items I might otherwise have missed. Richard Trottier suggested important revisions to the list of content categories. Fred Nick of the UW Center for Social Science Computation and Research wrote the computer program for the content index. Cathy Carruthers helped verify citations, edit the manuscript, and buck up the author's sometimes flagging spirits. Carol Widrig typed the manuscript. Margery Lang, editor for the School of International Studies, worked devotedly to mold the manuscript into a useful and attractive volume. That this book exists at all owes much to these people and many others besides. I am grateful to all of them. I also owe a debt to all those associated with the CSEN program. Without financial support through CSEN, arranged by Professor Paul Brass, and encouragement from its personnel this bibliography would never have been completed. Without the intellectual stimulation they provided early in my graduate career it would never have been begun.

INTRODUCTION

Studies of ethnicity and ethnic groups have proliferated at an increasing rate during the past two decades. The political importance of ethnicity in the United States has made it a topic of both public and academic interest. Television commercials extol the immigrant heritage of most Americans ("I was born in America. This summer I'm going home to Japan/Italy/Poland, etc., for the first time."). Unlikely political movements have spun off the momentum of ethnic consciousness (e.g., Polish populism). Individuals have claimed the public spotlight either as spokesmen for or interpreters of the new ethnic consciousness (Michael Novak, Andrew Greeley, and Daniel Patrick Moynihan come to mind).

The new interest in ethnicity extends well beyond the United States. It is a world-wide phenomenon. In Canada, Québécois separatism is still a live issue and opinion favoring immigration restriction is mounting. In England, "race" emerged as a political issue in Enoch Powell's nationalist campaigns and it has resisted attempts to douse its emotional power (see Katznelson, listing no. 167). In France, schismatic ethnic movements have emerged, or re-emerged, in Brittany, Normandy, and elsewhere. Belgium, Italy, Spain, and Switzerland have all experienced resurgent ethnic movements in recent years. In Eastern Europe, the very integrity of Yugoslavia may be threatened by the death of President Tito and the resurgence of ethnic particularism. The same can be said for much of the rest of the world. Current international events often contain an ethnic element (e.g., ethnic diversity in Iran and instability in the postrevolutionary government, Soviet Central Asian nationalisms, tribesmen and refugees in Indochina, and so forth).

All this attention directed at ethnicity in its various manifestations has resulted in enormous amounts of information about ethnic phenomena, structures, and processes, but it has not been accompanied by a comparable increase in understanding of ethnicity. It is as part of the effort to integrate and systematize the materials available to students, teachers, and researchers of ethnicity that I have constructed this bibliography. I had three goals in mind: to present in one volume a representative selection of research from the different academic disciplines concerned with ethnicity; to highlight important theoretical contributions to the understanding of ethnicity; and to provide a convenient guide to the literature that can be used as a starting point by a wide range of users.

Before proceeding I should define the focus of the following discussion. *Ethnicity* denotes phenomena of ascription by birth circumstances to categories, groups, or quasi-groups not circumscribed by demographic characteristics (e.g., age or sex), and the behavioral characteristics of such categories, groups, or quasi-groups. This definition excludes gender categories and age grades, but it includes castes, nationalities, and racial groupings. The bibliography assumes no position on the question of whether *races,* because of their physical diacritica, or *nations,* because of their territorial referents, or *castes,* because of their occupational specification, differ so much from culturally demarcated *ethnic groups* that each grouping should be analyzed separately. I have specifically included in the bibliography sources arguing the different sides of this issue and otherwise attempting to describe the conceptual limits of "ethnicity."

In the rest of these introductory remarks, references to works included in the bibliographic listings are cited using their entry numbers. Only those works not included in the listings are included in the references beginning on page xxi.

A NOTE ON CONFUSION IN THE ETHNICITY LITERATURE

Kuhn (1970, pp. 16-17) writes, "No natural history can be interpreted in the absence of at least some implicit body of intertwined theoretical and methodological belief that permits selection, evaluation, and criticism." This truism holds no less for studies of ethnicity than for physics, chemistry, or geology. Kuhn (ibid.) also suggests that if such a body of belief is not contained in the investigative process itself then it must be supplied, "perhaps by a current metaphysic, by another science, or by personal or historical accident." In studies of ethnicity the fundamental beliefs governing the analytical process have, for the most part, been ideological and political.

At one level, ethnicity research has been constrained by norms inhering in the structure of academe. The rise of American social science in the early years of this century reflected an elite faith that scientific methods and knowledge could be used to solve social problems and thereby to enhance the harmonious working of American society (see Touraine 1974, pp. 31-46). Social sciences promised control over social phenomena just as natural sciences promised control over natural phenomena (Becker 1950, p. 290). Robert Park, the seminal figure in the American sociology of race relations, decided midway in his life that scientific methods held greater promise for ameliorating race problems than did appeals to moral or political consciousness. He turned from a career of advocacy journalism, exposing the evils of Belgian rule in the Congo and American racism at home, to lecturing his University of Chicago students that "their role was to be that of the calm, detached scientist who investigates race relations with the same objectivity and detachment with which the zoologist dissects the potato bug" (Burgess 1961, p. 17). Park's turn from public exhortation to scientific detachment foreshadowed a general turn toward social technology and belief in its efficacy among the elite that provided money and influenced policy for American higher education.

Government support of research in the social sciences has favored theoretical perspectives equating order with normality and viewing disorder as a deviation ameliorable through administrative action (see Mills 1960; Gouldner 1970; Andreski 1972, pp. 144-54; Horton 1976, pp. 23-24; Strasser 1976). Surveys have shown that social scientists are generally aware of the political and ideological contexts within which they work and that claims of "scientific objectivity" are widely distrusted (Friedrichs 1970, pp. 121-24). Reflective members of many disciplines have pointed out the contradiction between "objectivity" and politically motivated funding (see, e.g., Lynd 1939; Wilson and Wilson 1945; Mills 1960; Friedrichs 1970; Asad 1973; Melanson 1975; Cohen, 55). Even so, social scientists have neither surmounted nor eliminated the problem so that "social science theory is little more than a weathercock shifting with ideological winds" (van den Berghe 1967, p. 8). Because ethnicity has historically been a sensitive political issue, studies in this area have closely mirrored changes in the political environment.

In fact, investigations of ethnicity have usually been prompted less by scientific curiosity than by immediate policy concerns. Except during periods of rapid immigration, when "immigrant problems" prompted flurries of research, scholarly studies of ethnicity, in the United States at least, have proceeded sporadically. Prevailing theories assumed ethnicity to be a vestige of the premodern order destined to eventually disappear and most research has addressed what were considered intermittent aberrations in the disappearance process. As van den Berghe (280, pp. xi-xii) notes, "It took the reemergence of ethnic sentiment in such countries as Belgium, Great Britain, Spain, Canada, the United States, and even, to a lesser degree, the archetypical nation-state of France and the model multiethnic democracy of Switzerland, to shake the complacency of social scientists on the supposedly vanishing role of ethnic and racial particularism, and to expose the vacuity of the conventional wisdom on the topic." That conventional wisdom saw the United States as the developmental model for the world as a whole and exalted the American experience of immigrant assimilation to the status of world-wide trend. However, this understanding of the American experience depended more on assertions of what ought to have happened than on what actually did happen. "Despite the romantic and rhetorically attractive Zangwillian metaphor of the 'Melting Pot' ideal, the American historical reality reflects at best an uneven mixture of only partial and selective assimilation on the one hand, and various forms of either voluntary or coerced lack of assimilation on the other" (Bash 1979, p. 41).

The prevalence of the assimilation perspective in the face of glaring counterexamples, both in the United States and elsewhere, derived from its responsiveness to political factors both extrinsic and intrinsic to academia. Primary among the extrinsic factors was a normative commitment to social equilibrium and a pervasive faith, especially among those funding the universities, that assimilation would ultimately lead to this goal. It has been argued on detailed evidence that assimilation dominated American studies of ethnicity because

As a social policy option, assimilation has surely represented the Reformist Liberal solution for the "immigrant problem" in America and, until very recent years at least, for the "racial problem" as well. . . . What came to take shape as the Assimilationist Perspective in the sociology of racial and ethnic relations must be regarded as the product of sociologists who, consciously or not, transmuted their more-or-less liberal social persuasions into a sociological perspective. [Ibid., p. 161; emphasis in original]

Contrary views did exist; Dollard (778) and Cox (681) vividly analyzed anti-assimilative forces in American society, but political considerations so firmly entrenched the conventional wisdom that these findings could scarcely dent its influence. Normative goals and research conclusions became so intertwined that the major post-World War II review of research in interethnic relations took the title of the administrative goal that motivated it, *The Reduction of Intergroup Tensions* (Williams, 2273).

The prediction of inevitable assimilation can, in retrospect, be seen to have derived from an ideologically skewed reading of American history and its ethnocentric projection onto the world as a whole. It was only when events made it clear that ethnic particularism had not disappeared, and probably would not disappear in the foreseeable future, that faith in the conventional wisdom began to waver.

While ideological commitments explain the popularity of certain perspectives, they cannot explain the underdevelopment of systematic theory in ethnicity studies. In principle there is no contradiction between ideological commitment and rigorous theory. However, in the social sciences there is an apparent preference for vague, ambiguous, rhetorically neat formulations over less flashy but more adequately theoretical ones. Andreski (1972) cites Parsons's work as a prime example of an egregious tendency to exalt abstraction and obscurantism. Any number of examples of this tendency could be drawn from the ethnicity literature. If *assimilation* and *the melting pot* carried the day for liberals in the past, an equally vague but equally attractive phrase, *internal colonialism,* currently carries the day. Each of these concepts has a checkered lineage. *Assimilation* was borrowed from biology, where its meaning was clear. The notion of *internal colonialism* was taken from the rhetoric of black nationalism and analytical significance was attached to it only at second hand (Blauner, 38).

However, even the questionable origins of many concepts in ethnicity studies do not explain why they have not been systematically explicated in the literature. One finds an explanatory hint in Andreski's (1972, p. 93) comment that "You have only to look at the language of politics to see the advantage of vagueness and obscurity in the struggle for popularity, where the secret of success lies in appearing to be on everybody's side, and to leave oneself a way out of any commitment which becomes embarrassing." In other words, concepts, like politicians, are likely to become popular and to stay popular if they are sufficiently ambiguous to be accepted by a wide range of people who might well disagree if they met face to face. Ambiguity also provides some insurance against counterarguments. As Bash (1979, pp. 85-104) points out, assimilation had a clear meaning in biology but social scientists have used it as a metaphor to describe incredibly diverse phenomena, eroding its original meaning and leaving the concept hopelessly fuzzy. It has become impossible to test whether assimilation has taken place, in the United States or anywhere else. Finally, vague images allow scholars to show whose side they are on without the risk of overt political declarations and without violating the canon of neutrality.

With ill-conceived, ideologically imbued metaphors filling Kuhn's selective, evaluative, and critical functions, the data-theory interaction loses much of its analytical value. The governing concepts in most ethnicity studies are incapable of systematically informing inquiry. Such studies take refuge in the forms of scientific research. They reflect a fetish of technique in which methods of data collection and analysis are placed before the questions they are supposed to answer. Detailed expositions of hypotheses, variables, and data are brought to bear on such essentially trivial questions as "demographic correlates of race relations and the methodology of racial attitude scales" (van den Berghe, 280, p. 6). Unfortunately technical sophistication can say nothing about the explanatory value or meaning of research results (see Williams, 296, p. 134; Mills 1960, pp. 60-86). Research topics defined mainly to fit the latest software are likely to be neither informative nor interesting. For all their technical sophistication they lack a sufficient theoretical context to give their results meaning and importance. In his review of sociology studies of ethnicity, Williams (296, p. 126) bemoaned the lack of a theoretical base, "The several hundred books and articles reviewed for this chapter contain an appalling number of ad hoc variables and indicators." All this leaves the literature on ethnicity a theoretical quagmire. Each new increment makes it a larger aggregate of disconnected bits of information.

Exclusive adherence to a "scientific" research model inhibits the more flexible and speculative thinking that might eventually lead to integrative theory. Schermerhorn (244, p. 253) makes this point satirically by raising "the frightening thought that the Ph.D. dissertation may have subtly become the paradigm for research design in our generation." Focus on method at the expense of substance also lets social scientists preserve their "cloak of neutrality," a mask for political cowardice. As Andreski (1972, p. 116) puts it, "An excessive preoccupation with methodology provides an alibi for timorous quietism."

Not all the fault lies with students of ethnicity however. The phenomena themselves are dauntingly complex:

> We must note carefully the complex referents that are variously attached to the concepts "racial" and "ethnic." In their psychological aspects, ethnic relations are characterized by variations in salience, clarity, importance, hostility or positive affect, ambivalence, commitment, identification. In the cultural system, ethnicity may involve language, religious beliefs and practices, institutional norms and values, expressive styles, food preferences, and so on. Ethnic collectivities vary in size, interconnectedness, definiteness and strength of boundaries, relationships with allies and enemies, internal interdependence, degree and kind of social control of members. [Williams, 296, p. 125]

Each of these is itself conceptually complex and subject to ambiguous interpretation. The obstacles that must be overcome in developing adequate theories of ethnicity are considerable, even if they have been exacerbated by ideological intrusions and a restrictive research model.

This is not to say that studies of ethnicity have been without value, as they have helped debunk harmful "myths and stereotypes, erroneous assumptions, and superficial explanations" (ibid., p. 154). In addition van den Berghe (280, p. xii) notes the appearance, since the mid-1960s, of studies that are "less provincial, more comparative, more historical, and less exclusively the disciplinary province of sociology and social psychology." Among these he includes studies by Banton (16), Francis (103), Levine and Campbell (187), Mason (194), and Schermerhorn (244). Other recent contributions include studies of nationalism and nationality by Seton-Watson (248) and Young (302). There has also been progress in specifying and systematizing some of the vague concepts that run through the ethnicity literature. Notable examples include Schermerhorn's (244) work on stratification and ethnic power differentials, Rabushka and Shepsle (266) on instability in plural societies, Smooha's (259) outline for studying pluralism, and Levine and Campbell (187) on ethnocentrism. Blalock (37), Levine and Campbell (187), Kinloch (174), and Francis (103) list theoretically generated testable propositions on majority-minority relations, ethnocentrism, colonial racism, and prejudice and nation formation.

Case studies of ethnic phenomena have tended to become more theoretically focused in recent years. Instead of ad hoc descriptions of one or another ethnic group, detailed case studies aimed at testing well-articulated propositions are joining the literature with welcome frequency (e.g., Hechter, 141; Grove, 131). Controlled comparisons of ethnic groups have yielded valuable information (e.g., Brass, 45; Schermerhorn, 245). Students of ethnicity continue their critical function, and some recent contributions have been especially stimulating (e.g., Patterson, 217).

While no theoretical synthesis about ethnicity seems imminent, and proponents of different perspectives often argue past one another, increasing theoretization and study of fundamental questions promise to increase our understanding of ethnicity and ethnic phenomena (see Williams, 296, p. 131; Dex, 77). This promise may be a product of dynamic times in which the ideological pendulum swings fast enough to produce clear disagreements (see Andreski 1972; Bash 1979). If the growth of ethnicity theory is a product of transitory circumstances then academicians concerned with ethnicity may resettle into the complacent reliance on "conventional wisdom," which so stultified the field not long ago.

For the immediate future, however, ethnicity probably will be examined from a wide variety of perspectives, using a wide variety of data sources, all of which favors increased understanding. However, this same expansion makes it more difficult for any individual to gain familiarity with the whole literature. Valuable opportunities for cross-fertilization across disciplinary, geographical, theoretical, and topical boundaries may be missed because of specialization and the breadth of the literature. It is to aid comparative, integrative research and to help overcome the impediment of a diffuse, often incoherent literature, that this bibliography is offered. It is only with knowledge of what has already been done that future students of ethnicity and nationality can avoid repeating past mistakes and can go beyond rediscovering what already is known.

ORDERING THE LITERATURE

I have suggested some reasons why the social science literature on ethnicity is not internally organized. As a first step toward remedying this difficulty some organization must be imposed on the material already at hand. One frequently used method of introducing order into an intellectual domain involves defining a small number of binarily opposed variables and using these to construct a set of logically related categories. Elements of the literature are then identified according to the categories they occupy. Usually one or two metatheoretical oppositions are used for this purpose (e.g., order vs. conflict, progressive vs. conservative) (see Horton 1966; Strasser 1976). A similar approach involves using pairs of ideal types to define a conceptual space in which elements of the literature can then be approximately located. Van den Berghe (280) uses *liberal-radical* and *descriptive-deterministic* dimensions in this manner. Unfortunately, while each of these approaches clarifies the logical relationships between different studies, they both necessarily obscure most differences in theory, method, subject matter, and conclusion. As a result, such classifications reveal little about the potential uses of individual studies.

Reviews of the literature have typically followed more descriptive approaches. In his survey, Williams (296, p. 125) would have preferred to list sociology studies of ethnicity according to the variables they employed but that was impracticable given the state of the literature. Instead he classified studies according to the major institutions (family, economy, religion, education, polity, etc.) they concerned and the particular topics they addressed. Cohen (55), on the other hand, reviewed anthropology's rising interest in ethnicity as part of the changing focus of anthropological inquiry. Thus, while Williams described dispersed topical clusterings within sociology, Cohen described historical changes in the central thrust of ethnicity studies in anthropology.

Because no single discipline subsumes all ethnicity studies, single discipline reviews only cover pieces of the literature. Review essays also suffer from trying to adequately describe individual studies too concisely. They take on the impossible task of communicating the range of information useful to researchers and students of ethnicity, possibly including a study's theoretical underpinnings, the academic discipline from which it issues, the characteristics of the subject population, its methods, data sources, conclusions, and so on, all in one or two sentences.

Without knowing what potential users of this bibliography require, it is impossible to tell which information would be most helpful. Therefore, I have chosen to include as much detail in as economical a form as possible. To accomplish this goal, I constructed the area and content indexes contained in the appendixes. In the contents index, matrices function as cross indexes of sources and topics. In addition to identifying sources covering specific topics and theoretical positions, these arrays provide a visual profile of each listed source's contents. The area index classifies sources by continent, region, and country and, where the variety of sources warrants it, individual ethnic groups within a country. The index of contents was developed from Schermerhorn's (244, pp. 295-300) outline of data requirements for an ethnicity research program. He included primarily macrosociological and political data types, along with some related cultural elements (e.g., systems of etiquette reinforcing stratification, beliefs concerning political legitimacy, etc.). To this outline I added rubrics for identity, prejudice, and other themes more frequently found in anthropology, psychology, and other fields outside of sociology. Since this outline preceded the literature search, I had a listing of what ideally ought to be included, but I found much that I had not anticipated, and a number of additions to the original outline were required. I tried to fill as many of the ideal data categories as possible and only reluctantly deleted a few categories when it became clear that they were entirely unrepresented in the literature.

To the initial topic and data classifications I added four sets of categories identifying the form of research employed in a study (rubrics 2-5 in the index to contents). These indicate the sources of data, the scale of analysis, academic field, and theoretical orientation. Finally I added a category indicating good entry points into the field for the beginner, these being general texts and topical anthologies (rubric 1).

Most of the rubrics for content categories and subcategories should be self-explanatory. This may not be true for categories listed under rubric 5, "Theoretical Orientation." Given the underdeveloped theory, such classification was bound to be difficult. Even so, the importance of theoretical orientations for guiding studies made it imperative to attempt some classification. Lacking any clear alternative, I have labeled rubrics according to my perceptions of theoretical clusters or continuities in the literature. Some of the resulting rubrics do not denote theories, properly speaking. For instance, rubrics 5d (Identity) and 5e (Nationalism) refer to substantive domains, within which numerous theories coexist or compete. On the other hand, rubric 5a (Assimilation) denotes an orientation that has become more diffuse and less usable as its accreted meanings have multiplied (see Bash 1979). Nevertheless, many studies still make use of "assimilation," and theories of "ethnic identity" and "nationalism" are legion.

Regardless of their epistemological status these rubrics denote conceptual schemes that fulfill the selective, evaluative, and critical functions outlined by Kuhn. In that sense at least they are all theories.

While the terms are drawn from the literature, the list of rubrics does not exhaust the range of named theoretical perspectives found in it. Some perspectives are reducible to combinations of theoretical components, and these have been listed as such (e.g., Plural Society = Pluralism [5f] + Stratification [5i]; Marxian Conflict Theory = Conflict [5b] + Stratification [5i]). The major exception is rubric 5j (Internal colonialism). While it can be argued that it ought to be reduced (e.g., Internal colonialism = Nationalism [5e] + Pluralism [5f] + Stratification [5i]), such a reduction would belie the unity of works from this perspective.

For definitions of these theoretical subcategories the reader should consult the following exemplary sources for each: 5a (Assimilation), 119 and 124; 5b (Conflict or intergroup competition), 64, 71, and 220; 5c (Ecological), 21 and 57; 5d (Identity), 75 and 170; 5e (Nationalism), 248, 256, and 260; 5f (Pluralism), 16 and 67; 5g (Prejudice), 35 and 89; 5h (Situational), 148 and 206; 5i (Stratification), 244 and 301; 5j (Internal colonialism), 38 and 141. The listed orientations are not mutually exclusive. In some works they may not even be easily distinguishable. For each study, I have marked those rubrics that, in combination, best characterize its theoretical perspectives.

The literature represented by the listings is circumscribed as follows:

1. Only English language materials have been included, although research revealed significant publications in over forty languages. This additional literature would have substantially lengthened the bibliography, with questionable benefits. American library holdings of non-English language works in this field are fragmentary at best, and any sampling of this literature would have been arbitrary. It seemed wiser to restrict listings so that adequate representation could be assured, the size controlled, and usefulness increased.

2. Only published works through 1979 have been included; some portions of the unpublished literature are accessible through generally available indexes (e.g., *Dissertation Abstracts,* University Microfilms, Ann Arbor, published yearly).

3. I have excluded the immense "ethnic studies" literature on the grounds that it is mostly nonanalytical. Because ethnic studies take a parochial perspective, insisting on the uniqueness of each group's particular experience, they share the limitations of archaic ethnography (see Cohen, 55). They do not aim at a general understanding of ethnicity per se (see van den Berghe, 280, p. xii). This is not to deny their value as repositories of ethnographic and historical data, but they are tangential to this compilation.

I have specifically excluded from the listings biographies and autobiographies of ethnic group leaders, ethnic literature, ethnic literary history and criticism, ethnic folklore, music, dance and drama, ethnic newspapers and periodicals, and narrative histories. Bibliographies of such materials do exist and some have been included in the listings as an entry point to this allied literature. Particularly valuable is the two-volume guide to materials on American ethnic minorities compiled by Miller et al. (1538).

4. Ethnographies of individual groups have been excluded, except where the analysis illuminates specific aspects of ethnicity, such as boundary maintenance, interethnic relations, structures of ethnic identity, and so on. Decisions about whether to include particular works hinged on how central ethnicity was to their analysis. Thus such an exemplary document as Tamotsu Shibutani's (1978) study of demoralization among a Nisei army company in World War II was excluded, despite its value as a microcosmic study of ethnic solidarity and alienation.

5. Materials on international relations have been excluded as more properly belonging to the study of relations between states. Exceptions include studies of nationalism and nationalist movements (e.g., Seton-Watson, 248; Smith, 256; Snyder, 260), studies concerning the effect on the international system of intrastate ethnic or national interactions (e.g., Neuman, 209), and studies of the international consequences of intrastate ethnic and national conflicts (e.g., Bertelsen, 33; Suhrke and Noble, 266).

6. I have omitted studies aimed primarily at legislative or administrative questions (e.g., designs for remedial bilingual education, reparative job placement, evaluation of desegregation programs). Like the ethnic studies literature, this material is more valuable as a source of data and as an object of study than

as a field of study itself (see van den Berghe 280, p. xii). This criterion too generated some difficult and arguable decisions about which works to include and which to exclude.

Given these criteria, choices about what works to include still had to be made. Generally I adhered to the priorities and procedures listed below in making these decisions.

7. I have favored studies that, in my view, exemplify some trend or focus in the literature on ethnicity and nationality.

8. I have chosen studies of substantive or conceptual importance over those concerned primarily with methodology, so works detailing techniques of data gathering and analysis are deliberately underrepresented.

9. I have given preference to synthesizing or integrating studies over narrowly constructed ones. Literature reviews, comparative tests of different theories, and explicit attempts at theory building are deliberately overrepresented, especially in the annotated listings.

10. Because it is much easier to work backward than forward in a bibliographic search I have given preference to recent works. I have omitted older articles and books when they have been superseded or subsumed by more recent ones, so the pre-1960 listings are limited to exemplary contributions (e.g., Dollard, 778; Myrdal, 205; Cox, 681; Bettelheim and Janowitz, 35).

11. To compensate for my own biases and to assure that these listings represent contributions made by all academic disciplines concerned with ethnicity and nationality, I kept a tally of works consulted according to the disciplinary orientation of their authors. I attempted to make the listings approximately consonant with the numerical proportion of each discipline's contribution to the literature.

SUGGESTED USES

This bibliography is aimed at students, teachers, and researchers. Students new to studies of ethnicity can use it as a general guide to the literature. The area index lists the countries and regions covered in each listed entry. The index of contents lists topics covered, data types used, academic disciplines, theoretical orientations, and much other information. The matrix arrangement of the content keys provides a general picture of ethnicity as a field of study. The student can work from the indexes to the listings to find sources appropriate to particular interests or desired levels of knowledge. Of particular use to students should be introductory texts (rubric 1b).

Teachers should find the bibiliography useful for lesson planning, assembling reading lists, and answering student questions. Advanced students and researchers can use the indexes to extend their knowledge and find cases for comparative analysis. In addition unfilled cells in the content and area indexes may indicate neglected topics and suggest possible subjects for further study. As with any information source, ingenuity and imagination will enhance its usefulness. The contents index contains over 10^{21} unique topical combinations, so the possibilities are not easily exhausted.

BIBLIOGRAPHIC GUIDES TO THE CURRENT LITERATURE

In compiling these listings I examined several guides to segments of the social science literature. The following proved useful in finding sources on ethnicity.

Combined Retrospective Index Set to Journals in Sociology 1895-1974. Vol. 1. 1978. Washington, D.C., and Inverness, Scotland: Carrollton Press.

Index of Economic Articles. Published yearly under the auspices of the *Journal of Economic Literature* of the American Economics Association.

International Bibliography of Political Science. Prepared by the International Committee for Social Science Information and Documentation. Published yearly. London: Tavistock; Chicago: Aldine.

International Bibliography of the Social Sciences—Economics. Prepared by the International Committee for Social Science Information and Documentation. Published yearly. London: Tavistock; Chicago: Aldine.

Psychology Abstracts. Published bimonthly. Washington, D.C.: American Psychological Association.

Sage Race Relations Abstracts. Published quarterly for the Institute of Race Relations, London.

Social Sciences Citation Index. Published annually. Philadelphia: Institute for Scientific Information.

Social Sciences Index. Published quarterly. Bronx, N.Y.: H. W. Wilson. Supersedes Social Sciences and Humanities Index after March 1974.

Sociological Abstracts. Published bimonthly. Sociological Abstracts, Inc.

FORMAT

The listings are numbered consecutively throughout the two sections of the bibliography. The first section (308 entries) is annotated. The second section (numbers 309 through 2338) is without annotation. Below and to the left of each entry is a series of numbers and letters that identifies its contents. A key to the appropriate code immediately precedes the annotated section (p. 2) and the index to contents (p. 381). To the right is listed the geographical area or country covered, together (when relevant) with the particular group or groups with which the study is concerned. The indexes provide a cross reference for these area and group listings.

REFERENCES

Andreski, Stanislav
    1972. *Social Science as Sorcery.* London: Deutsch.
Asad, Talal, ed.
    1973. *Anthropology and the Colonial Encounter.* London: Ithaca Press.
Bash, Harry H.
    1979. *Sociology, Race and Ethnicity: A Critique of American Ideological Intrusions upon Sociological Theory.* New York: Gordon & Breach Science.
Becker, Howard
    1950. *Through Values to Social Interpretation.* Durham, N.C.: Duke University Press.
Burgess, Ernest W.
    1961. "Social Planning and Race Relations." In *Race Relations: Problems*

and Theory, Essays in Honor of Robert E. Park, edited by J. Masuoka and Preston Valien, pp. 13-25. Chapel Hill: University of North Carolina Press.

Friedrichs, Robert W.
   1970. *A Sociology of Sociology.* New York: Free Press.
Gouldner, Alvin W.
   1970. *The Coming Crisis of Western Sociology.* New York: Basic Books.
Horton, John
   1966. "Order and Conflict Theories of Social Problems as Competing Ideologies." *American Journal of Sociology* 71:701-13.
Kuhn, Thomas S.
   1970. *The Structure of Scientific Revolutions.* 2d ed. Chicago: University of Chicago Press.
Lynd, Robert S.
   1939. *Knowledge for What? The Place of Social Science in American Culture.* Princeton, N.J.: Princeton University Press.
Melanson, Philip H.
   1975. *Political Science and Political Knowledge.* Washington, D.C.: Public Affairs Press.
Mills, C. Wright
   1960. *The Sociological Imagination.* New York: Oxford University Press.
Shibutani, Tamotsu
   1978. *The Derelicts of Company K: A Sociological Study of Demoralization.* Berkeley and Los Angeles: University of California Press.
Strasser, Hermann
   1976. *The Normative Structure of Sociology: Conservative and Emancipatory Themes in Social Thought.* London: Routledge & Kegan Paul.
Touraine, Alain
   1974. *The Academic System in American Society.* New York: McGraw-Hill.
van den Berghe, Pierre L.
   1967. *Race and Racism: A Comparative Perspective.* New York: John Wiley & Sons.
Wilson, Godfrey and Monica Wilson
   1945. *The Analysis of Social Change: Based on Observations in Central Africa.* Cambridge: At the University Press.

ERRATUM

Chan Heng-chee (1104) has been listed under his given name rather than his family name. The error was discovered too late to be corrected in the listings. My apologies to the author.

ETHNICITY AND NATIONALITY

KEY TO REFERENCES

The figures and letters appearing to the left of each entry are keyed to the outline below and cross-referenced in the index to contents, p. 381. In the unannotated section, there are no subcategories for rubrics six (Demography) through seventeen (Religion).

For cross references to the theoretical and general works and to the geographical areas listed to the right of each entry, see the appendix.

1. *General coverage*
   a. Collection or anthology
   b. General textbook
2. *Data orientation*
   a. Bibliography
   b. Primary data
   c. Secondary data
   d. Sample survey
   e. Survey of literature
   f. Other or none
3. *Scale of study*
   a. Community study
   b. National study
   c. Interethnic comparison
   d. Cross-national comparison
   e. Other or none
4. *Academic field*
   a. Anthropology
   b. Economics
   c. Geography
   d. History
   e. Linguistics
   f. Political science
   g. Social psychology
   h. Sociology
   i. Other or unknown
5. *Theoretical orientation*
   a. Assimilation
   b. Conflict or intergroup competition
   c. Ecological
   d. Identity
   e. Nationalism
   f. Pluralism
   g. Prejudice
   h. Situational
   i. Stratification
   j. Internal colonialism
   k. Other or unknown
6. *Demography*
   a. Population data
   b. Spatial distribution
   c. Urban/rural distribution
7. *Migration*
   a. Emigration
   b. Immigration
   c. Internal migration
   d. Urbanization
8. *Economics*

   a. Income
   b. Occupations
   c. Socioeconomic development
   d. Market processes
9. *Stratification*
   a. Caste
   b. Class
   c. Intergroup ranking
   d. Intragroup ranking
   e. Social mobility
10. *Politics*
    a. National or local authority structure
    b. Intergroup competition or conflict
    c. Subordination domination
    d. Political movements
    e. Political parties and elections
    f. Leadership
    g. Police or military
11. *Beliefs, attitudes, and ideology*
    a. Ethnocentrism and intergroup attitudes
    b. World view or ideology
    c. Sterotyping
    d. Ideological bases of government policies
12. *Ethnic identity*
    a. Ancestry or origin
    b. Consciousness of identity
    c. Culture or customs
    d. Communal sentiment
    e. Language
    f. Race
    g. Religion
    h. Tribe
    i. Common values or ethos
13. *Education*
    a. Educational levels
    b. Values associated with education
14. *Family and kinship*
    a. Family structure or composition
    b. Extended kin networks
    c. Marriage
15. *Voluntary associations*
16. *Communication*
    a. Language
    b. Media
17. *Religion*

ANNOTATED ENTRIES

1 ABRAMSON, Harold J. 1973. *Ethnic Diversity in Catholic America.*
New York: John Wiley & Sons. Notes, bibliog., index. Using secondary
analysis of survey data Abramson characterizes the ethnic diversity of
American Catholics. Data are presented on immigration and immigrant
descendants, regional and urban-rural distributions, occupational patterns,
and educational levels of different Catholic ethnic groups. Since he is
particularly concerned with the persistence of ethnicity, Abramson
devotes most attention to ethnic marriage, its frequency and antecedents,
to the social structural and cultural uniqueness of different Catholic
groups, and to changes in religio-ethnic behavior. Ethnic endogamy is
treated as a function of religiosity and ethnic boundary maintenance.
Finally he presents a model using generational changes, socioeconomic
competition, and religiosity as determinants of future ethnic group
maintenance or assimilation.

2d/3c/4h/5a,d/6a,b,c/8b/11b
12a,c,g/13a/14c/17   US: Euro-Americans

2 ABRAMSON, Paul R. 1977. *The Political Socialization of Black Ameri-*
cans: A Critical Evaluation of Research on Efficacy and Trust. New
York: The Free Press. Bibliog. Reviewing studies concerning political
attitudes among black Americans, Abramson finds consistent results
showing that black children feel less effective politically and show less
trust for political leaders than do white children. He evaluates four explanations for the observed differences: (1) differences in political education in schools, (2) social deprivation of blacks, (3) differences in intelligence, and (4) a stronger recognition of political reality among blacks.
He favors explanations (2) and (4). Appendixes list survey findings,
research sites, measures of trust and efficacy, and assumptions underlying
and empirical consequences following from each of the four explanations.

2c/3e/4f,g/5g,k/11a,b,d   US: Afro-Americans

3

3   ADAM, Heribert, and Hermann Giliomee. 1979. *Ethnic Power Mobi-
     lized: Can South Africa Change?* New Haven and London: Yale University
     Press.   This cooperative study by a sociologist and a historian analyzes
     the dynamics of Afrikaner society and politics to assess possibilities for
     change in the system of racial domination labeled apartheid. In the intro-
     duction, Adam attempts to specify the costs of maintaining Afrikaner
     domination. A second chapter critically evaluates the literature on South
     Africa, examining the thesis of religiously induced prejudice (Calvinism),
     Fascist analogies, racism, plural society models, class formation, and the
     colonial analogy. Adam concludes that foreign interests permit the strat-
     egy of domination, a strategy unlikely to be openly opposed by regional
     interests (including the "front-line states") who share an interest in
     regional stability. He then analyzes the politics of Afrikaner ethnic mobi-
     lization to show how intragroup politics preclude the successful advocacy
     of more moderate and pragmatic political positions. Giliomee documents
     the growth of Afrikaner identity. Adam discusses the search for a new
     ideology under conditions of survival politics. Giliomee documents
     Afrikaner economic advances under National party rule since World
     War II. Adam discusses the interests behind Afrikaner power. Giliomee
     describes the actual workings of Afrikaner politics. Adam then analyzes
     the failure of political liberalism in South Africa, and discusses political
     alternatives.

     2c/3a,b/4d,h/5d,e,i,j/8a,b/9b,c,e/10a,b,c,d,e,f,g
     11b,d/12a,b,c,d,e,g,i/17   South Africa

4   ALLPORT, Gordon W. 1954. *The Nature of Prejudice.* Reading, Mass.:
     Addison-Wesley. Index.   Allport describes and compares psychological
     theories of intergroup prejudice in this theoretical compendium. He begins
     by noting the normality of prejudgment and its relation to the formation
     of in-groups and out-groups. Subsequent chapters cover studies of group
     differences, visibility and strangeness, cognition and group differences,
     sociocultural patterns of boundary maintenance, scapegoating and stereo-
     typing, and contact hypotheses. He also discusses developmental studies of
     prejudice among children, the psychodynamics of frustration, anxiety,
     guilt, and projection as factors in prejudice, and elements of character
     structure such as authoritarianism and tolerance. He briefly analyzes
     mechanisms for reducing intergroup tensions (e.g., law, social programs,
     etc.). Most of the theoretical propositions included in the extensive post-
     World War II literature on prejudice are found in this theoretical inventory.

     2e/3e/5g/9b,c/11a,b,c/12b,c,d,i   Theory

5.   ALLWORTH, Edward, ed. 1971. *Soviet Nationality Problems.* New
     York and London: Columbia University Press. Bibliog. essay.   This
     collection surveys Soviet policies toward minority nationalities and

analyzes the changing situation in the Soviet Union. An introductory section describes Czarist imperial policies (Raiff) and the historical development of the present policy (Kohn). Currently the Soviet Union follows a dichotomous policy of cultural integration (including coercive assimilation) combined with a federal political structure. Also covered are the political and legal aspects of intergroup relations in the USSR (Brzezinski and Hazard, respectively); the distribution and dispersal of minority nationalities (Lewis); characteristics of ethnic identities in the USSR (Rubel); and the status of Islamic nationalities and potential for pan-Islamic movements in the USSR (Bennigson). An outline for a sociological approach to Soviet minorities (Lamser) is included.

1a/2c/3b/4f,h/5a,e,k/6a,b,c/8b/9c,e/10a,c
11d/12b,c,e,g/16a/17   USSR: General

6   ALLWORTH, Edward, ed. 1973. *The Nationality Question in Soviet Central Asia.* New York: Praeger. App., bibliog., comments. The editor introduces this conference collection by noting a resurgence of nationalism in Soviet Central Asia. He lists theoretical propositions relating to this resurgence in an appendix (Allworth). Other papers discuss national literatures and the Soviet policy of convergence on a single superethnic national identity (Barrett); demographic and socioeconomic characteristics of minority nationalities (especially relative urban-rural distributions) and their effects on national identity maintenance (Clem); intermarriage and cultural convergence (Dunn and Dunn); Tajik identity (Rosen); an assessment of assimilation trends (Wixman); language, education availability, and selective pressure toward integration (Shorish); a comparison of Uzbek and Kirghiz leadership (Hanselmen); Bukharan politics and identity (Matley, Hanaway, Kocaoglu, and Becker); and a summation of "ethnic consciousness" in Soviet Central Asia (Wallerstein).

1a/2c/3b/4a,d,f,h,i/5a,d,e/6a,c/9c,e/10a,f
11b,d/12b,c,d,e,g/13b/16a   USSR: General

7   ALLWORTH, Edward, ed. 1977. *Nationality Group Survival in Multi-Ethnic States: Shifting Support Patterns in the Soviet Baltic Region.* New York: Praeger. Apps., notes, bibliog. The papers in this seminar collection analyze reasons for the survival of Baltic nationalities in the face of Soviet pressures toward assimilation. The introductory chapter (Allworth) specifies identity and physical factors, relativity factors, and regulatory factors as group supports in the nationality question. Subsequent chapters cover demographic and cultural elements promoting group solidarity and maintenance of intergroup difference in the Baltic republics (Parming); analyses by Soviet historians as an indicator of nationality dissatisfaction (Nyirady); economic progess, indigenous economic managers, privileged status, and nationality supports in the

Baltic region (Shyrock); political leaders and identity maintenance (Fleming); culture and religion as group supports in the face of Sovietization policies (Doersam); resources for group maintenance among politically disenfranchised Baltic Jews (Lederhendler); and measurement of social distance among Soviet ethnic groups.

2c/3a,b/4f,h/5a,d,e,g,j/6a/8c/9c/10a,c,d,f
11a,d/12b,c,e,g/13a,b/14c/16a,b/17   USSR: Baltics

8   ARGYLE, W. J. 1969. "European Nationalism and African Tribalism."
In *Tradition and Transition in East Africa,* edited by P. H. Gulliver,
pp. 41-57. Berkeley and Los Angeles: University of California Press.
Argyle analyzes historical changes in the use of the terms *tribe* and *nation.*
He argues that the meaning of tribe, as it is applied in Africa, is equivalent
to the eighteenth-century European social theorists' concept *nation.*
Consequently "tribalism" now is conceptually equivalent to "nationalism" then. In western Europe *nation* has taken on a predominantly
territorial meaning, as opposed to its earlier ethnic one. Argyle suggests
that African tribalism should be viewed in a developmental framework
as incipient nationalism.

                                                                              Africa
2c/3d,e/4a/5k/10a,d/11b/12b,c,d,h,i   Europe

9   ASHENFELTER, Orley, and Albert Rees, eds. 1973. *Discrimination in
Labor Markets.* Princeton, N.J.: Princeton University Press. Notes, comments.   This collection includes papers presenting a neoclassical theory
of economic discrimination (Arrow); correlating education and racial
discrimination (Welch); showing the interaction of trade unions and
discrimination (Ashenfelter); documenting sex discrimination in wages
(Bergmann); and discussing policy considerations surrounding employment discrimination.

1a/2d,e/3b/4b/5g,i/8a,b/13a   US: General

10   ASHMORE, Richard D., ed. 1976. "Black and White in the 1970s."
Journal of Social Issues, vol. 32, no. 2.   The social-psychological oriented
topics in this special journal issue include construction of attitude scales
through verbal reactions to interracial marriage and optimal approaches
to racial equality (Brigham, Woodmansee, and Cook); affluent white
symbolic racism (McConahay and Hough); behavioral and attitudinal
effects of black integration of white suburban neighborhoods (Hamilton
and Bishop); patterns of political support for George Wallace (Ross,
Vanneman, and Pettigrew); tokenism and reverse discrimination phenomena (Dutton); child attitudes showing cleanliness to be a stronger
determinant than race in shaping evaluative attitudes (Epstein, Krupat,
and Obudho); relative deprivation and black militancy (Abeles); urban

black attitudes (Turner and Wilson); changes in black and white political orientations from 1960 to 1973 (Schwartz and Schwartz); and an army study of a training program sensitizing whites to cultural cues and its effects on intergroup understanding.

US: Afro-Americans
1a/2d/3a/4g/5d,f,g/10d,e/11a,b,c/12b,f   Euro-Americans

11   AZRAEL, Jeremy R., ed. 1978. *Soviet Nationality Policies and Practices.* New York: Praeger. Notes.   These essays are concerned with the development, character, and functioning of the multiethnic USSR. Part 1, on regime perspectives, contains papers exploring the imperial dimension of the tsarist polity (Starr), and analyzing Soviet mechanisms for dealing with the national question (Carrere d'Encausse). Part 2, on non-Russian elites, includes a study of the Baltic German diaspora during the tsarist period (Armstrong), a comparison of the career of two Ukrainian "national Communists" (Bilinsky), and a study of Beria's use of national cadres in his drive for power after World War II (Fairbanks). Part 3, on policy making and planning, includes treatments of anti-Semitism as a part of official policy (Burg); language planning (Pool); and correlation of policies, sociodemographic changes, and rates of linguistic Russification (Silver). Part 4, on national identity, contains estimates of the effects of linguistic Russification on national identification (Anderson); a study of north Caucasian Sufi brotherhoods and their political effects (Bennigson); and a study of resurgent Russian nationalism (Wimbush). Part 5 treats emergent nationality problems in the USSR (Azrael).

1a/2c/3a,b,c/4f/5a,d,e,k/6a,b,c/7c/10a,b,c,d,e,f
11a,c,d/13b/16a,b/17   USSR: General

12   BAGLEY, Christopher. 1972. "Racialism and Pluralism: A Dimensional Analysis of Forty-eight Countries." *Race* 13:347-54.   Bagley constructs quantitative estimates of the amounts of "racialism" and "pluralism" present in forty-eight countries. "Racialism" here involves power differentials between ascriptive categories while "pluralism" involves cultural variation (e.g., linguistic and religious differences) without necessarily invidious implications. His sample countries are located on a two-dimensional space according to their relative racialism and pluralism, and the resulting clusters are characterized by their patterns of intergroup relations, propensities for communal violence, and so forth.

2d/3d/4h/5b,f,i/9c,e/10b,c/11a   General

13   BAHR, Howard M., Bruce A. Chadwick, and Robert C. Day, eds. 1972. *Native Americans Today: Sociological Perspectives.* New York: Harper. Bibliogs. This sociology reader includes a variety of topical papers on

Native Americans. Among these are general discussions of rural poverty, occupations, and health (Johnson); images of Indians and blacks in commonly used history texts (Bowker); and contrasts between constitutional guarantees of equal treatment and Native Americans' experiences of United States governance (MacMeekin). Two papers relating to education discuss values and performance of adolescent Sioux boys (Wax) and comparative measures of achievement motivation in Navaho and white student populations (Raboussin and Goldstein). Elements of urban migration and adaptation discussed include migration, relocation, and ethnic visibility of urban Indians (Bahr); interaction patterns and identity of Indians in the San Francisco Bay area (Ablon); associations and adjustments among Indians in Los Angeles (Price); and an analysis of education, income, and economic correlates of urban migration (Sorkin). Other topics include measures of assimilation among Spokane Indians (Roy); identity change among the northern California Hupa (Bushnell); comparison of ethnic values in two Eskimo villages (Parker); role modeling and acculturation rates among Navahos (Downs); family structure and delinquency (Minnis); and several aspects of social and political mobilization.

1a/2b,c,d/3a/4a,f,g,h,i/5d,f,g/6a,b,c/7c,d
8a,b/9c,e/10b,c,d,f/11a,b,d/12a,b,c,d,i/13a,b
14a,c/15/16b   US: Native Americans

14 BAILEY, Harry A., Jr. and Ellis Katz, eds. 1969. *Ethnic Group Politics.*
    Columbus, Ohio: Charles E. Merrill.   Part 1 of this collection of previously published articles includes a brief history of ethnic group presence in the United States (Handlin); an analysis of religious conflict (Herberg); and a summary of ambivalent American attitudes toward racial equality over the past two hundred years (Franklin). Part 2: analyses of group membership as an influence on voting (Campbell et al.); strategic aspects of participation by ethnic minorities in local politics (Lane); political socialization of black Americans (Marwick); Jewish voting in presidential elections (Fuchs); black voters in northern industrial cities (Glantz); and Catholic voters in the Democratic party (Greer). Part 3: studies of political machines and ethnic politics (Cornwell); a comparison of the political styles of two black congressmen (Wilson); and the accession of the middle class to political leadership in New Haven (Dahl). Part 4: studies of recent persistence of ethnic group politics in New Haven (Dahl); the persistence of ethnic identification and ethnic politics (Parenti); black nationalism (Assien-Udom); black power (Carmichael and Hamilton); and a summary of ethnic persistence in New York City (Glazer and Moynihan).

1a/2b,c/3a,b/4f/5a,b,e,f
9e/ 10d,e,f/12b,d   US: General

15 BAKER, Donald G., ed. 1975. *Politics of Race: Comparative Studies.* Lexington, Mass.: Lexington Books. Bibliogs., index. This collection of papers analyzes different aspects of race relations in English settler societies. Topics include a general survey of race relations (Baker); psychopolitical power patterns in Native American conflicts with whites (Gurian): black subordination in the United States before World War II (Williams); post-1945 black-white relations in the United States (Himes); Japanese and Chinese in the United States and Canada (Maykovich); Native American-white relations (Patterson); black people in Canada (Scott); race and politics in Australia (Pittock); Maori-white relations in New Zealand (Forster); conflict in South Africa (Adam); racial domination in Rhodesia (Murphee); and a summary of the ways whites in Anglo-settler societies have used power to subordinate natives and subsequent immigrants (Baker).

	US: Afro-Americans	Australia
	Asian Americans	Canada
	Native Ameri-	New Zealand
1a/2c/3b/4f,h/5b,i,j/9b,c	cans	South Africa
10a,b,c,d,f/11c,d		Zimbabwe

16 BANTON, Michael. 1967. *Race Relations.* New York: Basic Books. Bibliog. In this comprehensive study of the idea of race and cross-cultural studies of race relations, Banton includes discussions of processes of contact, symbiosis, immigration and acculturation, and integration. Theories of prejudice and conformity (from social psychology), social distance, industrialization and its effects on race relations, class organization, pluralism, and racist ideologies are examined. Comparative materials include descriptions and analyses of New World slavery, United States racism, South African apartheid, African universalistic religious movements, Rhodesian racism, Brazilian integration, and British race relations. The emphasis is largely empirical. Banton takes no consistent theoretical position and most current theories about race relations are described.

1b/2c,e/3b,c,e/4h/5a,f,g,i/6a,b/7b/8b/9c,e
10b,c,d/11a,b,c,d/12a,b,c,f,i/14a   General

17 BANTON, Michael. 1977. *The Idea of Race.* London: Tavistock. Bibliog., index. Banton presents an intellectual history of the concept of race. Chapters are devoted to the development of European thinking and self-concepts of racial types; the development of world spanning "racial" classifications (including a nice summary of Gobineau's contribution); Charles Kingsley and Victorian racial chauvinism; social Darwinism; Park and American sociological perspectives on race; the development of American theories about race (emphasizing contributions by Dollard and

Cox); recent studies of ethnogenesis; and a discussion of the idea of racism.

2e/3e/4h/5k/9a,c/10c/11a,b,c/12b,f   Theory

18   BARCLAY, William, Krishna Kumar, and Ruth P. Simms, eds. 1976.
      *Racial Conflict, Discrimination, and Power: Historical and Contemporary
      Studies.* New York: AMS Press. Bibliogs.   This collection of previously
      published articles, most of which are abridged, focuses on the colonial
      context of interracial contact and its consequences in the modern world.
      It combines aspects of "world-systems" models of capitalist imperial
      development, with "internal colony" models used to explain internal
      race relations in the United States and elsewhere. In the introductory
      section different theoretical approaches are surveyed (Horton) and an
      internal colony model is described (Johnson). Other topics include the
      historical circumstances of interracial contact and the development of
      race relations patterns (Cox); descriptions of the slave trade (Davidson);
      slavery's contribution to British economic development (Williams); labor
      demand and black migration in the United States (Baron); race relations
      models and social change (Tabb); the economics of racism (Reich); and
      black capitalism (Bluestone). Studies of race relations elsewhere in the
      world include treatment of labor demand and migration as factors in
      British race relations (Rose et al.); South African history (Atmore and
      Westlake); capitalism, cheap labor, and the development of apartheid in
      South Africa (Wolpe); the "Indian problem" in Latin America (Gunder-
      Frank); Indian population decline after contact (Moerner); the Yucatan
      hacienda system (Strickon); and Indian-Ladino relations in the Chiapas
      highlands (Stavenhagen). World stratification is analyzed using a structural
      theory of imperialism (Galtung and Segal).

      1a/2c/3a,b,d/4a,b,d,f,h/5a,b,e,f,i,j/9b,c,d,e
      10a,b,c/12f   General

19   BARTH, Ernest A.T. and Donald T. Noel. 1972. "Conceptual Frame-
      works for the Analysis of Race Relations: An Evaluation." *Social Forces*
      50:333-48. Bibliog.   This review of theoretical perspectives on ethnic
      differentiation and race relations includes Park's "race cycle," Parson's
      "consensus," "symbiotic interdependence," and "conflict" models.
      "Consensus" corresponds to "assimilation" and "symbiotic interde-
      pendence" corresponds to "ecological" in the theoretical listings used in
      this bibliography. Barth and Noel frame questions concerning emergence,
      stability, adaptation, and change in systems of ethnic and racial dif-
      ferentiation. They decide that each theoretical paradigm explains one of
      the processes best. The pairs are race cycle/emergence, consensus/per-
      sistence, interdependence/adaptation, and conflict/change.

      2e/3e/4h/5a,b,c,k (Race Cycle)
      8b/10b,c,d   Theory

20 BARTH, Fredrik. 1964. "Competition and Symbiosis in North East Baluchistan." *Folk* 6:15-22. This study includes an early but thorough statement of the "ecological" approach to ethnic differentiation. Barth argues that while environmental factors do not completely explain movements of Pathan agriculturalists, Powindah pastoralists, and Marri eclectics, their movements must satisfy basic ecological requirements, especially the maintenance of an adequate food supply for each group. Cultural patterns of exploiting biotic niches must include means of protecting those niches. Barth argues that the northward movement of the Baluchi-Pathan boundary can be explained as an adjustment to the differential carrying capacities of the niches under different patterns of exploitation. He correlates migrations and seasonal rounds with different patterns of ecological adaptation in Baluchistan. These factors are seen in "relations of niches and populations, the constraints of ownership forms, and the variations in capital and labor resources between households."

2b/3a/4a/5c/6a,b,c/7c/8a,b,d/12a,c/14b   Afghanistan

21 BARTH, Fredrik, ed. 1969. *Ethnic Groups and Boundaries.* Boston: Little, Brown. Notes, bibliog. This collection from a 1967 symposium at the University of Bergen exemplifies the "ecological" approach to ethnic diversity. In his introduction, Barth argues that any cultural difference can be used to distinguish between ethnic groupings. Differences in ecologically influenced value orientations impose different performance standards on population segments, these underlie boundaries between groups, and visible diacritica are attached to these groupings as a secondary process. Polyethnic social systems demarcate domains of influence, status, power, and so forth. Ethnicity depends, in this view, on the maintenance of boundaries between the different domains. Case studies cover socially stigmatized Lapps in northern Norway (Eidheim); identity change stimulated by movement between ecological niches in the western Sudan (Haaland); the failure of ethnic differentiation to emerge in an area of wide cultural variation (Blom); interethnic relations in southern Ethiopia (Knutsson); ethnic boundary dynamics in southern Mexico (Siverts); the maintenance of Pathan identity (Barth); and ethnic diversity in Laos (Izikowitz).

	Theory	
	Afghanistan	Mexico
1a/2b,e/3a/4a/5c/6a,b,c/7c/8b,d	Ethiopia	Norway
9c,d,e/10b,d,f/11a/12b,c,d,i	Laos	Sudan

22 BARTH, Fredrik. 1969. "Pathan Identity and Its Maintenance." In *Ethnic Groups and Boundaries,* edited by Fredrik Barth, pp. 117-34. Boston: Little, Brown. Here Barth argues that ethnic identity is articulated throughout all public behavior but that it is only relevant as an identity marker when it is contrasted to alternative identities in specific

situations. Such alternatives exist on all sides of Pathan territory and the choice of identity in boundary areas depends on the ability of the individual to exhibit the behavior required by communal performance standards. Behavioral possibilities in any situation are constrained by external factors (e.g., ecology, military and political competition, etc.), and actors are free to choose their identity according to their perceptions of the possibilities available in given situations. Barth illustrates these points with data from the Pathans.

2b/3a/4a/5c,h/6b,c/7c/9c,d,e
10a,f/12a,b,c,i   Afghanistan

23   BARTON, Josef J. 1975. *Peasants and Strangers: Italians, Rumanians, and Slovaks in an American City, 1890-1950*. Cambridge, Mass.: Harvard University Press. App., index. Barton describes, in detailed historical terms, the experiences of Italians, Romanians, and Slovaks in Cleveland. He devotes attention to immigration and settlement, the formation of ethnic communities, comparative trends in social mobility among the three groups, family structure and education as sources of mobility, and group differences between the generations.

                                                                    US: Italians
2c/3a/4d/5a,i/6b/7b,d/8b/9c,e   Romanians
11a,b/12c,d,e,g/13a,b/14b   Slovaks

24   BEAN, Frank D. and W. Parker Frisbie, eds. 1978. *The Demography of Racial and Ethnic Groups*. New York: Academic Press. Bibliogs., index. The papers in this collection treat different issues of demography with reference to ethnic and racial groups in the United States. They are intended to be relevant both to evolving theory in demography and to construction and evaluation of public policies. Following an introduction that surveys previous contributions in this area (Frisbie and Bean), substantive studies are made of school integration in the United States (Farley); association between residential and school segregation in the United States (Wilson and Taeuber); black movements to the suburbs and prospects for metropolis-wide integration (Frey); black migration from the south and its likely effects in the north (Lieberson); relative marital instability among Mexican Americans, Afro-Americans, and Euro-Americans concentrating on elements of socioeconomic stratification as explanatory variables (Frisbie, Bean, and Eberstein); racial-ethnic differences in labor force participation (Sullivan); differential fertility among majority and minority groups (Bean and Marcum); fertility response among white southerners to the *Brown* vs. *Board of Education* school desegregation decision in 1954 (Rindfulls, Reed, and St. John); indicators of family and household structure among American minorities

(Sweet); and three papers concerning ethnic mortality differences.

1a/2c,e/3b,c,e/4h/5a,g,i,k/6a,b,c/7c,d/9b,c,e
10a/12a,f/13a/14a,b   US: General

25   BEATTIE, C. and S. Crysdale, eds. 1974. *Sociology Canada: Readings.*
     Toronto: Butterworth. Notes. This introductory reader contains several
     articles dealing with ethnicity and nationality in Canada. Most have been
     published elsewhere. Specific topics treated concern dilemmas and contra-
     dictions in a multiethnic society (Porter); national, class, and ethnic
     tensions underlying French nationalism in Quebec (Guindon); accultura-
     tion of Italian immigrant girls in Canada (Danziger); young people's
     images of French-English relations in Canada (Johnstone); ethnography of
     Greek working-class immigrants in Toronto (Nagata); and comparison of
     aboriginal administration in Canada and the United States.

1a,b/2c/3a,b,d/4a,h/5a,b,d,g,i   Canada: General
7b/8a/9c/10a,d/11a,d   US: Native Americans

26   BECKER, Gary S. 1971. *The Economics of Discrimination.* 2d ed.
     Chicago and London: University of Chicago Press. Index. Becker's
     neoclassical economic theory of discriminatory behavior depends on
     "taste for discrimination" to explain the difference between expected
     rational behavior and the actual discriminatory behavior of employers,
     employees, residents, consumers, and so forth. Given this variable of
     irrationality, Becker uses neoclassical mathematics to predict different
     kinds of discrimination in different kinds of market situations, and
     their aggregate effects. He tests the model using some United States
     employment data. This is the seminal work in American neoclassical
     economic thought on discrimination.

2c/3e/4b/5k (Neoclassical Economics)
8a,b,d/9e   Theory

27   BELL, Wendell and Walter E. Freeman, eds. 1974. *Ethnicity and Nation-
     Building.* Beverly Hills, Calif.: Sage. Bibliogs. This collection of con-
     ference papers is divided into sections on theory, status, conflict, and old
     and new states. Particularly useful papers in the first section include a
     general review of theories of race relations (Kuper); an analysis of somatic
     norm images and national identities (Hoetink); comparison of Marxist and
     pluralist theories (Edelstein); and critical comments on theories currently
     in use (Enloe and Lewis). Specific topics treated in the section on status
     include Soviet nationalities policy (Barghoorn); status differentiation
     and ethnic conflict in Rwanda and Burundi (Lemarchand); and English
     and Afrikander status in South Africa (Butler). Contributions to the

section on conflict include analysis of conflict as a contributor to nation-building (Freeman); description of Palestinian relations with the Arab states (Forsythe and Taulbee); ethnic conflict in Pakistan (Levak); ethnicity and policy in southeast Asian states (Enloe); education and ethnic cleavage in Kenya and Ghana (McKown); racial polarization in Guyana (Landis); and a critical review of conflict and nation-building (Galey). Old and new states topics include conflict in Ulster (Power); Mojave-Apache internal and external conflicts (Coblentz); ethnicity, religion, and the American revolution (Alger); Basque Spain (Blanco); and critical comments (Safa).

	Theory	South Africa
	Burundi	Southeast Asia
	N. Ireland	Spain
1a/2b,c/3b/4f/5b,e,f,i,j/9c	Pakistan	USSR: General
10a,b,c,d/11d/12b,d,e,f,g	Rwanda	US: Native Americans

28   BENNETT, John W., ed. 1975. *The New Ethnicity: Perspectives from Ethnology.* 1973 Proceedings of the American Ethnological Society. St. Paul, Minn.: West. Bibliogs.   These proceedings include useful papers describing changing patterns of ethnic identity among American Hasidim (Levy); ethnic maintenance among Northern Ute Indians through behavioral adaptations to changing socioeconomic circumstances (Collins); a comparison of Catawba and Monhegan adaptation and acculturation (Hicks); ethnic groups and interethnic relations in the British Virgin Islands (Dirks); patterns of Dominican ethnicity and Dominican nationalism (Gonzalez); ethnicity and group relations in Guyana (Despres); ethnic change in Ecuadorian haciendas (Crespi); urban Indian identity in Kansas (Steele); change in Mississippi Choctaw identity (Thompson and Peterson); change in ethnic identity as a function of resource competition in the American south (Makielski); and a comparison of interethnic and interclass relations in a Canadian town (Robbins). Major themes throughout these papers are mechanisms for identity maintenance and manipulations of ethnic identity for resource competition.

	Canada	Guyana
1a/2b,c/3a,c/4a/5c,d,e,k	Dominican	US: Jews
6b,c/8a,b/9b,c/10d/11a,c,d	Republic	Native
12a,b,c,d,f,g/13a/14a	Ecuador	Americans

29   BERREMAN, Gerald D. 1975. "Bazar Behavior: Social Identity and Social Interaction in Urban India." In *Ethnic Identity,* edited by G. De Vos and L. Romanucci-Ross, pp. 71-105. Palo Alto, Calif.: Mayfield. Bibliog. In this paper Berreman addresses four topics: (1) recognized social categories; (2) stereotypes attached to those categories; (3) cues

used in identification and classification of individuals; and (4) relation of of the first three to patterns of interpersonal behavior. He argues that social categories can be defined componentially, as unique combinations of values on such dimensions as religion, caste, class, and so forth. What components, and consequently what identities, are relevant varies between situations. No category takes precedence in all social situations. Individuals select relevant identity attributes from an array of possible partial identities as their perception of the situation dictates. He briefly discusses changes in the dimensions relevant to some definitions of social status. All these are illustrated with data drawn from ethnographic observation of urban situations in north India.

2b/3a/4a/5d,h/7c,d/8b/9a,b,c,d,e
11a,b,c/12b,c,d,e,g   India

30   BERREMAN, Gerald D. 1972. "Race, Caste, and Other Invidious Distinctions in Social Stratification." *Race* 13:385-414. Notes.   Berreman reviews analytical models of different types of social stratification. He dismisses van den Berghe's contention that race is irrelevant to valued cultural differences and therefore must be inherently invidious. He argues that because of its emphasis on ancestry as a criterion for classification, ethnic stratification approximates a birth-ascription model. He argues further that racial stratification is not unique because racial categories are defined in social terms just as are other social strata. He concludes that, despite apparent differences between them, ethnic stratification and caste stratification are logically similar and are therefore comparable.

2e/3c/4a/5i/8b/9a,b,c,d,e
11a,c/12a/14a,c   Theory

31   BERRY, Brewton. 1963. *Almost White.* New York: Macmillan. Bibliog., index.   Berry presents a general study of mixed-race Americans, especially those for whom unambiguous racial identities do not exist. These are mostly groups with, or at least claiming, Native American ancestry. Often genealogies are unclear, which allows strategic manipulation of putative origins for political purposes. Among the topics Berry addresses are the locations and identities of American mestizo communities, what whites believe about such groups, what black attitudes toward them are, elements of interracial etiquette for ambiguously defined peoples, life cycles, schools, and the consequences of status ambiguity (especially violence and discrimination).

2b,c/3a/4h/5d,i/6a,b,c/9b,c,d,e/10b,c
11a,c/12a,b,c,f   US: Mestizos

32   BERRY, Brewton and Henry L. Tischler. 1978. *Race and Ethnic Relations.* 4th ed. Boston: Houghton Mifflin. Bibliog., index. The most recent edition of this textbook follows the earlier editions by briefly explaining theoretical points drawn from the literature and illustrating them through brief case descriptions. Part 1: General approaches to race and ethnic relations; the concept of race; race differences; and a summary of information on race and intelligence. Part 2: Different conditions of intergroup contact including migration, conflict patterns, and cycle theories. Part 3: Elements of inequality including techniques of dominance, social stratification, cleavages, and prejudice. Part 4: (under the title "Resolutions of Inequality") Assimilation, pluralism, amalgamation, segregation, annihilation, expulsion, and reactions to minority status.

1b/2c/3a,b,c/4h/5a,b,d,f,g,i,j/6a/7b
9b,e/10b,c/11a,c/12c,f   General

33   BERTELSEN, Judy S., ed. 1977. *Nonstate Nations in International Politics: Comparative System Analysis.* New York: Praeger. Bibliogs., index. Centering on the observation that groups not generally recognized as nations can and often do assert sovereignty and act in the international political system as if they were sovereign nations, the articles in this collection focus on the strategies adopted in particular cases. The analytical framework for each case study includes five categories, decision makers, goals, resources, environment, and components or missions. The focus is clearly on possibilities open to the elite. Cases covered are Palestinian Arabs (Bertelsen); the Zionist movement (Nachmias and Rockaway); Kurds (Benjamin); Basques (da Silva); Wales (Corrado); Croats in Yugoslavia (Remington); and the Navaho (Shepardson). A concluding article includes general observations by the editor (Bertelsen).

1a/2c/3a,b/4f/5e/10a,d,e,f/11b,d   General

34   BETEILLE, Andre. 1971. "Race, Caste, and Ethnic Identity." *International Social Science Journal* 23:519-35. According to Beteille both caste and race differentiation are special cases of social stratification. Both are characterized by cumulative inequality (i.e., status differences are added to differences in wealth and power), strict rules of category endogamy with occasional hypergamy, a high value on the "purity" of upper-level women, and idealization as physiological categories. In this view, social stratification derives from group identity formation, processes coincident with the growth of internal group solidarity. The specific groups bounded by racial and caste identities are equally problematic. Consciousness of differences is the key, regardless of whether ideology emphasizes physical or cultural differences.

2f/3e/4a/5k/9a,c,d,e/11a,b,c/12a,b,c,f/13a,c   Theory

35 BETTELHEIM, Bruno and Morris Janowitz. 1950. *Dynamics of Preju-dice.* New York: Harper & Row. Index. This landmark study in the social psychology of prejudice was carried out among American World War II veterans. Using extensive survey data, the authors analyze patterns of stereotyping; social status determination; anxiety and intolerance; emotional control and tolerance; conditions associated with the condoning of intolerance; and implications of their findings for social policy. The study includes descriptions of the methods employed and some compilations of primary data.

2d/3b,c/4g/5g/9b,c,d/11a,b,c/12d,e,f,i   US: General

36 BHARATI, Agehananda. 1972. *The Asians in East Africa.* Chicago: Nelson-Hall. Bibliog. This study describes the Asians living in Tanzania, Uganda, and Kenya (Ugandan Asians have since been expelled). Most East African Asians are descended from people brought in as tradesmen and bureaucrats during the British colonial regime. Chapters in this general book cover demographic patterns; caste and marriage patterns; Asian entrepreneurship; interpersonal relations; interethnic images; and the maintenance of Asian systems of belief and religious practice.

2b/3d/4a/5k/6a,c/7b/8b/9a,c,d,e/11a,b   Kenya   Uganda
12a,b,c,d,e,f,g,i/13a/14a,b,c/15/17   Tanzania

37 BLALOCK, Hubert M., Jr. 1967. *Toward a Theory of Minority-Group Relations.* New York: Wiley. Index. Blalock combines social psychological studies of prejudice with macrosocial studies of discrimination within a systems theoretic framework. He divides his discussion into chapters on socioeconomic factors in majority-minority relations and discrimination (including concepts of status goals and flexibility, status consciousness, prejudice and avoidance behavior); competition and discrimination (structural contexts of competition, white settlers and natives, middleman minorities, blacks and labor unions, and so forth); power and discrimination (resources, mobilization strategies); majority-minority proportions and discrimination (competition, numbers, power threats and numbers, competition vs. power theories and practical policy implications of the two); and conclusions. Blalock concentrates on formulating quantitatively testable hypotheses, ninety-seven of which are appended to the different chapters. The discussion is well organized and lucid.

2e/3e/4h/5b,g,i/6a/8b,d/9b,c,d/10a,b,c,d
11a,c/12b,c/13a   Theory

38 BLAUNER, Robert. 1969. "Internal Colonialism and Ghetto Revolt." *Social Problems* 16:393-408. Blauner formalizes the popular notion of

internal colonialism. He lists four essential components of the colonial complex: (1) forced entry of the colonized group; (2) coercive accultura- tion; (3) asymmetric power relations; and (4) racism. According to Blauner, these four features are distinctive of blacks in comparison to all other American groups. This distinctiveness is used to explain urban ghetto violence in the 1960s.

2c/3b/4h/5j/9c,e/10a,b,c,d/12b,f   US: Afro-Americans

39   BLOM, Jan-Peter. 1969. "Ethnic and Cultural Differentiation." In *Ethnic Groups and Boundaries,* edited by Fredrik Barth, pp. 74-85. Boston: Little, Brown.   Blom explains why ethnic differentiation has not occurred in southern Norway despite the presence of common structural features of plural societies and considerable cultural variation. Residents of mountain valleys and lowland agricultural areas have adapted to very different ecological niches. Regional differences are recognized by residents of both areas. Contacts between them are predominantly com- plementary and economic, but despite all these potential bases for dif- ferentiation, recognized ethnic boundaries have not developed. Blom argues that this results from the failure of codification of cultural dif- ferences to generate contrasting total identities, as opposed to partial identities.

2b/3a/4a/5c/6b,c/8b,d/9c,d/12b,c,i   Norway

40   BLOOM, Leonard. 1971. *The Social Psychology of Race Relations.* London: George Allen & Unwin. Bibliog., index.   Introductory chapters to this social psychological analysis of race relations critically analyze the notion of "race" and briefly summarize the history of Nazi racism. Subsequent chapters treat the growth of race awareness in children (processes of developing self-awareness and conceptualization of group differences); personality patterns and racial attitudes (family and racial attitudes, authoritarianism, reactions to minority status, race awareness, and abnormality); attitudes toward race in Britain, in South Africa, and a discussion of social psychology's potential effect on future race relations.

1b/2e/3e/4g/5g/11a,b,c/12a,b,c,f,i/13b/14a   Theory

41   BONACICH, Edna. 1972. "A Theory of Ethnic Antagonism: The Split Labor Market." *American Sociological Review* 37:547-59. Bibliog. Given a split labor market, one in which there is a large differential in labor price between groups for the same occupation, Bonacich theorizes that business will seek to replace higher paid labor by cheaper labor. Higher paid labor will seek to protect its position, generating antagonism toward the lower paid, usually ethnically or racially marked, group. Ethnic antagonism normally takes one of two forms, exclusion move-

ments or caste systems. Both represent victories for higher paid labor. Split labor markets develop from differences in resources (e.g., living standards, information, political power) and motives (e.g., fixed income goals, sojourning, fortune seekers, etc.), which often correlate with ethnicity.

2f/3e/4h/5i/8a,b,d/9a,b,c,e/10b   Theory

42   BONACICH, Edna. 1973. "A Theory of Middleman Minorities." *American Sociological Review* 38: 583-94. Bibliog.   Working from the concept of middleman minorities, Bonacich sets out a theory of social structural development of such positions. The key variable is the orientation of immigrants to their place of residence. She argues that middleman minorities typically go from sojourning to maintaining "stranger" identity for purposes of economic advantage. Ethnic exclusivity of such stranger groups tends to arouse hostility in host societies, resulting in coercive perpetuation of the stranger status with substantial bars to assimilation. To illustrate the model she uses Southeast Asian Chinese, Indians in East Africa, and Jews in Europe.

2c/3d/4h/5g,i/6b/7b/8b,d/9c/10b
11a,c/12a,b,c/15   Theory

43   BORRIE, W. D., ed. 1959. *The Cultural Integration of Immigrants.* Paris: UNESCO.   The introduction by Borrie is an extended theoretical discussion of immigration and assimilation. Included are analyses of state policies toward immigrants; economic and cultural integration; the roles of individuals, family and community, education and the mass media; and a statement of United Nations policy on immigration. Case studies in the rest of the volume examine intra-European migration (Zubrzucki); cultural assimilation of immigrants in Brazil (Naiva and Dieguis); immigrants in Israel (Isaac); and immigration and group settlement (Price). Conference recommendations and resolutions are included.

2b,e/3d/4i/5a,k/6a,b/7a,b,c/9e   Brazil   Israel
13a/14a/16b   Europe

44   BRAM, Joseph. 1965. "Change and Choice in Ethnic Identification." *Transactions of the New York Academy of Sciences,* ser. 2, 28:242-48. Bibliog.   Bram discusses the conceptual relationships between ethnicity and nationality, the former based on alleged common origin and asserted common destiny, and the latter on sovereignty over a delimited territory. He cites examples of movements between the two statuses (Wales and Estonia); loss of sovereignty causing a shift from national to ethnic identification (South Tyrol); and shifts in individual identity ("passing"). He notes the interplay of ethnic and national symbols in Canada and

Indonesia. While he grants ethnicity only a "dubious reality" he does not argue for completely discarding the term or concept.

2c/3d,e/4h/5d/9c,e/10b,c,d/12a,b,c   General

45   BRASS, Paul R. 1974. *Language, Religion and Politics in North India.* Delhi: Vikas. Bibliog., index.   Brass argues that nationality formation is a two-stage process. During the first, competing elites attach symbolic value to objective group characteristics, define group boundaries, create identity-chartering myths, and try to mobilize a group by communicating the myth. The second stage in nationality formation involves articulation and acquisition of political rights for the group. He argues further that the congruent cleavages often supposed to generate conflict may be created by an elite mobilizing group for political purposes. He suggests that in North India, religion tends to be the dominant mobilizing symbol and that a group's language may be changed to coincide with its religious distinctiveness. Similarly a caste group seeking enhanced social status may change its religious identification. These themes are explored through examination of three North Indian political movements, the short-lived Maithili language movement in north Bihar, Urdu and Muslim minority organization in Uttar Pradesh and Bihar, and language and religious politics in the Punjab. Objective differences between groups cannot be used to accurately predict the course of group development. Numerous other variables, including which of the elite is leading the group formation process, government policies toward minorities, the presence or absence of other similarly defined groups, and the character of intergroup relations all must be accounted for in any adequate appraisal of nationality formation.

2b,c/3b,c/4f/5e/6a/8c/9a,b,c,e/10a,b,c,d,e,f
11a/12b,d,e,g/13b/15/16a,b/17   India

46   BRASS, Paul R. 1976. "Ethnicity and Nationality Formation." *Ethnicity* 3:225-41. Bibliog.   Brass argues that regardless of cultural diacritica, internal solidarity and external differentiation of ethnic groups result from similar processes. He points out that potential cultural distinctions are always available but that they have different sociopolitical effects in different situations. He sets up a continuum of solidarity and differentiation, from ethnic category (no political significance) to ethnic community (exclusive ethnic communalism) to nationality (an ethnic group with national sovereignty, a sovereign unit in a federal system, or at least corporate control over local education). Elite competition provides the motive force for movement along the continuum from category to community. Access to political resources and effective political organization are critical variables in nationality formation. Brass lists conditions governing success prospects for different elite strategies and discusses

the effects of class structures on ethnic mobilization.

2c/3a,e/4f/5e,k/8b/10a,b,c,d,f/12d   Theory

47 BRIGGS, Vernon K., Jr., Walter Fogel, and Fred H. Schmidt. 1977.
    The Chicano Worker. Austin and London: University of Texas Press.
    Tables, bibliog., index. This volume examines Chicano labor in the
    United States. Background information provided includes population
    statistics, information on immigration and internal migration, and educa-
    tional characteristics of the Chicano labor force. The bulk of the study
    concerns characteristics of labor supply, income and earnings of Chicano
    workers, the structure of the job market, rural economy, and the relation-
    ship between Chicano labor and United States public policy needs. Dis-
    crimination against Chicano workers is documented in quantitative detail.

    2c/3b/4b,h/5i,k/6a,b,d/7b,c/8a,b,d/9b,c,e
    10c/11d/13a/14a   US: Mexican Americans

48 BURAWOY, Michael. 1974. "Race, Class and Colonialism." *Social and
    Economic Studies* 23:521-50. After criticizing pluralism and internal
    colonialism theories of racial stratification as overemphasizing super-
    structure and neglecting economics, Burawoy offers a theoretical treatise
    explaining how capitalist economics generates differential incorporation
    of subordinate populations. The theory is illustrated through South
    African history, showing processes of class formation, legislative alliance,
    and the development of a colonial superstructure.

    2c/3b,c/4f/5b,e,i,j/8c/9b,c/10a,b,c   Theory

49 BURKEY, Richard M. 1978. *Ethnic and Racial Groups: The Dynamics
    of Dominance.* Menlo Park, Calif.: Benjamin/Cummings. Notes, bibliog.,
    indexes. This text is divided into sections considering concepts and
    processes, and historical analysis of dominance in the United States. The
    first section presents definitions of terms; dimensions of differentiation
    and dominance; contact conditions and the origin of dominance; means
    of maintaining dominance (discrimination, racism, coercive conformity,
    etc.); and mechanisms for reducing or terminating dominance. Historical
    treatment of United States ethnic and racial dominance covers the origins
    of American ethnicity; origins of subordinate groups; discrimination and
    racism before 1945; subordinate group adaptation since 1945; social
    movements and government policies since World War II; contemporary
    dominance; and consideration of pluralist and integrationist alternatives
    for the future. The author favors assimilation as a solution.

    1b/2c/3b,e/4h/5a,b,f,g,i/8a/9c/10c/11a,b,d
    12a,b,c/13a   US: General

50   CAIN, Glen C. 1976. "The Challenge of Segmented Labor Market
      Theories to Orthodox Theory: A Survey." *Journal of Economic Literature*
      14: 1215-56. Bibliog.   This survey of segmented labor market (SLM)
      theories challenging the neoclassical and human capital models covers
      empirical, theoretical, and policy-related challenges to the orthodoxy.
      Cain shows the development of segmented labor market theories from
      Mill, through Marxian theory, institutionalists (Veblen, Thurow, etc.),
      and structuralists of the 1960s and 1970s. Finally he summarizes the
      various contributions to SLM theory and offers an appraisal; that it
      usefully highlights questions of class, structure, and power, and that
      it sensitizes academic economists to policy issues, but that it has not
      offered a substantial alternative to neoclassical theory in labor market
      analysis.

      2c,e/3e/4b/5i,k (Neoclassical Economics)
      8a,b,d,e/9b,e   Theory

51   CAMPBELL, Ernest Q., ed. 1972. *Racial Tensions and National Identity.*
      Proceedings of the Second Annual Vanderbilt Sociology Conference,
      November 4-6, 1970. Nashville: Vanderbilt University Press. Notes,
      bibliogs., index.   This conference collection includes an introduction
      (Campbell); a discussion of segmented societies in the Caribbean (Hoe-
      tink); an analysis of racial buffering in England from 1948 to 1968
      as illustrative of colonial relationships within England (Katznelson); a
      discussion of nationalism and political militancy among black Americans
      (Kilson); a history of racial tensions and national identity in Rhodesia
      (Samkange); analysis of color, class, and prejudice in Brazil (Saunders);
      a study of South Africa as a limiting case in the use of coercive legalism
      in conflict regulation (Turk); the adequacy of concepts of race and status
      group for explaining social conflict in post independence Africa (Waller-
      stein); and a study of communal coexistence and communal conflict in
      Malaysia (Esman).

      1a/2b,c/3a,b,e/4a,f,h/5b,e,i,j/9c,e/10a,b,c,d   General

52   CANADA, Royal Commission on Bilingualism and Biculturalism. 1967-
      1970. *Report of the Royal Commission on Bilingualism and Bicultural-
      ism.* 6 vols. Ottawa: Roger Duhamel, Queen's Printer.   The final report
      of the royal commission covers a wide range of issues in considerable
      detail. Vol. 1, *The Official Languages,* covers the distribution of English,
      French, and minor language speakers in Canada; the history and legal
      foundations of language rights in Canada; and a detailed analysis of
      governmental and educational policies needed to promote linguistic
      equality. Vol. 2, *Education,* discusses education in Quebec; French
      language schools in other provinces; official-language minority schools
      in bilingual and other districts; provision of teachers, higher education,

second language teaching; and education and cultural diversity in Canada. Vol. 3A, *The Work World,* examines socioeconomic status, income, education, occupation, and industrial ownership by language. In addition, occupation is correlated with ethnic origin, religion, education, and so forth. Factors contributing to socioeconomic disparities are analyzed. Part 2 of vol. 3A discusses language use in the federal administration, public service, and the armed forces. Vol. 3B, *The Work World Continued,* discusses language use in the private sector, barriers to equality, and policy recommendations. Vol. 4, *The Cultural Contributions of the Other Ethnic Groups,* covers immigration in demographic and historical perspective; economic, political, and social patterns; and processes of language and culture maintenance for non-English and non-French ethnic groups. Vol. 5, *The Federal Capital,* sets out a plan for the capital area in Ottawa. Vol. 6, *Voluntary Associations,* discusses objectives, activities, structures, and communicational patterns of such associations. Additional background papers prepared for the commission are referred to in the text.

2b,c/3b/4f,g,h/5a,b,e,g,i/6a,b,c/7b,c/8a,b
10a,b,e,g/11d/12a,e,g/13a,b/14a/15/16a,b   Canada: General

53   COHEN, Abner. 1969. *Custom and Politics in Urban Africa: A Study of Hausa Migrants in Yoruba Towns.* Berkeley and Los Angeles: University of California Press. Notes, bibliog., index. This ethnography of the Sabo quarter in Ibadan, Nigeria, focuses on the Hausa use of ethnicity in maintaining economic control. Hausa migrants dominate the long-distance cattle trade in Nigeria, as well as begging, thievery, and prostitution in Ibadan. Ethnic distinctiveness was in the past marked by Islam, but since most of the surrounding Yoruba began to convert to Islam, most Hausa men joined the Tijaniyya sect, a puritanical Sufi order, to maintain their local distinctiveness. Cohen describes in detail how the economic monopoly developed under conditions of British colonial rule, and how the institutions unique to the Hausa migrant community (the mosque, hierarchy of religious leadership, etc.) function to support that monopoly. Identity change, boundary crossing, and general patterns of ethnic polity construction are also analyzed.

2b/3a/4a/5b,c,d/6a,b/7c,d/8b,d/9e/10a,b,d
11a,b,c,d/12a,d,g,h/14a,b,c/15/17   Nigeria

54   COHEN, Abner, ed. 1974. *Urban Ethnicity.* London: Tavistock. Bibliogs., indexes. In the introductory essay to this collection, Cohen insists that ethnic symbols are objective in the sense that they exist outside the individual and eventually become obligatory and exercise constraint on individual behavior. He argues that ethnicity is a cultural phenomenon, the politicization of formally nonpolitical social and cul-

tural forms for instrumental action, for forming and maintaining informal organizations, for articulating group functions, and heuristically for simplifying complex social settings. Substantive papers in the collection include studies of perceptions of ethnic identity and behavior among insiders and outsiders in a Zambian community (Mitchell); a short essay on ethnicity's positive and negative influences on opportunities for status advancement in the United States (Hannerz); a study of the Pakistani community in Bradford, England (Dahya); comparison of congregational and interpersonal ideologies adopted by minorities as means of dealing with different modes of incorporation in African cities (Parkin); a micro-study of instrumental manipulation of ethnic identities among residents of a stratified housing estate in Kampala, Uganda (Grillo); a comparison of ethnicity's functions for locally born and in-migrant Mossi in Kumasi in the Ashanti region, Ghana (Schildkrout); a retrospective study of ethnicity and inequality in a southern Nigerian town ca. 1955 (Lloyd); an examination of expressions of ethnicity in Indonesia (Bruner); a study of an Israeli election campaign and resurgence of Tunisian Jewish festivals in Israel as expressions of political and cultural ethnicity (Deshen); a study of the changing significance of ethnic identity for a Rhodesian in Zambia during the gaining of independence (Boswell); and ethnic collectivity formation in the largely migrant town of Kigumba, Uganda (Charsley).

	US: General	Israel
	Britain: Pakistanis	Nigeria
1a/2b/3a,b/4a/5a,b,c,d,i/7c,d/8b/9b,c,e	Ghana	Uganda
10b,f/11c/12b,c,h/14a,b,c/15/17	Indonesia	

55   COHEN, Ronald. 1978. "Ethnicity: Problem and Focus in Anthropology." *Annual Review of Anthropology* 7:379-403. Lit. review, bibliog. Cohen attributes anthropology's increasing concern with ethnicity to two factors, recognition of difficulties in defining ethnographic units and heightened sensitivity to the political contextuality of identity. He proposes a synthetic definition of ethnicity, and reviews anthropological analyses of situational ethnicity; interethnic relations; factors governing the salience of ethnic identity; pluralism; and models of plural societies. The shift in anthropology toward emphasis on ethnicity must be seen, Cohen argues, in light of an ideological shift in western societies from a liberal democratic emphasis on individual rights to recognition that personal status and power are often governed by group membership.

2e/3e/4a/5b,c,d,f,h,i/9c/10b,c/11d/12a,b,c,i   Theory

56   COHEN, Ronald and John Middleton, eds. 1970. *From Tribe to Nation in Africa: Studies in the Incorporation Processes.* Scranton, Penn.: Chandler. Bibliogs., index. The introduction to this collection examines theories of interethnic relations, boundary maintenance, incorporation

processes in plural societies, political organization, and common values (Cohen and Middleton). Several papers consider the incorporation of immigrants or aliens, including cases of aliens among the Zambian Tonga (Colson) and political incorporation of non-Uyamwezi immigrants in Tanzania (Abraham). General incorporation processes are discussed with reference to the Alur (Southall) and the east African Mossi (Skinner). The effects of colonialism and expansion of the political field are analyzed with reference to the Lugbara of Uganda (Middleton), the Kanuri king-dom of Bornu (Cohen), and the tribe-caste interactions of vertical and horizontal incorporation in Rwanda (Maquet). Additional papers consider the ethnic composition of and intergroup relations in Kano in northern Nigeria (Paden) and the Transkei Bantustans in South Africa. Most of these papers dwell on the concept of "tribe" as a name for a bounded social universe and incorporation as a form of boundary crossing accom-panied by ritual, status change, and so forth. Processual themes are boundary formation, maintenance, change, and crossing.

1a/2b/3a,b/4a/5a,d,j/6a,b,c/7c,d/8b/9a,b,c,e
10a,c,d/11a,c,d/12a,b,c,d,e,g/14b   Africa

57   COLE, John W. and Eric R. Wolf. 1974. *The Hidden Frontier: Ecology and Ethnicity in an Alpine Valley.* New York: Academic Press. Apps., bibliog., index.   A detailed comparative study of two neighboring villages in the Italian Alps in which the history of Tyrolean identity and the effects of nationalism in the two villages are described. Because the two, Tret and St. Croix, were long politically separated even though they shared a single ecological niche, minute cultural differences between them gained heightened significance as means of distinguishing between them. The process described is one of ethnogenesis, the development and per-sistence of cultural boundaries; and the role of ideals and ideology in maintaining the boundaries in relevant political and economic contexts is described. The unique history of these two villages allows the authors to control for ecological variation in analyzing the developmental history of the ethnic boundary between them.

2b,c/3a/4a/5c/6a,b/8b/9b,c,d/10a,c/11b
12a,b,c,d,e,i/14a,b,c/16a   Italy

58   COLLINS, Thomas W. 1975. "Behavioral Change and Ethnic Main-tenance among the Northern Ute: Some Political Considerations." In *The New Ethnicity: Perspectives from Ethnology,* edited by John W. Bennet, pp. 59-74. 1973 Proceedings of the American Ethnological Society. St. Paul, Minn.: West. Bibliog.   Collins argues that economic development of the Uintah Basin (Ute reservation) has changed the social structure of the local community. Voluntary termination of tribal membership by mixed bloods (under five-eighths Ute), along with a

general increase in the economic resources available to Indians, has brought about a redistribution of occupations and a general increase in living standards. Political action based on the new situation emphasizes ethnic symbols, including language and hair style, for political purposes. Collins sees ethnicity clearly as group political strategy.

2b/3a/4a/5d/8a,b,c/9c,d,e/10b,d
12a,b,c,d/13a,b   US: Native Americans

59   COLSON, Elizabeth. 1968. "Contemporary Tribes and the Development of Nationalism." In *Essays on the Problem of Tribe,* edited by June Helm, pp. 201-6. Proceedings of the 1967 Annual Spring Meeting of the American Ethnological Society. Seattle: University of Washington Press. Bibliog. Colson develops the thesis that "contemporary African tribes are either new forms of political organization created for administrative purposes by the modern states within which they exist or they represent the emergence of self-conscious nationalist movements comparable to those of Europe and Asia." In other words, "tribalism" is not an indigenous African phenomenon, but is instead a modern development produced by adaptation to colonial administration and nationalist politics.

2f/3e/4a/5d,e/10a,c/11a/12b,h   Theory

60   CONNOR, Walker. 1972. "Nation-Building or Nation-Destroying?" *World Politics* 24:319-55. Connor begins his critique of nation-building studies by reviewing the social mobilization theories of Deutsch, showing fluctuations in his predictions about the interactions of mobilization and ethnic loyalty. Weaknesses in nation-building perspectives are attributed to confusion in the use of the concepts of nation and state; consistent underestimation of the emotional power of ethnic nationalism; an unwarranted exaggeration of the influence of materialism in history; unquestioned acceptance that intergroup contact increases awareness of commonalities rather than differences; improper analogizing from the United States experience; overestimating the potential effect of communication and transportation; interpreting a lack of ethnic strife as proof of national unity; failure to take account of changing historical conditions in comparing situations; failure to consider the possible pace of assimilation as significant in determining political outcomes; confusions between symptoms and causes, and normative predispositions on the part of nation-building analysts.

2c/3e/4f/5a,e/10d/11a,b/12b,d,i/16a   Theory

61   CONNOR, Walker. 1973. "The Politics of Ethnonationalism." *Journal of International Affairs* 27:1-21. An examination of nationalism, by which Connor means the movement toward self-determination by a self-

consciously defined group. He asserts that ethnic groups, self-defined communal groups that have the potential to become nations, can be readily discerned by the outside observer. While he does not indicate what characteristics can be used to identify ethnic groups, he constructs a list of ethnic groups in several nations, indicating that there may be some doubt as to which groups are likely to become nations and which are not. He also lists thirteen caveats regarding ethnicity and national consciousness.

2f/3e/4f/5e/10a,b,c,d   Theory

62   CONROY, Hilary and T. Scott Miyawaka, eds. 1972. *East Across the Pacific: Historical and Sociological Studies of Japanese Immigration and Assimilation.* Santa Barbara, Calif.: American Bibliographical Center-Clio Press. Bibliog.   A collection of historical and sociological essays on Japanese Americans. The initial section on Hawaii and the Pacific Islands includes articles concerning the first year of Japanese immigration to Hawaii (1868); on R.T. Irwin, the "czar" of Japanese immigration to Hawaii (Irwin and Conroy); and on the growth of Japanese entrepreneurship in the Marshall and Marianas Islands (Purcell). Discrimination against Japanese and the World War II internment are discussed in articles concerned specifically with Issei in California from 1890 to 1940 (Daniels); anti-Japanese riots in Vancouver, B.C., in 1907 (Sugimoto); conditions in the relocation camps (Rhoads); and a bibliographical essay on the wartime internment (Sugimoto). Assimilation and adaptation are discussed in articles concerning New York Issei founders of Japanese-American trade enterprises (Miyawaka); the peculiar economic and social success of Nisei in Los Angeles (Kagiwada); and intergenerational cultural and character differences between Issei, Nisei, and Sansei (Lyman).

1a/2b,c/3b/4d,h/5a,f,g/7b/8b/9e/11a,d/12a,c,e,i   US: Japanese

63   CORDASCO, Francesco and Eugene Bucchioni, eds. 1973. *The Puerto Rican Experience: A Sociological Sourcebook.* Totowa, N.J.: Rowman & Littlefield. Annotated bibliog.   Analytically useful articles in this collection cover U.S./Puerto Rican colonial relations (Myerson); comparison of attitude patterns between Puerto Rican immigrants to the U.S., nonmigrants, and return migrants to Puerto Rico (Sandis); a cost-benefit analysis of the migration (Senor and Watkins); and a number of articles concerning aspects of Puerto Rican immigrant ethnicity. These include ethnic displacement in East Harlem (Cordasco and Galatiato); changes in Puerto Rican family organization (Fitzpatrick); youth groups (Maldonado-Denis); political organization (Browning); and revolutionary potential in the Puerto Rican community (Young Lords Party).

1a/2b,c/3a/4f,h/5j/6a,b,c/7a,b/10a,d/11a,b
12b,c,e/13a/14a/15/16a   US: Puerto Ricans

64   COX, Oliver. 1976. *Race Relations: Elements and Social Dynamics.*
      Detroit: Wayne State University Press. Bibliog., index.   Cox's orientation
      emphasizes economic causation of ethnic and racial phenomena. He draws
      freely but eclectically from Marxist theory. His study includes an intro-
      ductory theoretical statement on capitalist labor exploitation, tenancy,
      dependency, and migration. Subsequent chapters are devoted to analysis
      of reparative employment programs; the place of black capitalism; the
      structure of black labor; demographic dimensions of the black population;
      ghetto social structure; intermarriage and maintenance of racial bound-
      aries; the black family; education and black nationalism; types of black
      protests; nationalist leadership, riots, police and alienation; and prospects
      for the future.

      2c/3b/4h/5b,i/8a,b,d/9b,c,d,e/10a,b,c,d
      11a,d/12f/13a,b/14a/15   US: Afro-Americans

65   CRESPI, Muriel. 1975. "When Indios Become Cholos: Some Conse-
      quences of the Changing Ecuadorian Hacienda." In *The New Ethnicity:
      Perspectives from Ethnology,* edited by John W. Bennett, pp. 148-66.
      1973 Proceedings of the American Ethnological Society. St. Paul, Minn.:
      West. Bibliog.   Crespi emphasizes the primacy of occupational roles in
      defining ethnic identities in highland Ecuador. Mobility is possible and
      ethnic identities are manipulated to take advantage of available oppor-
      tunities, but successful movement from Indio to Cholo or from Cholo to
      white identity depends on obtaining an occupation appropriate to the
      desired ethnic status. Pressures toward identity manipulation center on
      demographic economic changes in the highland hacienda system. Crespi
      describes an extreme case where ethnicity is coterminous with the division
      of labor. Manual laborers are defined as Indians, patrons as white, and so
      forth, regardless of their actual ancestry.

      2b/3a/4a/5d,i/6a,b,c/8b/9c,d,e/10b,c
      11a,c/12a,c,e,i/14a,b   Ecuador

66   DANIELS, Roger and Harry H.L. Kitano. 1970. *American Racism:
      Exploration of the Nature of Prejudice.* Englewood Cliffs, N.J.: Prentice-
      Hall. Apps., index.   A study of racial prejudice and discriminatory
      behavior, addressing the dominant two-category racial system in the
      United States, white vs. nonwhite. They consider its maintenance and
      costs, the dynamics of prejudice, discrimination, and segregation. Racist
      practices in the California mission system are described; Chinese, Japa-
      nese, Filipinos, Chicanos, and blacks as victims of racism; and recent
      racial discrimination against Chicanos and blacks. Daniels and Kitano
      consider racial boundaries in terms of population proportions, color,
      nationality, religion, political ideology, and culture as determinants of
      mobility. They suggest several hypotheses concerning pariah groups and

their relations to dominant social groups: (1) pariah groups will be targets of majority disapprobation; (2) similar psychological profiles will be found among members of pariah groups; (3) a majority position engenders feelings of superiority and a motive for boundary maintenance; and (4) extreme boundary impermeability generates revolutionary responses.

2c/3b/4h/5g,i/9c,e/10c/11a,c,d/12a,e,f,g   US: General

67   DASHEFSKY, Arnold. 1975. "Theoretical Frameworks in the Study of Ethnic Identity: Towards a Psychology of Ethnicity." *Ethnicity* 2:10-18. Characterization and analysis of four frameworks used for the analysis of ethnic phenomena in psychology and sociology: sociocultural, interactionist, group dynamicist, and psychoanalytic. Dashefsky lists major assumptions and theoretical propositions derived from these four frameworks.

2e/3e/4g/5k/9c/11a,b,c   Theory

68   DE LA GARZA, Rudolph O., Z. Anthony Kruszewski, and Tomas A. Arciniega, eds. 1973. *Chicanos and Native Americans: The Territorial Minorities.* Englewood Cliffs, N.J.: Prentice-Hall. The papers in this symposium collection concern political attitudes and actions of Chicanos and Native Americans, and institutional responses to their actions. Papers in the first section include a characterization and analysis of educators' stereotypes of Chicano students (Brischetto and Arciniega); a study of aspirations and opportunities for mobility among Chicano youth (Wright, Salinas, and Kuvlesky); an attempt to characterize American Indian values (Haddox); a sample of urban Indian attitudes toward protest and violence (Stauss, Chadwick, and Bahr); a summary study of La Raza Unida party (Gutiérrez); and analysis of interethnic political coalitions in the American southwest (Herzog). The institutional setting of political behavior is described in papers concerning Chicano views of planning in the Department of Labor's Manpower Program (Rankin); vocational training by the Bureau of Indian Affairs (Stauus and Clinton); Civil Rights Commission studies of Chicano education (Uranga); compensatory education models for minority schooling (Arciniega); and analysis of apparent "progressive retardation" of Native American students, attributing the phenomenon to "goal dissonance" between professional educators and their students (Lynch). While most of the articles concern specific institutional contexts, they illustrate the strategic dimensions of some United States minority political action.

1a/2b,d/3a/4f,h/5a,b,g,i/9e/10c,d/11d   US: Mexican Americans
12b,c,e,g/13b/16a   Native Americans

69   DESPRES, Leo A. 1967. *Cultural Pluralism and Nationalist Politics in British Guiana.* Chicago: Rand McNally. Bibliog., index. A detailed

study of cultural pluralism and ethnic politics in British Guiana (now Guyana). As relevant history to the development of a pluralistic society, Despres describes British colonial rule, treatment of indigenes, and importation of Africans, East Indians, Portuguese, and Chinese as plantation laborers. These groups were differentially incorporated into Guianese society and polity. Local sociocultural integration is discussed in terms of settlement patterns, family structure, kin networks, village economics, religious activities, education, voluntary associations, local government, and so forth. National institutions related to group integration include schools, media, trade unions and other labor organizations, corporations and cooperatives, government, and political organizations and parties. Despres concentrates on nationalist ideologies and ethnic factionalism in Guianese politics. He details attempts by the Peoples Progressive party to maintain a united nationalist front despite threats of ethnic particularism during the early 1960s. Political entrepreneurship by PPP leader Jagan and opposition PNC (Peoples National Congress) leader Burnham is the key to increasing ethnic political conflict according to Despres. He sees markets as integrative; politics and culture as divisive.

2b,c/3b/4a/5b,e,f/6b/8b/9c,d/10a,b,c,d,e
11d/12b,d,e,f/13b/14a/15/16a,b/17   Guyana

70   DESPRES, Leo A. 1975. "Ethnicity and Ethnic Group Relations in Guyana." In *The New Ethnicity: Perspectives from Ethnology,* edited by John W. Bennett, pp. 127-47. Proceedings of the American Ethnological Society. Minneapolis, Minn.: West. Bibliog.   In this updated version of his earlier work, Despres analyzes ethnic pluralism in Guyana as a function of differences in access to economic resources. Pertinent structural factors are a cultural division of labor (ethnically marked occupational specialization) and social stratification. Despres argues that ethnic identity is an "imperative status" but even so it varies according to situation and audience. Contrary to appearance, ethnic stratification is not due to a coincidence of race and class boundaries. Despres cites attachment of economic differences to categorical ethnic groups rather than to individuals as the main difference between systems of ethnic stratification and social classes.

2c/3b/5b,f,h,i/6a/8b/9b,c,e/10a,b/12a,c/14a   Guyana

71   DESPRES, Leo A., ed. 1975. *Ethnicity and Resource Competition in Plural Societies.* The Hague: Mouton. Bibliog., indexes.   The papers in this collection analyze ethnicity and competition for scarce resources. Two theoretically oriented papers consider resource competition, monopoly strategies, and varieties of socioracial diversity (Hoetink), and a partial model of resource competition and ethnic ascription (Despres). Case studies analyze the partial incorporation of Cuna Indians in Panama

(Holloman); Quechua ethnicity in Ecuador (Whitten); ethnicity and class in highland Peru (van den Berghe); competitive interethnic relations in Nigeria (Otite); interethnic conflicts over resource distribution in postcolonial societies in Africa (Skinner); and the surprising lack of competition between Tibetan refugees and local people in South India (Goldstein).

	Theory	
1a/2b,c,e/3a,b,e/4a,h/5b,c,d,f,i/6a,b/8c,d	Africa	India
9a,b,c,e/10a,b,d,e,f/11a,b,d/12b,d,g,i/15	Latin America	

72 DEUTSCH, Karl W. 1966. *Nationalism and Social Communication: An Inquiry into the Foundations of Nationality.* 2d ed. Cambridge: MIT Press. Bibliog., index. Deutsch moves from an initial consideration of approaches to nationalism (geographic, economic, political) to consideration of factors affecting consciousness of nationality. The defining criterion of a "people" in his model is complementarity of communication habits. In this theory communicative facility underlies cultural community, profoundly affects possibilities for social action, and is measurable. Assimilation, the primary process Deutsch assumes to be at work in nationality formation, is analyzed as a function of social mobilization, the spread of nationalist/modernist consciousness, and social mobilization in turn can be affected by controllable socioeconomic characteristics such as income, communication networks, language use, and so forth. In this formulation nationality formation involves adoption of a more universal reference frame for social action, a process primarily of assimilation of diverse peoples to a national culture.

	Theory
2c,e/3d/4f/5a,e/8a,c,d/9b,e/10d,f	
11b,d/12c,e,i/16a,b	General

73 DEUTSCH, Karl W. 1979. *Tides Among Nations.* New York: Free Press. Notes, bibliogs., index. The chapters in this collection, which have all been published previously, represent Deutsch's work on national integration. Part 1 provides an overview, with chapters discussing processes of national development; language elements in European nationalism; economic competition and nationalistic intolerance; race discrimination within and among nations; and relations between social mobilization and political development. Part 2 examines some elements of nation building in detail, including the propensity to international transactions; shifts in the balance of international communication; and the general use of effective social distance and political development. Part 3 includes case studies of national integration, with particular attention to symbols of political community; central European integration problems (ca. 1954); western European integration (ca. 1962); arms control and integration in western Europe (ca. 1966); and a general discussion of national integration. General perspectives on nationalism and the world include prospects

for peace based on a projective marginal cost model for lost human life vs. prospective marginal gains from wars; world political effects of limited growth and continuing inequality; and prospects for industrial countries.

2c,d,e/3d,e/4f/5b,e,k/8d,e/9b,e
10a,b,c/11b/13b/16a,b   Theory

74 DEVEREUX, George. 1975. "Ethnic Identity: Its Logical Foundations and Its Dysfunctions." In *Ethnic Identity,* edited by G. DeVos and L. Romanucci-Ross, pp. 42-70. Palo Alto, Calif.: Mayfield. Bibliog. An analysis of the dissociative or differentiating aspects of ethnic identity, in which the author distinguishes between ethnic identity as a logical classification and ethnic personality as a stereotypic behavioral model. Both differentiation of identity and behavioral stereotypes can either be functional or dysfunctional, in Devereux's view, according to whether they help the individual positively adapt to social situations. Identity function and dysfunction are illustrated through reference to fifty-six individual cases drawn from a variety of cultures.

2b,f/3e/4a/5d,i/11b,c/12a,d,i   Theory

75 DEVOS, George and Lola Romanucci-Ross, eds. 1975. *Ethnic Identity. Cultural Continuities and Change.* Palo Alto, Calif.: Mayfield. Notes, bibliogs., index. In the introductory chapter to this collection, DeVos defines "ethnic group" as a self-perceived grouping of people adhering to a unique set of cultural traditions. Components of that tradition vary but they serve both as symbols of group uniqueness and objective differences. "Ethnicity" is defined as a subjective sense of continuity in belonging. Allegiance to the ethnic group indicates past-oriented identity based on putative common origin or experience. The orientation ties one to a supportive group as a means of coping with insecurity regarding self worth. The articles generally share the psychological/cultural orientation of the editors. They examine ethnicity as a functional adaptation that sometimes misfires, resulting in pathological maladjustments (Devereux); situationally chosen partial identity in urban Indian social situations (Berreman); and as a type of "cultural totemism" (Schwartz). The relationship of ethnicity to "national character" is discussed for overseas Chinese (Rin); the English (Gorer); Americans (Mead); and Italians (Romanucci-Ross). Ethnic identity and religion and their relations to political conflict in Sri Lanka are analyzed (Obeyesekere). Ethnic ascendancy and alienation are discussed for Africa (Uchendu); Egypt (El-Hamamsy); and modern Japan (Wagatsuma). Minority status and ethnic identity in Vilnius, Lithuania, are described (Milosz), along with a general analysis of color in identification processes (Raveau). The concluding chapter summarizes findings. The editors list instrumental and affective attributes of ethnicity derived from TAT (Thematic Apperception Test)

data. All themes concern development and maintenance of personal social and cultural identities. Affiliation to some sort of group is asserted to be a basic need that motivates expenditure of energy to develop and maintain group solidarity. Because ethnicity provides integration of identity (past-oriented) and personal goals (future-oriented), politicization of ethnicity, a process of goal change, often requires reformulation of identity. This threatens the psychological basis for ethnicity, security in continuity. The implications of this contradiction are not discussed.

1a/2b,c,f/3a,b,e/4a,g/5d,g/9a,c,e/10d,f
11a,b,c,d/12a,b,c,d,i/14a/16a/17   General

76. DEVOS, George and Hiroshi Wagatsuma, eds. 1966. *Japan's Invisible Race: Caste in Culture and Personality*. Berkeley and Los Angeles: University of California Press. Notes, bibliog., index.   This book examines occupational castes in general, and the specific case of the pariah Burakumin in Japan. Part 1, The Japanese case: histories of untouchability in Japan (Price); growth and transformation of the nineteenth-century emancipation movement (Totten and Wagatsuma); postwar political militance (Wagatsuma); analysis of the influences of religion and education in bringing about changes in the social standing of outcaste groups (Wagatsuma); an ethnographic study of the ecology of Buraku communities (Wagatsuma and DeVos); a community study of the Kyoto Buraku (Sasaki and DeVos); studies of the social persistence of outcaste groups (Donoghue); attitudes toward Burakumin in a progressive farming community (Cornell); other occupationally defined groups (Norbeck); Burakumin in the United States and their positions in the Japanese-American community (Ito); socialization, self-perception, and Burakumin status (DeVos and Wagatsuma); group solidarity and individual mobility (DeVos and Wagatsuma); minority status and attitudes toward authority (DeVos and Wagatsuma).   Part 2, A general discussion of caste systems: the structure and function of caste systems (Berreman); concomitants of caste organization (Berreman); the psychological elements essential to maintenance of caste systems (DeVos); elements toward a cross-cultural psychology of caste behavior (DeVos).

1a/2b,c,d,e/3a,e/4a,g/5c,d,g,i/6a,b/8b/9a,c,e
10a,d/11a,c/12a/13b/15/17   Japan

77 DEX, Shirley. 1979. "Economists' Theories of the Economics of Discrimination." *Ethnic and Racial Studies* 2:90-108. Bibliog. Dex classifies economists' theories of discrimination as neoclassical, institutional ("dual labor market theory"), and radical. She surveys the literature surrounding each type and sets out its major assumptions and propositions. The neoclassical school issues from the work of Becker who assumes some nonpecuniary motive ("taste") impinging on a free market model of the

economy. "Dual labor market theory" assumes there is some institutional separation of labor markets, each operating under a separate set of administrative rules, with diacritical selectors restricting mobility between sectors. Radical economic analysis founders on overly powerful assumptions about actors' motives, and an overly global orientation, according to the author. Because none of the theories clearly generates testable hypotheses, Dex sees little hope of ever being able to choose between them. She does suggest that the questions they do generate appear to be quite different, and so these may not be competing theories at all.

2e/3e/4b/5b,f,i,j,k (Neoclassical Economics)
8b,c,d/9b,c   Theory

78   DINNERSTEIN, Leonard and David W. Reimers. 1975. *Ethnic Americans: A History of Immigration and Assimilation.* New York: Dodd, Mead. Apps., bibliog. An examination of immigration patterns and trends of immigrant assimilation into American society. It assesses conditions leading to emigration from Europe and elsewhere, the pull of United States industrial expansion during periods of rapid immigration, transportation methods used by immigrants, and the specific ethnic character of the different waves of immigration. The immigration portion of the book is substantiated with quantitative material. Assimilation is treated more impressionistically. A bibliographical essay covers sources on immigration, American ethnic groups, nativism and immigration restrictions, ethnic mobility, and assimilation.

2c/3b/4d/5a/6a,b/7a,b/8b/9c,e
10b/11a,d/12a,b,f,g   US: General

79   DIRKS, Robert. 1975. "Ethnicity and Ethnic Group Relations in the British Virgin Islands." In *The New Ethnicity: Perspectives from Ethnology,* edited by John W. Bennett, pp. 95-109. 1973 Proceedings of the American Ethnological Society. St. Paul, Minn.: West. Bibliog. According to Dirks, changes in the labor market have modified behavioral characteristics expected of different ethnic categories in the British Virgin Islands. Immigrant laborers are stigmatized in terms similar to those used to refer to the institutional poor in the United States. Dirks argues that pejorative stereotypes accurately describe immigrant behavior patterns in the Virgin Islands. Since these are not typical behaviors in their home areas, he concludes that they reflect immigrant adaptations to the competitive labor markets they are entering for the first time.

2b/3b/4a/5c/7c/8b/9c,e/11a,c/12a,c,d,i/14a   Virgin Islands

80   DRAGIC, Nada, ed. 1974. *Nations and Nationalities of Yugoslavia.* Belgrade: Madjunarodna Politika. Bibliog. These papers were prepared

for a United Nations conference on national minorities. Topics covered include the ethnic composition of the Yugoslav population and the demographic characteristics of each national segment (Breznik and Sentic); nationalism and the origins of the Socialist Federal Republic of Yugoslavia (Lukac); mechanisms of self-management and ideals of equality in Yugoslav politics (Hadzivasilev); a regional survey of economic activity in the country, showing the socioeconomic foundations of claimed equality of distribution (Joncic); Yugoslav federal policy toward national languages (Zajmi); government policies toward national minorities (Devetak); policies on education, culture, and science (Varga); and internationality relations in Yugoslavia (Bilandzic). The descriptions of policies reflect official stances and ideal goals rather than actual operations and outcomes, but much useful information in national minorities in Yugoslavia can be obtained from these articles.

2b,c/3b/4f/5f/6a,b/9e/10a,d
11d/13a/16a   Yugoslavia

81   DRESANG, Dennis L. 1974. "Ethnic Politics, Representative Bureaucracy, and Development Administration: The Zambian Case." *American Political Science Review* 68:1605-17. Dresang analyzes ethnic politics as a competition for government-allocated development resources. Regional and ethnic differences in social mobilization have resulted in power differentials between groups and unequal resource allocations in Zambia. Bemba dominate the government bureaucracy and the Copperbelt receives the bulk of developmental resources. Dresang supports his argument through quantitative data documenting inequities in distribution of jobs and resources. Integrating theories of political entrepreneurship with pluralist theories of political balance, he predicts that Bemba dominance will be undermined as opposition coalitions emerge. Eventually, he argues, the bureaucracy will evolve toward self-regulating equilibrium.

2b,c/3b/4f/5b,i/6c/8b,c/9c/10b,c,e   Zambia

82   DREYER, June Teufel. 1976. *China's Forty Millions: Minority Nationalities and National Integration in the Peoples Republic of China.* Cambridge, Mass., and London: Harvard University Press. Bibliog., index. A detailed study of China's policies toward national minorities with introductory chapters that summarize policies during the empire, the republic, and the Marxist-Leninist analysis of minorities presented to China through the example of the USSR. Dreyer then examines postrevolution policies: the early years, 1949-55; years of radical experimentation, 1956-58; reaction, 1958-65; the Cultural Revolution, 1966-69; post-cultural Revolution, 1970-75. She finds a consistent emphasis on integration of national minorities through Sinification and modernization, but signifi-

cant variations in the policies used to promote these goals.

2c/3b/4f/5k/6a/8b/9c,e/10a,c/11a,d/12a,b,c,f   China (PRC)

83   DUCHACEK, Ivo D., ed. 1977. "Federalism and Ethnicity." *Publius: The Journal of Federalism*. vol. 7, no. 4. Notes.   This special-topic issue includes an introduction setting out types of federal governmental structures incorporating ethno-territorial communities (Duchacek); descriptive articles on elite accommodation of ethnic minorities in Switzerland (Glass); devolution and ethnic nationalism in the United Kingdom (Lazer); ethnicity and American federalism (Glazer); ethnic and territorial aspects of federalism in the USSR (Armstrong); the evolution of Yugoslav federalism (Berg); internal colonialism and federalism as means of conflict management in national development strategies (Enloe); internationalism in Quebec (Painchaud); and federalism, security, and the survival of small republics (Stevens).

	Britain: General	US: General
	Canada: Québécois	Yugoslavia
2c/3b/4f/5b,e,f,j/10a,b,c,f	Switzerland	USSR: General

84   DURAN, James J. 1974. "The Ecology of Ethnic Groups from a Kenyan Perspective." *Ethnicity* 1:43-64. Bibliog.   Duran uses an ecological approach derived from the work of Mitchell, Deutsch, and Barth to examine ethnicity in Lumbwa, an ethnically plural Kenyan highland town. He describes functional interactions of ethnic groups in Lumbwa, interethnic marriage in the town, and attitudes toward it among the different groups. He sees ethnic groups as new political units generated to fill the power vacuum left by the departure of the colonial administration. In areas like Lumbwa new types of confrontation are taking place as individuals come to interact with each other in novel social settings. Ethnic affiliation is a rational response to a situation where personal rights depend on group backing. Ethnic groups tend to form according to a process optimizing resources for political competition.

2b/3a/4a/5c/6b,c/8b/9c,d,e/10b,c/12c,e,h   Kenya

85   DURRENBERGER, E. Paul. 1975. "Understanding a Misunderstanding: Thai-Lisu Relations in Northern Thailand." *Anthropological Quarterly* 48:106-20. Bibliog.   Specific cases show how Thai and Lisu stereotypes of each other contribute to, and are a result of, their experiences of interaction with each other. Sterotypic behavioral expectations form a basis for action by members of each group and, since the stereotypes do not conform to images group members have of themselves, the results are misunderstanding and mutually negative outgroup images. The author relates Thai and Lisu beliefs about contracts, obligations, power, honor,

and so forth to specific cases of interaction across ethnic boundaries. These occur in such contexts as marketing a corn harvest, visits to state and private hospitals, and a visit by a traveling injection doctor.

2b/3a/4a/5c,d,k/9c/11a,b,c/12c,d,i   Thailand

86   DU TOIT, Brian M., ed. 1978. *Ethnicity in Modern Africa.* Boulder, Colo.: Westview Press. Introd., bibliog.   Papers covering a range of areas of Africa and a variety of aspects of ethnicity: ethnic affiliation in Tanzania (Guillotte); ethnic tensions in Uganda (Mazrui); language policies in sub-Saharan African countries (Landman); Ituri pygmy ethnic identification (Turnbull); location and ethnicity in Tanzania (Newman); urban ethnicity in Windhoek, Namibia (Pendleton); urban ethnicity in South Africa (Du Toit and Pendleton); women's voluntary associations as counterethnic forces in African cities (Little); Nigerian ethnic voluntary associations (Skinner); a case study of a "tribal fight" in a Namibian mine compound (Gordon); the developmental history of Afrikaner ethnicity (Coetzee); coloureds in South Africa (Adams); economic hostility to Indians in South Africa (Pachai); and an appraisal of future trends in southern African ethnicity (Nussey). These articles are mostly case studies.

1a/2b/3a,b,d/4a,d,f/5a,c,d,f,g/6b/9c,e/10a,b,d,f
11a,d/12a,b,c,d,e,f,g,h/15/16a   Africa

87   DWORKIN, Anthony Gary and Rosalind J. Dworkin, eds. 1976. *The Minority Report: An Introduction to Racial, Ethnic, and Gender Relations.* New York: Praeger. Bibliog., index.   An introductory sociology text on minority relations that includes an editors' introduction and collected papers. The introduction discusses problems in defining minorities, and decides on three dimensions of status: the distributive (concerning property, prestige, and power); the organizational (focusing on social institutions), and the social-psychological (concentrating on the effect of social structures on the individual) (Dworkin and Dworkin). Minority status is seen as inherently unstable, an intermediate status ultimately tending toward resolution either in separation or assimilation. The authors categorize nine United States minorities according to their standing on the above dimensions. Each subsequent chapter includes a literature survey with critical comments, documentation, and suggestions for further reading. Substantive papers examine five sociological perspectives (historical, organizations and movements, demographic, socioeconomic, and structural) on Afro-American experience (Jackson); the history, organization, distribution, and political activities of Mexican Americans (Rivera); Puerto Rican history, cultural adjustment, and adaptation (Molina); the history of Native Americans in the United States and their contemporary sociopolitical situations (Stauss, Chadwick, and Bahr); Japanese-American history, population, culture, and social structure

(Ima); Chinese-American history, demography, community organization, stereotypes, occupations, and integration problems (Li); Irish history and assimilation, and women as an American minority (Dworkin).

1a,b/2b,c/3b/4h/5a,b,f,g,i,j,k/6a,b/7b/8b/9c/10a,b,c,d
11a,c,d/12a,b,c,d,e,f,g,i/13a,b/14a/15   US: General

88   EHRLICH, Allen S. 1971. "History, Ecology, and Demography in the British Caribbean: An Analysis of East Indian Ethnicity." *Southwestern Journal of Anthropology* 27:166-80. Bibliog. A comparison of the social situations of East Indian immigrants in various Caribbean areas to find the determinants of relative persistence of cultural distinctions. In Jamaica and elsewhere ecology and demography are cited as the key factors. The dispersal of Indians on plantations in Jamaica and subsequent dilution of intraethnic communication caused dissolution of ethnic solidarity and a loss of cultural uniquenesss. In Trinidad, Guyana, and elsewhere, ecological restrictions generated dense concentrations of indentured laborers, mostly East Indians. In these situations, ethnic distinctions have persisted. Even in Jamaica recognition of ethnic boundaries persists, but cultural markers are much less visible than elsewhere in the Caribbean.

2b,c/3b/4a/5c/6a,b,c/7b,c/8b,d/12b,c,g,i   Caribbean

89   EHRLICH, Howard J. 1973. *The Social Psychology of Prejudice.* New York: Wiley. Bibliog., indexes. An overview of American studies of prejudice with an inventory of propositions contained in these studies. The literature on prejudice is divided into studies treating cognitive, connative, affective, and social dimensions. Under each of these dimensions analyses of more specific topics are summarized and evaluated. Within the cognitive dimension these include stereotype formation and social psychological determinants of dispositions toward prejudice. The connative dimension subsumes social distance, personal distance, and marginality. Affect covers structures of prejudice, language, norms, and cognitive determinants of affective states. The social dimension includes socialization and supporting mechanisms for prejudice, nuclear family forms, child-rearing practices, attitudes toward self and others, and reference group orientations. Ehrlich also comments on social change and its effects on dispositions toward prejudice. Each chapter includes a list of major hypotheses and propositions derived from the literature.

2e/3e/4g/5g/11a,b,c,d/12b,d,e,i/13a   Theory

90   EIDHEIM, Harald. 1969. "When Ethnic Identity is a Social Stigma." In *Ethnic Groups and Boundaries,* edited by Fredrik Barth, pp. 39-57. Boston: Little, Brown. Eidheim describes the distinctions between

people identified as Lapps and those identified as Norwegians in coastal fjord areas of northern Norway. Though language is the only readily apparent cultural distinction between the groups, ethnic identities are pervasive and binding. Eidheim argues that Norwegian is the only valid identity for public interactions. Lapps have to act out this identity but are less adept at doing so than are Norwegians. In this situation of unequal power, performance standards are imposed on the stigmatized group by dominant outsiders. Public behavior is subject to constraints of impression management in terms of these imposed standards.

2b/3a/4a/5d,g,i/6a,b,c/9c,e/10b,c,d/11a,b
12a,b,c,e/13a   Norway

91 EISENSTADT, S. N. and Stein Rokkan, eds. 1973. *Building States and Nations*. 2 vols. Beverly Hills and London: Sage. Notes, indexes. The first volume in this massive collection covers models and data resources and the second contains analyses by region. Of particular interest in volume 1 is an extensive selected bibliography organized by theme and country (Rokkan, Saelen, and Warmbrum). Volume 2 contains papers concerning the building of consociational nations using the Netherlands and Switzerland as example (Daalder); comparison of peripheral nationalisms in Spain (Linz); contrasts between types of nationalism in the Balkans (Pasic); nationalism in Canada (McRae); the Caribbean (Bell); Brazilian regional contrasts (Schwartzman); varieties of dependency in Latin America (Michelena); Japan and Korea (Watanuki); the Indian subcontinent (Mukherjee); Southeast Asia (Heng-chee Chan and Evers); the Maghreb (Zghal); Nigeria (Himmelstrand); and several papers covering nation building in regions of Africa (Goody, Foltz, Gellar, Mazrui).

1a/2a,b,c/3b/4a,d,f/5e,i/9b/10a,b,c,d,f
11b,d/12a,b,d   General

92 EL-HAMAMSY, Lalia Shukry. 1975. "The Assertion of Egyptian Identity." In *Ethnic Identity*, edited by G. DeVos and L. Romanucci-Ross, pp. 276-306. Palo Alto, Calif.: Mayfield. Bibliog. The author analyzes the development of national identity through a case study of Egypt. She argues that Egyptian identity developed in opposition to political and military domination by outsiders, especially after European conquest by Napoleon in the late eighteenth century. The development of Egypt as an independent nation with a leading position in the Arab world was largely a process of cultural emblemization leading to a unitary conception of political identity. The national identity is defined through loyalty to common key symbols. Interaction between Egypt and other Arab states has added new dimensions to this identity. The author offers some

ideas about the likely future course of Egyptian identity.

2c/3b/4a/5d,e/10d,f/11b,d/12b,c,g,i/16a   Egypt

93   ELLIOTT, Jean Leonard, ed. 1979. *Two Nations, Many Cultures: Ethnic Groups in Canada.* Scarborough, Ontario: Prentice-Hall of Canada. App., notes, bibliogs.   This anthology includes an introduction distinguishing between the politically recognized nations in the Canadian federation and the many culturally distinct ethnic groups that live in it (Elliott). Part 1, Native Peoples, includes a general survey of the "fourth world" in Canada (Manuel and Posluns); a declaration by the Dene of the Northwest Territories; a statement on Inuit land rights; a discussion of Canada from the native point of view (Adams); a survey of urban Indians in British Columbia (Stanbury); and a case study of a court challenge to acts guaranteeing Indian civil rights in Canada (Cardinal). Part 2, the French in Quebec, has a brief summary of the position of Quebec in the federal system of Canadian government (Rioux); a discussion of the evolution of nationalism in Quebec (Lee); a comparison of English and French cognitive styles (Richer and Laporte); a comparative study of educational aspirations of Montreal postsecondary school students (Denis); analysis of the emergence of Franco-Ontarians as an ethnic collectivity (Lee and Lapointe); a community study of the French in Toronto (Maxwell); a study of Acadian women (Sealy); and a history of cultural pluralism in the prairie provinces (Jaenen). Part 3, non-English groups in English Canada, includes a history of Canadian immigration (Elliott); a discussion of multiple ethnic identity in Canada (Nagata); minority churches (Millett); a study of assimilation of Icelandic Canadians (Matthiasson); a survey of Spanish- and Portuguese-speaking immigrants in Canada (Anderson); Italians in Toronto (Harney); Polish Canadians (Matejko); Ukrainian ethnicity in rural Saskatchewan (Anderson); the entrance status of Czech and Slovak women (Horna); Jewish immigration to Canada (Shaffir); immigration and racial prejudice in Canada (Richmond); prejudice against West Indian women from Montserrat; recent East Indian immigration from Fiji to British Columbia (Buchignani); postwar Japanese immigrants and job transferability (Ujimoto); tradition and change in Chinese family and community life in Canada (Johnson); and a discussion of Arab immigration (Abu-Laban).

1a/2b,c/3a,b/4a,d,g,h/5a,d,e,f,g,j/6a,b/7b/8b
10a,d,e/11a/12a,b/13b/14a/16a/17   Canada: General

94   ENLOE, Cynthia H. 1973. *Ethnic Conflict and Political Development.* Boston: Little, Brown. Index.   Enloe treats a variety of topics in this wide-ranging book. In introductory chapters she points out ethnicity's political salience, covers subjective and objective definitions of "ethnic group," surveys varieties of ethnic pluralism (tribal, national, racial),

and analyzes the relationships between class and ethnicity. Following an analysis of developmental and reactionary ideologies (e.g., Marxism and African socialism, respectively) she argues that universal political ideologies are hostile to particulate ethnic identities. She also considers the effects of state structures on ethnic politics, state systems in transition (e.g., Pakistan, Yugoslavia), ethnic representation in unitary states, political development of ethnic groups, communal underdevelopment and class conflict, and so forth. She presents a phase model of revolutions (cause, mobilization, warfare, consolidation) and argues that ethnic factors in revolutions can significantly shape their outcomes. She concludes that resurgent ethnicity may challenge the legitimacy of modernity, the goal underlying government policies in Third World nations, and further argues that a major shift in the structure of intra- and international relations may occur in the near future. Ideology and political structure are the key variables in her model.

2e/3d/5b,f/8c/9b,c,d,e/10a,b,c,d/11d   General

95   ESMAN, Milton Jacob, ed. 1977. *Ethnic Conflict in the Western World.* Ithaca, N.Y.: Cornell University Press. The introductory section to this conference collection includes essays placing first world ethnonationalism in historical perspective (Connor); showing the place of ethnonationalism in prevailing political theories, noting the false predictions made by those theories and offering explanations for their inaccuracy (Lijphart); and a general description of regionalism in Western Europe (Schienman). Case studies describe Basque separatism in Spain (Greenwood); federalization in Belgium (Zolberg); the class origins of ethnic activists in France (Berger); French/English consociational relations in Canada (Brazeau and Clotier); conflict management by the political center in Northern Ireland (Schmitt); English-Scottish relations and the struggle for control of North Sea oil (Esman); ethnic conflict in the south Tyrol (Katzenstein); an appraisal of the applicability of consociational theory to Switzerland (Steiner and Obler); and a description of divisive ethnicity in Yugoslavia (Bridge). The editor's summary uses the case studies to illustrate ethnicity as a normatively powerful basis for political mobilization, replacing other established institutions (e.g., religion) in that role. It also lists apparent preconditions for effective political mobilization in industrial societies.

	Belgium	N. Ireland
	Canada	Scotland
	Europe	Spain
1a/2b,c/3b/4f/5b,e/9c/10a,b,c,d,e,f	France	Switzerland
11b,c/12b,d,e,g/16a	Italy	Yugoslavia

96   FALLERS, Lloyd, ed. 1967. *Immigrants and Associations.* The Hague: Mouton. These collected articles describe the operations and functions

of voluntary associations in immigrant communities. All the articles were originally published in the journal *Comparative Studies in Society and History*. The first, which prompted publication of the others, cites the inability of kin and other networks to provide adequate organizational bases for immigrant Chinese in nineteenth-century Singapore. The author shows how secret societies, surname groupings, occupational guilds, and other voluntary associations provided a necessary framework for community organization (Freedman). Other articles describe the similar operations of religious associations during that same period (Topley); Chinese social life in Madagascar (Tche-Hao); Lebanese economic and social activities in West Africa and their political consequences (Winder); and voluntary associations among the Ibo in the Efik community of Calabar in southern Nigeria that function in ways similar to those described by the authors for Singapore (Morrill).

1a/2b/3a/4a,d/5b,c/8b,d
9c,e/10a,d,f/12a,b,c,d,e,g,h   Nigeria   Singapore
14a,b/15/16a   West Africa   Madagascar

97   FEAGIN, Joe R. 1978. *Racial and Ethnic Relations*. Englewood Cliffs, N.J.: Prentice Hall. Notes, index. This introductory text contains two introductory chapters followed by individual examinations of major American ethnic groups. The two chapters list definitions and delineations of concepts and a discussion of intergroup contact processes and their outcomes. Patterns of adaptation following interethnic contact are grouped into two major models, assimilation and power-conflict (internal colonialism). Each ethnic group is discussed in a single chapter. Most chapters include treatment of contact modes; stereotypes; economic and political effectiveness of the group; ethnic group effects on basic American institutions; and ethnic modes of adaptation to American society (assimilation or conflict).

1b/2c/3b/4h/5a,b,f,g,j/7b,c/8a,b/9c,d
10a,b,c,d/11a,b/13a,b/17   US: General

98   FENTON, Edwin. 1975. *Immigrants and Unions, A Case Study: Italians and American Labor, 1870-1920*. New York: Arno Press. Source analysis, bibliog. This reprinted 1957 Ph.D. dissertation contains a detailed analysis of the interaction of immigrant Italians (who were primarily of peasant origin) and urban American labor organizations from 1870 to 1920, the most active years of Italian immigration. After a general description of Italian-American life during the period (including population statistics, social structure, the padrone system, reactions to patronage), Fenton surveys conditions in different trades, especially those containing a large number of Italians. He covers unskilled workers, barbers, pianomakers, shoe and textile workers, members of the building trades, stoneworkers, and

garment workers. He concentrates on attempts by Italians in all these occupations to organize during the period immediately following the largest wave of Italian immigration. The data on occupations are extensive.

2c/3a,b/4d/5k/6a,b,c/7b/8b,d/9b,c,e/10b/11a   US: Italians

99   FISHMAN, Joshua A. et al. 1966. *Language Loyalty in the United States*. The Hague: Mouton. Bibliogs., index. This volume concerns maintenance of non-English languages among immigrant ethnic groups in the United States. It begins with statistics on nativity and mother tongue of the American population. Subsequent topics include non-English ethnic publishers and newspapers (1910-60); foreign language broadcasting; mother-tongue retention in ethnic parishes; organizations and leadership interest in language maintenance; German-American, Franco-American, Spanish-American, and Ukrainian efforts at language maintenance; a review of articles on language maintenance in the United States; discussion of policies for reinforcement of foreign language maintenance; and a summary conclusion.

2b/3b/4e/5a,d,k/6a/7b/11b/12e/16a,b   US: General

100   FISHMAN, Joshua A. 1972. *Language and Nationalism: Two Integrative Essays*. Rowley, Mass.: Newbury House. Notes, bibliog., index. In his examination of nationalism, Fishman stresses "authenticity" of group identity and its behavioral correlates. Since authenticity is nearly always established through reference to a primordial past, it stands in a dialectical relationship to modernization, the structural dynamic that creates the setting for nationalism. Pervasive social and economic change, the emergence of ambivalent elites, urbanization, and changing modes of sociocultural integration are seen as determinative factors underlying nationalism. In his essay on nationalism, language, and language planning (part 2), Fishman discusses language as a medium of nationalism and as a message of nationalism through its symbolic primordiality, its embodiment of authenticity, and its use as a diacriticon of identity. Language planning must take these factors into account, using language as a basis for unity and authenticity but at the same time promoting modernization.

2c/3d,e/4e/5d,e/10d/11b,d/12a,b,e/16a   Theory

101   FITZPATRICK, Joseph P. 1971. *Puerto Rican Americans: The Meaning of Migration to the Mainland*. Englewood Cliffs, N.J.: Prentice-Hall. Notes. Fitzpatrick examines the migration of Puerto Ricans to the mainland United States, and especially to New York City. He describes the demographics of the migration and also of the contract labor programs that motivate much of the population movement. He analyzes

the relevance of current theories of ethnic identity to the particular situation of Puerto Ricans. The results of the migration are examined in a community study of Puerto Ricans in New York City, showing settlement patterns; occupational profiles; community organization; family structures; racism and discrimination faced by Puerto Ricans (both in Puerto Rico and New York); religion; schools and education patterns; implications of bilingualism; the welfare system; patterns of mental illness; health delivery systems; and drug abuse.

2b,c/3a/4h/5f,i/6a,b,c/7a,b/8b/9c,e/10b,c,d
11a,c/13a,b/14a,b/15/16a/17   US: Puerto Ricans

102   FOSTER, Brian L. 1974. "Ethnicity and Commerce." *American Ethnologist* 1:437-48. Bibliog.   Foster uses the relations between the Mon and Thai in Thailand to examine hypotheses concerning marginal minority peoples as traders. He argues that culturally marginal commercial traders may exploit their strangeness to avoid cultural values inimical to commerce, and to invoke those values amenable to profitable transactions. Thai values discourage commerce and Mon traders have the advantage of not being judged by these values. As a group, Mon are stigmatized for their nonconformity, but group judgments don't interfere with individual Mon traders. Value judgments that would disrupt Mon activities if applied to individuals are displaced to the group as a whole. A number of cases are cited to support the hypothesis. Foster draws from his evidence general implications of ethnic marginality for commercial relations, entrepreneurship, and deviance. He categorizes processes by which potential value conflicts are avoided into (1) ritualization, (2) social categorization, and (3) displacement of responsibility.

2b/3a/4a/5c/6b/8b,d/11a,b,c/12a,c   Thailand

103   FRANCIS, E. K. 1976. *Interethnic Relations: An Essay in Sociological Theory.* New York: Elsevier. Bibliog., index.   This extensive theoretical treatise analyzes ethnicity in a range of structural contexts. Ethnicity is defined as belief in common descent and a sense of common identity and solidarity. Generally moving from less to more differentiated macrosocial contexts, Francis begins with a discussion of tribal societies and African empires. He moves from there to analysis of ethnie (ethnic group) and polity, with consideration of imperial relations, preludes to nation formation, nationalism and nation states, and national problems. The final level of differentiation treats ethnicity and interethnic relations in industrial societies with a discussion of ethnicity at the level of local communities, migration and annexation as ethnic group formation processes, ethnic categories, and assimilation. A fourth section treats interethnic relations in colonial situations, with specific discussion of nation building and tribalism in Africa, Mexico as a new state, and racial segrega-

tion and nationalism in South Africa. A final section lists 103 propositions developed from the text analyses. Francis views ethnicity as a function of evolving political structures.

2c/3d/4h/5b,e,f,i,j/7b/9c   General
10a,b,c,d,f/11a,d/12a,d,h,i   Theory

104   FRANKLIN, John Hope, ed. 1968. *Color and Race.* Boston: Beacon Press. Bibliog., index.   Descriptive papers in this collection on color, identity, and intergroup relations treat such diverse topics as social perceptions of skin color in Japan (Wagatsuma); race and descent as social categories in India (Beteille); color, class, and culture in Britain (Little); race, color, and class in Central America and the Andes (Pitt-Rivers); color perceptions in Brazil (Fernandes); and race and color in the West Indies (Laventhal).

		Theory	
		Brazil	India
1a/2c/3b/4d,f,g/5d,g/9c,d,e		Britain	Japan
10a,b,c/12a,b,c,g,i		Caribbean	Latin America

105   FRIDERES, James S. 1975. "Prejudice Towards Minority Groups: Ethnicity or Class." *Ethnicity* 2:34-42.   Frideres analyzes Canadian survey data to see whether controlling for social class reduces or otherwise alters the stereotypic negative images held of ethnic minorities. Other factors, including religion, language, and cultural maintenance are also isolated. While controlling for these latter factors has varying effects, depending on the object ethnic group, controlling for social class has no effect on reported images and attitudes. Frideres concludes that prejudicial attitudes toward ethnic minorities focus on different factors depending on the group, but that class (measured as socioeconomic status) is not a significantly consistent factor in stereotypes held of minorities.

2d/3b/4h/5g/9b/11c   Canada: General

106   FRIED, Morton H. 1968. "On the Concepts of 'Tribe' and 'Tribal Society.'" In *Essays on the Problem of Tribe,* edited by June Helm, pp. 3-20. Proceedings of the 1967 Annual Spring Meeting of the American Ethnological Society. Seattle: University of Washington Press.   After noting the inability of anthropologists to define diacritica that consistently and accurately distinguish between groups at the level of "tribe" (or "ethnic group"), Fried examines proposed definitions of these terms. He finds that most definitions emphasize linguistic, cultural, and political factors, and that these emphases haven't changed significantly in over fifty years. Most definitions lack clarity. Those that are clear are too restrictive and produce too many exceptions. Fried argues that "tribes"

are often the result of colonial pressure on indigenous peoples to organize politically, and that they are not indigenous political units. He concludes that the term is a pejorative artifact of colonial "divide and rule" politics and, in the absence of compelling reasons to continue using it, it should be discarded.

2e/3e/4a/5k/10c/12h   Theory

107   FURNIVALL, John Sydenham. 1939. *Netherlands India: A Study of Plural Economy.* Cambridge: At the University Press. Bibliog., index. This history of colonialism in the Netherlands East Indies covers the early competition among Europeans for control of the spice trade, consolidation of colonial sovereignty and commercial exploitation of native labor, and finally the development of an ethnically stratified plural economy. While the early colonial presence in the region was mercantile, Furnivall concentrates on the development of governmental administration after 1800. He discusses the importance of compulsory and coerced labor, the overlord positions of Europeans, and the restrictions on native entrepreneurship that encouraged domination of local trade by Chinese and Bengali immigrants. He argues that a succession of different programs for colonial administration, alternately dominated by demands for profits and by liberal (laissez-faire and native protection) sentiments, all contributed to development of a plural economic structure. This structure is defined by ethnic division of labor reinforced by social and cultural factors militating against assimilation or integration. Recent theories of "plural societies" draw heavily from Furnivall's conception of plural economy. Furnivall also discusses the ethnic bases of nationalist movements in the Indies up to 1930.

2b,c/3b,e/4i (Administrator)/5f,i/6a,b/8b,c,d
9b,c,e/10a,b,c/11d/13a   Indonesia

108   GALLO, Patrick J. 1974. *Ethnic Alienation: The Italian-Americans.* Rutherford, N.J.: Farleigh Dickinson University Press. Bibliog., index. Gallo's study analyzes political alienation of Italian Americans. He argues that Italians perceive themselves as politically powerless and so become alienated from the political system. He characterizes Italian Americans in terms of residential patterns; subsociety orientation (lack of residential mobility, closed value structure, rejection by the larger society); familism; social structure; urbanization; structural assimilation; ethnicity and religion; and class elements in their political behavior. He particularly notes the lack of Italian-American political organization and their relatively small impact on national politics in the United States. His data on perceptions and attitudes come from a small number of interviews but these results are supported and generalized through observations of

voting behavior.

2b,c/3a/4f/5k/6a,b,c/7b/8b/9b,e/10c/11a,b,c/14a,b,c/17   US: Italians

109   GARCIA, F. Chris, ed. 1974. *La Causa Politica: A Chicano Politics Reader*. Notre Dame, Ind.: University of Notre Dame Press. This reader contains academic articles, journalistic commentaries, and Chicano polemics. Garcia divides the foundations of Chicano politics into sociohistorical, psychological, and organizational bases. The sociohistorical basis is illustrated with studies of Anglo racism as a cause of Chicano political mobilization (Guzman), and the recent history of Chicano power movements (Cuellar). The psychological base is shown in an analysis of Tucson voting behavior (Freeman), political socialization of Chicano children (Garcia), and a study of Chicano consciousness and political attitudes (Gutiérrez and Hirsch). The organizational base is described in accounts of community political organization and Chicano leadership (Tirado), and Mexican-American political behavior in Texas (McCleskey and Merrill). Conventional accommodation politics are illustrated in studies of contacts between Chicanos and welfare agencies (Grebler, Moore, and Guzman), in Chicano responses to government service allocations (Comer, Steinman, and Welch), and in several analyses of local electoral movements. Nonconventional politics are seen in internal colony analyses (Barrera, Munoz, and Ornelas), separatist politics, radicalism, in accounts of the 1970-71 Chicano-police riots in East Los Angeles (Morales), and in the manifesto of the Brown Berets. Articles on future prospects are also included (Cuellar, Guzman, and Shickley).

1a/2b/3a/4f/5b/9b,c,e/10a,b,c,d,e,f,g
11a,c/12a,b,e,f/15/16a   US: Mexican Americans

110   GARCIA, F. Chris and Rudolph A. de la Garza. 1977. *The Chicano Political Experience: Three Perspectives*. North Scituate, Mass.: Duxbury Press. Index. The "three perspectives" are models used to analyze Chicano political experience: "pluralist," "elitist," and "internal colonialism." Subjects covered include Chicano identity; political culture; social and political resources; organizations and interest groups; voting patterns; coalitions and party participation; leadership; strategies of change; and future political prospects. The authors conclude that successes in local political movements offer support for the pluralist model and its optimistic predictions, while the elitist model accounts much better for Chicano powerlessness at the national level. Internal colonialism is useful descriptively but the authors complain that it does not suggest future directions for Chicano movements and is not very useful as a result.

2c/3a/4f/5a,i,j/9c,d,e/10a,b,c,d,e,f/11d/15   US: Mexican Americans

111   GEERTZ, Clifford. 1963. "The Integrative Revolution: Primordial
      Sentiments and Civil Politics in the New States." In *Old Societies and
      New States,* edited by C. Geertz, pp. 105-57. New York: Free Press.
      Geertz articulates the primordialist view that solidarities based on assumed
      blood ties, race, language, religion, and custom challenge the integrity of
      new states in the Third World. Modernization, the process of social
      mobilization, often sharpens rather than reduces primordial sentiments.
      In this article Geertz summarizes a number of cases of subnational com-
      munal solidarity. The common feature he finds in these is the aggregation
      of pre-existing primordial groups in new states and the problems of
      establishing national identities to supersede the traditional ones.

      2c/3e/4a/5d/10d/12a,b,c,d,e,f,g,h,i   General

112   GELFAND, Donald E. and Russell D. Lee, eds. 1973. *Ethnic Conflicts
      and Power: A Cross-National Perspective.* New York: John Wiley & Sons.
      Bibliogs.   The collected papers in this volume center on ethnic conflicts
      seen from the perspective of the sociology of conflict (a la Simmel and
      Dahrendorf). Part 1, class and ethnic conflicts: conflict studies in the
      sociology of knowledge (Gelfand); ethnic stratification (Noel); caste as
      social process (Berreman); theories of revolution and race relations
      (Kuper); and class struggle (DuBois). Part 2, hostility, tensions, and
      ethnic relations: covert hostility and displaced aggression (Johnson);
      twentieth-century black violence (Meir and Rudwick); the southern
      student sit-ins (Oppenheimer); the 1967 Chinese-Malay riots in Penang,
      Malaysia (Snider); and blacks and Pakistanis in Britain (White). Part 3,
      conflicts, boundary maintenance, and cohesion: American nativism from
      1905 to 1915 (Higham); Jewish communality and identity (Friedmann);
      Jews in Poland compared with the Chinese in the Philippines (Eitzen);
      the Burakumin in Japan (Donoghue); Asians against Africans in Kenya
      (Morris); Israeli Black Panthers (Elon); and conflict and stratification in
      Haiti (Fleurant). Part 4, the shape of intergroup conflict: South Africa
      (van den Berghe); Mormons vs. gentiles (MacMurray and Cunningham);
      blacks vs. Jews in New York City (Gans); the sociology of confrontation
      (van der Kroef); and an articulation of the internal colony model (Casa-
      nova). Part 5, conflicts and alliances: political strategies adopted by
      minorities, including black mass politics (Hill); black power as a rhetorical
      focus (Conant); racial integration (Gelfand); and protest as a political
      resource (Lipsky). Part 6, conflict and social change: identification
      of vulnerable points in systems of domination in constructing strategies
      for change (Miller); New York's Puerto Rican barrio as an internal colony
      (Maldonado-Denis); Mexican Americans as an internal colony (Moore);
      Watts after the 1965 riots (Boskin); politics of dissent as a means of
      winning minority rights (Piven and Cloward); conflict between American
      Indians and the federal government (Deloria); Québécois nationalism

(Corbett); and tradition and change in American Chinatowns (Lee).

1a/2b,c/3a,b/4a,d,f,h/5a,b,c,e,f,i,j/8a/9a,b,c,e
10a,b,c,d/11a,d/12a,b,c,h   General

113   GHAI, Dharam P., ed. 1965. *Portrait of a Minority: Asians in East Africa.* London: Oxford University Press. These symposium papers include a comparative history of Asians in Kenya and Tanzania (Singh); a survey of social features of the Asian community, including persistence and change in caste systems, ethnic subcommunities, cleavages, religious community movements, and cultural conservatism (Bharati); analysis of politics among East African Asians (Tandon); an economic survey noting employment patterns, income distributions, and sectoral concentrations of Asian economic activities (Ghai); a summary of patterns in education (Rattansi and Abdullah); and a brief analysis of future prospects for Asians in East Africa.

1a/2b,c,d/3a,b,d/4f,h/5f/6b/8a,b,d/9a,b,c,d,e
10a,b/12a,b,c,d,f,g,i/13a,b/15   East Africa

114   GILES, Howard, ed. 1977. *Language, Ethnicity and Intergroup Relations.* London: Academic Press. Bibliogs., indexes. Collected papers, beginning with an introductory essay by the editor, followed by: a study of language and ethnicity from a phenomenological perspective with emphasis on language as a symbol embodying perceived birthright and as a medium for dynamically expressing identity (Fishman); the symbolic role of language in the context of Anglo-Chicano social relations (Ryan and Corranza); an analysis of persuasiveness that shows that use of an outgroup language by ingroup members can be more influential than use of the ingroup language (Cooper, Fishman, Lown, Schaier, and Seckbach); a survey of Québécois students showing that acquisition of an outgroup language can detract from feelings of ingroup solidarity (Taylor, Meynard, and Rheault); a report of an experiment that shows that when their identity was threatened, Welsh subjects either increased or decreased the Welshness of their speech depending on their valuation of group membership and Welsh culture (Bourhis and Giles); a study of responses to ethnic humor showing that language-related humor impinges on identity feelings among young children (Chapman, Smith, and Foot); a study of Albanian immigrants to Greece showing the maintenance of ingroup solidarity but lessening significance of language in identity maintenance (Trudgill and Tzavaras); a study of vernacular channeling in Nairobi where adolescents are progressively polarized into class-distinguished English and Swahili speakers (Parkin); a survey of British newspaper headlines correlating descriptive (often subtly pejorative) labels with politics and prejudice (Husband); a short discussion of educational policies affecting language

use by migrant workers in Europe (Verdoodt); analysis of the use of bilingual education in the United States to encourage ultimate assimilation (Edwards); an account of Québécois imposition of French on the Greek community in Montreal and Greek reactions (Smith, Tucker, and Taylor); and a synthetic theory of language in intergroup relations emphasizing social categorization, psychological distinctiveness, identity positiveness, language use as expressive of evaluation, and structural variables of intergroup contact. Although the authors come from several different fields, their orientation is social-psychological, as they are all concerned with personal identity, its maintenance and expression in social contexts.

1a/2b,d/3a/4e,g,h/5d,f/9b,c,e/11b,c,d
12a,b,e/13a,b/16a,b   General

115   GIST, Noel P. 1972. "The Anglo-Indians of India." In *The Blending of Races,* edited by N. Gist and A.G. Dworkin, pp. 39-59. New York: John Wiley & Sons. Bibliog.   Anglo-Indians comprise a marginal minority throughout South Asia, both socially and culturally. Gist describes the circumstances under which this marginality developed, especially the preferential treatment given the "racially linked" Anglo-Indians after the Sepoy Mutiny in 1857. The special status enjoyed by Anglo-Indians, along with protection and preferential employment, were lost at independence following World War II. Gist documents adjustments to changing postindependence circumstances, including loss of employment security; growth of self awareness and ethnic organization; attempts at social mobility; educational change; and emigration. He includes survey data on stereotypes of Anglo-Indians among Indian students and on Anglo-Indian self images. This chapter is a lucid discussion of redefinition of identity in adaptation to altered circumstances.

2c,d/3a/4h/5d,g/6a,b,c/8b/9b,c,e/10b,d
11a,c/12a,b,d/13a,b/15   India

116   GIST, Noel P. and Anthony Gary Dworkin, eds. 1972. *The Blending of Races: Marginality and Identity in World Perspective.* New York: John Wiley & Sons. Bibliogs., index.   These symposium papers concern mixed-race peoples and their relations with the dominant societies of which they are parts. In an introductory chapter the editors review theories of marginality from Simmel to Park and onward. Marginality is presented as a social-psychological-cultural condition, an essential part of some social structures. In their paradigm for studies of marginal peoples, Gist and Dworkin isolate three dimensions: cultural, social, and political (legal). Values along these dimensions are listed for twelve marginal peoples. In addition to the introduction, there are chapters on "coloured" people in Durban, South Africa (Dickie-Clark); Anglo-Indians in India (Gist); Burghers in Ceylon (Fernando); Eurasians in Hawaii (Wittermans);

"coloureds" in Guyana (Gouveia); part-aborigines in Australia (Watts); Métis in northern Canada (Slobodin); Chicanos in Los Angeles (Dworkin); American Indian mestizos (Berry); mixed marriages in Hawaii (Hormann); mixed-race peoples in Brazil (Pierson); and race mixture in Tristan da Cunha (Munch).

	Australia	South Africa
	Brazil	Sri Lanka
	Guyana	Tristan da Cunha
1a/2b/3a/4a,h/5d,f,k/6a,b,c	India	US: Mestizos
8b/9a,d,e/10b,c,d		Mexican Amer-
11a,c/12a,b,c,f/13a		icans

117   GITTLER, Joseph N., ed. 1977. "Ethnic Minorities in the United States: Perspectives from the Social Sciences." *International Journal of Group Tensions,* vol. 7, nos. 3 and 4. Bibliogs.   This special-topic journal issue begins with a definitional essay stressing common values and symbols as diacritical characteristics for ethnic groups (Gittler). Subsequent articles include: a psychological study comparing personal adaptation, measured by life-satisfaction and mental health, between members of Euro-American immigrant groups (Cohler and Lieberman); a discussion of changing educational and occupational demography for Euro-American groups (Greeley); a summary of the experience of American law and justice by Afro-Americans (Parker); and summary articles on the contributions to studies of American minorities in different academic disciplines—political science (Cooley), economics (Deyrup), anthropology (Macklin), and sociology (Steinberg).

1a/2a,b,c,d/3a,b,c/4a,b,f,g,h,i (Law)/5a,d,f,g
6a/8b/9e/11a/12a,b,c/13a/14c/16a   US: General

118   GLAZER, Nathan. 1971. "Blacks and Ethnic Groups: The Difference and the Political Difference It Makes." *Social Problems* 18:444-61. Bibliog.   Glazer dwells on the problematic character of ethnic labels. He argues that although they persist, such labels change in meaning and importance and occasionally disappear entirely. In the more usual case, assimilation takes place, a process through which the stigmatized conditions attached to the labels are dropped. Glazer examines Blauner's distinction between blacks and "white" ethnic groups. He finds high residential segregation between some nonracial groups, and finds also that the position of blacks in northern cities is comparable to that of European immigrants when duration of residence is taken into account. He concludes that there are no inherent differences between racial and ethnic groups.

2e/3b/4h/5a/7b/9c,e/10b,c/11a,c/12a,c,f/13a   US: General

119   GLAZER, Nathan and Daniel Patrick Moynihan. 1970. *Beyond the Melting Pot.* 2d ed. Cambridge, Mass.: MIT Press. Index. This study compares the positions of major ethnic groups in New York City: blacks, Puerto Ricans, Jews, Italians, and Irish. Blacks are described in terms of their numbers, jobs, education, characteristic family organization, housing, and political orientations. The authors emphasize contrasts between blacks and the European groups. Puerto Ricans are described in terms of their migration, relations with Puerto Rico, income, childhood experience, and culture. Jews are described through reference to their occupations, community economic base, education and values associated with it, neighborhoods and integration, culture, and possible futures for the Jewish community. Elements of Italian life described include the community structure, family influences, religion, Democratic party politics, Catholicism, occupations, and local neighborhoods. Irish are described in terms of their migration, Democratic party politics, Catholicism, images associated with them, assimilation, the decline of their political power, and the future prospects for New York as a result of these changes. The importance of ethnicity in New York events is supported with qualitative and quantitative data. The authors speculate about the future of New York City politics given anticipated changes in the ethnic composition of the city and changes in interethnic relations between the constituent groups. Tabular data on country of origin, population, and group-specific occupation data are appended.

	US: Afro-Americans	Jews
2b/3a/4h/5a,b,g/6a,b,c/7b/8a,b	Irish	Puerto Ricans
9b,c/10d,e,f/13a,b/14a/15/17	Italians	

120   GLAZER, Nathan and Daniel Patrick Moynihan, eds. 1975. *Ethnicity: Theory and Experience.* Cambridge, Mass.: Harvard University Press. Index. These theoretical and empirical papers are oriented toward comparative ethnic studies. In an introductory chapter the editors point out the recent political salience of ethnicity in the United States, and they argue that a new theoretical framework is needed to understand it. Theoretical chapters concern: basic group identities (Isaac); some general comments on changes in the meaning of ethnicity in the United States (Parsons); elements toward a general theory of racial and ethnic group relations (Gordon); structures of ethnic identity, boundaries, and identity change (Horowitz); and ethnicity and social change (Bell). Empirical studies concern: subnations in western Europe (Peterson); comparison of Irish-American and Italian-American behavior patterns (Greeley and McCready); American politics and neoethnicity among blacks (Kilson); Canadian ethnic pluralism (Porter); a choice model for ethnic allegiance in the Caribbean (Patterson); Peruvian ethnic stratification (Bouricaud); communal conflict in southeast Asia (Esman); military and ethnic stratification in Uganda (Mazrui); nationality problems in the USSR (Pipes);

ethnicity and language demands in India (Das Gupta); and national security and policies toward minorities in China (Pye). The papers are fairly general and represent the standard analyses for the various areas they cover, but the collection does serve well as an introduction to the field.

1a,b/2c/3b,e/4f,g,h/5a,c,d,f/8c,d/9b,c,d,e   Theory
10a,b,c,d,e,f/11b,c,d/12b,c,e,f/16a   General

121   GOLDHAGEN, Erich, ed. 1968. *Ethnic Minorities in the Soviet Union.* New York: Praeger. Most articles in this collection on USSR minority nationalities emphasize the relations of minorities to the state. Topics include: Jewish geographical distributions, occupations, Armenians, Ukrainian urbanization, language distributions, and measures of social mobilization of different minorities (Armstrong); economic relations between the Soviet republics, with quantitative data supporting a picture of Russian imperialism and the maintenance of colonial relations of exploitation between metropolitan Russia and the other republics (Holubnychy); language policies and their goals (Ornstein); movements for Ukrainian assimilation and countermovements for Ukrainian nationalism (Bilisky); changes in Armenian cultural patterns with special attention to family patterns, religion, language, and housing (Matossian); nationalism in the Baltic republics (Pennar); demographic and cultural trends among Turkic peoples (Vakar); Soviet publications in Yiddish (Brumberg and Brumberg); and the legal position of Jews in the USSR (Korey). Although these analyses are somewhat dated they reflect concerns repeatedly treated in the more recent literature on Soviet minority nationalities. Most are quite detailed.

1a/2c/3b/4f,h/5a,d,e,i,j/6a,b,c/7c,d/8b,c/9c,d,e
10a,e/11d/12b,c,e,g/13a,b/14a,b/15/16a,b   USSR: General

122   GOMEZ, Rudolph, Clements Cottingham, Jr., Russell Endo, and Kathleen Jackson, eds. 1974. *The Social Reality of Ethnic America.* Lexington, Mass.: D.C. Heath. Notes, bibliogs. This collection is divided into sections on Afro-Americans, American Indians, Japanese Americans, and Mexican Americans. The first section, Afro-Americans: political activities, with specific attention to historical changes in black political patterns, 1900-40 (Kilson); the implications of minority psychology for social action (Poussaint); a critical evaluation of coalition politics as a vehicle for black aspirations (Carmichael and Hamilton); efforts to cultivate black ethnicity as a political vehicle (Kilson): and a survey of blacks elected to city councils (Kramer). The second section, American Indians: federal encroachment on water rights and consequent impairment of reservation development (Veeder); a brief account of the Pacific Northwest fishing rights dispute (American Friends Service Committee); and

a description of rising Indian political activism (Deloria). The third section, Japanese Americans: four papers describing and analyzing immigrant experience and the World War II internment; employment and education (Peterson); community structure, religion, and voluntary associations (Kitano); and Japanese ethnic enterprise (Light). Articles on Mexican Americans document discrimination (Glick) and describe an "internal colony" model of American society (Moore). Most of these chapters are excerpts or abridgements of already published works.

US: Afro-Americans
Japanese Americans
1a/2c/3a,b/4f,g,h/5b,g,i,j/9b,c,e   Mexican Americans
10a,b,c,d,e,f/11a,c/15   Native Americans

123   GORDON, David M., ed. 1977. *Problems in Political Economy: An Urban Perspective*. 2d ed. Lexington, Mass.: D.C. Heath. Notes, Bibliogs. Those selections concerning race, discrimination, segregation, education, and so forth, reflect on ethnicity. Of particular interest are short explanations of dual labor-market theory (Piore); a theory of labor market segmentation (Reich, Gordon, and Edwards); a summary of the economic situation of American blacks (Jhabvala); analytical papers on discrimination and the free market (Friedman); a liberal explanation of relations between racism and capitalism (Bergmann); a comparison of economic theories of racism (Cherry); a radical model of racism under capitalism (Reich); an empirical examination of labor-market segregation by race (Baron and Hymer); and a critique of gradualist solutions to discrimination (Jhabvala).

1a/2c/3b/4b/5b,i,j/8a,b,d/9b/10b,c/11d   Theory

124   GORDON, Milton M. 1964. *Assimilation in American Life: The Role of Race, Religion, and National Origin*. New York: Oxford University Press. In this study of assimilation as a process of intergroup relations, Gordon discusses definitions of ethnic groups in the United States, along with concepts of subsociety and subculture. He categorizes social-science definitions of assimilation into Anglo-conformity, melting pot, and pluralist variants. Conditions of structural pluralism, ideological orientations, and psychological conditions are the primary variables in his popular, but vaguely articulated model. Using his framework, Gordon briefly analyzes blacks, Jews, Catholics, and white Protestants as American ethnic groups. He assesses the implications of the pluralist perspective for government policy options.

2d,e/3e/4h/5a,f/7b/11a   US: General

125   GOSSETT, Thomas F. 1963. *Race: The History of an Idea in America.*

Dallas: Southern Methodist University Press. Bibliog. Gossett presents a detailed history of the idea of "race" in the United States. Drawing the strains of American race theories from their European origins, Gossett traces their growth and development through eighteenth- and nineteenth-century anthropology, the rise of Social Darwinism, and more recent dominant social theories. He places the development of race ideologies in historical context, showing how social and political movements produced changes in popular ideologies. Among the movements he considers are the eighteenth-century social gospel; manifest destiny; frontier expansion; confrontation with American Indians; reconstruction and change in the status of American blacks; nativism and anti-immigration agitation; Anglo-Saxon imperialism around the turn of the century; and recrudescent Nazi racist doctrine. He shows the evolution of current thought on "race" lucidly and simply.

2e/3c/4d/5k/10b,c/11a,b,c,d/12f   US: General

126 GREBLER, Leo, Joan W. Moore, and Ralph C. Guzman. 1970. *The Mexican-American People: The Nation's Largest Minority.* New York: Free Press. Notes, apps., bibliog., index.   This report of a five-year-long (1963-68) study of Mexican Americans in five southwest states includes a comprehensive description of their history in the United States, socioeconomic conditions, attitudes, political behavior, social institutions, and so forth. The book has been criticized as uncritical of oppression, and nonanalytical in general, but it provides by far the most comprehensive available picture of Mexican Americans in the United States.

2b,d/3a/4c,d,e,f/5a,d,f,i
6a,b,c/7a,b,c,d/8a,b,d/9b,c,e
10a,b,c,d,e,f/11a,b,c,d/12a,b,e,g
13a,b/14a,b,c/15/16a/17   US: Mexican Americans

127 GREELEY, Andrew M. 1974. *Ethnicity in the United States: A Preliminary Reconnaissance.* New York: Wiley. Bibliogs.   This is a preliminary summary analysis of National Opinion Research Center Survey data on ethnicity among European immigrant groups. Basic data compilations include breakdowns of religio-ethnic composition and distribution of the United States population (by region, urban area, education level, occupation, income, etc.) and educational and economic differences between the major religio-ethnic groups. A number of questions are tested using these data: the adequacy of cultural heritage as a predictor of attitudes and behavior (here cultural heritage is used as a proxy for ethnicity, controlling for religion); ethnicity vs. religion as explanatory factors for observed behavior patterns; comparison of patterns of ethnic political participation; persistent ethnic variation in patterns of family composition (McCready);

ethnic origins of American scientists and engineers; political attitudes among ethnic groups (Nee, Curry, and McCready); comparison of Jewish and Polish reactions to urban unrest; ethnic segmentation within the white Anglo-Saxon Protestant category (differences by denomination); the white ethnic political movement; discussion of different perspectives for studying American ethnicity; and a summary conclusion of findings. The perspective taken here is largely social psychological. Differences are measured on attitude scales.

2d/3b,c/4h/5a,d,f/6a,b/8a,b/9e
11a,b,c/12c,d,g/13a,b/14a   US: Euro-Americans

128 GREELEY, Andrew M. and William C. McCready. 1974. "Does Ethnicity Matter?" *Ethnicity* 1:73-89. Bibliog. In this article the authors compare character and behavior traits of Irish and Italian immigrants to the United States with profiles of home-country Irish and Italians taken from the anthropological and sociological literature to see whether cultural and personality themes are maintained in immigrants over several generations. Predicted differences between Irish and Italians were generally confirmed, but not necessarily in the expected directions on all dimensions.

                                                                          US: Irish
2d/3c/4h/5d/11a,b/12c/14a   Italians

129 GRIGULEVICH, I. R. and S. Y. Doslov, eds. 1974. *Races and Peoples: Contemporary Ethnic and Racial Problems.* Moscow: Progress Publishers. The selections in this volume were taken from Soviet ethnographic journals, the yearbook *Rasi i narody* (Races and peoples), and (in a few cases) were commissioned for this particular book. Theoretical problems treated include the definition and use of the term *ethnos* in Soviet social science (Bromley); the distinction between human races and populations (Cheboksarov); and the geographical distribution of genes responsible for racial discrimination and modes of race formation (Alexeyev). Chapters covering the USSR treat the history of Soviet nationalities policies (Kamanev); national processes (ethnic and socioeconomic transformations) in the USSR (Bromley and Kozlov); and the development of national culture in the USSR (Arutunyan). Elements considered for foreign countries include nationalist movements within developed capitalist countries (Kolpakov and Soroko-Tsyupa); national processes in other Asian countries (Bruk, Cheboksarov, and Chesnov); ethnicity in modern Africa (Ismagilova); and ethnicity in Oceania (Puchkov). Articles on racism consider racialism as an imperialist ideology (Fedoseyev); legislation against racial discrimination (Shebanov); anthropological theory and racism (Averkiyeva); and South African revolutionism (Butlitsky).

1a/2c,e/3b,e/4a,h,i/5b,e,g,i/8c/10a,b,c
11a,b,c/12a,c,f/13b/14c/16a   General

130 GROVE, D. John. 1974. *The Race vs. Ethnic Debate: A Cross-National Analysis of Two Theoretical Approaches.* Center on International Race Relations, Graduate School of International Studies, University of Colorado, Studies in Race and Nations, vol. 5, no. 4. Grove groups race and ethnic relations theories into five categories: assimilation; plural society; power-conflict; stratification; and Marxian. He emphasizes the distinction between ethnic and racial differentiation, arguing that racial distinctions are inherently invidious, whereas ethnic ones need not be. His tests show that the political consequences of ethnic and racial pluralism are different. He concludes that racial distinctions are the most basic dimension of stratification and exploitation, followed by the division of labor, followed finally by ethnic distinctions. According to Grove, these conclusions support the Marxian theory of ethnic and racial relations.

2c,d/3d/4h/5a,b,f,i,j/8b/9c/10b,c   Theory

131 GROVE, D. John, ed. 1979. *Global Inequality: Political and Socio-economic Perspectives.* Boulder, Colo.: Westview Press. Bibliogs. Several papers in this conference collection concern resource distribution along ethnic or racial lines: the dominant neoclassical approach in economics to American class and race stratification and recent political-economy approaches challenging it are characterized (Tabb); empirical tests include a cross-national study purporting to show that bureaucratic states tend to increase ethnic and racial equality as measured by income, employment status, education, political representation, and so forth (Grove); a cross-cultural survey of ethnic inequality (Singh); a survey explaining income and education differentials in Third World countries by spatial distortion of population and consequent unequal access to education (van der Mehden), and subregional inequality and Welsh nationalism (Corrado and Rockman).

1a/2b,c,d,e/3b,d/4b,h/5i/6b,c/8a,b/9b,c,e/10d/13a   General

132 GUILLAUMIN, Collette. 1971. "The Popular Press and Ethnic Pluralism: The Situation in France." *International Social Science Journal* 23:576-93. Guillaumin shows both the existence of marked and unmarked ethnic categories in French mass media and their ideological uses. The treatment of majority and minority members is notably different, although the differences are not immediately apparent. The discussion sensitizes readers to invidious press practices.

2d/3b/4h/5g/9c/11a,c/12c/16b   France

133 GUMPERZ, John J. 1962. "Types of Linguistic Communities." *Anthropological Linguistics* 4:28-40. Bibliog. Gumperz relates degrees of intralanguage variation to relative complexities of social organization in different societies. Different elements of linguistic usage (e.g., bi-

lingualism, loyalty to primary language, and so forth) are correlated with communication requirements (e.g., trade, ritual, administration, and so forth). These requirements inhere in social structures, according to Gumperz, much in the same way that specialized argots (occupational, religious, administrative) develop with reference to specific social settings. The basic point of his argument is that linguistic distinctions are functional as well as symbolic.

2f/3e/4e/5k/12d,e,i/16a   Theory

134   GUTKIND, P. C. W., ed. 1970. *The Passing of Tribal Man in Africa.* Leiden: E.J. Brill. Bibliog., index.   The papers in this collection concern the concept, application, and theory of tribes and tribalism in Africa. A variety of viewpoints are represented, from those who accept the social reality of tribes in modern Africa to those who do not accept that they ever did exist. The latter view sees tribalism as incipient nationalism.

1a/2b,c/3d/4a,f/5d,e/9c,e/10a,b,c,d/11a,d/12a,b,c,i   Africa

135   HAALAND, Gunnar. 1969. "Economic Determinants in Ethnic Processes." In *Ethnic Groups and Boundaries,* edited by F. Barth, pp. 58-73. Boston: Little, Brown.   Haaland describes the interaction between Fur (millet cultivators) and Baggara (nomadic pastoralists) in the western Sudan. He argues that interactions between members of these contiguous groups are predicated on complementary goods and services brought to economic transactions. Identity change from Fur to Baggara is analyzed in terms of social adaptations necessary for a subsistence pattern that demands maximization of capital in cattle, a feature very different from the Fur pattern. Ambiguities in identity definitions are analyzed through the question of when a Fur becomes a Baggara. The behavioral expectations of participants in social situations are the final criteria of ethnic identity, according to Haaland. A Fur has become a Baggara when members of both groups expect that individual to act like a Baggara. Haaland concludes that behavioral expectations do not necessarily correlate with cultural differences (e.g., language) but that they do closely relate to economic and ecological circumstances.

2b/3a/4a/5c/6b/8b,d/9c,e/11a,b,c/12c,i/14a,b,c   Sudan

136   HACKENBERG, Robert A. 1967. "The Parameters of an Ethnic Group: A Method for Studying the Total Tribe." *American Anthropologist* 69:478-92. Bibliog. Hackenberg describes a method for obtaining, classifying, retrieving, and utilizing base-line data on all individuals in a society. He thereby avoids sampling problems entirely. Of interest to ethnicity studies is his use of language, social groupings, and cultural traits as potentially distinctive criteria for group membership. Using

these, he argues, one can discern accurately the substance and boundaries of an ethnic group. The assumptions underlying his method, the techniques he employs, and his results are illustrated through application to Papago Indians.

2d/3a/4a/5d/6a,b/12a,c,e,h   US: Native Americans

137   HANDLIN, Oscar. 1972. *Boston's Immigrants: A Study in Accultura-tion*. Rev. ed. New York: Atheneum. Notes, app., bibliog., index.   This history of Boston during the period of rapid immigration (1790-1880) describes the changing social milieu of the city; the process of immigrant arrival; their economic and physical adjustments; ideological conflicts between native Bostonians and (largely Irish) immigrants; the growth of communal consciousness; intergroup conflicts; and the appearance of stability in the post-Civil War years. The last period was characterized by transition of political leadership from the old elite to immigrant-descended members of the middle class.

2c/3a/4d/5a,b/6a/7b/8b/9b,e/10a,b,d,e,f/11a   US: Euro-Americans

138   HAUGEN, Einar. 1972. *Ecology of Language*. Stanford, Calif.: Stanford University Press. Bibliog.   Useful papers in this retrospective collection of Haugen's work (1938-72) include studies of bilingualism in Norway; language planning and national identity in modern Norway; mutual intelligibility and language gaps in Scandinavia; relations between language, dialects, and national boundaries; disabilities of bilinguals; and theoretical discussion of the ecology of language.

2b/3e/4g/5e/11d/12e/16a   Norway

139   HECHTER, Michael. 1971. "Towards a Theory of Ethnic Change." *Politics & Society* 2:21-45.   Hechter considers procedures of theory building and sets out requirements for an adequate theory of ethnic change. He first considers national integration, dividing it into cultural, structural, and political factors. Comparing social, cultural, and internal colony theories of integration, he constructs a perspective emphasizing cultural and social consequences of power differentials.

2f/3e/4h/5b,f,i,j/9b,c,e/10a,b,c/11d/12b,e   Theory

140   HECHTER, Michael. 1974. "The Political Economy of Ethnic Change." *American Journal of Sociology* 79:1151-78. Bibliog.   Using examinations of British voting records, Hechter compares the adequacy of "functional-ist" and "reactive" theories of ethnic solidarity in predicting political behavior. The reactive model predicts that where cultural division of labor persists in industrial society, ethnic solidarity will also persist. Func-

tionalist theory predicts that ethnic solidarity should decrease with industrialization. Hechter concludes that the reactive model provides better predictions of voting patterns in Celtic fringe areas of Britain over the period from 1855 to 1966.

2c/3b/5i,j/7c,d/8b,c/9b,e/10a,c,d,e/12e,i   Britain: General

141   HECHTER, Michael. 1975. *Internal Colonialism: The Celtic Fringe in British National Development, 1536-1966.* Berkeley and Los Angeles: University of California Press. Notes, index.   Working from a theory of ethnic change that emphasizes core-periphery differences in national development as generative of ethnic boundaries, Hechter traces the expansion of the British state to include the Celtic fringe. He notes the governmental insistence on English cultural superiority and traces the development of economic specialization in peripheral areas. The political and cultural consequences of incorporation of peripheral areas into the English polity were subordination and dependency, prime characteristics of a colony. This process is also described during the period of industrialization. The relative maintenance of cultural differences in peripheral areas is examined, as are regional voting patterns and resurgent nationalist movements in Celtic regions. The theoretical chapters in this book were previously published as journal articles.

2c/3b/4h/5j/8c,d/9b,c,e/10a,b,c,d,e,f   Britain   Scotland
11d/12e,g/13b/16a/17   Ireland   Wales

142   HECHTER, Michael. 1976. "Ethnicity and Industrialization: On the Proliferation of the Cultural Division of Labor." *Ethnicity* 3:214-24. Bibliog.   Hechter argues against structural-functional analyses that purport to show that with industrialization and increasing social differentiation, social attachments and foci of group formation will move from particularistic to universalistic grounds. He argues that industrialization may produce culturally marked social strata, a complex he calls a "cultural division of labor." Working from center-periphery economic systems models, he argues that where there is occupational specialization in urban areas (the metropolitan core) there is a corresponding drop in lower-class wage rates in peripheral areas. This is the social analogue of the economic monopolist, with different segments of the population marked by cultural distinctions monopolizing different occupational segments, thus partially negating the effects of labor competition.

2c/3e/4h/5b,i,j/7c/8b,c,d/9b,c/10a,c   Theory

143   HECHTER, Michael. 1978. "Group Formation and the Cultural Division of Labor." *American Journal of Sociology* 84:293-318. Bibliog.   In this paper Hechter distinguishes between determinants affecting class and

status group solidarity. After an initial discussion of group formation in general, he uses United States census samples to test relations between occupational specialization of ethnic groups, their positions in the U.S. system of social stratification (using mean occupational prestige as a proxy), and group solidarity (measured by relative group endogamy). The first two variables are predicted to determine the third and the prediction is generally confirmed. Comparative measures of class vs. ethnic endogamy indicate these identities are competitive, with strength of class endogamy inversely related to ethnic endogamy. Examination of Australian voting data supports the argument that ethnic stratification and ethnic occupational specialization will be negatively correlated with conscious class formation. In all these arguments the central concept is the cultural division of labor, the distribution of culturally marked groups differentially through the occupational structure. Hechter notes the limitations of his data and the predictive limits of the model.

Australia
2c,e/3c,d,e/4h/5j/8b/9b,c/11c/14c   US: General

144   HECHTER, Michael and Margaret Levi. 1979. "The Comparative Analysis of Ethnoregional Movements." *Ethnic and Racial Studies* 2:260-74. Surveying ethnoregional movements in Western Europe, the authors suggest preliminary answers to questions of what social bases underlie such movements; how their varying intensity in different countries can be explained; and what accounts for the timing of ethnoregional political mobilization. They argue that the answer to the first question will be found in hierarchical and segmental relations in peripheral regions. Hierarchical relations are often found in regions that have developed as internal colonies. Segmental relations, in which groups in the periphery develop monopolistic control over economic and occupational niches, often produce interactive groups, in which nearly all social transactions are contained within the bounded group. The second question finds answer in the internal organizational capacity of groups. This is affected by what tolerance central states have for cultural and political diversity, the completeness of culturally distinct institutions, and the group's historical success in producing rewards and benefits for its members. Timing of movements is explained by changing state policies and alterations in the world system that change the resources available to the elite.

2c,e/3e/4h/5j/8b,c/9b,e/10a,b,c,d/12c,d   Theory

145   HEISLER, Martin O., ed. 1977. *Ethnic Conflict in the World Today.* Annals of the American Academy of Political and Social Science, no. 433. Topics covered include: cultural movements and ethnic change (Horowitz); description of ethnic conflict in Quebec (McRoberts); in Belgium (Heisler); in Northern Ireland (Terchek); in the USSR (Rakowska-

Harmstone); in Yugoslavia (Bertsch); and in China (Dreyer). Additional articles compare separatism in the American south and Quebec (Levine); discuss ethnicity, regionalism, and development politics in South Asia (Das Gupta); analyze the role of police and militaries in ethnic conflict (Enloe); comparatively survey cases of ethnic violence (Hewitt); and compare policies toward Kurds in several central Asian countries (Harris).

2b,c/3b/4d,f/5b/9a,c/10a,b,c,d,f,g/16a/17   General

146   HENRY, Francis, ed. 1976. *Ethnicity in the Americas.* The Hague: Mouton. Comments, bibliogs.   These ethnology conference papers on ethnicity in the New World are collected into sections on Canada, the Caribbean and Latin America, and the United States. An introductory essay defines ethnicity as a cultural system oriented around an ideology of disengagement and value differentiation from the dominant culture (Aronson). Canadian topics include: ethnic policies (Burnet); urban ethnicity in Toronto (Richmond); black consciousness in Nova Scotia (Clairmont and Magill); an ethnoreligious group (Dunn); and Chinese in Canada (Chow). Caribbean and Latin American topics are: Jews in Latin America (Hotzberg); Bermuda ethnic politics (Ryan); Guyanese ethnic politics (Silverman); Indian ethnic fiestas in Colombia (Friedmann); immigrant adjustment in Jamaica (Taylor); Rastafarian attitudes toward race in Jamaica (Yawney); and the social history of the Rastafarian movement (Chivannes). The section on the United States includes West Indian radicalism in the United States (Forsythe); black humanism (Aschenbrenner); black adaptive strategies (Mithun); resurgent American Indian ethnicity (Talbert); and comparison of black and Chicano ethnic linkages.

	Canada	South America
1a/2b/3a,b/4a/5a,b,d,f,g	Caribbean	US: General
10b,d/11d/12b,c,d,f,g		Mesoamerica

147   HERNANDEZ, Carrol A., Marsha J. Haug, and Nathaniel N. Wagner, eds. 1976. *Chicanos: Social and Psychological Studies.* 2d ed. St. Louis: C.V. Mosby. Annotated bibliog.   Introductory sections to this collection include: ethnic pride and socioeconomic prejudice against Chicanos (Casavantes); Mexican-American family patterns (Murillo); militancy and ethnic attitudes in Crystal City, Texas (Gutiérrez and Hirsch); and a "psychological history" of Mexican Americans (Alvarez). Articles on society and justice include: a blatantly racist court record from Santa Clara, Calif. (Judge Gerald S. Chargin); analysis of Chicano-police riots (Morales); reports on the administration of justice in the southwest (U.W. Civil Rights Commission); analysis of the costs of Chicano identity in terms of labor force participation (Poston and Alvarez); and description of prejudice and discrimination against Chicanos (Padilla and Ruiz). Remaining sections in the book emphasize personality studies (social

motives, perceptions of control, stereotypes and self conceptions, psychological research on Chicanos); education (bilingualism and measures of intelligence, cognitive styles and cultural democracy); and mental health (racism in mental health measures, cultural problems in psychotherapy, language and therapy success, bilingualism and perceptions of mental illness, mental health care delivery systems, folk beliefs and mental health, etc.).

1a,b/2b,c/3a/4g,h/5a,b,g/9c,e/10a,c,d/11a,c
12b,c,d,e,f/13a,b/14a/16a   US: Mexican Americans

148   HICKS, George L. and David I. Kertzer. 1972. "Making a Middle Way: Problems of Monhegan Identity." *Southwestern Journal of Anthropology* 28:1-24. Bibliog. This article analyzes the reassertion of Monhegan (Native American) identity subsequent to the redefinition of American Indian legal status in the 1930s. The authors describe strategic projections of identity in situations where it is preferable to avoid the stigma of inclusion in the general category of "blacks." At other times, Monhegans assert white identity. According to the authors, tribe, church, and pow wow (annual meeting) are three separate factors in group organization and identification. Ceremonies are used to attract public attention. Cultural symbols are manipulated openly according to situational perceptions.

2b/3a/5d,h/6a,b/8b/9c,e/10b,d/12a,b,c/13a,b   US: Native Americans

149   HICKS, George L. and Philip E. Leis, eds. 1977. *Ethnic Encounters: Identities and Contexts.* North Scituate, Mass.: Duxbury Press. Notes, bibliog., index. The papers in this collection are organized into an introduction, discussions of identity and ethnicity, and analysis of ethnicity and social life. The introduction summarizes and evaluates the ethnicity literature (Hicks). Papers on identity and ethnicity analyze political motives in organization of Haitian ethnic organizations in the United States (Schiller); East Indian adaptation on St. Vincent (Stone); language use and ethnic difference in the Cape Verde Islands (Machado); and similarities in adaptive strategies adopted by Catawba and Monhegan Indians in the United States (Hicks). In the second section, community studies include description of the insular Japanese community in Bolivia (Thompson); conflicting interpretations of roles for American technicians on Ecuador sugar plantations (Lang); ethnic encounters between Yankees, Portuguese, and Italians in a New England town (Swiderski); and ethnic segmentation on St. Barthélemy in the Caribbean (Morrill). On leaders and mediators, an analysis of brokerage roles in a New England Portuguese community (Trueblood); of entrepreneurship among Portuguese immigrants in a Canadian city (Brettell); and general discussion of brokerage in the social ecology of minority groups (De'Ath and Padbury). The final section, on contexts of inequality, includes studies of caste and ethnicity

in West Bengal as flexible adaptation to economic development (Fried-lander); north-south distinctions in Italy and the organization of a Com-munist quarter in Bologna (Kertzer); and analysis of Portuguese and Italian roles in planning a parade in a New England town (Leis).

1a/2b,c,e,f/3a,b,e/4a/5a,b,c,d,g,h,i,j/7b/8b
9a,b,c,e/10a,e,f/12b,e/14c/16a/17   General

150 HOETINK, Hermannus. 1967. *The Two Variants in Caribbean Race Relations.* London: Oxford University Press. Bibliog. Hoetink discusses at length two patterns of race relations, "Iberian" and "Northwest Euro-pean." These are supposed to have been produced by different cultural inputs during the period of European domination in Latin America. He discusses the social structures that rose from colonial influences, especially cultural integration and racial stratification in newly indepen-dent states. The different social and cultural forms resulting from the differences in Iberian and northwest European colonial systems produce different prognoses for national integration in the areas governed by the two variants.

2c/3d/4a/5f,i/9c/11a,b,c/12f/16a   Caribbean

151 HOETINK, Hermannus. 1972. "National Identity, Culture, and Race in the Caribbean." In *Racial Tensions and National Identity,* edited by E. Campbell, pp. 17-44. Nashville: Vanderbilt University Press. App., bibliog. Hoetink rejects economic imperialism and colonial legacies as sufficient explanations of Caribbean social structures. He uses a plural society model to analyze recent violence in the Caribbean. According to his argument, Africanism, both as an ideological mystique and as a poli-tical movement, promotes vertical solidarity, cohesion of a social segment crossing class lines. Cultural discontinuity is a function of symbolic inter-action in this view. Where social conditions produce vertical segmenta-tion, cultural pluralism will follow. The argument is illustrated by exam-ples from several Caribbean societies.

2c/3b/4a/5f,i/10a,b,c/11d/12a,b,c   Caribbean

152 HOLLOMAN, Regina E. and Serghei A. Arutiunov, eds. 1978. *Perspec-tives on Ethnicity.* The Hague: Mouton. Notes, bibliogs., indexes. This collection is notable for its substantial inclusion of Soviet theoretical and substantive work on ethnicity. Section 1, theoretical issues, includes: an overview essay on studies of ethnicity (Holloman); a characterization of Soviet approaches to ethnicity in ethnographic studies (Arutiunov and Bromley); a theoretical discussion of typologies of ethnic communities (Bromley); and a discussion of psychotopology (Maruyama). Section 2, ethnicity as identity, includes: a discussion of endogenous anthropological

research (Maruyama); an analysis of headhunting as an ethnically defining symbol among the Jivaro (Silverts); analysis of opposition as a component of ethnic self-consciousness (Porshnev); characterization of ethnicity and family in the Soviet Union (Gantskaja and Terenteva); changing family life in rural Byelorussia (Bondarchik and Sobolenko); interethnic families in the middle Volga Republic of the Soviet Union (Busygin and Zorin); analysis of black-white marriage trends in Chicago (Roberts); and examination of changing patterns of ethnic identity and prestige in East Africa (Arens). Section 3, contact, acculturation, and boundary maintenance, includes: studies of region, religion, and language as elements in acculturation of Marathi-speakers in Tamilnadu, India (Apte); ethnically contrasting value orientations in Hungarian peasant communities (Andrasfalvy); a mapping of Nigerian ethnic groups (Gandonu); characterization of the Chinese community in Canada before 1947 and examination of recent changes in it (Chow); study of Tuli-Chinese ethnic boundaries in Yunnan, southwest China (Tweddell); objective definition of Jewish groups (Zenner); policy study of language use in India (Gupta); study of cultural brokers in Chiapas, Mexico (Salovesh); correlation of class and ethnic consciousness among Mapuche Indians in Chile (Berdichewsky); problems of identifying ethnic processes (Kozlov); examination of peculiarities of ethnonational development in postcolonial third world countries (Maretin); contemporary ethnic processes in Siberia (Gurvich); socialism and ethnicity in the USSR (Kulichenko); and the development of interethnic relations in the Ukraine (Naulko).

1a/2b,c/3a,b,e/4a/5c,d,h,k/8c,d/11b,c,d   Theory
12b,c,d,e,f,g,h,i/13b/14a,c/16a/17   General

153   HORAK, Stephen M. 1961. *Poland and Her National Minorities, 1919-1939*. New York: Vantage Press. App., bibliog., index.   In this historical study of Polish state formation and national minorities during the interwar period, Horak presents an analysis of events leading to formation of the Polish state in 1918 and of the subsequent annexation of minority areas. Subsequent chapters detail institutional safeguards for the rights of minorities (e.g., constitutions, treaties, etc.), the demographic structure of Poland, and the struggle of Poles against the national minorities during this period (e.g., pogroms, boycotts, discrimination, etc.).

2c/3b/4d/5b,f,g/6a,b,c/8b/9c,e/10a,b,c,d,e
11a,d/12a,b,c,e,g/13a   Poland

154   HSU, Francis L. K. 1971. *The Challenge of the American Dream: The Chinese in the United States*. Belmont, Calif.: Wadsworth. Bibliog., index.   Hsu describes Chinese-American ways of life in general terms. Elements in his description include language, family and kinship forms, local associations, religion, patterns of friendship and hospitality, ado-

lescence, prejudice, Americanization, and Chinese identity. His theme is that Chinese and American cultures are synthesized in Chinese-American cultural and social patterns.

2b,c/3a/4a/5a/9c,d,e/10a/11a,b/12a,b,c,d,e,g,i
13a,b/14a,b/15/17   US: Chinese

155   HUNT, Chester L. and Lewis Walker. 1974. *Ethnic Dynamics: Patterns of Intergroup Relations in Various Societies.* Homewood, Ill.: Dorsey Press. Bibliog., index.   This textbook presents a variety of case studies of intergroup relations, drawn from Europe, the USSR, Africa, Southeast Asia, the United States, the Middle East, and so on. Themes of the case studies include strategic approaches to eliminating ethnicity (genocide, assimilation, etc.), and to coping with it (various types of pluralism). Chap. 4, on marginal trading peoples, provides an introduction to Indians and Chinese in Africa and the Philippines. The format allows for quick area comparisons.

1b/2c/4h/5a,b,f/8b/9b,c,e/10b,c,d
11d/12b,c,e,f   General

156   HYMES, Dell. 1968. "Linguistic Problems in Defining the Concept of Tribe." In *Essays on the Problem of Tribe,* Proceedings of the 1967 Annual Spring Meeting of the American Ethnological Society, edited by June Helm, pp. 23-48. Seattle: University of Washington Press.   Hymes describes the difficulties of using language as a criterion for mapping cultures. Hymes argues that to do so one must assume (1) ethnological units exist discretely; (2) communication discontinuities match other sociocultural boundaries; (3) language is the only relevant communication medium; and (4) cultural-linguistic boundaries persist in time. Hymes examines these assumptions using case examples and concludes that such boundaries often don't persist in time, that linguistic and culturally defined units often don't coincide, and that linguistic-cultural units are often impossible to delimit in the first place. He presents, in very orderly fashion, a critique of assumptions, theory, and methods used in mapping of cultures using language. Since language is the primary criterion used in "objective" definitions of ethnic groups, Hymes's argument severely injures any such attempt. He includes references to most important papers in the controversy of "objective" vs. "subjective" definitions of ethnic groups.

2f/3e/4e/5d/6b/12a,c,e/16a   Theory

157   ICHIHASHI, Yamato. 1932. *Japanese in the United States.* Stanford, Calif.: Stanford University Press. Bibliog.   This early study of Japanese Americans emphasizes occupations and Japanese legal status in the United States. Statistics on population and occupational distribution are included

with labor participation in the agrarian sector a primary concern. Ichihashi discusses alien land laws, the Exclusion Law, and other discriminatory legislation—the interests underlying it and its effects on the Japanese community.

2b,c/3a/4h/5a,g,i/6a,b,c/7b/8b/9c,e/10b,c,d
11a,d/12a,b   US: Japanese

158   ISAACS, Harold R. 1975. *Idols of the Tribe: Group Identity and Political Change.* New York: Harper & Row. Notes, index.   Isaacs presents an eclectic and impressionistic account of bases for group identity and their impacts in different societies. He argues that the characteristics individuals take as primordial markers of their own identity are those that are elevated to group identity markers. These include body, name, language, history and origins, religion, and nationality. Isaacs illustrates elements of identity through anecdotal cases and references to the academic literature.

2b/3c,d/4h/5d/10b,d/11a,b,c/12a,b,e,f,g/16a/17   General

159   ISAJIW, Wsevolod W. 1974. "Definition of Ethnicity." *Ethnicity* 1:111-24.   Isajiw describes three empirical foci of ethnicity: European, North American, and tribal experiences. He claims that these three foci are different and roughly correspond to ethnicity in terms of nationality, subculture, and discrete cultural units. He compares objective and subjective definitions of ethnicity found in the literature. He lists arguments for and against inclusion of race and religion as elements of ethnicity. He also samples definitions of ethnicity and shows a frequency distribution of attributes used to define ethnicity. Finally he suggests a general definition of ethnicity and definitions specifically applicable to the North American variant.

2e/3e/4h/5k   Theory

160   JOHNSON, Colleen Leahy and Frank Arvid Johnson. 1975. "Interaction Rules and Ethnicity: The Japanese and Caucasians in Honolulu." *Social Forces* 52:542-66. Bibliog.   This article considers cultural factors contributing to ethnic segmentation in Honolulu. It emphasizes sets of interaction rules, with Japanese *enryo* rules ("distance consideration") contrasted with *haole* (Caucasian) familiarity. Instances of intergroup interaction are presented and their effects on attitudes and intergroup relations are discussed.

2b/3a/4a/5c/6a,b/9b,e/11a,b/12b,c,e,f   US: Japanese

161   JONES, James M. 1972. *Prejudice and Racism.* Reading, Mass.: Addison-

Wesley. Bibliog. This introduction to social psychological perspectives on racism and prejudice covers the history of race relations in the United States; perspectives on prejudice (definitions, attitude studies, stereotyping, development of racial attitudes in children, behavioral research, and theories of race prejudice—historical, sociocultural, situational, psychodynamic, phenomenological); studies of racism (definitions, individual, institutional, education, justice, and cultural); and summary conclusions. Emphasis is on invidious cultural differences maintained by discriminatory socioeconomic structures that constrain psychological orientations.

1b/2c/3b/4g/5g/9c,e/11a,b,c/12b,c,f,i/13b/16b   US: General

162   KANG, Tai S., ed. 1976. "Ethnic Relations in Asia." *Journal of Asian Affairs*, vol. 1, no. 2. Bibliogs. Topics treated in this special journal issue include: Shanghai as a haven for Jewish refugees (Kranzler); Chinese-aborigine relations on Taiwan (Nettleship); attitudes of the Japanese Supreme Court toward Koreans in Japan (Suh); relations between Orang Asli (indigenous minorities) and other Malaysians (Raffie'i); the emergency resettlement of Chinese in Malaya (Humphrey); intergroup contact through voluntary associations in Southeast Asia (Pederson); the position of Chinese in the political economy of post-World War II Southeast Asia (Huang); identity problems of former elite minorities (Wright); Indians in Burma (Mahajani); and a discussion of ethnic diversity and its implications for political stability in South Asia (Singh).

1a/2b/3a,b/4d,f/5d,f,i/6a/9b,d/10a,c/15   Asia

163   KAPLAN, H. Roy, ed. 1977. *American Minorities and Economic Opportunity*. Itasca, Ill.: F. E. Peacock. Indexes, bibliogs. The essays in this collection examine the economic positions of American minorities. Most survey the available literature on minority force labor participation and work commitment. None is specifically theoretical. Essays examine: changes in the American economic structure (1900-1970) and the positions of minorities in the work environment (Golden and Tautsky); the economic position of black Americans (Landry); work-related values among Mexican Americans (Benitez); concepts of work and situational demands on New York City Puerto Ricans (Padilla); poverty and work among American Indians (Jorgensen); working women in America (Levine); labor force participation by workers over age 45 (Cain); prospects for equality in the world of work (Kaplan); and reflections on the work ethic in contemporary America (Willhelm). Most articles draw heavily on quantitative material and all contain substantial bibliographies.

                                                              US: Afro-Americans
                                                              Mexican Americans
1a/2c/3a,b/4a,b,h/5g,i/6c/7d   Native Americans
8a,b,c,d/9e/10d/11c,d/13a,b   Puerto Ricans

164 KASFIR, Nelson. 1976. *The Shrinking Political Arena: Participation and Ethnicity in African Politics, with a Case Study of Uganda.* Berkeley: University of California Press. Bibliog. Following a general discussion of political participation and political development, Kasfir considers the effects ethnicity has on these processes. He especially considers class and ethnic effects in Africa, with illustrative data drawn from Uganda. His case study includes a history of ethnic political participation (indirect colonial rule, differential modernization of ethnic groups, nationalist political parties), studies of different ethnic political movements, linkages between different ethnic groups and the government, ethnic criteria in leadership selection (both elective and professional appointive), and government policies toward ethnicity under Obote and Amin. The last section concerns restriction of political participation ("departicipation") in African politics as a means of national integration.

2b,c/3b/4f/5f,i/6a,b/8b/9b,c,e/10a,b,c,d,e,f/12b,c,e   Uganda

165 KATZ, Zev, Rosemarie Rogers, and Fredric Harned, eds. 1975. *Handbook of Major Soviet Nationalities.* New York: Free Press. Bibliogs., apps., index. Each of these seventeen articles summarizes information on one nationality. Following an introduction, Part 1 covers the three major Slavic groups: Russians (Spechler), Ukrainians (Szporluk), and Byelorussians (Zaprudnik). Part 2 covers the Baltic peoples: Estonians (Taagepera), Latvians (Harned), and Lithuanians (Harned). Part 3, the Transcaucasus area, includes Armenians (Matossian), Georgians (Dobson), and Azerbaidzhanis (Huddle). Part 4, central Asian peoples, covers Kazakhs (Katz), Kirghiz (Hetmanek), Turkmen (Murat), Uzbeks (Carlisle), and Tadziks (Rakowska-Harmstone). Part 5, on other nationalities, covers Jews (Katz), Tatars (Burbiel), and Moldavians (Fischer-Galati). Each article follows a general format divided into sections on general information (territory, economy, history, demography, culture, and external relations), media (language data, local media, educational institutions, cultural and scientific institutions), and national attitudes (factors forming national attitudes, views of scholars on national attitudes, and recent manifestations of nationalism). Tables compare the included nationalities: demographic characteristics, language use, party organizations, economics, education, books and periodicals, and indexes of identity vitality, using as variables economic development, sociocultural development, and composite indexes of development.

1a/2c/3a,b/4c,d,f,h,i/5a,e,i/6a,b,c/7d/8a,b,c
9e/10a,d,e/11d/12b,c,g/13a,b/16a,b/17   USSR: General

166 KATZNELSON, Ira. 1972. "The Politics of Racial Buffering in England, 1948-68: Colonial Relationships in the Mother Country." In *Racial Tensions and National Identity,* edited by E. Campbell, pp. 63-87. Nashville: Vanderbilt University Press. Bibliog. Voluntary third-world mi-

grants to Britain have faced a situation that fits a model of internal colonialism, according to Katznelson. To support the point he examines parliamentary action since 1950 that has progressively restricted immigration and the avenues through which immigrants can be assimilated into British society. He argues that there is a tacit consensus regarding restrictions on immigrant mobility in England. Recent trends in this direction have been toward the erection of buffer institutions by which social distance and stratification can be maintained.

2c/3b/4f/5j/6a/7b/9c,e/10b,c/15   Britain: General

167   KATZNELSON, Ira. 1973. *Black Men, White Cities: Race, Politics, and Migration in the United States, 1900-30, and Britain, 1948-68.* London and New York: Oxford University Press. Notes, index. This book examines the political responses to black migration and political relationships formed in early periods of interracial contact in northern cities of the United States and in the United Kingdom. Introductory sections survey recent research, articulate a power-stratification model as a special type of Weberian stratification model, and consider the immigrant-colonial amalgam character of black social positions in the northern United States and of immigrants in Britain. Analysis of the American situation considers parameters of national participation, institutional parallelism in New York City, black politics in Chicago, and an overview of northern political linkages. Analysis of the British situation considers the prepolitical consensus and fundamental debate on race, the institutionalization of a consensus position on the question, Nottingham as a limiting case of institutionalized integration for immigrants into Britain, and the creation of buffer institutions separating immigrants from the British polity. Conclusions of the comparison emphasize structural similarities in responses of the liberal democracies to immigrant groups. Reactions in both cases involved creation of indirect institutional linkages between political authorities and potential partisan immigrants that provided a means by which the groups could be socially controlled, and that operated to maintain a racist status quo. Liberal morality diffused and dissipated responsibility for continuing racist discrimination in both countries.

2c/3a,d/4f/5b,f,i,j/7b,c,d/9b,e   Britain: General
10a,c,e,f/11a,b,d/13a   US: Afro-Americans

168   KATZNELSON, Ira., ed. 1973. "Special Issue: The Politics of Race." *Race,* vol. 14, no. 4. This issue contains articles developing a formal Marxian analysis of behavioral-legal racism in capitalist societies (Nikolinakos); an outline of relations of race, class, and power in England (Sivanandan); and an extended analysis of neocolonialism and race relations, drawing data from New Guinea and the Pacific Rim region to

use in evaluating imperialism theories of economic development and interethnic relations (Zable).

1a/2b,c/3b,e/4b,f,h/5b,i,j/8a,b,d   Britain: General
9b/10a,b,c/11d   Papua New Guinea

169   KAYAL, Philip M. and Joseph M. Kayal. 1975. *The Syrian-Lebanese in America: A Study in Religion and Assimilation.* Boston: Twayne. Bibliog. This book is concerned with Eastern-rite Arab Christians in the United States. It gives an introduction to Arab Christianity in Lebanon and Syria (including Melkites, Maronites, Catholics, Syrian Orthodox, and Protestants); a background of Christian groups in the Middle East; description of migration to the United States (including its causes and demographic outlines); analysis of the spread and settlement of Arab Christian immigrants: measures of their social mobility, economic success, and its effects on ethnic identity; confrontation and integration between Syrian and American churches; and analysis of future prospects for Syrian-American ethnicity. The relative importance of different factors in this complex ethnic situation is assessed.

2c/3a/4h/5a,b/7b,c/8b/9e/11b   US: Lebanese
12a,b,c,d,e,f,g,i/14a/15   Syrians

170   KEYES, Charles F. 1976. "Towards a New Formulation of the Concept of Ethnic Group." *Ethnicity* 3:202-13. Bibliog.   Keyes argues that ethnicity is not a purely subjective phenomenon, but that it entails particular kinds of ideas, specifically shared belief in common origin in terms of descent, place of birth, or biological features. He discusses concepts in other cultures comparable to this meaning of ethnicity. The salience of descent beliefs depends on their facility in conceptually structuring intergroup relations, these being based on modes of exchange of messages (communication), goods (economics), or personnel (marriage alliance). Groups using ethnicity to orient themselves to primordial identities are asserted to arise in certain types of political-economic contexts.

2b,c/3f/4a/5d/8b/11b/12a,b,c,e,f,g/14c   Theory

171   KHAN, Verity Saifullah, ed. 1979. *Minority Families in Britain: Support and Stress.* London: Macmillan. Bibliog., index.   This collection focuses on institutional sources of stress for minority families in Britain and networks of persons from which they derive support. Groups and topics studied include: patronage, kinship, and other supports in the Cypriot community (Oakley); migration and social stress among Mirpuris (Khan); stress points for a West African couple in London (Goody and Groothues) ethnicity and adolescent identity conflicts among native white, Asian,

and Caribbean teenagers (Weinreich); conflict and change among second-generation South Asians (Ballard); classroom stress and school achievement among West Indian adolescents (Driver); ethnic minorities and social services (Ballard); and problems of addressing Asians through the psychiatric services (Rack).

Britain: Africans
Cypriots
1a/2b/3a/4a,i(Psychiatry)/5a,h   Indians
7a,b,d/11b,d/12b,d,i/13b   Pakistanis

172   KILSON, Martin. 1972. "Dynamics of Nationalism and Political Militancy Among Negro Americans." In *Racial Tensions and National Identity,* edited by E. Campbell, pp. 97-114. Bibliog. Nashville, Tenn.: Vanderbilt University Press. Kilson defines nationalism as the manipulation of ethnicity for political goals. He argues that this strategy will be adopted by leaders deficient in ordinary political resources. The motive for group organization is competition for scarce economic resources. Black militancy is seen as a grass-roots movement supplanting black leaders who are perceived as having been co-opted by inimical interests. The movement has come to depend on resources supplied by whites but apparently this does not threaten its legitimacy as representing the black community. Ideological polarization is used as a strategy to achieve institutional homogenization within the black community. Kilson's argument has a dialectical format.

2c/3b/4f/5e/8b,d/9c,e/10c,d,f/11d/12b,f,i   US: Afro-Americans

173   KING, Robert R. 1973. *Minorities under Communism: Nationalities as a Source of Tension among Balkan Communist States.* Cambridge, Mass.: Harvard University Press. Apps., bibliog., index. King considers the political impact of national minorities after World War II in Balkan Communist states. In his introductory chapters he discusses nationalism and Communist theory of nationalities, redefinition of state boundaries following World War II, and the subordination of national to political interests among Balkan Communists seeking Soviet support. Subsequent chapters concern the Hungarian revolution (and the fear among Hungarian minorities of Magyar irredentism); interpretations of Balkan census figures; territorial autonomy and cultural rights in Slovakia, Yugoslavia, and Romania; debates over interpretations of the history of the Hungarian successor states, Macedonia, and Bessarabia; and prospects for the future of Balkan national identities.

2c/3b,d/4f/5d,e/6a/9c/10a,b,c,d/11d/12a,b,c,e   Balkans

174   KINLOCH, Graham. 1974. *The Dynamics of Race Relations: A Socio-*

logical Analysis. New York: McGraw-Hill. Bibliogs., indexes. Kinloch develops an axiomatic-deductive theory of race relations and emphasizes the social structural factors underlying racism. He divides the book according to procedures he uses in theory building, beginning with identification of problems in race-relations analysis; definition of concepts; and examination of psychological, social psychological, and sociological approaches to race relations. His theory represents a synthesis of these approaches, in a colonial model. This model emphasizes colonial political structures, their psychological correlates (for both colonists and colonized), and their historical consequences. The model is used to explain differences between race relations in the United States and South Africa and also between race relations in Brazil and Hawaii. The model is also applied to explain the statuses of different minorities in the United States. The colonial structure model is articulated through 23 propositions and 253 potentially testable theorems listed in an appendix.

2c,e/3b,c,d/4h/5b,g,i,j/9b,c,e/10a,b,c/11a,b,c,d/12f   Theory

175   KITANO, Harry H.L. 1976. *Japanese Americans: The Evolution of a Subculture.* 2d ed. Englewood Cliffs, N.J.: Prentice-Hall. App., bibliog. Kitano traces changes in Japanese-American society and culture, relating these to changes in the sociohistorical context of American society. He focuses on Japanese-American strategies of accommodation to American society. He considers ethnicity, generation, and class as social parameters of individual identity. His discussion includes a summary of nineteenth-century Japanese immigration; description of occupations (farming, restrictions imposed by alien land laws, chain migration to urban occupations); educational forms; anti-Japanese legislation; discriminatory social practices, and so forth. Other chapters are devoted to Japanese-American family life before World War II (family structure, social control, extended kin links); community structure (voluntary associations, religion, community leadership); the wartime internment and concentration-camp effects; and conditions after World War II. The latter discussion is structured in the same way as the prewar data (occupations, family, community, and so forth). Kitano describes Japanese-American culture in terms of norms and values, deviance and social control, mental illness, and so forth. Japanese in Hawaii are discussed in a separate chapter. His concluding analysis relates residence, generation, and social structural variables to social and cultural assimilation.

2b,c/3a/4h/5a,g/6a,b,c/7b/8b/9b,c,d,c/10a,c,d
11a,c/12a,b,c,d,f,i/13a,b/14a,b,c/15   US: Japanese

176   KRAUSZ, Ernest. 1971. *Ethnic Minorities in Britain.* London: Mac-Gibbon & Kee. Bibliog., index. This general study of minorities in Britain includes material on Cypriots, West Indians, African blacks,

Indians and Pakistanis, Irish, Jews, Poles, and other East Europeans. Minority numbers, geographical distributions, demographic characteristics, and population projections are included along with summary histories of their presence in Britain. Specific topics include responses to immigration (organized action, protest, legislative measures, elements of prejudice); social conditions of immigrants (housing, employment, social mobility, development and change in urban situations); and intergroup relations (using models of pluralism, power-conflict, etc.). Krausz concludes with a discussion of prospects for future relations between groups.

2c/3b/4h/5a,b,f,i/6a,b,c/7b/8b/9c,e/10b,c,d
11a/12b,c,e,f,g,i/13a/15   Britain: General

177   KREJCI, Jaroslav. 1978. "Ethnic Problems in Europe." In *Contemporary Europe: Social Structures and Cultural Patterns,* edited by S. Giner
and M.S. Archer, pp. 124-71. London: Routledge & Kegan Paul. Notes,
bibliog.   Krejci surveys ethnic problems of national identification in
Europe. He classifies ethnic minorities throughout the continent according
to their values on dimensions of territoriality, political status, history,
cultural base, language, national consciousness, and population. He then
analyzes these factors as encouraging or inhibiting separatist movements
and assesses prospects for reintegration of minorities into European
national polities.

2c/3c,d/4h/5b,e/6a/10a,d/12b,c,e,f,g/16a   Europe

178   KUNSTADTER, Peter, ed. 1967. *Southeast Asian Tribes, Minorities, and
Nations.* 2 vols. Princeton, N.J.: Princeton University Press. Notes, bibliog.   Relationships of ethnic minorities to governments are the primary
focus of essays in this volume. The introductions to each country characterize its sociopolitical contexts for ethnicity. The general introductory
essay characterizes the range of such contexts for ethnic groups in the
region (Kunstadter). It considers historical trends (e.g., migration, in-
vasion, etc.), forms of government, the impact of colonialism, demographics, variations in religion, language, and so forth. Terms are defined
and the notions of social and cultural boundaries are examined. The
introduction to the section on Burma discusses the colonial growth of
Burma to include groups other than ethnic Burmese and independence
movements among such groups (especially Shan and Karens). Linguistic
designations and their relations to self-ascriptive ethnic categories in Burma
are discussed (Kunstadter). The introduction to China notes that although
national minorities comprise only a small portion of the Chinese population (about 6 percent) they occupy strategic border areas and security
considerations have strongly influenced Chinese government policies
toward them (Kunstadter). The political positions of tribal people in
India are described (Kunstadter). The military situation in Laos sets the

context for ethnicity in that country with different appeals to ethnic consciousness being made by Pathet Lao and Royal Laotian forces and a general decrease in the ability of highland peoples to escape involvement because of the pervasive militarization of the countryside (Halpern and Kunstadter). Pluralism in Malaysia involves complex interactions of religious, linguistic, political, and territorial affinities (Kunstadter). Political issues tend to be expressed in ethnic terms and outlying areas (e.g., Sarawak and Sabah) frequently assert both political and cultural independence. The introduction to Thailand once again considers difficulties in objectively defining ethnic groups, given the variety of positions different minorities occupy in the social structure of Thailand. Thai government policies are examined, especially with regard to highland tribes (Kunstadter). Historical factors in lowland-highland political relations dominate the introduction to Vietnam (Kunstadter). Some of the essays on specific topics are also of use in studying ethnicity. These include papers on situational attributes of identity among ethnic minorities in Burma (Lehman); political changes and their effects on Kachin identity (la Raw); political administration of lowland peoples and highland tribes in Assam (Burling); growing ethnic consciousness as a result of central government administration in Sarawak, Malaysia (Harrisson); changes in the position of highland Muruts in Sabah, North Borneo (Ley); Thai-Haw (Yunnanese Chinese) interactions in Northern Thailand (Mote); the integration system (adoption and purchase) of the Iu Mien (Yao or Man) in Northern Thailand (Kandre); and changes in the ecological interaction of Lua and Skaw Karens in Maehongson Province, northwestern Thailand (Kunstadter).

1a/2b,c/3a,b/4a/5a,b,c,d,f,h,i,j/6a,b,c/7a,b,c,d/8d/9a,b,c,e
10a,b,c,d,e,f/11a,b,d/12a,b,c,d,e,g,h,i/14a,c/15/16a/17   Southeast Asia

179   KUPER, Leo. 1971. "Political Change in Plural Societies: Problems in Racial Pluralism." *International Social Science Journal* 23:594-607. Bibliog.   Kuper contrasts Marxian and Durkheimian theories that predict eventual interracial solidarity with plural society models that anticipate no such development. He reviews the development of plural society theory, and discusses noncoincidence of racial and class boundaries and the problems that causes for Marxian theory. He argues that differential incorporation is the pluralist equivalent of class inequality in Marxian models. Unlike Marxism, plural society models cannot predict directions of change.

2f/3e/4h/5a,b,i,j/8b/9b,c/10b,c,d/11b,d   Theory

180   KUPER, Leo. 1973. *Race, Class, and Power: Ideology and Revolutionary Change in Plural Societies*. Chicago: Aldine. Bibliog., index.   Kuper presents a study of ideologies of cultural differences, conceptions of

race structure and social strata, ideologies of violence among subordinate minorities, and on the theme "black is beautiful" as a political ideology. Chapters on revolutionary change include analyses of several revolutions to determine their effect on race relations; analysis of change in white settler societies; theories of revolution and race relations (examined with reference to Rwanda and Zanzibar); and present an alternative to Marxist models of revolutionary change.

2b,c/3d/4h/5b,e/8b/9c/10a,b,c,d/11b,d   Africa

181 KUPER, Leo. 1977. *The Pity of It All: Polarisation of Racial and Ethnic Relations.* Minneapolis: University of Minnesota Press. Bibliog., index. Noting that sectional conflict often seems to follow the irresistible logic of an "infernal machine," Kuper compares conflicts in Algeria, Zanzibar, Rwanda, and Burundi to discern the mechanism and process of the machine. In the events leading up to the Algerian revolution, Kuper sees the failure of evolutionary forms, the inevitability of violence in accomplishing radical reforms, and the existence of key points at which the outcome might have been altered but for the logic of repression that dictated ever increasing levels of violence. Burundi offers an even stronger case of polarization in which the only goal for both Hutu and Tutsi appears to have been genocide for their opponents as a condition for their own survival. In a general examination of polarized ethnic and racial conflict, Kuper emphasizes uncompromising dualistic polarizing ideologies (e.g., Marxist revolutionary ideologies such as that articulated by Fanon, and conflict rhetoric of the Right, such as Social Darwinism), the interaction of action-reaction systems to form escalating cycles of polarization (illustrated in all of his case studies), and the elimination of the middle ground as a critical step to generation of unrestrained violence. His conclusions about polarization processes are offered as a set of general laws, and the choice between reform or genocide is shown to exist for several countries (Kuper concentrates on South Africa).

	Algeria	South Africa
2c/3d/4h/5b/9a,b,e	Burundi	Zanzibar
10a,b,c,d,e,f,g/11b,d	Rwanda	

182 KUPER, Leo and M. G. Smith, eds. 1969. *Pluralism in Africa.* Berkeley and Los Angeles: University of California Press. Notes, bibliog., index. This collection begins with theoretical papers on plural societies, tracing the origin and development of this theoretical perspective (Kuper); defining institutional and political conditions of pluralism (Smith); and theoretically relating pluralism and polity with relative cultural and social homogeneity and relative democracy (van den Berghe). Case studies cover pluralism in precolonial African societies (Smith); violent and nonviolent change in plural societies (Kuper); social pluralism in French

African colonies (Alexandre); Northern Rhodesia and Zambia (Davidson); Asians in South Africa and Uganda (H. Kuper); and pluralism in Zanzibar (Lofchie). General perspectives are presented on national integration (Mazrui); pluralism in the history of Africa (Thompson); and tribal areas in South and Central Africa (Gluckman). Concluding chapters concern developments in the analytic framework of pluralism (Smith), and polarization and prospects for depluralization (Kuper).

1a/2b,c/3a,b,e/4a,d,f,h/5b,f,i/9a,b,e/10a,b,c/11d   Africa

183   LANCASTER, C. S. 1971. "The Economics of Social Organization in an Ethnic Border Zone: The Goba (Northern Shona) of the Zambezi Valley." *Ethnology* 10:445-65. Bibliog. Zambezi Valley Shona live in lowland areas where tse-tse flies produce high mortality rates for cattle. Since they cannot accumulate the wealth in cattle needed to live up to the regional patrilineal ideal (which requires high bridewealth payments in cattle), they are stigmatized. Shona frequently try to escape their stigma by passing as Tonga to gain access to higher altitude areas where cattle can survive. If they are successful they adopt the patrilineal pattern. Here economic factors strongly influence possibilities for ethnic identity, and help define boundaries between the groups.

2b/3a/4a/5c/6a,b/7c/8b,c/9b,c,d,e/10a/11a,b/12a,c/14a,b   Zambia

184   LEACH, Edmund R. 1960. "The Frontiers of Burma." *Comparative Studies in Society and History* 3:49-68. Bibliog. Leach argues that ecological and political factors define frontier zones better than precise linguistic or cultural boundaries between groups. He explicitly omits language as a possible basis for mapping ethnic zones. He argues that the main cultural influences in Burma have been ecologically channeled, with Chinese influence predominating among hill peoples and Indian influence on valley peoples. The primary interests motivating expansion of great culture interests into Burma were different in the two cases. Chinese interests were primarily commercial; India was concerned with religious and political assimilation of Burma. Similarly the Chinese and Indian cultural models imposed on Burma were different, bureaucratic and charismatic, respectively. Interactions between hill and valley peoples are shown to follow the two models. In this way the cyclical *gumsa-gumlao* interaction of Shan and Kachins in Burma is explained historically.

2b,c/3a/4a/5c/6b/10a/12a,c,i   Burma

185   LEACH, Edmund R. 1962. "Introduction: What Should We Mean by Caste?" In *Aspects of Caste in South India, Ceylon, and Northwest Pakistan,* edited by E.R. Leach, pp. 1-10. Cambridge: At the University Press. Bibliog. Leach surveys major theoretical positions on "castes"

since Weber. He specifically addresses the question of whether caste should be seen primarily as an element of social structure or of culture. He considers it an element of culture and criticizes the social definition of castes as imperative status groups (à la Weber). Social definitions, in his view, allow caste to be conceptually merged with class and ethnicity. The result is confusion since castes and classes have functionally opposite effects (classes compete for resources, caste systems guarantee resource distribution).

2e/3e/4a/5i/8b/9a,c,e/11a,b,d/12a,b,c,d,g/14a,b   Theory

186   LEACH, Edmund R. 1964. *Political Systems of Highland Burma.* 2d ed. London: G. Bell & Sons. Bibliog., index. This book contains a classic anthropological analysis of alternate models of social organization and ideology among Kachins of northeastern Burma. The theme is their adaptation to the adjoining Shan social system. It includes a clear discussion of ambiguities in Burmese ethnic categories, centering on the Kachin, a commonly accepted ethnic category subsuming people who speak several mutually unintelligible languages. Leach considers all meaningful action as ritual and expressive of social systems. He discusses movement across ethnic boundaries through symbols and associated rituals. He argues that although rates of change in group composition, migrations, political changes, and so forth ultimately depend on ecology (highland vs. lowland ecological adaptations), the entire system of interrelated ethnic groups is acted out through everyday social relations. He discusses specific cases of transition from Kachin to Shan ethnic identity.

2b/3a/4a/5c/6a,b/8b/9c,d,e/10a,b/11a,b,c,d/12a,c,d/14a,b   Burma

187   LEVINE, Robert A. and Donald T. Campbell. 1972. *Ethnocentrism: Theories of Conflict, Ethnic Attitudes, and Group Behavior.* New York: John Wiley & Sons. Bibliog. This extensive review of theories of intergroup relations concentrates on attitudes as factors in hostility and intergroup tension. The authors deliberately simplify many theories in the interest of generating testable hypotheses. Their discussion includes an innovative description of field methods that incorporates a useful field manual for research in intergroup relations. They offer conclusions concerning the effect of competition over scarce resources, reciprocation of hostility, accentuation of group differences in stereotyping, and intergroup relations and societal complexity (especially complexity of the division of labor). These conclusions are tentative but suggestive.

1b/2e/3c/4a,g/5g/8d/9c,e/10b,c/11a,b,c/12a,b,c,i   Theory

188   LIEBERSON, Stanley. 1961. "A Societal Theory of Race and Ethnic Relations." *American Sociological Review* 26:902-10. Lieberson at-

tempts to modify Park's "race cycle" model to account for varying outcomes in race relations around the world. The characteristics of initial contact are strongly determining factors of subsequent intergroup relations in his model. Primary variables include relative numbers, relative technological sophistication, the time course of penetration, and economic circumstances governing migration and initial contact. These control whether subsequent interaction will result in conflict or assimilation. The presence of a third or of multipule ethnic groups is also a factor. Lieberson finds that where indigenous populations are subordinate, conflict is the likely outcome; where indigenous groups are superordinate, assimilation is much more likely.

2e/3c/4h/5a,b/6a/7b/8b/9c,e/10b,c/12a,f   Theory

189 LIJPHART, Arend. 1972. *Democracy in Plural Societies: A Comparative Exploration.* New Haven and London: Yale University Press. Index. Lijphart presents a theoretical exploration of plural societies and examines the applicability of consociational models in analyzing new postcolonial states. The consociational model is described in terms of grand alliances between separate social segments, the preconditions for a workable consociational system, consociational elements in nonconsociational democracies of various types, and analyses of how such systems work in Lebanon, Malaysia, Cyprus, and Nigeria. Out of these descriptions Lijphart extracts factors affecting the success probabilities of consociational systems. Consociation is seen as a product of colonial amalgamation of distinct groups into political units. Despite historical failures, Lijphart expresses optimism about the ability of consociational systems to cope with ethnic plurality in new states.

	Theory	
2c/3d/4f/5a,b,f/9c/10a,b,c,d,e,f	Cyprus	Malaysia
11b,d/16a/17	Lebanon	Nigeria

190 LYMAN, Stanford M. 1974. *Chinese Americans.* New York: Random House. Bibliog. Lyman offers general coverage of Chinese Americans, including discussion of the Chinese diaspora; community organizations in China and their analogs in Chinese-American communities (e.g., clans, Hui Kuan, secret societies, etc.); the anti-Chinese movement in the United States; ghetto encapsulation; and institutional racism. Specific facets of the Chinese community treated in this essay include prostitution, gambling, illegal immigration, and consolidation of the immigrant elite. Also discussed are class mobility, and the new alienation and rising ethnic consciousness of Chinese Americans.

2c/3a/4h/5g,i/6a,b/7b/8b/9b,c,d,e/10b,c,d,f
11a,b/12a,b,c,d,f,g,i/14a,b/15   US: Chinese

191   LYNCH, Owen. 1969. *The Politics of Untouchability: Social Mobility and Social Change in a City of India.* New York: Columbia University Press. Bibliog., index.   In analyzing political movements among Indian untouchables, Owen utilizes a social structural theoretical perspective drawn from Weber, Srinivas, and Bailey. He defines socioeconomic classes as ranked imperative status groupings, and castes as imperative status groups culturally and structurally differentiated. He examines Sanskritization as a strategic means of competing for valued resources. His analysis diverges sharply from earlier models in viewing caste mobility as a group political strategy. He argues that an economic hierarchy is the basis for caste rankings.

      2b/3a/4f/5i/6a,b/8b,d/9a,b,c,d,e/11a,b,d/12a,b,c,d,g,i   India

192   MACKIE, J.A.C., ed. 1976. *The Chinese in Indonesia.* Honolulu: University Press of Hawaii. Bibliog., index.   The five essays in this volume discuss different aspects of overseas Chinese society in Indonesia. The introduction includes a sketch of population characteristics, description of Chinese legal status in Indonesia, their economic roles, and Sino-Indonesian relations (Mackie). Other papers cover Chinese political activity in Indonesia in historical perspective (Coppel); the anti-Chinese outbreaks of 1959-68 (Mackie); the role of Chinese in the Sumatran rubber industry and changes in the ethnic division of labor in that industry in the post-World War II period (Thomas and Panglaykim), and comparison of the position of Chinese in Indonesia with their positions in other Southeast Asian countries (Gungwu).

      2b/3a/4h/5c,e,f/6a,b/8b,c,d/9c,e
      10a,b,c,d,e/11a,c,d/16a   Indonesia

193   MARSHALL, Ray. 1974. "The Economics of Racial Discrimination: A Survey." *Journal of Economic Literature* 12:849-71. Bibliog.   Marshall describes the major theoretical approaches to discrimination in economics. He argues that neoclassical approaches that follow Becker's analysis have great difficulty explaining the persistence of wage differentials. Dual labor-market theories are still undeveloped, since they describe discriminatory market structures but fail to explain their origins or how they operate. Radical theories combine the structural arguments of dual labor-market theories with Marxian class conceptions. In a critique of the neoclassical model, Marshall argues that this model rests on the empirically untenable assumption that competition erodes discrimination and group interests. Further, this model is not formulated in empirically testable fashion. Marshall suggests a bargaining model as a more adequate theoretical explanation and policy guide.

      2e/3e/4b/5b,c,f/8a,b,d/9b   Theory

194 MASON, Philip. 1970. *Patterns of Dominance*. London: Oxford University Press. Bibliog., index. Mason presents a theoretical discussion of inequality, especially concerning its origins and the forms by which it is expressed. His discussion moves from a brief history of ideas concerning equality to analysis of modes of contact and conquest (including classification of societies according to the proportions of dominants and dominated population segments, pre-European empires, and the European imperial expansion), to descriptions of particular systems of inequality (castes, religious groups, and tribes in India, dominant whites in southern Africa, Spanish America, the Caribbean, and Brazil), to concluding remarks. He covers political, psychological, and economic elements of intergroup relations.

1b/2c,e/3d/4h/5i/9a,b,c,d,e/10a,b,c/11a,b,d/12a,b,c,f,g   General

195 MAYO, Patricia Elton. 1974. *The Roots of Identity: Three Nationalist Movements in Contemporary European Politics*. London: Allen Lane. Bibliog., index. Mayo examines three nationalist movements in peripheral regions of Western European states. She documents the economic regression of Brittany, following its annexation to France, multiple governmental policies toward the periphery (all inimical to Breton aspirations), and the development of modern Breton nationalism. Her description of Welsh history follows similar lines, though Welsh nationalism has been a continuing ideological current from the eighteenth century to the present. Nationalist aspirations are embodied in the Plaid Cymru party, unlike Breton nationalism, to which all major parties appeal, especially those of the Left. Unequal development, economic dependency, depopulation, and interference by central authorities characterize the Basque provinces in Spain and France. Political repression has been extreme in Spain; neglect is more the case in France. The proper framework for analysis and solution of regional nationalist movements is the political-economic region, according to Mayo. The critical location of Brittany in Anglo-French trade, and of the Basque areas in Franco-Spanish trade make these areas politically critical but potentially responsive to change within the context of the European Economic Community.

2b,c/3d/4f/5e,i,j/7a/8c,d   France   Wales
9c/10a,c,d,e/12b/16a   Spain

196 MAZRUI, Ali A. 1969. *Post Imperial Fragmentation: The Legacy of Ethnic and Racial Conflict*. Center on International Race Relations, Graduate School of International Affairs, University of Denver, Studies in Race and Nations, vol. 1, no. 2. Mazrui analyzes racial and ethnic fragmentation of newly independent nations as a direct consequence of European imperialism. Panethnic nationalist movements grew up in opposition to European colonial domination, but they could only tempo-

rarily contain the ethnic conflicts encouraged by colonial administrations. The movements have broken up, national identity has fragmented, and there has been a steady "retribalization" in much of the Third World, especially in Africa. Mazrui sees the solution in economic nationalism, independence from and denial of European economic influence. He asserts that when economic independence is established, cultural independence can be asserted, with increasing probabilities of constructing viable national identities.

2f/3e/4f/5b,i/9c,e/10a,b,c,d/11d/12f,i   Theory

197   MELSON, Robert and Howard Wolpe. 1970. "Modernization and the Politics of Communalism: A Theoretical Perspective." *American Political Science Review* 64:1112-30.   The authors define communalism as an ideology binding together groups covering the full range of demographic characteristics: sharing common culture, subsuming entire life cycles of individuals, and internally differentiated by wealth, class, and power. Propositions concerning politics in such groups are tested using Nigeria as a case study. Fourteen propositions are listed under the general headings: (1) competitive communalism; (2) institutional communalism; (3) communal transformations; and (4) communal compartmentalization. Variables used to test the propositions include social mobilization (amounts and relative rates); imbalances in wealth, status, and power; segregation; participation in associations; mass vs. elite political participation; intergroup boundary specifications; possibilities of intergroup alliance; complexity of social identities; and contextualization of social identities. Relations between these variables are fairly clearly specified. The tests conducted here may be useful for comparative analysis.

2c,e/3b,e/4f/5d,e,f/9b,c,d/10b,c,d/11a/12a,b,c,d/15   Nigeria

198   MILLER, Kent S. and Ralph Mason Dreger, eds. 1973. *Comparative Studies of Blacks and Whites in the United States.* New York and London: Seminar Press. Bibliogs., indexes.   Papers in this collection summarize and review research comparing American blacks and whites in several areas. Chapters cover black-white differences in experimental responses (Sattler); behavior-genetic analyses and biosocial consequences (Hirsch); biological and medical differences (Molina); comparison of language abilities (Baratz); comparisons of intelligence (Dreger); self-concepts and attitudes (Christmas); comparative effects of early integration programs (Gottfried); desegregation effects (Roberts and Horton); educational achievement (Kirkpatrick); social perceptions and attitudes (Johnson); family organization (Jackson); mental health (See and Miller); crime (Savitz); and political behavior (Clarke).

1a/2c,e/3c/4g,h,i/5k/8b/9b,c,e   US: Afro-Americans
10d,f/11a,b,c,d/12i/13a,b/14a/16a   Euro-Americans

199 MINDEL, Charles H. and Robert W. Habenstein, eds. 1976. *Ethnic Families in America: Patterns and Variations.* New York: Elsevier. Bibliogs. In this comparison of American ethnic family patterns, the editors define ethnicity in terms of continuing cultural traditions. Group survival then depends largely on the effectiveness of families as agents of socialization and enculturation. The collection of papers is divided topically and periodically. Following an introduction, several papers describe family patterns among groups that immigrated to the United States prior to 1920: Polish Americans (Lopata); Japanese Americans (Kitano and Kikuma); Italian Americans (Femminella and Quadegno); Catholic Irish Americans (Biddle); and Chinese Americans (Huang). More recently arrived groups (post-1920) include Arab Americans (Elkholy); Greek Americans (Hourvetaris); and Puerto Ricans (Fitzpatrick). Other papers describe historically subjugated but politically volatile minorities such as Afro-Americans (Staples); Native Americans (Price); and Mexican Americans (Alvirez and Bean). The final topical section discusses socioreligious minorities such as the Amish (Huntington); working-class Franco-Americans (French); Jews (Farber, Mindel, and Lazerwitz); and Mormons (Campbell). The editors offer a summary conclusion. Each selection includes information on homeland family patterns, trends in the United States (including family demography), and patterns of adaptation and change in family structures.

1a/2b/3a/4a,g,h/5k/6a/7a,b/9e/12a,b,c,g,i/14a,b,c   US: General

200 MITCHELL, J. Clyde. 1974. "Perceptions of Ethnicity and Ethnic Behavior." In *Urban Ethnicity,* edited by A. Cohen, pp. 1-35. London: Tavistock. Bibliog. This paper includes a summary of Mitchell's research in the Rhodesian Copperbelt, and proposes a theoretical paradigm for interpreting it. He regards ethnic categories as epistemological devices for making order out of the complex populations in the mining communities of the Copperbelt. His analysis of the categorization phenomenon includes a discussion of social and perceptual distance between tribal categories in the Rhodesian communities. He includes discussion of "super-tribalism," the formation of new, unprecedentedly inclusive ethnic categories. He discusses theoretical perspectives on ethnicity as common-sense interpretations for behavior, as an analytical explanation for behavior, and ethnic groups as analytical constructs.

2d/3c/4a/5d/6b/7d/8b/9c,e/12a,b,i/14a/15   Zimbabwe

201 MOERMAN, Michael. 1965. "Ethnic Identity in a Complex Civilization: Who Are the Lue?" *American Anthropologist* 67:1215-30. Bibliog. Moerman argues that the inability to discern clear cultural discontinuities can be a difficult analytical problem in areas where cultural variation appears to approach continuity. Definition of group boundaries using substantive criteria becomes a futile task because any two criteria delimit

different groups of people. Moerman discusses these problems with reference to the Lue, a group for which the label "Lue" serves as a self-ascriptive label and a label for their language, but which does not coincide with substantial cultural differences. Moerman argues that ethnicity is impermanent and information can be gained by observing shifts in identity; that nonmembers vary in their use of ethnic labels and uniformity of label usage may signal unity among the outside group; that group members vary in the terms they use to denote themselves; and that an ethnosemantic approach is needed to understand ethnic labels and categories.

2b/3a,e/4a/5d/11a,b,c/12a,b,c,d,e,i   Thailand

202   MOORE, Joan W., with Alfred Cuellar. 1970. *Mexican Americans.* Englewood Cliffs, N.J.: Prentice-Hall. Bibliog.   Topics addressed in this general study of Mexican Americans include Anglo images of Chicanos; their historical background; dynamics of immigration; border states and the legal positions of Mexican Americans; a profile of Chicano population characteristics; educational attainments; income; subjection to prejudice and segregation; family organization; class and social mobility; maintenance of language and culture (and ethnic boundary maintenance); and political mobilization.

2b,c/3a/4h/5g,i/6a,b,c/7b/8a,b/9c,e/10a,c,d
11a,c,d/12b,c,d,f,g/13a/14a,b/16a   US: Mexican Americans

203   MÖRNER, Magnus, ed. 1970. *Race and Class in Latin America.* New York and London: Columbia University Press. Notes, index.   This conference collection concerns aspects of immigration, stratification, and politics in Latin American countries. Part 1, the abolition of slavery and its aftermath, examines the integration of blacks in Mexican national society (Beltran); the passing of Afro-Uruguayans from caste to class society (Rama); and the abolitionist movement in Brazil (Graham). Part 2, immigration, stratification, and race relations, includes papers studying immigration and "mestizaje" (cultural coalescence) in nineteenth-century Peru (Vasquez); stratification, immigration, and race in the nineteenth-century Dominican Republic (Hoetink); and immigration and race relations in São Paulo (Fernandes). Part 3, change in Indo-America during the nineteenth and twentieth centuries, includes: studies of "mestizaje" (in this case "miscegenation"), in Mexico (Navarro); impacts of economic change on middle American Indians (Nash); and official "indigenismo" in Peru in 1920 (Chevalier). Part 4, an appraisal of the state of knowledge and tasks ahead, includes: essays on historical research (Mörner); race and class as explanation for politics (Anderson); Brazilian race relations research (Ianni); and a geographer's view (Sternberg).

1a/2c/3a,b,e/4a,c,d,f/5a,i/7b/8c,d   Mesoamerica
9a,b,c/10c,d/12c,f   South America

204 MUNCH, Peter A. 1972. "Race and Social Relations in Tristan da Cunha." In *The Blending of Races,* edited by N. Gist and A. G. Dworkin, pp. 265-84. Bibliog. New York: John Wiley & Sons. Bibliog. This isolated island in the south Atlantic has a racially mixed population of under 200 operating under an ideology of economic communalism, political anarchy, and complete social equality. Progressive isolation and increasing poverty on the island following the end of shipping by sail and South Atlantic whaling brought a general self-image of inferiority and subsequent development of correlation between skin lightness and relative social prestige. By 1938 stereotypes of laziness and industriousness had become attached to dark and light-skinned persons, respectively. Since World War II economic conditions have improved, and the seafaring skills of Tristan residents have become marketable and a fairly steady source of income. Under these conditions Munch reports that internal divisions in the population have been subordinated to the communal ideology. Incipient racism has receded.

2b/3a/4h/6a/8b/9c,d/11a,c/12a,b,f,i/14a   Tristan da Cunha

205 MYRDAL, Gunnar. 1944. *An American Dilemma: The Negro Problem and Modern Democracy.* New York: Harper & Brothers. Notes, apps., bibliog., index. This final report of a massive Carnegie Corporation study on the position of black Americans includes information on a wide range of topics. The initial section concerns the incompatibility of stratification by race, prejudice, and discrimination with American ideals. Subsequent sections concern beliefs about, and evidence on, racial differences; the demographic and migratory characteristics of the black population; a history of the economic position of blacks in America; income, housing, segregation and labor market controls; and the effects of the war economy on economic chances for blacks. Also included are studies of the politics of racialism in the United States; the justice system and blacks' experience of it; discrimination; social stratification; leadership and concerted action; the Negro church, schools, press, community characteristics; and comments on possible social programs to alleviate the dilemma of the title.

2b,c,d/3a,b/4b,h/5g,i,j/6a,b,c/7c/8a,b/9a,b
10a,b,c,d,f/11a,c,d/12f/13a,b/14a/15/16b/17   US: Afro-Americans

206 NAGATA, Judith A. 1974. "What is a Malay? Situational Selection of Ethnic Identity in a Plural Society." *American Ethnologist* 1:331-50. Bibliog. According to Nagata, ethnic pluralism is extreme in Malaysia, as it subsumes not only economic differentation between Malays, Indians, Chinese (the official races) and indigenous groups, but also includes obvious intergroup competition for power. Chinese comprise 34 percent of the population and possess a concentrated economic base. Census and legal definitions of precisely who is a Malay vary according to whether

Chinese power is an issue or not. Nagata describes situational determinants of identity choice, along with the structural limits of identity choice.

2b/3a/4a/5f,h/9c/10a,b,d/11a/12a,b,c,d,f   Malaysia

207   NAGATA, Judith A., ed. 1975. *Pluralism in Malaysia: Myth and Reality.* Contributions to Asian Studies, vol. 7. Leiden: E.J. Brill. Bibliogs.   This collection of eight papers on Malaysian pluralism begins with a summary of definitions and theories on ethnicity, stratification, Malaysian institutional pluralism, and alternatives to pluralist perspectives (Nagata). Subsequent papers include: comparison of pluralist models used to describe Malaysia and Caribbean nations and discussion of the conceptual confusion caused by failure to distinguish between them (Banks); description of ethnic identity and social relations in central Borneo in terms of levels of ethnic boundary demarcation and the contents of ethnic labels (Rousseau); analysis of the different names used by Semai to classify elements of their social environment (Dentan); discussion of economic sectorization, rural economic development, government policies, and interethnic relations in West Malaysia (Purcal); analysis of party formation and pluralism in West Malaysian politics (Tennant); description of South Indian plantation workers as a forgotten minority in terms of the socio-economic structure of the estates on which they work and live, their education, social mobility, and pluralism (Colletta); and an analysis of perceptions of class and ethnic inequalities by Malays, Chinese, and Indians, and expressions of class differences in ethnic terms (Nagata). Group interests and socioeconomic complexity are discussed in each of these papers.

1a/2b,c/3b/4a,f,h/5d,f,i/6a,b,c/8a,b/9b,c,d,e/10a,b,c,d,e
11a,b/12a,b,c,d,e,g,i/13a,b/14a,b,c/15/16a,b   Malaysia

208   NAROLL, Raoul. 1968. "Who the Lue Are." In *Essays on the Problem of Tribe.* Proceedings of the 1967 Annual Spring Meeting of the American Ethnological Society, edited by June Helm, pp. 72-79. Seattle: University of Washington Press. Bibliog.   Naroll defends his objective "cultunit" method of defining ethnic groups as useful for comparative purposes if not for descriptive ones. He responds to Moerman's argument that the Lue are an ethnic group not bounded by statistically observable discontinuities in cultural traits by arguing that while native ethnic labels are useful in some cases they are not adequate for comparative purposes. He cites some groups who have no names for themselves at all as destructive of Moerman's argument that native labels should define the units of description and comparison. Relying on sociolingustics, he sets out a method for finding objective group boundaries.

2e/3a,e/4a/5k/6a,b/8b/12c,e/14a,b/16a   Theory

209 NEUMAN, Stephanie G., ed. 1976. *Small States and Segmented Societies: National Political Integration in a Global Environment.* New York:
Praeger. Notes, index. These eight essays analyze factors affecting
national integration in a number of countries. An introductory essay
examines the lack of definitional clarity in the use of "integration" as
an analytical concept, means of measuring integration as a variable, normative biases implicit in political theories, and the effect of international
factors on national integration (Neuman). Other essays consider the role
of international factors in the failure of integration in Cyprus (Pollis);
internal and external factors involved in the crisis of Pakistan (Inayatullah);
corporation theory, political change, and integration in Zaire (MacGaffey);
Marxism as an integrating ideology in Yugoslavia (Legters); integration in
the German Democratic Republic (Hanhardt and Sharp); ethnicity and
Philippine-Malaysian relations (Noble); and racial segmentation, stratification, and political conflict in Guyana (Smith).

	Cyprus	Pakistan
	Guyana	Philippines
1a/2b,c/3b,e/4a,f/5a,b,e,f,i	G.D.R.	Yugoslavia
9c,e/10a,b,c,d,f	Malaysia	Zaire

210 OBEYESEKERE, Gananath. 1975. "Sinhalese-Buddhist Identity in Ceylon." In *Ethnic Identity,* edited by G. DeVos and L. Romanucci-Ross,
pp. 231-58. Palo Alto, Calif.: Mayfield. Bibliog. Obeyesekere describes
the historical development of connections between Sinhalese ethnic and
Buddhist identities. He sees this as consolidating opposition to non-
Buddhist invaders of Ceylon, including the British in the late eighteenth
century. The historical charter for Sinhalese identity is provided by
religious myth, legend, and political history. The development of Ceylon
as a religiously defined ethnic polity is seen in the life history of Anagarika
Dharmapala, leader of the Sinhalese independence movement, whose early
identification with British Christians eventually was superseded by a
return to familial Buddhist orientations. He generalized this past-oriented
identity in leading the independence movement to a moral (Buddhist)
redefinition of the Sinhalese community. Since 1956 Ceylon (now Sri
Lanka) has been defined as a political-ethnic-religious unit. Ethnic and
religious identity are nearly synonymous.

2b/3b/4a/5d,e/9c,d,e/10b,d,f/11a,b,d/12a,b,c,d,g,i/13a,b   Sri Lanka

211 OLORUNSOLA, Victor A., ed. 1972. *The Politics of Cultural Subnationalism in Africa.* Garden City, N.Y.: Doubleday. Index. Five
case studies of cultural subnationalism in African countries, each analyzing the political positions, patterns of participation, and resources for
political power of the contending groups. Essays discuss ethnic particularism in Nigeria (Olorunsola); Uganda (Kasfir); Sierra Leone (Simpson);

Congo-Kinshasa (Turner); and Kenya (Rothchild). Each paper includes information on occupational distributions, social stratification, and political participation.

	Kenya	Uganda
1a/2c/3b/4f/5b,i/6a/8b	Nigeria	Zaire
9c,e/10a,c,d,e/12b,c,g	Sierra Leone	

212   OTTENBERG, Simon. 1976. "Ethnicity in a Nigerian Town and Its Environs." *Ethnicity* 3:275-303. Bibliog. Ottenberg describes the history of Abakaliki, Nigeria, and changing interethnic relations there. He argues that economic and political factors are crucial to the current interethnic situation in the town. British colonial policy dictated the style of development. The British used Ibo as government workers and housed them on government land, segregating Ibo from other groups. Prior to World War II there was a clear division of labor between British, Ibo, and northern Nigerians. Since the end of the war economic growth and commercialization have been accompanied by the growth of ethnically based political parties. This has further separated Ibo and northerners. Population migration has inevitably involved the town in conflicts originating elsewhere in the country, and conflict developed locally along ethnic lines.

2b,c/3a/4a/5b/6a,b,c/7c,d/8b,c/9c/10b,c/12a,b,c,g/14a   Nigeria

213   PARENTI, Michael. 1967. "Ethnic Politics and the Persistence of Ethnic Identification." *American Political Science Review* 61:717-26.   Parenti examines the persistence of ethnic voting patterns among second- and third-generation descendants of immigrants who are, to all appearances, fully assimilated to American society. Parenti distinguishes between acculturation and assimilation. He argues that culture change takes place among immigrants but that their relations to immigrant community social structures persist. Support for this asserted persistence of structural differences between groups is found in persistent ethnic occupational concentrations, religious affiliations, and ethnic institutions. He argues that identification with ethnicity persists even when cultural diacritica are minimal. Identity maintenance and political manipulation are considered mutually dependent and mutually reinforcing variables.

2c,e/3e/4f/5d,f/8b/10c/12a,b,c/15   US: Euro-Americans

214   PARK, Robert Ezra. 1950. *Race and Culture*. Glencoe, Ill.: The Free Press. Index.   This collection of papers by Park, seminal figure in modern American perspectives on ethnic and race relations, includes representative selections from his previous publications. Topics treated are the theory of race relations and case studies of it (Southern American race-relations

etiquette, the race cycle in Hawaii, Africans in Brazil, assimilation of secondary groups); racial attitudes (bases for prejudice, concepts of social distance, etc.); cases of prejudice and discrimination (racism and Japanese Americans, education and prejudice, etc.); and marginality (migrant personality and culture conflicts). Park sets out his "race cycle" model of intergroup relations. This sets four types of interactions (competition, conflict, accommodation, assimilation) as a natural sequence of intergroup relations from contact to coalescence.

1a/2c/3e/4h/5a,b,g,i/9c,e/11a,b,c/12c,f/13a   General

215   PARKIN, David J. 1969. "Tribe as Fact and Fiction in an East African City." In *Tradition and Transition in East Africa*, edited by P.H. Gulliver, pp. 273-96. Berkeley and Los Angeles: University of California Press. Bibliog.   Parkin compares the effect of tribal factors in the domestic, contractual (public), and friendship domains. He finds that in Kampala economic competition between Ganda and Luo is openly apparent, that members of both groups use "tribal" explanations as opposed to "class" explanations for intergroup hostility. Social stratification tends to follow class lines. Relations between friends and neighbors are indirectly related to ethnic identity through economic stratification and differential residence patterns (although strict residential segregation is not found). Parkin makes three main points: (1) ethnocentrism is stronger among lower class persons; (2) explanations of conflict vary according to the socioeconomic status of the informant; and (3) domestic relations are relatively unaffected by status and class but do vary according to tribe, especially with regard to women's social roles and relative status.

2b/3a/4a/5b/6a,b/8b/9b,c,d,e/10b,c,d/12c,d,h,i/14a,b/15   Uganda

216   PASCAL, Anthony H., ed. 1972. *Racial Discrimination in Economic Life*. Lexington, Mass.: Lexington Books. Bibliogs.   The greater portion of this collection consists of empirically oriented papers documenting race differences in income in the United States (Wohlstetter and Coleman); the effects of minimum wages by race, age, and sex (Kasters and Welch); the economics of racial discrimination in baseball (Pascal and Rapping); and the process of "neighborhood tipping" in generating residential segregation (Schelling). Other papers survey economic models of employment discrimination (Arrow); delineate formal mathematical models of racial discrimination in the labor market (Arrow); and present a mathematical model of information, job search, and prejudice (McCall).

1a/2b,d/3b/4b/5g,k/8a,b,d/9b   US: General

217   PATTERSON, Orlando. 1977. *Ethnic Chauvinism: The Reactionary Impulse*. New York: Stein & Hill. Notes, index.   This general exploration

of ethnicity and its political meaning in the modern world begins with a discussion of six types of ethnic groups that existed in the classical (ancient) world. According to Patterson the only peculiarly modern type of ethnic group is the nation or national group. Drawing examples from different world regions and times, Patterson defines colonial, symbiotic, sovereignal, national, adaptive, and revivalist groups. Using Caribbean Chinese as a case example, Patterson argues that economic motives underlie identity and that people will choose whatever identity is best suited to their short-term economic purposes. The revival of ethnicity in the United States is, according to his argument, tied to the economic crisis and is one aspect of group strategies evolved for dealing with it. The primary option to particularistic ethnicity is, he argues, an open universalistic egalitarian culture. Ethnic movements are reactionary against such a culture. In a second section, Patterson examines the particular and the universal in Western thought and decides that all great revolutionary movements have been universal. Particularism is associated politically with fascism. Finally he argues that resurgent ethnicity is a core symptom of a reactionary denial of the universal values of the Enlightenment.

2c/3e/4h/5a,f,i,k/10d,f/11a,b,c,d   General

218   PETTIGREW, Thomas F., ed. 1975. *Racial Discrimination in the United States.* New York: Harper & Row.   Nearly all the articles in the anthology have been previously published. The first section contains a historical summary of discrimination against blacks in the United States (DuBois), and a survey and summary of trends in race-relations work (Pettigrew). Part 2, housing discrimination, contains: an overview of housing discrimination and policies encouraging it (Abrams); a quantitative characterization of mid-1960s segregation (Clemence); analysis of segregation policies in a southern industrial city (Lowi); a survey evaluating discrimination in southern California apartment rentals (Johnson, Parker, and Mateljan); notation of differences between black and European immigrant housing patterns (Taeuber and Taeuber); and analysis of ethnic attitudes toward race and housing (Pettigrew). Part 3, discrimination in employment, education, and income, contains: the implications of housing segregation for maintaining systems of collective inequality (Roof); a summary of black unemployment trends (National Committee against Discrimination in Housing); discrimination in government employment (U.S. Commission on Civil Rights); black male occupational mobility (Duncan); black-white occupational differences assuming no discrimination (Lieberson and Fuguitt); the effects of school integration on black occupational achievement (Crain); arguments for school integration (Pettigrew); a summary economic perspective on poverty and discrimination (Thurow); and analysis of trends indicating progress for blacks during the 1960s (Farley and Hermalin). Part 4, discrimination in politics, crime, and so forth, notes: the overvictimization of blacks by criminals

(Wolfgang and Cohen); black powerlessness in policy-making positions (Flaming, Palen, Ringlien, and Taylor); and differential trends in equality indicators between blacks and whites (Palmore and Whittington). Part 5, human costs of discrimination, includes: evidence of decreasing black trust in government (Institute for Social Research); comments of Harlem drug addicts (Clark); and an account of a murdered Chicago teenager (Hunt). Part 6, proposed remedies, include proposals for incentives to upgrade impoverished workers (Thurow); a metropolitan educational park (Pettigrew); a negative income tax (Tobin); and a characterization of institutional racism (Friedman).

1a/2b,c,d/3b/4b,d,h/5g,i/6b/8a,b/9b,c,e/10c/11d/13a,b   US: General

219   PIERSON, Donald. 1972. "Brazilians of Mixed Racial Descent." In *The Blending of Races,* edited by N. Gist and A.G. Dworkin, pp. 237-65. New York: John Wiley & Sons. Bibliog.   Pierson argues that mixed-descent Brazilians are more of a statistical aggregate than a socially recognized category. They are more numerous than any other Brazilian group as a result of persistent intermarriage. Pierson argues that now racial categories in Brazil are artifacts of occupational distinctions rather than classifications of perceived physical differences. Supposedly class is already more important than race as a basis for social classification in Brazil and Pierson expects it to become even more dominant as intermarriage moves Brazil toward physical homogeneity.

2b/3b/4h/5f,g/6a,b/8b/9b,c/11a/12a,f/13a,b/14a   Brazil

220   PINKNEY, Alphonso. 1975. *Black Americans.* 2d ed. Englewood Cliffs, N.J.: Prentice-Hall. Bibliog., index.   This general study of Afro-Americans includes discussions of their history (slavery, emancipation, reconstruction, Jim Crow discrimination, and twentieth-century race relations developments); characteristics of their population (numbers, fertility, mortality, age and sex distributions); their socioeconomic status (educational attainment, occupational distribution, employment characteristics and income); the growth of rural and urban black communities, social institutions (family patterns, politics, religion); social deviance (crime and delinquency, mental illness, drug addiction); contributions to American culture (art, literature, dance, and values); their assimilation into American society; and prospects for their future.

2c/3b/4h/5a,g,i/6a,b,c/8b
9c/10c,d/12b,f,g,i/13a/14a/15   US: Afro-Americans

221   PLAX, Martin. 1974. "On Group Behavior and the Ethnic Factor in Politics." *Ethnicity* 1:295-316.   Plax argues that ethnic groups operate politically as a special type of faction. He examines the semantics of

ethnic labels, and notes that ethnic group names are generally collectively plural nouns that depend on the presence of identifiable characteristics to key their application. However potential diacritica often don't generate consistent groupings. Plax opts for subjective definitions of ethnic groups as a way out of this dilemma. He defines groups as aggregations of individuals who are collectively identified and who consciously identify themselves as a group. Conscious self identification provides a basis for faction formation in politics.

2e/3e/4f/5b,d/10b,c,d/12a,b,d,i   Theory

222 PRATT, Henry J., ed. 1974. *Ethno-Religious Politics.* Cambridge, Mass.: Schenkman. This collection of reprinted essays on ethnic politics in the United States is divided into five sections. Part 1, the organizational component in ethnic political action, contains: treatments of social forces involved in group identification or withdrawal from ethnic political participation (Yinger); dynamics of ethnic identification (Glaser); the organization of Protestant minority-group interests in New York City (Pratt); family-church-community as an organizational triad among Irish (Litt); black clergy as agents of political action (Washington); super-territorial organizations among Polish Americans (Znaniecki and Thomas); and the NAACP (Lomax). Part 2, ethnic factors in partisan politics, includes: studies of the rise of Senator John Pastore (Lubell); the development and persistence of ethnic voting (Wolfinger); ethnic politics and persistent ethnic identification (Parenti); sources of Jewish liberalism (Fuchs); the future of Jewish liberalism (Litt); and black-Jewish conflict in New York City (Gans). Part 3, ethnic group demands and public policy, covers: two essays on community control (Gittell and Berube, Wilson); two studies of policy toward Mexican Americans (Pritchett, Rowan); and a history of American immigration policies. Part 4, mass protest, includes: a history of American communism (Draper); a study of the radical Right (Lipset); a brief survey of black power (Graham); an autobiographical excerpt from Bernadette Devlin (Devlin); and comments on the odds facing urban black guerrillas (Oppenheimer). Part 5, general interpretations of American ethnic politics, includes: two comparisons of black and white ethnic experiences (Sindler, Glazer); two analyses of black family organization as pathological (Moynihan, Payton); and histories of discrimination against Irish immigrants in Boston (Handlin) and Detroit (Vinyard).

1a/2c/3a,b/4d,f/5b,i,k/9c,e/10b,c,e,f/11d/12b/15   US: General

223 PRICE, Charles A. 1963. *Southern Europeans in Australia.* New York: Oxford University Press. Bibliog. This detailed quantitative study of southern Europeans in Australia contains information on the geographical origins of southern European immigrants; their social and political back-

grounds (settlement patterns, nucleated vs. dispersed villages, language affinities, family patterns, religion, regional and national loyalties); the migration (migration processes and chain migration); settlement in Australia (employment backgrounds, occupations assumed, distribution of immigrants, migration chains and settlement patterns, generational change in social characteristics of immigrants); ethnic groups and assimilation (national policies, British-Australian attitudes toward Australians of southern European origin, economic assimilation, and tendencies toward intermarriage by generation); and concluding remarks. Compilations of data and statistics used in this analysis are contained in a companion volume (see Price, 1963, in the unannotated section). This companion volume includes detailed quantitative information on migration, settlement, generational change, intermarriage, duration of residence, occupations, relations between region of origin and region of settlement, and other variables for each southern European immigrant group.

2c/3b/4h/5k/6a,b,c/7a,b,c/8a,b/9e/10a
12a,c,f,g,i/14a,b,c/16a   Australia

224   PURCELL, Victor. 1965. *The Chinese in Southeast Asia.* 2d ed. London: Oxford University Press. App., bibliog., index.   This is the standard work on overseas Chinese in Southeast Asia. For each country (Burma, Thailand, Vietnam, Cambodia, Laos, Malaysia, Singapore, Sarawak, Indonesia, and the Philippines) Purcell provides a survey of population characteristics for Chinese residents (including information on numbers, spatial distributions, etc.). He also describes the historical relationships between the Chinese and other groups in these nations. His central concerns are the social and economic positions of the overseas Chinese.

2b,c/3a,d/4h/5f,i/6a,b,c/7b
8b/9b,c,e/10b,d/12a,c,e,g   Southeast Asia

225   RABUSHKA, Alvin. 1974. *A Theory of Racial Harmony.* Columbia: University of South Carolina Press. Bibliogs., index.   Rabushka presents a theoretical study in the political economy of race relations. He argues that individuals, as members of racial groups, gain or lose economically according to the marginal value of their productivity. Groups with low values compensate politically by gaining control over public resources and reallocating them to their advantage, thus generating interracial conflict. According to this model, the greater the amount of government control over resource allocation, the greater the potential for racial conflict. All government action is therefore potentially divisive. The normative implications of Rabushka's theory are that government actions are valued by individual groups according to the particular gains or losses imposed on each of them. Market-resource allocations are not group specific and

therefore, according to this theory, do not generate divisive evaluation.

2f/3e/4f/5k/8d/10a/11d/12f   Theory

226   RABUSHKA, Alvin and Kenneth A. Shepsle. 1972. *Politics in Plural Societies: A Theory of Democratic Instability.* Columbia, S.C.: Merrill. Bibliog., index.   Plural societies are defined here as those societies exhibiting cultural sections and coincident cohesive political sections. The authors present a general theoretical model to account for the relative instability of such societies. They draw on decision theory, preference measures of utility, risk, uncertainty, intensity measures, and the relationship between political entrepreneurship and issue salience. Starting from assumptions that ethnic preferences are intense and nonnegotiable, that intracommunal preference perceptions are uniform, and that intercommunal relations are characterized by conflict, the authors construct a theory of political entrepreneurship to explain the salience of ethnic issues. Key variables in this theory are the structure of access to public resources, and means of influencing public decision making (e.g., violence, electoral machinations, etc.). Case examples are classified according to their intergroup relations type, and the theory is used to explain the patterns of ethnic politics found in them. Types and case examples are competitive (Guyana, Belgium, Trinidad and Tobago, Malaysia); majority dominance (Ceylon, Northern Ireland, Mauritius, Rwanda, Zanzibar); minority dominance (South Africa, Rhodesia, Burundi); and fragmented societies (Lebanon, Zaire, Sudan, Nigeria, Yugoslavia). Switzerland is examined as a potential counterexample (but judged insignificant). The authors propose solutions to plural conflicts in terms of denial or restriction of independent decision-making authority; restrictions on political competition; reduction of the scope of government; creation of homogeneous societies; and creation of permanent external enemies.

2e/3d,e/4f/5b,f/9c/10a,b,c,d,e,f/11d/12a,c,f,g,i   General

227   REX, John. 1970. *Race Relations in Sociological Theory.* New York: Schocken.   Rex describes various theories of race relations in terms of their position in general sociological theory. He includes a discussion of racist ideologies, along with conceptual analysis of analytical perspectives on race relations. Although he does not articulate any personal paradigm, his presentation appears generally sympathetic to conflict theories and to Marxian variants.

2e/3e/4h/5b,j/9c,e/10b,c,d/11a,b,d/12a,c,f   Theory

228   RHOODIE, Nie, ed. 1978. *Intergroup Accommodation in Plural Societies: A Selection of Conference Papers with Special Reference to the Republic of South Africa.* London: Macmillan & Co.   Useful papers in

this collection cover a variety of topics: a discussion of forms of group identity (national, ethnic, tribe, region, subnation, etc.) and use of these terms (Connor); Islamic-Arabism vs. pluralism in the Middle East (Ma'oz); patterns of intergroup accommodation in Southeast Asia (van der Kroef); the role of mass news media in plural societies (Sussman); pluralism in the politics of Pakistan (Nasir); and several papers directed at specific policy questions in South Africa.

1a/2c/3b/4f,h/5e/9c/11a,c,d/12b/16b   General

229   RICHERT, Jean Pierre. 1974. "The Impact of Ethnicity on the Perception of Heroes and Historical Symbols." *Canadian Review of Sociology and Anthropology* 11:156-63. In this follow-up to government reports on bilingualism and biculturalism in Canada, Richert tries to determine whether Anglophone and Francophone children in Quebec differ significantly in their perceptions of historical figures. After analyzing textbooks, interviews with elementary-age children, and children's essays, Richert concludes that ethnocentrism is more pronounced among Francophone children and that it increases with age. He concludes that where history is perceived very differently by members of different groups, historical symbols can be divisive rather than integrative.

2d/3b/4g/5d/11a,b,c/12a,c,e,f/16a,b   Canada: Québécois

230   ROBBINS, Edward. 1975. "Ethnicity or Class? Social Relations in a Small Canadian Industrial Community." In *The New Ethnicity: Perspectives from Ethnology,* 1973 Proceedings of the American Ethnological Society, edited by John W. Bennett, pp. 285-304. St. Paul, Minn.: West. Robbins assesses the relative importance of ethnic identity and class (defined as occupational status) as determinants of social relations in a small single-industry (iron-ore extraction) town in Labrador. He argues that class is the superordinate identity and that, when ethnicity becomes divisive or competitive, it reflects the underlying social reality of class inequalities.

2b/3a/4h/5i/6a/8a,b/9b,c/12b,d,i   Canada: General

231   ROBERTSON, Ian and Phillip Whitten, eds. 1978. *Race and Politics in South Africa.* New Brunswick, N.J.: Transaction Books. These papers examine a range of issues concerning South African institutional structures, political dynamics, and race relations. Background papers concern degrees and kinds of race relations in South Africa (van den Berghe); a political sociological analysis of South Africa as a pragmatic race oligarchy (Adam); and radical resistance to white domination (Daniel). On institutions of apartheid, chapters examine the Bantustans (Vigne); the churches (Carstens); the educational system (Robertson);

apartheid medical treatment (Mechanic); and the law and justice system (Sachs). On relations between South Africa and the rest of the world, articles analyze South Africa's strategic geopolitical position (Legum and Legum); foreign investment in South Africa (Lock); external liberation movements (Stokes); and United States policies toward South Africa (Easum). Alternate projections for the future are offered in a final chapter. Prognoses include evolution toward detente and coexistence (Gandar), toward increasing conflict (Howe), and toward a United States of South Africa (Munger).

1a/2b,c/3b/4f,h,i/5b,e,g,i,j/6c/7d/8d
9c,e/10a,c,d,f,g/17   South Africa

232 ROSE, E.J.B. and Associates. 1969. *Colour and Citizenship: A Report on British Race Relations.* London: Oxford University Press. Apps., bibliog., index.   This is a comprehensive discussion of the results of the Institute of Race Relations Survey (1962-68). Introductory sections are followed by sections on coloured immigration to Britain (chapters discuss sending societies, the Caribbean and Guyana, India and Pakistan, post-World War II migration, labor demand and labor flow before and after immigration control); census data (analyses of London population figures, numbers and distributions of "coloured" people in England and Wales in 1966); changes in the demography of minority groups 1961-66 (housing and changes in it, employment, patterns of household expenditures); government policies and practices (the fall of laissez-faire immigration, housing and education, industrial relations, health and welfare, law enforcement, churches, political interest groups, analysis of the effects of different policies); immigrant responses to British politics (adaptation or withdrawal for West Indians, Pakistanis, and Indians, second-generation responses, and emerging leadership); legislation against discrimination; public attitudes of race prejudice (reporting on an attitude survey and evaluation of results); current trends in race relations (conservatism and recrudescent racism); and projections for the future (numbers of minority members, their economic and social effects). The study also includes policy recommendations on law, housing, education, employment, welfare, police, community relations, public education, and immigration policies.

2b,d/3b/4f,g,h/5f,i,k/6a,b,c/7b/8b/9b,c,e/10a,b,c,d,f
11a,d/12a,b,c,f,i/13a,b/14a,b/15/16b   Britain: General

233 ROSE, Jerry D. 1976. *Peoples: The Ethnic Dimension in Human Relations.* Chicago: Rand McNally College. Bibliog., indexes.   This introductory text offers a concise and fairly thorough coverage of sociological perspectives on ethnicity. Chapters are devoted to ethnic identity, ac-

culturation and revitalization, ethnic community coherence and cleavage, ethnic distance, stratification (both origins and mechanisms for maintenance), and dynamics of group identity, organization, and behavior. Most cases used to illustrate theoretical points are drawn from outside the United States.

1b/2c/3d/4h/5b,f,g,i/8a,b/9c,d,e/10a,c,d/11a/12c,d   General

234 ROSS, E. Lamar, ed. 1978. *Interethnic Communication.* Southern Anthropological Society Proceedings, no. 12. Athens: University of Georgia Press. Bibliog., notes. These collected conference papers include a summary introduction (Ross); an analysis of intercultural communication patterns between native English speakers and immigrant Indians in London (Gumperz); a mathematical model and method for analyzing the role of language as a bond within and between ethnic groups (Lieberson); an analysis of cases of intercultural misunderstanding (Yousef); an analysis of factionalism and misunderstandings among Portuguese in a New England community (Smith); a discussion of communication problems in community organization (Molina); a description of linguistic usage, political content, and national language policies operating in a Tanzanian community (Guillotte); an analysis of missionaries as a medium of intercultural communication among the Eastern Cherokee (French); a discussion of Acadian nationalism in the context of industrial society (Fox, Aull, and Cimino); and a discussant's summary of the conference papers (Helms).

	Brazil	South Africa
1a/2b,c,e,f/3a,e/4a,e,h/5b,d,f,k/7b	Britain: General	
10a,b,d/12d,e/16a/17	US: Afro-Americans	

235 ROTHMAN, Jack, ed. 1976. *Issues in Race and Ethnic Relations: Theory, Research and Action.* Itasca, Ill.: R.E. Peacock. This is an issue-oriented combination of previously published articles, new contributions, and editor's comments. The introduction reviews theories of ethnicity for their policy implications, especially as they provide for evaluations of alternate policies (Rothman). Sections on issues treat equality vs. preferential treatment, with analyses of racial reparations (Bolner); favoritism in hiring (Gilbert and Eaton); trends toward equality (Palmore and Whittington); and minority employment (Galbraith et al.). Other sections cover integration vs. local control in education, coalitions vs. independent action as minority political strategies, white ethnics as victims of oppression, and conflict vs. consensus as group relations strategies. The issues are current and the presentation of them is well organized.

1a/2f/3b/4b,f,h,i/5f,i,k/8b/9c,e/10b,c,d
11a,d/12a,b,c,f/13a   US: General

236   RUNCIMAN, W. G., ed. 1972. "Special Issue: Race and Social Stratification." *Race,* vol. 13, no. 4.   Articles in this special journal issue treat various aspects of racial and ethnic stratification. These include the logical content of social science concepts of race, caste, and ethnic stratification, treating them all as special types of social stratification and also as types drawn from the general category of ascriptive statuses (Berreman); a comparison of historical dynamics in race stratification in the United States, Brazil, and South Africa (Dunning); perspectives on ethnic stratification from psychological anthropology (DeVos); correlations between race, racism, and relative deprivation in the urban United States (Pettigrew and Vanneman); analyses of stratification patterns in plural new states and their relations to internal political conflict (West); and a survey of definitions of race and ethnicity, settling on low feasible social mobility as uniquely distinctive of racial groupings (Runciman).

                                                                  Brazil   South Africa
      1a/2b,e/3b,e/4a,d,g,h/5b,g,i/9a,b,c,e   Britain: General
      10a,b,c/11a,d/12a,f   US: Afro-Americans

237   RYAN, Joseph A., ed. 1973. *White Ethnics: Their Life in Working-Class America.* Englewood Cliffs, N.J.: Prentice-Hall. Bibliog.   This collection of papers on resurgent white American ethnicity begins with articles defining what ethnics are (Greeley), analyzing the demographic, religious, and class components of the white ethnic movement (Weed), and defining political commitment to the movement (Novak). Some of the personal identity-influencing facets of ethnicity covered in this collection are Italian-American family history (Gambino); Catholicism and immigrant experiences (Loperato); Italian peer-group neighborhoods (Gans); and policies tending to stabilize white ethnic neighborhoods (Aderbato and Krickus). Public aspects of white ethnic experience analyzed include elementary education and identity (Covello); ethnicity and blue collar class identity (Tyler); ethnic political behavior (Wolfinger); and Slavic political patterns (Levy and Kramer).

      1a/2b,c/3a,b/4d,g,h/5a,f,g/6a,b/8b/10b,c,d,e,f
      11a,b/12a,b,c,g,i/13a,b/14a,b   US: Euro-Americans

238   SAFA, Helen I., and Brian M. Du Toit, eds. 1975. *Migration and Development: Implications for Ethnic Identity and Political Conflict.* The Hague: Mouton. Bibliogs., indexes.   Useful papers in this conference collection include analyses of kinship, ethnic identity, and chain migration as factors in the Galician migration to Switzerland (Buechler and Buechler); ethnicity and American Indian migration (Hodge); West Indian ethnicity in Great Britain and its difference from ethnic identity in the Caribbean islands (Midgett); racial and ethnic identification in Afro-American and Afro-Caribbean in-migrant communities (Green); ethnic differentiation

among Jews in Israel (Heller); migration and racial/ethnic consciousness in Barbados and perceptions of home and emigrant societies in the United States and England (Sutton and Makiesky); ethnic identity, group boundaries, political economy, and Quechuan identity in the Ecuadorian jungle interior (Whitten); and comments on the papers (Sutton). Other articles on inequality, power, and development treat such specific topics as class and social inequality among the West Nigerian Yoruba (Lloyd); plantations and labor mobility in Guyana and Trinidad (Richards); Bantustans and labor migration in South Africa (Magubane); affinity, interests and urban networks as factors in migration in sub-Saharan Africa (Gugler); and comments (Bryce-Laport).

1a/2b,c/3a,b/4a/5a,b,d,f,i/6b,c/7b,c,d/8b/9b,c,d,e
10b,c,d/11a,c,d/12a,b,c,d,e,f,g/13a/14b/15   General

239   SAID, Abdul and Luiz R. Simmons, eds. 1976. *Ethnicity in an International Context*. New Brunswick, N.J.: Transaction Books. Index.   A theoretical introduction (Said and Simmons) notes the world-wide political importance of ethnicity both in intrastate and international relations, argues the importance of taking ethnic subnationalism into account in the formulation of United States foreign policy, and speculates on "neo-ethnic" behavior in the postindustrial age. The other theoretical paper in this collection treats ethnic mobilization in light of communication theory, a development of work by Deutsch (Mowlana and Robinson). Case studies address the relationship between black consciousness in the United States and American policies toward Africa (Obatala); the French nationalist movement in Quebec (Morf); the changing status of Jewish minorities in light of Latin American nationalist movements (Horowitz); ethnonationalism in western Europe and its political significance (Connor); ethnicity in Yugoslavia (Stavrou); ethnic autonomy in the USSR (Rakowska-Harmstone); ethnicity operating in the strategic international location of Cyprus (Kitromilides and Coulumbis); the growth of the English-speaking black population in both hemispheres and its likely political and cultural consequences (Mazrui); and language policies in India and their significance for national development (Sharma).

			Mesoamerica
	Canada:	South Amer-
	Québécois	ica
1a/2b,e/3b,e/4f,g,h,i/5b,e,g,k	Cyprus	USSR: General
10a,b,c,d/11d/12b,d,e/16a	India	Yugoslavia

240   SAMORA, Julian, ed. 1966. *La Raza: Forgotten Americans*. Notre Dame, Ind.: University of Notre Dame Press. Bibliog., index.   This collection on Chicanos includes the history of Mexican Americans in the southwest (Sanchez); the church as an organizational focus for Chicano

communities (Wagner); increasing local, state, and national Chicano political mobilization (Martinez); migrant workers and legislation concerning them (Scholes); equal opportunities for Chicanos in employment, housing, education, law, and justice (Glick); middle-class growth and community participation among Chicanos in Los Angeles (Sheldon); and Chicano population characteristics (Barrett).

1a/2b,c/3a/4a,d,f,h/5a,d,i/6a,b/7b/8b/9c
10b,c,d/12c,e,f,i/13a/15/16a   US: Mexican Americans

241   SANDHU, Kernial Singh. 1969. *Indians in Malaya: Some Aspects of Their Immigration and Settlement.* Cambridge: At the University Press. App., bibliog., index. This detailed study of Indian immigration to Malaya includes its causes, recruitment of migrants, laws regarding migraion and policy practice, and the characteristics of the migration flow. Sangdhu describes the population structure of the Malayan Indian community, its dynamics, and its proportions in the national population. Patterns of spatial distribution are described in detail (with numerous maps), and urbanization trends are analyzed. Chapters are devoted to setttlement characteristics, urban and rural, and the ethno-linguistic composition of the Indian population, the economic position of Indians, occupational profiles, analysis of estate holdings, agricultural and governmental positions, forestry, mining, manufacturing, communications, commerce, finance, and so forth, and participation in Malayan politics.

2b,c/3a,b/4c,h/5k/6a,b,c/7a,b,c,d
8a,b,c/9a,b,c,e/10c,e/12a,b,c,e   Malaysia

242   SAUNDERS, John. 1972. "Class, Color, and Prejudice: A Brazilian Counterpoint." In *Racial Tensions and National Identity,* edited by E. Campbell, pp. 141-65. Nashville: Vanderbilt University Press. Bibliog. Saunders refutes the common image of contemporary Brazil as free from all racial prejudice. He cites studies of stereotypes and attitude surveys, pejorative uses of racial labels, etiquette barriers, restrictions on social mobility, economic stratification by race, and other deviations from the ideal of racial democracy. A commenting paper is appended.

2b,c/3b/4h/5g/9b,c,d,e/11a,c,d/12a,f   Brazil

243   SAVARD, Jean-Guy and Richard Vigneault, eds. 1975. *Multilingual Political Systems: Problems and Solutions.* Québec: Les Presses de L'Université Laval. Notes, bibliogs. The first section of this collection includes contributions on the political significance of linguistic conflicts (Deutsch); dilemmas for democracy in multinational states (Kloss); language, nations, and democracy (Rustow); the widespread use of English and racial boundaries of its use in Africa (Mazrui); occupational structures, multilingualism,

and social change (Simon); a method for measuring language diversity in a nation or in regions within it (Lieberson and O'Connor); the political consequences of stress induced by language shifting in multilingual societies and structural means of reducing such stress (Laponce); and corporate federalism as means of coping with linguistic politics (Friedrich). Also included in this section are French-language papers on models and indexes of power, attraction, and pressure of languages in contact (Mackey), and possibilities for territorial solutions to the problem of multilingualism (Donneur). Case studies cover the applicability of consociational models to Canada (McRae); a detailed survey of political styles and language use in Canada (Meidel); multilingual politics in Spain (Linz); a history of Belgian linguistic ideologies (Zolberg); "official" languages in Israel, their status in law and police attitudes toward them (Fishman and Fisherman); political, cultural, and economic factors operating on individual identity choices through language use in British Honduras (LePage); India as a multilingual federation (Katre); and a general description of Asian multicultural federations (Watts). French-language papers in this section cover controlling factors in use of French in work activities in Quebec (Brazeau); and conditions for a national culture in Lebanon given bilingualism (Abou).

	Belgium	India
	British Honduras	Israel
1a/2b,d/3a,b,e/4d,e,f/5a,d,e	Canada:	Lebanon
10a,b,c,e/12d,e/15/16a	Québécois	Spain

244 SCHERMERHORN, Robert A. 1970. *Comparative Ethnic Relations.* New York: Random House. App., bibliog., index. Schermerhorn presents a theoretical and methodological treatise on the sociology of interethnic relations. In the introduction he characterizes and evaluates general trends in sociology. He reviews systems-analysis and power-conflict theories of ethnic relations and suggests that they are dialectically related. He analyzes structural types of integration, intergroup sequences and racism, and intergroup sequences and pluralism, as factors determining patterns of intergroup relations. He finds that different world regions are characterized by different contexts for intergroup relations, and he classifies structural types. Finally he builds a theoretical and analytical paradigm for a comparative approach to ethnic relations research. References are contained in chapter bibliographies.

1b/2c,e/3d,e/4h/5a,e,f,i/6a,b/7b,c/8a,b/9a,b,c,d   Theory
10a,b,c,d/11a,b,c/12a,c/13a,b/14a,b/15/16b   General

245 SCHERMERHORN, Robert A. 1978. *Ethnic Plurality in India.* Tucson: University of Arizona Press. Bibliogs. This study of ten ethnic minority categories in India classifies them according to "intergroup sequences"

or processes of their formation and inclusion in the social system. "Scheduled castes" are analyzed as resulting from pariah group formation, "scheduled tribes" as a case of emerging indigenous isolates; Jains and Sikhs as the result of religious cleavage; Muslims, Christians, and Anglo-Indians as results of colonization and conquest; and Jews, Parsis, and Chinese from migration. The history, characteristics, and position in Indian society of each minority is examined. Schermerhorn discusses such topics as the mobility of scheduled castes; economic encapsulation of scheduled tribes; Parsi entrepreneurship; Muslim political movements; family patterns among Anglo-Indians, and the effect of Sino-Indian conflicts on Chinese in India. Given the many ethnic categories in India, transitions between types are frequent, and Schermerhorn discusses the processes of type change. In particular he discusses the transformation of several scheduled tribes into scheduled castes. The final chapter offers a summary perspective on ethnic plurality in India.

2b,d/3b/4h/5b,c,f/6a,c/7b/8b,c,d/9a,c,e
10a,b,c,d,f/11b,d/12a,b,e,f,g,h/14a/15/16a   India

246   SCHWARTZ, Norman B. 1971. "Assimilation and Acculturation: Aspects of Ethnicity in a Guatemalan Town." *Ethnology* 10:291-310. Bibliog. Schwartz analyzes cultural change among Mayeros in the Guatemalan highlands. From 1870 to 1960 this Indian group underwent substantial cultural change as it imitated Ladino cultural forms. Only among older Mayeros does language now serve to distinguish them ethnically. Most cultural diacritica are unclear. Nevertheless the two groups are still recognized as distinct and there exists a high degree of stereotyping between them. Ethnic identity is determined by descent reckoning, and genealogical records are carefully maintained. Ethnicity is said to remain relevant in domains requiring social performance, but not where technical performance takes precedence. Schwartz says economics is irrelevant to ethnicity, but he also says Mayeros are stereotyped as lazy, shiftless, and unable to handle money.

2b/3a/4a/5a,g/6b/8b/9c/10a/11a,b/12a,b,c,e,i/14a,b   Guatemala

247   SCHWARTZ, Theodore. 1975. "Cultural Totemism: Ethnic Identity Primitive and Modern." In *Ethnic Identity,* edited by G. DeVos and L. Romanucci-Ross, pp. 106-31. Palo Alto, Calif.: Mayfield. Analyzing data from Melanesian island societies, Schwartz sees ethnic group formation as a classificatory artifact of mental operations in the same way that totemic classifications are mental operations. He asserts that the totemic attitude in Melanesia that imparts significance to differences between groups derives from a primordial cultural diversity based on migration and settlement patterns and argues that ethnic groups function as fictive associations where organizational infrastructures do not exist.

Key differences between categories are connected with the totemic attitude. Allegiance to key symbols emphasizes the substance of group identity rather than relative positions of groups in social or conceptual structures.

2b/3a/4a/5d/10a/11a/12a,b,i   Admiralty Islands

248 SETON-WATSON, Hugh. 1977. *Nations and States: An Enquiry into the Origins of Nations and the Politics of Nationalism.* Boulder, Colo.: Westview Press. Notes, bibliog., indexes. This historical essay on nationalism and national development examines the different types of political movements that have led to the formation of nation states. Chapters cover old continuous nations in Europe (the British, French, Swiss, Russians); movements for national unity in Europe (Germany, Italy, Greece, Pan-Slavism); multinational empires and new nations in Europe (Hungarians, Romanians, Ukrainians); European nations overseas (United States, Latin America, South Africa, Australia); Muslim empires and modern nations in West Asia and North Africa (Iran, the Arab nation); East Asian empires, colonies, and nations (Chinese, Japanese, India, Pakistan, Southeast Asia); colonial empires and new nations in Africa, racism in the Americas and South Africa, diaspora nations (Jews, overseas Indians, Chinese, and Malaysians); class and nation, nationalism and ideological movements (liberalism, socialism, fascism, communism), and the relations of nations, states, and the human community.

2c/3b,d,e/4d,f/5b,e,g,j/8c/9b,c,e/10a,b,c,d,e,f,g
11b,d/12a,b,d,e,f,i/16a/17   General

249 SHEPHERD, George W., Jr. and Tilden J. LeMelle, eds. 1970. *Race Among Nations: A Conceptual Approach.* Lexington, Mass.: Heath, Lexington Books. Bibliog. This volume brings together conceptual studies intended as background for comparative research programs. Introductory papers include a historical description of the development of race relations studies (Rose); a suggested research program including hypotheses (Deutsch); and a systems framework for the analysis of white dominance systems. Of particular note is an extensive bibliography classified into theoretical studies; area studies; American ethnic studies; race and United States institutions; foreign views of United States race problems: race in United States foreign policy; and race, national minorities, human rights, and the United Nations.

1a/2a,c/3e/4f/5b,k/10a,b,c/11d   Theory

250 SHIBUTANI, Tamatsu and Kian M. Kwan. 1965. *Ethnic Stratification: A Comparative Approach.* New York: Macmillan. This introductory text on ethnic relations covers the field generally. The authors define

ethnicity as fictive common descent, and discuss different aspects of groupings along this dimension, including identity, ethnic stratification, cultural symbols, variations in patterns of interethnic relations, and so forth. Their theoretical perspective is drawn from sociology and anthropology (especially Cooley and Linton). A variety of cases is used to illustrate their points. Parts 4 and 5, on disjunctive and integrative ethnic movements, are particularly useful.

1b/2c/3e/4h/5d,i/9a,b,c,d,e/11a,d/12a,b,c,e,f,g,h/13a/16a   General

251   SILVER, Brian. 1974. "Social Mobilization and the Russification of Soviet Nationalities." *American Political Science Review* 68:45-66. Silver presents an analysis of assimilation to Russian cultural patterns throughout the Soviet Union, using nationality and language as indicators of national identity. His hypotheses concern the relation of social mobilization to Russian cultural patterns, especially language use. Specific variables employed include urbanization, degrees of contact with Russians, and sex. Complex variables are also employed. Quantitative tests confirm the expected relationships (that high values on all variables will be associated with Russianization). He adds comments concerning religiosity as a factor in resistance to Russianization, especially among Islamic nationalities.

2c/3b/4f/5a/6b,c/9c/11d/12a,c,e,g   USSR: General

252   SIMMONDS, George W., ed. 1977. *Nationalism in the USSR and Eastern Europe in the Era of Brezhnev and Kosygin.* Detroit: University of Detroit Press. Notes.   This symposium collection begins with introductory papers appraising research on ethnic politics in the USSR (Rakowska-Harmstone); analyzing demographic trends among Soviet nationalities and their political implications (Clem); and summarizing minority policies and evidences of ethnic consciousness in Eastern Europe since 1964 (Isajiw). Studies of Soviet minorities examine social bases for Ukrainian change since 1964 (Isajiw); Ukrainian resistance against Russification (Sawczuk); Ukrainian culture (Stepanenko); religion and nationalism in the contemporary Ukraine (Bociukow); demographic and industrial features of Byelorussia (Kipel); political developments in Byelorussia (Zaprudnik); Estonian nationalism (Parming); group demands and group consciousness in Latvia (Dreifelds); cautions about using aggregate statistics to analyze political conditions in Latvia (Penikis); recent political developments in Lithuania (Remcikis); pressure on Lithuanian culture (Landbergis); Azerbaidzhan nationalism (Hegaard); Armenian ethnic consciousness in historical perspective (Dadrian); Moldavian politics (Spector); a general overview of Central Asian nationalism (Rakowska-Harmstone); Kazakh nationalism (Hetmanek); Uzbekistan politics (Critchlow); Turkmen nationalism (Murat and Simmonds); Jews in the Soviet Union (Gitelman); Jews in

Poland (Rozenbaum); comments on anti-Semitism (Specter); and a discussion of anti-Semitism as official Soviet policy. Papers on Eastern Europe discuss Poland's international position (Dziewanowski); Polish politics during the 1960s (Piekalkiewicz); recent Polish nationalism (Chrypinski); Slovak nationalism (Kirschbaum); comments on Slovak nationalism (Stolarik); recent constitutional changes in Czechoslovakia (Mikus); official nationalism in Hungary (Pastor); Hungarians in the Communist successor states (Homonnay); comments on official Hungarian nationalism (Dreisziger); nationalism in Yugoslavia (MacKenzie); Croatian nationalism (Raditsa); nationalism in Albania (Pano); the events surrounding dismissal of the Albanian minister of defense (Prifti); Romanian nationalism (Fischer); and comments on U.S.-Soviet trade (Dobriansky).

1a/2c/3a,b/4b,d,f,h,i/5b,e   Eastern Europe
10a,b,c,d,e,f/11a,d/16a/17   USSR: General

253   SINHA, Surajit. 1965. "Tribe-Caste and Tribe-Peasant Continua in Central India." *Man in India* 45:57-83. Bibliog. Sinha defines the positions of central Indian hill tribes in terms of tribe-caste and tribe-peasant continua. He argues that movement from the tribal pole to the caste and peasant ends of the continua involves a progression toward ethnic heterogeneity in social interaction, role specification, social stratification, and intensification of relationships with metropolitan centers. Sinha sees castes as ethnic groups, since they are constituent parts of larger systems, as are peasants. Tribes are defined as autonomous sociopolitical units. Sinha sees castes as sociocultural subgroupings found only in complex societies.

2b/3a/4a/5i/6a,b,c/8b/9a,c,e/10b,c/11a,d/12a,b,c,d,i   India

254   SKINNER, G. William. 1958. *Leadership and Power in the Chinese Community in Thailand.* Ithaca, N.Y.: Cornell University Press. Bibliog., index. Skinner studies the community structure and leadership patterns of the Chinese community in Thailand in great detail. Using interview and survey data he analyzes the community structure and leadership in terms of sources of leaders (associations, schools, press, national politics), economic power (occupations, structures of economic control, elites in business), power structures, assimilation and leadership, stability and change in community structure and leadership, politics, and group security. The analyses of economics and Chinese associations are particularly well documented with quantitative data. Skinner analyzes the organizational resources potentially available to minority ethnic communities.

2b,c/3a/4a/5k/8a,b/9c,d,e
10a,b,f/12a,c,d,e,g/15   Thailand

255   SKINNER, G. William. 1968. "Overseas Chinese Leadership: Paradigm for a Paradox." In *Leadership and Authority,* edited by Gehan Wijeyewadene, pp. 191-207. Singapore: University of Malaya Press.   Skinner analyzes the effects of indirect rule of overseas Chinese communities in Southeast Asia. One effect of this system of administration was to put community leaders in marginal positions with regard both to their own communities and to colonial administrations. The paradox to which Skinner refers is that leadership in such marginal situations is only effective if the positions are legitimized from within the minority community, but sanctions and rewards for leadership come from the outside administration. Political results of this paradox are illustrated with cases from recent Southeast Asian history.

      2b/3a/4a/5d,i/8b/9b,d/10a,b,f/12a,b,d,i/14a   Southeast Asia

256   SMITH, Anthony D. 1971. *Theories of Nationalism.* New York: Harper & Row. Apps., notes, bibliog., index.   Part 1 of this book reviews academic theories of nationalism. Smith criticizes intellectualist history that sees nationalism as primarily an idea. He also notes the devotion of most sociologists to the process of modernization and their placement of nationalism in their models as part of that process. He rejects colonial explanations as overly simplistic, and discards "marginal-man" identity theories as psychologically reductionist. He favors a theory emphasizing the dislocation of the intelligentsia in the process of industrialization and nationalism as a means for its pursuit of class (or group) interest. He constructs a theory based on dual legitimation, the tension among dislocated intellectuals demanding both reinstatement of their former exalted position and assimilation to the upper stratum of industrial society. This produces the paradoxical forward-backward looking character of ethnonationalist movements. Nationalism, in this theory, is a particularist strategy adopted after the failure of reform and assimilation strategies. Smith illustrates his arguments with examples drawn from a wide variety of societies.

      2c,e/3e/4f/5e/10d,f/11b,d/12a,e,f/17   Theory

257   SMITH, Anthony D. 1979. "Towards a Theory of Ethnic Separatism." *Ethnic and Racial Studies* 2:21-37.   Smith argues that neither differential development nor "internal colonialism" adequately explain ethnic, as opposed to territorial, separatism. Ethnic markers, such as language and religion, are involved but in different ways with different consequences in different situations. Ethnic revivals are explained as functions of education, aspirations, and political mobilization in the specific context of bureaucratic states. Ethnicity functions as a symbolic system used by the intelligentsia for mobilizing political support across class lines. Ethnic mobilization is classified into three processual stages: communalist,

autonomist, and separatist. Each of these denotes the goal of the elite at different stages of a movement's development. Transition between stages is a function of politics, especially the response of central governments to ethnically embodied demands.

2f/3e/4f/5b,d,e,j/10a,c,d,f/11b,d/12b,d   Theory

258   SMOCK, David R. and Audrey C. Smock. 1975. *The Politics of Pluralism: A Comparative Study of Lebanon and Ghana.* New York: Elsevier. Bibliog., index. The authors compare politics in Lebanon and Ghana, two states of comparable size, plural ethnic composition, extensive internal migration, and residential interpenetration. Despite their similarities, Ghana and Lebanon differ radically in that the prime cleavages in Ghana are ethnic and in Lebanon they are religious, and in that government policies in Ghana neglect communal conflict while those in Lebanon reflect almost obsessive concern with communal conflict. The two countries are compared through their histories, sociocultural characteristics, social structures, politics, and economic systems. The authors conclude that religion and ethnicity do not differ in their potential for generating salient social cleavages, that separation does not impede intercommunal understanding, and that political structures influence communal identities by determining politically expedient levels of communal identification. In general, the authors argue, the more inclusive the politically relevant communal identity, the greater the potential for intergroup conflict. Influences of language and length of residence on politics are also analyzed.

2b,c/3d/4f/5b,e,f/9e   Ghana
10a,b,c/11a,d/12b,c,e,g   Lebanon

259   SMOOHA, Sammy. 1978. *Israel: Pluralism and Conflict.* Berkeley and Los Angeles: University of California Press. Apps., notes, bibliog., index. This detailed structural analysis of Israeli society includes a critique of pluralist theories and a conceptual scheme derived from them that includes consideration of setting, pluralism, inequality, cohesion, and change. Each variable is given operational definitions. In addition, three models of Israeli society (i.e., nation-building, colonial, pluralist) are examined. Substantive chapters treat the historical background and current social contexts of intergroup relations among Ashkenazim, Sephardim, and Arabs, intergroup inequality, Oriental-Ashkenazi inequality, conflict and integration, continuity and change, and concluding comments comparing the differing impacts of Oriental-Ashkenazi-Arab social cleavages.

2c,d/3b/4h/5a,b,f,i,j/6a/7b
8a,b/9b,c,e/10a,c/12g/13a/17   Israel

260 SNYDER, Louis L. 1976. *Varieties of Nationalism: A Comparative Study.* New York: Holt, Rinehart & Winston. Bibliog., index. This general study proceeds from consideration of definitions and a brief intellectual history of the idea of nationalism, through a history of its emergence as politically important in eighteenth-century England and France, nineteenth-century unification drives in Germany and Italy, empire-breaking in Austria-Hungary, and the "new nationalisms." These are shown in fragmenting "mini-nationalisms" in Europe, tribalism in Africa, Asian nationalism, American and Russian "messianic" nationalism, pan-national movements, transnational agglomerates, and speculation about future trends.

2a,c/3b,d,e/4d/5e/10a,b,d/11b,d/12a,b,d   General

261 SRINIVAS, M. N. 1956. "A Note on Sanskritization and Westernization." *Far Eastern Quarterly* 15:481-96. Bibliog. Srinivas relates the homogenization of Indian cultures through adoption of the high status Sanskritic traditions to upward social mobility, nationalistic reaction to British colonial rule, and so forth. He sees Westernization as a subsequent movement for those already highly Sanskritized. Brahmins seem to lead both movements. Srinivas shows how different groups manipulate their cultural traditions to enhance or maintain their social positions. Changes in Hindu caste mythology are used to show this process in action.

2b/3b/4a,d,i/5a,d,i/8b/9a,b,c,d,e/10a
11a,b/12a,b,c,e,g,i/13a,b/16a   India

262 SRINIVAS, M. N. 1966. *Social Change in Modern India.* Berkeley: University of California Press. Bibliog. Srinivas here expands his earlier essays on the subject of disjunctive identities, ideologies, and ritual. He analyzes the mutually reinforcing relationship between religious rituals and secular hierarchies and discusses the origins and development of caste ideology and its relationship to actual rankings. His conclusion is that cultural change involves emulation of the dominant caste in a region, regardless of its ranking. The over-all correspondence of local caste rankings to the pan-Indian varnic hierarchy remains problematic as it varies by region. There is a general tendency to reduce extreme disparities between the theory and the practice. Stigmatized groups (scheduled castes) here appear to use political strategies similar to those adopted elsewhere by stigmatized ethnic groups.

2b/3b/4a/5a/6b/8b/9c,e/10a,b,c,d/11a,b/12a,d,i/13a,b   India

263 STEIN, Howard F. and Robert F. Hill. 1977. *The Ethnic Imperative: Examining the New White Ethnic Movement.* University Park and London: Pennsylvania State University Press. Stein and Hill explore psycho-

social aspects of ethnicity. They distinguish between an unconscious "behavioral ethnicity" formerly prevailing in the United States and a currently dominant "ideological ethnicity." The difference in meanings of ethnicity correlates, in their analysis, with changing social circumstances faced by immigrants and their descendants, especially conflicts between rising expectations and unfulfilled ambitions. The authors conclude that the new ethnicity focuses on a counterculture ideology of separateness and is self-condemnatory since it emphasizes fear of the dominant cultural tradition. It is thus maladaptive and subordinates personal identity to an inadequate and essentially negative communal identification. A psychodynamic model of nativist movements is also included along with notes.

2c/3b/4g/5d/9a/10d/11a,b,c/12b,d,g,i   US: Euro-Americans

264   SUE, Stanley and Harry H. L. Kitano, eds. 1973. "Asian Americans: A Success Story?" *Journal of Social Issues,* vol. 29, no. 2. Bibliogs.   In this special journal issue devoted to Asian Americans, topics include a political economic analysis of the Japanese-American evacuation and internment (Miyamoto); socioeconomic mobility among Japanese Americans (Levine and Montreso); Japanese-American intermarriage with other groups (Tinker, Nakamura, and Kitano); stereotyping of Japanese and Chinese (Sue, Kitano, and Yee); changes in Chinese-American social roles (Fong); psychological studies of Japanese- and Chinese-American college students (Sue and Frank); mental illness among Chinese Americans (Berk and Hirata); Japanese-American youth political activism (Maykovitch); and conditions for elderly Asian Americans (Kalish and Moriwaki). Although the title refers to Asian Americans, Filipinos, Koreans, and other Asian groups are not covered.

1a/2b,c,d/3a/4g,h/5a,d,g,i/6a,b,c/7b/8b/9b,c,d,e   US: Chinese
10b,c,d,f/11a,b/12a,b,c,f,i/13a,b/14a,b/16a,b   Japanese

265   SUGAR, Peter F. and Ivo J. Lederer, eds. 1969. *Nationalism in Eastern Europe.* Seattle and London: University of Washington Press. Index. This conference collection includes an introduction describing the roots of Eastern European nationalism with emphasis on how the meaning of "nationalism" was changed during the borrowing of it from Western Europe (Sugar). Included also are historical studies of nationalism in Albania (Zavalani); Bulgaria (Pundeff); Czechoslovakia (Zacek); Greece (Xydis); Hungary (Barany); Poland (Brock); Romania (Fischer-Galati); and Yugoslavia (Lederer). Most of these studies concern the historical development of Eastern European nation-states in the breakup of colonial empires. However the position of minority groups is specifically addressed in the papers on Czechoslovakia and Yugoslavia and the paper on Hungary briefly discusses government concern for the position

of ethnic Magyars outside Hungary.

1a/2c/3b,d/4d/5e/9c/10a,b,c,d,f/12c,d,e   Eastern Europe

266 SUHRKE, Astri and Lela Garner Noble, eds. 1977. *Ethnic Conflict in International Relations*. New York: Praeger. Index. The papers collected in this volume discuss the implications of local ethnic conflicts for relations between nations. Following an editors' introduction that sets ethnic conflict on a resource allocation-separatism continuum (Suhrke and Noble), case studies describe international involvements in ethnic conflicts in Northern Ireland (Carroll); Cyprus (Black); Iraq's Kurdish rebellion (Harris); Lebanon (Meo); the Eritrean-Ethiopian conflict (Ethiopiawi); Kazakhs in China (Dreyer); and Muslims in the Philippines and Thailand (Suhrke and Noble). A concluding chapter classifies and analyzes the cases.

	China	Lebanon
	Cyprus	N. Ireland
1a/2b,c/3d/4f/5b	Ethiopia	Philippines
10b,c,d/11d/12a,b	Iraq	Thailand

267 SVENSSON, Frances. 1973. *The Ethnics in American Politics: American Indians*. Minneapolis, Minn.: Burgess. Bibliog. This is a short treatise on American-Indian relations with political authority and their participation in American politics. Svensson defines "Indian" racially, culturally, and socially. She discusses Indian relations with the United States government, constitutional provisions, removal, the Allotment Act (1887), Citizenship Act (1924), Reorganization Act (1934), Termination, and Public Law 280 as signal points in American-Indian relations with the government. She also discusses Indian organizations (Society of American Indians, National Congress of American Indians), and political movements (Red Power, National Indian Youth Congress, etc.).

2c/3b/4f/5b,f,i,j/10a,c,d,f/11d/12a,b,c,d,f,i   US: Native Americans

268 SZWED, John F. 1975. "Race and the Embodiment of Culture." *Ethnicity* 2:19-33. Szwed draws on data regarding Elizabethan English racist attitudes toward the Irish to support the thesis that racial distinctions and discriminations are embodiments of culture and have little to do with actual physical difference. Fictions of racial purity are maintained as means of keeping distance between groups. Szwed indicts antiracist anthropologists (especially Boas) for arguing against racism by denying the cultural variety that underlies the ideology. He concludes with a plea for fair valuation of cultural variety.

2c/3e/4a/5g/9c/11a,b,c/12b,c,f,i   Theory

269 TAYLOR, Ronald L. 1979. "Black Ethnicity and the Persistence of Ethnogenesis." *American Journal of Sociology* 84:1401-23. Bibliog. After criticizing the prevalent assumption that black American experiences radically differ from those of immigrant group members, Taylor draws on the theoretical literature on ethnicity to show the structural conditions in the urban north that generate a continuing process of ethnogenesis. Particularly salient variables are migration, urbanization, and intergroup conflict. Occupational concentration and residential segregation have been crucial factors in the generation of immigrant and black ethnic communities. These structural conditions underlie the commonalities of experience embodied in the focus on roots, ethnic symbols, and putative common culture. Taylor argues that black ethnicity in the United States devolved from essentially the same causes as European immigrant ethnicity.

2c,e/3a/4h/5d,i/8b/9e/10b/12b,d   US: Afro-Americans

270 TROSPER, Ronald L. 1976. "Native American Boundary Maintenance: The Flathead Indian Reservation." *Ethnicity* 3:256-74. Bibliog. Trosper presents a historical study of boundary maintenance by Kootenai-Salish tribes on the Flathead reservation in Montana. In particular he discusses the use of blood quanta as the single defining criterion for tribal membership. The boundary definitions changed according to different federal policies toward Indians at different periods of time. Federal authorities and Indian tribes both maneuvered for economic and political advantage. Indian definitions of identity are seen as adaptive to the power structure presented by government policies. Their variable policies seek to maximize their interests in a variable social and political context.

2b,c/3a/4b/5d,k/8a/10a,c,d/12a   US: Native Americans

271 TUMIN, Melvin M. with Arnold Feldman. 1969. "Social Class and Skin Color in Puerto Rico." In *Comparative Perspectives on Race Relations,* edited by M. Tumin, pp. 197-214. Boston: Little, Brown. Tumin notes that skin-color distinctions are recognized in Puerto Rico, using the white, mixed, and black classifications common throughout the Caribbean. However the patterns of self definition Tumin observes do not match predictions based on a light-dark preference continuum. His discussion is based on survey data gathered on perceptions of respect, opportunity, general attitudes according to color and class of respondent, educational level, and so forth.

2b,d/3b/4h/5g/9b,c/11a,b,c/12f   Puerto Rico

272 TUMIN, Melvin and Walter Plotch, eds. 1977. *Pluralism in a Democratic Society.* New York: Praeger. Apps., notes, bibliogs. This collection of

conference papers includes a historical summary of American attitudes toward cultural pluralism, moving from early twentieth-century assimilation to current emphases on ethnic studies programs (Glazer); a personal vision of the effect of ethnic consciousness on the individual (Novak); a discussion of political life and cultural pluralism (Apter); the findings of political socialization research about respect for ethnic diversity (Torney and Tesconi); a cognitive-developmental analysis of respect for persons and childhood ethnic prejudice (Davidson); implications of child-development research for teaching respect for cultural diversity (Sigel and Johnson); and two papers concerning design of curricula with cultural pluralism as a focus (Jaramillo, Banks).

1a/2c,d/3b/4a,g,h,i(Education)/5g/9b/11a,b,c,d/13b   US: General

273   TURNER, Jonathan H. and Royce Singleton, Jr. 1978. "A Theory of Ethnic Oppression: Toward a Reintegration of Cultural and Structural Concepts in Ethnic Relations Theory." *Social Forces* 56:1001-18. Notes, bibliog.   Borrowing extensively from Bonacich's work on split labor market theory and ethnic antagonism, the authors suggest that ethnic antagonism, grounded in political exclusion or castelike immobility, is likely to contradict social norms or ideals emphasizing equality and/or mobility. Members of detached social segments of the population (i.e., those not threatened by market penetration of lower price labor), are likely to hold progressive beliefs undermining exclusive or caste systems. In response to the exposure of contradictions, the high wage segment of the system is likely to adjust the system by which its interests are protected, and to adjust its associated racist-ethnicist ideology to conceal the contradictions. The resulting succession of dominant racist or ethnicist beliefs is shown in periodic changes in economic and political structures of oppression, dominant beliefs about blacks, and progressive beliefs about blacks in the United States from colonial times to the present.

2c/3b,e/4f/5i/8a,d/9a,c,e/10b,c/11b,d   Theory

274   UCHENDU, Victor C. 1975. "The Dilemma of Ethnicity and Polity Primacy in Black Africa." In *Ethnic Identity*, edited by G. DeVos and L. Romanucci-Ross, pp. 265-75. Palo Alto, Calif.: Mayfield.   Uchendu discusses four levels of group identity in Africa, local (ethnic), national, racial, and continental. He argues that different identities are invoked in response to different situations and that there has been considerable conflict between them. Switching between identities is not simply a situational orientation, but involves a psychological expansion or contraction of the reference frames used by individuals. Such psychological shifts require considerable self-redefinition and have substantial personal as well as political implications.

2c/3b/4a/5d,h/10a,b/11a,b,c,d/12a,c,h,i   Africa

275 VAN DEN BERGHE, Pierre L. 1970. "Distance Mechanisms of Stratification." In *Readings in Race and Ethnic Relations,* edited by A. H.
Richmond, pp. 210-19. Oxford: Pergamon Press. According to van
den Berghe, social distance, expressed socially or spatially, is the key to
all forms of authority, hierarchy, or stratification. Etiquette and segregation are two basic mechanisms of hierarchization in caste (especially
racial caste) situations. Etiquette and segregation vary inversely to each
other and can have very different consequences for intergroup relations.
If both of these mechanisms fail to maintain distance between groups,
then race (or caste) must diminish in importance as a factor in social
life. Examples are drawn from South Africa and the United States.

South Africa
2b/3d/4h/5i/9c,e/11a,c,d/12a,i US: Afro-Americans

276 VAN DEN BERGHE, Pierre L. 1970. *Race and Ethnicity: Essays in
Comparative Sociology.* New York: Basic Books. This retrospective
collection of van den Berghe's work includes analyses of various aspects
of intergroup relations in the United States, Guatemala, South and East
Africa, and Fiji. The empirical material is wide ranging. Of particular use
are the analyses of social distance, hypergamy, and ethnicity in highland
Chiapas and Guatemala. These use case material to illustrate clearly
articulated theoretical positions.

1a/2b/3d/4h/5f,i/6b/8b/9b,c,d,e/10a,b,c,d/11a/12b,c,f,i/14c General

277 VAN DEN BERGHE, Pierre L., ed. 1972. *Intergroup Relations: Sociological Perspectives.* New York: Basic Books. Index. This is a collection
of articles originally published in the *American Sociological Review*
(1939-69) on intergroup relations. It is organized into sections that
illustrate American sociological thought on intergroup relations for the
period covered. A number of theoretical papers are included (Frazier,
Walker, Lieberson). Articles on the ethnography of racial and ethnic
relations include treatment of triracial isolates in Robeson County,
North Carolina (Johnson); race relations in the upper Rio Grande area
(Francis); cultural and linguistic pluralism in Switzerland (Mayer); and
description of Jamaican pluralism (Broom). Other topics covered include
analysis of the African diaspora and cultural survivals (the Herskovitz-
Frazier debate); group exogamous marriages among Jews (Barron), Pana-
manians (Biesanz), and in Hawaii (Schmitt); race and ethnic attitudes in
São Paulo (Bastide and van den Berghe); race and alienation (Middleton);
situational patterning of interracial attitudes (Kohn and Williams); American southerners and northern racism (Killian); black visibility (Kephart);
demography and the ecology of racism (Glenn and Cutright); Japanese-
American family change as a response to oppression (Bloom); power
structures in the black community (Barth and Abu-Laban); leadership
patterns in subordinate groups (Watson and Samora); racial humor (Burma);

intergroup humor in general (Barron); jazz as acculturation (Slotkin); and evaluation of skin color in all-black school classes (Seeman).

1a/2b/3a,b,d/4h/5f,g,h,i/8b/9b,c,e/10b,c,f
11a,b/12a,b,c,e,f,i/13a/14a/16a   General

278   VAN DEN BERGHE, Pierre L. 1976. "Ethnic Pluralism in Industrial Societies: A Special Case?" *Ethnicity* 3:242-55. Bibliog. Van den Berghe argues that ethnicity results from a combination of subjective and objective factors. Interethnic relations are governed by conditions of contact (conquest vs. peaceful immigration), the degree of assimilation between groups, and combinations of these two factors. He uses historical examples from Europe to show how particular intergroup events produce lasting consequences for intergroup relations. Other relevant variables include the territorial integrity of different groups and mechanisms of communal incorporation. Van den Berghe uses these variables to evaluate the prospects for nation formation by various ethnic groups, and to evaluate separatism as a political strategy.

2e/3d/4h/5a,b,f,i/7b/10a,c/11a,d/12a,e,g   General

279   VAN DEN BERGHE, Pierre L. 1978. "Race and Ethnicity: A Socio-biological Perspective." *Ethnic and Racial Studies* 1:401-11. Bibliog. Van den Berghe argues that both ethnicity and race are extensions of the idiom of kinship and that ethnic and race sentiments are extended forms of kin selection. Natural selection, in this theory, generates a cooperative orientation favoring kin over nonkin. Close kin cooperation increases the probability that an individual's genetic characteristics will be transmitted to future generations. Cultural signals are used to identify quasi-kin and thus cultural diacritica come to denote ethnic superfamilies. Race becomes a social factor when large morphologically distinct populations meet, a recent development, according to van den Berghe. Racial and ethnic groups are thus cooperative ingroups and also transacting and genetically competing outgroups.

2f/3e/4h/5k(Sociobiology)/11a/12a,d,f/14b,c   Theory

280   VAN DEN BERGHE, Pierre L. 1978. *Race and Racism: A Comparative Perspective.* 2d ed. New York: John Wiley & Sons. Bibliog. This edition replicates the 1967 edition except for a new introduction. Van den Berghe advances ideal characterizations of paternalistic and competitive race relations. He uses these to compare the historical developments of race relation in Mexico, Brazil, the United States, and South Africa. Similarities and differences between these cases are analyzed in terms of social and cultural pluralism. Population proportions of dominant and subordinate social groups, religion, the nature of the indigenous culture, and

changes in the social infrastructures of dominant groups are held to be the dominant factors affecting the development of different intergroup relations. The concluding chapter presents a general theory of pluralism.

1b/2c/3d/4h/5f,i/6a,b/8b/9c,e	Brazil	South Africa
10a,b,c,d/11a/12c,d,f,i/14a,c	Mexico	US: Afro-Americans

281 VAN DEN BERGHE, Pierre L. and George P. Primov. 1977. *Inequality in the Peruvian Andes: Class and Ethnicity in Cuzco.* Columbia: University of Missouri Press. Apps., glossary, bibliog., index. This detailed case study of stratification in the Peruvian Andes takes a regional perspective, with Cuzco the metropolitan center surrounded by dependent rural areas. Following an introductory chapter on class and ethnicity in plural societies, the analysis covers description of the research setting (geographically, demographically, in terms of infrastructure); the history of inequality in Peru from the Incas to the present; political structures (government, military and police, schools, church, patronage networks and power); economic structures (loci of economic control, haciendas, cooperatives, town and local markets, the transport system, regional metropolises and economic elite, regional links to national and world economics); cultural dynamics (the Indian-Mestizo continuum, social definitions of class and ethnicity, Spanish vs. Quechua language use); the institutional framework of class and ethnic relations (dependence and religion, the "compadrazgo" system of ritual kinship, marriage, the market system, army, police, judiciary, schools, municipal and central government bureaucracies); rural towns; market towns; metropolitan regional centers; and summary conclusions.

2b/3b/4a,h/5c,f,i/6a,b,c/8b,d/9b,c,d,e/10a,c,f,g
11a,d/12a,c,d,e,f,g,i/13a/14a,b/16a,b/17   Peru

282 VERMA, Gajendra K. and Christopher Bagley, eds. 1979. *Race, Education and Identity.* London: Macmillan. Bibliog., index. The editors' introduction to this collection summarizes arguments on four issues: (1) recent empirical attacks on the scientific racism of Jensen et al.; (2) labeling used in education that works to the disadvantage of nonwhite students; (3) encapsulation of blacks in schools for retarded or other subnormals students; and (4) alienation and identity of blacks in multi-racial school settings (Verma and Bagley). Chapter topics include the effects of cultural differences on student perceptions of black and white school teachers (Landis and McGrew); comparison of rates of rote and conceptual learning between racial groups (Stones); antecedents of scholastic success among West Indian children in London (Bagley, Bart, and Wong); educational effects of different home and school languages (Macnamara); ethnic identification and self-rejection (Weinreich); pupil self-esteem (Bagley, Malick, and Verma); and two papers on adjustment

problems of transracially adopted children (Bagley and Yong; Costin and Wattenberg). Each paper contains a critical summary of the relevant literature.

1a/2d,e/3b/4g,h,i(Education)/5d,f,g/9c
11a,c/12a,b,c,e,f/13a,b/16a   Britain: General

283   VON FURSTENBERG, George M., Ann R. Horowitz, and Bennett Harrison, eds. 1974. *Patterns of Racial Discrimination.* 2 vols. Lexington, Mass.: Lexington Books. Notes, bibliogs., indexes. These two volumes examine discriminatory patterns in housing (vol. 1) and in employment and income (vol. 2). Part 1 of volume 1 includes papers contributing to a debate over the interaction of housing segregation and employment discrimination given the dispersal of urban jobs. The papers review the argument (Kain); empirically criticize the argument that ghetto concentration of blacks isolates them from growing suburban job markets (Harrison); analyze the effects of housing quality and consumption patterns on blacks' economic activities (Bell); study the effects of accessibility and segregation on employment of urban poor (Hutchinson); and offer a policy agenda on employment and location of black households (Harrison). Part 2, on racial discrimination in housing, includes studies of equilibrium and disequilibrium theories of racial housing markets (pt. 2A) and papers addressing the question of whether blacks pay more for housing (pt. 2B). Comparison of theories includes a review of the literature and an argument that segregation is the result of equilibrium market processes (Muth); an argument that institutional factors prevent cross-race equilibration from taking place (Quigley); an empirical study of segregation in the area east of San Francisco Bay and demonstration of its substantial market imperfections (Straszheim); an examination of income and race on home-mortgage delinquency rates in Pittsburgh (Von Furstenberg and Green); and policy recommendations (Straszheim). On the question of whether blacks pay more for housing, contributions include a review of issues (Lapham); an argument based on New York City data that housing prices are essentially the same for blacks and whites (Olsen); and a critique of the preceding paper with evidence that if quality factors are taken into account discriminatory price differences do appear (Mieszkowski). Volume 2, on employment and income discrimination, is divided into consideration of theoretical perspectives and measures of racial inequality. Part 1, on theories of racial discrimination, includes a survey of theories explaining income differences (Stiglitz); a micro-simulation of a labor market as a means of studying black-white differences (Bergmann); alternative theories of labor-market discrimination (Freeman); a description of federal civil rights enforcement policies for the 1970s (Lyle); a political-economic synthesis of labor-market discrimination (Alexis); analysis of uncertainty and discrimination (Pleeter); a comparative test of discrimination hypotheses supporting white em-

ployee discrimination as explanatory (Chiswick); articulation of an employee discrimination model (Bell); and a critique of these contributions (Schiller). Chapters in part 2 concern patterns and causes of changes in white-nonwhite income differentials, 1947-72 (Horowitz); factors involved in changing relative earning for black workers during the 1960s (Vroman); trends in distribution of family incomes within and between racial groups (Horowitz); black-white differences in returns to schooling (Welch); and racial differences in variation in rates of return from schooling and implications for relative rates of human capital investment (Chiswick).

1a/2b,c/3a,b,c/4b/5i,k (Neoclassical Economics)   Theory
6b/8a,b,d/9e/13a,b/14a   US: General

284   WAGATSUMA, Hiroshi. 1969. "The Social Perception of Skin Color in Japan." In *Comparative Perspectives on Race Relations,* edited by M. Tumin, pp. 124-39. Boston: Little, Brown. Bibliog.   Given traditional identification of whiteness with beauty in Japanese culture, Japanese contact with fair-skinned Europeans had interesting effects. Japanese standards of beauty were justified by denigrating other Caucasoid characteristics (e.g., smelly skin, coarse texture, etc.). Wagatsuma documents these reactions in Japanese art, literature, and popular media. Stereotypes of blacks held by native and expatriate Japanese are also discussed.

2c/3b/4g/5d,g/9c,d/11a,b,c/12a,b,f,i   Japan

285   WAGATSUMA, Hiroshi. 1975. "Problems of Cultural Identity in Modern Japan." In *Ethnic Identity,* edited by G. DeVos and L. Romanucci-Ross, pp. 307-34. Palo Alto, Calif.: Mayfield. Bibliog.   Wagatsuma reviews historical changes in Japanese perceptions of identity since 1868. He argues that assimilation of European and American technology and accompanying cultural influences has radically altered the Japanese sociocultural milieu. Progressive and traditional definitions of the meaning of Japanese identity have alternated. Wagatsuma analyzes the various meanings as personal adjustments to realities of interactions across ethnic boundaries. He also includes comments on current conflicts in Japanese ethnic definitions.

2c/3b/4g/5d/11a,b,c/12a,b,c   Japan

286   WALKER, Deward E., Jr., ed. *The Emergent Native Americans: A Reader in Culture Contact.* Boston: Little, Brown. Bibliog.   Through examination of interaction between Native Americans and European groups, Walker constructs a reader illustrating many aspects of culture contact. The initial theoretical paper delineates concepts of acculturation and assimilation. Useful papers on policies of native administration concern pluralism and American Indians (Manners) and Canada's treaty admin-

istration system (Harper). Population decline and recovery are discussed in papers analyzing the 1830-33 California-Oregon epidemic and its effects on Indian populations (Cook); Cherokee population and its geographic distribution (Wahrhaftig); and Nez Perce intermarriage, distribution of blood quanta, and the implications of these for cultural maintenance (Walker). Other papers concern technoeconomic changes brought about by contact, religious innovation as reaction to contact and conquest with particular reference to peyote cults (Stewart); early changes in social relations, Naragansett survival through adopted culture traits (Boissevain); the social characteristics of relocated Indians in San Francisco (Ablon); and adaptive strategies of migrant Indians in Los Angeles (Price).

1a/2a,c,d/3a/4a,h/5a,f,g,i,j/6a,b,c/7c,d/8a,b,c/9c,e
10a,c,d,e/11a,b,d/12a,b,c,f,g/13a/14a,b,c/15/17   US: Native Americans

287   WALLERSTEIN, Immanuel. 1972. "Social Conflict in Post-Independence Black Africa: The Concepts of Race and Status-Group Reconsidered." In *Racial Tensions and National Identity,* edited by E. Campbell, pp. 207-26. Nashville, Tenn.: Vanderbilt University Press. Bibliog.   Using an inclusive definition of status group drawn from Weber, Wallerstein argues that ethnic and religious groups, castes, and nations are all examples of this phenomenon. All are affinities based on criteria ostensibly predating the social context within which they are activated. Each functions as a base for group organization in competition for scarce resources. Status is thus both retrogressive and progressive, a strategy of both offense and defense. In ultimate conflict situations, boundaries of status groups will tend to coincide with their infrastructural bases, class inequalities. Wallerstein thus argues that both tribalism and race conflict are ideological epiphenomena of class. They are phenomenally distinct from class because races, tribes, and ethnic groups are, by definition, groups, while classes are not. Examples are drawn from Africa.

2c/3e/4h/5b/10b,c,d/11a/12a,d,f,i   Africa

288   WALLMAN, Sandra, ed. 1979. *Ethnicity at Work.* London: Macmillan. Notes, bibliog., index.   These essays examine ethnicity in work contexts. The introductory essay points out uneven ethnic distributions in almost all occupational settings and the differing perceptions of and behavior in work settings characteristic of ethnically different persons (Wallman). Case studies consider occupational concentration and identity manipulation among English gypsies (Okely); processes resulting in occupational concentration of English Jews in professions consistent with group value orientations (Kosmin); chain migration of Macedonians into the Toronto restaurant trade with entry as dishwashers and the goal of owning an independent restaurant (Herman); Sikh brokerage in

British foundries (Brooks and Singh); alteration of ethnic boundaries by South Asian women to meet the exigencies of different work situations (Khan); manipulation of identity in bureaucratic contexts (Flett); the impact of noneconomic (i.e., ethnic) factors on occupational mobility in a New Zealand company (Macrae); factors limiting use of ethnicity as a resource in Toronto casual labor (Stymeist); and a placement of ethnic economic activity within over-all economic dependency structures.

	Britain:	Canada:
	Asians	General
1a/2b,c,d/3b,c,e/4a,c,h/5c,i	Gypsies	New Zealand
7b/8b,d/9b,e/11c/12c,i/14b	Jews	

289   WATSON, James L., ed. 1977. *Between Two Cultures: Migrants and Minorities in Britain.* Oxford: Basil Blackwell. Bibliog. These twelve anthropological essays describe social and cultural adjustments of different immigrant groups in England. Watson sees the conflicting cultural demand facing children of immigrants as a consistent theme in these studies, hence the book's title. Each author treats his/her case differently. Among the topics covered are the developmental history of the Sikh community in Britain (Ballard and Ballard); maintenance of social links between Mirpuri Pakistani immigrants and their home region in Pakistan (Khan); Montserrat economic dependence on migration to Britain and its social and cultural consequences on the home island (Philpott); change processes among Jamaican migrants (Foner); child fosterage and the education imperative among West African immigrants (Goody and Groothues); Hong Kong Chinese control of the London catering trade and maintenance of cultural and ethnic boundaries (Watson); the Polish exile community (Patterson); patterns of Italian migration to London (Palmer); maintenance of Greek Cypriot identity (Constantinides); and relations between Turkish Cypriots and other groups (Ladbury). Most of these papers fit a community study model, discussing a range of topics for each group.

	Britain:	Jamaicans
	Africans	Montserratians
	Chinese	Pakistanis
1a/2b/3a/4a/5c,f/7a,b/8b/9b,c,e	Cypriots	Poles
11b/12a,d,g,i/13b/14a,b,c/15/16a	Italians	Sikhs

290   WAX, Murray L. 1971. *Indian Americans: Unity and Diversity.* Englewood Cliffs., N.J.: Prentice-Hall. Apps., bibliogs., index. This general discussion of Native Americans includes chapters on historical and ecological backgrounds of modern Indians; demographic characteristics of Indian populations in the United States, Canada, and Spanish America; Indian-white relations (missions, traders, Bureau of Indian Affairs, termi-

nation policies); contemporary Plains reservation communities (their legal background, ecology, sociopolitical organization, internal stratification, urbanization, economy, education); the Oklahoma Cherokee (tribal nonreservation people, their population, income, education, language use); pan-Indianism (religious movements—Handsome Lake, Ghost Dance, Native American church, and political nationalism); Indians in cities (in Alaska, urban Iroquois enclaves, Sioux in Rapid City, S.D.); ideologies of Indian-white relations (genocide, innate inferiority, melting-pot ideals, cultural pluralism, etc.); and problems of community and Indian identity.

2b,c/3b/4h/5d,e,f,g,i,j/6a,b,c/7c,d/8b/9c,e/10a,b,c,d
11a,c,d/12a,b,c,d,e,f,g,h,i/13a,b/14a,b/15/16a/17   US: Native Americans

291   WEINSTEIN, Warren and Robert Schrire. 1976. *Political Conflict and Ethnic Stereotypes: A Case Study of Burundi.* Syracuse, N.Y.: Maxwell School of Citizenship and Public Affairs, Syracuse University. This study of ethnic political conflict in Burundi defines ethnicity in terms of common descent. The particular conflict at issue is that between Hutu majority agriculturalists and the Tutsi minority in Burundi. The discussion includes a historical survey of relations between the two groups; an analysis of the distribution of elite positions in Burundi politics by ethnic group; and a detailed analysis of the 1972 Hutu revolt and Tutsi counter-revolt, which together resulted in several hundred thousand deaths in that country.

2b,c/3b/4f/5b/10a,b,c,d,e,f,g/12a,c   Burundi

292   WEINSTOCK, S. Alexander. 1969. *Acculturation and Occupation: A Study of the 1956 Hungarian Refugees in the United States.* The Hague: Martinus Nijhoff. This survey of Hungarians who emigrated as a result of the 1956 revolution shows that occupation is a stronger predictor than age, sex, or religion in the assimilation of the immigrants to American life. High status occupations apparently facilitated acculturation. Those variables secondarily related to occupation (e.g., occupational mobility, educational level, etc.) also correlated strongly. Numerous other variables were also tested. The author concludes that those factors of personality adapted for success in industrial society led to success in both Hungary and the United States and facilitated a relatively quick transition between the two cultures. This study also supports the argument that the substantive (cultural) content of ethnic identity tends to be more important among lower socioeconomic classes.

2d/3a/4g/5a,d/6a,b/7b/8b/9e/11b/12b,c,g,i/13a,b/14a/15 US: Hungarians

293   WEST, Katherine. 1972. "Stratification and Ethnicity in 'Plural' New States." *Race* 13:487-95. West relates ethnicity with political align-

ments in new states. She sees ethnicity as an important factor in determining perceptions and interpretations of political decisions in pluralistic
states. Where bounded ethnic groups exist, there is no middle ground in
decision making. All decisions are divisive, since they will inevitably be
interpreted as favorable to one or another of the competing groups.
Stratification and ethnic boundary maintenance contribute to politicization of ethnicity.

2f/3d/4f/5b,i/9c,e/10b,c,d/11a,d/12a/16a,b   Theory

294   WILKIE, Mary. 1977. "Colonials, Marginals, and Immigrants: Contribu-
      tions to a Theory of Ethnic Stratification." *Comparative Studies in
      Society and History* 19:67-95.   By integrating functionalist and Marxian
      theories of social stratification, Wilkie tries to construct a stratification
      model capable of encompassing all types of interethnic relations. She
      sets out three idea-type situations that generate different kinds of inter-
      ethnic relations. The *colonial* situation is characterized by a perfect
      coincidence between race and class, a full integration of social structure
      and economic interests. Peoples in *marginal* situations are not economi-
      cally integrated, are often accorded special protected status, and are
      often subject to strong pressure to assimilate. *Immigrants* nearly always
      ultimately assimilate, and class and ethnic interest are more fluid in
      this than in the other two situations. The interaction of these three
      situations depends on conditions of economic growth. Wilkie's thesis is
      that societies originating in these three situations develop in character-
      istically different ways.

      2c/3e/4h/5a,c,i,j/7b,d/8b,c,d/9c,e/10a,c   Theory

295   WILLIAMS, Robin M., Jr. 1972. *Mutual Accommodation: Ethnic
      Conflict and Cooperation.* Minneapolis: University of Minnesota Press.
      Bibliog.   In this review and appraisal of the state of American interethnic
      relations in the 1970s, Williams takes a positive view, emphasizing mu-
      tually satisfactory outcomes of recent ethnic and racial conflicts. He
      sees conflict resolution as an overreaching process and so develops his
      case by looking at specific aspects of it. These include cases of school
      desegregation planning, political and legal inducements to compliance
      with government social goals, the effects of using coercive constraints,
      and prospects for an end to ethnic conflict in the United States. Each
      chapter in this book contains a set of testable propositions on the topic
      covered in that chapter, and the effects of specific government programs
      and recent legal cases are examined in some detail.

      2c/3b/4h/5a,k(Consensus)/8a/10a,b,d/11d/13b   US: General

296   WILLIAMS, Robin M., Jr. 1975. "Race and Ethnic Relations." *Annual*

Review of Sociology 1:125-64. Bibliog.   Williams reviews the sociological literature on ethnicity and race relations and characterizes research trends in the field.   His review is divided into: general description of the field; recent developments in research and theory building (changes in activity, major controversies, findings, and hypotheses); substantive findings (family, stratification, mobility, education, economy, housing, residential segregation, contact effects, religion, politics, civil disorder, conditions associated with protest and revolt, political strategies, beliefs, and values); issues of method and theory; and concluding remarks.

2e/3a,b,c,d/4h/5a,b,g,i/6b/8a,b/9b,c,e/10b,d,g
11a,b,d/12d,e,f,g/13a/14a,b,c/15/16a/17   General

297   WILSON, William J. 1973. *Power, Racism, and Privilege: Race Relations in Theoretical and Socio-historical Perspectives.* New York: Macmillan. Bibliog., index.   Wilson critically discusses current theories of racial status differentiation and intergroup conflict. His approach is structural and centers on how social structures generate and tolerate certain minority responses to them. He uses social structural analysis to analyze United States slavery, segregation and ideas of biological racism, competitive race relations and protest, the situation in South Africa, and to draw comparison between South African and American race relations.

2c,e/3b,d/4h/5b,f,i/8b   South Africa
9c/10b,c,d/11a/12c,f   US: Afro-Americans

298   WOLFF, Hans. 1959. "Intelligibility and Inter-Ethnic Attitudes." *Anthropological Linguistics* 1:34-41. Bibliog.   Though he was concerned primarily with the general linguistic problems of determining mutual intelligibility, Wolff noted in his Nigerian research that there appeared to be a connection between interethnic attitudes and whether people said they could understand each other. Responses to his survey questions on intelligibility puzzled him. Speakers of what appeared objectively to be mutually intelligible dialects claimed not to be able to understand each other. He also found numerous instances of nonreciprocal intelligibility, and further study revealed that intelligibility tended to correspond to relative prestige rankings of ethnic groups. Individuals generally could understand dialects of those with higher prestige, but not the dialects of persons lower in prestige than they. Claims for unintelligibility may indicate ethnically based movements toward political autonomy.

2b/3b/4e/5d,i/9c/10a/11a/12e,i/16a   Nigeria

299   WOLFF, Hans. 1967. "Language, Ethnic Identity and Social Change in Southern Nigeria." *Anthropological Linguistics* 9:18-25. Bibliog.   Following on his earlier research, Wolff surveyed the Niger Delta area of

Nigeria. He found that coastal people often did not acquire proficiency in the local language, even if they moved to inland hinterlands. Kalabari and Nembe were the dominant language groups under colonial administration and personal and place names in inland areas were often recorded in those languages. New ethnic identity in inland areas coincided with movement away from bilingualism in coastal languages. Many interior people now are bilingual in Igbo. Wolff concluded that assertion of economic and political identity tended to be accompanied by redefinition of linguistic identity.

2b/3a/4e/5d,i/6b/8b/9c,e/10b,c,d/11a/12b,e/16a   Nigeria

300   YANCEY, William L., Eugene P. Ericksen, and Richard N. Juliani. 1976. "Emergent Ethnicity: A Review and Reformulation." *American Sociological Review* 41:391-403. Bibliog.   The authors argue against cultural heritage as the principal antecedent and defining characteristic for American ethnic groups. Instead they assert that structural conditions of American cities and the position of immigrant groups in American social structures are the preeminent independent variables. The topics covered in this analysis are the conditions of ethnic cultural emergence; social forces promoting ethnic solidarity and identification; and generation of different forms of ethnic culture as social conditions change. Occupational concentrations of ethnic cohorts, consequent residential concentration, segregation and ethnic endogamy, and community development are all discussed. Tests for salience of ethnicity are suggested.

2c,f/3b/4h/5f,i/6b,c/7d/8a,b/9c/11a/12b,c,d,i/14a   US: General

301   YETMAN, Norman R. and C. Hoy Steele, eds. 1971. *Majority and Minority: The Dynamics of Racial and Ethnic Relations.* Boston: Allyn & Bacon.   This collection contains only previously published articles. Theoretical papers are taken from Nod, Heston, Lieberson, and van den Berghe. Regional perspectives on intergroup relations are given through case studies of Central America (Pitt-Rivers); blacks in the United States and Britain (Singham); comparison of Jews in Poland and Chinese in the Philippines (Eitzen); gypsies in Czechoslovakia (Ulc); and apartheid in South Africa (Legum). Also included are articles treating the history of American minorities, including specific discussion of American slavery (Bryce-Laport); the federal government and free blacks from 1790 to 1860 (Litwack); enduring ghettos (Osofrey); American Indian history (Lurie); and the evolution of American racism (Higham). Patterns of intergroup contact are analyzed, with specific reference to assimilation (Gordon); resurgent ethnicity (Glazer and Moynihan); Japanese Americans (Caudill and de Vason); Mexican Americans in southern California (Penalosa); American Indians and the education system (Lesser); and the black psyche (Poussaint). Politics and discrimination are described by

papers on black rage (Boesel et al.); public beliefs in race (Schuman); black powerlessness in Chicago (Baron); Sioux politics without power (Thomas); police-youth encounters (Piliavin and Briar); Mexican Americans and the administration of justice (U.S. Civil Rights Commission); class and justice (Wright); housing segregation (Greer and Greer); employment discrimination (Hill); early education and racism (Baratz and Baratz); federal programs for American Indians (Wax and Wax); textbook stereotypes of Indians (Henry); black athletes (Yetman and Eitzen); and several articles on black revolution (Skolnick, Killian, Merck and Griego, and Gans). The reader is a representative sample of the general literature.

1a,b/2e/3a,b,d/4a,f,g,h/5a,b,g,i,j/6b/10c,d/12a,b,c,d,f/13a   General

302   YOUNG, Crawford. 1976. *The Politics of Cultural Pluralism.* Madison: University of Wisconsin Press. Index.   This general study of cultural pluralism and its political impacts is illustrated by a large number of well-done case studies. Introductory chapters cover the literature on cultural diversity and political development; a discussion of types of cultural pluralism (nationalism, tribal, social class, relativity of identity, variation in identity, types of differentiation); state, nation, and nationalism (as the arena for cultural pluralism); patterns of identity change and cultural mobilization; symbols; threats; and identity. Subsequent chapters develop these concepts in case studies of Zaire; a comparison of Uganda and Tanzania; comparison of Nigeria and India; comparison of Indonesia and the Philippines; the Arab world; Latin American Indians; Biafra; Bangladesh; and the southern Sudan (comparison of secessionist movements). A concluding chapter draws general conclusions from the case studies.

1b/2c/3d/4f/5e,f/10a,b,c,d,e,f,g/11a,d/12a,b,e,g   General

Anonymous works, listed chronologically

303   1971. "Dimensions of the Racial Situation." *International Social Science Journal,* vol. 23, no. 4.   This special topic journal issue includes a summary of the African experience of ethnicity in light of colonialism, segmentation, and integration (van den Berghe); an analysis of race and caste as types of social stratification (Beteille); a summary of educational problems deriving from intergroup conflicts (Bowker); a discussion of changes in the Nanyang (southern seas) Chinese trade position in Southeast Asia (Tjwan); a comparison of the adequacy of Marxist, Durkheimian, and plural society theories for explaining current social conditions, especially the persistence of ethnic and racial segmentation and the failure of interethnic and interracial solidarity to emerge (Kuper); a discussion of differential treatment of ethnic groups in the French press with notations of semantic marking (Guillaumin); and addresses on prospects for change

in the "racial situation" (Gluckman, Levi-Strauss).

	Africa
1a/2b,e/3b/4a,d,h,i/5b,f,i/9a,b,c,d,e	France
10b,c/11c,d/12b,f/16a	Southeast Asia

304 1971. "Nationalism and Separatism." *Journal of Contemporary History,*
vol. 6, no. 1.   The articles in this topical journal issue describe unsatisfied
nationalist movements. Following a general introduction on nationalism
(Seton-Watson); case studies consider movements for Basque and Catalan
nationalism in Spain (Payne); the situation of German speakers in Romania (Catellan); attempts to build a sense of Lebanese identity (Salibi);
Kurdish nationalism in Iraq and Iran (Edmonds); separatism in the southern Sudan (Gray); the Protestant-Catholic conflict in Northern Ireland
(Beckett); Scottish nationalism (Bedd and Stewart); the historical background of Welsh nationalism (Morgan); and conflicts between ideas of
"nation" prevalent in French and English Canada (Spry). All the movements are treated in historical perspective.

	Canada: Québécois	Romania
	Iran	Scotland
	Iraq	Spain
1a/2c/3b/4d/5e/10a,c,d,e	Lebanon	Sudan
11d/12b,e,g/17	N. Ireland	Wales

305 1975. *Social Dynamics,* vol. 1, no. 1. Notes, bibliogs.   This journal
issue contains eight articles on racial and ethnic relations. Three of them
develop theoretical approaches to the question, the first describing the
pluralist approach and distinguishing types of minorities (ethnic, national,
racial), according to their social positions (van den Berghe), the second
presenting a critique of the pluralist approach (Bekker); and the third
analyzing the role of third parties in ethnic conflicts (Hare). Four papers
deal with South Africa, including a summary of research in South Africa
(Welsh); a discussion of impediments to research on race relations in
South Africa (Lever); an analysis of industrialization and its implications
for continued racial stratification in that country (Cilliers); and an analysis
of changing attitudes toward "passing" in a colored community (Unter-
halter). The final article describes ethnic inequalities in Israel (Smooha
and Peres).

1a/2b,c,e/3b,e/4h/5d,f,g,j/7b/8a	Israel
9a,b,c,e/10a,d/11a,b,d/13a	South Africa

306 1976. "Symposium on Racial and Ethnic Relations in the Armed Forces."
Armed Forces and Society, vol. 2, no. 2. Notes, bibliog.   Five articles
make up the symposium portion of this journal issue. An introduction

contains a brief description of the positions of Africans and Coloureds
in the South African armed forces as well as summarizing the other
articles (Grundy). The other papers describe African elements in Portu-
gal's armies in Africa from 1961 to 1974 (Wheeler); the construction of
a multiethnic army by Nkrumah in Ghana in 1957 to 1966 and its subsequent political roles (Adekson); racial and ethnic relations in the Cuban
armed forces (Dominguez); and efficiency, responsibility, and equality
as dimensions of military staffing strategies, using data from Burma,
Malaysia, and the United States to illustrate these factors (Guyob).

	Angola Guinea
	Burma Malaysia
1a/2c/3b/4f/5k/8b/9c/10g	Ghana Mozambique

307   1978. "The National Question: A Special Issue on Quebec." *Canadian
Review of Sociology and Anthropology*, vol. 15, no. 2. Bibliog.   This
collection includes an address by then Minister of State for Cultural
Development Camille Laurin supporting Canadian Parliament Bill 101,
the French Language Charter, along with responsive commentaries concerning Anglophone and Francophone perceptions of national identity
(Breton); class associations in the development of Canadian national
identity (Jackson); a positive Anglophone response to the bill (Rioux);
and a direct attack on the "mythology of nationalism" in Quebec (Ossen-
berg). Substantive topics covered in the issue include the relation of
institutional completeness (institutional parallelism) to conflict between
ethnolinguistic communities (Breton); a detailed dimensional analysis
of public opinion data on Quebec separatism (Ornstein, Stevenson, and
Williams); English Canadian reactions to Québécois nationalism (Laczko);
and relationship between the underdevelopment of Quebec and the
nationalist movement (Guindon). The issue reflects English academic
points of view on separatist politics in Canada.

1a/2a,b,d/3b/4a,h/5b,f/9c/10b,c,d	Canada: English
11a,d/12e/13b/16a	Québécois

308   1979. "Special Issue: Internal Colonialism." *Ethnic and Racial Studies*,
vol. 2, no. 3. Notes, bibliog.   This special topic issue contains theoretical
discussions of the notion of internal colonialism and case studies used to
illustrate and evaluate it. The theory is set out in a general discussion
of comparative analyses of ethnoregional movements (Hechter and Levi).
Case studies examine the position of Brittany in France (Reece); Quebec
in Canada (McRoberts); colonial relationships and industrial development
in Alaska (Ritter); center-periphery relations and the development of the
regional party system in Finland (Alapuro); a comparison of internal
colonial and clientage politics models in explaining Christian Democratic
voting patterns in southern Italy (Palloni); and a historical analysis of

colonialism in the Austro-Hungarian Empire, with particular attention to the position of Transylvania as a semiperipheral region (Verdery). A summary introduction reviews the literature and brings out the salient points of the articles.

1a/2c/3a,e/4d,f,h/5j/7c,d/8b,c,d 9b,c,e/10a,c,d,e,f/12b,e/13b/16a

Canada: Québécois Italy
Finland Romania
France US: General

UNANNOTATED ENTRIES

309 ABBOTT, Simon, ed. 1971. *The Prevention of Racial Discrimination in Britain.* London: Oxford University Press.

    1a/2b,c/3b/4h/5g/6/7/8/9/10/13   Britain: General

310 ABLON, Joan. 1971. "Retention of Cultural Values and Differential Urban Adaptation: Samoans and American Indians in a West Coast City." *Social Forces* 49: 385-93.

    2b/3c/4a/5a/7/12   US: Native Americans, Samoans

311 ABRAHAMS, R.G. 1970. "The Political Incorporation of Non-Nyam-wezi Immigrants in Tanzania." In *From Tribe to Nation in Africa: Studies in Incorporation Processes,* edited by Ronald Cohen and John Middleton, pp. 93-115. Scranton, Penn.: Chandler.

    2b/3a/4a/5a/7/12   Tanzania

312 ABRAHAMSON, Harold J. 1975. "The Religioethnic Factor and the American Experience: Another Look at the Three Generations Hypothesis." *Ethnicity* 2: 163-77.

    2c/3c/4d/5a/12   US: Euro-Americans

313 ACUNA, Rudolfo. 1972. *Occupied America: The Chicano's Struggle Toward Liberation.* San Francisco: Canfield Press.

    2c/3a/4d,f/5b/10   US: Mexican Americans

314 ADAM, Heribert. 1971. *Modernizing Racial Domination: South Africa's Political Dynamics.* Berkeley: University of California Press.

    2c/3b/4h/5b,f,j/9/10   South Africa

315 ——. 1975. "Conflict and Change in South Africa." In *Politics of Race: Comparative Studies,* edited by Donald G. Baker, pp. 211-43. Lexington, Mass.: Lexington Books.

2c/3b/4h/5b,i/9/10 South Africa

316 ——. 1977. "When the Chips are Down: Confrontation and Accommodation in South Africa." *Contemporary Crises* 1:417-35.

2c/3b/4h/5b/10 South Africa

317 ADAMS, Barbara, Judith Okely, David Morgan, and David Smith. 1975. "Gypsies: Current Policies and Practices." *Journal of Social Policy* 4:129-50.

2b/3a/4a,h/5k/7/10 Britain: Gypsies

318 ADAMS, R.C. 1978. "The Coloureds of South Africa." In *Ethnicity in Modern Africa,* edited by Brian M. Du Toit, pp. 253-70. Boulder, Colo.: Westview Press.

2b,c/3a/4a/5d/9/12 South Africa

319 ADEKSON, J. 'Bayo. 1978. "Ethnicity, the Military, and Domination: The Case of Obote's Uganda, 1962-71." *Plural Societies* 9:85-110.

2c/3b/4f/5i/10 Uganda

320 ——. 1979. "Ethnicity and Army Recruitment in Colonial Plural Societies." *Ethnic and Racial Studies* 2:151-65.

2c/3d/4f/5k/10 Africa

321 AGARWAL, N. N. 1969. *Soviet Nationalities Policy.* Agra: Sri Ram Mehra.

2c/3b/4f/5k/10/11 USSR: General

322 AIGNER, Dennis J. and Glen C. Cain. 1977. "Statistical Theories of Discrimination in Labor Markets." *Industrial and Labor Relations Review* 30:175-87.

2e/3e/4b/5k(Neoclassical Economics)/8 Theory

323 AKINSOLA, Akiwowo A. 1963. "The Sociology of Nigerian Tribalism." *Phylon* 25:155-63.

2b/3b/4h/5f/10/12   Nigeria

324   ALAPURO, Risto. 1979. "Internal Colonialism and the Regional Party System in Eastern Finland." *Ethnic and Racial Studies* 2:341-59.

2c/3a/4d/5j/7/8/9/10   Finland

325   ALBA, Richard D. 1976. "Social Assimilation among American Catholic National-Origin Groups." *American Sociological Review* 41:1030-46.

2d/3c/4h/5a/12/14   US: Euro-Americans

326   ——. 1978. "Ethnic Networks and Tolerant Attitudes." *Public Opinion Quarterly* 42:1-16.

2d/3c/4g/5a/11/12   US/General

327   ——. 1979. "Patterns of Interethnic Marriage among American Catholics." *Social Forces* 57:1124-40.

2c/3c/4h/5d,k/12/14   US: Euro-Americans

328   ALDERMAN, Geoffrey. 1975. "Not Quite British: The Political Attitudes of Anglo-Jewry." In *The Politics of Race,* edited by Ivor Crewe, pp. 188-211. British Political Sociology Yearbook, vol. 2. New York: John Wiley & Sons.

2c,d/3a/4f/5d/10/11/12   Britain: Jews

329   ALDRICH, Howard E. 1973. "Employment Opportunities for Blacks in the Black Ghetto: The Role of White-Owned Business." *American Journal of Sociology* 78:1403-25.

2d/3a/4h/5 k/8/9   US: Afro-Americans

330   ALERS, M.H. 1973. "The Development of Pluralism in Surinam." *Plural Societies* 4, no. 3:53-65.

2b/3b/4i/5f,g,i/6/8/9/10/12   Surinam

331   ALEXANDER, Jack. 1977. "The Culture of Race in Middle-Class Kingston, Jamaica." *American Ethnologist* 4:413-35.

2d/3a/4a/5d,g/11   Jamaica

332   ALFORD, Harold J. 1972. *The Proud Peoples: The Heritage and Culture*

of Spanish-Speaking Peoples in the United States. New York: David McKay.

2c/3a/4h/5d/12/14   US: Latin Americans

333 ALGER, Janet Merrill. 1974. "The Impact of Ethnicity and Religion on Social Development in Revolutionary America." In *Ethnicity and Nation-Building,* edited by Wendell Bell and Walter E. Freeman, pp. 327-39. Beverly Hills, Calif.: Sage.

2c/3b/4d/5i/10/17   US: General

334 ALI, Ahmed. 1978. "Ethnicity and Politics in Fiji." *Australian and New Zealand Journal of Sociology* 14:149-53.

2b/3b/4h/5b/10   Fiji

335 ALISJABHANA, S. Takdir. 1971. "Language Policy, Language Engineering and Literacy in Indonesia and Malaysia." *Current Trends in Linguistics* 8:1025-38.

2c/3d/4e/5k/16   Indonesia; Malaysia

336 ALLEN, Irving Lewis. 1975. "WASP—From Sociological Concept to Epithet." *Ethnicity* 2:153-62.

2c/3b/4h/5k/11   US: Euro-Americans

337 ALLEN, James P. 1977. "Recent Immigration from the Philippines and Filipino Communities in the United States." *Geographical Review* 67: 195-208.

2c/3a/4c/5k/6/7/12   US: Filipinos

338 ALLEN, Sheila. 1970. "Immigrants or Workers." In *Race and Racialism,* edited by Sami Zubaida, pp. 99-126. London: Tavistock.

2d/3b/4h/5k/8/9/15   Britain: General

339 ——. 1971. *New Minorities, Old Conflicts: Asians and West Indian Migrants in Britain.* New York: Random House.

2b,c/3a/4h/5a,b,g/7/8/9/10   Britain: Asians, West Indians

340 ——. 1971. "Race and the Economy: Some Aspects of the Position on Non-Indigenous Labor." *Race* 13:165-78.

2c/3b/4h/5i/8/10   Britain: General

341   ALLOWAY, David N. and Francesco Cordasco. 1970. *Minorities and the
      American City: A Sociological Primer for Educators.* New York: David
      McKay.

1b/2c/3b/4h/5a,b/8/9/10/13/14   US: General

342   ALLWORTH, Edward. 1968. "The Nationality Idea in Czarist Central
      Asia." In *Ethnic Minorities in the Soviet Union,* edited by Erich Gold-
      hagen, pp. 229-50. New York: Frederick A. Praeger.

2c/3b/4f/5k/11/12   USSR: General

343   ——. 1971. "Materials for Soviet Nationality Study: The Problem of
      Bibliography." In *Soviet Nationality Problems,* edited by Edward All-
      worth, et al., pp. 241-72. New York: Columbia University Press.

2a/8/10/11   USSR: General

344   ——. 1973. "Regeneration in Central Asia." In *The Nationality Question
      in Soviet Central Asia,* edited by Edward Allworth, pp. 3-18. New York:
      Praeger.

2c/3b/4f/5d,e/6/12/13   USSR: Central Asians

345   ——. 1975. "Mainstay or Mirror of Identity—The Printed Word in
      Central Asia and Other Soviet Regions Today." *Canadian Slavonic Papers*
      17:436-62.

2c/3b/4f/5d/12/16   USSR: Central Asians

346   ——. 1975. *Soviet Asia: Bibliographies.* New York: Praeger.

2a   USSR: Iranians, Mongolians, Turkics

347   ——. 1977. "Flexible Defenses of a Nationality." In *Nationality Group
      Survival in Multi-Ethnic States: Shifting Support Patterns in the Soviet
      Baltic Region,* edited by Edward Allworth, pp. 1-23. New York: Praeger.

2e/3b/4f/5e/10/11   USSR: Estonians, Latvians, Lithuanians

348   ALMIROL, Edwin B. 1978. "Economic Strategies and Ethnic Alterna-
      tives." *Human Relations* 31:363-74.

2b/3a/4i/5d,i/8/12   Mexico

349 ALMQUIST, Elizabeth McTaggart. 1979. *Minorities, Gender, and Work.* Lexington, Mass.: Lexington Books.

2c,d/3c/4h/5a,c,f,g/8/10

US: Afro-, Asian-, Latin-, Native Americans

350 ALPERS, Edward A. 1974. "Ethnicity, Politics, and History in Mozambique." *Africa Today* 21:39-52.

2b/3b/4f/5e/10

Mozambique

351 ALTMAN, Jon C. and John Nieuwenhuysen. 1979. *The Economic Status of Australian Aborigines.* Cambridge: At the University Press.

2c/3b/4b/5k/6/8/9/10

Australia

352 ALVERSON, Hoyt S. 1974. "Minority Group Autonomy and the Rejection of Dominant Group Racial Mythologies: The Zulu of South Africa." *African Studies* 33:3-24.

2d/3a/4a/5d/9/11

South Africa

353 AMELUNXEN, Clemens. 1972. "Greenland's Plural Society Problems." *Plural Societies* 3:3-12.

2c/3b/4i/5f/10/12

Greenland

354 AMERSFOORT, Hans Van. 1978. "'Minority' as a Sociological Concept." *Ethnic and Racial Studies* 1:218-34.

2e/3e/4h/5f,i/9/10

Theory

355 AMFITHEATROF, Erik. 1973. *The Children of Columbus: An Informal History of the Italians in the New World.* Boston: Little, Brown.

2c/3a/4d/5a,d/7/10

US: Italians

356 ANDERSON, Barbara A. 1978. "Some Factors Related to Ethnic Re-identification in the Russian Republic." In *Soviet Nationality Policies and Practices,* edited by Jeremy R. Azrael, pp. 309-33. New York: Praeger.

2c/3b/4h/5d/12

USSR: Russians

357 ANDERSON, Charles H. 1970. *White Protestant Americans: From*

National Origins to Religious Group. Englewood Cliffs, N.J.: Prentice-Hall.

2c/3a/4h/5d/12   US: Euro-Americans

358   ANDERSON, David D. and Robert L. Wright, eds. 1971. *The Dark and Tangled Path: Race in America.* Boston: Houghton Mifflin.

1a/2c/3b/4d/5k/10/11   US: Afro-, Chinese-, Native Americans

359   ANGEL, Marc D. 1974. *The Sephardim of the United States: An Exploratory Study.* New York: Union of Sephardic Congregations.

2b/3a/4h/5d/17   US: Jews

360   ANIMASHASUN, G. K. 1963. "African Students in Britain." *Race* 5: 38-47.

2b/3a/4h/5k/13   Britain: Africans

361   Anti-Apartheid Movement. 1974. *Racism and Apartheid in Southern Africa.* Paris: UNESCO Press.

2c/3b/4i/5b,f,j/9/10   Namibia; South Africa

362   ARAM, M. 1974. *Peace in Nagaland: Eight Year Story: 1964-1972.* New Delhi: Arnold-Heinemann.

2b,c/3a/4d/5b/10   India

363   ARCHER, Dane and Mary Archer. 1971. "Maoris in Cities." *Race* 13: 179-86.

2b/3a/4h/5k/7   New Zealand

364   ARFA, Hassan. 1966. *The Kurds: A Historical and Political Study.* London: Oxford University Press.

2c/3a/4d/5b,d,e/10   Iran; Iraq; Turkey

365   ARLES, J-P. 1971. "The Economic and Social Promotion of Scheduled Castes and Tribes in India." *International Labor Review* 103:29-64.

2c/3b/4i/5i/8/13   India

366 ——. 1971. "Ethnic and Socio-Economic Patterns in Malaysia." *International Labor Review* 104:527-53.

2c/3b/4i/5k/6/8/9/13 Malaysia

367 ARMSTRONG, John A. 1968. "The Ethnic Scene in the Soviet Union: The View of the Dictatorship." In *Ethnic Minorities in the Soviet Union*, edited by Erich Goldhagen, pp. 3-49. New York: Frederick A. Praeger.

2c/3b/4f/5k/6/7/9/10/16 USSR: General

368 ——. 1978. "Mobilized Diaspora in Tsarist Russia: The Case of the Baltic Germans." In *Soviet Nationality Policies and Practices*, edited by Jeremy R. Azrael, pp. 63-104. New York: Praeger.

2c/3a/4f/5i/9/10/12 USSR: Baltic Germans

369 ARNEZ, John A. 1971. *Slovenian Community in Bridgeport, Conn.* New York and Washington: Studia Slovenica.

2b/3a/4d,h/5a,d/12/16/17 US: Slovenes

370 ARTIBISE, Alan F. J. 1976. "Patterns of Population Growth and Ethnic Relationships in Winnipeg, 1874-1974." *Social History* 9:297-335.

2c/3a/4d/5k/6 Canada: General

371 ASHWORTH, Georgina. 1977. *World Minorities*, vol. 1. Sudbury: Quartermaine House.

2c/3a/4i/5i/9/10/11 General

372 ASUNCION-LANDÉ, Nobleza. 1971. "Multilingualism, Politics, and 'Filipinism.'" *Asian Survey* 11:677-92.

2c/3b/4i (Speech)/5d,e/10/16 Philippines

373 ASWAD, Barbara C., ed. 1974. *Arabic Speaking Communities in American Cities.* New York: Center for Migration Studies.

1a/2b,c/3a/4h/5a,d,g/6/8/10/12 US: Arabs

374 AUSTIN, B. William. 1975. "Why Ethnicity Is Important to Blacks." *Urban League Review* 1:13-17.

2c/3a/4i/5k/12   US: Afro-Americans

375   AVERY, Donald. 1979. *"Dangerous Foreigners": European Immigrant Workers and Labour Radicalism in Canada 1896-1932.* Toronto: McClelland & Stewart.

2c/3b/4d/5b,i/7/8/9/10/11   Canada: Euro-Canadians

376   AVNI, Haim. 1971-72. "Argentine Jewry: Its Socio-Political Status and Organizational Patterns." *Dispersion and Unity* 12:128-62; 13-14:161-208; 15-16:158-215.

2c/3a/4h/5k/6/7/8/9/10   Argentina

377   AZRAEL, Jeremy R. 1978. "Emergent Nationality Problems in the USSR." In *Soviet Nationality Policies and Practices,* edited by Jeremy R. Azrael, pp. 363-90. New York: Praeger.

2c/3b/4f/5k/6/8/10   USSR: General

378   BADALIAN, I. A. 1977. "Some Methodological Aspects of Ethnic Problems in the Works of Contemporary Western Sociologists and Ethnographers." *Soviet Sociology* 16:49-69.

2e/3e/4h/5k   Theory

379   BADDELEY, Josephine. 1977. "The Church and the Coffeehouse: Alternative Strategies of Urban Adaptation among Greek Migrants to Auckland." *Urban Anthropology* 6:217-36.

2b/3a/4a/5d/7/12/15   New Zealand

380   BAGENAL, Philip H. 1970. *The American Irish and Their Influence on Irish Politics.* Reprint, 1892 ed. London: Kegan Paul, Trench.

2c/3b/4d,f/5k/7/10   US: Irish

381   BAGLEY, Christopher. 1969. "A Survey of Problems Reported by Indian and Pakistani Immigrants in Britain." *Race* 11:65-76.

2c/3a/4h/5f,g/7/9/11   Britain: Indians, Pakistanis

382   ——. 1970. "Race Relations and Theories of Status Consistency." *Race* 11:267-88.

2e/3e/4h/5d,i/9   Theory

383 ——. 1970. "Relation of Religion and Racial Prejudice in Europe." *Journal for the Scientific Study of Religion* 9:219-25.

2d/3d/4h/5g/11/17   Britain: General; Netherlands

384 ——. 1972. "Pluralism, Development, and Social Conflict in Africa." *Plural Societies* 3, no. 2:13-32.

2d/3d/4h/5f/10/11/12   Africa

385 ——. 1973. *The Dutch Plural Society: A Comparative Study in Race Relations.* London: Oxford University Press.

2b,d/3b/4h/5g/7/9/10/11   Netherlands

386 ——. 1973. "Race Relations and the Press: An Empirical Analysis." *Race* 15:59-89.

2b/3b/4h/5g/16   Britain: General

387 BAILEY, F.G. 1961. "Tribe and Caste in India." *Contributions to Indian Sociology* 5:7-19.

2c/3b/4a/5i/9   India

388 BAIRD, Charles W. 1885. *History of the Huguenot Emigration to America.* 2 vols. New York:Dodd, Mead.

2c/3a/4d/5k/7   US: Huguenots

389 BAIRD, Frank L., ed. 1977. *Mexican Americans: Political Power, Influence, or Resource.* Texas Tech University Graduate Studies no. 14. Lubbock: Texas Tech Press.

1a/2b,c/3a/4f/5b/9/10   US: Mexican Americans

390 BAKER, Donald G. 1975. "Politics, Power and Race Relations." In *Politics of Race: Comparative Studies,* edited by Donald G. Baker, pp. 1-22. Lexington, Mass.: Lexington Books.

2c/3e/4f/5b/9/10   Theory

391 ——. 1975. "Race Relations in Comparative Perspective." In *Politics of Race: Comparative Studies,* edited by Donald G. Baker, pp. 277-305. Lexington, Mass.: Lexington Books.

2c/3d/4f/5b,i/9/10/11   General

392 ——. 1975. "Stress, Threat Perception and Siege Culture Responses in Anglo-Fragment Societies." *International Review of Modern Societies.* 5:164-72.

                                                     Canada: English; South Africa
2c/3d/4h/5b/10/11   US: Euro-Americans; Zimbabwe

393 ——. 1978. "Race and Power: Comparative Approaches to the Analysis of Race Relations." *Ethnic and Racial Studies* 1:316-35.

2c,e/3e/4h/5b/9/10   Theory

394 BALAKRISHNAN, T.R. 1976. "Ethnic Residential Segregation in the Metropolitan Areas of Canada." *Canadian Journal of Sociology* 1:481-98.

2c/3b/4h/5k/6   Canada: General

395 BALDWIN, S.L. 1970. *Must the Chinese Go?* Reprint, 1890 ed. New York: H.B. Elkins.

2c/3a/4d/5g/7   US: Chinese

396 BALL, Richard E., George J. Warheit, Joseph S. Vandiver, and Charles E. Holtzer III. 1979. "Kin Ties of Low-Income Blacks and Whites." *Ethnicity* 6:184-96.

2d/3c/4h/5k/14   US: Afro-, Euro-Americans

397 BALLARD, Roger and Catherine Ballard. 1977. "The Sikhs: The Development of South Asian Settlements in Britain." In *Between Two Cultures: Migrants and Minorities in Britain,* edited by James L. Watson, pp. 21-56. Oxford: Basil Blackwell.

2c/3a/4a/5d/7/12/14/15   Britain: Indians

398 BANERJEE, Kalyan Kumar. 1969. *Indian Freedom Movement Revolutionaries in America.* Calcutta: Jijnasa.

2c/3a/4d/5b/7/10   US: East Indians

399 BANKS, David J., ed. 1976. *Changing Identities in Modern Southeast*

Asia. The Hague: Mouton.

1a/2b,c/3a/4a/5d/9/10/11/12/14/16/17   Malaysia;
Singapore; Thailand

400   BANKS, James A. 1975. *Teaching Strategies for Ethnic Studies.* Boston: Allyn & Bacon.

2a   US: General

401   BANNICK, Christian John. 1971. *Portuguese Immigration to the United States: Its Distribution and Status.* Reprint, 1916 ed. San Francisco: R & E Research Associates.

2c/3a/4d/5a/6/7   US: Portuguese

402   BANTON, Michael. 1953. "The Changing Position of the Negro in Britain." *Phylon* 14:74-83.

2c/3b/4h/5i/9   Britain: Africans, West Indians

403   ——. 1960. "Social Distance: A New Appreciation." *Sociological Review,* n.s., 8:169-83.

2d/3a/4h/5g/9/11   Africa

404   ——. 1966. "Race as a Social Category." *Race* 8:1-16.

2e/3e/4h/5d,g,h/9/11/12   Theory

405   ——. 1969. "White and Coloured in Britain." In *Comparative Perspectives on Race Relations,* edited by Melvin Tumin, pp. 63-80. Boston: Little, Brown.

2c,d/3b/4h/5b,i/9/11/13   Britain: Africans, West Indians

406   ——. 1970. "The Concept of Racism." In *Race and Racialism,* edited by Sami Zubaida, pp. 17-34. London: Tavistock.

2e/3e/4a/5g/11   Theory

407   ——. 1972. *Racial Minorities.* London: Fontana.

1b/2e/3e/4h/5a,b,f/9   General

408   ——. 1979. "Analytical and Folk Concepts of Race and Ethnicity."
       Ethnic and Racial Studies 2:127-38.

       2c/3e/4a/5k/11/12   Theory

409   ——. 1979. "It's Our Country." In *Racism and Political Action in
       Britain,* edited by Robert Miles and Annie Phizacklea, pp. 223-46. Lon-
       don: Routledge & Kegan Paul.

       2e/3b/4h/5b,d,e,g/11   Britain: General

410   —— and Jonathan Harwood. 1975. *The Race Concept.* New York:
       Praeger.

       2c/3e/4h/5k/11   Theory

411   BARANY, George. 1969. "Hungary: From Aristocratic to Proletarian
       Nationalism." In *Nationalism in Eastern Europe,* edited by Peter F. Sugar
       and Ivo J. Lederer, pp. 259-309. Seattle and London: University of Wash-
       ington Press.

       2c/3b/4d/5e/10/11   Hungary

412   ——. 1974. "'Magyar Jew or Jewish Magyar'? To the Question of Jewish
       Assimilation in Hungary." *Canadian-American Slavic Studies* 8, no. 1:
       1-44.

       2b/3a/4d/5a/10/12   Hungary

413   BARGHOORN, Frederick C. 1974. "Soviet Dissenters on Soviet Nation-
       ality Policy." In *Ethnicity and Nation-Building,* edited by Wendell Bell
       and Walter E. Freeman, pp. 117-33. Beverly Hills, Calif.: Sage.

       2c/3b/4j/5k/10/11/12   USSR: Jews, Tatars, Ukrainians

414   BARKOW, Jerome H. 1976. "The Generation of an Incipient Ethnic
       Split: A Hausa Case (Nigeria)." *Anthropos* 71:857-67.

       2b/3a/4a/5f/12   Nigeria

415   BARNETT, Marguerite Ross. 1974. "Creating Political Identity: The
       Emergent South Indian Tamils." *Ethnicity* 1:235-65.

       2b,c/3a/4f/5b,e/6/8/9/10/11/12/15/16   India

416 ——. 1976. *The Politics of Cultural Nationalism in South India.* Princeton, N.J.: Princeton University Press.

2b/3b/4f/5e/10   India

417 BARNOUW, Victor. 1966. "The Sindhis, Mercantile Refugees in India: Problems of Their Assimilation." *Phylon* 27:40-49.

2b/3a/4a/5a/8/9/11   India

418 BARON, Harold M. 1975. "Racial Domination in Advanced Capitalism: A Theory of Nationalism and Divisions in the Labor Market." In *Labor Market Segmentation,* edited by Richard C. Edwards, Michael Reich, and David M. Gordon, pp. 173-216. Lexington, Mass.: D.C. Heath.

2e/3e/4h/5b,i/8/9   Theory

419 BARON, Salo Wittmayer. 1971. *Steeled by Adversity: Essays and Addresses on American Jewish Life.* Philadelphia: Jewish Publication Society.

2c/3a/4d/5a,g/6/7/8/11/12/13/15/17   US: Jews

420 BARRON, Milton, ed. 1958. *American Minorities.* New York: Alfred A. Knopf.

1a,b/2c,e/3b/4d/5a/7/9/12   US: General

421 ——, ed. 1967. *Minorities in a Changing World.* New York: Alfred A. Knopf.

1a/2c/3b/4a,f,h/5a,b,g,i/8/9/10/11/14   General

422 ——, ed. 1972. *The Blending American: Patterns of Intermarriage.* Chicago: Quadrangle Books.

                                                                        Panama
1a/2b,c,d/3b/4g,h/5a/6/9/12/14/17   US: General

423 BARRY, Brian. 1975. "The Consociational Model and Its Dangers." *European Journal of Political Research* 3:393-412.

2c/3d/4f/5f/10   N. Ireland; Canada: Québécois

424 ——. 1975. "Political Accommodation and Consociational Democracy."

British Journal of Political Science 5:477-505.

2c/3d,e/4f/5f/10   Theory

425   BARTH, Fredrik. 1964. "Ethnic Processes on the Pathan-Baluch Boundary." In *Indo-Iranica,* pp. 13-20. Weisbaden: Harrassowitz.

2b/3a/4a/5c/10/12/16   Iran

426   BARTLETT, Vernon. 1969. *The Colour of Their Skin.* London: Chatto and Windus.

2c/3a,b/4g/5g/9/11   Theory

427   BARTON, Josef J. 1978. "Eastern and Southern Europeans." In *Ethnic Leadership in America,* edited by John Higham, pp. 150-75. Baltimore and London: Johns Hopkins University Press.

2c/3c/4d/5k/10   US: Croatians, Czechs, Romanians, Slovaks, Slovenes

428   BASSAND, Michel. 1975. "The Jura Problem." *Journal of Peace Research* 12:139-50.

2b/3a/4h/5e/10/12   Switzerland

429   BASTIDE, Roger. 1961. "Dusky Venus, Black Apollo." *Race* 3:10-18.

2e/3e/4g/5g/11   Theory

430   BATES, Robert H. 1970. "Approaches to the Study of Ethnicity." *Cahiers d'Etudes Africaines* 10:546-61.

2d/3a/4f/5b,d/9/10/12   Zambia

431   ——. 1974. "Ethnic Competition and Modernization in Contemporary Africa." *Comparative Political Studies* 6:457-84.

2a,c/3d/4f/5b,i/8/9/10   Africa

432   BATES, Timothy Mason. 1973. *Black Capitalism: A Quantitative Analysis.* New York: Praeger.

2c,d/3b/4b/5k/8   US: Afro-Americans

433 BAUGHMAN, E. Earl. 1971. *Black Americans: A Psychological Analysis.* New York and London: Academic Press.

2c/3b/4g/5k/11/12/13/14 US: Afro-Americans

434 BAUREISS, Gunter. 1971. "The Chinese Community of Calgary." *Canadian Ethnic Studies* 3:43-56.

2b/3a/4h/5d/6/8/12/13/16/17 Canada: Chinese

435 BAYTON, J.A., L.B. McAlister, and J. Hamer. 1956. "Race-Class Stereotypes." *Journal of Negro Education* 25:75-78.

2d/3a/4g/5g/9/11 US: General

436 BEAGLEHOLE, J. H. 1967. "The Indian Christians: A Study of a Minority." *Modern Asian Studies* 1:59-80.

2b/3a/4h/5d,i/9/12/17 India

437 BEALE, Calvin L. 1973. "Migration Patterns of Minorities in the United States." *American Journal of Agricultural Economics* 55:938-46.

2c/3c/4h/5k/7 US: Afro-, Mexican-, Native Americans

438 BEAN, Frank D. and John P. Marcum. 1978. "Differential Fertility and the Minority Group Status Hypothesis: An Assessment and Review." In *The Demography of Racial and Ethnic Groups,* edited by Frank D. Bean and W. Parker Frisbie, pp. 189-211. New York: Academic Press.

2c/3c/4h/5j,k/6/7/14 US: General

439 BEARDSLEY, Theodore S., Jr. 1976. "The Hispanic Impact upon the United States." In *The Immigrant Experience in America,* edited by Frank J. Coppa and Thomas J. Curran, pp. 9-43. Boston: Twayne.

2c/3a/4d/5k/6/10/11/13/16 US: Latin Americans

440 BEATTIE, Christopher, Jacques Désy, and Stephen Longstaff. 1972. *Bureaucratic Careers: Anglophones and Francophones in the Canadian Public Service.* Ottawa: Information Canada.

2b/3c/4h/5f,g/8/9/16 Canada: English, Québécois

441   BECKER, Tamar. 1973. "Black Africans and Black Americans on an American Campus: The African View." *Sociology and Social Research* 57:168-81.

      2b/3a/4h/5d/12   US: Africans, Afro-Americans

442   BECKETT, J.C. 1971. "Northern Ireland." *Journal of Contemporary History* 6:121-34.

      2c/3b/4d/5e/10   N. Ireland

443   BEE, Robert and Ronald Gingerich. 1977. "Colonialism, Classes, and Ethnic Identity: Native Americans and the National Political Economy." *Studies in Comparative International Development* 12:70-93.

      2c/3b/4i/5b,d,j/9/10/12   US: Native Americans

444   BEEMAN, Richard R. 1971. "Labor Force and Race Relations: A Comparative View of the Colonization of Brazil and Virginia." *Political Science Quarterly* 86:609-36.

      2c/3d/4d/5g,i/8/9/10   Brazil; US: General

445   BEER, William R. 1976. "Language and Ethnicity in France." *Plural Societies* 7:85-94.

      2c/3b/4h/5f/12/16   France

446   ——. 1977. "The Social Class of Ethnic Activists in Contemporary France." In *Ethnic Conflict in the Western World,* edited by Milton J. Esman, pp. 143-58. Ithaca and London: Cornell University Press.

      2d/3b/4f/5i/8/9/10   France

447   BEGG, H.M. and J.A. Stewart; 1971. "The Nationalist Movement in Scotland." *Journal of Contemporary History* 6:135-52.

      2c/3b/4d/5e/10   Scotland

448   BEIJBOM, Ulf. 1971. *Swedes in Chicago: A Demographic and Social Study of the 1846-1880 Immigration.* Stockholm: Laromedelsforlagen.

      2c/3a/4d/5k/6/7/8/15/16   US: Swedes

449 BELL, Daniel. 1975. "Ethnicity and Social Change." In *Ethnicity: Theory and Experience,* edited by Nathan Glazer and Daniel Patrick Moynihan, pp. 141-74. Cambridge, Mass.: Harvard University Press.

2e/3e/4h/5d,e,i/9/10/11/12   Theory

450 BELL, Wendell. 1973. "New States in the Caribbean: A Grounded Theoretical Account." In *Building States and Nations: Analyses by Region,* vol. 2, edited by S.N. Eisenstadt and Stein Rokkan, pp. 177-208. Beverly Hills, Calif.: Sage.

2c/3e/4h/5e/6/9/10/11   Caribbean

451 ——. 1974. "Ethnicity, Decisions of Nationhood, and Images of the Future." In *Ethnicity and Nation-Building,* edited by Wendell Bell and Walter E. Freeman, pp. 283-300. Beverly Hills, Calif.: Sage.

2c/3e/4h/5e/10   General

452 BELLINI, James. 1975. "European Migrant Labor: Present and Future Conditions." *New Community* 4:5-18.

2c/3d/4h/5k/7/8   Europe

453 BELTRÁN, Gonzalo Aguirre. 1970. "The Integration of the Negro into the National Society of Mexico." In *Race and Class in Latin America,* edited by Magnus Mörner, pp. 11-27. New York and London: Columbia University Press.

2c/3a/4a/5a/9/12   Mexico

454 BENDER, Eugene I. and George Kagiwada. 1968. "Hansen's Law of 'Third-Generation Return' and the Study of American Religio-Ethnic Groups." *Phylon* 29:360-70.

2e/3e/4d/5a/11/12   US: Euro-Americans

455 BENEDICT, Burton. 1961. *Indians in a Plural Society: A Report on Mauritius.* Colonial Research Studies no. 34. London: Her Majesty's Stationery Office.

2b/3b/4a/5f,i/9   Mauritius

456 ——. 1962. "The Plural Society in Mauritius." *Race* 3:65-78.

2b/3b/4a/5 f,i/9/10   Mauritius

457 ——. 1962. "Stratification in Plural Societies." *American Anthropologist*
64:1235-46.

2b,c/3e/4a/5f,i/9   Theory

458 ——. 1965. *Mauritius: The Problems of a Plural Society.* London: Pall
Mall Press.

2b/3b/4a/5f,i/8/9/10   Mauritius

459 BENEDICT, Ruth. 1942. *Race and Racism.* London: Routledge & Kegan
Paul.

2e/3e/4a/5g/11/12   Theory

460 BENITEZ, Joseph Spielberg. 1977. "Dimensions for the Study of Work-
Related Values in Mexican-American Culture: An Exploratory Essay."
In *American Minorities and Economic Opportunity,* edited by H. Roy
Kaplan, pp. 109-47. Itasca, Ill.: F.E. Peacock.

2c/3a/4a/5d/9/11/12   US: Mexican Americans

461 BENKIN, Richard L. 1978. "Ethnicity and Organization: Jewish Communities in Eastern Europe and the United States." *Sociological Quarterly*
19:614-25.

2c/3d/4h/5d/12/15   Eastern Europe; US: Jews

462 BENNETT, George. 1969. "Tribalism in Politics." In *Tradition and
Transition in East Africa: Studies of the Tribal Element in the Modern
Era,* edited by P. H. Gulliver, pp. 59-87. Berkeley and Los Angeles: Uni-
versity of California Press.

2c/3d/4a/5b,k/10   Kenya; Tanzania; Uganda

463 BENNIGSEN, Alexandre. 1971. "Islamic or Local Consciousness among
Soviet Nationalities?" In *Soviet Nationality Problems.* edited by Edward
Allworth, et al., pp. 168-82. New York: Columbia University Press.

2c/3a/4 f/5d,e/6/12/17   USSR: Central Asians, Transcaucasians

464 BENNOUNE, Mahfoud. 1975. "The Maghribian Migrant Workers in
France." *Race and Class* 17:39-56.

2c/3b/4a/5b,i/7/8/9   France

465 BENSIMON-DONATH, Doris. 1971. "Social Integration of North African Jews in Israel." *Dispersion and Unity* 12:68-100.

2c,d/3b/4h/5a/6/7/11/14   Israel

466 BERBIEL, Gustav. 1975. "The Tatars and the Tatar ASSR." In *Handbook of Major Soviet Nationalities*, edited by Zev Katz, Rosemarie Rogers, and Frederic Harned, pp. 390-414. New York: Free Press.

2c/3a/4i/5k/6/8/10/11/13/16   USSR: Tatars

467 BERGER, Suzanne. 1972. *Peasants against Politics: Rural Organization in Brittany, 1911-1967.* Cambridge, Mass.: Harvard University Press.

2c/3a/4f/5e,j/8/10   France

468 ———. 1977. "Bretons and Jacobins: Reflections on French Regional Ethnicity." In *Ethnic Conflict in the Western World*, edited by Milton J. Esman, pp. 159-78. Ithaca and London: Cornell University Press.

2c/3a/4f/5b,j/9/10   France

469 BERKHOFER, Robert F., Jr. 1978. "Native Americans." In *Ethnic Leadership in America*, edited by John Higham, pp. 119-49. Baltimore and London: Johns Hopkins University Press.

2c/3a/4f/5k/10   US: Native Americans

470 BERNHEIMER, Charles S., ed. 1971. *The Russian Jew in the United States.* Reprint, 1905 ed. Philadelphia: John C. Winston.

1a/2c/3b/4d/5a,d/7/12   US: Jews

471 BERREMAN, Gerald D. 1960. "Cultural Variability and Drift in the Himalayan Hills." *American Anthropologist* 62:774-94.

2b/3a/4a/5c/6/8/9/10/12/14   India

472 ———. 1966. "Concomitants of Caste Organization." In *Japan's Invisible Race*, edited by George DeVos and Hiroshi Wagatsuma, pp. 308-24. Berkeley and Los Angeles: University of California Press.

2e/3e/4a/5i/9   Theory

473 ———. 1966. "Structure and Function of Caste Systems." In *Japan's Invisible Race*, edited by George DeVos and Hiroshi Wagatsuma, pp. 277-307. Berkeley and Los Angeles: University of California Press.

2e/3e/4a/5i/9   Theory

474   BERRY, Brewton. 1960. "The Myth of the Vanishing Indian." *Phylon*
      20:51-57.

2c/3a/4h/5k/6/10   US: Native Americans

475   ——. 1972. "America's Mestizos." In *The Blending of Races: Marginality
      and Identity in World Perspective,* edited by Noel P. Gist and Anthony
      Gary Dworkin, pp. 191-212. New York: Wiley-Interscience.

2c/3a/4h/5d/9/12   US: Mestizos

476   BERTSCH, Gary K. 1973. "The Revival of Nationalisms." *Problems of
      Communism* 22, no. 6:1-15.

2c/3b/4f/5e/9/10/11   Yugoslavia

477   ——. 1974. *Value Change and Political Community: The Multinational
      Czechoslovak, Soviet, and Yugoslav Cases.* Sage Professional Papers,
      Comparative Politics Series, vol. 5. Beverly Hills and London: Sage.

                                                         Czechoslovakia; USSR:
2d/3d/4f/5d,e/10/11/12   General; Yugoslavia

478   BESSAC, Frank. 1968. "Cultunit and Ethnic Unit—Processes and Sym-
      bolism." In *Essays on the Problem of Tribe.* Proceedings of the 1967
      Annual Spring Meeting of the American Ethnological Society, edited by
      J. Helm, pp. 58-67. Seattle: University of Washington Press.

2e/3e/4a/5d/11/12/16   Theory

479   BETTELHEIM, Bruno and Morris Janowitz. 1964. *Social Change and
      Prejudice.* New York: Free Press of Glencoe.

2e/3e/4g/5g/11   US: General

480   BHAR, Supriya. 1972. "Malaysian Culture and the English Educated
      Class." *Sociological Bulletin* 21:1-16.

2b/3a/4h/5d,i/9/13   Malaysia

481   BHATTACHARYA, D. K. 1968. "The Anglo-Indians in Bombay: An
      Introduction to their Socio-Economic and Cultural Life." *Race* 10:163-72.

2b/3a/4h/5k/10/12/14   India

482   BIDDISS, Michael D. 1966. "Gobineau and the Origins of European Racism." *Race* 7:255-70.

2c/3e/4d/5k/11   Theory

483   BIENAN, Henry. 1974. *Kenya: The Politics of Participation and Control.* Princeton, N.J.: Princeton University Press.

2c/3b/4f/5e,i/10   Kenya

484   BIESANZ, John. 1950. "Race Relations in the Canal Zone." *Phylon* 11:23-30.

2b/3b/4i/5k/9/11   Panama

485   BILINSKY, Yaroslav. 1968. "Assimilation and Ethnic Assertiveness among Ukrainians of the Soviet Union." In *Ethnic Minorities in the Soviet Union,* edited by Erich Goldhagen, pp. 147-84. New York: Frederick A. Praeger.

2c/3a/4f/5a/6/9/10/12/13/16   USSR: Ukrainians

486   ——. 1978. "Mykola Skrypnyk and Petro Shelest: An Essay on the Persistence and Limits of Ukrainian National Communism." In *Soviet Nationality Policies and Practices,* edited by Jeremy R. Azrael, pp. 105-43. New York: Praeger.

2c/3a/4f/5e/10   USSR: Ukrainians

487   BILLE, John H. 1971. *A History of the Danes in America.* Reprint, 1896 ed. San Francisco: R & E Research Associates.

2c/3a/4d/5k/12/14/17   US: Danes

488   BILLIGMEIER, Robert Henry. 1974. *Americans from Germany: A Study in Cultural Diversity.* Belmont, Calif.: Wadsworth.

2c/3a/4d/5a,d,f/10/11   US: Germans

489   BINGHAM, John and Theodore Weissbach, eds. 1972. *Racial Attitudes in America: Analyses and Findings of Social Psychology.* New York: Harper & Row.

1a/2c,d/3b/4g/5g/11   US: Afro-, Euro-Americans

490   BIRCH, Anthony II. 1978. "Minority Nationalist Movements and Theories of Political Integration." *World Politics* 30:325-44.

2c/3e/4f/5b,e,f,i,j/10   Britain; Ireland; N. Ireland

491   BIRMINGHAM, Stephen. 1973. *Real Lace: America's Irish Rich.* New York: Harper & Row.

2c/3a/4d/5i/9/14   US: Irish

492   BISKUP, R. 1968. "White-Aboriginal Relations in Western Australia: An Overview." *Comparative Studies in Society and History* 10:447-57.

2b/3a/4i/5g,i/10/11   Australia

493   BJORK, Kenneth O. 1976. "The Norwegians in America: 'Giants in the Earth.'" In *The Immigrant Experience in America,* edited by Frank J. Coppa and Thomas J. Curran, pp. 63-94. Boston: Twayne.

2c/3a/4d/5a/7/17   US: Norwegians

494   BLACK, Merle. 1978. "Racial Composition of Congressional Districts and Support for Federal Voting Rights in the American South." *Social Science Quarterly* 59:435-50.

2c/3a/4f/5k/6/10   US: General

495   BLACK, Naomi. 1977. "The Cyprus Conflict." In *Ethnic Conflict in International Relations,* edited by Astri Suhrke and Lela Garner Noble, pp. 43-67. New York: Praeger.

2c/3b/4f/5b/10   Cyprus

496   BLAIR, Philip M. 1972. *Job Discrimination and Education: An Investment Analysis: A Case Study of Mexican-Americans in Santa Clara County, California.* New York: Praeger.

2d/3a/4b/5g,i/8/9/13   US: Mexican Americans

497   BLAIR, William C. 1952. "Spanish-Speaking Minorities in a Utah Mining Town." *Journal of Social Issues* 8:4-9.

2b/3a/4i/5i/8/9   US: Mexican Americans

498   Blasco, Pedro Gonzalez. 1974. "Modern Nationalism in Old Nations as a

Consequence of Earlier State-Building: The Case of Basque-Spain."
In *Ethnicity and Nation-Building,* edited by Wendell Bell and Walter E.
Freeman, pp. 341-73. Beverly Hills, Calif.: Sage.

2c/3a/4h/5e/6/7/8/9/10/16   Spain

499 BLAU, Joseph. 1976. *Judaism in America.* Chicago and London: University of Chicago Press.

2b,c/3a/4h/5d,g/7/9/11/12/17   US: Jews

500 BLAUNER, Robert. 1972. *Racial Oppression in America.* New York:
Harper & Row.

2c,e/3b/4h/5b,h,i,j/8/9/10   US: General

501 BLEDA, Sharon Estee. 1978. "Intergenerational Differences in Patterns
and Bases of Ethnic Residential Similarity." *Ethnicity* 5:91-107.

2d/3c/4h/5a/6   US: General

502 ——. 1979. "Socioeconomic, Demographic, and Cultural Bases of
Ethnic Residential Segregation." *Ethnicity* 6:147-67.

2e/3c/4h/5k/6   US: General

503 BLEGEN, Theodore C. 1931-40. *Norwegian Migration to America.*
2 vols. Northfield, Minn.: The Norwegian-American Historical Association.

2c/3a/4d/5a/7/9/10/11/12/15/16/17   US: Norwegians

504 BLOOD, Hilary. 1957. "Ethnic and Cultural Pluralism in Mauritius."
In *Ethnic and Cultural Pluralism in Intertropical Countries,* pp. 356-62.
Brussels: INCIDI.

2c/3b/4i/5f/9/10   Mauritius

505 BLOOM, Leonard. 1948. "Concerning Ethnic Research." *American
Sociological Review* 13:171-82.

2e/3e/4g/5a,g   Theory

506 ——. 1967. "The Coloured People of South Africa." *Phylon* 28:139-50.

2c/3b/4h/5d,i/9/10/11   South Africa

507   BLU, Karen I. 1979. "Race and Ethnicity: Changing Symbols of Domi-
      nance and Hierarchy in the United States." *Anthropological Quarterly*
      52:77-85.

      2c/3e/4a/5d,i/9/11/12   US: General

508   BOCOCK, Robert J. 1971. "The Ismailis in Tanzania: A Weberian
      Analysis." *British Journal of Sociology* 22:365-80.

      2b/3a/4h/5d,i/9/10   Tanzania

509   BODNAR, John E., ed. 1973. *The Ethnic Experience in Pennsylvania.*
      Lewisburg, Penn.: Bucknell University Press.

      1a/2c/3a/4d/5k/7/8/9/15   US: General

510   BOGINA, Sh. 1968. "Review of N. Glazer and D.P. Moynihan's *Beyond
      the Melting Pot.*" *Soviet Sociology* 6:56-60.

      2f/3e/4h/5a,f/11   Theory

511   BOISSEVAIN, Jeremy. 1971. *The Italians of Montreal: Social Adjust-
      ment in a Plural Society.* New York: Arno Press.

      2b/3a/4a/5f,i/8/9/10/14   Canada: Italians

512   BONACICH, Edna. 1975. "Small Business and Japanese American
      Ethnic Solidarity." *Amerasia Journal* 3:96-112.

      2d/3a/4h/5k/8/9/10/17   US: Japanese

513   ——. 1976. "Advanced Capitalism and Black/White Relations in the
      United States: A Split Labor Market Interpretation." *American Socio-
      logical Review* 41:34-51.

      2c/3b/4h/5b,i/8/9   US: Afro-Americans

514   BORALE, P.T. 1968. *Segregation and Desegregation in India: A Socio-
      Legal Study.* Bombay: Manaktalas.

      2c/3b,d/4i(Law)/5g,i/9/10/13   India

515   BORHEK, J.T. 1970. "Ethnic-Group Cohesion." *American Journal of
      Sociology* 76:33-46.

      2d/3a/4h/5d/6/8/12/13   Canada: General

516 BOROWIEC, Walter A. 1974. "Perceptions of Ethnic Voters by Ethnic Politicians." *Ethnicity* 1:267-78.

2d/3b/4h/5k/10   US: General

517 BOSWELL, David M. 1974. "Independence, Ethnicity, and Elite Status." In *Urban Ethnicity,* edited by Abner Cohen, pp. 311-36. London: Tavistock.

2b/3a/4a/5d/9/12   Zambia

518 BOTTOMLEY, Gill. 1976. "Ethnicity and Identity among Greek Australians." *Australian and New Zealand Journal of Sociology* 12:118-25.

2b/3a/4h/5d/12   Australia

519 BOTTOMS, A.-E. 1967. "Delinquency amongst Immigrants." *Race* 8: 357-84.

2c/3b/4h/5k/11   Britain: General

520 BOURAIN, Anne Marie. 1976. "Ethnic Problems of Swedish Finns and Finnish Finns: Present Situation." *Plural Societies* 7, no. 1:63-67.

2c/3b/4i/5d/12/16   Finland

521 BOURHIS, Richard Y., Howard Giles, and Henri Tajfel. 1973. "Language as a Determinant of Welsh Identity." *European Journal of Social Psychology* 3:447-60.

2d/3b/4g/5d/12/16   Wales

522 BOURRICAUD, Francois. 1975. "Indian, Mestizo and Cholo as Symbols in the Peruvian System of Stratification." In *Ethnicity: Theory and Experience,* edited by Nathan Glazer and Daniel Patrick Moynihan, pp. 350-87. Cambridge, Mass.: Harvard University Press.

2c/3b/4i/5i/9/12   Peru

523 BOYD, Monica. 1974. "The Changing Nature of Central and Southeast Asian Immigration to the United States: 1961-1972." *International Migration Review* 8:507-19.

2b/3b/4i/5k/7/8   US: Asians

524 BRACEY, John H., August Meier, and Elliott Rudwick, eds. 1971.

Free Blacks in America, 1800-1860. Belmont, Calif.: Wadsworth.

1a/2c/3a/4d/5k/9/11/12   US: Afro-Americans

525   BRAIN, James L. 1973. "The Tutsi and the Ha: A Study in Integration."
      Journal of Asian and African Studies 8:39-49.

2b/3d/4i/5b,i/6/9/10   Burundi; Rwanda

526   BRAITHWAITE, Lloyd. 1953. "Social Stratification in Trinidad." *Social
      and Economic Studies* 2:5-175.

2b/3a/4a/5i/9   Trinidad

527   ——. 1960. "Social Stratification and Cultural Pluralism." *Annals of the
      New York Academy of Sciences* 83:816-31.

2e/3e/4a/5f,i/9   Theory

528   BRAND, Jack. 1978. *The National Movement in Scotland.* London:
      Routledge & Kegan Paul.

2c/3b/4f/5e/8/10/16   Scotland

529   BRAROE, Niels Winther. 1965. "Reciprocal Exploitation in an Indian-
      White Community." *Southwestern Journal of Anthropology* 21:166-78.

2b/3a/4a/5c/9/10   Canada: Euro-, Native Canadians

530   ——. 1975. *Indian and White: Self-Image and Interaction in a Canadian
      Plains Community.* Stanford: Stanford University Press.

2b/3a/4a/5g/11/12   Canada: Euro-, Native Canadians

531   BRASS, Paul R. and Pierre L. van den Berghe. 1976. "Ethnicity and
      Nationality in World Perspective." *Ethnicity* 3:197-201.

2e/3e/4f,h/5d,e/9/10/12   General

532   BRAZEAU, Jacques and Edouard Cloutier. 1977. "Interethnic Relations
      and the Language Issue in Contemporary Canada: A General Appraisal."
      In *Ethnic Conflict in the Western World,* edited by Milton J. Esman, pp.
      204-27. Ithaca and London: Cornell University Press.

2c/3b/4f/5b,f/10/11/16   Canada: Québécois

533 BRETON, Raymond. 1978. "Stratification and Conflict between Ethno-
linguistic Communities with Different Social Structures." *Canadian
Review of Sociology and Anthropology* 15:148-57.

2e/3e/4h/5b,f/9/10   Theory

534 —— and Maurice Pinard. 1960. "Group Formation among Immigrants:
Criteria and Processes." *Canadian Journal of Economics and Political
Science* 26:465-77.

2b/3a/4f,h/5d,k/7/12/15   Canada: General

535 BRETELL, Caroline Bieler. 1977. "Ethnicity and Entrepreneurs: Portuguese Immigrants in a Canadian City." In *Ethnic Encounters: Identities
and Contexts,* edited by George L. Hicks and Philip E. Leis, pp. 169-80.
North Scituate, Mass.: Duxbury Press.

2b/3a/4a/5k/7/8   Canada: Portuguese

536 BREUGELMANS, R. 1970. "Dutch and Flemings in Canada." *Canadian
Ethnic Studies* 2:83-115.

2c/3a/4d/5a/7/15/16   Canada: Dutch, Flemings

537 BREWER, Marilynn and Donald T. Campbell. 1976. *Ethnocentrism and
Intergroup Attitudes: East African Evidence.* New York: John Wiley &
Sons.

2c/3c/4a/5g/11   East Africa

538 BRIDGE, Susan. 1977. "Some Causes of Political Change in Modern
Yugoslavia." In *Ethnic Conflict in the Modern World,* edited by Milton J.
Esman, pp. 343-68. Ithaca and London: Cornell University Press.

2c/3b/4f/5f/10   Yugoslavia

539 BRIER, Alan and Barrie Ashford. 1975. "The Theme of Race in British
Social and Political Research." In *The Politics of Race,* edited by Ivor
Crewe, pp. 2-25. *British Political Sociology Yearbook,* vol. 2. New York:
John Wiley & Sons.

2e/3b/4h/5g,j, k/10/11   Britain: General

540 —— and Stephen Tansey. 1974. "Ethnic Diversity and Political At-

titudes in a Nigerian University." *Youth and Society* 6:151-78.

2d/3c/4h/5a,k (Consensus)/11   Nigeria

541 BRIGGS, John W. 1978. *An Italian Passage: Immigrants to Three American Cities, 1890-1930.* New Haven and London: Yale University Press.

2c/3a/4d/5c,f/6/7/8/9/10/11/12/13/14/15/16   US: Italians

542 BRIGHAM, John C. and Theodore A. Weissbach, eds. 1972. *Racial Attitudes in America: Analyses and Findings of Social Psychology.* New York: Harper & Row.

1a/2c,d/3b/4g/5g/9/11/13   US: Afro-Americans

543 BRINTNALL, Douglas E. 1979. "Race Relations in the Southeastern Highlands of Mesoamerica." *American Ethnologist* 6:638-52.

2b,c/3a/4a/5d,f,i/9/10/12   Guatemala

544 BROADBENT, Elizabeth. 1972. *The Distribution of Mexican Populations in the U.S.* Reprint, 1941 ed. San Francisco: R & E Research Associates.

2c/3a/4i/5k/6/7   US: Mexican Americans

545 BROCK, Peter. 1969. "Polish Nationalism." In *Nationalism in Eastern Europe,* edited by Peter F. Sugar and Ivo J. Lederer, pp. 310-72. Seattle and London: University of Washington Press.

2c/3b/4d/5e/10/11/16   Poland

546 BROOKS, Dennis and Karamjit Singh. 1979. "Pivots and Presents: Asian Brokers in British Foundries." In *Ethnicity at Work,* edited by Sandra Wallman, pp. 93-112. London: Macmillan.

2b/3a/4a/5k/8   Britain: Sikhs

547 BROWN, Carolyn Henning. 1978. "Ethnic Politics in Fiji: Fijian-Indian Relations." *Journal of Ethnic Studies* 5:1-18.

2b/3b/4h/5b/10   Fiji

548 BROWN, F.J. and J.S. Roucek, eds. 1937. *Our Racial and National Minorities.* New York: Prentice-Hall.

1a,b/2c/3b/4h/5a,h/9/11   US: General

549 BROWN, Thomas N. 1966. *Irish-American Nationalism, 1870-1890.* Philadelphia: J.P. Lippincott.

2c/3a/4d/5e/10   US: Irish

550 BROWNE, William P. and Michael Davis. 1976. "Community Control and the Reservation: Self-Interest as a Factor Limiting Reform." *Ethnicity* 3:368-77.

2b/3a/4i/5k/10   US: Native Americans

551 BRUNCKER, Ernest. 1970. *German Political Refugees in the United States during the Period from 1815-1860.* Reprint, 1904 ed. San Francisco: R & E Research Associates.

2b/3a/4d/5k/7   US: Germans

552 BRUNER, Edward M. 1961. "Urbanization and Ethnic Identity in North Sumatra." *American Anthropologist* 63:508-21.

2b/3a/4a/5c/6/7/10/12/14/15   Indonesia

553 ———. 1972. "Batak Ethnic Associations in Three Indonesian Cities." *Southwestern Journal of Anthropology* 28:207-29.

2b/3a/4a/5d/6/11/12/14/15   Indonesia

554 ———. 1974. "The Expression of Ethnicity in Indonesia." In *Urban Ethnicity,* edited by Abner Cohen, pp. 251-80. A.S.A. Monographs, no. 12. London: Tavistock.

2b/3c/4a/5k/6/10/12   Indonesia

555 BUECHLER, Hans C. and Judith-Maria Buechler. 1975. "Los Suizos: Galician Migration to Switzerland." In *Migration and Development: Implications for Ethnic Identity and Political Conflict,* edited by Helen I. Safa and Brian M. Du Toit, pp. 17-29. The Hague: Mouton.

2b/3a/4a/5d/7/8/12   Switzerland

556 BUENKER, John D. and Nicholas C. Burkel, eds. 1977. *Immigration and Ethnicity: A Guide to Information Sources.* Detroit, Mich.: Gale Research.

2a/7   US: General

557 BULLOCK, Charles S., III, and Harell Rodgers, Jr. 1975. "Black Workers

and the Labor Market: A Programmatic Evaluation." *International Journal of Group Tensions* 5:196-218.

2c/3b/4h/5i/8   US: Afro-Americans

558   BURG, Steven L. 1978. "The Calculus of Soviet Antisemitism." In *Soviet Nationality Policies and Practices*, edited by Jeremy R. Azrael, pp. 189-222. New York: Praeger.

2c/3a/4f/5g,i/9/10/11   USSR: Jews

559   BURGER, Henry G. 1970. "The Furnivall Effect (Ethnic Disinvolvement) versus Compensatory Education." *Urban Education* 5:238-52.

2c/3e/4i/5d,i/13   US: General

560   BURGESS, Thomas. 1970. *Greeks in America.* Reprint, 1913 ed. San Francisco: R & E Research Associates.

2b,c/3a/4d/5k/7/8/10   US: Greeks

561   BURLING, Robbins. 1967. "Tribesmen and Lowlanders of Assam." In *Southeast Asian Tribes, Minorities, and Nations*, edited by Peter Kunstadter, pp. 215-29. Princeton, N.J.: Princeton University Press.

2c/3a,b/4a/5f/9/10/11/12/16   India

562   BURMA, John H., ed. 1970. *Mexican-Americans in the United States: A Reader.* New York: Schenkman.

1a/2c,d/3a/4a,d,f,g,h,i/5a,b,g,i,j/8/9/10
11/12/13/14/15/16/17   US: Mexican Americans

563   BURTON, Frank. 1978. *The Politics of Legitimacy: Struggles in a Belfast Community.* London: Routledge & Kegan Paul.

2b/3a/4a,f/5b,i,j/9/10/11   N. Ireland

564   BUSCH, Peter A. 1974. *Legitimacy and Ethnicity: A Case Study of Singapore.* Lexington, Mass.: Lexington Books.

2b,c,d/3b/4f/5d,e,g,i/10/11   Singapore

565   BUSHNELL, J.H. 1968. "From American Indian to Indian American." *American Anthropologist* 70:1108-16.

2c/3a/4a/5d/10/12   US: Native Americans

566 BUSTIN, Edouard. 1975. *Lunda Under Belgian Rule: The Politics of Ethnicity.* Cambridge, Mass., and London: Harvard University Press.

2c/3b/4f/5e/10/11   Zaire

567 BUTLER, Jeffrey E. 1974. "Social Status, Ethnic Division, and Political Conflict in New Nations: Afrikaners and Englishmen in South Africa." In *Ethnicity and Nation-Building,* edited by Wendell Bell and Walter E. Freeman, pp. 147-69. Beverly Hills, Calif.: Sage.

2c/3b/4d/5b,d,i/9/10/12   South Africa

568 BUTLER, John Sibley and Kenneth L. Wilson. 1978. "The American Soldier Revisited: Race Relations and the Military." *Social Science Quarterly* 59:451-67.

2d/3a/4h/5g/11   US: General

569 BUTTERWORTH, Eric. 1964. "Aspects of Race Relations in Bradford." *Race* 6:129-41.

2d/3a/4f/5g/6/7/8/9/10/12   Britain: Pakistanis

570 ——. 1967. "The Presence of Immigrant School Children: A Study of Leeds." *Race* 8:247-62.

2d/3a/4h/5g/7/13   Britain: General

571 CABRERA, Ysidro Arturo. 1972. *A Study of American and Mexican-American Culture Values and their Significance in Education.* Reprint, 1963 ed. San Francisco: R & E Research Associates.

2b/3a/4i/5k/13   US: Euro-, Mexican Americans

572 CAFFERTY, Pastora San Juan. 1975. "Puerto Rican Return Migration: Its Implications for Bilingual Education." *Ethnicity* 2:52-65.

2b/3b/4h/5k/7/13/16   Puerto Rico; US: Puerto Ricans

573 CAHN, Edgar S., ed. 1969. *Our Brother's Keeper: The Indian in White America.* New York: New Community Press.

1a/2c/3b/4a, f,h/5g/10/11   US: Native Americans

574   CAMEJO, Acton. 1971. "Racial Discrimination in Employment in the
        Private Sector in Trinidad and Tobago: A Study of the Business Elite
        and the Social Structure." *Social and Economic Studies* 20:294-318.

        2d/3b/4h/5g/8/9   Trinidad and Tobago

575   CAMERON,   David. 1974. *Nationalism,   Self-Determination   and   the
        Quebec Question.* Canada: Macmillan.

        2e/3e/4d/5e/10/11/12   Canada: Québécois

576   CAMPBELL, Angus. 1971. *White Attitudes Toward Black People.* Ann
        Arbor: Institute for Social Research, University of Michigan.

        2d/3a/4g/5g/9/11   US: Afro-, Euro-Americans

577   CANADA, Royal Commission on Chinese and Japanese Immigration. 1978.
        Report of the Royal Commission on Chinese and Japanese Immigration.
        Reprint, 1902 ed. New York: Arno Press.

        2b/3b/4d/5g,i/6/7/8/10/11   Canada: Chinese, Japanese

578   ——, Royal Commission on Chinese Immigration. 1978. *Report of the
        Royal Commission on Chinese Immigration: Report and Evidence.* Reprint,
        1885 ed. New York: Arno Press.

        2b,c/3b/4d/5g,i/6/7/8/10/11   Canada: Chinese; US: Chinese

579   CANFIELD, Robert L. 1973. "The Ecology of Rural Ethnic Groups and
        the Spatial Dimension of Power." *American Anthropologist* 75:1511-28.

        2b/3a/4a/5c/6/7/8/9/12   Afghanistan

580   CARDONA, Luis Antonio. 1974. *The Coming of the Puerto Ricans.*
        Washington: UNIDOS.

        2b,c/3a/4h/5k/7   US: Puerto Ricans

581   CAREY, Iskandar. 1976. "The Administration of the Aboriginal Tribes
        of Western Malaysia." In *Changing Identities in Modern Southeast Asia,*
        edited by David J. Banks, pp. 43-69. The Hague: Mouton.

        2b,c/3b/4a/5k/10/12   Malaysia

582 CARLISLE, Donald S. 1975. "Uzbekistan and the Uzbeks." In *Handbook of Major Soviet Nationalities,* edited by Zev Katz, Rosemarie Rogers, and Frederic Harned, pp. 283-314. New York: Free Press.

2c/3a/4f/5k/6/8/10/11/13/16   USSR: Uzbeks

583 CARLISLE, Rodney. 1975. *The Roots of Black Nationalism.* Port Washington, N.Y.: Kennikat Press.

2c/3b/4d/5e/10/12   US: Afro-Americans

584 CARLSON, Lewis H. and George A. Colburn. 1972. *In Their Place: White America Defines Her Minorities, 1850-1950.* New York: Wiley.

2c/3b/4d/5g/9/11   US: General

585 CARRÈRE D'ENCAUSSE, Hélène. 1978. "Determinants and Parameters of Soviet Nationality Policy." In *Soviet Nationality Policies and Practices,* edited by Jeremy R. Azrael, pp. 39-59. New York: Praeger.

2c/3b/4f/5k/10/11   USSR: General

586 ——. 1978. "Party and Federation in the USSR: The Problem of the Nationalities and Power in the USSR." *Government and Opposition* 13:133-50.

2c/3b/4d,f/5e/10   USSR: General

587 CARROLL, Terence G. 1977. "Northern Ireland." In *Ethnic Conflict in International Relations,* edited by Astri Suhrke and Lela Garner Noble, pp. 21-42. New York: Praeger.

2c/3b/4f/5b/10   N. Ireland

588 CARTER, Lewis F. 1968. "Racial-Caste Hypogamy: A Sociological Myth?" *Phylon* 29:347-50.

2c/3b/4h/5i/9/14   US: General

589 CASELLI, Ron, comp. 1974. *The Minority Experience: A Basic Bibliography of American Ethnic Studies.* Santa Rosa, Calif.: Sonoma County Office of Education.

2a   US: Afro-, Euro-, Mexican-, Native Americans

590   CASHMAN, Marc and Barry Klein, eds. 1976. *Bibliography of American Ethnology*. Rye, N.Y.: Todd.

    2a   US: General

591   CASTELLS, Manuel. 1975. "Immigrant Workers and Class Struggle in Advanced Capitalism: The Western European Experience." *Politics and Society* 5:33-66.

    2c/3e/4i/5i/7/8/9   Europe

592   CASTLES, Godula and Stephen Castles. 1971. "Immigrant Workers and Class Structure in France." *Race* 12:303-16.

    2c/3b/4i/5i/7/8/9   France

593   CASTLES, Stephen and Godula Kosack. 1973. *Immigrant Workers and Class Structure in Western Europe*. London: Oxford University Press.

    2c/3e/4h/5i/7/8/9/10/11   Western Europe

594   CATELLAN, Georges. 1971. "The Germans of Rumania." *Journal of Contemporary History* 6:52-75.

    2c/3a/4d/5e/10   Romania

595   CATER, John and Trevor Jones. 1979. "Ethnic Residential Space: The Case of Asians in Bradford." *Tijdschrift voor economische en sociale geografie* 70:86-97.

    2c/3a/4c/5k/7/8/9/10   Britain: Asians

596   CHADNEY, James G. 1977. "Demography, Ethnic Identity, and Decision Making: The Case of the Vancouver Sikhs." *Urban Anthropology* 6:187-204.

    2b/3a/4h/5d/6/12/15   Canada: Indians

597   CHADWICK, Bruce and Joseph A. Stauss. 1975. "The Assimilation of American Indians into Urban Society: The Seattle Case." *Human Organization* 34:359-69.

    2d/3a/4h/5a/8/11/12/14   US: Native Americans

598   CHADWICK-JONES, J.K. 1965. "Italian Workers in a British Factory." *Race* 6:191-98.

2b/3a/4h/5i/7/8/9   Britain: Italians

599 CHAN, Chai-Hon. 1978. "Political Change, Education, and Group
     Identity: Guyana and Malaysia." In *The Mixing of Peoples: Problems of
     Identity and Ethnicity*, edited by Robert I. Rotberg, pp. 69-104. Stam-
     ford, Conn.: Greylock.

2c/3d/4h/5f,i/9/10/12/13/16   Malaysia

600 CHANDRA, Kananur V. 1973. *Racial Discrimination in Canada: Asian
     Minorities*. San Francisco: R & E Research Associates.

2b,c/3b/4h/5g/9/11   Canada: Asians

601 CHANDRAS, Kanahur V., ed. 1978. *Racial Discrimination against Nei-
     ther-White-nor-Black American Minorities*. San Francisco: R & E Research
     Associates.

1a/2c/3a,b/4a/d,h,i   US: Chinese-, East Indian-, Japanese-,
(Education)/5g,i/9/10/11   Mexican-, Native Americans, Puerto Ricans

602 CHARSLEY, S.R. 1974. "The Formation of Ethnic Groups." In *Urban
     Ethnicity*, edited by Abner Cohen, pp. 337-68. A.S.A. Monographs,
     no. 12. London: Tavistock.

2e/3e/4a/5d/7/12   Uganda

603 CHASE, Allan. 1977. *The Legacy of Malthus: The Social Costs of the
     New Scientific Racism*. New York: Alfred A. Knopf.

2c/3e/4i/5g,k/11   Theory

604 CHAUBE, Shibani Kinkar. 1975. "Interethnic Politics in Northeast
     India." *International Review of Modern Sociology* 5:193-200.

2c/3a/4h/5k/9/10   India

605 CHAUHAN, I. S. 1965. "Fiji Today: Political Process and Race Relations
     in a Plural Society." *Sociological Bulletin* 14:70-85.

2b/3b/4h/5f/10   Fiji

606 CHEBOKSAROV, N. N. 1970. "Problems of the Typology of Ethnic
     Units in the Works of Soviet Scholars." *Soviet Anthropology and Archae-
     ology* 9:127-53.

2e/3b/4a/5k/10/12   USSR: General

607   CHIMBOS, Peter D. 1974. "Ethnicity and Occupational Mobility: A Comparative Study of Greek and Slovak Immigrants in 'Ontario City.'" *International Journal of Comparative Sociology* 15:57-67.

2d/3c/4h/5i/7/8/9   Canada: Greeks, Slovaks

608   CHIN, Ai-Li. 1978. "Being Chinese-American: The Reshaping of Identity and Relationships in One Generation" In *The Mixing of Peoples: Problems of Identity and Ethnicity,* edited by Robert I. Rotberg, pp. 131-50. Stamford, Conn.: Greylock.

2b/3a/4i/5d/12/14   US: Chinese

609   CHIN, Rocky. 1971. "New York Chinatown Today: Community in Crisis." *Amerasia Journal* 1:1-24.

2b/3a/4i/5k/6/8/10/12   US: Chinese

610   CHING, Frank. 1976. "The Asian Experience in the United States." In *The Immigrant Experience in the United States,* edited by Frank J. Coppa and Thomas J. Curran, pp. 192-214. Boston: Twayne.

2c/3a/4d/5b,g/7/10/11   US: Asian Americans

611   CHISWICK, Barry R. 1973. "Racial Discrimination in the Labor Market: A Test of Alternative Hypotheses." *Journal of Political Economy* 81: 1330-52.

2d/3b/4b/5b,i,k(Neoclassical Economics)/8/9   US: General

612   ——. 1978. "The Effect of Americanization on the Earnings of Foreign-born Men." *Journal of Political Economy* 86:897-921.

2c/3b,c/4b/5a/8/9   US: General

613   CHITEPO, Herbert. 1970. "The Passing of Tribal Man: A Rhodesian View." In *The Passing of Tribal Man in Africa,* edited by P.C.W. Gutkind, pp. 10-15. Leiden: E.J. Brill.

2b/3b/4i/5b,i/10/12   Zimbabwe

614   CHOY, Bong-youn. 1979. *Koreans in America.* Chicago: Nelson-Hall.

2c/3a/4d/5k/7/8/9/10/11/12/13/15/17   US: Koreans

615 CHRISTIAN, John, Nicholas J. Gadfield, Howard Giles, and Donald M. Taylor. 1976. "The Multidimensional and Dynamic Nature of Ethnic Identity." *International Journal of Psychology* 11:281-91.

2d/3a/4g/5d,h/11/12   Wales

616 CHRISTIANSEN, John B. 1979. "The Split Labor Market Theory and Filipino Exclusion: 1927-1934." *Phylon* 40:66-74.

2c/3a/4d/5b,i/8/9/10   US: Filipinos

617 CHURCH, Avery G. 1978. "Personal Control, Delay of Gratification, Ethnic Stereotypes, and Self-Concepts for Anglo and Navaho High School Seniors." *Psychology* 15:30-42.

2d/3c/4g/5g/11   US: Euro-, Native Americans

618 CHURCHILL, Charles W. 1975. *The Italians of Newark: A Community Study.* New York: Arno Press.

2b/3a/4h/5k/6/8/10/12/14/16   US: Italians

619 CLARK, David. 1979. "Politics and Business Enterprise: Limits on the Scope of Ethnicity." In *Ethnicity at Work,* edited by Sandra Wallman, pp. 173-90. London: Macmillan.

2c/3e/4h/5i/8/12   Theory

620 CLARK, Kenneth B. 1967. *Dark Ghetto: Dilemmas of Social Power.* New York: Harper & Row.

2c/3a/4h/5b/9/10   US: Afro-Americans

621 CLARK, Margaret, Sharon Kaufman, and Robert C. Pierce. 1976. "Explorations of Acculturation: Toward a Model of Ethnic Identity." *Human Organization* 35:231-38.

2e/3e/4a/5a,d/12   US: General

622 CLARKE, John Henrick. 1976. "Black Americans: Immigrants against Their Will." In *The Immigrant Experience in America,* edited by Frank J. Coppa and Thomas J. Curran, pp. 172-91. Boston: Twayne.

2c/3a/4d/5i/9   US: Afro-Americans

623   CLAUDE, Inis L. 1955. *National Minorities: An International Problem.* Cambridge, Mass.: Harvard University Press.

      2c/3b/4f/5k/10   General

624   CLEM, Ralph Scott. 1973. "The Impact of Demographic and Socioeconomic Forces Upon the Nationality Question in Central Asia." In *The Nationality Question in Soviet Central Asia,* edited by Edward Allworth, pp. 35-44. New York: Praeger.

      2c/3b/4c/5k/6   USSR: Central Asians

625   ——, ed. 1975. *The Soviet West: Interplay between Nationality and Social Organization.* New York: Praeger.

      1a/2c/3b/4f/5a,d,e/6/10/12/16   USSR: Estonians; Latvians, Lithuanians

626   CLISSOLD, Stephen. 1965. "The Indian Problem in Latin America: Changing Attitudes in the Andean Republics." *Race* 7:47-58.

      2c/3d/4i/5f,g/10/11   South America

627   CLOSE, M.E., G.C. Kinloch, and L. Schlemmer. 1971. "The Afrikaners as an Emergent Minority: An Alternative View." *British Journal of Sociology* 22:200-208.

      2b/3a/4h/5d/12   South Africa

628   COBLENTZ, Harry S. 1974. "Internal and External Conflict of an American Indian Community." In *Ethnicity and Nation-Building,* edited by Wendell Bell and Walter E. Freeman, pp. 315-25. Beverly Hills, Calif.: Sage.

      2b/3a/4i/5k/10/11   US: Native Americans

629   COETZEE, J.H. 1978. "Formative Factors in the Origins and Growth of Afrikaner Ethnicity." In *Ethnicity in Modern Africa,* edited by Brian M. Du Toit, pp. 235-52. Boulder, Colo.: Westview Press.

      2c/3a/4a/5d/9/12   South Africa

630   COHEN, Abner. 1974. *Two Dimensional Man: An Essay on the Anthropology of Power and Symbolism in Complex Society.* Berkeley and Los Angeles: University of California Press.

2c/3e/4a/5b,e,i/9/10/11/12   Theory

631   COHEN, David Steven. 1974. *The Ramapo Mountain People.* New Brunswick, N.J.: Rutgers University Press.

2b/3a/4a/5d,g,i/6/8/9/11/12/14/17   US: Mestizos

632   —— and Jack P. Greene, eds. 1972. *Neither Slave nor Free: The Freedman of African Descent in the Slave Societies of the New World.* Baltimore and London: Johns Hopkins University Press.

1a/2c/3d/4d/5k/9/11   Mesoamerica; North America; South America

633   COHEN, Erik. 1972. "The Black Panthers and Israeli Society." *Jewish Journal of Sociology* 14:93-109.

2b/3a/4h/5b/9/10   Israel

634   ——. 1977. "Expatriate Communities." *Current Sociology,* vol. 24, no. 3.

2a,c,e/3a/4h/5k/6/7/9/14   General

635   ——. 1977. "Recent Anthropological Studies of Middle Eastern Communities and Ethnic Groups." In *Annual Review of Anthropology,* vol. 6, edited by B.J. Siegal et al., pp. 315-47. Palo Alto, Calif.: Annual Reviews.

2a,c,e/3e/4a/5a,b,c,d,e,f,g,i,j/9/10/11/12   Middle East

636   COHEN, Hayyim. 1971-72. "Sephardi Jews in the United States: Marriage with Ashkenazim and Non-Jews." *Dispersion and Unity* 13-14:151-60.

2d/3a/4h/5d/11/14   US: Jews

637   COHEN, Percy. 1968. "Ethnic Group Differences in Israel." *Race* 9:303-10.

2c/3b/4b/5f,h/6/9/10/12/13   Israel

638   COHEN, Steven Martin. 1974. "The Impact of Jewish Education on Religious Identification and Practice." *Jewish Social Studies* 36:316-26.

2d/3a/4h/5d/12/13/17   US: Jews

639   ——. 1977. "Socioeconomic Determinants of Intraethnic Marriage and Friendship." *Social Forces* 55:997-1010.

2d/3a/4h/5a/12/14   US: General

640   —— and Robert E. Kapsis. 1978. "Participation of Blacks, Puerto Ricans, and Whites in Voluntary Associations: A Test of Current Theories." *Social Forces* 56:1053-71.

2d/3c/4h/5k/15   US: Afro-, Euro-Americans, Puerto Ricans

641   —— and Robert E. Kapsis. 1977. "Religion, Ethnicity, and Party Affiliation in the U.S.: Evidence from Pooled Electoral Surveys, 1968-1972." *Social Forces* 56:637-53.

2c/3b/4h/5d/10   US: General

642   COLBY, Benjamin N. 1966. *Ethnic Relations in the Chiapas Highlands of Mexico.* Santa Fe: Museum of New Mexico Press.

2b/3a/4a/5f,i/8/9   Mexico

643   ——. 1966. "The Ixil Maya, A Culture Variation Study in Guatemala." *El Palacio* 73:26-38.

2b/3a/4a/5d,f   Guatemala

644   —— and Pierre L. van den Berghe. 1961. "Ethnic Relation in South-Eastern Mexico." *American Anthropologist* 63:772-92.

2b/3a/4a,h/5f/8/9   Mexico

645   —— and Pierre L. van den Berghe. 1969. *Ixil Country: A Plural Society in Highland Guatemala.* Berkeley: University of California Press.

2c/3a/4a,h/5f,i/9/10   Guatemala

646   COLE, Leonard A. 1977. "Blacks and Ethnic Political Tolerance." *Polity* 9:302-20.

2d/3b/4f/5k/11   US: Afro-Americans

647   COLEMAN, Andrew M. 1972. "'Scientific' Racism and the Evidence on Race and Intelligence." *Race* 14:137-53.

2c,e/3e/4i/5k/11   General

648 COLEMAN, Terry. 1972. *Passage to America: A History of Emigrants from Great Britain and Ireland to America in the Mid-Nineteenth Century.* London: Hutchinson.

2c/3a/4d/5k/7 US: English, Irish, Scottish, Welsh

649 COLLINS, Sydney. 1955. "The British-Born Coloured." *Sociological Review*, n.s., 3:77-92.

2b/3a/4h/5g,h,i/9/11 Britain: Africans, West Indians

650 COLSON, Elizabeth. 1970. "The Assimilation of Aliens among Zambian Tonga." In *From Tribe to Nation in Africa: Studies in Incorporation Processes,* edited by Ronald Cohen and John Middleton, pp. 35-54. Scranton, Penn.: Chandler.

2b/3a/4a/5a/12 Zambia

651 COMEAU, Larry R. and Leo Driedger. 1978. "Ethnic Opening and Closing in an Open System: A Canadian Example." *Social Forces* 57: 600-620.

2b/3a/4h/5k(Systems Theory)/12 Canada: General

652 COMISSAO DE RECENSEAMENTO DA COLONIA JAPANESA. 1964. *The Japanese Immigrant in Brazil: Statistical Tables.* Tokyo: University of Tokyo Press.

2d/3a/4i/5k/6/7/8/9/10/13/14/16/17 Brazil

653 COMMUNITY RELATIONS COMMISSION. 1975. *Race Relations in Britain: A Select Bibliography.* London: Community Relations Commission.

2a/7/8/11/13 Britain: General

654 COMPARATIVE POLITICS SEMINAR, University of London, 1974-1975. 1976. *Collected Seminar Papers on the Politics of Separatism, October 1974-June 1975.* London: Institute of Commonwealth Studies.

1a/2b,c/3b/4f/5e/10 General

655 CONNOR, John W. 1977. *Tradition and Change in Three Generations of Japanese Americans.* Chicago: Nelson-Hall.

2d/3a/4g/5d/11/14 US: Japanese

656   CONNOR, Walker. 1967. "Self-Determinism: The New Phase." *World Politics* 20:30-53.

2c/3e/4f/5e/10/11   General

657   ——. 1969. "Ethnology and the Peace of South Asia." *World Politics* 22:51-86.

2c/3d/4f/5b/6/10   South Asia

658   ——. 1976. "The Political Significance of Ethnonationalism within Western Europe." In *Ethnicity in an International Context,* edited by Abdul Said and Luiz R. Simmons, pp. 110-33. New Brunswick, N.J.: Transaction Books.

2c/3e/4f/5e/10/11   Europe

659   ——. 1977. "Ethnonationalism in the First World: The Present in Historical Perspective." In *Ethnic Conflict in the Western World,* edited by Milton J. Esman, pp. 19-45. Ithaca and London: Cornell University Press.

2e/3e/4f/5e/11   General

660   ——. 1978. "A Nation is a Nation, is a State, is an Ethnic Group is a. . . ." *Ethnic and Racial Studies* 1:377-400.

2e/3e/4f/5k   Theory

661   CONQUEST, Robert, ed. 1967. *Soviet Nationalities Policy in Practice.* New York: Praeger.

1a/2c/3b/4f/5f,j/10/11   USSR: General

662   CONSTANTINIDES, Pamela. 1977. "The Greek Cypriots: Factors in the Maintenance of Ethnic Identity." In *Between Two Cultures: Migrants and Minorities in Britain,* edited by James L. Watson, pp. 269-300. Oxford: Basil Blackwell.

2b/3a/4a/5d/7/8/10/13/14/15/17   Britain: Cypriots

663   COOK, Ramsay, ed. 1969. *French-Canadian Nationalism: An Anthology.* Toronto: Macmillan.

1a/2c/3a/4d/5e/10/11   Canada: Québécois

664   COOMBS, H.C. 1972. "The Employment Status of Aborigines." *Australian Economic Papers* 11, no. 18:8-18.

2b/3b/4b/5i/8   Australia

665 COOPER, Mark N. 1974. "Plural Societies and Conflict:Theoretical
     Considerations and Cross-National Evidence." *International Journal of
     Group Tensions* 4:403-30.

2d/3d,e/4f/5b,f/9/10/12   General

666 ——. 1974. "Racialism and Pluralism as Dimensions of Nations: A
     Further Investigation." *Race* 3:370-82.

2d/3d/4f/5f,i/9/10/12   General

667 COOPER, Paulette, ed. 1972. *Growing Up Puerto Rican.* New York:
     Arbor House.

1a/2b/3a/4h/5d/12/14   US: Puerto Ricans

668 COPPA, Frank J. 1976. "Those Who Followed Columbus: The Italian
     Migration to the United States of America." In *The Immigrant Experience
     in America,* edited by Frank J. Coppa and Thomas J. Curran, pp. 115-46.
     Boston: Twayne.

2c/3a/4d/5a,g/7/10/16/17   US: Italians

669 —— and Thomas J. Curran. 1976. "From the Rhine to the Mississippi:
     The German Emigration to the United States." In *The Immigrant Ex-
     perience in America,* edited by Frank J. Coppa and Thomas J. Curran,
     pp. 44-62. Boston: Twayne.

2c/3a/4d/5a/7/10/17   US: Germans

670 —— and Thomas J. Curran, eds. 1976. *The Immigrant Experience in
     America.* Boston: Twayne.

1a/2c/3a/4d,h/5a/7/9/10/11/12   US: General

671 CORDASCO, Francesco, ed. 1975. *Studies in Italian American Social
     History.* Totowa, N.J.: Rowman & Littlefield.

1a/2b,c/3a/4c,d,h,i/5a,d/10/11/12/14   US: Italians

672 —— and Eugene Bucchioni, eds. 1974. *The Italians: Social Background
     of an American Group.* Clifton, N.J.: August M. Kelley.

1a/2b,c/3a/4d,h/5k/6/7/8/9/10/11
12/13/14/15/16/17   US: Italians

673   —— and Rocco G. Galatiato. 1970. "Ethnic Displacement in the Interstitial Community: The East Harlem Experience." *Phylon* 31:302-12.

2c/3a/4h/5a/7   US: Afro-Americans, Jews, Italians, Puerto Ricans

674   CORNELIUS, Wayne A. 1978. *Mexican Migration to the United States: Causes, Consequences, and U.S. Responses.* Cambridge, Mass.: Migration and Development Study Group, Center for International Studies, Massachusetts Institute of Technology.

2c/3a/4h/5k/7/8/10   US: Mexican Americans

675   CORNELL, John B. 1964. "Ainu Assimilation and Cultural Extinction: Acculturation Policy in Hokkaido." *Ethnology* 3:287-304.

2b/3a/4a/5d,g/10/11   Japan

676   CORRADO, Raymond B. 1975. "Nationalism and Communalism in Wales." *Ethnicity* 2:360-81.

2b/3b/4f/5e/10/12   Wales

677   CORTÈS, Carlos E., Arlin I. Ginsberg, Alan W.F. Green, and James A. Joseph, eds. 1976. *Three Perspectives on Ethnicity: Blacks, Chicanos, and Native Americans.* New York: G.P. Putnam's Sons.

1a/2b,c/3a/4d,h   US: Afro-, Mexican-,
5a,b,g,i/9/10/11   Native Americans

678   CORWIN, Arthur F., ed. 1978. *Immigrants—and Immigrants: Perspectives on Mexican Labor Migration to the United States.* Westport, Conn.: Greenwood Press.

1a/2c/3a/4b,d/5b,i,j/7/8/9/10/12   US: Mexican Americans

679   COTRAN, Eugene. 1969. "Tribal Factors in the Establishment of the East African Legal Systems." In *Tradition and Transition in East Africa,* edited by P.H. Gulliver, pp. 127-46. Berkeley and Los Angeles: University of California Press.

2c/3d/4f/5f/10/11/12   East Africa

680   COVELLO, Leonard. 1967. *The Social Background of the Italo-American School Child.* Leiden: E.J. Brill.

2c/3a/4d,h/5d/13   US: Italians

681   COX, Oliver C. 1948. *Caste, Class, and Race: A Study in Social Dynamics.* New York: Doubleday.

2c/3b/4h/5b,i/8/9/10   US: Afro-Americans

682   ——. 1971. "The Question of Pluralism." *Race* 12:385-400.

2f/3e/4h/5b,f/8   Theory

683   ——. 1974. "Jewish Self-Interest in 'Black Pluralism.'" *The Sociological Quarterly* 15:183-98.

2c/3a/4h/5i/10/11   US: Afro-Americans, Jews

684   CRAIN, Robert L. and Carol Sachs Weisman. 1972. *Discrimination, Personality, and Achievement: A Survey of Northern Blacks.* New York and London: Seminar Press.

2d/3b/4g/5g/9/11/12/14   US: Afro-Americans

685   CREWE, Ivor, ed. 1975. "The Politics of Race." *British Political Sociology Yearbook,* vol. 2. New York: Wiley.

1a/2c/3b/4f,h/5b,i,j/10/11   Britain: General

686   CROSS, Malcolm. 1971. "On Conflict, Race Relations, and the Theory of the Plural Society." *Race* 12:477-94.

2e/3e/4h/5b,f,h,i/10   Theory

687   ——. "Colonialism and Ethnicity: A Theory and Comparative Case Study." *Ethnic and Racial Studies* 1:37-59.

2c/3d/4h/5b,d,i,j/9/10   Guyana; Trinidad

688   CROSS, Robert D. 1978. "The Irish." In *Ethnic Leadership in America,* edited by John Higham, pp. 176-97. Baltimore and London: Johns Hopkins University Press.

2c/3a/4d/5k/10/17   US: Irish

689   CROWLEY, Daniel J. 1957. "Plural and Differential Acculturation in

Trinidad." *American Anthropologist* 59:817-24.

2b/3b/4a/5a,f/12   Trinidad

690   CUEVA-JARAMILLO, Juan. 1978. "Ethnocentrism and Culture Conflicts: The Anthropology of Acculturation." *Cultures* 5:19-31.

2c/3e/4i/5b,g,i/11/12   Mesoamerica; South America

691   CULIN, Stewart. 1970. *The I Hing or "Patriotic Uprising," Chinese Secret Societies, Customs of Chinese in America.* Reprint, 1887 ed. Philadelphia: Stewart Culin.

2b/3a/4i/5k/15   US: Chinese

692   CUMMINGS, Scott. 1977. "Racial Prejudice and Political Orientations among Blue-Collar Workers." *Social Science Quarterly* 57:907-20.

2d/3a/4h/5g/8/11   US: General

693   CURRAN, Thomas J. 1976. "From 'Paddy' to the Presidency: The Irish in America." In *The Immigrant Experience in America,* edited by Frank J. Coppa and Thomas J. Curran, pp. 95-114. Boston: Twayne.

2c/3a/4d/5b,g,i/10/13/17   US: Irish

694   CURTHOYS, Ann and Andrew Markus, eds. 1978. *Who Are Our Enemies? Racism and the Working Class in Australia.* Neutral Bay, New South Wales: Hale and Iremonger.

1a/2c/3b/4d/5b,i/8/9/10/11   Australia

695   CURTIS, Lynn A. 1975. *Violence, Race, and Culture.* Lexington, Mass.: Lexington Books.

2d/3b/4i/5k/10/11/12   US: Afro-Americans

696   CZENANOWSKI, Jan. 1961. "Race and Nationality in Europe." *Race* 3: 68-79.

2c/3d/4h/5d,e/11   Europe

697   DAALDER, Hans. 1971. "On Building Consociational Nations: The Cases of the Netherlands and Switzerland." *International Social Science Journal* 23:355-70.

2c/3d/4f/5f/10/16   Netherlands; Switzerland

698 ——. 1973. "Building Consociational Nations." In *Building States and Nations: Analyses by Region,* vol. 2, edited by S.N. Eisenstadt and Stein Rokkan, pp. 14-31. Beverly Hills, Calif.: Sage.

2c/3d/4f/5f/10   Netherlands; Switzerland

699 DADRIAN, Vahakn N. 1969. "Inter-Ethnic Conflicts in the Soviet Transcaucasus with Particular Reference to Armenia." *International Review of History and Political Science* 6:79-92.

2c/3b/4f/5b,e/9/10   USSR: Armenians

700 ——. 1975. "A Typology of Genocide." *International Review of Modern Sociology* 5:201-12.

2c/3e/4h/5b/10   General

701 DAHYA, Badr U. D. 1965. "Yemenis in Britain: An Arab Migrant Community." *Race* 6:177-90.

2b/3a/4h/5k/7   Britain: Yemenis

702 ——. 1973. "Pakistanis in Britain: Transients or Settlers?" *Race* 14: 241-78.

2b/3a/4h/5k/7   Britain: Pakistanis

703 ——. 1974. "The Nature of Pakistani Ethnicity in Industrial Cities in Britain." In *Urban Ethnicity,* edited by Abner Cohen, pp. 77-118. A.S.A. Monographs, no. 12. London: Tavistock.

2e/3a/4h/5k/6/7/8   Britain: Pakistanis

704 DAHYA, Zaynab. 1965. "Pakistani Wives in Bradford." *Race* 6:311-21.

2b/3a/4i/5k/14   Britain: Pakistanis

705 DAMROSZ, Jerzy. 1978. "Social Change and Ethnic Processes in Contemporary Poland." *Polish Sociological Bulletin,* no. 1, pp. 71-80.

2c/3b/4h/5d/7/12   Poland

706 DANE, J.K. and B. Eugene Griessman. 1972. "The Collective Identity of Marginal Peoples: The North Carolina Experience." *American Anthropologist* 74:694-704.

2b/3a/4a/5d/12   US: Mestizos

707 DANIELS, Roger. 1977. *The Politics of Prejudice: The Anti-Japanese Movement in California and the Struggle for Japanese Exclusion.* 2d ed. Berkeley and Los Angeles: University of California Press.

    2c/3a/4d/5b,g/7/8/9/10/11   US: Japanese

708 ——. 1978. "The Japanese." In *Ethnic Leadership in America,* edited by John Higham, pp. 36-63. Baltimore and London: Johns Hopkins University Press.

    2c/3a/4h/5k/10/15   US: Japanese

709 DARROCH, A. Gordon. 1979. "Another Look at Ethnicity, Stratification and Social Mobility in Canada." *Canadian Journal of Sociology* 4:1-26.

    2d/3b/4h/5a,i/8/9   Canada: General

710 —— and W.G. Marston. 1972. "Ethnic Differentiation: Ecological Aspects of a Multidimensional Concept." In *Readings in Race and Ethnic Relations,* edited by A.H. Richmond, pp. 107-28. Oxford: Pergamon Press.

    2d/3a/4h/5c/6/7/12   Canada: General

711 DAS GUPTA, Jyotirindra. 1970. *Language Conflict and National Development: Group Politics and Language Policy in India.* Berkeley: University of California Press.

    2b,c/3b/4f/5b,e/10/16   India

712 ——. 1975. "Ethnicity, Language Demands, and National Development." *Ethnicity* 1:65-72.

    2c/3e/4f/5e,f/10/11/16   Theory

713 ——. 1975. "Ethnicity, Language Demands, and National Development in India." In *Ethnicity: Theory and Experience,* edited by Nathan Glazer and Daniel Patrick Moynihan, pp. 466-88. Cambridge, Mass.: Harvard University Press.

    2c/3b/4f/5b/10/12/16   India

714 DASHEVSKY, A. 1972. "And the Search Goes On: The Meaning of Religico-Ethnic Identity and Identification." *Sociological Analysis* 33: 239-45.

    2e/3e/4g,h/5d/12   Theory

715 —— and H. M. Shapiro. 1974. *Ethnic Identification among American Jews.* Lexington, Mass.: Lexington Books.

2b,d/3a/4g,h/5d/12   US: Jews

716 DA SILVA, Milton M. 1977. "Modernization and Ethnic Conflict: The Case of the Basques." *Comparative Politics* 7:227-51.

2b/3b/4f/5b,e,i/6/8/9/10/11/16/17   Spain

717 DAVID, Wilfred L. 1972. *The Economics of Racial Discontent: Black America in Development and Perspective.* Center on International Race Relations, Graduate School of International Studies, University of Denver, Studies in Race and Nations, vol. 4, study no. 1.

2c/3a/4b,h/5b,i,j/8/9/10   US: Afro-Americans

718 DAVIDSON, Basil. 1969. "Pluralism in Colonial African Societies: Northern Rhodesia/Zambia." In *Pluralism in Africa,* edited by Leo Kuper and M.G. Smith, pp. 211-45. Berkeley and Los Angeles: University of California Press.

2c/3b/4d/5f,i/8/9/10   Zambia; Zimbabwe

719 DAVIDSON, Chandler. 1972. *Biracial Politics: Conflict and Coalition in the Metropolitan South.* Baton Rouge: Louisiana State University Press.

2c/3a/4f/5i/10   US: Afro-Americans

720 DAVIES, E. Hudson. 1968. "Welsh Nationalism." *Political Quarterly* 39:322-32.

2c/3b/4f/5e/10   Wales

721 DAVIES, Howard B. 1978. *Toward a Marxist Theory of Nationalism.* New York and London: Monthly Review Press.

2c,e/3e/4f/5b,e/9/10/11   General

722 DAVIS, Jerome. 1969. *The Russian Immigrant.* Reprint, 1922 ed. New York: Arno Press.

2d/3a/4h/5a/6/7/8/10/11/12/15/16/17   US: Russians

723 DAVIS, Kingsley. 1969. "The Demography of Caste." In *Comparative Perspectives on Race Relations,* edited by M. Tumin, pp. 91-107. Boston:

Little, Brown.

2c/3b/4h/5i/9/11/12   India

724   DAVIS, Lenwood G. 1978. *The Black Family in the United States: A Selected Bibliography of Annotated Books, Articles, and Dissertations on the Black Family in America.* Westport, Conn.: Greenwood Press.

2a/14   US: Afro-Americans

725   DAVISON, R.B. 1963. "The Distribution of Immigrant Groups in London." *Race* 5:56-69.

2c/3b/4h/5k/6   Britain: General

726   DAWSON, Betty. 1968. "No Place Back Home: A Study of Jamaicans Returning to Kingston, Jamaica." *Race* 9:499-510.

2b/3a/4h/5d/7   Britain: Jamaicans; Jamaica

727   DAWSON, John. 1964. "Race and Intergroup Relations in Sierra Leone," pt. 1. *Race* 6:83-99.

2c/3b/4g/5g,i/6/9/10/11/12/13   Sierra Leone

728   ——. 1965. "Race and Intergroup Relations in Sierra Leone," pt. 2. *Race* 6:217-31.

2c/3b/4g/5g,i/6/8/10/11/12/13   Sierra Leone

729   DEAKIN, Nicholas. 1964. "Residential Segregation in Britain: A Comparative Note." *Race* 6:18-26.

2c/3b/4h/5i/6/9   Britain: General

730   ——. 1970. "Race, the Politicians, and Public Opinion: A Case Study." In *Race and Racialism,* edited by Sami Zubaida, pp. 127-49. London: Tavistock.

2d/3a/4h/5g/10/11   Britain: General

731   DE'ATH, Colin E. and Peter Padbury. 1977. "Brokers and the Social Ecology of Minority Groups." In *Ethnic Encounters: Identities and Contexts,* edited by George L. Hicks and Philip E. Leis, pp. 181-200.

North Scituate, Mass.: Duxbury Press.

2f/3e/4a/5c,k/9/10/12   Theory

732   DEGLER, Carl N. 1959. "Slavery and the Genesis of American Race Prejudice." *Comparative Studies in Society and History* 2:49-66.

2c/3b/4d/5g/9/11   US: Afro-Americans

733   ——. 1971. *Neither Black nor White: Slavery and Race Relations in Brazil and the United States*. New York: Macmillan.

2c/3d/4d/5g,i/9/10/11   Brazil; US: Afro-Americans

734   DEJONG, Gerald F. 1975. *The Dutch in America, 1609-1974.* Boston: Twayne.

2c/3a/4d/5k/6/7/8/9/10/12/14/16/17   US: Dutch

735   DEKMEJIAN, Richard Hrair. 1978. "Consociational Democracy in Crisis: The Case of Lebanon." *Comparative Politics* 10:251-65.

2c/3b/4f/5b,f/10   Lebanon

736   DELF, George. 1963. *Asians in East Africa.* London: Oxford University Press.

2c/3d/4i/5k/8/9   East Africa

737   DELORIA, Vine, Jr. 1970. *We Talk, You Listen.* New York: Macmillan.

2c/3a/4i/5b,d/10/11   US: Native Americans

738   DEMEDTS, Andre. 1972. "The French Netherlands." *Plural Societies*, 3, no. 1:19-37.

2b/3b/4h/5d,f/10/11   Netherlands

739   DENCH, Geoff. 1975. *Maltese in London: A Case Study in the Erosion of Ethnic Consciousness.* London and Boston: Routledge & Kegan Paul.

2b,c/3a/4h/5a,d,i/6/7/8/9/11/12/14/17   Britain: Maltese

740   DENTAN, R.K. 1976. "Ethnics and Ethics in Southeast Asia." In

Changing Identities in Modern Southeast Asia, edited by David J. Banks, pp. 71-81. The Hague: Mouton.

2e/3e/4a/5k/11   Theory

741   DENTON, Trevor. 1975. "Canadian Indian Migrants and Impression Management of Ethnic Stigma." *Canadian Review of Sociology and Anthropology* 12:65-71.

2b/3a/4a/5h/7/11   Canada: Native Canadians

742   DE REUCK, Anthony and Julie Knight, eds. 1966. *Caste and Race: Comparative Approaches.* London: J & A Churchill.

1a/2c/3b,d/4a,f,g,h/5i/9/11   Theory

743   DESAI, Rashmi. 1963. *Indian Immigrants in Britain.* London: Oxford University Press.

2b/3a/4h/5k/6/7/8/9/10/11/12/13/14/15/17   Britain: Indians

744   DESBARATZ, Jacqueline. 1979. "Thai Migration to Los Angeles." *Geographical Review* 69:302-18.

2b,c/3a/4c/5k/7   US: Thais

745   DESHEN, Shlomo A. 1970. *Immigrant Voters in Israel: Parties and Congregations in a Local Election Campaign.* Manchester, England: Manchester University Press.

2b,c/3a/4h/5k/10   Israel

746   ——. 1972. "Ethnicity and Citizenship in the Ritual of an Israeli Synagogue." *Southwestern Journal of Anthropology* 28:69-82.

2b/3a/4h/5d/11/12/17   Israel

747   ——. 1974. "Political Ethnicity and Cultural Ethnicity in Israel during the 1960s." In *Urban Ethnicity,* edited by Abner Cohen, pp. 281-309. A.S.A. Monographs, no. 12. London: Tavistock.

2b/3b/4a/5d/10/12   Israel

748   ——. 1975. "Ritualization of Literacy: The Works of Tunisian Scholars in Israel." *American Ethnologist* 2:251-59.

2b/3a/4h/5d,i/12/13/16   Israel

749 ——. 1976. "Ethnic Boundaries and Cultural Paradigms: The Case of Southern Tunisian Immigrants in Israel." *Ethos* 4:271-94.

2b/3a/4h/5d/10/12   Israel

750 DESPRES, Leo A. 1964. "The Implications of Nationalist Policies in British Guiana for the Development of Cultural Theory." *American Anthropologist* 66:1051-77.

2b/3b/4a/5e,f/10/11   Guyana

751 ——. 1968. "Anthropological Theory, Cultural Pluralism, and the Study of Complex Societies." *Current Anthropology* 9:3-26.

2e/3e/4a/5f   Theory

752 ——. 1969. *Protest and Change in Plural Societies.* Montreal: Center for Developing-Area Studies, McGill University.

2b,c/3d/4a/5f/9/10/11   General

753 ——. 1975. "Ethnicity and Ethnic Group Relations in Guyana." In *The New Ethnicity: Perspectives from Ethnology.* 1973 Proceedings of the American Ethnological Society, edited by John W. Bennett, pp. 127-47. St. Paul: West.

2b/3b/4a/5b,f,i/8/9/10   Guyana

754 ——. 1975. "Ethnicity and Resource Competition in Guyanese Society." In *Ethnicity and Resource Competition in Plural Societies,* edited by Leo A. Despres, pp. 87-117. The Hague: Mouton.

2b/3b/4a/5b,f,i/6/8/9/10/12   Guyana

755 ——. 1975. "Toward a Theory of Ethnic Phenomena." In *Ethnicity and Resource Competition in Plural Societies,* edited by Leo A. Despres, pp. 187-207. The Hague: Mouton.

2e/3e/4a/5b,d,i/9/10   Theory

756 DEUTSCH, Karl W. and Richard L. Merritt. 1970. *Nationalism and National Development: An Interdisciplinary Bibliography.* Cambridge, Mass.: MIT Press.

2a/6/8/10/13/16   General

757 DEVOS, George. 1966. "Essential Elements of Caste: Psychological

Determinants in Structural Theory." In *Japan's Invisible Race: Caste in Culture and Personality*, edited by George DeVos and Hiroshi Wagatsuma, pp. 332-52. Berkeley and Los Angeles: University of California Press.

2c/3e/4a/5i/8/9/11/14/17   Theory

758   ——. 1966. "Toward a Cross-Cultural Psychology of Caste Behavior." In *Japan's Invisible Race: Caste in Culture and Personality*, edited by George DeVos and Hiroshi Wagatsuma, pp. 353-84. Berkeley and Los Angeles: University of California Press.

2e/3e/4a/5g,i/9/11   Theory

759   ——. 1972. "Social Stratification and Ethnic Pluralism: An Overview from the Perspective of Psychological Anthropology." *Race* 13:435-40.

2e/3e/4a/5f,g,i/9/11   Theory

760   —— and Hiroshi Wagatsuma. 1966. "Group Solidarity and Individual Mobility." In *Japan's Invisible Race: Caste in Culture and Personality*, edited by George DeVos and Hiroshi Wagatsuma, pp. 241-57. Berkeley and Los Angeles: University of California Press.

2b/3a/4a,g/5d,g/9/11   Japan

761   —— and Hiroshi Wagatsuma. 1966. "Minority Status and Attitudes toward Authority." In *Japan's Invisible Race: Caste in Culture and Personality*, edited by George DeVos and Hiroshi Wagatsuma, pp. 258-72. Berkeley and Los Angeles: University of California Press.

2c/3a/4a,g/5k/9/10/13   Japan

762   —— and William O. Weatherall. 1974. *Japan's Minorities: Burakumin, Koreans, and Ainu.* London: Minority Rights Group.

2b,c/3b/4a,h/5g,i/9/10/11   Japan

763   DEW, Edward. 1972. "Surinam: The Test of Consociationalism." *Plural Societies* 3:35-56.

2b/3b/4f/5f/6/10   Surinam

764   ——. 1974. "Surinam—The Struggle for Ethnic Balance and Identity." *Plural Societies* 5:3-17.

2b/3b/4f/5b/10   Surinam

765 ——. 1978. *The Difficult Flowering of Surinam: Ethnicity and Politics in a Plural Society.* The Hague: Martinus Nijhoff.

2b,c/3b/4f/5b,e/6/7/9/10   Surinam

766 DEY, Mukul K. 1962. "The Indian Population of Trinidad and Tobago." *International Journal of Comparative Sociology* 3:245-53.

2c/3b/4h/5k/6/9   Trinidad and Tobago

767 DIAMOND, Stanley. 1970. "Reflections on the African Revolution: The Point of the Biafran Case." In *The Passing of Tribal Man in Africa,* edited by P.C.W. Gutkind, pp. 16-27. Leiden: E.J. Brill.

2c/3b/4a/5b,d/9/10/11/12   Nigeria

768 DICKIE-CLARK, H.F. 1972. "The Coloured Minority of Durban." In *The Blending of Races: Marginality and Identity in World Perspective,* edited by Noel P. Gist and Anthony Gary Dworkin, pp. 25-38. New York: Wiley-Interscience.

2c/3a/4h/5i/9/10/15   South Africa

769 DICKSON, R.J. 1966. *Ulster Emigration to Colonial America, 1718-1755.* London: Routledge & Kegan Paul.

2c/3a/4d/5k/7   US: Scotch-Irish

770 DINER, Hasia R. 1977. *In the Almost Promised Land: American Jews and Blacks, 1915-1935.* Westport, Conn.: Greenwood Press.

2c/3a/4d/5b/9/10/11   US: Afro-Americans, Jews

771 DINNERSTEIN, Leonard and Frederic Cole Jaher, eds. 1977. *Uncertain Americans: Readings in Ethnic History.* New York: Oxford University Press.

1a,b/2c/3b/4d/5k/9/10/11   US: General

772 DISHMAN, Robert. 1978. "Cultural Pluralism and Bureaucratic Neutrality in the British Caribbean." *Ethnicity* 5:274-99.

2b/3d/4i/5b,f/10   Caribbean

773 DOBBY, E.H.G. 1952. "Resettlement Transforms Malaya: A Case-

History of Relocating the Population of an Asian Plural Society." *Economic Development and Cultural Change* 1:163-89.

2b/3b/4i/5k/6/7/8   Malaysia

774 DOBSON, Richard B. 1975. "Georgia and the Georgians." In *Handbook of Major Soviet Nationalities,* edited by Zev Katz, Rosemarie Rogers, and Frederic Harned, pp. 161-88. New York: Free Press.

2c/3a/4h/5k/6/8/10/11/13/16   USSR: Georgians

775 DOERSAM, Christopher. 1977. "Sovietization, Culture, and Religion." In *Nationality Group Survival in Multi-Ethnic States: Shifting Support Patterns in the Soviet Baltic Regions,* edited by Edward Allworth, pp. 148-93. New York: Praeger.

2c/3b/4f/5d/12/16/17   USSR: Estonians, Latvians, Lithuanians

776 DOLCE, Philip C. 1976. "The McCarran-Walter Act and the Conflict over Immigration Policy During the Truman Administration." In *The Immigrant Experience in America,* edited by Frank J. Coppa and Thomas J. Curran, pp. 215-32. Boston: Twayne.

2c/3b/4d/5k/10/11   US: General

777 DOLGIN, Janet L. 1977. *Jewish Identity and the JDL.* Princeton, N.J.: Princeton University Press.

2b/3a/4a/5d/10/11/12/15   US: Jews

778 DOLLARD, John. 1937. *Caste and Class in a Southern Town.* New York: Harper.

2b,c/3a/4h/5b,i/8/9/10/11   US: Afro-Americans

779 DONOGHUE, John. 1966. "The Social Persistence of an Outcaste Group." In *Japan's Invisible Race: Caste in Culture and Personality,* edited by George DeVos and Hiroshi Wagatsuma, pp. 137-52. Berkeley and Los Angeles: University of California Press.

2b/3a/4a/5i/9/11   Japan

780 DOORNBOS, Martin R. 1976. "Ethnicity, Christianity, and the Development of Social Stratification in Colonial Ankole, Uganda." *The International Journal of African Historical Studies* 9:555-75.

2c/3b/4d/5i/9/10/11/17   Uganda

781   DOROSHKIN, Milton. 1969. *Yiddish in America: Social and Cultural Foundations.* Cranbury, N.J.: Associated University Presses.

2c/3a/4d/5k/6/11/12/15/16   US: Jews

782   DOROTICH, Daniel A. 1978. "Ethnic Diversity and National Unity in Yugoslav Education: The Socialist Autonomous Province of Vojvodina." *Compare* 8:81-92.

2c/3b/4f/5f/6/13/16   Yugoslavia

783   DOSTAL, Walter, ed. 1972. *The Situation of the Indian in South America: Contributions to the Study of Inter-Ethnic Conflict in the Non-Andean Regions of South America.* Geneva: World Council of Churches.

1a/2a,b,c/3b/4a,i/5a,b,i,j/6/8/9/10/11/17   South America

784   DOTSON, Floyd and Lillian Dotson. 1963. "Indians and Coloureds in Rhodesia and Nyasaland." *Race* 5:61-75.

2b/3a/4i/5g,i/9/11   Zambia

785   DRAKE, St. Clair. 1966. "The 'Colour Problem' in Britain: A Study in Social Definitions." *Sociological Review,* n.s., 3:197-216.

2c/3b/4g/5d,g/9/11   Britain: General

786   DREYER, June Teufel. 1971. "China's Minority Nationalities: Traditional and Party Elites." *Pacific Affairs* 43:506-30.

2c/3b/4d,f/5k/10   China (PRC)

787   ——. 1975. "Go West Young Han: The Hsia Fang Movement to China's Minority Areas." *Pacific Affairs* 48:353-69.

2c/3b/4f/5b/7/10   China (PRC)

788   ——. 1977. "The Kazakhs in China." In *Ethnic Conflict in International Relations,* edited by Astri Suhrke and Lela Garner Noble, pp. 146-77. New York: Praeger.

2c/3a/4f/5b/10   China (PRC)

789   DRIEDGER, Leo. 1976. "Ethnic Self-Identity: A Comparison of In-

group Evaluations." *Sociometry* 39:131-41.

2d/3a,c/4g,h/5d/12   Canada: General

790 ——. 1977. "Toward a Perspective on Canadian Ethnic Pluralism:
Ethnic Identity in Winnipeg." *Canadian Journal of Sociology* 4:77-95.

2d/3a/4h/5d,f/6/9/11/12/14   Canada: General

791 ——. 1978. *The Canadian Ethnic Mosaic: A Quest for Identity.* Toronto:
McClelland & Stewart.

1a/2b,c/3a/4a,g,h/5c,d,e,g,i
6/7/8/11/12/16/17   Canada: General

792 ——. 1978. "Ethnic Boundaries: A Comparison of Two Urban Neighborhoods." *Sociology and Social Research* 62:193-211.

2b/3a/4h/5c/6/11/12   Canada: General

793 ——. 1979. "Maintenance of Urban Ethnic Boundaries: The French
in St. Boniface." *Sociological Quarterly* 20:89-108.

2c/3a/4h/5c/6/10/11/12/13/16/17   Canada: Québécois

794 —— and Glenn Church. 1974. "Residential Segregation and Institutional
Completeness." *Canadian Review of Sociology and Anthropology* 11:30-
52.

2d/3c/4h/5c,f/6/7/15   Canada: General

795 —— and Jacob Peters. 1977. "Identity and Social Distance: Towards
Understanding Simmel's 'The Stranger.'" *Canadian Review of Sociology
and Anthropology* 14:158-73.

2d/3c/4h/5d,i/11/12   Canada: General

796 DRUCKER, Henry. 1978 (?). *Breakaway: The Scottish Labour Party.*
Edinburgh: EUSPB.

2b/3a/4f/5k/10   Scotland

797 DRUMMOND, Robert. 1977. "Nationalism and Ethnic Demands: Some
Speculations on a Congenial Note." *Canadian Journal of Political Science*
10:375-89.

2e/3e/4f/5e/10   Theory

798 DSYUBA, Ivan. 1974. *Internationalism or Russification? A Study in the Soviet Nationalities Problem.* New York: Monad Press.

2b/3b/4i/5a,j/9/10/11/16   USSR: General

799 DUNN, Ethel and Stephen P. Dunn. 1973. "Ethnic Intermarriage as an Indicator of Cultural Convergence in Soviet Central Asia." In *The Nationality Question in Soviet Central Asia,* edited by Edward Allworth, pp. 45-58. New York: Praeger.

2c/3b/4a/5a/14   USSR: Central Asians

800 DUNN, James A., Jr. 1972. " 'Consociational Democracy' and Language Conflict: A Comparison of the Belgian and Swiss Experiences." *Comparative Political Studies* 5:3-39.

2c/3d/4f/5f/10/16/17   Belgium; Switzerland

801 ———. 1974. "The Revision of the Constitution in Belgium: A Study in the Institutionalization of Ethnic Conflict." *Western Political Quarterly* 27:143-63.

2c/3b/4f/5f/10   Belgium

802 DUNN, L. C. et al. 1975. *Race, Science and Society.* Paris: UNESCO Press.

1a/2c/3e/4a,f,g,h/5f,g,i,k/8/9/11/12   General

803 DUNN, Stephen P. and Ethel Dunn. 1967. "Soviet Regime and Native Culture in Central Asia and Kazakhstan: The Major Peoples." *Current Anthropology* 8:147-208.

2c/3b/4a/5f/8/10/11/12/13/14   USSR: General

804 DUNNING, Eric. 1972. "Dynamics of Racial Stratification: Some Preliminary Observations." *Race* 13:415-34.

2c/3e/4h/5i/9   Theory

805 DURRENBERGER, Paul. 1974. "The Regional Context of the Economy of a Lisu Village in Northern Thailand." *Southeast Asia* 3:569-75.

2b/3a/4a/5c/8/12   Thailand

806   DU TOIT, Brian M. 1978. "Ethnicity, Neighborliness, and Friendship among Urban Africans in South Africa." In *Ethnicity in Modern Africa,* edited by Brian M. Du Toit, pp. 143-74. Boulder, Colo.: Westview Press.

2d/3a/4a/5d,g/11/12   South Africa

807   DUTTER, Lee E. 1977. "Eastern and Western Jews: Ethnic Divisions in Israeli Society." *Middle East Journal* 31:451-68.

2d/3c/4f/5f/9/10/12   Israel

808   DWORKIN, Anthony Gary. 1972. "The Peoples of La Raza: The Mexican-Americans of Los Angeles." In *The Blending of Races: Marginality and Identity in World Perspective,* edited by Noel P. Gist and Anthony Gary Dworkin, pp. 167-90. New York: Wiley-Interscience.

2c/3a/4h/5k/6/8/9/10/12/13/14   US: Mexican Americans

809   EAMES, Edwin and Howard Robboy. 1978. "The Wulfranian and the Punjabi: Conflict, Identity, and Adaptation." *Anthropological Quarterly* 51:207-20.

2b/3a/4a/5a,b,c/7/8/12/17   Britain: Pakistanis

810   EASTMAN, Carol. 1971. "Who are the Waswahili?" *Africa* 41:228-35.

2b/3a/4a/5d/12/16   East Africa

811   ——. 1975. "Ethnicity and the Social Scientist: Phonemes and Distinctive Features." *African Studies Review* 18:29-38.

2b/3a/4a/5d/12/16   Kenya

812   EDEL, M. M. 1965. "African Tribalism: Some Reflections on Uganda." *Political Science Quarterly* 80:357-72.

2c/3b/4f/5b,f,i/10   Uganda

813   EDELSTEIN, Joel C. 1974. "Pluralist and Marxist Perspectives on Ethnicity and Nation-Building." In *Ethnicity and Nation-Building,* edited by Wendell Bell and Walter E. Freeman, pp. 45-57. Beverly Hills, Calif.: Sage.

2e/3e/4h/5b,f,i/8/9   Theory

814   EDLEFSON, John B., Khalida Shal, and Mohsin Farooqi. 1960.
      "Makranis, the Negroes of West Pakistan." *Phylon* 21:124-30.

2b/3a/4a/5g,i/8/9   Pakistan

815   EDMONDS, C. J. 1971. "Kurdish Nationalism." *Journal of Contemporary History* 6:87-107.

2c/3a/4d/5e/10   Iran; Iraq; Turkey

816   EDMONDS, Juliet. 1968. "Religion, Intermarriage and Assimilation:
      The Chinese in Malaya." *Race* 10:57-68.

2b/3a/4a/5a/12/14/17   Malaysia

817   EDMONDSON, Locksley. 1974. "Caribbean Nation-Building and the
      Internationalization of Race: Issues and Perspectives." In *Ethnicity and
      Nation-Building,* edited by Wendell Bell and Walter E. Freeman, pp. 73-
      86. Beverly Hills, Calif.: Sage.

2c/3e/4f/5k/9/10   Caribbean

818   EDWARDS, J. R. 1976. "Current Issues in Bilingual Education." *Ethnicity* 3:70-81.

2c/3e/4i/5k/13/16   US: General

819   EDWARDS, Reginald. 1978. "Language, Politics and Ethnicity as
      Educational Variables: The Quebec Case." *Compare* 8:15-29.

2b/3b/4i/5k/10/13/16   Canada: Québécois

820   EGERTON, John. 1969. *Cubans in Miami: A Third Dimension in Racial
      and Cultural Relations.* Nashville, Tenn.: Race Relations Information
      Center.

2b/3a/4h/5f,i/8/9/11   US: Cubans

821   EISINGER, Peter K. 1978. "Ethnic Political Transition in Boston,
      1884-1933: Some Lessons for Contemporary Cities." *Political Science
      Quarterly* 93:217-39.

2c/3a/4f/5b/10   US: General

822   EITZEN, D. Stanley. 1968. "Two Minorities: The Jews of Poland and
      the Chinese of the Philippines." *Jewish Journal of Sociology*, n.s., 10:
      221-40.

2c/3c,d/4h/5f,i/9/10/11   Philippines; Poland

823   ELKHOLY, Abdo A. 1966. *The Arab Moslems in the United States.*
      New Haven, Conn.: College and University Press.

2b/3a/4i/5d,i/9/12   US: Arabs

824   ELLIOTT, Jean Leonard, ed. 1971. *Immigrant Groups. Minority Ca-
      nadians 1.* Scarborough, Ontario: Prentice-Hall.

1a/2b,c/3a/4a,h/5a,b,d,f,i
9/13/14/16/17   Canada: General

825   ——, ed. 1971. *Native Peoples. Minority Canadians 2.* Scarborough,
      Ontario: Prentice-Hall.

1a/2b,c/3a/4a,h/5g,i/6/8/9/10/11   Canada: Native Canadians

826   ELLMAN, Yisrael. 1970. "The Economic Structure and Characteristics
      of American Jewry." *Dispersion and Unity* 11:101-46.

2c/3a/4h/5k/8   US: Jews

827   EMERSON, Rupert. 1960. *From Empire to Nation: The Rise to Self-
      Assertion of Asian and African Peoples.* Boston: Beacon Press.

2c/3d/4f/5b,d,e/9/10/16/17   General

828   ENLOE, Cynthia H. 1973. "Ethnicity and the Myth of the Military in
      African Development." *Ufahamu* 4:35-56.

2c/3e/4f/5k/10   Africa

829   ——. 1974. "Foreign Policy and Ethnicity in 'Soft States': Prospects
      for Southeast Asia." In *Ethnicity and Nation-Building,* edited by Wendell
      Bell and Walter E. Freeman, pp. 223-31. Beverly Hills, Calif.: Sage.

2c/3e/4f/5d,e/10/12   Southeast Asia

830   ——. 1975. "Ethnic Factors in the Evolution of the South African Military." *Issue: A Quarterly of Africanist Opinion* 5:21-28.

2c/3b/4f/5j,k/10/11   South Africa

831   ——. 1976. "Civilian Control of the Military: Implications in the Plural Societies of Guyana and Malaysia." In *Civilian Control of the Military: Theory and Cases from Developing Countries,* edited by Claude E. Welch, Jr., pp. 65-98. Albany: State University of New York Press.

2b/3d/4f/5 f,i,k/9/10   Guyana; Malaysia

832   ——. 1978. "Ethnicity, Bureaucracy, and State-Building in Africa and Latin America." *Ethnic and Racial Studies* 1:336-51.

2c/3e/4f/5b,e,f,i/10   Africa; Mesoamerica; South America

833   ——. 1978. "The Issue Saliency of the Military-Ethnic Connection: Some Thoughts on Malaysia." *Comparative Politics* 10:267-85.

2b/3b/4f/5k/10   Malaysia

834   ——. 1979. "Development Viewed from the Palace: Political Scientists Look at Southeast Asian Ethnic Politics." *Ethnicity* 6:1-9.

2c/3e/4f/5b/10   Southeast Asia

835   EPSTEIN, A. L. 1958. *Politics in an Urban African Community.* Manchester, England: Manchester University Press.

2b/3a/4a/5b,c,d,h,i/6/7/8/9   Zambia

836   ——. 1969. *Matupit: Land, Politics, and Change among the Tolai of New Britain.* Berkeley and Los Angeles: University of California Press.

2b/3a/4a/5a,c,d/6/7/8/9/10
11/12/14/15   New Britain

837   ——. 1970. "Autonomy and Identity: Aspects of Political Development in the Gazelle Peninsula." *Anthropological Forum* 2:427-43.

2b/3a/4a/5b,d/10/12   New Britain

838   ——. 1978. *Ethos and Identity: Three Studies in Ethnicity.* London: Tavistock.

2b,c/3a/4a/5d/11/12   Papua New Guinea; US: Jews; Zambia

839   ERICKSON, Charlotte. 1972. *Invisible Immigrants: The Adaptation of English and Scottish Immigrants in Nineteenth Century America.* Coral Gables, Fla.: University of Miami Press.

2c/3a/4d/5a/12   US: English, Scottish

840   ESMAN, Milton J. 1972. "Malaysia: Communal Coexistence and Mutual Deterrence." In *Racial Tensions and National Identity,* edited by Ernest Q. Campbell, pp. 227-43. Nashville, Tenn.: Vanderbilt University Press.

2c/3b/4f/5b/6/8/9/10   Malaysia

841   ——. 1975. "Communal Conflict in Southeast Asia." In *Ethnicity: Theory and Experience,* edited by Nathan Glazer and Daniel Patrick Moynihan, pp. 391-419. Cambridge, Mass.: Harvard University Press.

2c/3e/4f/5b/10   Southeast Asia

842   ——. 1977. "Perspectives on Ethnic Conflict in Industrialized Societies." In *Ethnic Conflict in the Western World,* edited by Milton J. Esman, pp. 371-90. Ithaca and London: Cornell University Press.

2e/3e/4f/5k/10   Theory

843   ——. 1977. "Scottish Nationalism, North Sea Oil, and the British Response." In *Ethnic Conflict in the Western World,* edited by Milton J. Esman, pp. 251-86. Ithaca and London: Cornell University Press.

2c/3b/4f/5b,i/9/10   Scotland

844   ETEROVICH, Adam S. 1966. *Jugoslavs in Los Angeles 1733-1900.* San Francisco: R & E Research Associates.

2c/3a/4d/5k/8/10/15   US: Yugoslavs

845   ——. 1971. *Croatians from Dalmatia and Montenegrin Serbs in the West and South 1800-1900.* San Francisco: R & E Research Associates.

2c/3a/4d/5k/6/7/8   US: Croatians, Serbs

846   ——. 1971. *Yugoslav Survey of California, Nevada, Arizona, and the South 1800-1900*. San Francisco: R & E Research Associates.

2c/3a/4d/5k/7/15   US: Yugoslavs

847   ETHIOPIAWI. 1977. "The Eritrean-Ethiopian Conflict." In *Ethnic Conflict in International Relations,* edited by Astri Suhrke and Lela Garner Noble, pp. 127-45. New York: Praeger.

2c/3a/4f/5b/10   Ethiopia

848   FALLERS, Lloyd A. 1974. *The Social Anthropology of the Nation-State*. Chicago: Aldine.

2b,c/3b/4a/5e/9/10   East Africa, Turkey

849   FARBER, Bernard, Leonard Gordon, and Albert J. Mayer. 1979. "Intermarriage and Jewish Identity: The Implications for Pluralism and Assimilation in American Society." *Ethnic and Racial Studies* 2:222-30.

2c/3a/4h/5a,f/12/14   US: Jews

850   FARLEY, Reynolds. 1970. *Growth of the Black Population: A Study of Demographic Trends*. Chicago: Markham.

2d/3a/4h/5k/6   US: Afro-Americans

851   ——. 1978. "School Integration in the United States." In *The Demography of Racial and Ethnic Groups,* edited by Frank D. Bean and W. Parker Frisbie, pp. 15-50. New York: Academic Press.

2c/3b/4h/5g,i/6/10/13   US: Afro-, Euro-Americans

852   FEAGIN, Joe R. and Nancy Fujitaki. 1972. "On the Assimilation of Japanese Americans." *Amerasia Journal* 1:13-30.

853   FEATHERMAN, David L. 1971. "The Socioeconomic Achievement of White Religio-Ethnic Subgroups: Social and Psychological Explana-

tions." *American Sociological Review* 36:207-22.

2d/3c/4g,h/5a,i/9/11/13   US: Euro-Americans

854   —— and Robert M. Hauser. 1976. "Changes in the Socioeconomic
Stratification of the Races, 1962-73." *American Journal of Sociology*
82:621-51.

2d/3b/4h/5i/9   US: Afro-, Euro-Americans

855   FEINGOLD, David A. 1976. "On Knowing Who You Are: Intraethnic
Distinctions among the Akha of Northern Thailand." In *Changing Iden-
tities in Modern Southeast Asia,* edited by David J. Banks, pp. 83-94.
The Hague: Mouton.

2b/3a/4a/5d/12   Thailand

856   FEINGOLD, Henry L. 1974. *Zion in America: The Jewish Experience
from Colonial Times to the Present.* New York: Twayne.

2c/3a/4d/5k/7/8/10/11/12   US: Jews

857   FEINSTEIN, Otto, ed. 1971. *Ethnic Groups in the City: Culture, Institutions, and Power.* Lexington, Mass.: Heath Lexington Books.

1a/2b,c/3b/4f/5a,e,f,h,i/9/10/13   US: Euro-Americans

858   FEIT, E. 1967. "Community in a Quandary: The South African Jewish
Community and Apartheid." *Race* 8:395-408.

2b/3a/4h/5d,i/9/10/11/12   South Africa

859   FELDSTEIN, Stanley, ed. 1971. *The Poisoned Tongue: A Documentary
History of American Racism and Prejudice.* New York: William Morrow.

2c/3b/4d/5g/11   US: General

860   FELLOWS, Donald Keith. 1972. *A Mosaic of America's Ethnic Minorities.* New York: Wiley.

1b/2c/3b/4h/5k   US: Afro-, Asian-, Mexican-, Native Americans,
6/8/12/13   Puerto Ricans

861   FENNELL, Valerie. 1977. "International Atlanta and Ethnic Group

Relations." *Urban Anthropology* 6:345-54.

2b/3a/4a/5k/10/11   US: General

862 FENTON, Mike. 1976. "Price Discrimination under Non-Monopolistic Conditions." *Applied Economics* 8:135-44.

2d/3a/4b/5k(Neoclassical Economics)/6/8   US: Afro-, Asian Americans

863 FERMI, Laura. 1971. *Illustrious Immigrants: The Intellectual Migration from Europe 1930-41.* Chicago: University of Chicago Press.

2c/3b/4d/5k/7   US: Euro-Americans

864 FERNANDES, Florestan. 1970. "Immigration and Race Relations in São Paulo." In *Race and Class in Latin America,* edited by Magnus Mörner, pp. 122-42. New York and London: Columbia University Press.

2c/3a/4d/5d,g/7/11   Brazil

865 FERNANDO, Tissa. 1972. "The Burghers of Ceylon." In *The Blending of Races: Marginality and Identity in World Perspective,* edited by Noel P. Gist and Anthony Gary Dworkin, pp. 61-78. New York: Wiley-Interscience.

2c/3a/4h/5i/8/9/11/12/13   Sri Lanka

866 FILIPINAS FOUNDATION, Inc. 1975. *Philippine Majority-Minority Relations and Ethnic Attitudes.* Makati: Filipinas Foundation, Inc.

2b,c,d/3b/4a,f,h/5g/11   Southeast Asia; Philippines

867 FINKELSTEIN, Louis, ed. 1971. *The Jews: Their History, Culture, and Religion.* 2 vols. 4th ed. New York: Schocken.

2b/3e/4d/5k/11/12/13   US: Jews

868 FISCHER-GALATI, Stephen. 1969. "Romanian Nationalism." In *Nationalism in Eastern Europe,* edited by Peter F. Sugar and Ivo J. Lederer, pp. 373-95. Seattle and London: University of Washington Press.

2c/3b/4d/5e/10   Romania

869 ——. 1975. "Moldavia and the Moldavians." In *Handbook of Major Soviet Nationalities,* edited by Zev Katz, Rosemarie Rogers, and Frederic

Harned, pp. 415-33. New York: Free Press.

2c/3a/4d/5k/6/8/10/11/13/16   USSR: Moldavians

870   FISHER, Maxine P. 1978. "Creating Ethnic Identity: Asian Indians in the New York City Area." *Urban Anthropology* 7:271-85.

2b/3a/4a/5d,h/7/8/9/12/15   US: East Indians

871   FISHER, Wesley A. 1977. "Ethnic Consciousness and Intermarriage: Correlates of Endogamy among the Major Soviet Nationalities." *Soviet Studies* 29:395-408.

2c/3c/4h/5d/12/14   USSR: General

872   FISHMAN, Joshua A., Charles A. Ferguson, and Jyotirindra Das Gupta, eds. 1968. *Language Problems of Developing Nations.* New York: Wiley.

1a/2c/3d/4e,f/5d,e,f/10/11/16   General

873   FISKE, Shirley. 1977. "Intertribal Perceptions: Navahos and Pan-Indianism." *Ethos* 5:358-75.

2d/3a/4g/5d,g/11   US: Native Americans

874   FITZGERALD, Stephen. 1973. *China and the Overseas Chinese.* New York: Cambridge University Press.

2c/3b/4f/5k/10/11   China (PRC)

875   FLANAGAN, Robert J. 1973. "Racial Wage Discrimination and Employment Segregation." *Journal of Human Resources* 8:456-71.

2d/3c/4b/5i/8   US: Afro-Americans

876   ——. 1973. "Segmented Market Theories and Racial Discrimination." *Industrial Relations* 12:253-73.

2e/3e/4b/5i/8   Theory

877   FLEMING, Judith. 1977. "Political Leaders." In *Nationality Group Survival in Multi-Ethnic States: Shifting Support Patterns in the Soviet Baltic Region,* edited by Edward Allworth, pp. 123-47. New York: Praeger.

2c/3b/4f/5e/10   USSR: Estonians, Latvians, Lithuanians

878 FLETT, Hazel. 1979. "Bureaucracy and Ethnicity: Notion of Eligibility to Public Housing." In *Ethnicity at Work,* edited by Sandra Wallman, pp. 135-52. London: Macmillan.

2b/3a/4a/5d,g/11/12   Britain: General

879 FOGEL, Walter. 1978. *Mexican Illegal Alien Workers in the United States.* Los Angeles: Institute of Industrial Relations, University of California.

2c/3a/4b/5b,i/8/10   US: Mexican Americans

880 FOLTZ, William J. 1973. "Political Boundaries and Political Competition in Tropical Africa." In *Building States and Nations: Analyses by Region,* vol. 2, edited by S. N. Eisenstadt and Stein Rokkan, pp. 357-83. Beverly Hills, Calif.: Sage.

2c/3e/4f/5e,f/10/11   Africa

881 ——. 1974. "Ethnicity, Status, and Conflict." In *Ethnicity and Nation-Building,* edited by Wendell Bell and Walter E. Freeman, pp. 103-16. Beverly Hills, Calif.: Sage.

2c/3e/4f/5b,d,f,i/9/10/11/12/16   General

882 FONER, Nancy. 1977. "The Jamaicans: Cultural and Social Change among Migrants in Britain." In *Between Two Cultures: Migrants and Minorities in Britain,* edited by James L. Watson, pp. 120-50. Oxford: Basil Blackwell.

2b/3a/4a/5k/8/11/13/14   Britain: Jamaicans

883 ——. 1978. *Jamaica Farewell: Jamaican Migrants in London.* Berkeley and Los Angeles: University of California Press.

2b/3a/4a/5d,g/7/8/9/13   Britain: Jamaicans

884 FONER, Philip S. 1974. *Organized Labor and the Black Worker 1619-1973.* New York: Praeger.

2c/3b/4d/5k/8/9/10   US: Afro-Americans

885 ——. 1978. *Essays on Afro-American History.* Philadelphia: Temple University Press.

2c/3a/4d/5g/9/10/11   US: Afro-Americans

886   FONG, Stanley L. M. 1973. "Assimilation and Changing Social Roles of Chinese Americans." *Journal of Social Issues* 29:115-27.

2b/3a/4h/5a/12   US: Chinese

887   FONSECA, A. 1971. "Law, Secularism, and Indian Minorities." *Social Action* 21:233-42.

2c/3b/4b/5a,d,e/11/12   India

888   FOON, Chew Sock. 1977. *Forever Plural: The Perception and Practice of Inter-Communal Marriage in Singapore.* Papers in International Studies, Southeast Asia Series, no. 45. Athens: Ohio University Center for International Studies, Southeast Asia Program.

2d/3b/4h/5f,g/11/14/17   Singapore

889   FORBES, Jack D. 1973. *Aztecas del Norte: The Chicanos of Aztlan.* Greenwich, Conn.: Fawcett.

2b,c/3a/4i/5b,d/9/10/11/12   US: Mexican Americans

890   FORD, Henry Jones. 1915. *The Scotch-Irish in America.* Princeton, N.J.: Princeton University Press.

2c/3a/4d/5a/7/8/10   US: Scotch-Irish

891   FORD, W. Scott. 1972. *Interracial Public Housing in Border City: A Situational Analysis of the Contact Hypothesis.* Lexington, Mass.: Lexington Books.

2d/3b/4d/5k/9/10   US: Afro-, Euro-Americans

892   FOREMAN, Scott. 1976. *From Africa to the United States and Then . . . . A Concise Afro-American History.* 2d ed. Glenview, Ill.: Scott, Foresman.

2c/3b/4d/5k/9/10   US: Afro-Americans

893   FORSTER, John. 1975. "Maori-White Relations in New Zealand." In *Politics of Race: Comparative Studies,* edited by Donald G. Baker, pp. 191-209. Lexington, Mass.: Lexington Books.

2c/3b/4h/5k/6/7/9/10   New Zealand

894   FORSYTHE, David P. and J. L. Taulbee. 1974. "The Palestinians and

the Arab States." In *Ethnicity and Nation-Building,* edited by Wendell Bell and Walter E. Freeman, pp. 187-202. Beverly Hills, Calif.: Sage.

2c/3e/4f/5b/10   Middle East

895   FORTES, Meyer. 1970. *The Plural Society in Africa.* Johannesburg: South African Institute of Race Relations.

2c/3e/4a/5f,g,i/9/10   Africa

896   FOX, Richard G., Charlotte Aull, and Louis Cimino. 1978. "Ethnic Nationalism and Political Mobilization in Industrial Societies." In *Interethnic Communication.* Southern Anthropological Society Proceedings, no. 12, edited by E. Lamar Ross, pp. 113-33. Athens: University of Georgia Press.

2b/3a,e/4a/5e/10/12   Canada: Acadians

897   FRANCIS, E.K. 1951. "Minority Groups—A Revision of Concepts." *British Journal of Sociology* 2:219-29.

2e/3e/4h/5f,g   Theory

898   ———. 1968. "The Ethnic Factor in Nation-Building." *Social Forces* 46:338-46.

2f/3e/4h/5a,d,e/10/11   Theory

899   FRANCK, Thomas M. 1960. *Race and Nationalism: The Struggle for Power in Rhodesia and Nyasaland.* New York: Fordham University Press.

2b,c/3b/4f/5b,e/10/11   Zambia; Zimbabwe

900   FRANDA, Marcus F. 1971. "Some Notes on the Internal Dynamics and Influence of the Indian Community in Ethiopia." *Indian Political Science Review* 5:111-26.

2b/3a/4f/5k/8/10/15/17   Ethiopia

901   FRAZIER, E. Franklin. 1957. *The Negro in the United States.* New York: Macmillan.

2c/3a/4h/5i,k/8/9/10/13/14/16/17   US: Afro-Americans

902   ———. 1957. *Race and Culture Contacts in the Modern World.* New

York: Alfred A. Knopf.

2c/3e/4d,h/5i,k/9/10   General

903 ——. 1968. *On Race Relations.* Chicago and London: University of Chicago Press.

2c/3b,d,e/4h/5h/9/11/14   General

904 FREEDMAN, Maurice. 1960. "The Growth of a Plural Society in Malaya." *Pacific Affairs* 33:158-68.

2b/3b/4a/5f/7/8/9   Malaysia

905 FREEMAN, Gary P. 1978. "Immigrant Labor and Working-Class Politics: The French and British Experience." *Comparative Politics* 11:24-41.

2b/3d/4f/5b,i/8/9/10   Britain: General; France

906 ——. 1979. *Immigrant Labor and Racial Conflict in Industrial Societies: The French and British Experience 1945-1975.* Princeton, N.J.: Princeton University Press.

2c/3b,d/4f/5b,e,f,g,h,j/7/8/9/10/11   Britain: General; France

907 FREEMAN, Richard B. 1976. *Black Elite: The New Market for Highly Educated Black Americans.* New York: McGraw-Hill.

2c,d/3b/4b/5k/8/11/13   US: Afro-Americans

908 FREEMAN, Walter E. 1974. "Functions of Ethnic Conflict and Their Contributions to National Growth." In *Ethnicity and Nation-Building,* edited by Wendell Bell and Walter E. Freeman, pp. 177-86. Beverly Hills, Calif.: Sage.

2e/3e/4h/5b,f,i/9/10   Theory

909 FRENCH, Laurence. 1978. "Missionaries among the Eastern Cherokee: Religion as a Means of Interethnic Communication." In *Interethnic Communication.* Southern Anthropological Society Proceedings, no. 12, edited by E. Lamar Ross, pp. 100-112. Athens: University of Georgia Press.

2b,c/3a/4a/5b,d/10/17   US: Native Americans

910 FRENDO, Henry J. 1975. "Language and Nationality in an Island Colony: Malta." *Canadian Review of Studies in Nationalism* 3:22-33.

2c/3a/4d/5e/10/11/12/16   Malta

911 FREUND, W. M. 1976. "Race in the Social Structure of South Africa, 1652-1836." *Race and Class* 18:53-67.

2c/3b/4d/5i/9/10/11/12   South Africa

912 FREY, William H. 1978. "Black Movement to the Suburbs: Potential and Prospects for Metropolitan-Wide Integration." In *The Demography of Racial and Ethnic Groups,* edited by Frank D. Bean and W. Parker Frisbie, pp. 79-117. New York: Academic Press.

2c/3b/4h/5k/6/7/9   US: Afro-, Euro-Americans

913 FRIDERES, James S. 1971. "Termination or Migration: The Hutterites— A Case Study." *Canadian Ethnic Studies* 3:17-24.

2c/3a/4h/5a,g/10   Canada: Hutterites

914 ———. 1978. "British Canadian Attitudes Toward Minority Ethnic Groups in Canada." *Ethnicity* 5:20-32.

2d/3a/4g/5g/9/11   Canada: English

915 FRIED, Morton H. 1975. *The Notion of Tribe.* Menlo Park, Calif.: Cummings.

2e/3e/4a/5d,f/10/11   Theory

916 FRIEDLANDER, Dov and Calvin Goldscheider. 1979. *The Population of Israel.* New York: Columbia University Press.

2c/3b/4h/5k/6/7/11   Israel

917 FRIEDLANDER, Eva. 1977. "Caste, Ethnicity, and Change in West Bengal." In *Ethnic Encounters: Identities and Contexts,* edited by George L. Hicks and Philip E. Leis, pp. 201-20. North Scituate, Mass.: Duxbury Press.

2b,c/3a/4a/5i/8/9   India

918 FRIESAN, John W. 1971. "Characteristics of Mennonite Identity:

A Survey of Mennonite and Non-Mennonite Views." *Canadian Ethnic Studies* 3:25-42.

2d/3a/4h/5d,g/11/12/13   Canada: Mennonites

919   FRISBIE, W. Parker and Frank D. Bean. 1978. "Some Issues in the
      Demographic Study of Racial and Ethnic Populations." In *The Demo-
      graphy of Racial and Ethnic Groups,* edited by Frank D. Bean and W.
      Parker Frisbie, pp. 1-14. New York: Academic Press.

2e/3e/4h/5k/6/12   Theory

920   ——, Frank D. Bean, and Isaac W. Eberstein. 1978. "Patterns of Marital
      Instability among Mexican Americans, Blacks, and Anglos." In *The
      Demography of Racial and Ethnic Groups,* edited by Frank D. Bean and
      W. Parker Frisbie, pp. 143-63. New York: Academic Press.

2c/3c/4h/5k/8/9/13/14   US: Afro-, Euro-, Mexican Americans

921   FUCHS, Lawrence, W., ed. 1968. *American Ethnic Politics.* New York:
      Harper Torchbooks.

1a/2a,c/3b/4f/5a,d,k/10/11   US: General

922   FUGITA, Steven S. and David J. O'Brien. 1977. "Economics, Ideology,
      and Ethnicity: The Struggle Between the United Farm Workers Union
      and the Nisei Farmers League." *Social Problems* 25:146-56.

2b/3a/4h/5b/8/9/10   US: Japanese, Mexican Americans

923   FURNIVALL, Joseph Sydenham. 1942. "The Political Economy of
      the Tropical Far East." *Journal of the Royal Central Asiatic Society*
      29:195-210.

2b,c/3e/4i/5f,i/8/9/10   Southeast Asia

924   ——. 1945. "Some Problems of Tropical Economy." In *Fabian Colonial
      Essays,* edited by Rita Hinden, pp. 161-84. London: Allen & Unwin.

2c/3e/4i/5f,i/8/9/11   Southeast Asia

925   ——. 1956. *Colonial Policy and Practice: A Comparative Study of
      Burma and Netherlands India.* New York: New York University Press.

2c/3d/4i/5c,f,i/6/8/10/11/12/13/15/16   Burma, Indonesia

926 GABRIEL, John and Gideon Ben-Tovim. 1979. "The Conceptualization of Race Relations in Sociological Theory." *Ethnic and Racial Studies* 2:190-212.

2e/3e/4h/5b,d,h,i   Theory

927 GABRIEL, Richard A. 1973. *The Ethnic Factor in the Urban Polity.* New York: MSS Information.

2d/3a/4f/5c,f/10   US: Irish, Italians

928 GAGALA, Ken. 1973. "The Dual Urban Labor Market: Blacks and Whites." *American Economist* 17:51-59.

2f/3b/4b/5i/8/9   US: Afro-, Euro-Americans

929 ——. 1973. "The Dual Urban Labor Market." *Journal of Black Studies* 3:350-70.

2e/3e/4b/5i/8/9   US: Afro-Americans

930 GAIGE, Frederick H. 1975. *Regionalism and National Unity in Nepal.* Berkeley: University of California Press.

2b/3b/4f/5b,f/10   Nepal

931 GALUSH, William. 1974. "American Poles and the New Poland: An Example of Change in Ethnic Orientation." *Ethnicity* 1:209-21.

2b/3a/4h/5d/12   US: Poles

932 GAMBINO, Richard. 1974. *Blood of My Blood: The Dilemma of the Italian Americans.* Garden City, N.Y.: Doubleday.

2b/3a/4i/5d,f,g/6/8/9/10/11/12/13/14   US: Italians

933 GAMIO, Manuel. 1969. *The Mexican Immigrant: His Life-Story.* Reprint, 1931 ed. Chicago: University of Chicago Press.

2b,c/3a/4i/5k/7/8/11/12/14/16/17   US: Mexican Americans

934 GANN, L. H. 1958. *The Birth of a Plural Society: The Development of Northern Rhodesia under the British South Africa Company, 1894-1914.* Manchester, England: Manchester University Press.

2c/3b/4d/5f,i/8/9/10/11   Zambia

935   GANS, Herbert J. 1962. *The Urban Villagers: Group and Class in the Life of Italian-Americans.* Glencoe, Ill.: Free Press of Glencoe.

2b/3a/4h/5d,i/9/10/12/13   US: Italians

936   GARBARINO, Merwyn S. 1971. "Life in the City:Chicago." In *The American Indian in Urban Society,* edited by Jack O. Waddell and O. Michael Watson, pp. 169-205. Boston: Little, Brown.

2b/3a/4a/5k/6/7/8/12/14/15   US: Native Americans

937   GARCIA, F. Chris, ed. 1973. *Chicano Political Readings.* New York: MSS Information.

1a/2b/3a/4f/5k/10/11/12   US: Mexican Americans

938   ――. 1973. *Political Socialization of Chicano Children: A Comparative Study with Anglos in California Schools.* New York: Praeger.

2d/3c/4f,h/5d/10/11/12/13   US: Euro-, Mexican Americans

939   GARZA, Catarino, ed. 1977. *Puerto Ricans in the U.S.: The Struggle for Freedom.* New York: Pathfinder Press.

1a/2c/3a/4f/5b,i/9/10   US: Puerto Ricans

940   GARZA, Edward D. 1972. *LULAC: League of United Latin-American Citizens.* Reprint, 1951 ed. San Francisco: R & E Research Associates.

2b/3a/4h/5k/15   US: Latin Americans

941   GELLAR, Sheldon. 1973. "State-Building and Nation-Building in West Africa." In *Building States and Nations: Analyses by Region,* vol. 2, edited by S. N. Eisenstadt and Stein Rokkan, pp. 384-426. Beverly Hills, Calif.: Sage.

2c/3e/4f/5e/10   Africa

942   GELLNER, Ernest. 1964. *Thought and Change.* Chicago: University of Chicago Press.

2c/3e/4f/5e/8/9/10/12   Theory

943   ――. 1977. "Ethnicity and Anthropology in the Soviet Union." *Archives Européennes de Sociologie* 18:201-20.

2c/3b/4a/5k/9/12   Theory

944   GELLNER, John and John Smerek. 1968. *The Czechs and Slovaks in Canada.* Toronto: University of Toronto Press.

2c/3a/4d/5k/7/15/16/17   Canada: Czechs, Slovaks

945   GEORGE, Vic and Geoffrey Millerson. 1967. "The Cypriot Community in London." *Race* 8:277-92.

2b/3a/4h/5f/6/7/8/12/14/15/16   Britain: Cypriots

946   GERHART, Gail M. 1978. *Black Power in South Africa: The Evolution of an Ideology.* Berkeley and Los Angeles: University of California Press.

2c/3b/4d/5b,e,j/9/10/11/12   South Africa

947   GERSON, Louis L. 1964. *The Hyphenate in Recent American Politics and Diplomacy.* Lawrence: University of Kansas Press.

2c/3b/4f/5k/10   US: General

948   GERTEINY, Alfred G. 1966. "The Racial Factor and Politics in the Islamic Republic of Mauritania." *Race* 8:263-76.

2b/3b/4a/5k/10   Mauritania

949   GILBERG, Trond. 1974. "Ethnic Minorities in Romania under Socialism." *East European Quarterly* 7:435-58.

2c/3e/4f/5f,i/6/8/13/16   Romania

950   GILES, Howard, Donald M. Taylor, and Richard Y. Bourhis. 1977. "Dimensions of Welsh Identity." *European Journal of Social Psychology* 7:165-74.

2d/3a/4g/5d/12/16   Wales

951   GILLIN, John. 1948. "Race Relations without Conflict, a Guatemalan Town." *American Journal of Sociology* 53:337-43.

2b/3a/4h/5f,i/9   Guatemala

952   GINGRAS, Francois-Pierre. 1975. "Interethnic Contacts and Militancy in the Quebec Independence Movement." *International Review of Modern Sociology* 5:156-63.

2c/3a/4h/5b,e/8/10/13   Canada: Québécois

953   GINSBERG, Philip. 1970. "The Chinese in the Philippine Revolution."
      Asian Studies 8:143-59.

2c/3a/4d/5e/10   Philippines

954   GINSBERG, Yona. 1975. *Jews in a Changing Neighborhood: The Study
      of Mattapan.* New York: The Free Press.

2b/3a/4h/5k/6/10/11/12   US: Jews

955   GIST, Noel P. 1967. "Cultural versus Social Marginality: The Anglo-
      Indians Case." *Phylon* 28:361-75.

2b/3a/4h/5d,g,i/9   India

956   GITTLER, Joseph D., ed. 1964. *Understanding Minority Groups.* New
      York: John Wiley & Sons.

1a/2b/3a/4h/5k/7/8/9/11/12   US: General

957   GLANZ, Rudolph. 1966. *Jew and Irish: Historic Group Relations and
      Immigration.* New York: Shulsinger Brothers.

2c/3a/4d/5k/7/10/11   US: Irish, Jews

958   ——. 1970. *Jew and Italian: Historic Group Relations and the New Im-
      migration.* New York: Shulsinger Brothers.

2c/3a/4d/5k/7/10/11   US: Italians, Jews

959   ——. 1970. *Studies in Judaica Americana.* New York: Ktav.

2c/3a/4d/5k/7/8/9/11/15   US: Jews

960   GLASER, Daniel. 1958. "Dynamics of Ethnic Identification." *American
      Sociological Review* 23:31-40.

2f/3e/4h/5d,h/12   Theory

961   GLASER, Richard. 1976. "The Greek Jews in Baltimore." *Jewish
      Social Studies* 38:321-36.

2b,d/3a/4h/5d/8/12/14   US: Jews

962 GLASGOW, Roy Arthur. 1970. *Guyana: Race and Politics among Africans and East Indians.* The Hague: Martinus Nijhoff.

2c/3b/4f/5b,i/8/9/10   Guyana

963 GLAZER, Nathan. 1978. "The Jews." In *Ethnic Leadership in America,* edited by John Higham, pp. 19-35. Baltimore and London: Johns Hopkins University Press.

2c/3a/4h/5k/10   US: Jews

964 GLENN, Norval D. and Charles M. Bonjean, eds. 1969. *Blacks in the United States.* San Francisco: Chandler.

1a/2b,c,d/3a/4b,d,f,g,h/5b,g,i
8/9/10/11/14   US: Afro-Americans

965 GLICK, Clarence E. 1970. "Interracial Marriage and Admixture in Hawaii." *Social Biology* 17:278-91.

2c/3a/4h/5k/14   US: General

966 GLICK, Paul C. 1970. "Intermarriage among Ethnic Groups in the United States." *Social Biology* 17:292-98.

2c/3b/4h/5k/14   US: General

967 GLOCK, Charles Y. and Ellen Siegelman, eds. 1969. *Prejudice U.S.A.* New York: Praeger.

1a/2c/3b/4g/5g/11/13/17   US: General

968 GLUCKMAN, Max. 1958. *An Analysis of a Social Situation in Modern Zululand.* Manchester, England: Manchester University Press.

2b/3a/4a/5f/9/12   South Africa

969 ———. 1962. "How Foreign Are You?" *Race* 4:12-21.

2f/3e/4a/5d,f/12   General

970 ———. 1965. "Tribalism in Modern British Central Africa." In *Africa: Social Problems of Change and Conflict,* edited by Pierre L. van den Berghe, pp. 346-60. San Francisco: Chandler.

2b/3e/4a/5d,e,f/9/10/12   Africa

971   ——. 1969. "The Tribal Area in South and Central Africa." In *Pluralism in Africa,* edited by Leo Kuper and M. G. Smith, pp. 373-409. Berkeley: University of California Press.

      2b/3e/4a/5d,e,f/9/10/11   Africa

972   GMELCH, Sharon Bohn and George. 1976. "The Emergence of an Ethnic Group: The Irish Tinkers." *Anthropological Quarterly* 49:225-38.

      2b/3a/4a/5d/8/12   Ireland

973   GOERING, John M. 1971. "The Emergence of Ethnic Interests: A Case of Serendipity." *Social Forces* 49:379-84.

      2d/3a/4h/5d/12   US: Irish, Italians

974   GOLDBERG, Harvey. 1977. "Introduction: Culture and Ethnicity in the Study of Israeli Society." *Ethnic Groups* 1:163-86.

      2c/3b/4a/5d,f,k/10/11/12   Israel

975   GOLDEN, Hilda H. and Curt Tausky. 1977. "Minority Groups in the World of Work." In *American Minorities and Economic Opportunity,* edited by H. Roy Kaplan, pp. 10-49. Itasca, Ill.: F. E. Peacock.

                                                         US: Afro-, Mexican-,
      2c/3b/4h/5i/8/9   Native Americans, Puerto Ricans

976   GOLDSTEIN, Melvyn C. 1975. "Ethnogenesis and Resource Competition among Tibetan Refugees in South India." In *Ethnicity and Resource Competition in Plural Societies,* edited by Leo A. Despres, pp. 159-86. The Hague: Mouton.

      2b/3a/4a/5b,d/10   India

977   GOLDSTEIN, Michael. 1971. *Minority Status and Radicalism in Japan.* Center on International Race Relations, Graduate School of International Studies, University of Denver, Studies in Race and Nations, vol. 3, study no. 4.

      2c,e/3a/4f/5b,i/9/10   Japan

978   GOLDSTEIN, Sidney and Calvin Goldscheuder. 1968. *Jewish Americans.* Englewood Cliffs, N. J.: Prentice-Hall.

      2d/3a/4h/5a/6/8/9/11/12/13/14   US: Jews

979   GOMEZ, David F. 1973. *Somos Chicanos: Strangers in Our Own Land.* Boston: Beacon Press.

   2b,c/3a/4f/5g/9/11   US: Mexican Americans

980   GONZALES, Alex S. 1974. *Minorities and the U.S. Economy.* Santa Barbara: University Library, University of California.

   2a/8   US: General

981   GONZALEZ, Nancie L. 1969. *The Spanish Americans of New Mexico: A Heritage of Pride.* Albuquerque: University of New Mexico Press.

   2b/3a/4a/5d/7/11/12   US: Mexican Americans

982   ———. 1975. "Patterns of Dominican Ethnicity." In *The New Ethnicity: Perspectives from Ethnology.* 1973 Proceedings of the American Ethnological Society, edited by John W. Bennett, pp. 110-23. St. Paul: West.

   2b/3b/4a/5f,g/6/7/10/12   Dominican Republic

983   GOODY, Esther N. and Christine Muir Groothues. 1977. "The West Africans: The Quest for Educations." In *Between Two Cultures: Migrants and Minorities in Britain,* edited by James L. Watson, pp. 151-80. Oxford: Basil Blackwell.

   2b/3a/4a/5k/7/8/9/13/14   Britain: Africans

984   GOODY, Jack. 1970. "Marriage Policy and Incorporation in Northern Ghana." In *From Tribe to Nation in Africa: Studies in Incorporation Processes,* edited by Ronald Cohen and John Middleton, pp. 114-49. Scranton, Penn.: Chandler.

   2b,d/3a/4a/5a/7/12/14   Ghana

985   ———. 1973. "Uniqueness in the Cultural Conditions for Political Development in Black Africa." In *Building States and Nations: Analyses by Region,* vol. 2, edited by S. N. Eisenstadt and Stein Rokkan, pp. 341-56. Beverly Hills, Calif.: Sage.

   2c/3e/4a/5e/8   Africa

986   GORDON, Albert I. 1964. *Intermarriage: Interfaith, Interracial, Interethnic.* Boston: Beacon Press.

2b/3b/4i/5k/12/14/17   US: General

987   GORDON, David M. 1972. *Theories of Poverty and Underemployment: Orthodox, Radical, and Dual Labor Market Perspectives.* Lexington, Mass: D.C. Heath.

2c,e/3e/4b/5b,g,i/8/9   Theory

988   GORDON, Leonard A. 1978. "Divided Bengal: Problems of Nationalism and Identity in the 1947 Partition." *Journal of Commonwealth and Comparative Politics* 16:136-68.

2c/3a/4d,f/5d,e/10/12   India; Pakistan

989   GORDON, Milton M. 1975. "Toward a General Theory of Racial and Ethnic Group Relations." In *Ethnicity: Theory and Experience,* edited by Nathan Glazer and Daniel Patrick Moynihan, pp. 84-110. Cambridge, Mass.: Harvard University Press.

2e/3e/4h/5a,b,g,i/9/10/11   Theory

990   ——. 1978. *Human Nature, Class, and Ethnicity.* New York: Oxford University Press.

1a/2c,e/3e/4h/5a,i,k/9/11/12   Theory

991   GORDON, Robert. 1978. "The Celebration of Ethnicity: A 'Tribal Fight' in a Namibian Mine Compound." In *Ethnicity in Modern Africa,* edited by Brian M. Du Toit, pp. 213-31. Boulder, Colo.: Westview Press.

2b/3a/4a/5b,d/12   Namibia

992   GORER, Geoffrey. 1975. "English Identity over Time and Empire." In *Ethnic Identity,* edited by G. DeVos and L. Romanucci-Ross, pp. 156-72. Palo Alto, Calif.: Mayfield.

2c/3b/4a/5d/8/9/12/13   Britain: English

993   GOUVEIA, Dennis Hilary. 1972. "The Coloreds of Guyana." In *The Blending of Races: Marginality and Identity in World Perspective,* edited by Noel P. Gist and Anthony Gary Dworkin, pp. 103-19. New York: Wiley-Interscience.

2c/3a/4i/5d,g/11/12   Guyana

994   GRAVES, Theodore D. 1967. "Psychological Acculturation in a Tri-

Ethnic Community." *Southwestern Journal of Anthropology* 23:337-50.

2b/3a/4a/5a,d,g,h/11 US: Mexican-, Native Americans

995 GRAY, Richard. 1971. "The Southern Sudan." *Journal of Contemporary History* 6:108-20.

2c/3b/4d/5e,f/9/10 Sudan

996 GREELEY, Andrew M. 1971. *Why Can't They Be Like Us? America's White Ethnic Groups*. New York: Dutton.

2c/3b/4h/5g/12 US: Euro-Americans

997 ———. 1972. *That Most Distressful Nation: The Taming of the American Irish*. Chicago: Quadrangle Books.

2c,d/3a/4h/5a/7/8/9/10/11/12/13/14/17 US: Irish

998 ———. 1974. "Political Participation among Ethnic Groups in the United States: A Preliminary Reconnaissance." *American Journal of Sociology* 80:170-204.

2d/3c/4h/5a/10 US: General

999 ———. 1976. "The Ethnic Miracle." *Public Interest,* no. 45, pp. 20-36.

2c/3b/4h/5a/7/8/9/12 US: General

1000 ———. 1976. *Ethnicity, Discrimination, and Inequality*. Beverly Hills, Calif.: Sage.

2d/3c/4h/5g,i/8/9/12/13/17 US: General

1001 ———. 1977. *The American Catholic: A Social Portrait*. New York: Basic Books.

2c,d/3a/4h/5a,d,g/8/9/10/11/12/13/17 US: Euro-Americans

1002 ———. and William C. McCready. 1975. "The Transmission of Cultural Heritages: The Case of the Irish and Italians." In *Ethnicity: Theory and Experience,* edited by Nathan Glazer and Daniel Patrick Moynihan, pp. 209-35. Cambridge, Mass.: Harvard University Press.

2d/3c/4h/5d/9/12/14 US: Irish, Italians

1003   GREEN, Alan G. 1976. *Immigration and the Postwar Canadian Economy.* Scarborough, Ont.: Macmillan.

       2c/3b/4b/5k/8/10   Canada: General

1004   GREEN, Samuel Swett. 1970. *The Scotch-Irish in America.* Reprint, 1895 ed. San Francisco: R & E Research Associates.

       2c/3a/4d/5a/8/12   US: Scotch-Irish

1005   GREEN, Vera. 1975. "Racial versus Ethnic Factors in Afro-American and Afro-Caribbean Migration." In *Migration and Development: Implications for Ethnic Identity and Political Conflict,* edited by Helen I. Safa and Brian M. Du Toit, pp. 83-96. The Hague: Mouton.

       2c/3a/4a/5d/7/12   Caribbean; US: Afro-Americans

1006   GREENE, Victor. 1975. *For God and Country: The Rise of Polish and Lithuanian Ethnic Consciousness in America 1860-1910.* Madison: State Historical Society of Wisconsin.

       2c/3a/4d/5d/6/7/11/12   US: Lithuanians, Poles

1007   GREENSTONE, J. David. 1975. "Ethnicity, Class, and Discontent: The Case of Polish Peasant Immigrants." *Ethnicity* 2:1-9.

       2b/3a/4h/5d,i/9/10   US: Poles

1008   GREENWOOD, Davydd J. 1977. "Continuity in Change: Spanish Basque Ethnicity as a Historical Process." In *Ethnic Conflict in the Western World,* edited by Milton J. Esman, pp. 81-102. Ithaca and London: Cornell University Press.

       2c/3a/4a/5k/8/9/10   Spain

1009   GREER, Colin, ed. 1974. *Divided Society: The Ethnic Experience in America.* New York: Basic Books.

       1a,b/2c/3a/4h/5a/7/8/9/13   US: General

1010   GREGERSON, Marilyn J. 1972. "The Ethnic Minorities of Vietnam." *Southeast Asia* 2:11-17.

       2c/3b/4a/5k/8/9/10/12/14/16/17   Vietnam

1011   GREGOROVICH, Andrew. 1972. *Canadian Ethnic Groups Bibliogra-*

phy. Toronto: Department of the Provincial Secretary and Citizenship of Ontario.

2a/6/7/9/16 Canada: General

1012 GREGORY, James R. 1976. "The Modification of an Interethnic Boundary in Belize." *American Ethnologist* 3:683-708.

2b/3a/4a,d/5c/8/9/12 Belize

1013 GREIF, Stuart W. 1975. "Political Attitudes of the Overseas Chinese of Fiji." *Asian Survey* 15:971-80.

2d/3a/4f/5k/10/11 Fiji

1014 GRIESSMAN, C. Eugene and Curtis T. Henson, Jr. 1975. "The History and Social Topography of an Ethnic Island in Alabama." *Phylon* 36:97-112.

2b/3a/4d,h/5d,g/8/9/10/11/12 US: Mestizos

1015 GRIFFIN, James. 1975. "Ethnonationalism and Integration: An Optimistic View." *Meanjin Quarterly* 34:240-49.

2c/3b/4f/5e/10 Papua New Guinea

1016 GRILLO, R. D. 1969. "The Tribal Factor in an East African Trade Union." In *Tradition and Transition in East Africa: Studies of the Tribal Element in the Modern Era,* edited by P. H. Gulliver, pp. 297-321. Berkeley and Los Angeles: University of California Press.

2b/3a/4a/5b,d/8/10/12 Uganda

1017 ———. 1974. "Ethnic Identity and Social Stratification on a Kampala Housing Estate." In *Urban Ethnicity,* edited by Abner Cohen, pp. 159-85. A.S.A. Monographs, no. 12. London: Tavistock.

2b/3a/4a/5d/6/9/12 Uganda

1018 GRIMSHAW, Allen D. 1962. "Factors Contributing to Colour Violence in the United States and Britain." *Race* 3:3-19.

2c/3d/4h/5b/10 Britain: General; US: General

1019 ———. 1969. *Racial Violence in the United States.* Chicago: Aldine.

1a/2c/3b/4d,h,i/5b/10 US: Afro-, Euro-Americans

1020   GROH, George W. 1972. *The Black Migration: The Journey to Urban America.* New York: Weybright and Telley.

2c/3b/4h/5k/6/7/8   US: Afro-Americans

1021   GROVE, D. John. 1974. "Differential Political and Economic Patterns of Ethnic and Race Relations: A Cross-National Analysis. *Race* 15:303-28.

2c/3d/4f,h/5f/10/16/17   General

1022   ——. 1977. "A Cross-National Examination of Cross-Cutting and Reinforcing Cultural Cleavages." *International Journal of Comparative Sociology* 18:217-27.

2c/3d/4f,h/5f/12   General

1023   ——. 1978. "A Test of the Ethnic Equalization Hypothesis: A Cross-National Study." *Ethnic and Racial Studies* 1:175-95.

2d/3d/4f,h/5i/8/9/13   General

1024   GRUNDY, Kenneth W. 1973. *Confrontation and Accommodation in Southern Africa: The Limits of Independence.* Berkeley and Los Angeles: University of California Press.

2c/3e/4f/5b,i/10   Southern Africa

1025   GUEST, Avery M. and James A. Weed. 1976. "Ethnic Residential Segregation: Patterns of Change." *American Journal of Sociology* 81: 1088-1111.

2c/3b/4h/5k/6   US: General

1026   GUILLEMIN, Jeanne. 1975. *Urban Renegades: The Cultural Strategy of American Indians.* New York and London: Columbia University Press.

2b/3a/4a/5a,c,d/8/9/10/12/14   US: Native Americans

1027   GUILLOTTE, Joseph V., III. 1978. "Citizens and Tribesmen: Variations in Ethnic Affiliation in a Multiethnic Farming Community in Northern Tanzania." In *Ethnicity in Modern Africa,* edited by Brian M. Du Toit, pp. 19-46. Boulder, Colo.: Westview Press.

2b/3a/4a/5d/7/10/12/14/17   Tanzania

1028 ——. 1978. "Ethnic Communication Circuits and Noise in a Rural Community in Tanzania." In *Interethnic Communication.* Southern Anthropological Society Proceedings, no. 12, edited by E. Lamar Ross, pp. 87-99. Athens: University of Georgia Press.

2b/3a/4a/5d,k/10/16   Tanzania

1029 GUINDON, Hubert. 1978. "The Modernization of Quebec and the Legitimacy of the Canadian State." *Canadian Review of Sociology and Anthropology* 15:227-45.

2c/3a/4h/5f,i/8/9/10/16   Canada: Québécois

1030 GULLIVER, P. H. 1969. "The Conservative Commitment in Northern Tanzania: The Arusha and Masai." *Tradition and Transition in East Africa,* edited by P. H. Gulliver, pp. 223-42. Berkeley and Los Angeles: University of California Press.

2b/3c/4a/5c/6/7/8/9/10/11/12/14   Tanzania

1031 ——, ed. 1969. *Tradition and Transition in East Africa: Studies of the Tribal Element in the Modern Era.* Berkeley and Los Angeles: University of California Press.

1a/2b/3a,b/4a/5d,e,f/10/12   East Africa

1032 GUMPERZ, John J. 1961. "Speech Variation and the Study of Indian Civilization." *American Anthropologist* 63:976-88.

2c/3b/4e/5d/6/12/16   India

1033 ——. 1966. "The Ethnology of Linguistic Change." In *Sociolinguistics,* edited by W. Bright, pp. 27-38. The Hague: Mouton.

2e/3e/4e/5d/16   Theory

1034 ——. 1978. "The Conversational Analysis of Interethnic Communication." In *Interethnic Communication.* Southern Anthropological Society Proceedings, no. 12, edited by E. Lamar Ross, pp. 13-31. Athens: University of Georgia Press.

2b/3a/4e/5k/16   Britain: Indians

1035 —— and Dell Hymes, eds. 1972. *Directions in Sociolinguistics: The Ethnography of Communication.* New York: Holt, Rinehart & Winston.

1a/2b,c/3a,b/4a,e/5d,h,k/16   General

1036 GURAK, Douglas T. 1978. "Sources of Ethnic Fertility Differences."
      Social Science Quarterly 59:295-310.

      2d/3c/4h/5k/6   US: General

1037 GURIAN, Jay P. 1975. "Psycho-Political Power Patterns in Native Amer-
      ican-White Conflicts." In *Politics of Race: Comparative Studies,* edited by
      Donald G. Baker, pp. 23-44. Lexington, Mass.: Lexington Books.

      2c/3a/4i/5d,i/8/9/10/11   US: Euro-, Native Americans

1038 GUTHIER, Steven L. 1977. "The Belorussians: National Identifications
      and Assimilation, 1897-1970." Pt. 1:1897-1939. *Soviet Studies* 24:37-61.

      2b,c/3a/4d/5a,e/12/16   USSR: Byelorussians

1039 ——. 1977. "The Belorussians: National Identification and Assimilation,
      1897-1970." Pt. 2:1939-1970. *Soviet Studies* 24:270-83.

      2b/3a/4d/5a,e/12/16   USSR: Byelorussians

1040 GUTKIND, Peter C. W. 1957. "Some African Attitudes to Multi-Racial-
      ism from Uganda, British East Africa." *Ethnic and Cultural Pluralism in
      Intertropical Countries,* pp. 338-55. Brussels: INCIDI.

      2d/3a/4a/5g/11   Uganda

1041 GUTTENTAG, Marcia. 1970. "Group Cohesiveness, Ethnic Organization
      and Poverty." *Journal of Social Issues* 26:105-32.

      2b/3a/4h/5d,i/8/9/12   Theory

1042 GUZMAN, Ralph C. 1976. *The Political Socialization of the Mexican
      American People.* New York: Arno Press.

      2c/3a/4f/5k/10   US: Mexican Americans

1043 GWARTNEY, James D. and Kenneth M. McCaffree. 1971. "Variance
      in Discrimination among Occupations." *Southern Economic Journal*
      38:141-55.

      2d/3b/4b/5i/8   US: General

1044 HABERFELD, Steven. 1973. "Strategies for Structural Change." *Race*
      14:443-63.

2b/3a/4i/5b,i/9/10/15   US: General

1045 HAGOPIAN, Elaine C. and Ann Paden, eds. 1969. *The Arab Americans: Studies in Assimilation.* Wilmette, Ill: Medina University Press International.

1a/2b/3a/4h/5a/6/8/12/14/15/16/17   US: Arabs

1046 HAIMAN, Miecislaus. 1939. *Polish Past in America 1608-1865.* Chicago: Polish Roman Catholic Union.

2c/3a/4d/5k/7/8/9/10/12/17   US: Poles

1047 HALLEY, Robert M., Alan C. Acock, and Thomas H. Greene. 1976. "Ethnicity and Social Class: Voting in the 1973 Los Angeles Municipal Elections." *Western Political Quarterly* 29:521-30.

2c/3a/4f/5k/9/10   US: General

1048 HALLIBURTON, R., Jr. 1975. "Black Slave Control in the Cherokee Nation." *Journal of Ethnic Studies* 3:23-36.

2c/3a/4d/5k/9   US: Native Americans

1049 HAMILTON, Howard D. 1975. "Political Ethos: The Evidence in Referenda Survey Data." *Ethnicity* 2:81-98.

2c/3a/4g/5k/10/11/12   US: General

1050 HAMMOND, Hailey Ross. 1963. "Race, Social Mobility and Politics in Brazil." *Race* 4:3-13.

2c/3b/4h/5i/9/10/11   Brazil

1051 HAMMOND-TOOKE, David. 1970. "Tribal Cohesion and the Incorporative Process in the Transkei, South Africa." In *From Tribe to Nation in Africa: Studies in Incorporation Processes,* edited by Ronald Cohen and John Middleton, pp. 217-41. Scranton, Penn.: Chandler.

2b/3a/4a/5d/9/11/13   South Africa

1052 HANBY, Victor J. 1977. "Current Scottish Nationalism." *Scottish Journal of Sociology* 1:95-110.

2c/3b/4f/5e/10   Scotland

1053 HANDLEMAN, Don. 1977. "The Organization of Ethnicity." *Ethnic*

Groups 1:187-200.

2c,e/3e/4a/5d/12/15   Theory

1054   HANDLIN, Oscar. 1952. *The Uprooted.* Boston: Little, Brown.

2c/3b/4d/5a/7/12   US: Euro-Americans

1055   ———. 1957. *Race and Nationality in American Life.* Boston: Little,
       Brown.

1b/2c/3b/4d/5a,f,i/7/9/11   US: General

1056   ———. 1959. *Immigration as a Factor in American History.* Englewood
       Cliffs, N.J.: Prentice-Hall.

2c/3b/4d/5a,b/7/8/10/15/17   US: General

1057   ———. 1959. *The Newcomers: Negroes and Puerto Ricans in a Changing
       Metropolis.* Cambridge, Mass.: Harvard University Press.

2b,c,d/3a/4d/5a/7/8/9/10/15   US: Afro-Americans, Puerto Ricans

1058   ———. 1971. *Adventure in Freedom: Three Hundred Years of Jewish Life
       in America.* Port Washington, N.Y.: Kennikat.

2c/3a/4d/5a/7/12/17   US: Jews

1059   ———, Brinley Thomas, et al. 1955. *The Positive Contribution by Immi-
       grants.* Paris: UNESCO.

2c/3d/4d/5a,k/7/8   General

1060   HANHAM, H. J. 1969. *Scottish Nationalism.* London: Faber & Faber.

2c/3b/4d/5e/10/11   Scotland

1061   HANHARDT, Arthur M., Jr. and William Sharp. 1976. "The German
       Democratic Republic and Socialist Integration." In *Small States and Seg-
       mented Societies: National Political Integration in a Global Environment,*
       edited by Stephanie G. Neuman, pp. 154-71. New York: Praeger.

2c/3b/4f/5e/10   German Democratic Republic

1062   HANNERZ, Ulf. 1969. *Soulside: Inquiries into Ghetto Culture and
       Community.* New York and London: Columbia University Press.

2b/3a/4a/5d/12   US: Afro-Americans

1063 ——. 1974. "Ethnicity and Opportunity in Urban America." In *Urban Ethnicity*, edited by Abner Cohen, pp. 37-76. A.S.A. Monographs, no. 12. London: Tavistock.

2c/3b/4a/5i/9/11/12   US: General

1064 HANSEN, Marcus Lee. 1961. *The Atlantic Migration, 1607-1860.* Rev. ed. New York: Harper & Row.

2c/3b/4d/5a/7   US: Euro-Americans

1065 HAREWOOD, Jack. 1971. "Racial Discrimination in Employment in Trinidad and Tobago (Based on Data from the 1960 Census)." *Social and Economic Studies* 20:267-93.

2c/3b/4h/5g/8/9   Trinidad and Tobago

1066 HARNED, Frederic T. 1975. "Latvia and the Latvians." In *Handbook of Major Soviet Nationalities,* edited by Zev Katz, Rosemarie Rogers, and Frederic Harned, pp. 94-117. New York: Free Press.

2c/3a/4i/5k/6/8/10/11/13/16   USSR: Latvians

1067 ——. 1975. "Lithuania and the Lithuanians." In *Handbook of Major Soviet Nationalities,* edited by Zev Katz, Rosemarie Rogers, and Frederic Harned, pp. 118-40. New York: Free Press.

2c/3a/4i/5k/6/8/10/11/13/16   USSR: Lithuanians

1068 HARRE, John. 1963. "The Background to Race Relations in New Zealand." *Race* 5:3-15.

2b,c/3a/4h/5g,i/6/8/9/10/12/13   New Zealand

1069 ——. 1966. "The Interracial Mixing of Young New Zealand Adults." *Race* 7:271-88.

2d/3b/4h/5d/14   New Zealand

1070 ——. 1966. *Maori and Pakeha: A Study of Mixed Marriages in New Zealand.* New York: Frederick A. Praeger.

2b/3a/4h/5k/14   New Zealand

1071 HARRIS, George S. 1977. "The Kurdish Conflict in Iraq." In *Ethnic Conflict in International Relations,* edited by Astri Suhrke and Lela Garner Noble, pp. 68-92. New York: Praeger.

2c/3b/4f/5b/10   Iraq

1072 HARRIS, Marvin. 1970. "Referential Ambiguity in the Calculus of Brazilian Racial Identity." *Southwestern Journal of Anthropology* 26: 1-14.

2d/3a/4a/5d,g/11/12   Brazil

1073 HARRIS, Rosemary. 1972. *Prejudice and Tolerance in Ulster: A Study of Neighbors and "Strangers" in a Border Community.* Totowa, N.J.: Rowman & Littlefield.

2b/3a/4a/5g/11/14/17   N. Ireland

1074 HARRISON, Barbara. 1971. *Outside Down Under: The History, Conditions, and Struggle of the Australian Aborigines.* Center on International Race Relations, Graduate School of International Studies, University of Denver, Studies in Race and Nations, vol. 3, study no. 1.

2b,c/3a/4d/5b,i/9/10/11   Australia

1075 HARRISON, Bennett. 1972. *Education, Training, and the Urban Ghetto.* Baltimore and London: Johns Hopkins University Press.

2c/3b/4b/5i/8/9/10/11/13   US: General

1076 HARRISON, Joseph. 1977. "Big Business and the Rise of Basque Nationalism." *European Studies Review* 7:371-91.

2c/3a/4d/5e/8/10   Spain

1077 HARRISSON, Tom. 1967. "Tribes, Minorities, and the Central Government in Sarawak, Malaysia." In *Southeast Asian Tribes, Minorities, and Nations,* edited by P. Kunstadter, pp. 317-52. Princeton, N.J.: Princeton University Press.

2b/3b/4a/5d,f/6/8/10/11   Malaysia

1078 HARTMANN, Edward George. 1967. *Americans from Wales.* Boston: Christopher.

2e/3a/4a,f/5a/6/7/12/15/16   US: Welsh

1079 HARTMANN, Paul and Charles Husband. 1974. *Racism and the Mass Media: A Study of the Role of the Mass Media in the Formation of White Beliefs and Attitudes in Britain.* Totowa, N. J.: Rowman & Little-field.

2d/3b/4g/5g/16   Britain: General

1080 HARVIE, Christopher. 1977. *Scotland and Nationalism: Scottish Society and Politics, 1707-1977.* London: George Allen & Unwin.

2c/3b/4d/5e/10   Scotland

1081 HASSAN, Riaz. 1970. "Class, Ethnicity, and Occupational Structure in Singapore." *Civilisations* 20:496-515.

2b/3b/4h/5i/8/9   Singapore

1082 ——. 1971. "Interethnic Marriage in Singapore: A Sociological Analysis." *Sociology and Social Research* 55:305-23.

2c/3b/4h/5k/14   Singapore

1083 ——. 1978. "National and Ethnic Identities in Southeast Asia." *Internationales Asienforum* 9:155-64.

2e/3e/4h/5d,e/12   Southeast Asia

1084 —— and Geoffrey Benjamin. 1976. "Ethnic Outmarriage Rates in Singapore: The Influence of Traditional Sociocultural Organization." In *Changing Identities in Modern Southeast Asia,* edited by David J. Banks, pp. 111-26. The Hague: Mouton.

2c,d/3b/4h/5k/14   Singapore

1085 HATT, Paul. 1948. "Class and Ethnic Attitudes." *American Sociological Review* 13:36-43.

2d/3a/4g,h/5g,i/9/11   US: General

1086 HAUG, Marie R. 1967. "Social and Cultural Pluralism as a Concept in Social System Analysis." *American Journal of Sociology* 73:294-304.

2e/3e/4h/5f   Theory

1087 HAUGEN, Einar. 1967. *The Norwegians in America.* New York: Teachers College Press.

2c/3a/4d/5a,d/7/8/9/10/12/13/16/17   US: Norwegians

1088 HAWKINS, Brett W. and Robert A. Lorinskas, eds. 1970. *The Ethnic Factor in American Politics.* Columbus, Ohio: Charles E. Merrill.

1a/2b,c/3b/4f/5f/10/11   US: General

1089 HAWKINS, John. 1978. "National-Minority Education in the People's Republic of China." *Comparative Education Review* 22:147-62.

2c/3b/4i(Education)/5a,f/13   China (PRC)

1090 HAWS, Robert, ed. 1978. *The Age of Segregation: Race Relations in the South, 1890-1945.* Jackson: University Press of Mississippi.

1a/2c/3a/4b,d,f/5i/8/9/10/11   US: Afro-Americans

1091 HAYS, William C. and Charles C. Mindel. 1977. "Parental Perceptions for Children: A Comparison of Black and White Families." *Ethnic Groups* 1:281-95.

2d/3c/4g/5k/11/14   US: Afro-, Euro-Americans

1092 HAZAREESINGH, K. 1966. "The Religion and Culture of Indian Immigrants in Mauritius and the Effect of Social Change." *Comparative Studies in Society and History* 8:241-57.

2b/3a/4a/5k/9/12/17   Mauritius

1093 HEARD, Kenneth A. 1961. *Political Systems in Multiracial Societies.* Johannesburg: South African Institute of Race Relations.

2c/3d/4f/5i/10/11   General

1094 HEATON, William R., Jr. 1977. "The Minorities and the Military in China." *Armed Forces and Society* 3:325-42.

2c/3b/4i/5f/10   China (PRC)

1095 HECHTER, Michael. 1973. "The Persistence of Regionalism in the British Isles, 1885-1966." *American Journal of Sociology* 79:319-42.

2c/3b/4h/5j/10   Britain: General

1096 ——. 1976. "Response to Cohen: Max Weber on Ethnicity and Ethnic Change." *American Journal of Sociology* 81:1162-68.

2e/3e/4h/5i/9/11/12   Theory

1097 HEILMAN, Samuel C. 1977. "Inner and Outer Identities: Sociological Ambivalence among Orthodox Jews." *Jewish Social Studies* 39:227-40.

2b/3a/4g/5d/12   US: Jews

1098 HEINEMAN, Benjamin W., Jr. 1972. *The Politics of the Powerless: A Study of the Campaign Against Racial Discrimination.* London: Oxford University Press.

2b/3a/4d,f/5b/10/11   Britain: General

1099 HELLER, Celia S. 1971. *New Converts to the American Dream? Mobility Aspirations of Young Mexican Americans.* New Haven, Conn: College & University Press.

2d/3a/4h/5k/9/11   US: Mexican Americans

1100 ——. 1975. "Ethnic Differentiation among the Jews of Israel." In *Migration and Development: Implications for Ethnic Identity and Political Conflict,* edited by Helen I. Safa and Brian M. Du Toit, pp. 97-111. The Hague: Mouton.

2c/3b/4a/5i/9   Israel

1101 HELM, June, ed. 1968. *Spanish-Speaking People in the United States.* Proceedings of the 1968 Annual Spring Meeting of the American Ethnological Society. Seattle: University of Washington Press.

1a/2b/3a/4a/5a,c,d,i/7/9/10/11/12   US: Latin Americans

1102 HENDERSON, Thomas McLean. 1976. *Tammany Hall and the New Immigrants: The Progressive Years.* New York: Arno Press.

2c/3b/4d/5k/10   US: Irish

1103 HENDRICKS, Glenn. 1974. *The Dominican Diaspora: From the Dominican Republic to New York City—Villagers in Transition.* New York: Teachers College Press.

2b,c/3a/4a/5k/6/7
8/10/12/13/14/15/17   US: Dominicans

1104 HENG-CHEE, Chan and Hans-Dieter Evers. 1973. "Nation-Building and National Identity in Southeast Asia." In *Building States and Nations:*

Analyses by Region, vol. 2, edited by S. N. Eisenstadt and Stein Rokkan, pp. 301-19. Beverly Hills, Calif.: Sage.

2c/3b/4f,h/5f/10/12   Singapore

1105 HENRIQUES, Fernando. 1975. *Children of Conflict: A Study of Inter-racial Sex and Marriage.* New York: E.P. Dutton.

2c/3e/4d/5b,g,k/14   Africa; Caribbean; India; US: Afro-, Euro-Americans

1106 HENRY, Frances. 1973. *Forgotten Canadians: The Blacks of Nova Scotia.* Don Mills, Ontario: Longman.

2b,d/3a/4a/5k/6/7/8/9/11/17   Canada: Afro-Canadians

1107 HEPBURN, A. C., ed. 1979. *Minorities in History.* New York: St. Martin's Press.

                                   Canada: Québécois; Cyprus; France;
1a/2c/3a,b/4d/5b,i/9/10/11   Ireland; US: Afro-Americans, English

1108 HEPPLE, Bob. 1968. "Ethnic Minorities at Work." *Race* 10:17-30.

2b,c/3b/4h/5g,i/8   Britain: General

1109 ——. 1968. *Race, Jobs and the Law in Britain.* London: Allen Lane, The Penguin Press.

2c/3b/4i/5g/8/10   Britain: General

1110 HERCULES, Frank. 1972. *American Society and Black Revolution.* New York: Harcourt Brace Jovanovich.

2c/3b/4d/5b/10   US: Afro-Americans

1111 HERMAN, Harry Vjekoslav. 1979. "Dishwashers and Proprietors: Macedonians in Toronto's Restaurant Trade." In *Ethnicity at Work,* edited by Sandra Wallman, pp. 71-90. London: Macmillan.

2b/3a/4a/5k/7/8   Canada: Macedonians

1112 HERMASSI, Elbaki. 1972. *Leadership and National Development in North Africa: A Comparative Study.* Berkeley and Los Angeles: University of California Press.

2b,c/3b,d/4f/5e/9/10/11   Algeria; Morocco; Tunisia

1113 HERSKOVITZ, Melville J. 1966. *The New World Negro.* Bloomington: Indiana University Press.

2b,c/3e/4a/5d/12 US: Afro-Americans

1114 HERTZBERG, Hazel W. 1971. *The Search for an American Indian Identity: Modern Pan-Indian Movements.* Syracuse, N.Y.: Syracuse University Press.

2b,c/3a/4i/5d/10/12 US: Native Americans

1115 HESS, Fjeril. 1970. *High Adventure: A Story of Slavic Pioneers in America.* Reprint, 1925 ed. San Francisco: R & E Research Associates.

2c/3a/4d/5k/7/8/10 US: Slavs

1116 HESS, Gary R. 1974. "The Forgotten Asian Americans: The East Indian Community in the United States." *Pacific Historical Review* 43:576-96.

2c/3a/4d/5k/7/10 US: East Indians

1117 HETMANEK, Allen. 1975. "Kirgizistan and the Kirgiz." In *Handbook of Major Soviet Nationalities,* edited by Zev Katz, Rosemarie Rogers, and Frederic Harned, pp. 238-61. New York: Free Press.

2c/3a/4i/5k/6/8/10/11/13/16 USSR: Kirghiz

1118 HICKS, George L. 1975. "The Same North and South: Ethnicity and Change in Two American Indian Groups." In *The New Ethnicity: Perspectives from Ethnology.* 1973 Proceedings of the American Ethnological Society, edited by John W. Bennett, pp. 75-94. St. Paul: West.

2b/3a/4a/5d/10/12 US: Native Americans

1119 ———. 1977. "Introduction: Problems in the Study of Ethnicity." In *Ethnic Encounters: Identities and Contexts,* edited by George L. Hicks and Philip E. Leis, pp. 1-20. North Scituate, Mass.: Duxbury Press.

2e/3e/4a/5a,b,c,d,g,i/9/10/12 Theory

1120 ———. 1977. "Separate but Similar: Adaptation by Two American Indian Groups." In *Ethnic Encounters: Identities and Contexts,* edited by George L. Hicks and Philip E. Leis, pp. 63-83. North Scituate, Mass.: Duxbury Press.

2c/3a/4a/5a,d/12   US: Native Americans

1121   HIGGS, Robert. 1977. *Competition and Coercion: Blacks in the American Economy 1865-1914.* Cambridge: At the University Press.

2c/3a/4b/5b,i/6/8   US: Afro-Americans

1122   HIGHAM, John. 1955. *Strangers in the Land: Patterns of American Nativism, 1860-1925.* New Brunswick, N.J.: Rutgers University Press.

2c/3b/4d/5g/10/11   US: General

1123   ——, ed. 1978. *Ethnic Leadership in America.* Baltimore: Johns Hopkins University Press.

1a/2b/3a/4c,d/5a,c,e/10/12/15   US: General

1124   HILL, Carole. 1975. "Adaptation in Public and Private Behavior of Ethnic Groups in an American Urban Setting." *Urban Anthropology* 4:333-47.

2b/3a/4a/5a,d/6   US: General

1125   HILLER, Harry H. 1977. "Internal Problem Resolution and Third Party Emergence." *Canadian Journal of Sociology* 2:55-75.

2d/3a/4f/5b/7/10   Canada: Québécois

1126   HIMES, Joseph S. 1973. *Racial Conflict in American Society.* Columbus, Ohio: Charles E. Merrill.

2c/3b/4h/5b/6/9/10   US: Afro-Americans

1127   HIMMELSTRAND, Ulf. 1969. "Tribalism, Nationalism, Rank-Equilibration, and Social Structure: A Theoretical Interpretation of Some Sociopolitical Processes in Southern Nigeria." *Journal of Peace Research* 6: 81-103.

2b/3b/4h/5i/9/10/11   Nigeria

1128   ——. 1973. "'Tribalism' Regionalism, Nationalism, and Secession in Nigeria." In *Building States and Nations: Analyses by Region,* vol. 2, edited by S. N. Eisenstadt and Stein Rokkan, pp. 427-67. Beverly Hills, Calif.: Sage.

2c/3a/4h/5b,f,i/7/8/9/10   Nigeria

1129 HIRATA, Lucie C. 1975. "Toward a Political Economy of Chinese America: A Study of Property Ownership in Los Angeles Chinatown." *Amerasia Journal* 3:76-95.

2b,c/3a/4h/5i/6/8/9   US: Asian Americans

1130 HIRSCH, Herbert. 1973. "Political Scientists and Other Camarades: Academic Myth-Making and Racial Stereotypes." In *Chicanos and Native Americans: The Territorial Minorities,* edited by Rudolph O. de la Garza et al., pp. 10-22. Englewood Cliffs, N. J.: Prentice-Hall.

2b,c,d/3a/4f/5g/10/11   US: Mexican Americans

1131 HODDER-WILLIAMS, Richard. 1974. "Afrikaners in Rhodesia: A Partial Portrait." *African Social Research* 18:611-42.

2c/3b/4d,f/5d,k/10/11   Zimbabwe

1132 HODGE, Robert W. 1973. "Toward a Theory of Racial Differences in Employment." *Social Forces* 52:16-31.

2e/3e/4h/5k (Neoclassical Economics)/8   Theory

1133 HODGE, William H. 1975. "Ethnicity as a Factor in Modern American Indian Migration: A Winnebago Case Study with Reference to Other Indian Situations." In *Migration and Development: Implications for Ethnic Identity and Political Conflict,* edited by Helen I. Safa and Brian M. Du Toit, pp. 31-56. The Hague: Mouton.

2b/3a/4a/5d/12   US: Native Americans

1134 HOETINK, Hermannus. 1967. "The Concept of Pluralism as Envisaged by M. G. Smith." *Caribbean Studies* 7:36-43.

2f/3e/4a/5f   Theory

1135 ——. 1971. *Caribbean Race Relations: A Study of Two Variants.* New York: Oxford University Press.

2c/3d/4a/5f,i/11   Caribbean

1136 ——. 1973. *Slavery and Race Relations in the Americas: An Inquiry into Their Nature and Nexus.* New York: Harper & Row.

2c/3d/4a,d/5f,g,i/9   Mesoamerica; North America; South America

1137   ———. 1974. "National Identity and Somatic Norm Image." In *Ethnicity and Nation-Building,* edited by Wendell Bell and Walter E. Freeman, pp. 29-44. Beverly Hills, Calif.: Sage.

2e/3e/4h/5d,i/9/11/12   Theory

1138   ———. 1975. "Resource Competition, Monopoly, and Socioracial Diversity." In *Ethnicity and Resource Competition in Plural Societies,* edited by Leo A. Despres, pp. 9-26. The Hague: Mouton.

2f/3e/4a/5b,i/9/10/12   Theory

1139   HOFFMAN, Abraham. 1974. *Unwanted Mexican Americans in the Great Depression: Repatriation Pressures, 1929-1939.* Tucson: University of Arizona Press.

2c/3b/4d/5g/7/8/10/11   US: Mexican Americans

1140   HOFFMAN, George W. 1973. "Migration and Social Change." *Problems of Communism* 22:16-31.

2c/3b/4c/5k/7/8/10   Yugoslavia

1141   HOFFMAN, Joan. 1975. *Racial Discrimination and Economic Development.* Lexington, Mass.: Lexington Books.

2c/3b/4b/5g,i/8/9   US: Afro-Americans

1142   HOGAN, Dennis P. and David L. Featherman. 1977. "Racial Stratification and Socioeconomic Change in the American North and South." *American Journal of Scoiology* 83:100-126.

2c/3b/4h/5i/8/9/13   US: Afro-Americans

1143   HOLLOMAN, Regina E. 1975. "Ethnic Boundary Maintenance, Readaptation, and Societal Evolution in the San Blas Islands of Panama." In *Ethnicity and Resource Competition in Plural Societies,* edited by Leo A. Despres, pp. 27-40. The Hague: Mouton.

2c/3a/4a/5c/8/9/10   Panama

1144   HOLMES, Colin, ed. 1978. *Immigrants and Minorities in British Society.* London: George Allen & Unwin.

1a/2b,c/3b/4d/5k/7/11   Britain: Chinese, Germans, Irish, Jews

1145   HOLUBNYCHY, Vsevolod. 1968. "Some Economic Aspects of Relations among the Soviet Republics." In *Ethnic Minorities in the Soviet Union,* edited by Erich Goldhagen, pp. 50-120. New York: Frederick A. Praeger.

2c/3b/4b/5 i/8/9/10/11   USSR: General

1146   HOLZBERG, Carol S. 1977. "The Social Organization of Jamaican Political Economy: Ethnicity and the Jewish Segment." *Ethnic Groups* 1:319-36.

2b/3a/4a/5d,i/8/9/10/12/15   Jamaica

1147   ——. 1977. "Social Stratification, Cultural Nationalism and Political Economy in Jamaica: The Myths of Development and the Anti-White Bias." *Canadian Review of Sociology and Anthropology* 14:368-80.

2b/3b/4h/5e,g,i/8/10   Jamaica

1148   HONDIUS, Frits W. 1968. *The Yugoslav Community of Nations.* The Hague: Mouton.

2c/3b/4d,f/5e/10   Yugoslavia

1149   HORMANN, Bernhard L. 1972. "Hawaii's Mixing People." In *The Blending of Races: Marginality and Identity in World Perspective,* edited by Noel P. Gist and Anthony Gary Dworkin, pp. 213-36. New York: Wiley-Interscience.

2c/3a/4h/5i/9/12/14   US: General (Hawaii)

1150   HOROWITZ, Donald L. 1971. "Three Dimensions of Ethnic Politics." *World Politics* 23:232-44.

2c/3e/4f/5i/10/12   Theory

1151   ——. 1973. "Direct, Displaced, and Cumulative Ethnic Aggression." *Comparative Politics* 6:1-16.

2b,c/3d/4f/5b/10   General

1152   ——. 1975. "Ethnic Identity." In *Ethnicity: Theory and Experience,* edited by Nathan Glazer and Daniel Patrick Moynihan, pp. 111-40. Cambridge, Mass.: Harvard University Press.

2c/3e/4f/5a,c,d/10/12   Theory

1153 HOROWITZ, Irving Louis. 1976. "Jewish Ethnicity and Latin American Nationalism." In *Ethnicity in an International Context,* edited by Abdul Said and Luiz R. Simmons, pp. 92-109. New Brunswick, N. J.: Transaction Books.

2c/3e/4h/5e/10/11/12   Mesoamerica; South America

1154 HOROWITZ, Michael M. 1974. "Barbers and Bearers: Ecology and Ethnicity in an Islamic Society." *Africa* 44:371-82.

2b/3a/4a/5c/8/12/14   Niger

1155 HOSOKAWA, Bill. 1969. *Nisei: The Quiet Americans.* New York: William Morrow.

2c/3a/4d/5d,g/9/11/12   US: Japanese

1156 ———. 1971. "The Cherishing of Liberty: The American Nisei." *Pacific Community* 2:391-401.

2c/3a/4d/5b,i/10/11   US: Japanese

1157 HOSOKAWA, Fumiko. 1978. *The Sansei: Social Interaction and Ethnic Identification among the Third Generation Japanese.* San Francisco: R & E Research Associates.

2b,d/3a/4h/5d/11/12/13
14/15/16/17   US: Japanese

1158 HOUCHINS, Lee and Chang-su Houchins. 1974. "The Korean Experience in America, 1903-1924." *Pacific Historical Review* 43:548-75.

2c/3a/4d/5k/7/8/10/13/15/16   US: Koreans

1159 HOURANI, Albert. 1969. "Race and Related Ideas in the Near East." In *Comparative Perspectives on Race Relations,* edited by Melvin Tumin, pp. 161-77. Boston: Little, Brown.

2c/3d/4g/5k/6/12   Middle East

1160 HOVANNISIAN, Richard G. 1974. "The Ebb and Flow of the Armenian Minority in the Middle East." *Middle East Journal* 28:19-32.

2b/3a/4d/5k/10/12   Middle East

1161 HOWARD, John R.. ed. 1970. *Awakening Minorities: American Indians,*

Mexican Americans, Puerto Ricans. Chicago: Aldine.

1a/2b,c/3a/4a,f,h/5b,d,e/10/11
US: Mexican-,
Native Americans, Puerto Ricans

1162 HUBLER, William Henry. 1978. *Koreans in Emlyn: A Community in Transition.* Philip Jaisohn Memorial Papers, no. 3. Elkins Park, Penn.: The Philip Jaisohn Memorial Foundation.

2d/3a/4i(Education)/5a/12/13
US: Koreans

1163 HUDDLE, Frank, Jr. 1975. "Azerbaidzhan and the Azerbaidzhanis." In *Handbook of Major Soviet Nationalities,* edited by Zev Katz, Rosemarie Rogers, and Frederic Harned, pp. 189-209. New York: Free Press.

2c/3a/4d/5k/6/8/10/11/13/16
USSR: Azerbaidzhanis

1164 HUGGINS, Nathan Irvin. 1978. "Afro-Americans." In *Ethnic Leadership in America,* edited by John Higham, pp. 91-118. Baltimore: Johns Hopkins University Press.

2c/3a/4h/5k/10/15
US: Afro-Americans

1165 HUGHES, Everett C. 1964. "Race Relations and the Sociological Imagination." *Race* 5:3-19.

2e/3e/4h/5h,i/9
Theory

1166 HUNDLEY, Norris, Jr., ed. 1976. *The Asian Americans: The Historical Experience.* Santa Barbara, Calif.: ABC-Clio.

1a/2c/3a/4d/5k/7/8
US: Chinese, East Indians,
Filipinos, Japanese, Koreans

1167 HUNT, Larry L. and Janet G. Hunt. 1975. "Race and the Father-Son Connection: The Conditional Relevance of Father Absence for the Orientations and Identities of Adolescent Boys." *Social Problems* 23:35-51.

2d/3a/4g/5d/14
US: Afro-Americans

1168 ——. 1977. "Religious Affiliation and Militancy among Urban Blacks: Some Catholic/Protestant Comparisons" *Social Science Quarterly* 57: 821-33.

2d/3a/4h/5d/10/11/17
US: Afro-Americans

1169   HUNTER, A. A. 1977. "A Comparative Analysis of Anglophone-Franco-phone Occupational Prestige Structures in Canada." *Canadian Journal of Sociology* 2:179-93.

       2d/3c/4h/5i/9/11/16   Canada: English, Québécois

1170   HUNTER, Guy, ed. 1965. *Industrialisation and Race Relations: A Symposium.* London: Oxford University Press.

       1a/2c/3b/4a,b,f,h/5i/8/9   General

1171   HURH, Won Moo. 1977. *Assimilation of the Korean Minority in the United States.* Philip Jaisohn Memorial Papers, no. 1. Elkins Park, Penn.: The Philip Jaisohn Memorial Foundation.

       2d/3a/4a/5a/7/9/11/12   US: Koreans

1172   ——. 1977. *Comparative Study of Korean Immigrants in the United States: A Typological Approach.* San Francisco: R & E Research Associates.

       2c/3c/4h/5a,g/11   US: Koreans

1173   HURSTFIELD, Jennifer. 1978. "'Internal' Colonialism: White, Black, and Chicano Self-Conceptions." *Ethnic and Racial Studies* 1:60-79.

       2d/3c/4g/5d/12   US: Afro-, Euro-, Mexican Americans

1174   HUSBANDS, Christopher T. 1979. "The 'Threat' Hypothesis and Racist Voting in England and the United States." In *Racism and Political Action in Britain,* edited by Robert Miles and Annie Phizacklea, pp. 147-83. London: Routledge & Kegan Paul.

       2c/3d/4f/5g/10/11   US: General; Britain: General

1175   HVIDT, Kristian. 1975. *Flight to America: The Social Background of 300,000 Danish Emigrants.* New York: Academic Press.

       2c/3a/4d/5k/7   US: Danes

1176   HYLON-SMITH, K. 1968. "A Study of Immigrant Group Relations in North London." *Race* 9:467-76.

       2b/3a/4h/5g/10/11   Britain: General

1177   IANNI, Octavio. 1972. "Race and Class in Latin America." In *Readings* in *Race and Ethnic Relations,* edited by Anthony H. Richmond, pp. 237-56. Oxford: Pergamon Press.

2c/3d/4h/5i/9   Mesoamerica; South America

1178 ICHIKAWA, Kenjiro. 1976. "Social and Cultural Change of Japanese and Chinese In Thailand." In *Changing Identities in Modern Southeast Asia,* edited by David J. Banks, pp. 147-54. The Hague: Mouton.

2c/3a,c/4a/5a,d/12   Thailand

1179 INAYATULLAH. 1976. "Internal and External Factors in the Failure of National Integration in Pakistan." In *Small States and Segmented Societies: National Political Integration in a Global Environment,* edited by Stephanie G. Neuman, pp. 84-120. New York: Praeger.

2c/3b/4f/5k/10   Bangladesh; Pakistan

1180 INBAR, Michael and Chaim Adler. 1977. *Ethnic Integration in Israel: A Comparative Study of Moroccan Brothers Who Settled in France and in Israel.* New Brunswick, N.J.: Transaction Books.

2d/3c,d/4h/5g,i/8/9/11/13   Israel; France

1181 INDRA, Doreen. 1979. "South Asian Stereotypes in the Vancouver Press." *Ethnic and Racial Studies* 2:166-89.

2b/3a/4h/5g/11/16   Canada: Indians

1182 INGLIS, Christine. 1972. "Chinese in Australia." *International Migration Review* 6:266-81.

2b/3a/4c/5k/6/8   Australia

1183 IORIZZO, Luciano J. and Salvatore Mondello. 1971. *The Italian-Americans.* New York: Twayne.

2c/3a/4d/5a,b,d,k/7/10/11/17   US: Italians

1184 IRBY, Charles C. 1978. "A Developmental Design for Understanding Ethnicity." *Explorations in Ethnic Studies* 1:3-15.

2f/3d/4i/5b,d,f,i,k   Theory

1185 IRELAND, Ralph R. 1975. "Apartheid and the Education of the Indian

Community in the Republic of South Africa." *Plural Societies* 6:3-18.

2c/3b/4h/5k/13   South Africa

1186 IRISH, Donald P. 1952. "Reactions of Caucasian Residents to Japanese American Neighbors." *Journal of Social Issues* 8:11-17.

2d/3a/4g/5g/11   US: Japanese

1187 IRVINE, William P. 1972. "Recruitment to Nationalism: New Politics or Normal Politics?" *Canadian Journal of Political Science* 5:503-20.

2d/3a/4f/5e,k/10   Canada: General

1188 ISAACS, Harold P. 1964. *India's Ex-Untouchables.* New York: John Day.

2b,c/3a/4f/5d,i/9/10   India

1189 ITO, Hiroshi. 1966. "Japan's Outcastes in the United States." In *Japan's Invisible Race: Caste in Culture and Personality,* edited by George DeVos and Hiroshi Wagatsuma, pp. 200-221. Berkeley and Los Angeles: University of California Press.

2b/3a/4a/5k/7/8/10/11/12/14   US: Japanese

1190 IZRAELI, Dafna Nundi. 1979. "Ethnicity and Industrial Relations: An Israeli Factory Case Study." *Ethnic and Racial Studies* 2:80-89.

2b/3a/4h/5d/8   Israel

1191 JACEK, Henry and Robert Cunningham. 1975. "Ethnic Conflict and Political Action: Political Parties and Voters in Urban Canada." *International Review of Modern Sociology* 5:143-55.

2c,d/3b/4f/5b,k/9/10/11   Canada: General

1192 JACKSON, John Arthur. 1963. *The Irish in Britain.* London: Routledge & Kegan Paul.

2c/3a/4h/5d,e/6/7/8/9/10/11/12/14/15   Britain: Irish

1193 JACKSON, John D. 1975. *Community and Conflict: A Study of French-English Relations in Toronto.* Toronto: Holt, Rinehart & Winston.

2b/3a/4h/5b/9/10   Canada: English, Québécois

1194 JACO, Daniel E. and George L. Wilbur. 1975. "Asian Americans in the
      Labor Market." *Monthly Labor Review* 98:33-38.

2d/3c/4h/5i/8   US: Chinese, Filipinos, Japanese

1195 JACOB, James E. 1975. "The Basques of France: A Case of Peripheral
      Ethnonationalism in Europe." *Political Anthropology* 1:67-87.

2b/3b/4a/5e/6/10/11   France

1196 JACOBS, Paul and Saul Landau. 1971. *To Serve the Devil.* 2 vols. New
      York: Random House.

2f(Documents)/3b   US: Afro-, Chinese-, Hawaiian-, Japanese-, Mexican-,
4i/5k/9/10/11   Native Americans, Puerto Ricans

1197 JACOBS, Wilbur R. 1972. *Dispossessing the American Indian: Indians
      and Whites on the Colonial Frontier.* New York: Charles Scribner's Sons.

2c/3a/4d/5b/10/11   US: Native Americans

1198 JAENSCH, Dean. 1976. "The Scottish Vote 1974: A Realigning Party
      System?" *Political Studies* 24:306-19.

2c/3b/4f/5e/10   Scotland

1199 JAKLE, John A. 1973. *Ethnic and Racial Minorities in North America:
      A Selected Bibliography of the Geographical Literature* (Council of Plan-
      ning Librarians, Exchange Bibliography nos. 459-60). Monticello, Ill.:
      Council of Exchange Librarians.

2a/4c   US: General; Canada: General

1200 JALKANEN, Ralph J., ed. 1969. *The Finns in North America: A Social
      Symposium.* Hancock: Michigan State University Press for Suomi College.

2b,c/3a/4d,h/5a,d/7/11/12/13/16/17   US: Finns

1201 JAMAL, Vali. 1976. "Asians in Uganda, 1880-1972: Inequality and Ex-
      pulsion." *Economic History Review* 29:602-16.

2c/3a/4d/5e/8/9/10   Uganda

1202   JANICS, Kalman. 1975. "Czechoslavakia's Magyar Minority: An Example of Diaspora Nationalism." *Canadian Review of Studies in Nationalism* 3:34-44.

    2b/3a/4f/5e/7/10/11/13/16   Czechoslovakia

1203   JAYWARDENA, Chandra. 1959. *Interim Report on a Study of Social Structure and Processes of Social Control amongst East Indian Sugar Workers in British Guiana.* Mona, Jamaica: Institute of Social and Economic Research, University College of the West Indies.

    2b/3a/4a/5b,i/8/9   Guyana

1204   ——. 1963. *Conflict and Solidarity in a Guianese Plantation.* London: Athlone Press.

    2b/3a/4a/5b,f,i/9/10   Guyana

1205   JEFFREY, Patricia. 1976. *Migrants and Refugees: Muslim and Christian Pakistani Families in Bristol.* Cambridge: At the University Press.

    2b/3a/4a/5a,c,d/7/12/14/15/17   Britain: Pakistanis

1206   JEFFRIES, Vincent. 1971. "Cultural Sources of Solidarity and Antagonism Toward Blacks." *Social Science Quarterly* 51:860-72.

    2d/3b/4h/5g/11   US: Afro-Americans

1207   JEROME, Dorothy. 1978. "Migrants or Settlers? The Ibo in London." *Africa* 48:368-79.

    2b/3a/4a/5d,k/7/8/9/13   Britain: Ibos

1208   JIOBU, Robert M. 1976. "Earnings Differentials between Whites and Ethnic Minorities: The Cases of Asian Americans, Blacks, and Chicanos." *Sociology and Social Research* 61:24-38.

                                  US: Afro-, Chinese-,
    2d/3c/4h/5i/8/13   Japanese-, Mexican Americans

1209   JIRYIS, Sabri. 1976. *The Arabs in Israel.* New York: Monthly Review Press.

    2c/3b/4i/5b,i/8/10/13   Israel

1210 JOCANO, F. Landa. 1970. "Filipinos in Hawaii: Problems in the Promised Land." *Philippine Sociological Review* 18:151-57.

2b/3a/4a/5k/8/12   US: Filipinos

1211 JOHNSON, Colleen Leahy. 1976. "The Principle of Generation among the Japanese in Honolulu." *Ethnic Groups* 1:13-35.

2b,d/3a/4h/5d/12/14   US: Japanese

1212 JOHNSON, Kenneth F. and Nina M. Ogle. 1978. *Illegal Mexican Aliens in the United States: A Teaching Manual on Impact Dimensions and Alternative Futures.* Washington, D.C.: University Press of America.

2b,c/3a/4i/5k/6/7/10   US: Mexican Americans

1213 JONES, Maldwyn A. 1960. *American Immigration.* Chicago: University of Chicago Press.

2c/3b/4d/5k/7   US: General

1214 JONES, Peter d'A. and Melvin Holli, eds. 1978. *The Ethnic Frontier: Group Survival in Chicago and the Midwest.* Grand Rapids, Minn: Wm. B. Erdmans.

1a/2c/3a/4d/5a,b,d/9/10/12   US: General

1215 JORGENSEN, Joseph G. 1971. "Indians and the Metropolis." In *The American Indian in Urban Society,* edited by Jack O. Waddell and O. Michael Watson, pp. 67-113. Boston: Little, Brown.

2c/3a/4a/5i/6/8/9/10   US: Native Americans

1216 ——. 1977. "Poverty and Work among American Indians." In *American Minorities and Economic Opportunity,* edited by H. Roy Kaplan, pp. 170-97.

2c/3a/4a/5i/8/9/10   US: Native Americans

1217 JORGENSEN-DAHL, Arnfinn. 1975. "Forces of Fragmentation in the International System: The Case of Ethnonationalism." *Orbis* 19:652-74.

2c/3e/4f/5b/10   General

1218 JUPP, James. 1969. "Immigrant Involvement in British and Australian

Politics." *Race* 10:323-40.

2c/3b,d/4f/5k/7/10   Australia; Britain: General

1219   JUSTUS, Joyce Bennett. 1978. "Language and National Integration: The Jamaican Case." *Ethnology* 17:39-52.

2b/3b/4a/5d,e/12/16   Jamaica

1220   JUTIKKALA, Eino. 1976. "Ethnic Problems of Swedish Finns and Finnish Finns: Historical Survey." *Plural Societies* 7:57-62.

2c/3b/4d/5d/11/12   Finland

1221   KALBACH, Warren E. 1970. *The Impact of Immigration on Canada's Population*. Ottawa: Dominion Bureau of Statistics.

2d/3b/4i/5k/6/7/8/10/14   Canada: General

1222   KALISH, Richard A. and Sharon Moriwaki. 1973. "The World of the Elderly Asian American." *Journal of Social Issues* 29:187-209.

2b/3a/4g/5d/6/14   US: Asian Americans

1223   KALLEN, Horace M. 1956. *Cultural Pluralism and the American Idea: An Essay in Social Philosophy*. Philadelphia: University of Pennsylvania Press.

2e/3e/4i(Philosophy)/5f/11   Theory

1224   KAMENETSKY, Ihor, ed. 1977. *Nationalism and Human Rights: Processes of Modernization in the USSR*. Littleton, Colo.: Libraries Unlimited.

1a/2c/3b/4f,h/5a,b,e,f/9/10/11   USSR: General

1225   KANDRE, Peter. 1967. "Autonomy and Integration of Social Systems: the Iu Mien ('Yao' or 'Man') Mountain Population and Their Neighbors." In *Southeast Asian Tribes, Minorities, and Nations*, edited by Peter Kunstadter, pp. 583-638. Princeton, N. J.: Princeton University Press.

2b/3a/4a/5c/6/8/9/11/12/14/17   Thailand

1226   ———. 1976. "Yao (Iu Mien) Supernaturalism, Language and Ethnicity." In *Changing Identities in Modern Southeast Asia*, edited by David J. Banks, pp. 171-97. The Hague: Mouton.

2b/3a/4a/5d/11/12/14/16   Burma; Laos; Thailand

1227   KANG, T. S., ed. 1979. *Nationalism and the Crisis of Ethnic Minorities in Asia.* Westport, Conn.: Greenwood Press.

1a/2c/3e/4a,d,f,h/5a,b,d,e/9/10/11/12/16   Asia

1228   KANNAN, C. T. 1972. *Inter-Racial Marriages in London.* London: C. T. Kannan.

                                        Britain: Africans, Indians,
2d/3a/4h/5g/12/14   Pakistanis, West Indians

1229   KANTROWITZ, Edward R. 1975. *Polish-American Politics in Chicago 1888-1900.* Chicago: University of Chicago Press.

2c/3a/4d,f/5k/7/10/12   US: Poles

1230   KANTROWITZ, Nathan. 1969. "Ethnic and Racial Segregation in the New York Metropolis." *American Journal of Sociology* 74:685-95.

2c/3a/4h/5i/6   US: General

1231   ———. 1973. *Ethnic and Racial Segregation Patterns in the New York Metropolis: Residential Patterns among White Groups, Blacks, and Puerto Ricans.* New York: Praeger.

2c/3a/4h/5i/6   US: General

1232   KAPLAN, Bernice A. and Gabriel W. Lasher. 1953. "Ethnic Identification in an Indian Mestizo Community." *Phylon* 14:179-90.

2b/3a/4a/5d/12   Mexico

1233   KAPLAN, H. Roy. 1977. "The Road Ahead: Prospects for Equality in the World of Work." In *American Minorities and Economic Opportunity*, edited by H. Roy Kaplan, pp. 279-318. Itasca, Ill.: F. E. Peacock.

2c/3b/4h/5g,i/9/10   US: General

1234   KARNI, Michael G., Matti E. Kaups, and Douglas J. Ollilia, Jr., eds. 1975. *The Finnish Experience in the Western Great Lakes Region: New Perspectives.* Turku, Finland: Institute for Migration.

1a/2c/3a/4d/5a,b,f/6/7/8   US: Finns

1235   KATZ, Zev. 1975. "The Jews in the Soviet Union." In *Handbook of Major Soviet Nationalities,* edited by Zev Katz, Rosemarie Rogers, and Frederic Harned, pp. 355-89. New York: Free Press.

       2c/3a/4i/5k/6/7/8/10
       11/12/13/16/17   USSR: Jews

1236   ——. 1975. "Kazakhstan and the Kazakhs." In *Handbook of Major Soviet Nationalities,* edited by Zev Katz, Rosemarie Rogers, and Frederic Harned, pp. 213-37. New York: Free Press.

       2c/3a/4i/5k/6/8/10/11/12/13/16   USSR: Kazakhs

1237   KATZENSTEIN, Mary Fainsod. 1977. "Preferential Treatment and Ethnic Conflict in Bombay." *Public Policy* 25:313-32.

       2d/3b/4f/5b,i/8/9/10   India

1238   ——. 1979. *Ethnicity and Equality: The Shiv Shea Party and Preferential Policies in Bombay.* Ithaca: Cornell University Press.

       2b/3a/4f/5b,i/6/8/9/10/11/12   India

1239   KATZENSTEIN, Peter J. 1977. "Ethnic Political Conflict in South Tyrol." In *Ethnic Conflict in the Western World,* edited by Milton J. Esman, pp. 287-323. Ithaca: Cornell University Press.

       2c/3a/4f/5b,e/8/9/10   Italy

1240   KATZMAN, Martin T. 1969. "Opportunity, Subculture and the Economic Performance of Urban Ethnic Groups." *American Journal of Economics and Sociology* 28:351-66.

       2c/3c/4b/5i/8/9   US: Euro-Americans

1241   ——. 1971. "Urban Racial Minorities and Immigrant Groups: Some Economic Comparisons." *American Journal of Economics and Sociology* 30:15-26.

       2b,c/3c/4b/5i/8/9   US: General

1242   KATZNELSON, Ira. 1973. "Participation and Political Buffers in Urban America." *Race* 14:465-80.

       2e/3b/4f/5b,i/9/10   US: General

1243 KAUFERT, Joseph M. 1977. "Situational Identity and Ethnicity among Ghanaian University Students." *Journal of Modern African Studies* 15: 126-35.

2d/3a/4a/5d,h/12   Ghana

1244 KAYAL, Philip M. 1973. "Religion and Assimilation: Catholic 'Syrians' in America." *International Migration Review* 7:409-26.

2b,c/3a/4h/5a/12/17   US: Syrians

1245 KAZLAS, Juozas A. 1977. "Social Distance among Ethnic Groups." In *Nationality Group Survival in Multi-Ethnic States: Shifting Support Patterns in the Soviet Baltic Region,* edited by Edward Allworth, pp. 228-56. New York: Praeger.

2d/3b/4f/5d/9/12   USSR: General

1246 KEECH, William R. 1972. "Linguistic Diversity and Political Conflict: Some Observations Based on Four Swiss Cantons." *Comparative Politics* 4:387-404.

2c/3c/4f/5b/10/12/16   Switzerland

1247 KEEFE, Susan Emley. 1979. "Urbanization, Acculturation, and Extended Family Ties: Mexican Americans in Cities." *American Ethnologist* 6:349-65.

2d/3a/4a/5a,k/14   US: Mexican Americans

1248 KELLSTEDT, Lyman A. 1974. "Ethnicity and Political Behavior: Inter-Group and Inter-Generational Differences." *Ethnicity* 1:393-415.

2d/3c/4h/5k/10   US: General

1249 KELLY, George Armstrong. 1969. "Belgium: New Nationalism in an Old World." *Comparative Politics* 1:343-65.

2c/3b/4f/5f/10/16   Belgium

1250 KELNER, Merrijoy. 1970. "Ethnic Penetration into Toronto's Elite Structure." *Canadian Review of Sociology and Anthropology* 7:128-37.

2b/3a/4h/5a,i/9   Canada: General

1251   KENDIS, Kaoru Oguri and Randall Jay Kendis. 1976. "The Street
       Boy Identity: An Alternate Strategy of Boston's Chinese-Americans."
       Urban Anthropology 5:1-18.

       2b/3a/4a/5d/8/12   US: Chinese

1252   KENNEDY, Stetson. 1959. *Jim Crow Guide to the USA: The Laws,
       Customs and Etiquette Governing the Conduct of Nonwhite and Other
       Minorities as Second-Class Citizens.* Westport, Conn.: Greenwood Press.

       2c/3b/4d/5g/11   US: General

1253   KENNEY, Bradford P., C. Edwin Vaughan, and Ronald E. Cromwell.
       1977. "Identifying the Socio-Contextual Forms of Religiosity among
       Urban Ethnic Minority Group Members." *Journal for the Scientific
       Study of Religion* 16:237-44.

       2d/3c/4h/5k/11/17   US: Afro-, Mexican Americans

1254   KENT, Donald Peterson. 1953. *The Refugee Intellectual: The American-
       ization of the Immigrants of 1933-1941.* New York: Columbia University
       Press.

       2c/3a/4h/5a/7   US: Euro-Americans

1255   KERTZER, David I. 1977. "Ethnicity and Political Allegiance in an
       Italian Communist Quartiere." In *Ethnic Encounters: Identities and Con-
       texts,* edited by George L. Hicks and Philip E. Leis, pp. 221-37. North
       Scituate, Mass.: Duxbury Press.

       2b,c/3b/4a/5b,i/9/10/17   Italy

1256   KERTZER, Morris N. 1967. *Today's American Jew.* New York: McGraw-
       Hill.

       2c/3a/4i/5k/12/17   US: Jews

1257   KEYES, Charles F. 1966. "Ethnic Identity and Loyalty of Villagers in
       Northeastern Thailand." *Asian Survey* 6:362-69.

       2b/3a/4a/5d/10/11/12   Thailand

1258   ——. 1971. "Buddhism and National Integration in Thailand." *Journal
       of Asian Studies* 30:551-68.

       2b/3b/4a/5k(Consensus)/10/11/17   Thailand

1259 ——. 1979. *Ethnic Adaptation and Identity: The Karen on the Thai Frontier with Burma.* Philadelphia: Institute for the Study of Human Issues.

1a/2b/3a/4a/5d/10/11/12/16/17   Thailand

1260 KHAN, Verity Saifullah. 1976. "Pakistani Women in Britain." *Journal of the Community Relations Commission* 5:1-10.

2b/3a/4g/5k/14   Britain: Pakistanis

1261 ——. 1977. "The Pakistanis: Mirpuri Villagers at Home and in Bradford." In *Between Two Cultures: Migrants and Minorities in Britain,* edited by James L. Watson, pp. 57-89. Oxford: Basil Blackwell.

2b/3a/4a/5d/7/12/14/15   Britain: Pakistanis

1262 ——. 1979. "Work and Network: South Asian Women in South London." In *Ethnicity at Work,* edited by Sandra Wallman, pp. 115-33. London: Macmillan.

2b/3a/4a/5d/8/12   Britain: Asians

1263 KHATENA, Joe. 1970. "Relative Integration of Selected Ethnic Groups in Singapore." *Sociology and Social Research* 54:460-65.

2d/3b/4h/5a/11   Singapore

1264 KIBBE, Pauline R. 1946. *Latin Americans in Texas.* Albuquerque: University of New Mexico Press.

2b/3a/4h/5i/8/9/11/13   US: Latin Americans

1265 KIKUMURA, Akemi and Harry H. L. Kitano. 1973. "Interracial Marriage: A Picture of the Japanese Americans." *Journal of Social Issues* 29:67-81.

2d/3a/4h/5d/14   US: Japanese

1266 KILSON, Martin. 1975. "Blacks and Neo-Ethnicity in American Political Life." In *Ethnicity: Theory and Experience,* edited by Nathan Glazer and Daniel Patrick Moynihan, pp. 236-66. Cambridge, Mass.: Harvard University Press.

2c/3a/4f/5d,e,i/10   US: Afro-Americans

1267   KIM, Hyung-chan, ed. 1977. *The Korean Diaspora: Historical and Sociological Studies of Korean Immigration and Assimilation in North America.* Santa Barbara, Calif.: ABC-Clio.

1a/2a,b,d/3a/4b,c,g,h/5a/6/7/8/12/15   US: Koreans

1268   KIM, Warren Y. 1971. *Koreans in America.* Seoul: Po Chin Chai.

2c/3a/4c/5a,g/7/9/12   US: Koreans

1269   KIMURA, Yukiko. 1968. "Locality Clubs as Basic Units of the Social Organization of the Okinawans in Hawaii." *Phylon* 29:331-38.

2b/3a/4a/5d/15   US: Japanese

1270   KING, Roger and Michael Wood. 1975. "The Support for Enoch Powell." In *The Politics of Race.* British Political Sociology Yearbook, vol. 2, edited by Ivor Crewe, pp. 239-62. New York: John Wiley & Sons.

2d/3b/4f/5k/10   Britain: General

1271   KINLOCH, Graham C. 1973. "Race, Socio-economic States and Social Distance in Hawaii." *Sociology and Social Research* 57:156-67.

2d/3c/4h/5g,i/9/11   US: General

1272   KITANO, Harry H. L. 1974. "Japanese Americans: The Development of a Middleman Minority." *Pacific Historical Review* 43:500-519.

2c/3a/4d,h/5 i/6/7/8/9/10   US: Japanese

1273   —— and Stanley Sue. 1973. "The Model Minorities." *Journal of Social Issues* 29:1-9.

2c/3a/4h/5d,g/9/12   US: Asian Americans

1274   KITROMILIDES, Paschalis M. and Theodore A. Coloumbi. 1976. "Ethnic Conflict in a Strategic Area: The Case of Cyprus." In *Ethnicity in an International Context,* edited by Abdul Said and Luiz R. Simmons, pp. 167-202. New Brunswick, N. J.: Transaction Books.

2c/3b/4f/5b/10   Cyprus

1275   KLAFF, Vivian Z. 1977. "Residence and Integration in Israel: A Mosaic of Segregated Peoples." *Ethnicity* 4:103-21.

2b/3c/4h/5i/6/7   Israel

1276 KLEIN, George. 1975. "The Role of Ethnic Politics in the Czechoslovak Crisis of 1968 and the Yugoslav Crisis of 1971." *Studies in Comparative Communism* 8:339-69.

2c/3d/4f/5k/8/9/10/11   Czechoslovakia; Yugoslavia

1277 KLEWAN, Helge. 1970. "Culture and Ethnic Identity: On Modernization and Ethnicity in Greenland." *Folk* 11-12:209-34.

2b/3b/4h/5d/9/10/12/13   Greenland

1278 KLEWAN, Inge. 1970. "Language and Ethnic Identity: Language Policy and Debate in Greenland." *Folk* 11-12:235-85.

2c/3b/4e/5f/9/10/11/12/13/16   Greenland

1279 KLOBUS-EDWARDS, Patricia, John N. Edwards, and David L. Klemmack. 1978. "Differences in Social Participation: Blacks and Whites." *Social Forces* 56:1035-52.

2d/3c/4h/5k/10/15   US: Afro-, Euro-Americans

1280 KLOSS, Heinz. 1967. "Bilingualism and Nationalism." *Journal of Social Issues* 23:39-47.

2c/3d/4f/5e/10/16   Europe

1281 KNOKE, David and Richard B. Felson. 1974. "Ethnic Stratification and Political Cleavage in the United States, 1952-68." *American Journal of Sociology* 80:630-42.

2c/3a/4h/5i/9/10   US: General

1282 KNOWLES, Louis L. and Kenneth Prewitt, eds. 1969. *Institutional Racism in America.* Englewood Cliffs, N. J.: Prentice-Hall.

1a/2c/3b/4h/5g,i/9/10/11   US: Afro-Americans

1283 KOHLER, David F. 1975. *Ethnic Minorities in Britain: Statistical Data.* London: Community Relations Commission.

2c/3b/4h/5k/6/7/8   Britain: General

1284 KOHN, Hans. 1944. *The Idea of Nationalism: A Study in Its Origins and*

Background. New York: Macmillan.

2c/3e/4d,f/5e/10/11   Theory

1285   KOLEHMAINEN, John I. 1968. *The Finns in America.* New York:
       Teachers College Press.

2c/3a/4d/5a,d/6/7/8/12/15/16   US: Finns

1286   KOLM, Richard. 1973. *Bibliography of Ethnicity and Ethnic Groups.*
       Rockville, Md.: National Institute of Mental Health.

2a   US: General

1287   KOOP, John Clement. 1960. "The Eurasian Population of Burma."
       Southeast Asia Studies Cultural Report Series no. 6. New Haven, Conn.:
       Yale University.

2c/3b/4a/5a,d,g,i/6   Burma

1288   KOREY, William. 1968. "The Legal Position of the Jewish Community
       of the Soviet Union." In *Ethnic Minorities in the Soviet Union,* edited by
       Erich Goldhagen, pp. 316-50. New York: Frederick A. Praeger.

2c/3a/4f/5k/10/11/17   USSR: Jews

1289   KOSLOV, V. I. 1978. "Changes in the Settlement and Urbanization of
       the Peoples of the USSR as Condition and Factors of Ethnic Processes."
       Soviet Sociology 17:26-53.

2c/3c/4h/5a/6/7   USSR: General

1290   KOSMIN, Barry. 1979. "Exclusion and Opportunity: Traditions of Work
       amongst British Jews." In *Ethnicity at Work,* edited by Sandra Wallman,
       pp. 37-68. London: Macmillan.

2b,c/3a/4i/5d,g/8/11/12   Britain: Jews

1291   KOTHARI, Rajni. 1971. "Introduction: Variations and Uniformities in
       Nation-Building." *International Social Science Journal* 23:339-54.

2c/3e/4i/5e,i/8/9/10   Theory

1292   KOTOK, Victor. 1971. "The Development of the National State System
       in the USSR." *International Social Science Journal* 23:371-83.

2c/3b/4i(Law)/5k/10 USSR: General

1293 KRAMER, Judith R. 1970. *The American Minority Community.* New York: Thomas Y. Crowell.

2c/3b/4h/5a,c,d,i/9/12/16 US: General

1294 KRANE, Ronald E., ed. 1979. *International Labor Migration in Europe.* New York: Praeger.

2d/3d/4b,h,i/5e,i/6/7/8/10/11 Europe; US: Mexican Americans

1295 KRAUSZ, Ernest. 1977. "The Religious Factor in Jewish Identification." *International Social Science Journal* 29:250-60.

2c/3a/4h/5d/12 Europe; Israel; US: Jews

1296 KRESSEL, Gideon M. 1977. "Ethnic Duality in a Kibbutz." *Ethnic Groups* 1:241-62.

2b/3a/4a/5b,d/9/10/12 Israel

1297 KRICKUS, Richard. 1976. *Pursuing the American Dream: White Ethnics and the New Populism.* Garden City, N. Y.: Anchor Press.

2c/3b/4f/5b/10 US: Euro-Americans

1298 KUMAGI, Gloria L. 1978. "The Asian Woman in America." *Explorations in Ethnic Studies* 1:27-39.

2c/3a/4i/5g,i/8/11/14 US: Asian Americans

1299 KUNG, S. W. 1975. *Chinese in American Life: Some Aspects of Their History, Status, Problems, and Contributions.* Westport, Conn.: Greenwood Press.

2c/3a/4h/5a/6/7/8/10/11/12/13/15 US: Chinese

1300 KUNSTADTER, Peter. 1967. "The Lau? and Skaw Karens of Maehongson Province, Northwestern Thailand." In *Southeast Asian Tribes, Minorities, and Nations,* edited by Peter Kunstadter, pp. 639-74. Princeton, N. J.: Princeton University Press.

2b/3a/4a/5c/6/7/8/9/10/11/12/13 Thailand

1301 KUNZ, Phillip R. 1968. "Immigrants and Socialisation: A New Look."

Sociological Review, n.s., 16:363-75.

2c/3b/4h/5a,k(Consensus)/7/11   Theory

1302   KUO, Chia-ling. 1977. *Social and Political Change in New York's China-town: The Role of Voluntary Associations.* New York: Praeger.

2b,c/3a/4a/5b,d/6/9/10/15   US: Chinese

1303   KUO, Eddie C. Y. 1974. "Bilingual Patterns of a Chinese Immigrant Group in the United States." *Anthropological Linguistics* 16:128-40.

2b/3a/4a,e/5k/16   US: Chinese

1304   —— and Riaz Hassan. 1976. "Some Social Concomitants of Interethnic Marriage in Singapore." *Journal of Marriage and the Family* 38:549-59.

2c/3b/4h/5k/6/9/14   Singapore

1305   KUPER, Hilda. 1947. *The Uniform of Color.* Johannesburg: Witwaters-rand University Press.

2c/3b/4a/5g,i/9/10/11/12   South Africa

1306   ——. 1969. " 'Strangers' in Plural Societies: Asians in South Africa and Uganda." In *Pluralism in Africa,* edited by Leo Kuper and M. G. Smith, pp. 247-82. Berkeley and Los Angeles: University of California Press.

2c/3c/4a/5f/6/7/8/9/12   South Africa; Uganda

1307   KUPER, Leo. 1963. "Racialism and Integration in South African Soci-ety." *Race* 4:26-31.

2b,c/3b/4a/5b,h,i/9   South Africa

1308   ——. 1965. "Religion and Urbanization in Africa." In *Religious Plural-ism and Social Structure, International Yearbook of Religion,* pp. 213-33. Cologne: Westdeutscher Verlag.

2c/3e/4a/5f/6/11/17   Africa

1309   ——. 1965. "Sociology: Some Aspects of Urban Plural Societies in Africa." In *The African World: A Survey of Social Research,* edited by Robert A. Lystad, pp. 107-30. New York: Praeger.

2c/3e/4a/5f,i/6/9   Africa

1310   ——. 1967. "Structural Discontinuities in African Towns: Some Aspects of Racial Pluralism." In *The City in Modern Africa,* edited by Horace Miner, pp. 127-50. New York: Praeger.

2b,c/3e/4a/5 i/6/9   Africa

1311.   ——. 1969. "Ethnic and Racial Pluralism: Some Aspects of Polarization and Depolarization." In *Pluralism in Africa,* edited by Leo Kuper and M. G. Smith, pp. 459-90. Berkeley and Los Angeles: University of California Press.

2c/3d/4a/5b,e,f/10   Africa

1312   ——. 1969. "Plural Societies: Perspectives and Problems." In *Pluralism in Africa,* edited by Leo Kuper and M. G. Smith, pp. 7-20. Berkeley and Los Angeles: University of California Press.

2e/3e/4a/5b,f,i/9/10   Theory

1313   ——. 1969. "Some Aspects of Violent and Nonviolent Political Change in Plural Societies." In *Pluralism in Africa,* edited by Leo Kuper and M. G. Smith, pp. 153-94. Berkeley and Los Angeles: University of California Press.

2e/3e/4a/5f,i/9/10/11   Theory

1314   ——. 1971. "Theories of Revolution and Race Relations." *Comparative Studies in Society and History* 13:87-107.

2c/3e/4h/5b/6/8/9/10/12   Theory

1315   ——. 1974. "On Theories of Race Relations." In *Ethnicity and Nation-Building,* edited by Wendell Bell and Walter E. Freeman, pp. 19-28. Beverly Hills, Calif.: Sage.

2e/3e/4a/5f,i   Theory

1316   KUROKAWA, Minako. 1971. *Minority Responses.* New York: Random House.

2c/3a,b/4h/5b/9/10/11   US: General

1317   ——. 1971. "Mutual Perceptions of Racial Images: White, Black and Japanese Americans." *Journal of Social Issues* 27:213-35.

2d/3a/4g/5d,g/11   US: Afro-Americans, Japanese, Euro-Americans

1318   LABOV, William. 1966. *The Social Stratification of English in New York City*. Washington, D.C.: Center for Applied Linguistics.

2b/3a/4e/5i/9/16   US: General

1319   LACZKO, Leslie. 1978. "English Canadians and Québécois Nationalism: An Empirical Analysis." *Canadian Review of Sociology and Anthropology* 15:206-17.

2d/3b/4h/5e/11/12/13/16   Canada: English

1320   LADBURY, Sarah. 1977. "The Turkish Cypriots: Ethnic Relations in London and Cyprus." In *Between Two Cultures: Migrants and Minorities in Britain*, edited by James L. Watson, pp. 301-31. Oxford: Basil Blackwell.

2b/3a/4a/5k/11/12   Britain: Cypriots

1321   LA FONTAINE, J. S. 1969. "Tribalism among the Gisu: An Anthropological Approach." In *Tradition and Transition in East Africa: Studies of the Tribal Element in the Modern Era*, edited by P. H. Gulliver, pp. 177-92. Berkeley and Los Angeles: University of California Press.

2b/3a/4a/5d/10/12   Kenya; Uganda

1322   LAGUERRE, John. 1976. "Afro-Indian Relations in Trinidad and Tobago." *Social and Economic Studies* 25:291-306.

2c/3b/4c/5k/10   Trinidad and Tobago

1323   LAGUMINA, Salvatore J. and Frank J. Cavaioli. 1974. *The Ethnic Dimension in American Society*. Boston: Holbrook Press.

2c/3a,b/4d/5a,d,f,g,i/7/10/12   US: General

1324   LAMBERT, John R. 1970. "Race Relations: The Role of the Police." In *Race and Racialism*, edited by Sami Zubaida, pp. 73-98. London: Tavistock.

2c/3b/4h/5k/10   General

1325   LAMBERT, Ronald D. 1975. *Nationalism and National Ideologies in Canada and Quebec: A Bibliography*. Waterloo, Ont.: Department of Sociology.

2a/5e/6/8/9/10/11   Canada: General

1326 LAMPE, Philip E. 1977. "Ethnic Identity among Minority Groups in Public and Parochial Schools." *Ethnic Groups* 1:337-52.

2d/3a,c/4g/5d,g/11/12   US: Afro-, Mexican Americans

1327 ——. 1977. "Religion and the Assimilation of Mexican Americans." *Review of Religious Research* 18:243-53.

2d/3a/4g/5a/13/17   US: Mexican Americans

1328 ——. 1978. "Ethnic Self-Referent and the Assimilation of Mexican Americans." *International Journal of Comparative Sociology* 19:259-70.

2d/3a/4g/5a/12   US: Mexican Americans

1329 LANCASTER, C. S. 1974. "Ethnic Identity, History, and 'Tribe' in the Middle Zambezi Valley." *American Ethnologist* 1:707-30.

2b/3a/4a/5d/12   Mozambique; Zambia

1330 LANDAU, Jacob M. 1969. *The Arabs in Israel: A Political Study.* London: Oxford University Press.

2b,c/3a/4f/5e/10/12/13/17   Israel

1331 LANDIS, Joseph B. 1973. "Racial Attitudes of Africans and Indians in Guyana." *Social and Economic Studies* 22:427-39.

2d/3b/4h/5g/11   Guyana

1332 ——. 1974. "Racial Polarization and Political Conflict in Guyana." In *Ethnicity and Nation-Building,* edited by Wendell Bell and Walter E. Freeman, pp. 255-67. Beverly Hills, Calif.: Sage.

2d/3b/4h/5b/8/9/10   Guyana

1333 LANDMAN, Ruth H. 1978. "Language Policies and Their Implications for Ethnic Relations in the Newly Sovereign States of Sub-Saharan Africa." In *Ethnicity in Modern Africa,* edited by Brian M. Du Toit, pp. 69-90. Boulder, Colo.: Westview Press.

2c/3d/4a/5k/13/16   Africa

1334 LANDON, Kenneth Perry. 1941. *The Chinese in Thailand.* London:

Oxford University Press.

2c/3a/4a/5k/6/8/9   Thailand

1335   LANDRY, Bart. 1977. "The Economic Position of Black Americans."
       In *American Minorities and Economic Opportunity,* edited by H. Roy
       Kaplan, pp. 50-108. Itasca, Ill.: F. E. Peacock.

       2c/3a/4h/5g,i/8/9/11/13   US: Afro-Americans

1336   LANE, David. 1975. "Ethnic and Class Stratification in Soviet Kazakh-
       stan, 1917-39." *Comparative Studies in Society and History* 17:165-89.

       2c/3a/4a/5i/9   USSR: Kazakhs

1337   LANG, Nicholas R. 1975. "The Dialectics of Decentralization: Eco-
       nomic Reform and Regional Inequality in Yugoslavia." *World Politics* 27:
       309-35.

       2c/3b/4f/5e,f,i/6/8/9/10/11   Yugoslavia

1338   LANG, Norris G. 1977. "Transplanted Technicians: Americans on an
       Ecuadorian Sugar Plantation." In *Ethnic Encounters: Identities and Con-
       texts,* edited by George L. Hicks and Philip E. Leis, pp. 103-18. North
       Scituate, Mass.: Duxbury Press.

       2b/3a/4a/5g,i/9   Ecuador

1339   LANPHIER, C. M. and R. N. Morris. 1974. "Structural Aspects of Dif-
       ferences in Income between Anglophones and Francophones." *Canadian
       Review of Sociology and Anthropology* 11:53-66.

       2d/3c/4h/5i/8/9/16   Canada: English, Québécois

1340   LA RAW, Maran. 1967. "Toward a Basis for Understanding the Minor-
       ities of Burma: The Kachin Example." In *Southeast Asian Tribes, Minor-
       ities, and Nations,* edited by Peter Kunstader, pp. 125-46. Princeton, N.J.:
       Princeton University Press.

       2b/3b/4a/5d,f/10/12/14   Burma

1341   LARRALDE, Carlos. 1976. *Mexican Americans: Movements and Lead-
       ers.* Los Alamitos, Calif.: Hwong.

       2c/3b/4d/5k/10   US: Mexican Americans

1342 LAVENDER, Abraham D. 1975. "Disadvantages of Minority Group Membership: The Perspective of a 'Nondeprived' Minority Group." *Ethnicity* 2:99-119.

2b/3a/4h/5g,i/9/11   US: Jews

1343 ——. 1975. "The Sephardic Revival in the United States: A Case of Ethnic Revival in a Minority-within-a-Minority." *Journal of Ethnic Studies* 3:21-32.

2b,c/3a/4h/5d/12/17   US: Jews

1344 ——, ed. 1977. *A Coat of Many Colors: Jewish Subcommunities in the United States*. Westport, Conn.: Greenwood Press.

1a/2b/3a/4i/5k/8/9/11/12   US: Jews

1345 —— and John M. Forsyth. 1976. "The Sociological Study of Minority Groups as Reflected by Leading Sociological Journals." *Ethnicity* 3:388-98.

2c/3e/4h/5k   US: General

1346 LAVONDES, Henri. 1971. "Language Policy, Language Engineering and Literacy in French Polynesia." *Current Trends in Linguistics* 8:1110-28.

2c/3b/4e/5k/10/11/16   French Polynesia

1347 LAWRENCE, Daniel. 1975. "Race, Elections and Politics." In *The Politics of Race*. British Political Sociology Yearbook, vol. 2, edited by Ivor Crewe, pp. 55-82. New York: John Wiley & Sons.

2c/3b/4f/5b,i/10/11   Britain: General

1348 LEAP, William L. 1974. "Ethnics, Emics, and the New Ideology: The Identity Potential of Indian English." In *Social and Cultural Identity: Problems of Persistence and Change*. Southern Anthropological Society Proceedings, no. 8, edited by Thomas K. Fitzgerald, pp. 51-62. Athens: University of Georgia Press.

2b/3a/4a/5d/12/16   US: Native Americans

1349 LEBAR, Frank M., ed. 1972. *Ethnic Groups of Insular Southeast Asia*. 2 vols. New Haven, Conn.: Human Relations Area Files Press.

2b,c/3a/4a/5d,k/6/10/12/14/16/17   Southeast Asia

1350 ——, G. C. Hickey, and J. K. Musgrave, eds. 1964. *Ethnic Groups of Mainland Southeast Asia.* New Haven, Conn.: Human Relations Area Files Press.

2b,c/3a/4a/5d,k/6/11/14/16/17   Southeast Asia

1351 LEDERER, Ivo J. 1969. "Nationalism and the Yugoslavs." In *Nationalism in Eastern Europe,* edited by Peter F. Sugar and Ivo J. Lederer, pp. 396-438. Seattle: University of Washington Press.

2/c/3b/4d/5e/10/12   Yugoslavia

1352 LEDERHENDLER, Eli M. 1977. "Resources of the Ethnically Disenfranchised." In *Nationality Group Survival in Multi-Ethnic States: Shifting Support Patterns in the Soviet Baltic Region,* edited by Edward Allworth, pp. 194-227. New York: Praeger.

2c/3a/4d/5k/12/14/17   USSR: Estonians, Latvians, Lithuanians

1353 LEE, Frank F. 1960. "Racial Patterns in a British City: An Institutional Approach." *Phylon* 21:40-50.

2b/3a/4h/5f,i/6/9/11   Britain: General

1354 LEE, Rose Hum. 1958. "The Stranded Chinese in the United States." *Phylon* 19:180-94.

2b/3a/4h/5d/6/7/8/9/12/13/14/16   US: Chinese

1355 ——. 1960. *The Chinese in the United States of America.* Hong Kong: Hong Kong University Press.

2b,c/3a/4h/5d,g,i/6/7/8/9/10/11/12/13/15   US: Chinese

1356 LEGTERS, Lyman H. 1976. "Ideology and Integration: Marxism in Yugoslavia." In *Small States and Segmented Societies: National Political Integration in a Global Environment,* edited by Stephanie G. Neuman, pp. 139-53. New York: Praeger.

2c/3b/4f/5e/10/11   Yugoslavia

1357 LEGUM, Colin. 1970. "Tribal Survivals in the Modern African Political System." In *The Passing of Tribal Man in Africa,* edited by P. C. W. Gutkind, pp. 102-12. Leiden: E. J. Brill.

2c/3c/4f/5k/8/9/12/13   Africa

1358 LEHMAN, F. K. 1967. "Ethnic Categories in Burma and the Theory of Social Systems." In *Southeast Asian Tribes, Minorities, and Nations,* edited by P. Kunstadter, pp. 93-124. Princeton, N. J.: Princeton University Press.

2c/3b/4a/5c,d/6/9/10/12/13   Burma

1359 LEIGH, Duane E. 1976. "Occupational Advancement in the Late 1960s: An Indirect Test of the Dual Labor Market Hypothesis." *Journal of Human Resources* 11:155-74.

2c/3a/4b/5i/8/9   US: Afro-Americans

1360 LEIS, Philip E. 1977. "Ethnicity and the Fourth of July Committee." In *Ethnic Encounters: Identities and Contexts,* edited by George L. Hicks and Philip E. Leis, pp. 239-58. North Scituate, Mass.: Duxbury Press.

2b/3a/4a/5d/10/12   US: Italians, Portuguese

1361 LE LOHE, M. J. 1975. "Participation in Elections by Asians in Bradford." In *The Politics of Race. British Political Sociology Yearbook,* vol. 2, edited by Ivor Crewe, pp. 84-122. New York: John Wiley & Sons.

2c,d/3a/4f/5k/10   Britain: Asians

1362 ———. 1979. "The Effects of the Presence of Immigrants upon the Local Political System in Bradford, 1945-77." In *Racism and Political Action in Britain,* edited by Robert Miles and Annie Phizacklea, pp. 184-203. London: Routledge & Kegan Paul.

2c/3a/4f/5k/10   Britain: General

1363 LEMARCHAND, René. 1972. "Political Clientelism and Ethnicity in Tropical Africa: Competing Solidarities in Nation Building." *American Political Science Review* 66:68-90.

2c/3d/4f/5e/10   Africa

1364 ———. 1974. "Status Differences and Ethnic Conflict: Rwanda and Burundi." In *Ethnicity and Nation-Building,* edited by Wendell Bell and Walter E. Freeman, pp. 135-46. Beverly Hills, Calif.: Sage.

2c/3d/4f/5b,i/9/10   Burundi, Rwanda

1365 LENDVAI, Paul. 1969. *Eagles in Cobwebs: Nationalism and Com-*

munism in the Balkans. Garden City, N. Y.: Doubleday.

2c/3d/4f/5e/10   Albania; Bulgaria; Romania; Yugoslavia

1366   ——. 1972. "National Tensions in Yugoslavia." *Conflict Studies,* no. 25.

2c/3b/4f/5 h/6/9/10   Yugoslavia

1367   LEON, Joseph J. 1975. "Sex-Ethnic Marriage in Hawaii: A Nonmetric
       Multidimensional Analysis." *Journal of Marriage and the Family* 37:
       775-81.

2c/3c/4h/5a/12/14   US: General

1368   LEONARD, Henry B. 1976. "Ethnic Conflict and Episcopal Power: The
       Diocese of Cleveland, 1847-1870." *Catholic Historical Review* 62:382-
       407.

2c/3a/4d/5b/10/17   US: General

1369   LEPAGE, R. B. 1964. *The National Language Question: Linguistic
       Problems of Newly Independent States.* London: Oxford University
       Press.

2c/3d/4e,f/5e,f/10/11/16   India; Malaysia

1370   LERNER, Richard M. and Christie J. Buehrig. 1975. "The Development
       of Racial Attitudes in Young Black and White Children." *Journal of
       Genetic Psychology* 127:45-54.

2d/3a/4g/5g/11   US: Afro-, Euro-Americans

1371   —— and Christine Schroeder. 1975. "Racial Attitudes in Young White
       Children: A Methodological Analysis." *Journal of Genetic Psychology*
       127:3-12.

2d/3c/4g/5g/11   US: Afro-, Euro-Americans

1372   LESTER, Anthony and Geoffrey Bindman. 1972. *Race and Law.* Lon-
       don: Longman.

2b/3b/4i(Law)/5k/9/10/11   Britain: General

1373   LETHBRIDGE, H. J. 1971. "A Chinese Association in Hong Kong: The
       Tung Wah." *Contributions to Asian Studies* 1:144-58.

2b/3a/4i/5k/15   Hong Kong

1374   LEVAK, Albert E. 1974. "Provincial Conflict and Nation-Building in Pakistan." In *Ethnicity and Nation-Building: Comparative, International, and Historical Perspectives*, edited by Wendell Bell and Walter E. Freeman, pp. 203-21. Beverly Hills, Calif: Sage.

2c/3b/4f/5b,i/10   Bangladesh; Pakistan

1375   LEVINE, Donald N. 1974. *Greater Ethiopia: The Evolution of a Multiethnic Society*. Chicago: University of Chicago Press.

2c/3b/4d/5f/9   Ethiopia

1376   LEVINE, Elaine Sue. 1976. *Ethnic Esteem among Anglo, Black, and Chicano Children*. San Francisco: R & E Research Associates.

2d/3c/4h/5d,g/11   US: Afro-, Euro-, Mexican Americans

1377   —— and Rene A. Ruiz. 1978. "An Exploration of Multicorrelates of Ethnic Group Choice." *Journal of Cross-Cultural Psychology* 9:179-90.

2d/3a/4g/5d,g/11/12   US: General

1378   LEVINE, Gene N. and Darrel M. Montrero. 1973. "Socioeconomic Mobility among Three Generations of Japanese Americans." *Journal of Social Issues* 29:33-48.

2d/3a/4h/5i/9   US: Japanese

1379   LEVINE, Stuart and Nancy O. Lurie, eds. 1968. *The American Indian Today*. Baltimore: Penguin.

1a/2b,c/3a/4a,h/5a,b,d,e,i
6/7/8/9/10/11/12   US: Native Americans

1380   LEVI-STRAUSS, Claude. 1971. "Race and Culture." *International Social Science Journal* 23:608-25.

2e/3e/4a/5d,g   Theory

1381   LEVITAN, Sar A., William B. Johnston, and Robert Taggart. 1975. *Minorities in the United States: Problems, Progress, and Prospects*. Washington, D. C.: Public Affairs Press.

                                              US: Afro-, Mexican-, Native Americans,
2c/3a,b/4b/5i/7/8/10/13   Puerto Ricans

1382   LEVY, Sydelle Brooks. 1975. "Shifting Patterns of Ethnic Identification
       among the Hassidim." In *The New Ethnicity: Perspectives from Ethnol-
       ogy.* 1973 Proceedings of the American Ethnological Society, edited by
       John W. Bennett, pp. 25-50. St. Paul: West.

       2b/3a/4a/5d/12   US: Jews

1383   LEWINS, Frank. 1976. "Ethnic Diversity within Australian Catholicism:
       A Comparative and Theoretical Analysis." *Australian and New Zealand
       Journal of Sociology* 12:126-35.

       2c/3c/4f/5d,e/12   Australia

1384   LEWIS, E. Glyn. 1977. "Migration and Language in the USSR." *Inter-
       national Migration Review* 5:147-79.

       2c/3b/4c/5k/7/16   USSR: General

1385   LEWIS, I. M. 1969. "Nationalism and Particularism in Somalia." In
       *Tradition and Transition in East Africa: Studies of the Tribal Element in
       the Modern Era,* edited by P. H. Gulliver, pp. 339-61. Berkeley and Los
       Angeles: University of California Press.

       2b,c/3b/4a/5e,f/10   Somalia

1386   LEWIS, Oscar. 1968. *A Study of Slum Culture: Backgrounds for La Vida.*
       New York: Random House.

       2b/3d/4a/5k/6/7/8/9/11/13/14   Puerto Rico; US: Puerto Ricans

1387   LEWIS, Robert A. 1971. "The Mixing of Russians and Soviet National-
       ities and its Demographic Impact." In *Soviet Nationality Problems,* edited
       by Edward Allworth et al., pp. 117-67. New York: Columbia University
       Press.

       2c/3b/4h/5k/6/7   USSR: General

1388   LEWIS, Russell E. 1976. "Controlled Acculturation Revisited: An Exam-
       ination of Differential Acculturation and Assimilation between the Hut-
       terian Brethren and the Old Order Amish." *International Review of
       Modern Sociology* 6:75-83.

       2b/3c/4h/5d/11   Canada: Hutterites; US: Amish

1389 LEY, C. H. 1967. "Muruts of Sabah (North Borneo)." In *Southeast Asian Tribes, Minorities, and Nations,* edited by Peter Kunstadter, pp. 353-65. Princeton, N. J.: Princeton University Press.

2b/3a/4a/5a,b,c,d/6/8/10/12   Malaysia

1390 LEYTON, Elliott. 1974. "Opposition and Integration in Ulster." *Man* 9: 185-98.

2b/3a/4a/5b/10   N. Ireland

1391 LI, Peter S. 1978. "The Stratification of Ethnic Immigrants: The Case of Toronto." *Canadian Review of Sociology and Anthropology* 15:31-40.

2d/3c/4h/5i/7/8/9/13   Canada: General

1392 LIDDLE, R. William. 1970. *Ethnicity, Party, and National Integration: An Indonesian Case Study.* New Haven, Conn.: Yale University Press.

2b/3b/4f/5d,e,f/10/11/12   Indonesia

1393 ——. 1972. "Ethnicity and Political Organization: Three East Sumatran Cases." In *Culture and Politics in Indonesia,* edited by Claire Holt, pp. 126-78. Ithaca, N.Y.: Cornell University Press.

2b/3a/4a/5b,d/10/15   Indonesia

1394 LIEBERMAN, Victor B. 1978. "Ethnic Politics in Eighteenth Century Burma." *Modern Asian Studies* 12:455-82.

2c/3b/4d/5b/10/11   Burma

1395 LIEBERSON, Stanley. 1963. *Ethnic Patterns in American Cities.* New York: Free Press of Glencoe.

2c/3a/4h/5i/6   US: General

1396 ——. 1970. *Language and Ethnic Relations in Canada.* New York: John Wiley & Sons.

2d/3b/4h/5d,f/6/8/10/16   Canada: General

1397 ——. 1970. "Stratification and Ethnic Groups." *Sociological Inquiry* 40: 172-81.

2e/3e/4h/5i/9   General

1398   ——. 1978. "The Anatomy of Language Diversity: Some Elementary Results." In *Interethnic Communication*. Southern Anthropological Society Proceedings, no. 12, edited by E. Lamar Ross, pp. 32-48. Athens: University of Georgia Press.

2f/3e/4h/5k/16   Theory

1399   ——. 1978. "Selective Black Migration from the South: A Historical View." In *The Demography of Racial and Ethnic Groups,* edited by Frank D. Bean and W. Parker Frisbie, pp. 119-41. New York: Academic Press.

2c/3b/4h/5k/6/7/13   US: Afro-Americans

1400   ——, Guy Dalto, and Mary Ellen Johnston. 1975. "The Course of Mother-Tongue Diversity in Nations." *American Journal of Sociology* 81:34-61.

2c/3d/4h/5k/6/10/16   General

1401   —— and Lynn K. Hansen. 1974. "National Development, Mother Tongue Diversity, and the Comparative Study of Nations." *American Sociological Review* 39:523-41.

2c/3d/4h/5k/16   General

1402   LIEBMAN, Charles S. 1973. *The Ambivalent American Jew: Politics, Religion, and Family in American Jewish Life.* Philadelphia: Jewish Publication Society of America.

2b/3a/4g/5k/11/12/17   US: Jews

1403   LIGHT, Ivan H. 1972 *The Ethnic Enterprise in America.* Berkeley and Los Angeles: University of California Press.

2c/3a/4h/5k/8/9   US: General

1404   LIGHTBODY, James. 1969. "A Note on the Theory of Nationalism as a Function of Ethnic Demands." *Canadian Journal of Political Science* 2: 327-37.

2e/3e/4f/5b,e/10   Theory

1405   LIJPHART, Arend. 1968. *The Politics of Accommodation: Pluralism and Democracy in the Netherlands.* Berkeley and Los Angeles: University of California Press.

2c/3b/4f/5e,f/10/16   Netherlands

1406   ———. 1977. "Political Theories and the Explanation of Ethnic Conflict
       in the Western World: Falsified Predications and Plausible Postdictions."
       In *Ethnic Conflict in the Western World,* edited by Milton J. Esman, pp.
       46-64. Ithaca, N.Y.: Cornell University Press.

2e/3e/4f/5k/10/11   Europe

1407   ———. 1979. "Religious vs. Linguistic vs. Class Voting: The 'Crucial Ex-
       periment' of Comparing Belgium, Canada, South Africa, and Switzer-
       land." *American Political Science Review* 73:442-58.

                                                      Belgium; Canada: General;
2d/3d/4f/5e,f,i/9/10/16/17   South Africa; Switzerland

1408   LIND, Andrew W., ed. 1973. *Race Relations in World Perspective.* Papers
       Read at the Conference on Race Relations in World Perspective, Honolulu,
       1954. Reprint. Westport, Conn.: Greenwood Press.

1a/2b,c/3b/4a,f,h/5b,f,i/9/10/11/13   General

1409   LINDMARK, Sture. 1971. *Swedish America 1914-1932: Studies in Eth-
       nicity with Emphasis on Illinois and Minnesota.* Uppsala, Sweden: Laro-
       medelsforlagen.

2c/3a/4d/5a/6/7/8/11/12/13/14/15/16/17   US: Swedes

1410   LINZ, Juan. 1973. "Early State-Building and Late Peripheral National-
       isms against the State: The Case of Spain." In *Building States and Nations:
       Analyses by Region,* vol. 2, edited by S. N. Eisenstadt and Stein Rokkan,
       pp. 32-116. Beverly Hills, Calif.: Sage.

2c/3b,d/4d,f/5e/6/9/10/16   Spain

1411   LITHMAN, Yngve George. 1978. *"The Community Apart: A Case Study
       of a Canadian Indian Reserve Community."* Stockholm Studies in Social
       Anthropology, vol. 6. Stockholm: Dept. of Social Anthropology, Univer-
       sity of Stockholm.

2b/3a/4a/5d,g,k/9/10/11/12   Canada: Native Canadians

1412   LITT, Edgar. 1970. *Beyond Pluralism: Ethnic Politics in America.* Glen-
       view, Ill.: Scott, Foresman.

2c/3b/4f/5b,e,f,i/9/10   US: General

1413   LITTLE, Kenneth. 1954. "The Position of Coloured People in Britain."
       Phylon 15:58-64.

       2c/3b/4a/5i/9/11   Britain: General

1414. ——. 1965. *West African Urbanization.* Cambridge: At the University
       Press.

       2b,c/3b/4a/5k/6/7/15   West Africa

1415   ——. 1978. "Countervailing Influences in African Ethnicity: A Less Ap-
       parent Factor." In *Ethnicity in Modern Africa,* edited by Brian M. Du
       Toit, pp. 175-89. Boulder, Colo.: Westview Press.

       2c/3e/4a/5k/15   Africa

1416   LLOYD, P. C. 1974. "Ethnicity and the Structure of Inequality in a
       Nigerian Town in the Mid-1950s." In *Urban Ethnicity,* edited by Abner
       Cohen, pp. 223-50. A.S.A. Monographs, no. 12. London: Tavistock.

       2c/3a/4a/5b/6/8/9/10   Nigeria

1417   LOCKHART, Audrey. 1976. *Some Aspects of Emigration from Ireland
       to the North American Colonies between 1660 and 1775.* New York:
       Arno Press.

       2c/3b/4d/5k/7   US: Irish

1418   LOCKWOOD, David. 1970. "Race, Conflict, and Plural Society." In
       Race and Racialism, edited by Sami Zubaida, pp. 57-72. London: Tavi-
       stock.

       2c/3a/4h/5b,i/9/10   US: Afro-Americans

1419   LOCKWOOD, William G. 1975. *European Moslems: Economics and Eth-
       nicity in Western Bosnia.* New York: Academic Press.

       2b/3a/4a/5c/6/8/10/12/14/17   Yugoslavia

1420   LOEB, Lawrence D. 1965. "Dhimmi Status and Jewish Roles in Iranian
       Society." *Ethnic Groups* 1:89-105.

       2b/3a/4a/5c/8/9/11   Iran

1421   LOEWAN, James W. 1971. *The Mississippi Chinese: Between Black and
       White.* Cambridge, Mass.: Harvard University Press.

2c/3a/4d/5d,g,i/6/7/8/9/10/11/12/14   US: Chinese

1422   LOFCHIE, Michael. 1969. "The Plural Society in Zanzibar." In *Pluralism in Africa*, edited by Leo Kuper and M. G. Smith, pp. 283-328. Berkeley and Los Angeles: University of California Press.

2c/3b/4a/5d,f,i/8/9/10/12/16/17   Tanzania

1423   LOH, Wallace D. 1975. "Nationalist Attitudes in Quebec and Belgium." *Journal of Conflict Resolution* 19:217-49.

2d/3d/4g/5e/10/11/12   Belgium; Canada: Québécois

1424   LONDON, Bruce and John Hearn. 1977. "The Ethnic Community Theory of Black Social and Political Participation: Additional Support." *Social Science Quarterly* 57:883-91.

2d/3a/4h/5d,k/12/15   US: Afro-Americans

1425   LONG, Norton E. 1975. "Ethos and the City: The Problem of Local Legitimacy." *Ethnicity* 2:43-51.

2b,c/3a/4h/5d,f/7/12   Theory

1426   LOPATA, Helen Znaniecki. 1976. *Polish Americans: Status Competition in an Ethnic Community*. Englewood Cliffs, N.J.: Prentice-Hall.

2c/3a/4h/5a,i/7/9/10/12/15/16   US: Poles

1427   LOPEZ, David E. 1978. "Chicano Language Loyalty in an Urban Setting." *Sociology and Social Research* 62:267-78.

2d/3a/4h/5a/16   US: Mexican Americans

1428   LOPEZ Y RIVAS, Gilberto. 1973. *The Chicanos: Life and Struggles of the Mexican Minority in the United States*. New York: Monthly Review Press.

2c/3a/4h/5i,j/6/7/8/9/10/11/12/13/17   US: Mexican Americans

1429   LOVOLL, Odd Sverre. 1975. *A Folk Epic: The Bygdelag in America*. Boston: Twayne.

2c/3a/4d/5k/12/16   US: Norwegians

1430   LUCAS, Henry S. 1955. *Netherlanders in America: Dutch Immigration to the United States and Canada, 1789-1950.* Ann Arbor: University of Michigan Press.

2c/3a/4d/5a,k/7/10/13/16   US: Dutch

1431   LUEBKE, Frederick. 1978. "The Germans." In *Ethnic Leadership in America,* edited by John Higham, pp. 64-90. Baltimore: Johns Hopkins University Press.

2c/3a/4d/5k/10/15   US: Germans

1432   LURIE, Nancy Oestreich. 1972. "Menominee Termination: From Reservation to Colony." *Human Organization* 31:257-70.

2b/3a/4a/5j/8/9/10   US: Native Americans

1433   LUSTICK, Ian. 1979. "Stability in Deeply Divided Societies: Consociationalism versus Control." *World Politics* 31:325-44.

2e/3e/4f/5f,j/10   Theory

1434   LYMAN, Stanford M. 1968. "Marriage and Family among Chinese Immigrants to America, 1850-1960." *Phylon* 29:321-30.

2c/3a/4a/5k/14   US: Chinese

1435   ——. 1970. *The Asian in the West.* Reno: Desert Research Institute, Western Studies Center, University of Nevada.

2b,c/3a/4h/5f/6/9/10/12/14/15   US: Chinese, Japanese

1436   ——. 1972. "Contrasts in the Community Organization of Chinese and Japanese in North America." In *Readings in Race and Ethnic Relations,* edited by Anthony H. Richmond, pp. 149-67. Oxford: Pergamon Press.

2b/3a,c/4a/5k/8/9/14/15   US: Chinese, Japanese

1437   ——. 1977. *The Asian in North America.* Santa Barbara, Calif.: ABC-Clio.

1a/2b,c/3a/4d/5d,g,i/6/8/9/10/11/12/14/15   US: Chinese, Japanese

1438   —— and William A. Douglass. 1973. "Ethnicity: Strategies of Collective and Individual Impression Management." *Social Research* 40:344-65.

2b/3e/4h/5d,h/12   General

1439 MACCORMICK, Neil, ed. 1970. *The Scottish Debate: Essays on Scottish Nationalism.* London: Oxford University Press.

1a/2c/3b/4b,d,f,i(Law)/5e/8/10   Scotland

1440 MACGAFFEY, Wyatt. 1976. "Corporation Theory and Political Change: The Case of Zaire." In *Small States and Segmented Societies: National Political Integration in a Global Environment,* edited by Stephanie G. Neuman, pp. 121-38. New York: Praeger.

2c/3b/4f/5f/10   Zaire

1441 MACHADO, Deirdre A. Meintel. 1977. "Language and Interethnic Relationships in a Portuguese Colony." In *Ethnic Encounters: Identities and Contexts,* edited by George L. Hicks and Philip E. Leis, pp. 49-62. North Scituate, Mass.: Duxbury Press.

2b/3a/4a/5d/10/12/13/16   Cape Verde Islands

1442 MACISCO, John J., Jr. 1968. "Assimilation of the Puerto Ricans on the Mainland." *International Migration Review* 2:7-18.

2b/3a/4h/5a/6/7/8   US: Puerto Ricans

1443 MACK, Raymond W. 1968. *Race, Class, and Power.* 2d ed. New York: Van Nostrand Reinhold.

2c/3e/4h/5b,j/8/9/10/11   General

1444 MACRAE, John. 1979. "Maoris, Islanders, and Europeans: Labour Mobility in New Zealand Industry." In *Ethnicity at Work,* edited by Sandra Wallman, pp. 155-71. London: Macmillan.

2b/3a/4b/5g/8   New Zealand

1445 MADAN, Raj. 1979. *Coloured Minorities in Great Britain: A Comprehensive Bibliography 1970-1977.* London: Aldwych Press.

2a/7/8/9/10/13/14/15/16   Britain: General

1446 MADAN, T. N. 1972. "Two Faces of Bengali Ethnicity: Muslim Bengali or Bengali Muslim." *Developing Economies* 10:74-85.

2b/3b/4f/5e/8/9/10   Bangladesh

1447 MADDOX, H. 1960. "The Assimilation of Negroes in a Dockland Area of Britain." *Sociological Review,* n.s., 8:5-16.

2c/3a/4h/5a/8/9/11   Britain: Africans, West Indians

1448   MAGUBANE, Bernard. 1969. "Pluralism and Conflict Situations in Africa: A New Look." *African Social Research* 7:529-54.

2c/3e/4h/5b,f/10   Africa

1449   ——. 1974. *The Continuing Class Struggle in South Africa.* Center on International Race Relations, Graduate School of International Studies, University of Denver, Studies in Race and Nations, vol. 6, study nos. 3-4.

2c/3b/4h/5b,i/9/10   South Africa

1450   ——. 1979. *The Political Economy of Race and Class in South Africa.* New York: Monthly Review Press.

2c/3b/4f/5b,i/8/9/10/11   South Africa

1451   MAKIELSKI, S. J., Jr. 1973. *Beleaguered Minorities: Cultural Politics in America.* San Francisco: W. H. Freeman.

2c/3b/4f/5b,e,f,i/10   US: General

1452   ——. 1975. "The Politics of Change: Southern Pluralism and Ethnic Identification." In *The New Ethnicity: Perspectives from Ethnology.* 1973 Proceedings of the American Ethnological Society, edited by John W. Bennett, pp. 197-214. St. Paul: West.

2c/3a/4f/5k/10   US: General

1453   MALCOLM, M. Vartan. 1969. *The Armenians in America.* Reprint, 1919 ed. Boston: Pilgrim Press.

2c/3a/4d/5a,d,k/6/7/8/9/10/11/12/16/17   US: Armenians

1454   MALDONADO, Edwin. 1979. "Contract Labor and the Origins of Puerto Rican Communities in the United States." *International Migration Review* 13:103-21.

2c/3a/4d/5k/7/8   US: Puerto Ricans

1455   MALIK, Yogendra K. 1969. "Agencies of Political Socialization and East Indian Ethnic Identification in Trinidad." *Sociological Bulletin* 18: 101-21.

2b/3a/4h/5b,d/10/12 Trinidad and Tobago

1456 MAMAK, Alexander. 1977. "Pluralism and Social Change in Suva City, Fiji: A Summary of Findings." *Plural Societies* 8:53-66.

2d/3a/4h/5f/8/9 Fiji

1457 MANGANO, Antonio. 1971. *Sons of Italy: A Social and Religious Study of the Italians in America.* Reprint, 1917 ed. New York: Missionary Education Movement of the U.S. and Canada.

2c/3a/4i/5a,d/7/12/14/16/17 US: Italians

1458 MANGAT, J. 1969. *A History of the Asians in East Africa.* London: Oxford University Press.

2c/3e/4d/5d,i/7/8/9 East Africa

1459 MANNING, Frank E. 1974. "Entertainment and Black Identity in Bermuda." In *Social and Cultural Identity: Problems of Persistence and Change.* Southern Anthropological Society Proceedings, no. 8, edited by Thomas K. Fitzgerald, pp. 39-50. Athens: University of Georgia Press.

2b/3b/4a/5d/12 Bermuda

1460 MAPP, Edward. 1974. *Puerto Rican Perspectives.* Metuchen. N.J.: Scarecrow Press.

2c/3a/4i/5g,i/9/11 US: Puerto Ricans

1461 MAPP, Roberta E. 1972. "Cross-National Dimensions of Ethnocentrism." *Canadian Journal of African Studies* 6:73-96.

2d/3d/4f/5g/11 Ghana; Kenya

1462 MAQUET, Jacques. 1970. "Rwanda Castes." In *Social Stratification in Africa,* edited by A. Tuden and L. Plotnicov, pp. 92-114. New York: Free Press.

2b/3b/4a/5i/8/9/12 Rwanda

1463 ——. 1970. "Societal and Cultural Incorporation in Rwanda." In *From Tribe to Nation in Africa: Studies in Incorporation Processes,* edited by Ronald Cohen and John Middleton, pp. 201-16. Scranton, Penn.: Chandler.

2b/3a/4a/5a,i/9 Rwanda

1464   MARCUS, Jacob R. 1970. *The Colonial American Jew, 1492-1776.* 3
       vols. Detroit: Wayne State University Press.

       2c/3a/4d/5a,d/7/10/17   US: Jews

1465   MARDEN, Charles F. and Gladyz Meyer. 1973. *Minorities in American
       Society.* 4th ed. New York: Van Nostrand.

       1b/2c/3b/4h/5a,d,f,i/7/8/9/10/11/12/14/17   US: General

1466   MARGER, Martin. 1978. "A Reexamination of Gordon's Ethclass."
       Sociological Focus 11:21-32.

       2e/3e/4h/5i/9/12   Theory

1467   MARKOWICZ, Harry and James Woodward. 1978. "Language and the
       Maintenance of Ethnic Boundaries in the Deaf Community." *Communica-
       tion and Cognition* 11:29-38.

       2b/3a/4e/5k/12/16   US: Deaf Persons

1468   MARQUAND, Leo. 1957. *South Africa's Colonial Policy.* Johannesburg:
       South African Institute of Race Relations.

       2c/3b/4f/5j/9/10/11   South Africa

1469   MARSHALL, Ray and Virgil L. Christian, Jr., eds. 1978. *Employment of
       Blacks in the South: A Perspective on the 1960's.* Austin: University of
       Texas Press.

       2b/3a/4b/5i/8/9   US: Afro-Americans

1470   MARSTON, Wilfred G. 1969. "Social Class Segregation within Ethnic
       Groups in Toronto." *Canadian Review of Sociology and Anthropology*
       6:65-79.

       2c/3a/4h/5i/6/9   Canada: General

1471   MARTIN, Elmer P. and Joanne Mitchell Martin. 1978. *The Black Ex-
       tended Family.* Chicago: University of Chicago Press.

       2b/3a/4a,h/5k/14   US: Afro-Americans

1472   MARTIN, James G. and Clyde W. Franklin. 1973. *Minority Group Rela-
       tions.* Columbus, Ohio: Charles E. Merrill.

1b/2c/3a,b,c/4h/5g/10/11   General

1473   MARTIN, Walter T. and Dudley T. Poston, Jr. 1977. "Differentials in the Ability to Convert Education into Income: The Case of the European Ethnics." *International Migration Review* 11:215-31.

2d/3c/4h/5g,i/8/13   US: Euro-Americans

1474   MARUNCHAK, Michael H. 1970. *The Ukrainian Canadians: A History.* Winnipeg: Ukrainian Free Academy of Sciences.

2c/3a/4d/5k/10/12/15/16/17   Canada: Ukrainians

1475   MASON, Philip. 1966. "Gradualism in Peru: Some Impressions on the Future of Ethnic Group Relations." *Race* 8:43-62.

2b/3b/4h/5a,k(Consensus)/9   Peru

1476   ——. 1970. *Race Relations.* London: Oxford University Press.

1b/2c/3e/4h/5a,g,h,i/9/10/11   General

1477   MAST, Robert. 1973. *Rethinking Race and Group Relations Work: From Philosophy to Practice.* Center on International Race Relations, Graduate School of International Studies, University of Denver, Studies in Race and Nations, vol. 5, study no. 2.

2e/3e/4h/5b,f,k(Consensus)   Theory

1478   MAST, Robert H. 1974. "Some Theoretical Considerations in International Race Relations." In *Ethnicity and Nation-Building,* edited by Wendell Bell and Walter E. Freeman, pp. 59-71. Beverly Hills, Calif.: Sage.

2e/3e/4h/5b,i/12   Theory

1479   MASUOKA, Jitsuichi and Preston Valien, eds. 1961. *Race Relations: Problems and Theory.* Chapel Hill: University of North Carolina Press.

1a,b/2c/3e/4h/5b,h,i/9/10/11   General

1480   MATEJKO, Alexander. 1976. "Blacks and Whites in Zambia." *Ethnicity* 3:317-37.

2b/3b/4i/5i/9/11   Zambia

1481 MATTHIASSON, Carolyn J. 1974. "Coping in a New Environment: Mexican Americans in Milwaukee, Wisconsin." *Urban Anthropology* 3: 262-77.

      2d/3a/4a/5c/8/14/15/16   US: Mexican Americans

1482 MATOSSIAN, Mary Kilbourne. 1968. "Communist Rule and the Changing Armenian Cultural Pattern." In *Ethnic Minorities in the Soviet Union,* edited by Erich Goldhagen, pp. 185-97. New York: Frederick A. Praeger.

      2c/3a/4h/5d/12/14   USSR: Armenians

1483 ———. 1975. "Armenia and the Armenians." In *Handbook of Major Soviet Nationalities,* edited by Zev Katz, Rosemarie Rogers, and Frederic Harned, pp. 143-60. New York: Free Press.

      2c/3a/4d/5k/6/8/10/11/13/16   USSR: Armenians

1484 MAXWELL, Neville. 1973. *India and the Nagas.* Report no. 17. London: Minority Rights Group.

      2c/3a/4i/5b/9/10   India

1485 MAXWELL, Thomas R. 1977. *The Invisible French: The French in Metropolitan Toronto.* Waterloo, Ontario: Wilfred Laurier University Press.

      2b,d/3a/4h/5d,f/6/8/10/12/13/16/17   Canada: Québécois

1486 MAYER, Adrian C. 1961. *Peasants in the Pacific: A Study of Fiji Indian Rural Society.* London: Routledge & Kegan Paul.

      2b/3a/4a/5k/8/9   Fiji

1487 ———. 1966. "The Significance of Quasi-Groups in the Study of Complex Societies." In *The Social Anthropology of Complex Societies.* A.S.A. Monographs no. 4, edited by Michael Banton, pp. 97-122. London: Tavistock.

      2e/3e/4a/5c,d,f   Theory

1488 MAYER, Kurt B. 1968. "The Jura Problem: Ethnic Conflict in Switzerland." *Social Research* 35:707-41.

      2b,c/3a/4d/5b/10/16/17   Switzerland

1489 MAYER, P. 1961. *Townsmen or Tribesmen: Conservatism and the Process of Urbanization in a South African City.* Cape Town: Oxford University Press.

2b/3a/4a/5a,d,i/7/12/15 South Africa

1490 MAYKOVICH, Minako Kurokawa. 1971. "Change in Racial Stereotypes among College Students." *Human Relations* 24:371-86.

2d/3a/4g/5g/11 US: General

1491 ——. 1972. "Stereotypes and Racial Images—White, Black, and Yellow." *Human Relations* 25:101-20.

2d/3e/4g/5g/11 US: General

1492 ——. 1973. "Political Activation of Japanese American Youth." *Journal of Social Issues* 29:167-85.

2d/3a/4g/5d,e,g/10/14 US: Japanese

1493 ——. 1975. "Japanese and Chinese in the United States and Canada." In *Politics of Race: Comparative Studies,* edited by Donald G. Baker, pp. 95-120. Lexington, Mass.: Lexington Books.

2c/3d/4h/5b,f,g,i/8/9/13 US: Chinese, Japanese

1494 MAZRUI, Ali A. 1969. "Pluralism and National Integration." In *Pluralism in Africa,* edited by Leo Kuper and M. G. Smith, pp. 333-49. Berkeley and Los Angeles: University of California Press.

2e/3e/4f/5e,f,i/9/10 Theory

1495 ——. 1970. "Political Hygiene and Cultural Transition in Africa." In *The Passing of Tribal Man in Africa,* edited by P. C. W. Gutkind, pp. 113-25. Leiden: E. J. Brill.

2c/3e/4f/5b/10/11/12 Africa

1496 ——. 1970. "Violent Contiguity and the Politics of Retribalization in Africa." *Journal of International Affairs* 23:89-105.

2c/3e/4f/5b/10 Africa

1497 ——. 1973. "Traditional Cleavages and Efforts of Integration in East

Africa." In *Building States and Nations: Analyses by Region*, vol. 2, edited by S. N. Eisenstadt and Stein Rokkan, pp. 469-93. Beverly Hills, Calif.: Sage.

2c/3e/4f/5d/8/10/12/16   East Africa

1498 ——. 1975. "Ethnic Stratification and the Military-Agrarian Complex: The Uganda Case." In *Ethnicity: Theory and Experience*, edited by Nathan Glazer and Daniel Patrick Moynihan, pp. 420-49. Cambridge, Mass.: Harvard University Press.

2c/3b/4f/5 i/9/10   Uganda

1499 ——. 1976. "The Afro-Saxons." In *Ethnicity in an International Context*, edited by Abdul Said and Luiz R. Simmons, pp. 203-17. New Brunswick, N. J.: Transaction Books.

2c/3e/4f/5k/12/16   General

1500 ——. 1978. "Ethnic Tensions and Political Stratification in Uganda." In *Ethnicity in Modern Africa*, edited by Brian M. Du Toit, pp. 47-68. Boulder, Colo.: Westview Press.

2c/3b/4f/5b/9/10/17   Uganda

1501 MCARTHUR, Marilyn. 1976. "The Saxon Germans: Political Fate of an Ethnic Identity." *Dialectical Anthropology* 1:349-64.

2b/3a/4a/5d/10/12   Romania

1502 MCBEATH, Gerald A. 1978. "Political Behavior of Ethnic Leaders." *Comparative Politics* 3:393-417.

2c/3d/4f/5k/10   Southeast Asia

1503 MCCAFFREY, Lawrence J. 1976. *The Irish Diaspore in America*. Bloomington: Indiana University Press.

2c/3a/4d/5a,d,e/7/10   US: Irish

1504 MCCOMBS, Vernon Monroe. 1970. *From Over the Border: A Study of the Mexicans in the United States*. Reprint, 1925 ed. San Francisco: R & E Research Associates.

2c/3a/4d/5k/7/8/11   US: Mexican Americans

1505 MCEVOY, Frederick D. 1977. "Understanding Ethnic Realities among the Grebo and Kru Peoples of West Africa." *Africa* 47:62-80.

2b/3a/4a/5d/12   West Africa

1506 MCFEE, M. 1968. "The 150% Man, A Product of Blackfeet Accultura-tion." *American Anthropologist* 70:1096-1103.

2b/3a/4a/5a,d/9/11/12   US: Native Americans

1507 MCKAY, James and Frank Lewins. 1978. "Ethnicity and the Ethnic Group: A Conceptual Analysis and Reformulation." *Ethnic and Racial Studies* 1:412-27.

2e/3e/4h/5k   Theory

1508 MCKENZIE, H. I. 1966. "The Plural Society Debate: Some Comments on a Recent Contribution." *Social and Economic Studies* 15:53-60.

2e/3e/4h/5f,i   Theory

1509 MCKOWN, Roberta E. 1974. "The Impact of Education on Ethnic Groups in Ghana and Kenya." In *Ethnicity and Nation-Building,* edited by Wendell Bell and Walter E. Freeman, pp. 233-54. Beverly Hills, Calif.: Sage.

2d/3d/4b/5i/8/9/13   Ghana; Kenya

1510 ——. 1975. "National Integration in Africa: Measurements and Corre-lates in Ghana and Kenya." *Canadian Review of Studies in Nationalism* 3:45-69.

2d/3d/4f/5a,e/11   Ghana; Kenya

1511 MCLEAN, Iain. 1977. "The Politics of Nationalism and Devolution." *Political Studies* 25:425-30.

2c/3b/4f/5e,k/10   Scotland

1512 MCNICKLE, D'Arcy. 1973. *Native American Tribalism: Indian Survivals and Renewals.* London: Oxford University Press.

2c/3a/4a/5d/10/11/12/13/16   US: Native Americans

1513 MCRAE, Kenneth D. 1973. "Empire, Language, and Nation: The Canadian Case." In *Building States and Nations: Analyses by Region,* vol. 2, edited by S. N. Eisenstadt and Stein Rokkan, pp. 144-76. Beverly Hills, Calif.: Sage.

2c/3b/4f/5e,f/8/10/12/16/17   Canada: General

1514   ——, ed. 1974. *Consociational Democracy: Political Accommodation in Segmented Societies.* Toronto: McClelland & Stewart.

                                                         Theory; Canada: General;
1a/2c/3b,d/4f/5f/10   Lebanon; Western Europe

1515   MCROBERTS, Kenneth. 1979. "Internal Colonialism: The Case of Quebec." *Ethnic and Racial Studies* 2:293-318.

2c/3a/4f/5b,j/8/9/10/12/13/16   Canada: Québécois

1516   MCWILLIAMS, Carey. 1964. *Brothers under the Skin.* Rev. ed. Boston: Little, Brown.

2c/3a/4d/5g,h,i/7/9/10/11   US: General

1517   ——. 1968. *The Mexicans in America.* New York: Teachers College Press.

2c/3a/4d/5a,i/6/7/8/9/11/12/13/14   US: Mexican Americans

1518   ——. 1968. *North from Mexico.* Reprint, 1948 ed. New York: Greenwood Press.

2c/3a/4d/5k/7   US: Mexican Americans

1519   MEDHURST, Kenneth. 1975. *The Basques.* Report no. 9. London: Minority Rights Group.

2c/3a/4i/5e/7/10/12/17   Spain

1520   MEISEL, John and Vincent Lemieux. 1972. *Ethnic Relations in Canadian Voluntary Associations.* Ottowa: Information Canada.

2b/3b/4h/5f/15/16   Canada: English, Québécois

1521   MEISTER, Richard J., ed. 1974. *Race and Ethnicity in Modern America.* Lexington, Mass.: D. C. Heath.

1a/2c/3b/4h/5a,f/12   US: General

1522   MELENDY, H. Brett. 1972. *The Oriental Americans.* New York: Twayne.

2c/3a/4d/5a,g/6/7/8/9/10   US: Chinese, Japanese

1523   ———. 1977. *Asians in America: Filipinos, Koreans, and East Indians.* Boston: Twayne.

2c/3a/4d/5g,i,k/7/8/10/11   US: East Indians, Filipinos, Koreans

1524   MENCARELLI, James and Steve Severin. 1975. *Protest 3: Red, Black, Brown Experience in America.* Grand Rapids, Mich.: Wm. B. Erdmans.

2c/3c/4f/5b/10   US: Afro-, Mexican-, Native Americans

1525   MENNERICK, Lewis A. 1968. "Ethnic Occupational Statuses." *Kansas Journal of Sociology* 4:53-64.

2c/3e/4h/5d/9/12   US: General

1526   MEO, Leila. 1977. "The War in Lebanon." In *Ethnic Conflict in International Relations,* edited by Astri Suhrke and Lela Garner Noble, pp. 93-126. New York: Praeger.

2c/3b/4f/5b/10/17   Lebanon

1527   MERANI, H. V. and H. L. van der Lann. 1979. "The Indian Traders in Sierra Leone." *African Affairs* 78:240-50.

2b/3a/4d/5k/8/9   Sierra Leone

1528   METZGER, L. Paul. 1971. "American Sociology and Black Assimilation: Conflicting Perspectives." *American Journal of Sociology* 76:627-47.

2e/3e/4h/5a,i/10/11   US: Afro-Americans

1529   MICAUD, Charles A. 1974. "Bilingualism in North Africa: Cultural and Sociopolitical Implications." *Western Political Quarterly* 27:92-103.

2c/3d/4f/5e,k/10/12/13/16   Tunisia

1530   MICHELENA, Jose A. Silva. 1971. "State Formation and Nation-Building in Latin America." *International Social Science Journal* 23:384-98.

2c/3e/4f/5e,i/8/9/10   Mesoamerica; South America

1531   MIDDLETON, John. 1970. "Political Incorporation among the Lugbara of Uganda." In *From Tribe to Nation in Africa: Studies in Incorporation Processes,* edited by Ronald Cohen and John Middleton, pp. 55-70. Scranton, Penn.: Chandler.

2b/3a/4a/5d/7/10/12   Uganda

1532 MILES, Robert and Annie Phizacklea. 1977. "Class, Race Ethnicity and Political Action." *Political Studies* 25:491-507.

2c/3b/4f/5i/9/10   Britain: Africans, Asians, West Indians

1533 ——. 1979. "Some Introductory Observations on Race and Politics in Britain." In *Racism and Political Action in Britain,* edited by Robert Miles and Annie Phizacklea, pp. 1-27. London: Routledge & Kegan Paul.

2e/3b/4h/5b,g/10/11   Britain: General

1534 MILLER, Abraham H. 1971. "Ethnicity and Political Behavior: A Review of Theories and an Attempt at Reformulation." *Western Political Quarterly* 24:483-500.

2d/3b/4f/5a/10   US: General

1535 ——. 1974. "Ethnicity and Party Identification: Continuation of a Theoretical Dialogue." *Western Political Quarterly* 27:479-90.

2d/3c/4f/5a/10   US: General

1536 MILLER, Michael V. 1975. "Chicano Community Control in South Texas: Problems and Prospects." *Journal of Ethnic Studies* 3:70-89.

2b/3a/4f/5e/10   US: Mexican Americans

1537 MILLER, Stuart Creighton. 1969. *The Unwelcome Immigrant: The American Image of the Chinese, 1785-1882.* Berkeley and Los Angeles: University of California Press.

2c/3a/4d/5g/11   US: Chinese

1538 MILLER, Wayne Charles. 1976. *A Comprehensive Bibliography for the Study of American Minorities.* 2 vols. New York: New York University Press.

2a/6/7/8/10/12/13/14/15/16/17   US: General

1539 MILNE, R. S. 1977. "Politics, Ethnicity and Class in Guyana and Malaysia." *Social and Economic Studies* 26:18-37.

2c/3d/4h/5f,i/9/10 Guyana; Malaysia

1540 MILNER, Henry. 1978. *Politics in the New Quebec.* Toronto: MacClelland & Stewart.

2c/3a/4f/5b,e/10 Canada: Québécois

1541 MITCHELL, J. Clyde. 1956. *The Kalela Dance: Aspects of Social Relationships among Urban Africans in Northern Rhodesia.* Rhodes-Livingstone Paper no. 26. Northern Rhodesia: Rhodes-Livingstone Institute.

2b/3a/4a/5d,f/7/12/15 Zambia

1542 ———. 1960. *Tribalism and the Plural Society: An Inaugural Lecture.* London: Oxford University Press.

2c/3e/4a/5e,f,i/10/12 Africa

1543 ———. 1970. "Race, Class, and Status in South Central Africa." In *Social Stratification in Africa,* edited by Arthur Tuden and Leonard Plotnicov, pp. 303-43. New York: Free Press.

2c/3e/4a/5i/8/9/10 Malawi; Zambia; Zimbabwe

1544 ———. 1970. "Tribe and Social Change in South Central Africa: A Situational Approach." In *The Passing of Tribal Man in Africa,* edited by P. C. W. Gutkind, pp. 83-101. Leiden: E. J. Brill.

2b/3b/4a/5h/8/9/10/11/12/15 Zambia

1545 ——— and A. L. Epstein. 1959. "Occupational Prestige and Social Status among Urban Africans in Northern Rhodesia." *Africa* 22:22-39.

2d/3a/4a/5i/8/9 Zambia

1546 MITTELMAN, James H. and Onker S. Marwah. 1974. *Asian Alien Pariahs: A Cross-Regional Perspective.* Center on International Race Relations, Graduate School of International Studies, University of Denver, Studies in Race and Nations, vol. 6, study no. 1.

2c/3d/4h/5g,i/7/8/9/10 East Africa; Southeast Asia

1547 MIYAMOTO, S. Frank. 1939. *Social Solidarity among the Japanese in Seattle.* Seattle: University of Washington Press.

2b/3a/4h/5d/8/9/12/14/15   US: Japanese

1548   ——. 1973. "The Forced Evacuation of the Japanese Minority During World War II." *Journal of Social Issues* 29:11-31.

2c/3a/4d/5k/9/10/11   US: Japanese

1549   MOERMAN, Michael. 1968. "Being Lue: Uses and Abuses of Ethnic Identification." In *Essays on the Problem of Tribe.* Proceedings of the 1967 Annual Spring Meeting of the American Ethnological Society, edited by June Helm, pp. 153-69. Seattle: University of Washington Press.

2b/3a/4a/5d,h/6/9/10/12/14   Thailand

1550   MOGULL, Robert G. 1972. "Discrimination in the Labor Market." *Journal of Black Studies* 3:237-49.

2d/3a/4i/5g,i/8/9   US: Afro-Americans

1551   MOLINA, Jose M. 1978. "Cultural Barriers and Interethnic Communication in a Multiethnic Neighborhood." In *Interethnic Communication.* Southern Anthropological Society Proceedings, no. 12, edited by E. Lamar Ross, pp. 78-86. Athens: University of Georgia Press.

2f/3e/4i(Community Organizer)/5f/10/12   Theory

1552   MOLNAR, Thomas. 1970. "Malaysia: Observations in a Bi-Racial Society." *Plural Societies* 1:41-52.

2c/3b/4h/5i/8/9   Malaysia

1553   MOLOHON, Kathryn T., Richard Paton, and Michael Lambert. 1979. "An Extension of Barth's Concept of Ethnic Boundaries to Include Both Other Groups and Developmental Stages of Ethnic Groups." *Human Relations* 32:1-17.

2e/3e/4a/5c,k   Theory

1554   MONTELL, Lynwood. 1972. "The Coe Ridge Colony: A Racial Island Disappears." *American Anthropologist* 74:710-19.

2b/3a/4a/5a/9   US: Mestizos

1555   MONTENEGRO, Marilyn. 1976. *Chicanos and Mexican-Americans: Ethnic Self-Identification and Attitudinal Differences.* San Francisco: R & E Research Associates.

2b/3a/4g/5d/9/11/12   US: Mexican Americans

1556   MONTIEL, Miguel, ed. 1978. *Hispanic Families: Critical Issues for Policy and Programs in Human Services.* Washington, D. C.: National Coalition of Hispanic Mental Health and Human Services Organizations.

1a/2b,c,d/3a/4i(Social Work)/5a,d,k/14   US: Latin Americans

1557   MOORE, Joan. 1970. "Colonialism: The Case of the Mexican Americans." *Social Problems* 17:463-72.

2c/3a/4h/5f,j/9/11   US: Mexican Americans

1558   MOORE, Robert. 1972. "Race Relations in the Six Counties: Colonialism, Industrialization, and Stratification in Ireland." *Race* 14:21-42.

2c/3a/4h/5i,j/8/9/10   N. Ireland

1559   MOQUIN, Wayne and Charles van Doren, eds. 1971. *A Documentary History of the Mexican Americans.* New York: Praeger.

2c/3a/4d/5k   US: Mexican Americans

1560   MORALES, Armando. 1972. *Ando Sangrando: A Study of Mexican-American Police Conflict.* Fair Lawn, N. J.: R. E. Burdick.

2b,c/3a/4h/5b/9/10   US: Mexican Americans

1561   MORALES, Royal R. 1974. *Makibaka: The Filipino American Struggle.* Los Angeles: Mountainview.

2c/3e/4i/5b,d,e/10   US: Filipinos

1562   MORF, Gustav. 1976. "Ethnic Groups and Developmental Models: The Case of Quebec." In *Ethnicity in an International Context,* edited by Abdul Said and Luiz R. Simmons, pp. 76-91. New Brunswick, N.J.: Transaction Books.

2c/3a/4f/5b,i/9/10   Canada: Québécois

1563   MORGAN, Kenneth O. 1971. "Welsh Nationalism: The Historical Background." *Journal of Contemporary History* 6:153-72.

2c/3b/4d/5e/10/13/16   Wales

1564   MORGAN, Ted. 1978. *On Becoming American.* Boston: Houghton Mifflin.

2b/3b/4i/5a/9/10/11/12   US: General

1565 MORGAN, W. J., ed. 1973. *The Welsh Dilemma: Some Essays on Nationalism in Wales.* Llandybie, Carmarthenshire, Wales: Christopher Davies.

1a/2c/3b/4d,i/5e/8/9/10/11/16/17   Wales

1566 MÖRNER, Magnus. 1970. "Historical Research on Race Relations in Latin America During the National Period." In *Race and Class in Latin America,* edited by Magnus Mörner, pp. 199-230. New York: Columbia University Press.

2c,e/3e/4d/5k/7/8/9/10/11   Mesoamerica; South America

1567 ——. 1978. "Immigration from the Mid-Nineteenth Century Onwards: A New Latin America." *Cultures* 5:56-75.

2c/3b/4d/5k/7   Mesoamerica; South America

1568 MORRILL, Warren T. 1977. "French Peasants in the Caribbean: St. Barthélemy." In *Ethnic Encounters: Identities and Contexts,* edited by George L. Hicks and Philip E. Leis, pp. 137-51. North Scituate, Mass.: Duxbury Press.

2b/3a/4a/5d/12/14/16   St. Barthélemy

1569 MORRIS, H. S. 1956. "Indians in East Africa: A Study in Plural Society." *British Journal of Sociology* 7:194-241.

2b/3e/4h/5f,i/8/9/11   East Africa

1570 ——. 1957. "The Plural Society." *Man* 57:124-25.

2e/3e/4a/5 f,i   Theory

1571 ——. 1966. Review of M. G. Smith, *The Plural Society in the British West Indies. Man,* n.s., 1:270-72.

2e/3e/4a/5 f,i   Theory

1572 ——. 1967. "Some Aspects of the Concept Plural Society." *Man,* n.s., 2:169-84.

2e/3e/4a/5f,i   Theory

1573 MORSE, Stanley J. 1976. "National Identity from a Social Psychological

Perspective: Two Brazilian Case Studies." *Canadian Review of Studies in Nationalism* 4:52-76.

2d/3a/4g/5d/12   Brazil

1574   ——. 1977. "Being a Canadian: Aspects of National Identity among a Sample of University Students in Saskatchewan." *Canadian Journal of Behavioral Science* 9:265-73.

2d/3a/4g/5d,e/12   Canada: General

1575   ——, J. W. Mann, and Elizabeth Nel. 1977. "National Identity in a 'Multi-Nation' State: A Comparison of Afrikaners and English Speaking South Africans." *Canadian Review of Studies in Nationalism* 4:225-46.

2d/3c/4f,g/5d,e/11/12   South Africa

1576   —— and Stanton Peele. 1974. " 'Coloured Power' or 'Coloured Bourgeoisie'? Political Attitudes among South African Coloureds." *Public Opinion Quarterly* 38:317-34.

2d/3b/4f,g/5i,k/9/11   South Africa

1577   MOWLANA, Hamid and Ann Elizabeth Robinson. 1976. "Ethnic Mobilization and Communication Theory." In *Ethnicity in an International Context,* edited by Abdul Said and Luiz R. Simmons, pp. 48-63. New Brunswick, N. J.: Transaction Books.

2c/3e/4f/5d,e/10   Theory

1578   MOYNIHAN, Daniel Patrick. 1979. "Patterns of Ethnic Succession: Blacks and Hispanics in New York City." *Political Science Quarterly* 94:1-14.

2c/3c/4f/5a/6/8/13   US: Afro-Americans; Puerto Ricans

1579   MUKHERJEE, R. 1973. "Diagnosing Processes of Nation-Building: An Overall Perspective and an Analysis of Development on the Indian Subcontinent." In *Building States and Nations: Analyses by Region,* vol. 2, edited by S. N. Eisenstadt and Stein Rokkan, pp. 266-300. Beverly Hills, Calif.: Sage.

2c/3b/4h/5e/10/12   India

1580   MULLARD, Chris. 1975. *On Being Black in Britain.* Washington, D.C.: Inscape.

2b/3b/4i/5d,h,i/9/10/11   Britain: Africans, West Indians

1581   MUNOZ, Alfred N. 1971. *The Filipinos in America.* Los Angeles: Mountainview.

2c/3a/4d/5d,g/7/9/11   US: Filipinos

1582   MURADOV, Gulam. 1974. "The USSR Experience in Solving the National Question and the Liberated Countries of the East." *Asian Survey* 14:289-306.

2c/3b/4d/5k/10   USSR: General

1583   MURAT, Aman Berdi. 1975. "Turkmenistan and the Turkmen." In *Handbook of Major Soviet Nationalities,* edited by Zev Katz, Rosemarie Rogers, and Frederic Harned, pp. 262-82. New York: Free Press.

2c/3a/4i/5k/6/8/10/11/13/16   USSR: Turkomen

1584   MURPHEE, Marshall W. 1975. "Race and Power in Rhodesia." In *Politics of Race: Comparative Studies,* edited by Donald G. Baker, pp. 245-76. Lexington, Mass.: Lexington Books.

2c/3b/4i/5i/6/9/10   Zimbabwe

1585   NACHMIAS, David and David H. Rosenbloom. 1978. "Bureaucracy and Ethnicity." *American Journal of Sociology* 83:967-74.

2d/3c/4h/5d/11/12   Israel

1586   NAG, Moni. 1968. "The Concept of Tribe in the Contemporary Context of India." In *Essays on the Problem of Tribe.* Proceedings of the 1967 Annual Spring Meeting of the American Ethnological Society, edited by June Helm, pp. 186-200. Seattle: University of Washington Press.

2c/3b/4a/5f,i/6/8/9/10/12   India

1587   NAGATA, Judith A. 1977. "Ethnic Differentiation within an Urban Muslim Mercantile Community in Malaysia." *Ethnicity* 4:380-400.

2b/3c/4a/5d,f,h/8/12   Malaysia

1588   NAGATA, Shuichi. 1971. "The Reservation Community and the Urban Community: Hopi Indians of Moenkopi." In *The American Indian in Urban Society,* edited by Jack O. Waddell and O. Michael Watson, pp. 115-59. Boston: Little, Brown.

2b/3a/4a/5k/8/9/14 US: Native Americans

1589 NAHIRNY, Vladimir C. and Joshua A. Fishman. 1965. "American Immigrant Groups: Ethnic Identification and the Problem of Generations." *Sociological Review* 13:311-26.

2c/3b/4h/5a/7 US: Euro-Americans

1590 NASH, Gary B. and Richard Weiss, eds. 1970. *The Great Fear: Race in the Mind of America.* New York: Holt, Rinehart & Winston.

2c/3b/4i/5g/9/11 US: General

1591 NASH, Manning. 1957. "The Multiple Society in Economic Development: Mexico and Guatemala." *American Anthropologist* 59:825-38.

2b/3d/4a/5c,f/8 Guatemala; Mexico

1592 ———. 1958. "Political Relations in Guatemala." *Social and Economic Studies* 7:65-75.

2a/3b/4a/5f,i/9/10 Guatemala

1593 ———. 1964. "Southeast Asian Society: Dual or Multiple." *Journal of Asian Studies* 23:417-31.

2c/3e/4a/5f,i/8/9 Southeast Asia

1594 NAVARRO, Moisés González. 1970. " 'Mestizaje' in Mexico During the National Period." In *Race and Class in Latin America,* edited by Magnus Mörner, pp. 145-69. New York: Columbia University Press.

2c/3b/4d/5a/12/14 Mexico

1595 NAYAR, Baldev Raj. 1966. *Minority Politics in the Punjab.* Princeton, N. J.: Princeton University Press.

2b,c/3a/4f/5k/6/10 India

1596 NEFZIGER, E. Wayne and William L. Richter. 1976. "Biafra and Bangladesh: The Political Economy of Secessionist Conflict." *Journal of Peace Research* 13:91-109.

2c/3d/4f/5b,e/8/9/10 Bangladesh; Nigeria

1597 NELSON, Donna. 1972. "Problems of Power in a Plural Society: Asians in Kenya." *Southwestern Journal of Anthropology* 29:255-64.

2b/3a/4a/5 i/9/10   Kenya

1598   NELSON, Sarah. 1975. "Protestant 'Ideology' Considered: The Case of 'Discrimination.'" In *The Politics of Race*. British Political Sociology Yearbook, vol. 2, edited by Ivor Crewe, pp. 155-87. New York: John Wiley & Sons.

2b/3b/4h/5g/11   N. Ireland

1599   NETTLEFORD, Rex. 1965. "National Identity and Attitudes to Race in Jamaica." *Race* 7:59-72.

2d/3b/4h/5e,g/11/12   Jamaica

1600   ——. 1972. *Identity, Race and Protest in Jamaica*. New York: William Morrow.

2b/3b/4h/5b,d,e/9/11   Jamaica

1601   NEUMAN, Brigitte, Richard Mezoff, and Anthony Richmond. 1973. *Immigrant Integration and Urban Renewal in Toronto*. Publications of the Research for European Migration Problems, no. 18. The Hague: Martinus Nijhoff.

2d/3a/4h/5k/6/8/14/15/17   Canada: General

1602   NEUMAN, Stephanie G. 1976. "Integration: Conceptual Tool or Academic Jargon?" In *Small States and Segmented Societies: National Political Integration in a Global Environment,* edited by Stephanie G. Neuman, pp. 1-43. New York: Praeger.

2e/3e/4f/5k/10   Theory

1603   NEWBURY, M. Catherine. 1978. "Ethnicity in Rwanda: The Case of Kinyaga." *Africa* 48:17-29.

2b/3a/4a/5 i/9/10   Rwanda

1604   NEWMAN, Dorothy K., Nancy J. Amidei, Barbara L. Carter, Dawn Day, William J. Kruvant, and Jack S. Russell. 1978. *Protest, Politics, and Prosperity: Black Americans and White Institutions, 1940-1975*. New York: Pantheon Books.

2c/3b/4b,d,f,i/5b,i,j/8/9/10/13   US: Afro-Americans

1605 NEWMAN, James L. 1978. "Place and Ethnicity among the Sandawe of Tanzania." In *Ethnicity in Modern Africa,* edited by Brian M. Du Toit, pp. 105-21. Boulder, Colo.: Westview Press.

2b/3a/4a/5d/6/12   Tanzania

1606 NEWMAN, William M. 1972. *American Pluralism: A Study of Minority Groups and Social Theory.* New York: Harper & Row.

2e/3e/4h/5a,f,g,i,j   Theory

1607 NG, Wing-Cheung. 1977. "An Evaluation of the Labor Market Status of Chinese Americans." *Amerasia Journal* 4:101-22.

2c/3a/4b/5i/8   US: Chinese

1608 NICHOLLS, David. 1974. *Three Varieties of Pluralism.* New York: St. Martin's Press.

2e/3e/4i/5f,i   Theory

1609 NICHOLS, Roger L. and George R. Adams, eds. 1971. *The American Indian: Past and Present.* New York: John Wiley & Sons.

1a/2c/3a/4a,d,f,h,i(Philosophy)
5b,i/8/9/10/12/17   US: Native Americans

1610 NIE, Norman H., Barbara Currie, and Andrew M. Greeley. 1974. "Political Attitudes among American Ethnics: A Study of Perceptual Distortion." *Ethnicity* 1:317-43.

2d/3c/4g,h/5g,k/10/12   US: Euro-Americans

1611 NNOLI, Okwudiba. 1974. "Socio-Economic Insecurity and Ethnic Politics in Africa." *African Review* 4:1-24.

2c/3e/4f/5b,i/8/9   Africa

1612 NOBLE, Lela Garner. 1975. "Ethnicity and Philippine-Malaysian Relations." *Asian Survey* 15:453-72.

2c/3d/4f/5b,d/10/12   Malaysia; Philippines

1613 ——. 1976. "Ethnicity and Philippine-Malaysian Relations." In *Small States and Segmented Societies: National Political Integration in a Global Environment,* edited by Stephanie G. Neuman, pp. 172-97. New York: Praeger.

2c/3d/4f/5k/10   Malaysia; Philippines

1614   NOEL, Donald T. 1968. "A Theory of the Origin of Ethnic Stratification." *Social Problems* 16:157-71.

       2c/3e/4h/5i/9   Theory

1615   NOGALES, Luis G. 1971. *The Mexican American: A Selected and Annotated Bibliography.* 2d ed. Stanford, Calif.: Stanford University.

       2a   US: Mexican Americans

1616   NORDLINGER, Eric A. 1972. *Conflict Regulation in Divided Societies.* Cambridge, Mass.: Center for International Affairs, Harvard University.

       2e/3e/4f/5b/9/10   Theory

1617   NORRIS, Katrin. 1962. *Jamaica: The Search for Identity.* London: Institute for Race Relations.

       2c/3b/4h/5d,e/11/12   Jamaica

1618   NORTHRUP, Herbert R., et al. 1970. *Negro Employment in Basic Industry: A Study of Racial Policies in Six Industries.* Philadelphia: Industrial Research Unit, Wharton School of Finance and Commerce, University of Pennsylvania.

       2b,c/3b/4b/5b,i/8/10   US: Afro-Americans

1619   NOVAK, Michael. 1971. *The Rise of the Unmeltable Ethnics: Politics and Culture in the Seventies.* New York: Macmillan.

       2c/3b/4h/5d/10/11/12   US: Euro-Americans

1620   ———. 1977. "Cultural Pluralism for Individuals: A Social Vision." In *Pluralism in a Democratic Society,* edited by Melvin Tumin and Walter Plotch, pp. 25-57. New York: Praeger.

       2e/3a/4h/5d,e/8/9/11   US: General

1621   NUGENT, Neill and Roger King. 1979. "Ethnic Minorities, Scapegoating, and the Extreme Right." In *Racism and Political Action in Britain,* edited by Robert Miles and Annie Phizacklea, pp. 28-49. London: Routledge & Kegan Paul.

       2c/3b/4h/5k/10/11   Britain: General

1622 NURGE, Ethel, ed. 1970. *The Modern Sioux: Social Systems and Reservation Culture.* Lincoln: University of Nebraska Press.

1a/2b/3a/4a,h/5d/10/12/14   US: Native Americans

1623 NUSSEY, Wilf. 1978. "The Future of Ethnicity in Southern Africa." In *Ethnicity in Modern Africa,* edited by Brian M. Du Toit, pp. 281-301. Boulder, Colo.: Westview Press.

2c/3e/4i/5k/9/10/12   Namibia; South Africa; Zimbabwe

1624 NYBLOM, Gosta, ed. 1948. *Americans of Swedish Descent: How They Live and Work.* Rock Island, Ill.: G. Nyblom.

2b/3a/4i/5k/8/12/13/14/15/17   US: Swedes

1625 OAKS, Priscilla. 1975. *Minority Studies: A Selected Annotated Bibliography.* Boston: G. K. Hall.

2a/6/7/9/10/13   US: Afro-, Asian-, Mexican-, Native Americans

1626 O'BALLANCE, Edgar. 1973. *The Kurdish Revolt: 1961-1970.* Hamden, Conn.: Archon Books.

2b,c/3a/4d/5b,e/10   Iran; Iraq; Turkey

1627 ———. 1977. *The Secret War in the Sudan: 1955-1972.* London: Faber & Faber.

2b,c/3b/4d/5b,e/10/11   Sudan

1628 OBATALA, J. K. 1976. "Black Consciousness and American Policy in Africa." In *Ethnicity in an International Context,* edited by Abdul Said and Luiz R. Simmons, pp. 64-75. New Brunswick, N.J.: Transaction Books.

2c/3b/4f/5k/10   US: Afro-Americans

1629 O'BRIEN, Rita Cruse. 1975. "Lebanese Entrepreneurs in Senegal: Economic Integration and the Politics of Protection." *Cahiers d'Etudes Africaines* 15:95-115.

2b/3a/4d/5k/8/10   Senegal

1630 OCHOA, Jorge A. Flores. 1974. "Mistis and Indians: Their Relations in a Micro-Region of Cuzco." *International Journal of Comparative Sociology* 15:182-92.

2b/3a/4a/5f,i/8/9/10   Peru

1631   O'CONNOR, Richard. 1968. *The German-Americans: An Informal History.* Boston: Little, Brown.

2c/3a/4d/5k/7/8/10/16/17   US: Germans

1632   OFFICER, James E. 1971. "The American Indian and Federal Policy." In *The American Indian in Urban Society,* edited by Jack O. Waddell and O. Michael Watson, pp. 9-65. Boston: Little, Brown.

2c/3a/4a/5i/9/10   US: Native Americans

1633   OGAWA, Dennis M. 1971. *From Japs to Japanese: The Evolution of Japanese-American Sterotypes.* Berkeley: McCutchan.

2b,c/3a/4g/5g/11   US: Japanese

1634   O'GRADY, Joseph P. 1973. *How the Irish Became Americans.* New York: Twayne.

2c/3a/4d/5a/8/10   US: Irish

1635   OJIAKU, Mazi Okoro. 1972. "European Tribalism and African Tribalism." *Civilisations* 22:387-403.

2c/3e/4f/5d,e/11/12   Theory

1636   O'KANE, James M. 1969. "Ethnic Mobility and the Lower Income Negro: A Socio-Historical Perspective." *Social Problems* 16:302-11.

2c/3a/4d/5i/8/9   US: Afro-Americans

1637   ——. 1975. "The Ethnic Factor in American Urban Civil Disorders." *Ethnicity* 2:230-43.

2c/3b/4h/5b/10   US: General

1638   OKELY, Judith. 1979. "Trading Stereotypes: The Case of English Gypsies." In *Ethnicity at Work,* edited by Sandra Wallman, pp. 17-34. London: Macmillan.

2b/3a/4a/5d/8/12   Britain: Gypsies

1639   OKPU, Ugbana. 1977. *Ethnic Minority Problems in Nigerian Politics: 1960-65.* Acta Universitatis Upsaliensis, Studia Historica Upsaliennsa, no. 88. Uppsala, Sweden: Academiae Upsaliensis.

2b,c/3b/4d,f/5b,e,i/8/9/10 Nigeria

1640 OLIVIER, M. J. 1971. "Ethnic Relations in South West Africa." *Plural Societies* 2:31-47.

2c/3b/4h/5i/9/10/11 Namibia

1641 OLSTED, R. and C. Wallenberg, eds. 1971. *Neither Separate nor Equal.* San Francisco: California Historical Society.

1a/2c/3a/4d/5g,i/8/9/11/13 US: General

1642 O'MALLEY, Patrick. 1973. "The Amplification of Maori Crime: Cultural and Economic Barriers to Equal Justice in New Zealand." *Race* 15: 47-58.

2b/3b/4a/5g/11 New Zealand

1643 ONWUKU, Chukwuemeka. 1975. "Ethnic Identity, Political Integration, and National Development: The Igbo Diaspora in Nigeria." *Journal of Modern African Studies* 13:399-413.

2b/3b/4h/5e/7/10/12 Nigeria

1644 OPELLO, Walter, Jr. 1975. "The Formation of Social Systems: The Frelimo Case." *Canadian Review of Studies in Nationalism* 2:297-316.

2c/3b/4f/5b/10 Mozambique

1645 OPLER, Marvin K. 1955. "The Influence of Ethnic and Class Subcultures on Child Care." *Social Problems* 3:12-20.

2c/3e/4a/5k/9/14 US: General

1646 OPPENHEIMER, Jonathan. 1977. "Culture and Politics in a Druze Community." *Ethnic Groups* 1:221-40.

2c/3a/4a/5d/10/12 Israel

1647 O'REILLY, F. D. 1977. "Ethnic Minorities in Thailand." *Plural Societies* 8:67-78.

2b/3b/4f/5f,i/7/10/11 Thailand

1648   ORNSTEIN, Jacob. 1968. "Soviet Language Policy: Continuity and Change." In *Ethnic Minorities in the Soviet Union,* edited by Erich Goldhagen, pp. 121-46. New York: Frederick A. Praeger.

2c/3b/4f/5k/13/16   USSR: General

1649   ——. 1978. "'Relational Bilingualism'—A New Approach to Linguistic-Cultural Diversity and a Mexican-American Case Study." *Ethnicity* 5:148-66.

2d/3a/4e/5k/16   US: Mexican Americans

1650   ORNSTEIN, Michael D., H. Michael Stevenson, and A. Paul M. Williams. 1978. "Public Opinion and the Canadian Political Crisis." *Canadian Review of Sociology and Anthropology* 15:158-205.

2d/3b/4h/5e/10/11/13/16   Canada: General

1651   OSTERMAN, Paul. 1975. "An Empirical Study of Labor Market Segmentation." *Industrial and Labor Relations Review* 28:508-21.

2d/3b/4b/5i/8/9   US: Afro-Americans

1652   OTITE, Onigu. 1975. "Resource Competition and Inter-Ethnic Relations in Nigeria." In *Ethnicity and Resource Competition in Plural Societies,* edited by Leo A. Despres, pp. 119-30. The Hague: Mouton.

2b/3b/4a/5b,d/6/9/12/14   Nigeria

1653   OWEN, Nancy H. 1975. "Land, Politics, and Ethnicity in a Carib Indian Community." *Ethnology* 14:385-93.

2b/3a/4a/5b/10/12   Caribbean

1654   PACHAI, Bridglal. 1978. "South African Indians and Economic Hostility." In *Ethnicity in Modern Africa,* edited by Brian M. Du Toit, pp. 271-80. Boulder, Colo.: Westview Press.

2c/3a/4a/5b/8/10   South Africa

1655   PADILLA, Elena. 1977. "Concepts of Work and Situational Demands on New York City Puerto Ricans." In *American Minorities and Economic Opportunity,* edited by H. Roy Kaplan, pp. 148-69. Itasca, Ill.: F. E. Peacock.

2c/3a/4i/5k/7/8/9/10   US: Puerto Ricans

1656   PAINE, Robert, ed. 1977. *The White Arctic: Anthropological Essays on Tutelage and Ethnicity.* Newfoundland Social and Economic Papers, no. 7. St. John: Memorial University of Newfoundland Institute of Social and Economic Research.

   1a/2b,c/3a/4a/5a,d,g,j/6/7/8/9
   10/11/12/13/14/15   Canada: Native Canadians

1657   PALLONI, Alberto. 1979. "Internal Colonialism or Clientelistic Politics? The Case of Southern Italy." *Ethnic and Racial Studies* 2:360-77.

   2c/3a/4f/5a,j/10   Italy

1658   PALMER, Ransford W. 1974. "A Decade of West Indian Migration to the United States, 1962-1972: An Economic Analysis." *Social and Economic Studies* 23:571-87.

   2c/3b/4b/5k/7/8   US: West Indians

1659   PALMER, Robin. 1977. "The Italians: Patterns of Migration to London." In *Between Two Cultures: Migrants and Minorities in Britain,* edited by James L. Watson, pp. 242-68. Oxford: Basil Blackwell.

   2c/3a/4a/5k/7   Britain: Italians

1660   PAREDES, Americo. 1963. "Texas' Third Man: The Texas-Mexican." *Race* 4:49-58.

   2b/3a/4i/5g,i/9/10   US: Mexican Americans

1661   PAREDES, J. Anthony. 1974. "The Emergence of Contemporary Eastern Creek Indian Identity." In *Social and Cultural Identity: Problems of Persistence and Change.* Southern Anthropological Society Proceedings, no. 8, edited by Thomas K. Fitzgerald, pp. 63-81. Athens: University of Georgia Press.

   2b,c/3a/4a/5d/10/12   US: Native Americans

1662   PARENTI, Michael John. 1975. *Ethnic and Racial Attitudes: A Depth Study of Italian Americans.* New York: Arno Press.

   2d/3a/4f/5d,k/10/11   US: Italians

1663   PARKIN, Andrew. 1977. "Ethnic Politics: A Comparative Study of Two Immigrant Societies, Australia and the United States." *Journal of Commonwealth and Comparative Politics* 15:22-38.

2e/3d/4f/5a/10   Australia; US: General

1664 PARKIN, David. 1974. "Congregational and Interpersonal Ideologies in Political Ethnicity." In *Urban Ethnicity*, edited by Abner Cohen, pp. 119-57. London: Tavistock.

2b/3c/4a/5b/8/10/12   Kenya; Nigeria

1665 PARMING, Tonu. 1977. "Roots of Nationality Differences." In *Nationality Group Survival in Multi-Ethnic States: Shifting Support Patterns in the Soviet Baltic Region,* edited by Edward Allworth, pp. 24-57. New York: Praeger.

2c/3c/4h/5d/6/12   USSR: General

1666 PARSONS, Talcott, 1975. "Some Theoretical Considerations on the Nature and Trends of Change of Ethnicity." In *Ethnicity: Theory and Experience,* edited by Nathan Glazer and Daniel Patrick Moynihan, pp. 53-83. Cambridge, Mass.: Harvard University Press.

2e/3e/4h/5d/12   Theory

1667 PAŠIĆ, NAJDAN. 1971. "Factors in the Formation of Nations in the Balkans and among the South Slavs." *International Social Science Journal* 23:399-420.

2c/3e/4f/5e/9/10/16   Yugoslavia

1668 ———. 1973. "Federalism and Relations between Nationalities and National Groups in Yugoslavia's Contemporary Period." *Journal of Constitutional and Parliamentary Studies* 7:1-17.

2b/3b/4f/5f/10   Yugoslavia

1669 ———. 1973. "Varieties of Nation-Building in the Balkans and among the Southern Slavs." In *Building States and Nations: Analyses by Regions,* vol. 2, edited by S. N. Eisenstadt and Stein Rokkan, pp. 117-41. Beverly Hills, Calif.: Sage.

2c/3e/4f/5e/10   Yugoslavia

1670 PATAI, Raphael. 1953. *Israel between East and West: A Study in Human Relations.* Philadelphia: Jewish Publication Society of America.

2c/3b/4i/5f,g,i/7/11   Israel

1671 PATEL, Hasu H. 1973. *Indians in Uganda and Rhodesia—Some Comparative Perspectives on a Minority in Africa.* Center on International Race Relations, Graduate School of International Studies, University of Denver, Studies in Race and Nations, vol. 5, study no. 1.

2c/3d/4f/5i/8/9/11   Uganda; Zimbabwe

1672 PATEL, Narsi. 1974. "Sociology of Indian Minorities in the Third World." *International Review of Modern Sociology* 4:19-34.

2c/3e/4h/5f,i/7/9/14/17   General

1673 PATTERSON, E. Palmer, II. 1975. "Indian-White Relations." In *Politics of Race: Comparative Studies,* edited by Donald G. Baker, pp. 121-41. Lexington Mass.: Lexington Books.

2c/3b/4d/5g,i/9/10   Canada: Euro-, Native Canadians

1674 PATTERSON, Orlando. 1968. "West Indian Migrants Returning Home." *Race* 10:69-78.

2b/3e/4i/5k/7   Jamaica

1675 ——. 1975. "Context and Choice in Ethnic Allegiance: A Theoretical Framework and Caribbean Case Study." In *Ethnicity: Theory and Experience,* edited by Nathan Glazer and Daniel Patrick Moynihan, pp. 305-49. Cambridge, Mass.: Harvard University Press.

2b,c/3d,e/4h/5h/9/10/12   Guyana; Jamaica

1676 PATTERSON, Sheila. 1977. "The Poles: An Exile Community in Britain." In *Between Two Cultures: Migrants and Minorities in Britain,* edited by James L. Watson, pp. 214-41. Oxford: Basil Blackwell.

2c/3a/4a/5k/6/7/8/10/13/14/15/17   Britain: Poles

1677 PAVLAK, Thomas J. 1976. *Ethnic Identification and Political Behavior.* San Francisco: R & E Research Associates.

2d/3b/4h/5g/10   US: General

1678 ——. 1977. "'White Ethnic Racism' Revisited: A Comparison of Racial Attitudes among Five Nationality Groups." *International Review of History and Political Science* 14:55-70.

US: Czechoslavaks, Irish, Lithuanians,

2d/3b/4f/5g/11   Mexican Americans, Poles

1679 PAYNE, Stanley G. 1971. "Catalan and Basque Nationalism." *Journal of Contemporary History* 6:15-51.

2b/3b/4d/5e/10   Spain

1680 ——. 1975. *Basque Nationalism*. Reno: University of Nevada Press.

2c/3a/4d/5e/10/11   Spain

1681 PEACH, Ceri. 1965. "West Indian Migration to Britain: The Economic Factors." *Race* 7:31-46.

2b/3a/4h/5k/7/8   Britain: West Indians

1682 ——. 1968. *West Indian Migration to Britain: A Social Geography*. London: Oxford University Press.

2c/3b/4c,h/5k/7/10   Britain: West Indians

1683 PEARSON, David G. 1978. "Race, Religiosity and Political Activism: Some Observations on West Indian Participation in Britain." *British Journal of Sociology* 29:340-57.

2d/3a/4h/5k/10/12/17   Britain: West Indians

1684 PEELE, Stanton and Stanley J. Morse. 1974. "Ethnic Voting and Political Change in South Africa." *American Political Science Review* 68:1520-41.

2d/3b/4f/5k/10   South Africa

1685 PEHOTSKY, Bessie Olga. 1970. *The Slavic Immigrant Woman*. Reprint, 1925 ed. San Francisco: R & E Research Associates.

2c/3a/4d/5k/7/14   US: Slavs

1686 PEIL, Margaret. 1974. "Ghana's Aliens." *International Migration Review* 8:367-82.

2b/3b/4a/5i/8/10   Ghana

1687 ——. 1975. "Interethnic Contacts in Nigerian Cities." *Africa* 45:107-22.

2d/3a/4a/5h/9/12/14   Nigeria

1688   PELISI, Bartolemes J. 1966. "Ethnic Patterns of Friendship." *Phylon*
       27:217-25.

       2b/3b/4h/5d/15   US: General

1689   PENDLETON, Wade C. 1978. "Urban Ethnicity in Windhoek." In *Ethnicity in Modern Africa*, edited by Brian M. Du Toit, pp. 125-42. Boulder,
       Colo.: Westview Press.

       2b/3a/4a/5d,i/6/8/10/12/13/14/15/17   Namibia

1690   PENG, Fred C. C., Robert Ricketts, and Nario Imamura. 1974. "The
       Socioeconomic Status of the Ainu: The Past in the Present." *American
       Ethnologist* 1:731-50.

       2b/3a/4a/5i/8/9/10/11   Japan

1691   PENNAR, Jaan. 1968. "Nationalism in the Soviet Baltics." In *Ethnic
       Minorities in the Soviet Union*, edited by Erich Goldhagen, pp. 198-217.
       New York: Frederick A. Praeger.

                                                         USSR: Estonians,
       2c/3a/4f/5e/6/10   Latvians, Lithuanians

1692   PERES, Yochanan. 1971. "Ethnic Relations in Israel." *American Journal
       of Sociology* 76:1021-47.

       2b/3b/4h/5f/9/11/12/13   Israel

1693   —— and Zepporah Levy. 1969. "Jews and Arabs: Ethnic Group Stereotypes in Israel." *Race* 10:479-92.

       2d/3c/4g/5g/11   Israel

1694   —— and Ruth Schrift. 1978. "Intermarriage and Interethnic Relations:
       A Comparative Study." *Ethnic and Racial Studies* 1:428-52.

       2d/3d/4h/5d,g/11/14   Israel; South Africa; US: General

1695   PERLO, Victor. 1975. *Economics of Racism U.S.A.: Roots of Black Inequality*. New York: International Publishers.

       2c/3b/4b/5b,i/8/9   US: Afro-Americans

1696   PETERSEN, William. 1971. *Japanese Americans: Oppression and Success*. New York: Random House.

2c/3a/4d/5a,g,i/9/10/11   US: Japanese

1697 ——. 1975. "On the Subnations of Western Europe." In *Ethnicity: Theory and Experience,* edited by Nathan Glazer and Daniel Patrick Moynihan, pp. 177-208. Cambridge, Mass.: Harvard University Press.

2b,c/3d/4h/5f/10/12/16   Belgium; Switzerland

1698 ——. 1976. "A Comparison of a Racial and a Language Subnation: American Negroes and Flemish." *Ethnicity* 3:145-73.

2c/3c,d/4h/5i/9/10/12/16   Belgium; US: Afro-Americans

1699 PHILIP, Alan Butt. 1975. *The Welsh Question: Nationalism in Welsh Politics 1945-1970.* Cardiff: University of Wales Press.

2c/3b/4f/5e/10/11   Wales

1700 PHILPOTT, Stuart B. 1977. "The Montserratians: Migration Dependency and the Maintenance of Island Ties with England." In *Between Two Cultures: Migrants and Minorities in Britain,* edited by James L. Watson, pp. 90-119. Oxford: Basil Blackwell.

2c/3a/4a/5k/7/8/9/10/14/15/17   Britain: Montserratians

1701 PHIZACKLEA, Anne-Marie. 1975. "A Sense of Political Efficacy: A Comparison of Black and White Adolescents." In *The Politics of Race,* edited by Ivor Crewe, pp. 123-54. British Political Sociology Yearbook. New York: John Wiley & Sons.

2d/3c/4f,g/5d,g/11   Britain: English, West Indians

1702 PHIZACKLEA, Annie and Robert Miles. 1979. "Working-Class Racist Beliefs in the Inner City." In *Racism and Political Action in Britain,* edited by Robert Miles and Annie Phizacklea, pp. 93-123. London: Routledge & Kegan Paul.

2d/3a/4h/5g,i/9/11   Britain: English

1703 PIENKOS, Donald E. 1974. "Foreign Affairs Perceptions of Ethnics: The Polish-Americans of Milwaukee." *Ethnicity* 1:223-35.

2d/3a/4h/5d,k/11   US: Poles

1704 ——. 1977. "Ethnic Orientation among Polish Americans." *International Migration Review* 11:350-62.

2d/3a/4h/5d/7/15   US: Poles

1705 PIERSON, James C. 1977. "Aboriginality in Adelaide: An Urban Context of Australian Aboriginal Ethnicity." *Urban Anthropology* 6: 307-28.

2b/3a/4a/5d/8/9/11   Australia

1706 PILL, Roisin. 1974. "Social Implications of a Bilingual Policy, with Particular Reference to Wales." *British Journal of Sociology* 25:94-107.

2c/3b/4f,h/5g/8/16   Wales

1707 PINEO, Peter C. 1977. "The Social Standing of Ethnic and Racial Groupings." *Canadian Review of Sociology and Anthropology* 14:147-57.

2d/3b/4h/5i/9/11   Canada: General

1708 PINKNEY, Alphonso. 1976. *Red, Black, and Green: Black Nationalism in the United States.* Cambridge: At the University Press.

2c/3a/4d/5b,e/10/12/13   US: Afro-Americans

1709 PIORE, Michael J. 1975. "Notes for a Theory of Labor Market Segmentation." In *Labor Market Segmentation,* edited by Richard C. Edwards, Michael Reich, and David M. Gordon, pp. 125-50. Lexington, Mass.: D.C. Heath.

2e/3e/4b,h/5i/8/9   Theory

1710 PIPES, Richard. 1975. "Reflections on the Nationality Problems in the Soviet Union." In *Ethnicity: Theory and Experience,* edited by Nathan Glazer and Daniel Patrick Moynihan, pp. 453-65. Cambridge, Mass.: Harvard University Press.

2c/3b/4d/5k/10/11/16   USSR: General

1711 PISANI, Andre du. 1977. "Reflections on the Role of Ethnicity in the Politics of Namibia." *Plural Societies* 8:79-95.

2b/3b/4f/5b/10   Namibia

1712 PITTOCK, A. Barrie. 1975. "Politics and Race in Australia." In *Politics of Race: Comparative Studies,* edited by Donald G. Baker, pp. 163-90. Lexington, Mass.: Lexington Books.

2c/3b/4i/5a,i/6/10   Australia

1713 PITT-RIVERS, Julian. 1969. "Mestizos or Ladinos?" *Race* 10:463-78.

2b/3e/4a/5d/9/12   Mesoamerica; South America

1714 PITTS, James P. 1974. "The Study of Race Consciousness: Comments on New Directions." *American Journal of Sociology* 80:664-87.

2c/3e/4g,h/5d,g,h/10/11   Theory

1715 PLAX, Martin. 1972. "On Studying Ethnicity." *Public Opinion Quarterly* 36:99-104.

2d/3b/4h/5d/12   US: General

1716 ——. 1976. "Towards a Redefinition of Ethnic Politics." *Ethnicity* 3:19-33.

2e/3e/4h/5k/10/11   Theory

1717 PLOTNICOV, Leonard. 1967. *Strangers to the City: Urban Man in Jos, Nigeria.* Pittsburgh: University of Pittsburgh Press.

2b/3a/4a/5d/6/7/8/11/12/14/15/17   Nigeria

1718 ——. 1970. "Rural-Urban Communication in Contemporary Nigeria: The Persistence of Traditional Social Institutions." In *The Passing of Tribal Man in Africa,* edited by P.C.W. Gutkind, pp. 66-82. Leiden: E.J. Brill.

2b/3b/4a/5k/6/7/8/11/12/14/15   Nigeria

1719 ——. 1972. "Who Owns Jobs? Ethnic Ideology in Nigerian Urban Politics." *Urban Anthropology* 1:1-13.

2b/3a/4a/5b,i/8/9/10/11   Nigeria

1720 —— and Myrna Silverman. 1978. "Jewish Ethnic Signalling: Social Bonding in Contemporary American Society." *Ethnology* 17:407-23.

2b/3a/4a/5h/12   US: Jews

1721 POLLIS, Adamantia. 1976. "International Factors and the Failure of Political Integration in Cyprus." In *Small States and Segmented Societies: National Political Integration in a Global Environment,* edited by Stephanie G. Neuman, pp. 44-83. New York: Praeger.

2c/3b/4f/5e/10   Cyprus

1722 POOL, Jonathan. 1972. "National Development and Language Diversity." In *Advances in the Sociology of Language,* vol. 1: *Selected Studies and Applications,* edited by Joshua A. Fishman, pp. 213-30. The Hague: Mouton.

2c/3d/4f/5f/8/16 General

1723 ———. 1978. "Soviet Language Planning: Goals, Results, Options." In *Soviet Nationality Policies and Practices,* edited by Jeremy R. Azrael, pp. 223-49. New York: Praeger.

2c/3b/4f/5a/10/13/16 USSR: General

1724 PORTER, John. 1966. *The Vertical Mosaic.* Toronto: University of Toronto Press.

2b,c/3b/4h/5f,i/9 Canada: General

1725 ———. 1975. "Ethnic Pluralism in Canadian Perspective." In *Ethnicity: Theory and Experience,* edited by Nathan Glazer and Daniel Patrick Moynihan, pp. 267-304. Cambridge, Mass.: Harvard University Press.

2c/3b/4h/5f/9/10/12 Canada: General

1726 PORTER, Judith D.R. 1971. *Black Child, White Child: The Development of Racial Attitudes.* Cambridge, Mass.: Harvard University Press.

2c/3e/4g/5g/11 Theory

1727 PORTERFIELD, Ernest. 1978. *Black and White Mixed Marriages.* Chicago: Nelson-Hall.

2c,d/3b/4h/5g,i,k/8/9/14 US: Afro-, Euro-Americans

1728 POSPIELOVSKY, D. 1974. "Nationalism as a Factor of Dissent in the Contemporary Soviet Union." *Canadian Review of Studies in Nationalism* 2:91-116.

2c/3b/4f/5e/10/11 USSR: General

1729 POSSONY, Stefan T. 1971. "Nationality and Boundary Problems in Central and East Asia." *Plural Societies* 2:3-28.

2c/3b/4f/5e/6/10/16 China (PRC)

1730 ———. 1975. "Communism and the National Question: Some Recent Developments." *Plural Societies* 6:51-68.

2c/3d/4f/5e/10/11   Eastern Europe

1731   ——. 1976. "Ethnomorphosis: Invisible Catastrophic Crime." *Plural Societies* 7:3-35.

2c/3b/4f/5a/10/11   USSR: General

1732   POTTER, George. 1960. *To the Golden Door: The Story of the Irish in Ireland and America.* Boston: Little, Brown.

2d/3a/4d/5k/7   US: Irish

1733   POTTER, Harold H. 1961. "Negroes in Canada." *Race* 3:39-56.

2c/3a/4h/5g/9/11   Canada: Afro-Canadians

1734   POWER, Paul F. 1974. "Conflict and Innovation in Ulster." In *Ethnicity and Nation-Building,* edited by Wendell Bell and Walter E. Freeman, pp. 301-14. Beverly Hills, Calif.: Sage.

2c/3b/4f/5b/10   N. Ireland

1735   PRANDY, Kenneth. 1979. "Ethnic Discrimination in Employment and Housing: Evidence from the 1966 British Census." *Ethnic and Racial Studies* 2:66-79.

2c/3b,e/4h/5g,i/8/9   Britain: General

1736   PRATT, Henry J. 1970. "Politics, Status and the Organization of Ethnic Minority Group Interests." *Polity* 3:222-46.

2b/3a/4f/5b,d,k/10/12/17   US: Euro-Americans

1737   PREMDAS, Ralph R. 1972. "Elections and Political Campaigns in a Racially Bifurcated State: The Case of Guyana." *Journal of Interamerican Studies and World Affairs* 14:271-96.

2c,d/3b/4f/5b/10   Guyana

1738   ——. 1973. "Competitive Party Organizations and Political Integration in a Racially Fragmented State: The Case of Guyana." *Caribbean Studies* 12:5-35.

2c/3b/4f/5b/10   Guyana

1739   ——. 1977. "Ethnonationalism, Copper, and Secession in Bougainville." *Canadian Review of Studies in Nationalism* 4:247-65.

2b/3a/4f/5b,e/8/10/11   Papua New Guinea

1740 PRICE, Charles A. 1963. *The Method and Statistics of Southern Euro-peans in Australia.* Canberra: Australian National University Press.

2c/3b/4h/5k/6/7/8/9/12/14   Australia

1741 PRICE, Daniel O. 1969. *Changing Characteristics of the Negro Popula-tion.* Washington, D.C.: U.S. Bureau of the Census.

2d/3b/4i(Demography)/5k/6/8/13   US: Afro-Americans

1742 PRICE, John. 1966. "A History of the Outcaste: Untouchability in Japan." In *Japan's Invisible Race: Caste in Culture and Personality,* edited by George DeVos and Hiroshi Wagatsuma, pp. 6-30. Berkeley and Los Angeles: University of California Press.

2c/3a/4a/5i/9   Japan

1743 ——. 1975. "U.S. and Canadian Indian Urban Ethnic Institutions." *Urban Anthropology* 4:35-52.

2b/3d/4a/5d/15   Canada: Native Canadians; US: Native Americans

1744 ——. 1976. "The Development of Urban Ethnic Institutions by U.S. and Canadian Indians." *Ethnic Groups* 1:107-31.

2c/3e/4a/5k/15   Canada: Native Canadians; US: Native Americans

1745 PRIMOV, George. 1974. "Aymara-Quechua Relations in Puno." *Inter-national Journal of Comparative Sociology* 15:167-81.

2b/3a/4a/5c,d/12   Peru

1746 PRINS, Jan. 1973. "Various Kinds of Nationalism in the Third World." *Plural Societies* 4:3-30.

2c/3d/4f/5e/10   Theory

1747 ——. 1977. "The Double Problem of the South Moluccan Minority." *Plural Societies* 8:3-48.

2c/3a/4d,f/5b,f/10   Indonesia

1748 PROCYK, Anna. 1973. "The Search for a Heritage and the Nationality Question in Central Asia." In *The Nationality Question in Soviet Central Asia,* edited by Edward Allworth, pp. 123-33. New York: Praeger.

2c/3a/4d/5d/12   USSR: General

1749 PRPIC, George J. 1978. *South Slav Immigration in America.* Boston: Twayne.

2c/3a/4d/5a/7   US: Yugoslavs

1750 PUNDEFF, Marin V. 1969. "Bulgarian Nationalism." In *Nationalism in Eastern Europe,* edited by Peter F. Sugar and Ivo J. Lederer, pp. 93-165. Seattle: University of Washington Press.

2c/3b/4d/5e/10/12/16/17   Bulgaria

1751 PURANIK, S.N. 1975. "The Problem of Communal Harmony in India." *Indian Political Science Review* 9:50-67.

2b/3b/4f/5b/10/17   India

1752 PURCELL, Theodore V. and Gerald F. Cavanaugh. 1972. *Blacks in the Industrial World.* New York: Free Press.

2d/3a,b/4i/5i,k/8   US: Afro-Americans

1753 PURCELL, Victor. 1948. *The Chinese in Malaya.* London: Oxford University Press.

2b,c/3a/4h/5d,f,i/8/9/10   Malaysia

1754 ——. 1962. "A Greater Malaysia? Its Possible Effects on Race Relations." *Race* 4:49-62.

2b/3b/4h/5b,g/6/8/9/10/12   Malaysia

1755 PYE, Lucian W. 1975. "China: Ethnic Minorities and National Security." In *Ethnicity: Theory and Experience,* edited by Nathan Glazer and Daniel Patrick Moynihan, pp. 489-512. Cambridge, Mass.: Harvard University Press.

2c/3b/4f/5k/10   China (PRC)

1756 QUALEY, Carlton C. 1938. *Norwegian Settlement in the United States.* Northfield, Minn.: Norwegian-American Historical Association.

2c/3a/4d/5k/6/7   US: Norwegians

1757 QUO, F.Q. 1971. "Ethnic Origin and Political Attitudes: The Case of

Orientals." *Canadian Ethnic Studies* 3:119-38.

2d/3a/4f/5k/10/11/12   Canada: Asian Canadians

1758   RABUSHKA, Alvin. 1969. "Integration in a Multi-Racial Institution: Ethnic Attitudes among Chinese and Malay Students at the University of Malaya." *Race* 11:53-64.

2d/3c/4f/5g/11/13   Malaysia

1759   ——. 1970. "The Manipulation of Ethnic Politics in Malaya." *Polity* 2:345-56.

2b/3b/4f/5b/10   Malaysia

1760   ——. 1971. "Integration in Urban Malaya: Ethnic Attitudes among Malays and Chinese." *Journal of Asian and African Studies* 6:91-107.

2d/3c/4f/5g/11   Malaysia

1761   RADECKI, Henry. 1976. "Ethnic Voluntary Organizational Dynamics in Canada: A Report." *International Journal of Comparative Sociology* 17:175-84.

2b/3c/4h/5d,f/15   Canada: General

1762   RADIN, Beryl. 1966. "Coloured Workers and British Trade Unions." *Race* 8:157-74.

2b/3a/4h/5i/8/9   Britain: General

1763   RADIN, Paul. 1935. *The Italians of San Francisco: Their Adjustment and Acculturation.* 2 pts. New York: Arno Press.

2b,c/3a/4a/5d,k/8/12/14/15/16/17   US: Italians

1764   RADLIAZOWSKI, Thaddeus. 1974. "The View from the Polish Ghetto: Some Observations on the First Hundred Years in Detroit." *Ethnicity* 1:125-50.

2c/3a/4d/5i/7/8/9   US: Poles

1765   RAGIN, Charles. 1977. "Class, Status, and 'Reactive Ethnic Cleavages': The Social Bases of Political Regionalism." *American Sociological Review* 42:438-50.

2d/3b/4h/5i/9/10   Theory

1766   RAITZ, Karl B. 1974. "Ethnic Maps of North America." *Geographical Review* 78:335-50.

       2a/3e/4c/5k/6   North America

1767   ——. 1979. "Themes in the Cultural Geography of European Ethnic Groups in the United States." *Geographical Review* 69:79-94.

       2e/3e/4c/5a/7/12/17   US: Euro-Americans

1768   RAKOWSKA-HARMSTONE, Teresa. 1974. "The Dialectics of Nationalism in the USSR." *Problems of Communism* 23:1-22.

       2c/3b/4f/5e/6/9/10/12   USSR: General

1769   ——. 1975. "Tadzhikistan and the Tadzhiks." In *Handbook of Major Soviet Nationalities,* edited by Zev Katz, Rosemarie Rogers, and Frederic Harned, pp. 315-51. New York: Free Press.

       2c/3a/4f/5k/6/8/10/11/13/16   USSR: Tadzhiks

1770   ——. 1976. "Ethnic Autonomy in the Soviet Union." In *Ethnicity in an International Context,* edited by Abdul Said and Luiz R. Simmons, pp. 150-66. New Brunswick, N.J.: Transaction Books.

       2c/3b/4f/5e/10/11   USSR: General

1771   RAMA, Carlos M. 1970. "The Passing of the Afro-Uruguayans from Caste Society into Class Society." In *Race and Class in Latin America,* edited by Magnus Mörner, pp. 28-50. New York: Columbia University Press.

       2c/3b/4h/5i/6/7/8/9   Uruguay

1772   RANSFORD, H. Edward. 1977. *Race and Class in American Society: Black, Chicano, Anglo.* Cambridge, Mass.: Schenkman.

       2c/3b/4h/5b,i,j/8/9/10/11   US: Afro-, Euro-, Mexican Americans

1773   RAO, V. Venkata. 1970. "Language Politics in India." *Indian Journal of Political Science* 31:203-21.

       2c/3b/4f/5b/10/16   India

1774   ——. 1976. *A Century of Tribal Politics in North East India, 1874-1974.* New Delhi: S. Chand.

2c/3b/4d,f/5b,i/10   India

1775 RATNAM, K.J. 1961. "Constitutional Government and the 'Plural Society.'" *Journal of South-East Asian History* 2:1-10.

2c/3e/4f/5f,i/10   Southeast Asia

1776 RAVEAU, F. H. M. 1975. "Role of Color in Identification Processes." In *Ethnic Identity,* edited by George DeVos and Lola Romanucci-Ross, pp. 353-59. Palo Alto: Mayfield.

2b/3e/4g/5d/11/12   France

1777 RAWKINS, Phillip M. 1978. "Outsiders as Insiders: The Implications of Minority Nationalism in Scotland and Wales." *Comparative Politics* 10:519-34.

2c/3b/4f/5e/8/9/10   Scotland; Wales

1778 RAYFIELD, J.R. 1976. "Maria in Markham Street: Italian Immigrants and Language-Learning in Toronto." *Ethnic Groups* 1:133-50.

2b/3a/4h/5a,d/16   Canada: Italians

1779 RAYSIDE, David M. 1978. "The Impact of the Linguistic Cleavage on the 'Governing' Parties of Belgium and Canada." *Canadian Journal of Political Science* 11:61-97.

2c/3d/4f/5f/10   Belgium; Canada: English, Québécois

1780 REAY, Marie. 1963. "Aboriginal and White Australian Family Structure: An Enquiry into Assimilation Trends." *Sociological Review,* n.s., 11: 19-47.

2b/3c/4a/5k/14   Australia

1781 ——, ed. 1964. *Aborigines Now.* Sydney: Angus & Robertson.

1a/2b/3a/4a,h/5a,b,d/6/10/12/14/15   Australia

1782 REDFIELD, Robert. 1956. "The Relations between Indians and Ladinos in Agua Escondida, Guatemala." *America Indigena* 16:253-76.

2b/3a/4a/5f,i/9   Guatemala

1783 REECE, Jack E. 1977. *The Bretons against France: Ethnic Minority*

Nationalism in Twentieth-Century Brittany. Chapel Hill: University of North Carolina Press.

2c/3a/4d/5e/10/11/12   France

1784 ——. 1979. "Internal Colonialism: The Case of Brittany." *Ethnic and Racial Studies* 2:275-92.

2c/3a/4d/5b,f,i,j/7/10/16   France

1785 REISLER, Mark. 1976. *By the Sweat of Their Brows: Mexican Immigrant Labor in the United States, 1900-1940.* Westport, Conn.: Greenwood Press.

2c/3a/4d/5i/7/8/10/11   US: Mexican Americans

1786 REITZES, Dietrich C. 1959. "Institutional Structure and Race Relations." *Phylon* 20:48-66.

2e/3e/4h/5g,i/9/11   Theory

1787 RENNER, H. 1976. "The National Minorities in Czechoslovakia after the Second World War." *Plural Societies* 7:23-41.

2c/3b/4d/5k/10/11   Czechoslovakia

1788 REX, John. 1959. "The Plural Society in Sociological Theory." *British Journal of Sociology* 10:114-24.

2e/3e/4h/5f,i/9   Theory

1789 ——. 1970. "The Concept of Race in Sociological Theory." In *Race and Racialism,* edited by Sami Zubaida, pp. 35-55. London: Tavistock.

2e/3e/4h/5g,i/9/11   Theory

1790 ——. 1971. "The Plural Society: The South African Case." *Race* 12: 401-14.

2c/3b/4h/5f,g,i/9/10   South Africa

1791 ——. 1973. *Race, Colonialism, and the City.* London and Boston: Routledge & Kegan Paul.

2c,e/3a,b,e/4h/5b,f,i,j/7/10/11   General

1792 ——. 1979. "Black Militancy and Class Conflict." In *Racism and Political*

Action in Britain, edited by Robert Miles and Annie Phizacklea, pp. 72-92. London: Routledge & Kegan Paul.

2c/3b/4h/5b,i/9/10   Britain: West Indians

1793   —— and Robert Moore. 1967. *Race, Community, and Conflict: A Study of Sparkbrook.* London: Oxford University Press.

2b/3a/4h/5b,f,i/7/10/15/17   Britain: General

1794   RHEE, Song Nai. 1973. "Jewish Assimilation: The Case of Chinese Jews." *Comparative Studies in Society and History* 15:115-26.

2c/3a/4d/5a/12   China (PRC)

1795   RICHMOND, Anthony H. 1967. *Post-War Immigrants in Canada.* Toronto: University of Toronto Press.

2c,d/3b/4h/5a/6/7/8/9/11/14   Canada: General

1796   ——, ed. 1972. *Readings in Race and Ethnic Relations.* Oxford: Pergamon Press.

1a,b/2b,c/3a,b/4h/5b,d,f,g,i/9/10/11   General

1797   ——. 1973. *Migration and Race Relations in an English City: A Study in Bristol.* London: Oxford University Press.

2d/3a/4h/5b,g,i/6/7/8/9/10/11   Britain: General

1798   ——. 1974. "Language, Ethnicity and the Problem of Identity in a Canadian Metropolis." *Ethnicity* 1:175-206.

2b/3a/4h/5d/12/16   Canada: General

1799   ——. 1978. "Migration, Ethnicity and Race Relations." *Ethnic and Racial Studies* 1:1-18.

2e/3e/4h/5k/7/9   Theory

1800   —— and G. Lakshmana Rao. 1976. "Recent Developments in Immigration to Canada and Australia." *International Journal of Comparative Sociology* 17:183-205.

2c/3d/4h/5k/6/7/8/11   Australia; Canada: General

1801   —— and Ravi P. Verma. 1978. "The Economic Adaptation of Immigrants: A New Theoretical Perspective." *International Migration Review* 12:3-38.

2c/3c/4h/5a,b,i/8/9   Canada: General

1802 RIESDESEL, Paul L. and T. Jean Blocker. 1978. "Race Prejudice, Status Prejudice, and Socioeconomic Status." *Sociology and Social Research* 62: 558-71.

2d/3a/4h/5g/9/11   US: Afro-Americans

1803 RIN, Hsien. 1975. "The Synthesizing Mind in Chinese Ethno-Cultural Adjustment." In *Ethnic Identity*, edited by George DeVos and Lola Romanucci-Ross, pp. 137-55. Palo Alto: Mayfield.

2c/3b/4g/5d/11/12   Southeast Asia; US: Chinese

1804 RINDFUSS, Ronald R., John Shelton Reed, and Craig St. John. 1978. "A Fertility Reaction to a Historical Event: Southern White Birthrates and the 1954 Desegregation Ruling." In *The Demography of Racial and Ethnic Groups,* edited by Frank D. Bean and W. Parker Frisbie, pp. 213-20. New York: Academic Press.

2c/3b/4h/5k/6   US: Euro-Americans

1805 RINGER, Benjamin. 1967. *The Edge of Friendliness.* New York: Basic Books.

2d/3a/4h/5f,g/9/11/12/15   US: Jews

1806 RIOUX, Marcel. 1978. *Quebec in Question.* Toronto: James Lorimer.

2c/3a/4h/5k/8/9/10   Canada: Québécois

1807 RITT, Leonard G. 1979. "Some Social and Political Views of American Indians." *Ethnicity* 6:45-72.

2d/3a/4g/5k/10/11   US: Native Americans

1808 RITTER, Kathleen V. 1979. "Internal Colonialism and Industrial Development in Alaska." *Ethnic and Racial Studies* 2:319-40.

2c/3a/4h/5j/8/9   US: Euro-, Native Americans

1809 ROBERTS, Michael. 1978. "Ethnic Conflict in Sri Lanka and Sinhalese Perspectives: Barriers to Accommodation." *Modern Asian Studies* 12:

353-76.

2b/3b/4d/5b,i/8/9/10   Sri Lanka

1810 ROBINSON, Gertrude Jack. 1974. "Mass Media and Ethnic Strife in Multi-National Yugoslavia." *Journalism Quarterly* 51:490-97.

2c/3b/4i/5b/10/16   Yugoslavia

1811 ROBINSON, Ira E., Donna K. Darden, and William R. Darden. 1972. *Cases in Crisis: Racial and Minority Conflicts.* Austin: University of Texas Press.

2c/3b/4d/5b/10/16   US: General

1812 RODRIGUEZ, Clara. 1975. "A Cost-Benefit Analysis of Subjective Factors Affecting Assimilation: Puerto Ricans." *Ethnicity* 2:66-80.

2b/3a/4b/5a/7/8   US: Puerto Ricans

1813 RODRIGUEZ, Olga, ed. 1977. *The Politics of Chicano Liberation.* New York: Pathfinder Press.

1a/2c/3a/4 f/5b,e/9/10   US: Mexican Americans

1814 ROFF, Margaret. 1969. "The Rise and Demise of Kadazan Nationalism." *Journal of Southeast Asian History* 10:326-43.

2c/3a/4d,f/5e/10   Malaysia

1815 ROGG, Eleanor Meyer. 1974. *The Assimilation of Cuban Exiles: The Role of Community and Class.* New York: Aberdeen Press.

2c/3a/4h/5a,i/9/15   US: Cubans

1816 ROGLER, Lloyd H. 1972. *Migrant in the City: The Life of a Puerto Rican Action Group.* New York: Basic Books.

2b/3a/4 h/5k/7/10/15   US: Puerto Ricans

1817 ROMANUCCI-ROSS, Lola. 1975. "Italian Ethnic Identity and Its Transformations." In *Ethnic Identity,* edited by George DeVos and Lola Romanucci-Ross, pp. 198-226. Palo Alto: Mayfield.

2b/3a/4a/5 d/8/9/10/12/14/16   Italy

1818 ROMERO, Fred E. 1979. *Chicano Workers: Their Utilization and Devel-*

opment. Monograph no. 8. Los Angeles: University of California, Los Angeles, Chicano Studies Center.

2c/3a/4b/5i/7/8/9   US: Mexican Americans

1819 RONEN, Dov. 1976. "Alternative Patterns of Integration in African States." *Journal of Modern African Studies* 14:577-96.

2b/3d/4f/5f/10   Africa

1820 ROOF, Wade Clark. 1972. "Residential Segregation of Blacks and Racial Inequality in Southern Cities: Toward a Causal Model." *Social Problems* 19:393-407.

2d/3a/4h/5i/6/8/9/13   US: Afro-Americans

1821 ——. 1978. " 'The Negro as an Immigrant Group'—Research Note on Chicago's Racial Trends." *Ethnic and Racial Studies* 1:452-64.

2d/3a/4h/5g,h/6/8/9/13   US: Afro-Americans

1822 ——, ed. 1979. *Race and Residence in American Cities.* Annals of the American Academy of Political and Social Science, no. 441.

1a/2c,d/3b/4f,h/5k/6/9   US: Afro-Americans

1823 ROSALDO, Renato, Robert A. Calvert, and Gustav L. Seligmann, eds. 1973. *Chicano: The Evolution of a People.* Minneapolis: Winston Press.

1a/2b,c/3a/4a,g,h/5a,b,d,g/6
7/9/10/11/12/14/15/16/17   US: Mexican Americans

1824 ROSE, Arnold M., ed. 1951. *Race Prejudice and Discrimination.* New York: Alfred A. Knopf.

1a,b/2c/3b/4g,h/5f,g/9/11/12/13   US: General

1825 ——. 1969. *Migrants in Europe: Problems of Acceptance and Adjustment.* Minneapolis: University of Minnesota Press.

2c/3d/4h/5d,g/7/10/11   Europe

1826 ——. 1972. "The American Blacks: Contexts of Ethnic Change." In *Social Change,* edited by Robert Nisbet, pp. 211-36. New York: Harper & Row.

2c/3a/4h/5k/10   US: Afro-Americans

1827   ROSE, Harold M. 1976. *Black Suburbanization: Access to Improved Quality of Life or Maintenance of the Status Quo?* Cambridge, Mass.: Ballinger.

2b/3b/4i/5k/6/7/13   US: Afro-Americans

1828   ROSE, Peter I. 1968. *The Subject Is Race: Traditional Ideologies and the Teaching of Race Relations.* London: Oxford University Press.

2e/3e/4h/5g/11   Theory

1829   ———, ed. 1969. *The Ghetto and Beyond: Essays on Jewish Life in America.* New York: Random House.

1a/2c/3a/4d,h/5k/9/12/13/14   US: Jews

1830   ———. 1970. "The Development of Race Studies." In *Race among Nations: A Conceptual Approach,* edited by George W. Shepherd, Jr., and Tilden LeMelle, pp. 23-59. Lexington, Mass.: Heath Lexington Books.

2e/3e/4h/5a,b,f,i   General

1831   ———, ed. 1972. *Nation of Nations: The Ethnic Experience and the Racial Crisis.* New York: Random House.

1a/2c/3b/4b,d,f,h/5a,b,f/9/10/11/12   US: General

1832   ———. 1974. *They and We: Racial and Ethnic Relations in the United States.* 2d ed. New York: Random House.

1b/2c/3e/4h/5a,f,i/9/10/11/12   US: General

1833   ———. 1977. *Strangers in Their Midst: Small-town Jews and Their Neighbors.* Mirrick, N.Y.: Richmond.

2c,d/3a/4d,h/5g/11/12   US: Jews

1834   ———, Stanley Rothman, and William J. Wilson, eds. 1973. *Through Different Eyes: Black and White Perspectives on American Race Relations.* New York: Oxford University Press.

1a/2b/3c/4d,g,h/5g/11/12   US: Afro-, Euro-Americans

1835   ROSE, Philip M. 1922. *The Italians in America.* New York: Arno Press.

2c/3a/4d/5a,d/6/7/8/10   US: Italians

1836   ROSEN, Barry M. 1973. "An Awareness of Traditional Tajik Identity
       in Central Asia." In *The Nationality Question in Soviet Central Asia,*
       edited by Edward Allworth, pp. 61-73. New York: Praeger.

       2c/3a/4f/5d/8/10/12   ～   USSR: Tadzhiks

1837   ROSEN, Bernard. 1959. "Race, Ethnicity, and the Achievement Syn-
       drome." *American Sociological Review* 24:47-60.

       2e/3e/4h/5k/9/11   US: General

1838   ROSEN, Gerald. 1974. "The Chicano Movement and the Politicization
       of Culture." *Ethnicity* 1:279-93.

       2c/3a/4f/5b,e/10   US: Mexican Americans

1839   ROSENSTOCK, Morton. 1976. "The Jews: From the Ghettos of Europe
       to the Suburbs of the United States." In *The Immigrant Experience in
       America,* edited by Frank J. Coppa and Thomas J. Curran, pp. 147-71.
       Boston: Twayne.

       2c/3a/4d/5k/7/8/11   US: Jews

1840   ROSENTHAL, Gilbert S., ed. 1970. *The Jewish Family in a Changing
       World.* New York: Thomas Yoseloff.

       1a/2c/3a/4h/5d/14/17   US: Jews

1841   ROSENWAIKE, Ira. 1973. "Interethnic Comparisons of Educational At-
       tainment: An Analysis Based on Census Data for New York City." *Amer-
       ican Journal of Sociology* 79:68-77.

       2c/3c/4h/5i/13   US: General

1842   ROSMAN, Abraham and Paula G. Rubel. 1976. "Nomad-Sedentary In-
       terethnic Relations in Iran and Afghanistan." *International Journal of
       Middle Eastern Studies* 7:545-70.

       2b/3c/4a/5c/8/12/14   Afghanistan; Iran

1843   ROSS, Aileen D. 1954. "Ethnic Group Contacts and Status Dilemma."
       Phylon 15:267-77.

       2c/3b/4h/5i/9   Canada: General

1844 ROSS, Arthur M. and Herbert Hill, eds. 1967. *Employment, Race, and Poverty.* New York: Harcourt, Brace & World.

1a/2c/3b/4b,f,h/5i/8/9/10   US: Afro-Americans

1845 ROSS, Carl. 1977. *The Finn Factor in American Labor, Culture, and Society.* New York Mills, Minn.: Parta Printers.

2c/3a/4d/5k/8/10/12   US: Finns

1846 ROSS, E. Lamar. 1978. "Interethnic Communication: An Overview." In *Interethnic Communication.* Southern Anthropological Society Proceedings, no. 12, edited by E. Lamar Ross, pp. 1-12. Athens: University of Georgia Press.

2e/3e/4a/5k/16   Theory

1847 ROSS, Jack C. and Raymond H. Wheeler. 1971. *Black Belonging: A Study of the Social Correlates of Work Relations among Negroes.* Westport, Conn.: Greenwood.

2d/3b/4h/5d/8/13/15   US: Afro-Americans

1848 ROSS, Marc Howard. 1975. "Political Alienation, Participation, and Ethnicity: An African Case." *American Journal of Political Science* 19: 291-311.

2c/3c/4f/5k/9/10/11   Kenya

1849 ROTBERG, Robert I. 1965. "Race Relations and Politics in Colonial Zambia: The Elwell Incident." *Race* 7:17-30.

2c/3a/4d/5b,i/10   Zambia

1850 ——, ed. 1978. *The Mixing of Peoples: Problems of Identity and Ethnicity.* Stamford, Conn.: Greylock.

1a/2b,c,e/3b,e/4a,f,g,h   Guyana; Japan; Malaysia;
5d,g/7/9/10/11/12   US: Chinese

1851 ROTHCHILD, Donald. 1968. "Kenya's Minorities and the African Crisis over Citizenship." *Race* 9:421-38.

2b,c/3b/4f/5e/9/10/11   Kenya

1852 ——. 1969. *Citizenship and National Integration: The Non-African Crisis in Kenya.* Center on International Race Relations, Graduate School of International Studies, University of Denver, Studies in Race and Nations, vol. 1, study no. 3.

2b,c/3b/4f/5e,i/10/11   Kenya

1853 ——. 1973. "Changing Racial Stratification and Bargaining Styles: The Kenya Experience." *Canadian Journal of African Studies* 7:419-31.

2b/3b/4d,f/5b,i/9/10   Kenya

1854 ROUCEK, Joseph S. 1961. "The Soviet Treatment of Minorities." *Phylon* 22:15-23.

2c/3b/4f/5g,i/10/11   USSR: General

1855 ROUT, Leslie B., Jr. 1976. *The African Experience in Spanish America: 1502 to the Present Day.* Cambridge: At the University Press.

2c/3e/4d/5a,i/7/9/10/12/13/14   Mesoamerica; South America

1856 ROWE, John. 1974. *The Hard-Rock Men: Cornish Immigrants and the North American Mining Frontier.* New York: Harper & Row.

2c/3a/4d/5k/7/8   US: English

1857 RUBEL, Paula G. 1971. "Ethnic Identity among the Soviet Nationalities." In *Soviet Nationality Problems,* edited by Edward Allworth et al., pp. 211-40. New York: Columbia University Press.

2c/3b/4a/5d/12   USSR: General

1858 RUBIN, Israel. 1975. "Ethnicity and Cultural Pluralism." *Phylon* 36: 140-48.

2e/3e/4h/5f/12   Theory

1859 RUBIN, Joan. 1968. *National Bilingualism in Paraguay.* The Hague: Mouton.

2b,d/3d/4a/5e,f/16   Paraguay

1860 RUBIN, Vera, ed. 1960. *Caribbean Studies: A Symposium.* Seattle: University of Washington Press.

1a/2b/3a,b/4a,h/5f/9/10   Caribbean

1861 ——. 1960. "Discussion of M. G. Smith's Social and Cultural Pluralism." *Annals of the New York Academy of Science* 83:780-85.

2e/3e/4a/5f,i   Theory

1862 ——, ed. 1960. "Social and Cultural Pluralism in the Caribbean." *Annals of the New York Academy of Sciences,* vol. 83, no. 5.

1a/2b,c/3a,b,c/4a,f/5f,i/9/10   Caribbean

1863 ——. 1962. "Cultural Politics and Race Relations." *Social and Economic Studies* 11:433-55.

2e/3e/4a/5b,f,h/10   Theory

1864 ——, R. A. J. van Lier, and Lloyd Braithwaite. 1962. "Pluralism in the Caribbean." In *Caribbean Studies Special Report 1962,* pp. 9-18. Caribbean Scholars' Conference, Institute of Caribbean Studies. San Juan: University of Puerto Rico.

2c/3e/4a/5f,i/9   Caribbean

1865 RUDOLPH, Joseph R., Jr. 1977. "Ethnic Sub-states and the Emergent Politics of Tri-level Interaction in Western Europe." *Western Political Quarterly* 30:537-57.

2c/3d/4f/5k/10   Europe

1866 RUNCIMAN, W. G. 1972. "Race and Social Stratification." *Race* 13: 497-509.

2c/3e/4h/5i/9/11/12/15   Theory

1867 RUSSELL, Margo and Martin Russell. 1979. *Afrikaners of the Kalahari: White Minority in a Black State.* Cambridge: At the University Press.

2b/3a/4a/5d,i/8/9/10/11/12/17   Namibia

1868 RUSSELL-WOOD, A. J. R. 1967. "Class, Creed, and Colour in Colonial Bahia: A Study in Prejudice." *Race* 9:133-58.

2c/3a/4d/5g,i/9/11   Brazil

1869 RUYLE, Eugene E. 1979. "Conflicting Japanese Interpretation of the Outcaste Problem (Buraku Mondai)." *American Ethnologist* 6:55-72.

2b/3a/4a/5b,i/9/11   Japan

1870   RYAN, Selwyn D. 1972. *Race and Nationalism in Trinidad and Tobago: A Study of Decolonization in a Multiracial Society.* Toronto: University of Toronto Press.

       2b,c/3b/4f/5e,g,j/9/10/11   Trinidad and Tobago

1871   SACKS, Stephen R. 1976. "Regional Inequality in Yugoslav Industry." *Journal of Developing Areas* 11:59-77.

       2c/3b/4b/5f,i/8/9   Yugoslavia

1872   SAID, Abdul Aziz, ed. 1977. *Ethnicity and US Foreign Policy.* New York: Praeger.

       1a/2b/3b/4f/5k/10   US: General

1873   —— and Luiz R. Simmons. 1976. "The Ethnic Factor in World Politics." In *Ethnicity in an International Context,* edited by Abdul Said and Luiz R. Simmons, pp. 15-47. New Brunswick, N.J.: Transaction Books.

       2c/3e/4f/5k/10   General

1874   SALA, Gary Clark. 1975. "Protest and the Ainu of Hokkaido." *Japan Interpreter* 10:44-65.

       2b,c/3a/4d,f/5b,g,i/10   Japan

1875   SALAMONE, Frank. 1975. "Becoming Hausa: Ethnic Identity Change and Its Implications for the Study of Ethnic Pluralism and Stratification." *Africa* 45:410-24.

       2b/3a/4a/5d,f,i/9/12   Nigeria

1876   ——. 1975. "The Serkawa of Yauri: Class, Status, or Party?" *African Studies Review* 18:88-101.

       2b/3a/4a/5c,d/8/12   Nigeria

1877   SALIBI, Kamal S. 1971. "The Lebanese Identity." *Journal of Contemporary History* 6:76-86.

       2c/3b/4d/5d/10/12   Lebanon

1878   SALLET, Richard. 1974. *Russian-German Settlement in the United States.* Fargo: North Dakota Institute for Regional Studies.

       2c/3a/4d/5c/6/7/8/12/15   US: Russian-Germans

1879 SALO, Matt T. 1979. "Gypsy Ethnicity: Implications of Native Categories and Interaction for Ethnic Classification." *Ethnicity* 6:73-96.

2b/3a/4a,g/5d/12   US: Gypsies

1880 SALOUTOS, Theodore. 1967. *The Greeks in America.* New York: Teachers College Press.

2c/3a/4d/5k/6/7/9/11/12/14/17   US: Greeks

1881 SALT, John and Hugh Clout, eds. 1976. *Migration in Post-War Europe: Geographical Essays.* London: Oxford University Press.

1a/2b,c/3e/4c/5k/7   Europe

1882 SALZMAN, Philip C. 1971. "National Integration of the Tribes in Modern Iran." *Middle East Journal* 25:325-36.

2b/3b/4a/5a/10   Iran

1883 SAMKANGE, Stanlake. 1972. "A Historical Perspective of Racial Tensions and National Identity in Rhodesia." In *Racial Tensions and National Identity,* edited by Ernest Q. Campbell, pp. 119-35. Nashville, Tenn.: Vanderbilt University Press.

2c/3b/4d/5b,e,i/9/10   Zimbabwe

1884 SAMORA, Julian. 1971. *Los Mojados: The Wetback Story.* Notre Dame, Ind.: University of Notre Dame Press.

2c/3a/4f/5d,g,i/7/10   US: Mexican Americans

1885 —— and Richard A. Lamanna. 1967. *Mexican-Americans in a Midwest Metropolis: A Study of East Chicago.* Mexican-American Study Project, Advance Report 8. Los Angeles: Division of Research, Graduate School of Business Administration, University of California, Los Angeles.

2b/3a/4h/5k/6/7/8   US: Mexican Americans

1886 SAMUELS, Frederick. 1969. "Colour Sensitivity among Honolulu's Haoles and Japanese." *Race* 11:203-12.

2d/3c/4g/5g/11   US: Euro-, Japanese Americans

1887 ——. 1970. *The Japanese and the Haoles of Honolulu: Durable Group Interaction.* New Haven, Conn.: College & University Press.

2b,d/3a/4h/5a,g,i/9/11/12   US: Euro-, Japanese Americans

1888   ——. 1970. "The Oriental In-Group in Hawaii." *Phylon* 31:148-56.

2b/3a/4h/5g,i/9/11   US: Asian Americans

1889   SANDBERG, Neil C. 1974. *Ethnic Identity and Assimilation: The Polish-American Community: Case Study of Metropolitan Los Angeles.* New York: Praeger.

2b,d/3a/4h/5a,d/12/15   US: Poles

1890   SANJEK, Roger. 1977. "Cognitive Maps of the Ethnic Domain in Urban Ghana: Reflections on Variability and Change." *American Ethnologist* 4: 603-22.

2b/3a/4a/5d/11/12   Ghana

1891   SANTOS, Milton. 1979. "Interdependencies in the Urban Economy." In *Ethnicity at Work,* edited by Sandra Wallman, pp. 216-26. London: Macmillan.

2e/3e/4c/5k/8/9   Theory

1892   SARHARDI, Ajit Singh. 1974. *Nationalisms in India: The Problem.* Delhi: Heritage.

2c/3b/4f/5e/10/11   India

1893   SARNA, Jonathan D. 1978. "From Immigrants to Ethnics: Toward a New Theory of 'Ethnicization.'" *Ethnicity* 5:370-78.

2e/3e/4h/5a,b,d/10   Theory

1894   SASAKI, Yuzuru and George DeVos. 1966. "A Traditional Urban Outcaste Community." In *Japan's Invisible Race: Caste in Culture and Personality,* edited by George DeVos and Hiroshi Wagatsuma, pp. 129-36. Berkeley and Los Angeles: University of California Press.

2b/3a/4a/5k/7/8/12   Japan

1895   SAXTON, Alexander. 1971. *The Indispensable Enemy: Labor and the Anti-Chinese Movement in California.* Berkeley and Los Angeles: University of California Press.

2c/3a/4d/5g/8/9/10/11   US: Chinese

1896 SAYIGH, Rosemary. 1977. "The Palestinian Identity among Camp Residents." *Journal of Palestine Studies* 6:3-22.

2b/3a/4h/5a,e/10/11/12 Lebanon

1897 ———. 1977. "Sources of Palestinian Nationalism." *Journal of Palestine Studies* 6:17-40.

2b/3a/4h/5b,d,e,f/9/10/12 Lebanon

1898 SAYWELL, John. 1977. *The Rise of the Parti Québécois, 1967-1976.* Toronto: University of Toronto Press.

2b,c/3a/4f/5e/10 Canada: Québécois

1899 SCARRIFF, James B. and John L. Hatter. 1970. *Racial and Ethnic Conflict in Zambia.* Center on International Race Relations, Graduate School of International Studies, University of Denver, Studies in Race and Nations, vol. 2, study no. 2.

2b,c/3b/4f/5b/10 Zambia

1900 SCHAEFER, Richard T. 1974. "Correlates of Racial Prejudice." In *Sociological Theory and Survey Research: Institutional Change and Social Policy in Great Britain,* edited by Timothy Leggatt, pp. 237-64. London: Sage.

2b,d/3b/4g/5g/11 Britain: General

1901 ———. 1975. "Regional Differences in Prejudice." *Regional Studies* 9:1-14.

2d/3b/4g/5g/11 Britain: General

1902 ———. 1976. "Indians in Great Britain." *International Review of Modern Sociology* 6:305-27.

2b/3a/4h/5k/7/8/9/10/11 Britain: Indians

1903 SCHEIN, Muriel D. 1975. "When Is an Ethnic Group: Ecology and Class Structure in Northern Greece." *Ethnology* 14:83-97.

2b/3c/4a/5c/8/9/10 Greece

1904 SCHEINMAN, Lawrence. 1977. "The Interfaces of Regionalism in Western Europe: Brussels and the Peripheries." In *Ethnic Conflict in the Western World,* edited by Milton J. Esman, pp. 65-78. Ithaca, N.Y.: Cornell University Press.

2c/3e/4f/5k/8/10   Europe

1905 SCHERMERHORN, R. A. 1959. "Minorities: European and American." *Phylon* 20:178-85.

2c/3e/4h/5b,f,k   Theory

1906 ———. 1964. "Toward a General Theory of Minority Groups." *Phylon* 25:238-46.

2e/3e/4h/5b,f,k   Theory

1907 ———. 1967. "Polarity in the Approach to Comparative Research in Ethnic Relations." *Sociology and Social Research* 51:235-40.

2f/3e/4h/5b/9/10   Theory

1908 ———. 1974. "Ethnicity in the Perspective of the Sociology of Knowledge." *Ethnicity* 1:1-14.

2e/3e/4h/5b,f,k   Theory

1909 SCHIAVO, Giovanni Ermenegildo. 1928. *The Italians in Chicago: A Study in Americanization.* New York: Arno Press.

2c/3a/4d/5a/11/12   US: Italians

1910 ———. 1947-49. *Italian-American History.* 2 vols. New York: Arno Press.

2c/3a/4d/5k/9/10/11/12/14/15   US: Italians

1911 ———. 1952. *Four Centuries of Italian-American History.* New York: Vigo Press.

2c/3a/4d/5k/7/10/11/14   US: Italians

1912 SCHILDKROUT, Enid. 1974. "Ethnicity and Generational Differences among Urban Immigrants in Ghana." In *Urban Ethnicity*, edited by Abner Cohen, pp. 187-222. A.S.A. Monographs, no. 12. London: Tavistock.

2b/3a/4a/5d/7/10/12   Ghana

1913 SCHILLER, Bradley R. 1971. "Class Discrimination vs. Racial Discrimination." *Review of Economics and Statistics* 53:263-69.

2d/3b/4b/5g,i/8/9   US: General

1914 SCHILLER, Nina Glick. 1977. "Ethnic Groups Are Made, Not Born: The Haitian Immigrant and American Politics." In *Ethnic Encounters: Identities and Contexts,* edited by George L. Hicks and Philip E. Leis, pp. 23-35. North Scituate, Mass.: Duxbury Press.

2b/3a/4a/5d,h/10/12   US: Haitians

1915 SCHLACHTER, Gail Ann. 1977. *Minorities and Women: A Guide to Reference Literature in the Social Sciences.* Los Angeles: Reference Services Press.

2a   US: Afro-, Asian-, Mexican-, Native Americans

1916 SCHMELZ, U. O. 1974. "New Evidence on Basic Issues in the Demography of Soviet Jews." *Jewish Journal of Sociology* 16:209-23.

2c/3a/4i(Demography)/5k/6   USSR: Jews

1917 SCHMITT, David E. 1977. "Ethnic Conflict in Northern Ireland: International Aspects of Conflict Management." In *Ethnic Conflict in the Western World,* edited by Milton J. Esman, pp. 228-50. Ithaca, N.Y.: Cornell University Press.

2c/3b/4f/5b/9/10   N. Ireland

1918 SCHMITT, Robert C. 1971. "Recent Trends in Hawaiian Interracial Marriage Rates by Occupation." *Journal of Marriage and the Family* 33:373-74.

2d/3a/4h/5k/8/9/14   US: General

1919 SCHNALL, David J. 1975. *Ethnicity and Suburban Local Politics.* New York: Praeger.

2d/3a/4f/5d,k/10/11/12/16   US: General

1920 SCHNEIDER, David M. 1969. "Kinship, Nationality and Religion in American Culture: Toward a Definition of Kinship." In *Forms of Symbolic Action.* Proceedings of the 1969 Annual Spring Meeting of the American Ethnological Society, edited by Robert F. Spencer, pp. 116-25. Seattle: University of Washington Press.

2e/3b/4a/5d/12   Theory

1921 SCHNEIDER, Mark. 1976. "Migration, Ethnicity, and Politics: A Comparative State Analysis." *Journal of Politics* 38:938-62.

2c/3e/4f/5k/7/10   US: General

1922   SCHNEIDER, William, Mark D. Berman, and Mark Schultz. 1974. "Bloc
       Voting Reconsidered: Is There a Jewish Vote?" *Ethnicity* 1:345-92.

       2c/3b/4f/5d/10   US: Jews

1923   SCHOEN, Robert. 1978. "Toward a Theory of the Demographic Impli-
       cations of Ethnic Stratification." *Social Science Quarterly* 59:468-81.

       2e/3e/4h/5i/6/9   Theory

1924   SCHOENFELD, Stuart. 1978. "The Jewish Religion in North America:
       Canadian and American Comparisons." *Canadian Journal of Sociology* 3:
       209-31.

       2d/3d/4h/5d/12/13/14/17   Canada: Jews; US: Jews

1925   SCHONEWEG, Egon. 1977. "Differences and Similarities in North
       African Nationalisms." *International Journal of Politics* 7:29-64.

       2c/3d/4f/5e/10   North Africa

1926   SCHOOLER, Carmi. 1976. "Serfdom's Legacy: An Ethnic Continuum."
       American Journal of Sociology 81:1265-86.

       2c/3c/4h/5a,d,i/9/11   US: Euro-Americans

1927   SCHUMAN, Howard and Shirley Hatchett. 1974. *Black Racial Attitudes:
       Trends and Complexities.* Ann Arbor: Survey Research Center, Institute
       for Social Research, University of Michigan.

       2d/3a/4g/5g,k/10/11   US: Afro-Americans

1928   SCHUTZ, Barry and Douglas Scott. 1975. "Patterns of Political Change
       in Fragment Regimes: Northern Ireland and Rhodesia." In *The Politics
       of Race,* edited by Ivor Crewe, pp. 26-54. British Political Sociology
       Yearbook, vol. 2. New York: John Wiley & Sons.

       2c/3d/4f/5b,i/9/10   N. Ireland; Zimbabwe

1929   SCHWARTZMAN, Simon. 1973. "Regional Contrasts within a Conti-
       nental-Scale State: Brazil." In *Building States and Nations: Analyses by
       Region,* vol. 2, edited by S. N. Eisenstadt and Stein Rokkan, pp. 209-31.
       Beverly Hills, Calif.: Sage.

       2c/3b/4f/5k/10   Brazil

1930 SCHWARZ, Henry G. 1971. *Chinese Policies Towards Minorities.* Bellingham: Western Washington State College Program in East Asian Studies.

2c/3b/4i/5k/6/10/11/12/13/16   China (PRC)

1931 SCHWARZ, John E. 1970. "The Scottish National Party: Nonviolent Separatism and Theories of Violence." *World Politics* 22:496-517.

2b/3d/4f/5e/8/10   Scotland

1932 SCOBIE, Edward. 1972. *Black Britannia: A History of Blacks in Britain.* Chicago: Johnson.

2c/3b/4d/5k/9/10   Britain: Africans

1933 SCOTT, Duncan. 1975. "The National Front in Local Politics: Some Interpretations." In *The Politics of Race,* edited by Ivor Crewe, pp. 214-38. British Political Sociology Yearbook, vol. 2. New York: John Wiley & Sons.

2b/3b/4f/5k/10   Britain: General

1934 SCOTT, Franklin D., ed. 1968. *World Migration in Modern Times.* Englewood Cliffs, N.J.: Prentice-Hall.

1a/2c/3e/4c/5k/7   General

1935 SCOTT, Nolvert P., Jr. 1975. "The Black Peoples of Canada." In *Politics of Race: Comparative Studies,* edited by Donald G. Baker, pp. 143-62. Lexington, Mass.: Lexington Books.

2c/3a/4g/5k/6/8/9/13   Canada: Afro-Canadians, West Indians

1936 SEGAL, Bernard A., ed. 1972. *Racial and Ethnic Minorities: Selected Readings.* 2d ed. New York: Thomas Y. Crowell.

1a,b/2c/3a,b/4d,f,h/5b,e,f,g,h,i/9/10/11/13/14   US: General

1937 ——. 1976. "A Mostly Open Door: Argentina's Jews and Argentine Pluralism." *Ethnicity* 3:82-97.

2b/3b/4a/5g/9/11   Argentina

1938 SEGAL, Ronald. 1968. *The Race War.* New York: Viking Press.

2e/3e/4i/5b/8/10   General

1939   SELLER, Maxine. 1977. *To Seek America: A History of Ethnic Life in the United States.* Englewood, N.J.: J. S. Ozer.

    2c,e/3b/4d/5a,f/7/9/10/15/16   US: General

1940   SELZER, Michael. 1968. "Who Are the Jews? A Guide for the Perplexed Gentile—and Jew." *Phylon* 29:231-44.

    2b/3a/4h/5d/12   US: Jews

1941   SENGSTOCK, Mary C. 1975. "Kinship in a Roman Catholic Ethnic Group." *Ethnicity* 2:134-52.

    2b/3a/4h/5k/14   US: Poles

1942   ——. 1977. "Social Change in the Country of Origin as a Factor in Immigrant Conceptions of Nationality." *Ethnicity* 4:54-70.

    2b/3a/4h/5d,e/7/12   US: Iraqis

1943   SENIOR, Clarence. 1965. *Puerto Ricans: Strangers—Then Neighbors.* Chicago: Quadrangle Books.

    2b,c/3a/4h/5a/6/7/8/9/12/13   US: Puerto Ricans

1944   SETON-WATSON, Hugh. 1971. "Unsatisfied Nationalisms." *Journal of Contemporary History* 6:3-14.

    2c/3e/4f/5e/10   General

1945   SHAFER, Boyd C. 1972. *Faces of Nationalism: New Realities and Old Myths.* New York: Harcourt Brace Jovanovich.

    2c/3e/4d/5e/10/11   General

1946   SHAMA, Avraham and Mark Iris. 1977. *Immigration without Integration: Third World Jews in Israel.* Cambridge, Mass.: Schenkman.

    2b,c/3b/4f/5a,b,i/7/10/11/12   Israel

1947   SHANNON, Lyle W. 1979. "The Changing World View of Minority Migrants in an Urban Setting." *Human Organization* 38:50-62.

    2d/3c/4a/5g/11   US: Mexican Americans

1948   SHARF, Andrew. 1963. "Nazi Racialism and British Opinion." *Race* 5:

15-24.

2c/3b/4g/5g/11 Britain: General

1949 SHARMA, Ajit Kumar. 1976. "Linguistic Nationalism and India's National Development." In *Ethnicity in an International Context,* edited by Abdul Said and Luiz R. Simmons, pp. 218-34. New Brunswick, N.J.: Transaction Books.

2c/3b/4f/5e/10/16 India

1950 SHARMA, B. S. 1973. *Politics of Tribalism in Africa Today.* Delhi: Department of African Studies, University of Delhi.

2c/3e/4f/5e/10/11/12 Africa

1951 SHAROT, Stephen. 1974. "Minority Situation and Religious Acculturation: A Comparative Analysis of Jewish Communities." *Comparative Studies in Society and History* 16:329-54.

2c/3d/4h/5f/6/9/11/12 General

1952 SHARP, Samuel L. 1975. "Ethnicity and Migration in Yugoslavia." *Studies in Comparative International Development* 10:63-70.

2c/3b/4b/5k/7/12/13 Yugoslavia

1953 SHAW, Douglas V. 1976. *The Making of an Immigrant City: Ethnic and Cultural Conflict in Jersey City, New Jersey, 1850-1877.* New York: Arno Press.

2c/3a/4d/5b/7/10 US: Irish

1954 SHEPHERD, George W., Jr., Cynthia Kahn, and Donald Seegmiller. 1970. "The Racial Factor in American Foreign Policy: A Selected Bibliography of the 1960s." In *Race among Nations: A Conceptual Approach,* edited by George W. Shepherd, Jr., and Tilden J. LeMelle, pp. 163-215. Lexington, Mass.: Heath Lexington Books.

2a General

1955 SHERMAN, C. Bezalel. 1965. *The Jew within American Society: A Study in Ethnic Individuality.* Detroit: Wayne State University Press.

2c/3a/4d,h/5d/12 US: Jews

1956   SHILS, Edward. 1957. "Primordial, Personal, Sacred, and Civil Ties." *British Journal of Sociology* 8:130-45.

       2e/3e/4h/5d/11/12   Theory

1957   SHIMKIN, Demitri B., Edith M. Shimkin, and Dennis A. Frate, eds. 1978. *The Extended Family in Black Societies.* The Hague: Mouton.

       1a/2b/3a,d/4a/5k/14   Caribbean; US: Afro-Americans; West Africa

1958   SHOKEID, Moshe. 1971. *The Dual Heritage: Immigrants from the Atlas Mountains in an Israeli Village.* Manchester, England: Manchester University Press.

       2b/3a/4a/5d/11/12   Israel

1959   SHOUP, Paul. 1968. *Communism and the Yugoslav National Question.* New York: Columbia University Press.

       2c/3b/4d,f/5e/6/8/10/11   Yugoslavia

1960   SHUVAL, Judith T. 1962. "The Micro-Neighborbood: An Approach to Ecological Patterns of Ethnic Groups." *Social Problems* 9:272-80.

       2f/3e/4h/5c/6/11/12   Israel

1961   SHYROCK, Richard. 1977. "Indigenous Economic Managers." In *Nationality Group Survival in Multi-Ethnic States: Shifting Support Patterns in the Soviet Baltic Region,* edited by Edward Allworth, pp. 83-122. New York: Praeger.

       2c/3b/4f/5k/8/9/10/12   USSR: General

1962   SIBAYAN, Bonifacio P. 1971. "Language Policy, Language Engineering and Literacy in the Philippines." *Current Trends in Linguistics* 8:1038-62.

       2c/3b/4e/5e/11/13/16   Philippines

1963   SIDER, Gerald M. 1976. "Lumbee Indian Cultural Nationalism and Ethnogenesis." *Dialectical Anthropology* 1:161-72.

       2b/3a/4a/5e/10   US: Native Americans

1964   SIDORSKY, David, ed. 1973. *The Future of the Jewish Community in America.* New York: Basic Books.

       1a/2c/3a/4i/5d/10/11/12/13/14   US: Jews

1965 SIGEL, Irving E. and James E. Johnson. 1977. "Child Development and Respect for Cultural Diversity." In *Pluralism in a Democratic Society,* edited by Melvin Tumin and Walter Plotch, pp. 169-206. New York: Praeger.

2e/3b/4g/5g/13/14 US: General

1966 SIH, Paul K. T. and Leonard B. Allen, eds. 1976. *The Chinese in America.* New York: St. John's University Press.

2c/3a/4i/5d,g,i/6/7/11/12/13 US: Chinese

1967 SILCOCK, T. H. 1969. "The Effects of Industrialisation on Race Relations in Malaya." In *Comparative Perspectives on Race Relations,* edited by Melvin Tumin, pp. 140-60. Boston: Little, Brown.

2c/3b/4h/5b,i/8/9/10/11/12 Malaysia

1968 SILVER, Brian. 1974. "The Impact of Urbanization and Geographical Dispersion on the Linguistic Russification of Soviet Nationalities." *Demography* 11:89-103.

2c/3b/4f/5a,f/6/12/16 USSR: General

1969 ———. 1974. "Levels of Sociocultural Development among Soviet Nationalities: A Partial Test of the Equalization Hypothesis." *American Political Science Review* 68:1618-37.

2c/3b/4f/5i/9 USSR: General

1970 ———. 1978. "Ethnic Intermarriage and Ethnic Consciousness among Soviet Nationalities." *Soviet Studies* 30:107-16.

2c/3c/4f/5d/12/14 USSR: General

1971 ———. 1978. "Language Policy and the Linguistic Russification of Soviet Nationalities." In *Soviet Nationality Policies and Practices,* edited by Jeremy R. Azrael, pp. 250-306. New York: Praeger.

2c/3b/4f/5a/6/10/13/16/17 USSR: General

1972 SIMEON, Richard, ed. 1977. *Must Canada Fail?* Montreal and London: McGill-Queen's University Press.

1a/2c,d/3b/4f/5e,k/10/11 Canada: General

1973 SIMMER, Edward, ed. 1972. *Pain and Promise: The Chicano Today.*

New York: New American Library.

2c/3c/4h/5b,d/9/10/11   US: Mexican Americans

1974 SIMMONS, Ozzie G. 1974. *Anglo-Americans and Mexican Americans in South Texas.* New York: Arno Press.

2c/3a/4h/5g,i/9/10   US: Euro-, Mexican Americans

1975 SIMMONS, R. D. G. Ph. 1961. *The Colour of the Skin in Human Relations.* Amsterdam: Elsevier.

2e/3e/4g/5g/11   General

1976 SIMPSON, George E. 1962. "Social Stratification in the Caribbean." *Phylon* 23:29-46.

2c/3e/4a/5i/9   Caribbean

1977 —— and J. Milton Yinger. 1972. *Racial and Cultural Minorities: An Analysis of Prejudice and Discrimination.* 4th ed. New York: Harper & Row.

1b/2c/3a,b,e/4a,h/5g/10/11/13/14/16   General

1978 SIMS, Harold D. 1972. "Japanese Postwar Migration to Brazil: An Analysis of Data Presently Available." *International Migration Review* 6:246-65.

2c/3b/4c/5k/6/7/8/13/14/16   Brazil

1979 SINGLETON, John. 1977. "Education and Ethnicity." *Comparative Education Review* 21:329-44.

2e/3e/4i(Education)/5k/9/10/12/13   Theory

1980 SINHA, M. R., ed. 1971. *Integration in India.* Bombay: Asian Studies Press.

1a/2b,c/3b/4a,b,d,e,f,g,h,i/5f,g/9/10/11/12/13/16/17   India

1981 SIVANANDAN, A. 1973. "Race, Class and Power: An Outline for Study." *Race* 14:383-91.

2e/3e/4f/5j/8/9/10   Theory

1982 ——. 1976. "Race, Class and the State: The Black Experience in Britain." *Race and Class* 17:347-68.

2c/3b/4h/5b,i,j/8/9/10   Britain: Africans

1983 SIVERTS, Henning. 1969. "Ethnic Stability and Boundary Dynamics in Southern Mexico." In *Ethnic Groups and Boundaries,* edited by Fredrik Barth, pp. 101-16. Boston: Little, Brown.

2b/3a/4a/5c/8/10/12/14/16   Mexico

1984 SKINNER, Elliott P. 1968. "Group Dynamics in the Politics of Changing Societies: The Problem of 'Tribal' Politics in Africa." In *Essays on the Problem of Tribe.* Proceedings of the 1967 Annual Spring Meeting of the American Ethnological Society, edited by June Helm, pp. 170-85. Seattle: University of Washington Press.

2c/3d/4a/5k/9/10/12/15   Africa

1985 ———. 1970. "Processes of Political Incorporation in Mossi Society." In *From Tribe to Nation in Africa: Studies in Incorporation Processes,* edited by Ronald Cohen and John Middleton, pp. 175-200. Scranton, Penn.: Chandler.

2b/3a/4a/5a/10/12   Ghana

1986 ———. 1975. "Competition within Ethnic Systems in Africa." In *Ethnicity and Resource Competition in Plural Societies,* edited by Leo A. Despres, pp. 131-57. The Hague: Mouton.

2c/3e/4a/5b/10   Africa

1987 ———. 1978. "Voluntary Associations and Ethnic Competition in Ouagadougou." In *Ethnicity in Modern Africa,* edited by Brian M. Du Toit, pp. 191-211. Boulder, Colo.: Westview Press.

2b/3a/4a/5b/10/15   Upper Volta

1988 SKINNER, G. William. 1957. *Chinese Society in Thailand.* Ithaca, N.Y.: Cornell University Press.

2b,c/3a/4a/5k/9/10/12/14/17   Thailand

1989 ———, ed. 1959. *Local, Ethnic, and National Loyalties in Village Indonesia: A Symposium.* Cultural Report Series, Southeast Asia Studies, no. 8. New Haven, Conn.: Yale University Press.

1a/2b,c/3b/4a,f/5e,f/10/11/12   Indonesia

1990   SKLARE, Marshall, ed. 1974. *The Jew in American Society.* New York: Behrman House.

       1a/2c/3a/4h/5k/6/7/11/12/14   US: Jews

1991   ——. 1974. "The Jew in American Sociological Thought." *Ethnicity* 1:151-73.

       2e/3e/4h/5k   US: Jews

1992   ——, ed. 1974. *The Jewish Community in America.* New York: Behrman House.

       1a/2b,c/3a/4h/5a,d/10/11/12/13/15/17   US: Jews

1993   —— and Joseph Greenblum. 1967. *Jewish Identity on the Suburban Frontier.* New York: Basic Books.

       2d/3a/4h/5a,d/6/8/9/10/11/12/13/14/15   US: Jews

1994   SLANN, Martin. 1973. "Jewish Ethnicity and the Integration of an Arab Minority in Israel: A Study of the Jerusalem Incorporation." *Human Relations* 26:359-70.

       2d/3a/4h/5a,f/10   Israel

1995   SLATER, Mariam K. 1976. "The Rule of Legitimacy and the Caribbean Family: A Case in Martinique." *Ethnic Groups* 1:36-87.

       2b/3a/4a/5k/14   Martinique

1996   SLOBODIN, Richard. 1972. "The Metis of Northern Canada." In *The Blending of Races: Marginality and Identity in World Perspective,* edited by Noel P. Gist and Anthony Gary Dworkin, pp. 143-66. New York: Wiley-Interscience.

       2b/3a/4a/5d/8/11/12/14   Canada: Métis

1997   SMALL, Sylvia. 1976. "Black Workers in Labor Unions—A Little Less Separate, a Little More Equal." *Ethnicity* 3:174-96.

       2c/3a/4h/5i/8/9/11   US: Afro-Americans

1998   SMILEY, Donald V. 1977. "French-English Relations in Canada and Consociational Democracy." In *Ethnic Conflict in the Western World,* edited by Milton J. Esman, pp. 179-203. Ithaca: Cornell University Press.

2c/3b/4f/5f/10   Canada: Québécois

1999   SMITH, Anthony D. 1972. "Ethnocentrism, Nationalism and Social Change." *International Journal of Comparative Sociology* 8:1-20.

2e/3e/4f/5e,f/11   Theory

2000   ——, ed. 1976. *Nationalist Movements.* London: Macmillan.

1a/2c/3b/4f/5e/9/10/16   General

2001   ——. 1978. "The Diffusion of Nationalism: Some Historical and Sociological Perspectives." *British Journal of Sociology* 29:234-48.

2e/3e/4d,f/5e/11   Theory

2002   SMITH, Burton. 1978. "The United States in Recent Canadian Nationalism." *World Affairs* 140:195-205.

2c/3b/4d/5e/10   Canada: General

2003   SMITH, David G. 1977. *Racial Disadvantage in Britain: The PEP Report.* New York: Penguin Books.

2d/3b/4h/5g,i/6/7/8/9/10/11   Britain: Asians, West Indians

2004   SMITH, M. Estellie. 1974. "Portuguese Enclaves: The Invisible Minority." In *Social and Cultural Identity: Problems of Persistence and Change.* Southern Anthropological Society Proceedings, no. 8, edited by Thomas K. Fitzgerald, pp. 81-90. Athens: University of Georgia Press.

2c/3a/4a/5d,h/7/12   US: Portuguese

2005   ——. 1978. "The Case of the Disappearing Ethnics." In *Interethnic Communication.* Southern Anthropological Society Proceedings, no. 12, edited by E. Lamar Ross, pp. 63-77. Athens: University of Georgia Press.

2b/3a/4a/5b,d/7/12   US: Portuguese

2006   SMITH, Michael Gordon. 1961. "The Plural Framework of Jamaican Society." *British Journal of Sociology* 12:249-62.

2b/3b/4a/5f,i/9/10   Jamaica

2007   ——. 1965. *The Plural Society in the British West Indies.* Berkeley and Los Angeles: University of California Press.

2b,c/3e/4a/5f,i/9/10   Caribbean

2008   ——. 1965. *Stratification in Grenada.* Berkeley and Los Angeles: University of California Press.

2b/3b/4a/5f,i/9/10   Grenada

2009   ——. 1969. "Institutional and Political Condition of Pluralism." In *Pluralism in Africa,* edited by Leo Kuper and M. G. Smith, pp. 27-66. Berkeley and Los Angeles: University of California Press.

2e/3e/4a/5f,i/9/10   Theory

2010   ——. 1969. "Pluralism in Precolonial African Societies." In *Pluralism in Africa,* edited by Leo Kuper and M. G. Smith, pp. 91-152. Berkeley and Los Angeles: University of California Press.

2c/3e/4a/5f,i/9/10   Africa

2011   ——. 1969. "Some Developments in the Analytic Framework of Pluralism." In *Pluralism in Africa,* edited by Leo Kuper and M. G. Smith, pp. 415-58. Berkeley and Los Angeles: University of California Press.

2e/3e/4a/5f,i/9/10   Theory

2012   SMITH, Raymond T. 1961. "Review of Social and Cultural Pluralism in the Caribbean." *American Anthropologist* 63:155-57.

2e/3e/4a/5f   Theory

2013   ——. 1962. *British Guiana.* London: Oxford University Press.

2b/3b/4a/5f,i/8/9/10   Guyana

2014   ——. 1976. "Race, Class, and Political Conflict in a Postcolonial Society." In *Small States and Segmented Societies: National Political Integration in a Global Environment,* edited by Stephanie G. Neuman, pp. 198-226. New York: Praeger.

2c/3b/4a/5b,i/9/10   Guyana

2015   SMITH, Timothy L. 1978. "Religion and Ethnicity in America." *American Historical Review* 83:1155-85.

2c/3b/4d/5a/12/17   US: General

2016 SMITH, Waldemar R. 1975. "Beyond the Plural Society: Economics and Ethnicity in Middle American Towns." *Ethnology* 14:225-44.

2c/3a,e/4a/5i/8/9 Mesoamerica

2017 SMOCK, Audrey C. 1971. *Ibo Politics: The Role of Ethnic Unions in Eastern Nigeria.* Cambridge, Mass.: Harvard University Press.

2b/3a/4a,f/5b,k/10/15 Nigeria

2018 SMOOHA, Sammy. 1975. "Pluralism and Conflict: A Theoretical Exploration." *Plural Societies* 6:69-89.

2e/3e/4h/5f Theory

2019 SMYTHE, Hugh and Yoshineasa Naitob. 1953. "The Eta Caste in Japan." *Phylon* 14:19-27, 157-62.

2c/3a/4d/5f,g,i/6/8/9/10/11/12 Japan

2020 SNYDER, Peter Z. 1971. "The Social Environment of the Urban Indian." In *The American Indian in Urban Society,* edited by Jack O. Waddell and O. Michael Watson, pp. 207-43. Boston: Little, Brown.

2b,d/3a/4a/5k/7/14/15 US: Native Americans

2021 SOEN, Dan. 1977. "Orientals, Westerners, and Ethnic Stratification in Israel." *Mankind Quarterly* 17:182-200.

2c/3b/4h/5i/6/8/9/13 Israel

2022 SOLAUN, Mauricio and Sidney Kronus. 1973. *Discrimination without Violence: Miscegenation and Racial Conflict in Latin America.* New York: Wiley.

2c/3e/4h/5g,i/10/14 Mesoamerica; South America

2023 SOLINGER, Dorothy J. 1977. "Minority Nationalities in China's Yunnan Province." *World Politics* 30:1-23.

2c/3a/4f/5a,b,e/10 China (PRC)

2024 SOON, Alice Tay Ehr. 1962. "The Chinese in Southeast Asia." *Race* 4:34-48.

2c/3a/4h/5c/6/8/9/10/12 Southeast Asia

2025   SOPER, Edmund Davison. 1947. *Racism: A World Issue.* New York: Negro Universities Press.

2c/3e/4d/5g/9/10/11   General

2026   SORKIN, Alan L. 1976. "The Economic and Social Status of the American Indian, 1940-1970." *Journal of Negro Education* 45:432-47.

2c/3a/4i/5i/8/9/13   US: Native Americans

2027   ——. 1978. *The Urban American Indian.* Lexington, Mass.: Lexington Books.

2c/3a/4i/5g,i,j/7/8/9/13/15/17   US: Native Americans

2028   SOTOMAYOR, Marta. 1977. "Language, Culture, and Ethnicity in Developing Self-Concept." *Social Casework* 58:195-203.

2e/3e/4i(Social Work)/5d/12/16   Theory

2029   SOUTHALL, Aidan. 1970. "Ethnic Incorporation among the Alur." In *From Tribe to Nation in Africa: Studies in Incorporation Processes,* edited by Ronald Cohen and John Middleton, pp. 71-92. Scranton, Penn.: Chandler.

2b/3a/4a/5a/12   Sudan

2030   ——. 1970. "The Illusion of Tribe." In *The Passing of Tribal Man in Africa,* edited by P. C. W. Gutkind, pp. 28-50. Leiden: E. J. Brill.

2c/3e/4a/5d/6/10/12   Africa

2031   ——. 1976. "Nuer and Dinka Are People: Ecology, Ethnicity and Logical Possibility." *Man* 11:463-91.

2b/3a/4a/5c/12   East Africa

2032   SOWELL, Thomas. 1975. *Race and Economics.* New York: David McKay.

2c/3b,e/4b,h/5g,i,k(Neoclassical Economics)/8/9/11   Theory

2033   ——. 1978. "Ethnicity in a Changing America." *Daedalus* 107:213-37.

2c/3b/4h/5a,f,g,i/6/8/10/11/13   US: General

2034   SOZON, Michael and The Romanian Research Group. 1979. "On Transylvanian Ethnicity." *Current Anthropology* 20:135-48.

2c/3b/4a/5a,b,i/10/12/13/16   Romania

2035   SPAULDING, E. Wilder. 1968. *The Quiet Invaders: The Story of the Austrian Impact upon America.* Vienna: Osterreischischer Bunderverlag.

2c/3a/4d/5a/6/7/8/12/15   US: Austrians

2036   SPECHLER, Dina Rome. 1975. "Russia and the Russians." In *Handbook of Major Soviet Nationalities,* edited by Zev Katz, Rosemarie Rogers, and Frederic Harned, pp. 9-20. New York: Free Press.

2c/3b/4f/5k/6/9/10/11   USSR: Russians

2037   SPECKMAN, J. D. 1963. "The Indian Group in the Segmented Society of Surinam." *Caribbean Studies* 3:2-17.

2b/3a/4a/5f,i/9   Surinam

2038   SPENCE, J. E. 1962. "The Political Implications of the South African Bantustan Policy." *Race* 3:20-30.

2c/3b/4f/5k/10/11   South Africa

2039   SPENCER, John. 1971. "Colonial Language Policies and Their Legacies in Sub-Saharan Africa." *Current Trends in Linguistics* 7:537-47.

2c/3e/4e/5e/11/16   Africa

2040   SPICER, Edward. 1971. "Persistent Cultural Systems: A Comparative Study of Identity Systems That Can Adapt to Contrasting Environments." *Science* 174:795-800.

2e/3e/4a/5d/12   Theory

2041   —— and Raymond H. Thompson. 1972. *Plural Society in the Southwest.* New York: Interbook.

2c/3a/4a/5f,i/8/9/10   US: Mexican Americans

2042   SPILERMAN, Seymour and Jack Habib. 1976. "Development Towns in Israel: The Role of Community in Creating Ethnic Disparities in Labor Force Characteristics." *American Journal of Sociology* 81:781-812.

2d/3b/4h/5i/6/7/8/9   Israel

2043 SPREITZER, Almer and Eldon E. Snyder. 1975. "Patterns of Variation within and between Ethnoreligious Groups." *Ethnicity* 2:125-33.

      2b,d/3c/4h/5d,g/11/12   US: General

2044 SPRY, Graham. 1971. "Canada: Notes on Two Ideas of Nation in Contradiction." *Journal of Contemporary History* 6:173-96.

      2c/3b/4d/5e,f/10   Canada: General

2045 SRINIVAS, M. N. 1952. *Religion and Society among the Coorgs of South India.* Oxford: At the Clarendon Press.

      2b/3a/4a/5d,i/8/9/10/11/12/14/16   India

2046 ——. 1962. *Caste in Modern India and Other Essays.* New York: Asia Publishing House.

      2c/3b,e/4a/5 i/8/9/10/11/12/14   India

2047 STAHL, Kathleen. 1969. "The Chagga." In *Transition and Tradition in East Africa,* edited by P. H. Gulliver, pp. 209-22. Berkeley and Los Angeles: University of California Press.

      2c/3c/4f/5d/6/8/9/10   Tanzania

2048 STANBURY, W. T. 1975. *Success and Failure: Indians in Urban Society.* Vancouver: University of British Columbia Press.

      2b,d/3a/4b/5d,g,i/6/7/8/12/13/14   Canada: Native Canadians

2049 STANLEY, Sam, ed. 1978. *American Indian Economic Development.* The Hague: Mouton.

      1a/2b,c/3a/4a,h/5b,i/8/9/10/11   US: Native Americans

2050 STARR, Paul D. 1978. "Ethnic Categories and Identification in Lebanon." *Urban Life* 7:111-42.

      2b/3a/4a/5d/12   Lebanon

2051 STAUSS, Joseph H., Bruce A. Chadwick, and Howard N. Bahr. 1973. "Red Power: A Sample of Indian Adults and Youth." In *Chicanos and Native Americans: The Territorial Minorities,* edited by Rudolph O. de la Garza et al., pp. 90-96. Englewood Cliffs, N.J.: Prentice-Hall.

      2d/3a/4h/5k/10/11   US: Native Americans

2052 STAVROU, Nikolaos A. 1976. "Ethnicity in Yugoslavia: Roots and Impact." In *Ethnicity in an International Context,* edited by Abdul Said and Luiz R. Simmons, pp. 134-49. New Brunswick, N.J.: Transaction Books.

2c/3b/4f/5e/10   Yugoslavia

2053 STEIN, Barry N. 1979. "Occupational Adjustment of Refugees: The Vietnamese in the United States." *International Migration Review* 13: 25-45.

2d/3a/4h/5k/7/8   US: Vietnamese

2054 STEIN, Howard F. 1975. "Ethnicity, Identity, and Ideology." *School Review* 83:273-300.

2e/3e/4a/5d/11/12   Theory

2055 STEINER, Jurg and Jeffrey Obler. 1977. "Does the Consociational Theory Really Hold for Switzerland?" In *Ethnic Conflict in the Western World,* edited by Milton J. Esman, pp. 324-41. Ithaca, N.Y.: Cornell University Press.

2c/3b/4f/5f/10   Switzerland

2056 STEINFIELD, Melvin, ed. 1973. *Cracks in the Melting Pot: Racism and Discrimination in American History.* New York: Glencoe Press.

1a/2c/3b/4d/5g,i/11   US: General

2057 STENDEL, Ori. 1973. *The Minorities in Israel: Trends in the Development of the Arab and Druze Communities, 1948-1973.* Jerusalem: The Israel Economist.

2b,c/3b/4i/5f/6/8/9/10/12/13/14/15/16/17   Israel

2058 STEPHENSON, Glenn V. 1972. "Cultural Regionalism and the Unitary State Idea in Belgium." *Geographical Review* 62:501-23.

2b/3b/4c/5f,k/8/10/16   Belgium

2059 STEWART, James B. and Thomas Hyclak. 1979. "Ethnicity and Economic Opportunity." *American Journal of Economics and Sociology* 38: 319-35.

2c/3c/4b/5g,i/8/9   US: General

2060 STONE, Linda. 1977. "East Indian Adaptation on St. Vincent." In *Eth-*

nic Encounters: Identities and Contexts, edited by George L. Hicks and Philip E. Leis, pp. 37-47. North Scituate, Mass.: Duxbury Press.

2c/3a/4a/5d/10/12/14   St. Vincent

2061   STOUT, Harry S. 1975. "Ethnicity: The Vital Center of Religion in America." *Ethnicity* 2:204-24.

2c/3b/4h/5d/12/17   US: Euro-Americans

2062   STREIB, Gordon F. 1974. "The Restoration of the Irish Language: Behavioral and Symbolic Aspects." *Ethnicity* 1:73-89.

2c/3b/4a/5d,e/10/11/12/16   Ireland

2063   STUART, Irving R. and Lawrence Edwin Abt, eds. 1973. *Interracial Marriage: Expectations and Realities.* New York: Grossman.

1a/2b,c,d,e/3a,b   Brazil; Cuba; Japan;
4a,g,h,i(Social Work, Psychiatry)   Puerto Rico; Trinidad;
5g,k/14   US: General, Afro-, Native Americans

2064   STUDLAR, Donley T. 1978. "Religion and White Racial Attitudes in Britain." *Ethnic and Racial Studies* 1:306-15.

2d/3c/4g/5g/11/17   Britain: General

2065   ——. 1979. "Racial Attitudes in Britain: A Causal Analysis." *Ethnicity* 6:107-22.

2d/3b/4g/5g/11   Britain: General

2066   STYMEIST, David. 1979. "Controlling the Job: Levels of Organization in Casual Labour." In *Ethnicity at Work,* edited by Sandra Wallman, pp. 193-212. London: Macmillan.

2b/3a/4a/5k/8   Canada: General

2067   SUBBA RAO, Koka. 1970. *Conflicts in Indian Polity.* Delhi: S. Chand.

2c/3b/4f/5b/10/11   India

2068   SUE, Stanley and Harry H. L. Kitano. 1973. "Stereotypes as a Measure of Success." *Journal of Social Issues* 29:83-98.

2d/3c,e/4g,h/5g/9/11   US: Asian Americans

2069 —— and Nathaniel Wagner, eds. 1973. *Asian Americans: Psychological Perspectives*. Ben Lomond, Calif.: Science and Behavior Books.

1a/2c/3a/4g,h/5a,d,g/6/9/10/11/12   US: Asian Americans

2070 SUGAR, Peter F. 1963. "The Nature of the Non-Germanic Societies under Hapsburg Rule." *Slavic Studies* 22:1-46.

2c/3d/4d/5b,i/10   Europe

2071 ——. 1969. "External and Domestic Roots of Eastern European Nationalism." In *Nationalism in Eastern Europe*, edited by Peter F. Sugar and Ivo J. Lederer, pp. 3-54. Seattle: University of Washington Press.

2c/3e/4d/5e/10/11   Eastern Europe

2072 SUHRKE, Astri. 1971. "The Thai Muslims: Some Aspects of Minority Integration." *Pacific Affairs* 43:531-47.

2b/3b/4f/5a,f,k/9/10   Thailand

2073 ——. 1975. "Irredentism Contained: The Thai-Muslim Case." *Comparative Politics* 7:187-204.

2b/3a/4f/5b/10   Thailand

2074 —— and Lela Garner Noble. 1977. "Muslims in the Philippines and Thailand." In *Ethnic Conflict in International Relations*, edited by Astri Suhrke and Lela Garner Noble, pp. 178-212. New York: Praeger.

2c/3d/4f/5b/10   Philippines; Thailand

2075 ——. 1977. "Spread or Containment: The Ethnic Factor." In *Ethnic Conflict in International Relations*, edited by Astri Suhrke and Lela Garner Noble, pp. 213-32. New York: Praeger.

2e/3e/4f/5b/10   Theory

2076 SULLIVAN, Teresa A. 1978. "Racial-Ethnic Differences in Labor Force Participation: An Ethnic Stratification Perspective." In *The Demography of Racial and Ethnic Groups*, edited by Frank D. Bean and W. Parker Frisbie, pp. 165-87. New York: Academic Press.

2c/3c/4h/5i/8/9   US: General

2077 SULTAN, Garip. 1968. "Demographic and Cultural Trends among

Turkic Peoples of the Soviet Union." In *Ethnic Minorities in the Soviet Union,* edited by Erich Goldhagen, pp. 251-73. New York: Frederick A. Praeger.

2c/3a/4h/5k/6/9/13/16   USSR: Central Asians, Transcaucasians

2078   SUNDBERG-WEITMAN, Brita. 1977. *Discrimination on Grounds of Nationality: Free Movement of Workers and Freedom of Establishment under the EEC Treaty.* Amsterdam: North-Holland.

2c/3e/4i(Law)/5g,k/7/10   Europe

2079   SUNG, Betty Lee. 1975. *Chinese American Manpower and Employment.* Washington, D.C.: U.S. Department of Labor Manpower Administration.

2b,c,d/3a/4i/5i/6/7/8/9/11/13   US: Chinese

2080   SUPELL, Robert and Clive Sneddon. 1965. "Colour Prejudice and Oxford Landladies." *Race* 6:322-33.

2d/3a/4g/5g/6/11   Britain: General

2081   SURYADINATA, Leo. 1976. "Indonesian Policies Toward the Chinese Minority under the New Order." *Asian Survey* 16:770-87.

2c/3b/4g/5k/10   Indonesia

2082   SUSOKOLOV, A. A. 1976. "The Influence on Interethnic Relations of Differences in the Educational Levels and Number of Ethnic Groups in Contact." *Soviet Sociology* 15:38-56.

2d/3b/4h/5f,g/12/13/16   USSR: General

2083   SUTTLES, Gerald D. 1968. *The Social Order of the Slum: Ethnicity and Territory in the Inner City.* Chicago: University of Chicago Press.

2b/3a/4h/5b,c,d,f/6/9/10   US: General

2084   SUTTON, Constance R. and Susan R. Makiesky. 1975. "Migration and West Indian Racial and Ethnic Consciousness." In *Migration and Development: Implications for Ethnic Identity and Political Conflict,* edited by Helen I. Safa and Brian M. Du Toit, pp. 113-44. The Hague: Mouton.

2b,c/3d/4a/5d,i/7/10/11   Britain: West Indians; US: West Indians

2085   SUZUKI, Bob H. 1977. "Education and the Socialization of Asian Americans: A Revisionist Analysis of the 'Model Minority' Thesis."

Amerasia Journal 4:23-51.

2b,c/3a/4i(Education)/5d/12/13   US: Asian Americans

2086   SUZUKI, Teiiti. 1969. *The Japanese Immigrant in Brazil: Narrative Part.* Tokyo: University of Tokyo Press.

2d/3a/4c/5k/6/7/8/9/13/16/17   Brazil

2087   SVENSSON, Tom G. 1976. *Ethnicity and Mobilization in Sami Politics.* Stockholm Studies in Social Anthropology, no. 4. Stockholm: Department of Social Anthropology, University of Stockholm.

2b/3a/4a/5b,i/9/10   Sweden

2088   SWARTZ, Marc J. 1979. "Religious Courts, Community, and Ethnicity among the Swahili of Mombasa: An Historical Study of Social Boundaries." *Africa* 49:29-41.

2c/3a/4a/5d/12   Kenya

2089   SWAY, Marlene. 1975. "Gypsies as a Perpetual Minority: A Case Study." *Humbolt Journal of Social Relations* 3:48-55.

2c/3a/4h/5d,k/9/12   General

2090   SWEET, James A. 1978. "Indicators of Family and Household Structure of Racial and Ethnic Minorities in the United States." In *The Demography of Racial and Ethnic Groups,* edited by Frank D. Bean and W. Parker Frisbie, pp. 221-59. New York: Academic Press.

2c/3c/4h/5k/6/14   US: General

2091   SWIDERSKI, Richard W. 1977. "Main Street and Church Road: Ethnic Relations in a New England Town." In *Ethnic Encounters: Identities and Contexts,* edited by George L. Hicks and Philip E. Leis, pp. 119-35. North Scituate, Mass.: Duxbury Press.

2b/3a/4a/5d/12   US: Italians, Portuguese

2092   SWIFT, Michael. 1962. "Malayan Politics: Race and Class." *Civilisations* 12:237-45.

2b,c/3b/4f/5i/9   Malaysia

2093   SWOBODA, Victor and Ann Sheehy. 1972. "Ethnic Pressures in the Soviet Union." *Conflict Studies,* no. 30.

2c/3b/4f/5b,e/9/10/12/17   USSR: General

2094   SZPORLUK, Roman. 1975. "The Ukraine and the Ukrainians." In
       Handbook of Major Soviet Nationalities, edited by Zev Katz, Rosemarie
       Rogers, and Frederic Harned, pp. 21-48. New York: Free Press.

2c/3a/4d/5k/6/8/10/11/12/13/16   USSR: Ukrainians

2095   SZYMANSKI, Albert. 1975. "Trends in Economic Discrimination
       against Blacks in the U.S. Working Class." *Review of Radical Political
       Economics* 7:1-21.

2c/3a/4f,h/5b,i/8/9   US: Afro-Americans

2096   ——. 1976. "Racial Discrimination and White Gain." *American Socio-
       logical Review* 41:403-14.

2e/3e/4h/5b,i/8/9   US: Afro-Americans

2097   TAAGEPERA, Rein. 1971. "The 1970 Soviet Census: Fusion or Crystal-
       lization of Nationalities." *Soviet Studies* 23:216-21.

2d/3b/4h/5d/6/16   USSR: General

2098   ——. 1975. "Estonia and the Estonians." In *Handbook of Major Soviet
       Nationalities,* edited by Zev Katz, Rosemarie Rogers, and Frederic Harned,
       pp. 75-93. New York: Free Press.

2c/3a/4f/5k/6/8/10/11/12/13/16   USSR: Estonians

2099   TABB, William K. 1970. *The Political Economy of the Black Ghetto.*
       New York: W. W. Norton.

2c/3a/4f/5b,g,i/8/9/10   US: Afro-Americans

2100   ——. 1971. "Capitalism, Colonialism, and Racism." *Review of Radical
       Political Economics* 3:90-106.

2c/3e/4b/5b,i,j/8/9   US: Afro-Americans

2101   ——. 1971. "Race Relations Models and Social Change." *Social Problems*
       18:431-43.

2e/3e/4f/5a,b,d,i   Theory

2102   TACHIKI, Amy, Eddie Wong, Franklin Odo, and Buck Wong, eds. 1971.

Roots: An Asian American Reader. Los Angeles: UCLA Asian American Studies Center.

1a/2b,c/3a/4i/5b,d,k/6/7/8/9/10/11/12   US: Asian Americans

2103   TAN, Allen L. and Grace E. de Vera. 1969. "Inter-ethnic Images between Filipinos and Chinese in the Philippines." *Asian Studies* 7:125-33.

2d/3c/4g,h/5g/11   Philippines

2104   TAPIA, Claude. 1974. "North African Jews in Belleville." *Jewish Journal of Sociology* 16:5-24.

2b/3a/4h/5k/6/8   France

2105   TASHJIAN, James H. 1970. *The Armenians of the United States and Canada.* Reprint, 1947 ed. Boston: Armenian Youth Federation at Hairenik Press.

2c/3a/4d/5a,d,k/6/7/8/12/13/17   Canada: Armenians; US: Armenians

2106   TATSUNO, Sheridan. 1971. "The Political and Economic Effects of Urban Renewal on Ethnic Communities: A Case Study of San Francisco's Japantown." *Amerasia Journal* 1:33-51.

2b/3a/4i/5k/10/11   US: Japanese

2107   TATZ, Colin M. 1972. *Four Kinds of Dominion: Comparative Race Relations in Australia, Canada, New Zealand, and South Africa.* Armidale, Australia: University of New England.

                    Australia; Canada: General;
2c/3d/4f/5i/8/9/10/11   New Zealand; South Africa

2108   TAX, Sol. 1942. "Ethnic Relations in Guatemala." *America Indigena* 2:43-48.

2b/3b/4a/5f,i/8/9/11   Guatemala

2109   TAYLOR, Philip. 1971. *The Distant Magnet: European Emigration to the USA.* New York: Harper & Row.

2a/3b/4d/5a,k/7   US: Euro-Americans

2110   TAYLOR, Stan. 1979. "The National Front: Anatomy of a Political Movement." In *Racism and Political Action in Britain,* edited by Robert

Miles and Annie Phizacklea, pp. 124-46. London: Routledge & Kegan Paul.

2c/3b/4f/5g/10/11   Britain: General

2111   TESKE, Raymond H. C. and Bardin H. Nelson. 1976. "An Analysis of Differential Assimilation Rates among Middle-Class Mexican Americans." *Sociological Quarterly* 17:218-35.

2d/3a/4h/5a/12/14   US: Mexican Americans

2112   TESSLER, Mark A. 1975. "Secularism in the Middle East? Reflections on Recent Palestinian Proposals." *Ethnicity* 2:178-203.

2c/3a/4a/5k/10/11/17   Israel

2113   ———. 1978. "The Identity of Religious Minorities in Non-Secular States: Jews in Tunisia and Morocco and Arabs in Israel." *Comparative Studies in Society and History* 20:359-73.

2d/3d/4a/5d/9/12   Israel; Morocco; Tunisia

2114   ———, William M. O'Barr, and David H. Spain. 1973. *Tradition and Identity in Changing Africa.* New York: Harper & Row.

2b,c/3a,b/4a/5d/11/12   Africa

2115   THOMAS, Colin J. and Colin H. Williams. 1978. "Language and Nationalism in Wales: A Case Study." *Ethnic and Racial Studies* 1:235-58.

2d/3b/4f/5e/10/16   Wales

2116   THOMAS, Ladd. 1974. "Bureaucratic Attitudes and Behavior as Obstacles to Political Integration of Thai Muslims." *Southeast Asia* 3:545-68.

2d/3a/4f/5g/11   Thailand

2117   THOMAS, W. I. and Flojan Znaniecki. 1918. *The Polish Peasant in Europe and America.* Chicago: University of Chicago Press.

2b,c/3a/4h/5a/6/7/9/11/12/14   US: Poles

2118   THOMPSON, Bobby and John H. Peterson, Jr. 1975. "Mississippi Choctaw Identity: Genesis and Change." In *The New Ethnicity: Perspectives from Ethnology.* 1973 Proceedings of the American Ethnological

Society, edited by John W. Bennett, pp. 179-96. St. Paul: West.

2b,c/3a/4a/5d/12   US: Native Americans

2119   THOMPSON, Edgar T. and Everett C. Hughes, eds. 1958. *Race: Individ-ual and Collective Behavior.* Glencoe, Ill.: The Free Press.

1a,b/2c/3b/4h/5h,i/9/11   General

2120   THOMPSON, Leonard. 1969. "Historical Perspectives of Pluralism in Africa." In *Pluralism in Africa,* edited by Leo Kuper and M. G. Smith, pp. 351-71. Berkeley and Los Angeles: University of California Press.

2c/3e/4d/5f,i/9/16   Africa

2121   THOMPSON, Richard. 1961. "Community Conflict in New Zealand: A Case Study." *Race* 3:28-38.

2b/3a/4h/5b/10/11   New Zealand

2122   ——. 1969. "Race Relations in New Zealand." In *Comparative Perspectives on Race Relations,* edited by Melvin Tumin, pp. 178-96. Boston: Little, Brown.

2c/3b/4h/5g,i/6/9/11/12   New Zealand

2123   THOMPSON, Stephen I. 1974. "Survival of Ethnicity in the Japanese Community of Lima, Peru." *Urban Anthropology* 3:243-61.

2b/3a/4a/5d,f/10/12   Peru

2124   ——. 1977. "Separate but Superior: Japanese in Bolivia." In *Ethnic Encounters: Identities and Contexts,* edited by George L. Hicks and Philip E. Leis, pp. 89-110. North Scituate, Mass.: Duxbury Press.

2b/3a/4a/5i/7/9/12   Bolivia

2125   THOMPSON, Virginia and Richard Adloff. 1955. *Minority Problems in Southeast Asia.* Stanford, Calif.: Stanford University Press.

2c/3d/4f/5b/6/9/10/12   Southeast Asia

2126   THONG, Lee Boon. 1977. "Malay Urbanization and the Ethnic Profile of Urban Centres in Peninsular Malaysia." *Journal of Southeast Asian Studies* 8:224-34.

2c/3a/4h/5k/6   Malaysia

2127   THORBURN, H. G. 1971. "French in the New Brunswick Civil Service:
       Ethnic Participation and Language Use." *Canadian Ethnic Studies* 3:23-54.

2d/3a/4h/5g,i/8/9/10/11   Canada: Québécois

2128   THORNDIKE, Robert L. 1977. "Content and Evaluation in Ethnic
       Stereotype." *Journal of Psychology* 96:131-40.

2d/3c/4g/5d,g/11   US: General

2129   TICE, Robert D. 1974. "Administrative Structure, Ethnicity, and Nation-
       Building in the Ivory Coast." *Journal of Modern African Studies* 12:211-
       29.

2b/3b/4f/5e/10   Ivory Coast

2130   TILLETT, Lowell. 1977. "The National Minorities Factor in the Sino-
       Soviet Dispute." *Orbis* 21:241-60.

2c/3e/4d,f/5b/10   China (PRC); USSR: General

2131   TINKER, Hugh. 1977. *Race, Conflict and the International Order: From
       Empire to United Nations.* London: Macmillan.

2c/3d/4f/5b/10   General

2132   TINKER, John N. 1973. "Intermarriage and Ethnic Boundaries: The
       Japanese American Case." *Journal of Social Issues* 29:49-66.

2b/3a/4h/5d/12/14   US: Japanese

2133   TJWAN, Go Gien. 1971. "The Changing Trade Position of the Chinese
       in Southeast Asia." *International Social Science Journal* 23:564-75.

2c/3a/4b/5c/8/9/10/11/12/13/14   Southeast Asia

2134   TOBIAS, Stephen F. 1977. "Buddhism, Belonging and Detachment—
       Some Paradoxes of Chinese Ethnicity in Thailand." *Journal of Asian Stud-
       ies* 36:303-25.

2b/3a/4a/5d/11/12/17   Thailand

2135   TODD, D. and J. S. Brierley. 1977. "Ethnicity and the Rural Economy:
       Illustrations from Southern Manitoba, 1961-1971." *Canadian Geographer*

21:237-49.

2c/3a/4c/5k/6/8 Canada: General

2136 TOLL, William. 1977. "American Jewish Families: The Occupational Basis of Adaptability in Portland, Oregon." *Jewish Journal of Sociology* 19:33-47.

2c/3a/4h/5c/6/8/14 US: Jews

2137 ——. 1978. "Fraternalism, and Community Structure on the Urban Frontier: The Jews of Portland, Oregon—A Case Study." *Pacific Historical Review* 47:369-403.

2c/3a/4d/5k/8/12/15 US: Jews

2138 TOMASI, Lydio F. 1972. *The Italians in America: The Progressive View, 1891-1914.* New York: Center for Migration Studies.

2c/3a/4d/5a,d/9/10 US: Italians

2139 ——. 1977. "The Italian Community in Toronto: A Demographic Profile." *International Migration Review* 11:486-513.

2c/3a/4i/5k/6/7/8/13 Canada: Italians

2140 TOMASI, Silvano M., ed. 1977. *Perspectives in Italian Immigration and Ethnicity.* Proceedings of the Symposium held at Casa Italiana, Columbia University, May 21-23, 1976. New York: Center for Migration Studies.

1a/2e/3e/4c,d,e,h/5k/6/7
8/10/14/15/16/17 Canada: Italians; US: Italians

2141 —— and Madeline H. Engel, eds. 1970. *The Italian Experience in the United States.* Staten Island, N.Y.: Center for Migration Studies.

1a/2b,c/3a/4h/5a/6/7/8/9/10/11/12/13/15/17 US: Italians

2142 TOPLIN, Robert Brent. 1971. "Reinterpreting Comparative Race Relations: The United States and Brazil." *Journal of Black Studies* 2:135-55.

2c/3d/4h/5i,k/9 Brazil; US: Afro-Americans

2143 TORNEY, Judith V. and Charles A. Tesconi, Jr. 1977. "Political Socialization Research and Respect for Ethnic Diversity." In *Pluralism in a*

Democratic Society, edited by Melvin Tumin and Walter Plotch, pp. 95-132. New York: Praeger.

2e/3e/4h/5g/10/11   US: General

2144   TOTTEN, George O. and Hiroshi Wagatsuma. 1966. "Emancipation: Growth and Transformation of a Political Movement." In *Japan's Invisible Race: Caste in Culture and Personality*, edited by George DeVos and Hiroshi Wagatsuma, pp. 33-67. Berkeley and Los Angeles: University of California Press.

2c/3a/4f,g/5i/9/10   Japan

2145   TOWNSEND, L. T. 1970. *The Chinese Problem*. Reprint, 1876 ed. Boston: Lee & Shepherd.

2c/3a/4d/5b,g,i/11   US: Chinese

2146   TREJO, Arnulfo D. 1975. *Bibliografia Chicana: A Guide to Information Sources*. Detroit: Gale Research.

2a   US: Mexican Americans

2147   TRENT, John. 1974. "The Politics of Nationalist Movement—A Reconsideration." *Canadian Review of Studies in Nationalism* 2:157-71.

2e/3e/4f/5e/10   Theory

2148   TRUEBLOOD, Marilyn A. 1977. "The Melting Pot and Ethnic Revitalization." In *Ethnic Encounters: Identities and Contexts*, edited by George L. Hicks and Philip E. Leis, pp. 153-67. North Scituate, Mass.: Duxbury Press.

2b/3a/4a/5a,d/7/12   US: Italians, Portuguese

2149   TRYGGVASON, Gustav. 1971. "The Effect of Intergroup Conflict in an Ethnic Community." *Canadian Ethnic Studies* 3:85-115.

2b/3a/4h/5k/10/15   Canada: General

2150   TUDEN, Arthur and Leonard Plotnicov, eds. 1970. *Social Stratification in Africa*. New York: The Free Press.

1a/2b,e/3a,b/4a/5i/8/9/10   Africa

2151   TUMIN, Melvin. 1949. "Reciprocity and Stability of Caste in Guatemala."

American Sociological Review 14:17-25.

2b/3b/4g/5i/8/9   Guatemala

2152 ——, ed. 1969. *Comparative Perspectives on Race Relations.* Boston: Little, Brown.

1a,b/2c/3b,d/4a,g,h/5g,i,k/6/8/9/10/11   General

2153 TURK, Austin T. 1972. "The Limits of Coercive Legalism in Conflict Regulation: South Africa." In *Racial Tensions and National Identity,* edited by Ernest Q. Campbell, pp. 171-98. Nashville, Tenn.: Vanderbilt University Press.

2c/3b/4h/5i,j/9/10   South Africa

2154 TWADDLE, Michael. 1969. "'Tribalism' in Eastern Uganda." In *Tradition and Transition in East Africa: Studies of the Tribal Element in the Modern Era,* edited by P. H. Gulliver, pp. 193-208. Berkeley and Los Angeles: University of California Press.

2b,c/3a/4a/5d/10/12   Uganda

2155 TYLER, Gus, ed. 1975. *Mexican-Americans Tomorrow: Educational and Economic Perspectives.* Albuquerque: University of New Mexico Press.

1a/2c/3a/4b,d,h/5k/6/7/8/12/13/15   US: Mexican Americans

2156 UCHENDU, Victor C. 1970. "The Passing of Tribal Man: A West African Experience." In *The Passing of Tribal Man in Africa,* edited by P. C. W. Gutkind, pp. 51-65. Leiden: E. J. Brill.

2b/3a/4a/5d/11/12   Nigeria

2157 ULLMAN, Albert D. 1960. "Ethnic Differences in the First Drinking Experience." *Social Problems* 8:45-56.

2b/3c/4h/5k/12   US: General

2158 ULRICH-ATENA, Ela. 1976. "National Linguistic Minorities: Bilingual Basic Education in Slovenia." *Prospects* 6:430-38.

2c/3a/4e,i(Education)/5f/13/16   Yugoslavia

2159 UNITED NATIONS Commission on Human Rights. 1950. *Definition* and *Classification of Minorities.* Lake Success, N.Y.: UN.

2e/3d/4i/5k/12   Theory

2160   UNITED NATIONS Economic Commission for Africa. 1963. *Economic and Social Consequences of Discriminatory Practices.* New York: UN.

2c/3e/4i/5h,i/8/9/10   Africa

2161   UNITED NATIONS Educational, Scientific, and Cultural Organization. 1961. *Race and Science.* New York: Columbia University Press.

1a/2c/3e/4a,g,h/5g/11   General

2162   UNITED NATIONS Education, Scientific, and Cultural Organization. 1974. *Race as News.* Paris: UNESCO Press.

2c,d/3b,e/4g,h/5g/11/16   Britain: General; France

2163   UNITED STATES Bureau of the Census. 1975. *The Social and Economic Status of the Black Population in the United States 1974.* Current Population Reports, Special Studies, series P-23, no. 54. Washington, D.C.: U.S. Government Printing Office.

2d/3a/4i(Demography)/5k/6/8/10/13/14   US: Afro-Americans

2164   UNITED STATES Bureau of the Census. 1979. *The Social and Economic Status of the Black Population in the United States: An Historical View, 1790-1978.* Current Population Reports, Special Studies, series P-23, no. 80. Washington, D.C.: U.S. Government Printing Office.

2c,d/3a/4i(Demography)/5k/6/8/10/13/14   US: Afro-Americans

2165   UNIVERSITY LEAGUE for Social Reform. 1966. *Nationalism in Canada,* edited by Peter Russell. Toronto: McGraw-Hill.

1a/2b/3b/4d,f/5e/7/10/12   Canada: General

2166   USSACH, Steven Samuel. 1975. "The New England Portuguese: A Plural Society within a Plural Society." *Plural Societies* 6:47-58.

2c/3a/4d/5k/7/12   US: Portuguese

2167   VAKAR, Nicholas P. 1968. "The Belorussian People: Between Nationhood and Extinction." In *Ethnic Minorities in the Soviet Union,* edited by Erich Goldhagen, pp. 218-28. New York: Frederick A. Praeger.

2c/3a/4i/5a/12/16   USSR: Byelorussians

2168 VALENTINE, C.A. 1975. "Voluntary Ethnicity and Social Change: Classism, Racism, Marginality, Mobility, and Revolution with Special Reference to Afro-Americans and other Third World Peoples." *Journal of Ethnic Studies* 3:1-27.

2e/3c/4a/5b,f,i/9/12   Theory

2169 VAN DEN BERGHE, Pierre L. 1960. "Hypergamy, Hypergenation, and Miscegenation." *Human Relations* 13:83-91.

2e/3e/4h/5i/9/14   Theory

2170 ———. 1962. "Indians in Natal and Fiji: A 'Controlled Experiment,' in Culture Contact." *Civilisations* 12:75-84.

2b/3d/4h/5f,i/8/9/11   Fiji; South Africa

2171 ———. 1963. "Racialism and Assimilation in Africa and the Americas." *Southwestern Journal of Anthropology* 19:424-32.

2c/3e/4a/5a,f,g,i   Africa; Mesoamerica; North America; South America

2172 ———. 1964. *Caneville: The Social Structure of a South African Town.* Middletown, Conn.: Wesleyan University Press.

2b/3a/4h/5f,i/8/9/15   South Africa

2173 ———. 1964. "Towards a Sociology of Africa." *Social Forces* 43:11-18.

2c/3e/4h/5f/9   Africa

2174 ———. 1965. *South Africa: A Study in Conflict.* Middletown, Conn.: Wesleyan University Press.

2b/3b/4h/5b,f,i/9/10/11   South Africa

2175 ———. 1967. "Language and Nationalism in South Africa." *Race* 9:36-46.

2b/3b/4h/5e/10/16   South Africa

2176 ———. 1969. "Pluralism and the Polity: A Theoretical Exploration." In *Pluralism in Africa,* edited by Leo Kuper and M. G. Smith, pp. 67-84. Berkeley and Los Angeles: University of California Press.

2e/3e/4h/5f   Theory

2177 ——. 1970. "Pluralism and Conflict Situations in Africa: A Reply to Magubane." *African Social Research* 9:681-89.

2e/3e/4h/5b,f   Africa

2178 ——. 1970. "Race, Class, and Ethnicity in South Africa." In *Social Stratification in Africa,* edited by Arthur Tuden and Leonard Plotnicov, pp. 345-71. New York: Free Press.

2c/3b/4h/5i/8/9   South Africa

2179 ——. 1971. "Ethnicity: The African Experience." *International Social Science Journal* 23:507-18.

2c/3d/4h/5f/9/10/11/12   Africa

2180 ——. 1971. "Pluralism at a Nigerian University: A Case Study." *Race* 12:429-42.

2c/3a/4h/5f,i/9/13   Nigeria

2181 ——. 1973. "Pluralism." In *Handbook of Social and Cultural Anthropology,* edited by John J. Honigmann, pp. 959-78. Chicago: Rand McNally.

2e/3e/4h/5f   Theory

2182 ——. 1974. *Class and Ethnicity in Peru.* Leiden: E. J. Brill.

2b/3b/4h/5b,d,f,i/8/9/11   Peru

2183 ——, ed. 1974. "Special Number on Class and Ethnicity in Peru." *International Journal of Comparative Sociology,* vol. 15, nos. 3-4.

1a/2b/3b/4h/5d,f,i/8/9   Peru

2184 ——. 1975. "Ethnicity and Class in Highland Peru." In *Ethnicity and Resource Competition in Plural Societies,* edited by Leo A. Despres, pp. 71-85. The Hague: Mouton.

2b/3a/4a/5d,i/9/12   Peru

2185 ——. 1976. "The African Diaspora in Mexico, Brazil, and the United States." *Social Forces* 54:530-45.

2c/3e/4h/5k/7/9/10/11   Brazil; Mexico; US: Afro-Americans

2186   VAN DER KROEF, Justus M. 1976. "Religion, Ethnicity, and Communist Tactics in Southeast Asia's Plural Societies." *Plural Societies* 7: 3-25.

    2b/3d/4f/5k/10   Southeast Asia

2187   VAN DER MERWE, Hendrik W. and Basil Kivedo. 1975. "Recent Trends in Coloured-White Contact Patterns and Attitudes in South Africa." *International Review of Modern Sociology* 5:173-84.

    2c/3b/4h/5g/11   South Africa

2188   VAN DER PLANK, P. H. 1975. "Language and Nationalism: A Historical Review on the Role of Language in Nationalistic Ideologies." *Plural Societies* 6:9-16.

    2c/3d/4e/5e/11/16   Europe

2189   VANDERZANDEN, James W. 1972. *American Minority Relations.* 3d ed. New York: Ronald Press.

    1b/2c/3b/4h/5a,b,f,g,i/9/10/11   US: General

2190   VAN DYKE, Vernon. 1977. "The Individual, the State, and Ethnic Communities in Political Theory." *World Politics* 29:343-59.

    2c,e/3e/4f/5d,e,f/11   Theory

2191   VAN LIER, R. A. J. 1950. *The Development and Nature of Society in the West Indies.* Amsterdam: Royal Institute for the Indies.

    2b,c/3a/4a,d,f/5f,i/9/10   Caribbean

2192   ——. 1971. *Frontier Society: A Social Analysis of the History of Surinam.* The Hague: Martinus Nijhoff.

    2c/3b/4d/5b,f,i/7/8/9/10   Surinam

2193   VANNEMAN, Reeve D. and Thomas F. Pettigrew. 1972. "Race and Relative Deprivation in the Urban United States." *Race* 13:461-86.

    2b,c/3b/4g/5d,g/9/10   US: Afro-Americans

2194   VARDYS, V. Stanley. 1975. "Modernization and Baltic Nationalism." *Problems of Communism* 24:32-48.

    2c/3d/4f/5e/6/10/12/14/16   USSR: Estonians, Latvians, Lithuanians

2195 VASQUEZ, Mario C. 1970. "Immigration and 'Mestizaje' in Nineteenth-Century Peru." In *Race and Class in Latin America,* edited by Magnus Mörner, pp. 73-95. New York: Columbia University Press.

2c/3b/4d/5k/7   Peru

2196 VAUGHAN, James H., Jr. 1970. "Caste Systems in the Western Sudan." In *Social Stratification in Africa,* edited by Arthur Tuden and Leonard Plotnicov, pp. 59-92. New York: Free Press.

2b/3a/4a/5i/8/9/11/12   Sudan

2197 VECOLI, Rudolph J. 1972. "European Americans: From Immigrants to Ethnics." *International Migration Review* 6:403-34.

2c/3b/4h/5a/7/10   US: Euro-Americans

2198 VELTMAN, Calvin J. 1977. "The Evolution of Ethno-Linguistic Frontiers in the United States and Canada." *Social Science Journal* 14:47-58.

2c,e/3d/4h/5f/16   Canada: General; US: General

2199 VERDERY, Katherine. 1979. "Internal Colonialism in Austria-Hungary." *Ethnic and Racial Studies* 2:378-99.

2c/3e/4d/5j/8/9/10   Austria; Hungary

2200 VILLACORTA, Wilfredo V. and Charles McCarthy, S. J., eds. 1976. "The Chinese in ASEAN Countries: Changing Roles and Expectations." *Philippine Sociological Review,* vol. 24, nos. 1-4.

1a/2a,b,d/3a/4f,h/5a,e/8/9/10/11   Southeast Asia

2201 VILLAMEZ, Wayne J. and John D. Kasarda. 1977. "The Impact of Regional Destination on Black Migrant Income." *Social Science Quarterly* 57:767-83.

2d/3a/4h/5k/7/8   US: Afro-Americans

2202 VINCENT, Joan. 1974. "The Structuring of Ethnicity." *Human Organization* 33:375-79.

2e/3e/4a/5d,i   Theory

2203 VINOGRADOV, Amal. 1974. "Ethnicity, Cultural Discontinuity and Power Brokers in Northern Iraq: The Case of the Shabak." *American*

Ethnologist 1:207-18.

2b/3a/4a/5c/8/9/10/17   Iraq

2204 VINYARD, Jo Ellen McNergney. 1976. *The Irish on the Urban Frontier: Nineteenth Century Detroit.* New York: Arno Press.

2c/3a/4d/5a,f/8/9   US: Irish

2205 VIRGIL, Maurilio. 1978. *Chicano Politics.* Washington, D.C.: University Press of America.

2c/3a/4f/5b/10/12/15   US: Mexican Americans

2206 VON HAGEN, Victor Wolfgang. 1976. *The Germanic People in America.* Norman: University of Oklahoma Press.

2c/3a/4d/5a,d/7/12/16/17   US: Germans

2207 VREELAND, H. H. 1958. "The Concept of Ethnic Groups as Related to Whole Societies." In *Report of the Ninth Annual Round Table Meeting on Linguistics and Language Studies,* edited by W. M. Austin, pp. 81-88. Monograph Series on Languages and Linguistics, no. 11. Washington, D.C.: Georgetown University Press.

2e/3e/4e/5k/11/12   Theory

2208 VRGA, Djuro J. and Frank J. Fahey. 1969. "Structural Sources of Ethnic Factionalism." *Social Science* 44:12-19.

2d/3a/4h/5k/7/12/17   US: Serbs

2209 WADDELL, J. O. and A. M. Watson, eds. 1971. *The American Indian in Urban Society.* Boston: Little, Brown.

1a/2b/3a/4a/5d,k/7/8/10/13   US: Native Americans

2210 WAGATSUMA, Hiroshi. 1966. "Non-Political Approaches: The Influences of Religion and Education." In *Japan's Invisible Race: Caste in Culture and Personality,* edited by George DeVos and Hiroshi Wagatsuma, pp. 88-109. Berkeley and Los Angeles: University of California Press.

2c/3a/4g/5g/9/11/13/17   Japan

2211 ——. 1966. "Postwar Political Militance." In *Japan's Invisible Race: Caste in Culture and Personality,* edited by George DeVos and Hiroshi

Wagatsuma, pp. 68-87. Berkeley and Los Angeles: University of California Press.

2c/3a/4g/5b,i/9/10   Japan

2212   ——. 1978. "Identity Problems of Black Japanese Youth." In *The Mixing of Peoples,* edited by Robert I. Rotberg, pp. 117-29. Stamford, Conn.: Greylock.

2b/3a/4g/5d,g/11/12   Japan

2213   —— and George DeVos. 1966. "The Ecology of Special Buraku." In *Japan's Invisible Race: Caste in Culture and Personality,* edited by George DeVos and Hiroshi Wagatsuma, pp. 113-28. Berkeley and Los Angeles: University of California Press.

2c/3a/4a,g/5i/6/8/14   Japan

2214   WAGENHEIM, Kal. 1975. *A Survey of Puerto Ricans on the U.S. Mainland in the 1970's.* New York: Praeger.

2d/3a/4h/5k/6/7/8/12/13/14/16   US: Puerto Ricans

2215   WAGLEY, Charles. 1960. "Discussion of Social and Cultural Pluralism." *Annals of the New York Academy of Sciences* 83:777-80.

2e/3e/4a/5f   Theory

2216   ——. 1969. "From Caste to Class in North Brazil." In *Comparative Perspectives on Race Relations,* edited by M. Tumin, pp. 47-62. Boston: Little, Brown.

2b/3b/4a/5i/8/9/11/12   Brazil

2217   ——, ed. 1972. *Race and Class in Brazil.* New York: Russell & Russell.

1a/2b/3a,b/4a,h/5g,i/9/11   Brazil

2218   —— and Marvin Harris. 1958. *Minorities in the New World: Six Case Studies.* New York: Columbia University Press.

2c/3a,d/4a/5g,i   Brazil; Canada: Québécois; Martinique;
8/9/10/11/12/14   Mexico; US: Afro-Americans, Jews

2219   WAGNER, Nathaniel N. and Marsha J. Haug, eds. 1971. *Chicanos: Social and Psychological Perspectives.* St. Louis, Mo.: C. V. Mosby.

1a/2b,c,d/3a/4a,g,h/5a,d,g,i/6/7/8
9/10/11/12/13/14/15   US: Mexican Americans

2220   WAI, Dunston M. 1978. "Sources of Communal Conflicts and Secession-
       ist Politics in Africa." *Ethnic and Racial Studies* 1:286-305.

       2c/3b/4f/5b,f,i/9/10/11   Africa

2221   WALD, Benji. 1974. "Bilingualism." *Annual Review of Anthropology*
       3:301-21.

       2e/3e/4a,e/5d,k/16   Theory

2222   WALLERSTEIN, Immanuel, ed. 1966. *Social Change: The Colonial
       Situation.* New York: Wiley.

       1a/2c/3e/4d,h/5i/9/10/11   General

2223   ——. 1973. "Imperialism and Capitalism: Are the Workers the Most
       Oppressed Class?" *Insurgent Sociologist* 3:25-28.

       2e/3e/4h/5b,i/9/11   Theory

2224   ——. 1973. "The Two Modes of Ethnic Consciousness: Soviet Central
       Asia in Transition." In *The Nationality Question in Soviet Central Asia,*
       edited by Edward Allworth, pp. 168-75. New York: Praeger.

       2f/3b/4h/5d,i/9/10/12   USSR: Central Asians

2225   WALLIMAN, Isidor. 1974. "Toward a Theoretical Understanding of
       Ethnic Antagonism: The Case of Factory Workers in Switzerland."
       Zeitschrift für Soziologie 3:84-94.

       2c/3b/4h/5b,i/8/9/10   Switzerland

2226   WALSH, James P., ed. 1976. *The Irish: America's Political Class.* New
       York: Arno Press.

       1a/2c/3a/4d/5d,k/10   US: Irish

2227   WARGELIN, John. 1972. *The Americanization of the Finns.* San Fran-
       cisco: R & E Research Associates.

       2c/3a/4h/5a/6/7/8/12/13/14/15/16   US: Finns

2228   WARNER, W. Lloyd and Lee Srole. 1945. *The Social Systems of Ameri-*

can *Immigrant Groups*. New Haven, Conn.: Yale University Press.

2b/3a/4h/5a/6/8/9/14/15/16/17   US: Euro-Americans

2229   WARREN, Jim. 1978. "Who Were the Balingingi Samal? Slave Raiding and Ethnogenesis in Nineteenth Century Sulu." *Journal of Asian Studies* 37:477-90.

2c/3a/4d/5d/10/12   Philippines

2230   WARREN, Max. 1964. "Christian Minorities in Muslim Countries." *Race* 6:41-51.

2c/3e/4i/5i/9/11/12/17   General

2231   WASHBURN, Wilcomb E. 1975. *The Indian in America*. New York: Harper & Row.

2c/3a/4d/5b,i,k/9/10/12   US: Native Americans

2232   WASSERMAN, Paul and Jean Morgan, eds. 1976. *Ethnic Information Sources of the United States*. Detroit, Mich.: Gale Research.

2a   US: General

2233   WATANUKI, Joji. 1971. "State Formation and Nation-Building in East Asia." *International Social Science Journal* 23:421-34.

2c/3d/4f/5e/10   China (PRC); Japan; Korea

2234   WATSON, G. Llewellyn. 1973. "Social Structure and Social Movements: The Black Muslims in the U.S.A. and the Ras-Tafarians in Jamaica." *British Journal of Sociology* 24:188-204.

2b/3d/4h/5b,i/9/10   Jamaica; US: Afro-Americans

2235   ——. 1974. "Patterns of Black Protest in Jamaica: The Case of the Ras-Tafarians." *Journal of Black Studies* 4:329-43.

2b/3a/4h/5b/10/17   Jamaica

2236   WATSON, James L. 1977. "The Chinese: Hong Kong Villagers in the British Catering Trade." In *Between Two Cultures: Migrants and Minorities in Britain,* edited by James L. Watson, pp. 181-213. Oxford: Basil Blackwell.

2b/3a/4a/5k/7/8/15   Britain: Chinese

2237   ——. 1977. "Introduction: Immigration, Ethnicity, and Class in Britain."
        In *Between Two Cultures: Migrants and Minorities in Britain,* edited by
        James L. Watson, pp. 1-20. Oxford: Basil Blackwell.

2e/3b/4a/5k/7/9/12   Britain: General

2238   WATSON, Peter. 1974. *Psychology and Race.* Chicago: Aldine.

2c,e/3e/4g/5d,g,i/9/11   General

2239   WATTS, Betty H. 1972. "The Part-Aborigines of Australia." In *The
        Blending of Races: Marginality and Identity in World Perspective,* edited
        by Noel P. Gist and Anthony Gary Dworkin, pp. 121-42. New York:
        Wiley-Interscience.

2c/3a/4i(Education)/5k/6/8/11/12/13/14   Australia

2240   WATTS, Ronald L. 1970. *Multicultural Societies and Federalism.* Ot-
        towa: Information Canada.

2e/3d,e/4f/5f/10/11   Theory

2241   WAX, Rosalie H. and Robert K. Thomas. 1961. "American Indians and
        White People." *Phylon* 22:305-17.

2c/3b/4a/5k/9/10/11   US: Native Americans

2242   WEBB, Keith. 1977. *The Growth of Nationalism in Scotland.* Glasgow:
        Molendinar Press.

2c/3b/4d/5e/10   Scotland

2243   WEBER, David J., ed. 1973. *Foreigners in Their Native Land: Historical
        Roots of the Mexican American.* Albuquerque: University of New Mexico
        Press.

1a/2c/3a/4d/5g/7/11   US: Mexican Americans

2244   WEBSTER, Staten W. 1972. *Knowing and Understanding the Socially
        Disadvantaged: Ethnic Minority Groups.* Scranton, Penn.: Intext.

                                                     US: Afro-, Asian-, Mexican-, Native
2c/3a/4h/5k/8/9/13   Americans, Puerto Ricans

2245   WEED, Perry L. 1972. *Ethnicity and American Group Life: A Bibliography.* New York: Institute of Human Relations.

       2a   US: General

2246   ——. 1973. *The White Ethnic Movement and Ethnic Politics.* New York: Praeger.

       2c/3b/4f/5b/10/12   US: Euro-Americans

2247   WEIL, Shalva. 1977. "Names and Identity among the Bene Israel." *Ethnic Groups* 1:201-19.

       2b,c/3b/4a/5d/12   Israel

2248   WEINER, Myron. 1978. "Sons of the Soil: Migration, Ethnicity, and Nativism in India." In *The Mixing of Peoples,* edited by Robert I. Rotberg, pp. 151-77. Stamford, Conn.: Greylock.

       2c/3b/4f/5k/7/9/10/11/16   India

2249   THE WEINER LIBRARY, London. 1971. *Prejudice: Racist-Religious-Nationalist.* London: Valentine, Mitchell.

       2a/11   General

2250   WEINSTEIN, Warren and Robert Schrire. 1975. "Ethnic Strategies and the Primacy of Ethnic Survival: The Case of Burundi." *International Review of Modern Sociology* 5:185-92.

       2c/3b/4f/5b/10   Burundi

2251   WEISBROD, Robert G. 1975. "Israel and the Black Hebrew Israelites." *Judaism* 24:23-38.

       2b/3a/4h/5d/7/9/11/12/17   Israel

2252   WEISER, Marjorie P. K., ed. 1978. *Ethnic America.* New York: H. W. Wilson.

       1a/2c/3b/4i/5a,b,f,g,i/12/13/14   US: General

2253   WEISS, Melford S. 1974. *Valley City: A Chinese Community in America.* Cambridge, Mass.: Schenkman.

       2b/3a/4h/5k/6/7/8/9/10/11/12/13/14/15   US: Chinese

2254   WELCH, Michael R. 1977. "Review of the Polls: Ethnicity and Religious Affiliation." *Journal for the Scientific Study of Religion* 16:193-95.

　　　　2d/3c/4h/5d/12/17　　　　　　　　　　US: Euro-Americans

2255   WELLMAN, Barry. 1971. "Social Identities in Black and White." *Sociological Inquiry* 41:54-66.

　　　　2d/3c/4h/5d/12　　　　　　　　　US: Afro-, Euro-Americans

2256   WENZEL, Lawrence A. 1968. "The Rural Punjabis of California: A Religio-Ethnic Group." *Phylon* 29:245-56.

　　　　2b/3a/4a/5k/6/8/9/14　　　　　　　　　US: East Indians

2257   WEPPNER, Robert S. 1971. "Urban Economic Opportunities: The Example of Denver." In *The American Indian in Urban Society,* edited by Jack O. Waddell and O. Michael Watson, pp. 245-73. Boston: Little, Brown.

　　　　2b,d/3a/4a/5i/8/9　　　　　　　　　US: Native Americans

2258   WERLING, Joan. 1968. *History of Slavs in America.* San Francisco: R & E Research Associates.

　　　　2c/3a/4d/5k/7　　　　　　　　　　　　US: Slavs

2259   WESTON, J. S. 1969. "The Australian Aboriginal: What White Australians Know and Think About Him—A Preliminary Survey." *Race* 10: 411-34.

　　　　2d/3b/4g/5g/11　　　　　　　　　　　　Australia

2260   WHITAKER, Ben, ed. 1973. *The Fourth World: Victims of Group Oppression.* New York: Schocken Books.

　　　　1a/2b/3a,b/4i/5a,f,g,j　　　　Brazil; Ethiopia; Ireland; Japan; N. Ireland;
　　　　6/8/9/10/11/12/17　　　　　　Sudan; USSR: General; Zimbabwe

2261   WHITE, Naomi Rosh. 1978. "Ethnicity, Culture and Cultural Pluralism." *Ethnic and Racial Studies* 1:139-53.

　　　　2e/3e/4i/5f　　　　　　　　　　　　　　Theory

2262   WHITELY, W. H. 1969. "Language Choice and Language Planning in East Africa." In *Tradition and Transition in East Africa,* edited by P. H.

Gulliver, pp. 105-25. Berkeley and Los Angeles: University of California Press.

2c/3d/4c/5f/12/13/16   East Africa

2263   WHITTEN, Norman E., Jr. 1975. "Jungle Quechua Ethnicity: An Ecuadorian Case Study." In *Ethnicity and Resource Competition in Plural Societies,* edited by Leo A. Despres, pp. 41-69. The Hague: Mouton.

2b/3a/4a/5b,d,i/10/11/12   Ecuador

2264   —— and John F. Szwed, eds. 1970. *Afro-American Anthropology: Contemporary Perspectives.* New York: Free Press.

1a/2b,c/3a,d/4a/5k/6/8/10/11/12/14   US: Afro-Americans

2265   WILCOX, Jerry and Wade Clark Roof. 1978. "Percent Black and Black-White Status Inequality: Southern versus Nonsouthern Patterns." *Social Science Quarterly* 59:421-34.

2c/3b/4h/5i/6/9   US: Afro-Americans

2266   WILD, R. and C. Ridgeway. 1970. "The Job Expectations of Immigrant Workers." *Race* 11:323-34.

2d/3b/4h/5k/7/8/9/11   Britain: General

2267   WILEY, Norbert F. 1967. "The Ethnic Mobility Trap and Stratification Theory." *Social Problems* 15:147-59.

2e/3e/4h/5i/9   US: General

2268   WILLIAMS, Colin H. 1976. "Cultural Nationalism in Wales." *Canadian Review of Studies in Nationalism* 4:15-37.

2b/3b/4f/5e/10/12/16   Wales

2269   WILLIAMS, J. Allen, Jr. and Louis St. Peters. 1977. "Ethnicity and Socioeconomic Status as Determinants of Social Participation: A Test of the Interaction Hypothesis." *Social Science Quarterly* 57:892-98.

2d/3a/4h/5k/15   US: Afro-Americans

2270   WILLIAMS, John E. and J. Kenneth Morland. 1976. *Race, Color, and the Young Child.* Chapel Hill: University of North Carolina Press.

2c/3e/4a,g/5g/11/12   Theory

2271   WILLIAMS, Lea E. 1966. *The Future of the Overseas Chinese in Southeast Asia.* New York: McGraw-Hill.

   2c/3a/4i/5b,i/8/9/10   Southeast Asia

2272   WILLIAMS, Loretta J. 1975. "Black Subordination in Colonies and Nations: 1619-1945." In *Politics of Race: Comparative Studies,* edited by Donald G. Baker, pp. 45-71. Lexington, Mass.: Lexington Books.

   2c/3b/4h/5b,i/9/10   US: Afro-Americans

2273   WILLIAMS, Robin M., Jr. 1947. *The Reduction of Intergroup Tensions: A Survey of Research on Problems of Ethnic, Racial, and Religious Group Relations.* New York: Social Science Research Council.

   2c,e/3e/4h/5a,b,e,f,g/6/9/10   General

2274   ——. 1964. *Strangers Next Door: Ethnic Relations in American Communities.* Englewood Cliffs, N.J.: Prentice-Hall.

   2d/3a/4h/5g/9/11   US: General

2275   WILLIE, Charles V. 1972. *Black/Brown/White Relations: Race Relations in the 1970s.* New Brunswick, N.J.: Transaction Books.

   1b/2b,c/3b/4f,h/5b,g,i/9/10/13   US: Afro-Americans

2276   WILLIS, R. 1968. "Ethnic and National Images: Peoples vs. Nations." *Public Opinion Quarterly* 32:186-201.

   2c/3e/4g/5d,g/11   General

2277   WILLMOTT, Donald Earl. 1960. *The Chinese of Semarang: A Changing Minority Community in Indonesia.* Ithaca, N.Y.: Cornell University Press.

   2b/3a/4a/5k/8/9/10/11   Indonesia

2278   WILLMOTT, W. E. 1969. "Congregations and Associations: The Political Structure of the Chinese Community in Phnom-Penh, Cambodia." *Comparative Studies in Society and History* 11:282-301.

   2b/3a/4a/5k/6/8/10/12/14/15   Kampuchea

2279   WILSON, Franklin D. and Karl E. Taeuber. 1978. "Residential and School Segregation: Some Tests of Their Association." In *The Demography of Racial and Ethnic Groups,* edited by Frank D. Bean and W. Parker Frisbie, pp. 51-78. New York: Academic Press.

2c/3b/4h/5g,i/6/9/13   US: Afro-, Euro-, Latin Americans

2280   WILSON, Godfrey. 1942. *An Essay on the Economics of Detribalization in Northern Rhodesia.* Rhodes-Livingstone Papers, nos. 5-6. Livingstone, Northern Rhodesia: Rhodes-Livingstone Institute.

2b/3b/4a/5f,j/8/9/10/11   Zambia

2281   WIMBUSH, S. Enders. 1978. "The Great Russians and the Soviet State: The Dilemmas of Ethnic Dominance." In *Soviet Nationality Policies and Practices,* edited by Jeremy R. Azrael, pp. 349-60. New York: Praeger.

2c/3b/4f/5e/10/11   USSR: Russians

2282   WINSTON, Henry. 1977. *Class, Race and Black Liberation.* New York: International.

2f/3e/4i/5b,j/8/9/10   US: Afro-Americans

2283   WIRT, Frederick M. 1979. "The Stranger within My Gate: Ethnic Minorities and School Policy in Europe." *Comparative Education Review* 23:17-40.

2e/3d/4i(Education)/5a,f,i/10/12/13   Europe

2284   WISE, Jennings C. 1971. *The Red Man in the New World Drama: A Politico-Legal Study with a Pageantry of American Indian History.* New York: Macmillan.

2c/3a/4d/5k/10   US: Native Americans

2285   WITTERMANS, Elizabeth. 1964. *Interethnic Relations in a Plural Society.* Groningen: J. B. Wolters.

2b/3a/4h/5f,g/9/10/14   US: General

2286   ——. 1972. "The Eurasians of Indonesia." In *The Blending of Races: Marginality and Identity in World Perspective,* edited by Noel P. Gist and Anthony Gary Dworkin, pp. 79-102. New York: Wiley-Interscience.

2c/3a/4a/5d/9/10/12   Indonesia

2287   WITTKE, Carl. 1956. *The Irish in America.* Baton Rouge: Louisiana State University Press.

2c/3a/4d/5a/6/7/8/9/10/11/12/14/15/16/17   US: Irish

2288 ——. 1967. *The Germans in America.* New York: Teachers College Press.

2c/3a/4d/5k/7/9/11/12/14   US: Germans

2289 ——. 1967. *We Who Built America: The Saga of the Immigrant.* Rev. ed. Cleveland: Press of Case Western Reserve University.

2c/3b/4d/5k/6/7/9/11/12/15   US: Euro-Americans

2290 ——. 1968. *The Irish in America.* New York: Teachers College Press.

2c/3a/4d/5k/7/9/10/11/12/14   US: Irish

2291 WIXMAN, Ronald. 1973. "Recent Assimilation Trends in Soviet Central Asia." In *The Nationality Question in Soviet Central Asia,* edited by Edward Allworth, pp. 73-85. New York: Praeger.

2c/3b/4c/5a/6/16   USSR: Central Asians

2292 WOLLHEIM, O. D. 1963. "The Coloured People of South Africa." *Race* 5:25-41.

2b/3a/4h/5f,g/6/8/9/10/11/12/13   South Africa

2293 WOLPE, Harold. 1970. "Industrialism and Race in South Africa." In *Race and Racialism,* edited by Sami Zubaida, pp. 151-79. London: Tavistock.

2c/3b/4h/5i,j/8/9/10/11   South Africa

2294 ——. 1975. "The Theory of Internal Colonialism: The South African Case." In *Beyond the Sociology of Development: Economy and Society in Latin America and Africa,* edited by Ivar Oxaal, Tony Barnett, and David Booth, pp. 229-52. London: Routledge & Kegan Paul.

2c/3b/4f/5b,f,j,k/8/9/10   South Africa

2295 WONG, Bernard. 1977. "Elites and Ethnic Boundary Maintenance: A Study of the Roles of Elites in Chinatown, New York City." *Urban Anthropology* 6:1-22.

2b/3a/4a/5d/10/15   US: Chinese

2296 ——. 1978. "A Comparative Study of the Assimilation of the Chinese in New York City and Lima, Peru." *Comparative Studies in Society and History* 20:335-58.

2b/3d/4a/5a/6/8/12   Peru; US: Chinese

2297   WOYCHENKO, Ol'ha. 1967. *The Ukrainians in Canada.* Canada Ethnie
       4. Winnipeg: Trident Press.

       2c/3a/4d/5k/6/7/8/10/12/13/15/17   Canada: Ukrainians

2298   WRIGHT, David E., Esteban Salinas, and William P. Kuvlesky. 1973.
       "Opportunities for Social Mobility for Mexican-American Youth." In
       Chicanos and Native Americans: The Territorial Minorities, edited by
       Rudolph O. de la Garza et al., pp. 43-60. Englewood Cliffs, N.J.: Prentice-
       Hall.

       2d/3a/4g,h/5a,d/11   US: Mexican Americans

2299   WRIGHT, Erik Olin. 1978. "Race, Class, and Income Inequality."
       American Journal of Sociology 83:1368-97.

       2c/3c/4h/5i/8/9   US: General

2300   WRIGHT, Franklin W. 1974. *The African Dimension in Latin American
       Societies.* New York: Macmillan.

       2b,c/3d/4d/5k/8/9/10/11/12   Mesoamerica; South America

2301   WURM, Stephen A. 1971. "Language Policy, Language Engineering, and
       Literacy in New Guinea and Australia." *Current Trends in Linguistics* 8:
       1025-38.

       2c/3d/4e/5k/10/11/16   Australia; Papua New Guinea

2302   WYSZOMIRSKI, Margaret J. 1975. "Communal Violence: The Arme-
       nians and the Copts as Case Studies." *World Politics* 27:430-55.

       2c/3c/4d/5b/9/10   Egypt; USSR: Armenians

2303   XYDIS, Stephen G. 1969. "Modern Greek Nationalism." In *Nationalism
       in Eastern Europe,* edited by Peter F. Sugar and Ivo J. Lederer, pp. 207-
       58. Seattle: University of Washington Press.

       2c/3b/4d/5e/10   Greece

2304   YAFFE, Sam. 1968. *The American Jews.* New York: Random House.

       2c/3a/4d/5k/9/11/12/13/14   US: Jews

2305   YANAGISAKO, Sylvia Junko. 1975. "Two Processes of Change in
       Japanese-American Kinship." *Journal of Anthropological Research*

31:196-224.

2b/3a/4a/5k/14   US: Japanese

2306   YANCEY, William L., Leo Rigsby, and John D. McCarthy. 1972. "Social
        Position and Self-Evaluation: The Relative Importance of Race." *American Journal of Sociology* 78:338-59.

2d/3a/4g,h/5d/9/12   US: General

2307   YEE, Albert H. 1973. "Myopic Perceptions and Textbooks: Chinese
        Americans' Search for Identity." *Journal of Social Issues* 29:99-113.

2b/3a/4h/5d/11/12/13   US: Chinese

2308   YIN, Robert K., ed. 1973. *Race, Creed, Color, or National Origin: A
        Reader on Racial and Ethnic Identities in American Society.* Itasca, Ill.:
        F. E. Peacock.

1a/2c/3b/4h/5d,g/11/12   US: General

2309   YINGER, J. Milton and George Eaton Simpson, eds. 1978. *American
        Indians Today.* The Annals of the American Academy of Political and
        Social Science, no. 436.

1a/2b,c/3a/4a,d,f/5a,d/6/7/8/10/11/12/17   US: Native Americans

2310   YOUNG, Jared J. 1977. *Discrimination, Income, Human Capital Investment, and Asian Americans.* San Francisco: R & E Research Associates.

2c/3b/4b/5g,i/8/9   US: Asian Americans

2311   YOUNG, Warren L. 1973. "Minority Group Participation in the US and
        UK Armed Forces: An Overview." *Plural Societies* 4:3-55.

2d/3d/4b/5k/9/10   Britain: General; US: General

2312   YOUSEF, Fathi S. 1978. "Communication Patterns: Some Aspects of
        Nonverbal Behavior in Intercultural Communication." In *Interethnic
        Communication.* Southern Anthropological Proceedings, no. 12, edited
        by E. Lamar Ross, pp. 49-62. Athens: University of Georgia Press.

2b/3e/4a/5d/16   Theory

2313   YUAN, D. Y. 1966. "Chinatown and Beyond: The Chinese Population in
        Metropolitan New York." *Phylon* 27:321-32.

2b/3a/4h/5d,i/6/8/9   US: Chinese

2314   ZABLE, Arnold. 1973. "Neo-Colonialism and Race Relations: New
       Guinea and the Pacific Rim." *Race* 14:393-441.

2c/3e/4f/5b,i/8/9/10/15   Papua New Guinea

2315   ZACEK, Joseph F. 1969. "Nationalism in Czechoslovakia." In *National-
       ism in Eastern Europe,* edited by Peter F. Sugar and Ivo J. Lederer,
       pp. 166-206. Seattle: University of Washington Press.

2c/3b/4d/5e/10   Czechoslovakia

2316   ZALENY, Carolyn. 1974. *Relations between the Spanish-Americans
       and Anglo-Americans in New Mexico.* New York: Arno Press.

2b/3a/4i/5g,h,i/9/11   US: Euro-, Latin Americans

2317   ZAPRUDNIK, Jan. 1975. "Belorussia and the Belorussians." In *Hand-
       book of Major Soviet Nationalities,* edited by Zev Katz, Rosemarie Rogers,
       and Frederic Harned, pp. 49-71. New York: Free Press.

2c/3a/4d/5k/6/8/10/11/12/13/16   USSR: Byelorussians

2318   ZAVALANI, T. 1969. "Albanian Nationalism." In *Nationalism in
       Eastern Europe,* edited by Peter F. Sugar and Ivo J. Lederer, pp. 55-92.
       Seattle: University of Washington Press.

2c/3b/4d/5e/10   Albania

2319   ZENNER, Walter P. and Maurice N. Richter, Jr. 1972. "The Druzes as
       a Divided Minority Group." *Journal of Asian and African Studies* 7:
       193-203.

2c/3a/4d/5k/10   Israel; Lebanon; Syria

2320   ZGHAL, Abdelkader. 1973. "Nation-Building in the Maghreb." In
       Building States and Nations: Analyses by Region, vol. 2, edited by S. N.
       Eisenstadt and Stein Rokkan, pp. 322-40. Beverly Hills, Calif.: Sage.

2c/3d/4b/5e/10/12   Algeria; Morocco; Tunisia

2321   ZINMAN, Rosalind. 1978. "Selected Bibliography on Quebec." *Cana-
       dian Review of Sociology and Anthropology* 15:246-51.

2a/6/8/9/10   Canada: Québécois

2322 ZOLBERG, Aristide R. 1977. "Splitting the Difference: Federalization without Federalism in Belgium." In *Ethnic Conflict in the Western World*, edited by Milton J. Esman, pp. 103-42. Ithaca: Cornell University Press.

2c/3b/4f/5f/10/16/17 Belgium

2323 ZUBAIDA, Sami, ed. 1970. *Race and Racialism*. London: Tavistock.

1a/2b,e/3a,b,e/4h/5f,g,i,j/8/9/10/11 Britain: General; South Africa

2324 ZUREIK, Elia T. 1976. "Transformation of Class Structure among the Arabs in Israel: From Peasantry to Proletariat." *Journal of Palestine Studies* 6:39-66.

2b/3a/4h/5j/8/9/10 Israel

2325 ———. 1979. *The Palestinians in Israel: A Study in Internal Colonialism*. London: Routledge & Kegan Paul.

2b,c/3b/4h/5b,e,g,i,j/6/7/8/9/10/11/13 Israel

2326 ZWICK, Peter. 1976. "The Marxist Roots of National Communism." *Canadian Review of Studies in Nationalism* 3:127-45.

2e/3e/4f/5e Theory

Anonymous works, listed chronologically

2327 1968. "Black America." *Social Science Quarterly*, vol. 49, no. 3.

1a/2b,d/3a/4h/5k/6/8/9/10/11 US: Afro-Americans

2328 1969. *Canadian Ethnic Studies*, vol. 1, no. 1.

2a Canada: General

2329 1970. *Canadian Ethnic Studies*, vol. 2, no. 1.

2a Canada: General

2330 1970. "Editorial: Pluralism in Africa." *Plural Societies* 1:10-34.

2c/3b,c/4f/5b,f,g,i/10/12 Africa

2331 1970. *Indian Voices: The First Convocation of American Indian Scholars*. San Francisco: The Indian Historian Press.

1a/2c/3a/4i/5d,k   US: Native Americans

2332   1971. "Regional Variations in Nation-Building." *International Social Science Journal,* vol. 23, no. 3.

1a/2c/3b,d,e/4a,b,d,f,h,i(Law)/5e/8/9/10/11/12   General

2333   1973. "Political Integration in Multinational States." *Journal of International Affairs,* vol. 27, no. 1.

1a/2c/3b/4f   Canada: Québécois; Czechoslovakia; India;
5a,e,i/9/10   Israel; Malaysia; USSR: General

2334   1973. "The Sudan: A New Era." *Africa Today,* vol. 20, no. 3.

1a/2b/3b/4f,i/5b,e/10/11/12   Sudan

2335   1974—. "Annotated Bibliography of Works in Nationalism: A Regional Selection." *Canadian Review of Studies in Nationalism,* vol. 1, continuing.

2a/10   General

2336   1975. "Bibliography of Studies on the Politics of Race in Britain." In *The Politics of Race.* British Political Sociology Yearbook, vol. 2, edited by Ivor Crewe, pp. 279-95. New York: John Wiley & Sons.

2a/8/9/10   Britain: General

2337   1975. "The Ethnic Factor." *Society,* vol. 12, no. 2.

1a/2b/3a,b/4h   Africa; Burundi; US: Gypsies,
5b,d/10/12/16   Jews, Native Americans

2338   1976. "Ethnic and Religious Minorities in the Middle East." *Middle East Review,* vol. 9, no. 1.

1a/2b/3b/4i/5a,f,i/9/10/12/16/17   Middle East

APPENDIX

Index to General and Theoretical Works

Index to Geographical Areas

Index to Contents

In the following matrices, the annotated entries (numbers 1 to 308) are cross referenced according to all seventeen categories and subcategories in this key. The unannotated entries (numbers 309 to 2338) are similarly indexed, except that no subcategories are given for categories six through seventeen.

NUM	AUTHOR	DATE	1 AB	2 ABCDEF	3 ABCDE	4 ABCDE	5 ABCDEFGHI	6 ABC	7 ABCD	8 ABCD	9 ABCDE	10 ABCDEFG	11 ABCD	12 ABCDEFGHI	13 AB	14 ABC	15 ABC	16 AB	17
1	ABRAMSON, HAROLD J	1973		*	*	*	*	***		*		*******	**	**	*	*			*
2	ABRAMSON, PAUL R	1977			**								**	*****	*				*
3	ADAM, HERIBERT ET AL	1979		*		*	**				**	*	***	****				**	*
4	ALLPORT, GORDON W	1954					*	***								*			
5	ALLWORTH, EDWARD ED	1971	*	*	*	*	*	***				*	*	****		*		*	*
6	ALLWORTH, EDWARD ED	1973	*	*	**	*	***	***		*		**	**	****	**	*		**	
7	ALLWORTH, EDWARD ED	1977		*	*	*	***	**			**	**	**	***	**	*		***	
8	ARGYLE, M J	1969		**	*	**	**					*	*	**	*				
9	ASHENFELTER, D ET AL EDS	1973	*	**	*	*	***	*		**									
10	ASHMORE, RICHARD D ED	1976	*	*	*	*	*	***			**	**	***	**	*	*			
11	AZRAEL, JEREMY R ED	1978	*	*	***	*	**	***			*	******	***	**	*	*		**	*
12	BAGLEY, CHRISTOPHER	1972		*	**	*	*	*			*	**	*	***					
13	BAHR, HOWARD M ET AL EDS	1972		***	**	**	***	**			**	*		***	**	**	*	*	
14	BAILEY H A JR ET AL EDS	1969	*	*	**	**	****	**		**		***	**	****	**	**		*	
15	BAKER, DONALD G ED	1975	*	*	*	*	**	**		*	**	***	**	**	*				
16	BANTON MICHAEL	1967														*			
17	BANTON MICHAEL	1977		*	*	*	*	*	***		*	******	****	***					
18	BARCLAY, WILLIAM ET AL ED	1976	*	*	**	*	**	***			**	**	**	**	**			**	
19	BARTH, ERNEST A T ET AL	1972		*	***	*	*	*			****	***	*	***	**	**		*	
20	BARTH FREDRIK	1964	*	*	*	*	**	***		*	**	***	**	*	*	*			
21	BARTH, FREDRIK ED	1969	*	*	*	**	*	***						*					
22	BARTH, FREDRIK	1969		**	**	*	*	**			*	*	***	***	**	**			
23	BARTON, JOSEF J	1975		*	**	*	*	*		*	**	*		***	**	**			
24	BEAN, FRANK D ET AL EDS	1978		**	***	*	***	**		**	*	*	**	***	**	**			
25	BEATTIE C ET AL EDS	1974	**	*	**	*	**	***		*	**		*	*					
26	BECKER, GARY S	1971	*	*	*		*	*	*		*			**					
27	BELL, WENDELL ET AL EDS	1974	*	**	**	**	**	**			****	****	***	****	*				
28	BENNETT, JOHN W ED	1975	*	**	*	*	***	**		**	***	**	**	***	*	*			
29	BERREMAN, GERALD D	1975		*	*		*	*			*****	***	**	****					
30	BERREMAN, GERALD D	1972		*		*		*		**	**	**	*	**					
31	BERRY BREWTON	1963	*	**	***	*	**	***			*	**	***	***	*	*			
32	BERRY, BREWTON ET AL	1978		**	**	*	**	*		*	***	**	***	**		*	*		
33	BERTELSEN, JUDY S ED	1977	*	*	*	**		*			***	**	***	***					
34	BETEILLE, ANDRE	1971						*					*						
35	BETTELHEIM, BRUNO ET AL	1950		*		*	***				*	****		***	*				*
36	BHARATI, AGEHANANDO	1972	*		**	*		**			***		**	*******	**	***			
37	BLALOCK, HUBERT M JR	1967		*	*	*		*		***	**	****	**	**	*				
38	BLAUNER, ROBERT	1969		*			***	**			**	****	*	***	*	*			
39	BLOOM, JAN-PETER	1969		**	*	**	*				**		*	*					
40	BLOOM, LEONARD	1971	*	*		*		**				*		***		*	*		
41	BONACICH, EDNA	1972		*	*	*	**	*		***	**	*	*	***					
42	BONACICH, EDNA	1973		*		*	**	**		**	*			**		*		*	
43	BORRIE, W D ED	1959		**	**	**						***		**			*	*	
44	BRAM, JOSEPH	1965																	
45	BRASS, PAUL R	1974		**	*	*	*	*			*	*****		**	*	*	*	**	*
46	BRASS, PAUL R	1976		*	*		**	*			*	*****	*	***			*	**	

NUM	AUTHOR	DATE	1 AB	2 ABCDEF	3 ABCDE	4 ABCDEFGHI	5 ABCDEFGHIJK	6 ABC	7 ABCD	8 ABCD	9 ABCDE	10 ABCDEFG	11 ABCD	12 ABCDEFGHI	13 AB	14 ABC	15 ABC	16 AB	17
47	BRIGGS, VERNON K JR ET AL	1977		*	*	*	*	***	**	**	*	*		*	*	*			
48	BURAWOY, MICHAEL	1974		*	**		**			*	**	***	**	***		*			
49	BURKEY, RICHARD M	1978		*	*	*	*			**	*	*							**
50	CAIN, GLEN C	1976	*	**	**	**	**												
51	CAMPBELL, ERNEST Q ED	1972	*	**	**	***	**	**		**	*	****	**	***					
52	CANADA, ROYAL COMMISSION	1970		*	*		**	***	**	**	**	**	*	*		***	**	**	**
53	COHEN, ABNER	1969					***	**	**		*		****	*		***	*	*	
54	COHEN, ABNER ED	1974	*	*	**		***		**	**		*	*	**		***	**	**	
55	COHEN, RONALD	1978				***	*					**	*	*****		*	*		**
56	COHEN, RONALD ET AL EDS	1970	*	*	**	*	*	***	**	**	**	*	**	*****	**	***	*	*	
57	COLE, JOHN W ET AL	1974	*	**	**	*		**			***	**	*	*****	**				
58	COLLINS, THOMAS W	1975					**				**	*		**			*		
59	COLSON, ELIZABETH	1968		*										*					
60	CONNOR, WALKER	1972			**	**	*				*	**	**	*		**	**		*
61	CONNOR, WALKER	1973		*	*	*	*				*	*	*	**					
62	CONROY, HILARY ET AL EDS	1972	*	**	*	*	*	***	**	*	*	***	*	*	**		*	*	
63	CORDASCO, F ET AL EDS	1973	*	**	*	*	**	***	**	**	***	***	*	**	**	**	**	**	
64	COX, OLIVER	1976		*	*		*				**	*	*	*					
65	CRESPI, MURIEL	1975	*	*	*	*		***				****	**	***	*				*
66	DANIELS, ROGER ET AL	1970		*	*		*				*	**	*	*					
67	DASHEFSKY, ARNOLD	1975		*	*	*	*					****	**	*				**	
68	DE LA GARZA, R K ET AL EDS	1973	*	**	**	**	**	**	**	*	*	*****	**	***	**	**	**	**	
69	DESPRES, LEO A	1967		**	*		**	*		**	**	*	*	*					
70	DESPRES, LEO A	1975		**	*	**	*	**			*	**	*	***	**	**	*	*	
71	DESPRES, LEO A ED	1975	*	*	*	*	***	*			*	*	**	*					
72	DEUTSCH, KARL W	1966		**	*		*			**	*	*	*					**	
73	DEUTSCH, KARL W	1979		***	**		**			**	**	**	**	**		*	**	**	
74	DEVEREUX, GEORGE	1975		*	*	*	*	*		*	*		*	*				*	
75	DE VOS, GEORGE ET AL EDS	1975	*	***	**	**	***	**	**	*	*	**	****	****	*	*	*		**
76	DE VOS, GEORGE ET AL EDS	1966		****	*	*	**		*	*	**	*	**	*					
77	DEX, SHIRLEY	1979		*	*	*	***	***	**	*	**	***	**	**	*	*			
78	DINNERSTEIN, L ET AL	1975		*	*		*				*	**	**	**					
79	DIRKS, ROBERT	1975		**	*	*		**			**	*	*	**		*	*	**	
80	DRAGIC, NADA ED	1975		**	*		**				*			*					
81	DRESANG, DENNIS L	1974		**	*	*		*			*	*	*	***					
82	DREYER, JUNE TEUFEL	1976		*	*	*		*			*	***	*	*					
83	DUCHACEK, IVO D ED	1977					**	**	**		**	**	**	**		*			
84	DURAN, JAMES J	1974		*	*	**	**				*		*	*					
85	DURRENBERGER, E PAUL	1975		*	*		*				*		**	**					
86	DU TOIT, BRIAN M ED	1978		*	*	*	**	*		*	**	*	**	****	*	*	**		
87	DWORKIN, A G ET AL EDS	1976	**	**	*	*	**	***	**	**	*	***	*	***	*				
88	EHRLICH, ALLEN S	1971		**		*		**	**	*	*	***	****	**					
89	EHRLICH, HOWARD J	1973			*	**					*	*	***	*.*	**				**
90	EIDHEIM, HARALD	1969		***	*	*	**					****	*	**					
91	EISENSTADT, S N ET AL EDS	1973	*		*	*		**	**		*	*	**	**		*	*		
92	EL-HAMAMSY, LAILA SHUKRY	1975		*	*	*		*			*	*	*	**	*	*	*	*	

NUM	AUTHOR	DATE	1 AB	2 ABCDEF	3 ABCDE	4 ABCDEFGHI	5 ABCDEFGHIJK	6 ABC	7 ABCD	8 ABCD	9 ABCDE	10 ABCDEFG	11 ABCD	12 ABCDEFGHI	13 AB	14 ABC	15	16 AB	17
93	ELLIOTT, JEAN LEONARD ED	1979																	
94	ENLOE, CYNTHIA H	1973																	
95	ESMAN, MILTON JACOB ED	1977																	
96	FALLERS, LLOYD ED	1967																	
97	FEAGIN, JOE R	1978																	
98	FENTON EDWIN	1975																	
99	FISHMAN, JOSHUA A ET AL	1966																	
100	FISHMAN, JOSHUA A	1972																	
101	FITZPATRICK, JOSEPH P	1971																	
102	FOSTER, BRIAN L	1974																	
103	FRANCIS, E K	1976																	
104	FRANKLIN, JOHN HOPE ED	1968																	
105	FRIDERES, JAMES S	1975																	
106	FRIED, MORTON H	1968																	
107	FURNIVALL, JOHN SYDENHAM	1939																	
108	GALLO, PATRICK J	1974																	
109	GARCIA, F CHRIS ED	1974																	
110	GARCIA, F CHRIS ET AL	1977																	
111	GEERTZ, CLIFFORD	1963																	
112	GELFAND, D E ET AL EDS	1973																	
113	GHIA, DHARAM P ED	1965																	
114	GILES, HOWARD ED	1977																	
115	GIST, NOEL P	1972																	
116	GIST, NOEL P ET AL EDS	1972																	
117	GITTLER, JOSEPH N ED	1977																	
118	GLAZER, NATHAN	1971																	
119	GLAZER, NATHAN ET AL	1970																	
120	GLAZER, NATHAN ET AL EDS	1975																	
121	GOLDHAGEN, ERICH ED	1968																	
122	GOMEZ, RUDOLPH ET AL EDS	1974																	
123	GORDON, DAVID M ED	1977																	
124	GORDON, MILTON M	1964																	
125	GOSSETT, THOMAS F	1963																	
126	GREBLER, LEO ET AL	1970																	
127	GREELEY, ANDREW M	1974																	
128	GREELEY, ANDREW M ET AL	1974																	
129	GRIGULEVICH, I R ET AL ED	1974																	
130	GROVE, D JOHN	1974																	
131	GROVE, D JOHN ED	1979																	
132	GUILLAUMIN, COLLETTE	1971																	
133	GUMPERZ, JOHN J	1962																	
134	GUTKIND, P C W ED	1970																	
135	HAALAND, GUNNAR	1969																	
136	HACKENBERG, ROBERT A	1967																	
137	HANDLIN, OSCAR	1972																	
138	HAUGEN, EINAR	1972																	

NUM	AUTHOR	DATE	1 AB	2 ABCDEF	3 ABCDE	4 ABCDEFGHI	5 ABCDEFGHI	6 ABC	7 ABCD	8 ABCD	9 ABCD	10 ABCDEFG	11 ABCD	12 ABCDEFGHI	13 AB	14 ABC	15 AB	16 AB	17
139	HECHTER, MICHAEL	1971			*	*	*				* *	* * *		* *					*
140	HECHTER, MICHAEL	1974		*	* *		*			* *	* *	* * * *	*	*				*	
141	HECHTER, MICHAEL	1975		* *	* * *		*				* *	* * * * *		* * *		*			
142	HECHTER, MICHAEL	1976		* *	* * *	*	*				* *	* * *	*						*
143	HECHTER, MICHAEL	1978		* *	*	*	*	* *		*	* *	* * *	*	* *				*	
144	HECHTER, MICHAEL ET AL	1979		* *	*		* *	*				* * * *		* *					
145	HEISLER, MARTIN O ED	1977		* *	* *		* *					* *						*	*
146	HENRY, FRANCIS ED	1976	*	* *	* *	* *	* *				*		*	* * * * *	* *			* *	
147	HERNANDEZ, C A ET AL EDS	1976	* *	* *	*		* *			* *	*	* *	* *	* * * * *	* *	*			
148	HICKS, GEORGE L ET AL	1972		* *	*	*	*	* *		* *	*	*		* * *	* *	*			
149	HICKS, GEORGE L ET AL EDS	1977	*	* *	* *	* *	* * * *	* * *			* * *	*	* *	* *		*			*
150	HOETINK, HERMANNUS	1967		*			* *			* *			* * *	* *					
151	HOETINK, HERMANNUS	1974		*	*	*	*					* * *	*	* * *					
152	HOLLOMAN, R É ET AL EDS	1978	*	* *	* *	* *	* *	* * *		* *	*	* * *	* *	* * * * * *	*	*		*	
153	HORAK, STEPHEN M	1961		*	* *	*	*		*	*		* * * * *		* * *					
154	HSU, FRANCIS L K	1971	*	* *	*		* *	* *			* * *	*	* *	* * *	* *	* *	*		*
155	HUNT, CHESTER L ET AL	1974	*	* *	*	*	*	*		*	* * *	* * * *	* *	* * *	* *	*		*	
156	HYMES, DELL	1968		*			* *	*			*			* * *					
157	ICHIHASHI, YAMATO	1932		* *	* *							* * *	* *	* * *				*	
158	ISAACS, HAROLD R	1975	*	*	* *	* *	*	* * *		* *	*	* * *	*	* * *		*	*		*
159	ISAJIW, WSEVOLOD W	1974	*	* *	* *	* *	*		*			*	* *						
160	JOHNSON, COLLEEN L ET AL	1975		*	*	* * *	* *	* *			* * *	* * *	* *	* *		*	*		
161	JONES, JAMES M	1972	*	*	*	* * *	*	*			* *	* * *	* *	* *	*				
162	KANG, TAI S ED	1976		*	*	*	*	* * *			* *	* * *		* *					
163	KAPLAN, H ROY ED	1977		* *	* *	* *	*	* *		*	* * * *	*	* *		* *		*	*	
164	KASFIR, NELSON	1976		* *	*	* * *	* *	* *			*	* * * * * *		* *				* *	*
165	KATZ, ZEV ET AL EDS	1975		*	*	* *	* *	* * *	*	*	* *	*	*	* *				*	
166	KATZNELSON, IRA	1972		*	* *	*	*	*	* *	* *	*	* *	*	* *					
167	KATZNELSON, IRA	1973		*	* *	*	*			* *	*	* *	* *						
168	KATZNELSON, IRA ED	1973		* *	* *		* *	* * *	* *		*	* *	* *	* *			*		
169	KAYAL, PHILIP M ET AL	1975		*	*	*	* *	* *		* *	*	*	*	* * * * * * *			*		
170	KEYES, CHARLES F	1976		* *	*	* *	* *		* *		* *	* * * *	* *	* * *	*	*		* *	
171	KHAN, VERITY S ED	1979	*	*	*		* *		* *		*	*	* *	* * *	*		*		
172	KILSON, MARTIN	1972		*	* *	*	* *			*	*	*		* * *					
173	KING, ROBERT R	1973		*	*	*						*	* *	* * *					
174	KINLOCH, GRAHAM	1974		* *	* * *	*	* *	* * *		*	*	* * * *	* * * *	* *	*	*	*	* *	*
175	KITANO, HARRY H L	1976		* *	*	*	* *	* * *		*	* * * *	* * *	* *	* * * *	* *	* * *	* *		
176	KRAUSZ, ERNEST	1971		* *	*	*	* *	* * *		*	* *	* * *	* *	* * *	*	*		*	
177	KREJCI, JAROSLAV	1978		*	*	* *	*	*		*	* *	* * * * * * *	*	* * *					
178	KUNSTADTER, PETER ED	1967	*	* *	*	* *	* * * *	* * *		*	*	* * * *	* *	* * *	* * *	*	*	* *	
179	KUPER, LEO	1971		* *	*	*	*				* * * *	* *	* *	* * * *	* *	* * *			
180	KUPER, LEO	1973		* *	*	* *	*			*	*	* * *	* *	* * *	*				
181	KUPER, LEO	1977		* *	*	* *	*				* *	* * *	*	* * *					
182	KUPER, LEO ET AL EDS	1969	*	*	* *	* *	*	* *			* * * * *	* * * * * * *	* *	* *				* *	
183	LANCASTER, C S	1971		* *	*	* *	*				*	*		* *	* *		*		
184	LEACH, EDMUND, R	1960		* *	*		*												

NUM	AUTHOR	DATE	1 AB	2 ABCDEF	3 ABCDE	4 ABCDEFGHI	5 ABCDEFGHIJK	6 ABC	7 ABCD	8 ABCD	9 ABCDE	10 ABCDEFG	11 ABCD	12 ABCDEFGHI	13 AB	14 ABC	15	16 AB	17
185	LEACH, EDMUND R	1962																	
186	LEACH, EDMUND R	1964																	
187	LEVINE, ROBERT A ET AL	1972																	
188	LIEBERSON, STANLEY	1961																	
189	LIJPHART, AREND	1972																	
190	LYMAN, STANFORD M	1974																	
191	LYNCH, OWEN	1969																	
192	MACKIE, J A C ED	1976																	
193	MARSHALL, RAY	1974																	
194	MASON, PHILIP	1970																	
195	MAYO, PATRICIA ELTON	1974																	
196	MAZRUI, ALI A	1969																	
197	MELSON, ROBERT ET AL	1970																	
198	MILLER, KENT S ET AL EDS	1973																	
199	MINDEL, C H ET AL EDS	1976																	
200	MITCHELL, J CLYDE	1974																	
201	MOERMAN, MICHAEL	1965																	
202	MOORE, JOAN W ET AL	1970																	
203	MORNER, MAGNUS ED	1970																	
204	MUNCH, PETER A	1972																	
205	MYRDAL, GUNNAR	1944																	
206	NAGATA, JUDITH A	1974																	
207	NAGATA, JUDITH A ED	1975																	
208	NAROLL, RAOUL	1968																	
209	NEUMAN, STEPHANIE G ED	1976																	
210	OBEYESEKERE, GANANATH	1975																	
211	OLORUNSOLA, VICTOR A ED	1972																	
212	OTTENBERG, SIMON	1976																	
213	PARENTI, MICHAEL	1967																	
214	PARK, ROBERT EZRA	1950																	
215	PARKIN, DAVID J	1969																	
216	PASCAL, ANTHONY H ED	1972																	
217	PATTERSON, ORLANDO	1977																	
218	PETTIGREW, THOMAS F ED	1975																	
219	PIERSON, DONALD	1972																	
220	PINKNEY, ALPHONSO	1975																	
221	PLAX, MARTIN	1974																	
222	PRATT, HENRY J ED	1974																	
223	PRICE, CHARLES A	1963																	
224	PURCELL, VICTOR	1965																	
225	RABUSHKA, ALVIN	1974																	
226	RABUSHKA, ALVIN ET AL	1972																	
227	REX, JOHN	1970																	
228	RHOODIE, NIC ED	1978																	
229	RICHERT, JEAN PIERRE	1974																	
230	ROBBINS, EDWARD	1975																	

NUM	AUTHOR	DATE	1 AB	2 ABCDEF	3 ABCDE	4 ABCDEFGHI	5 ABCDEFGHIJK	6 ABC	7 ABCD	8 ABCD	9 ABCDE	10 ABCDEFG	11 ABCD	12 ABCDEFGHI	13 AB	14 ABC	15	16 AB	17
231	ROBERTSON, I ET AL EDS	1978	*	**	*	***	***	*	*	*	*	* **	*	***	*	**	*	*	*
232	RUSE, E J B ET AL	1969		*	*	***	***	***		**	*	***		***	**	**	*	*	
233	ROSE, JERRY D	1976	*	**		*	***		*	*		**		**				*	*
234	ROSS, E LAMAR ED	1978	*	** **	*	**	*		*			**			*				
235	ROTHMAN, JACK ED	1976	*		*	**	*				*	***	**	***	*				
236	RUNCIMAN, W G ED	1972	*	**	**	**	*	***	***		***	***	*	***					
237	RYAN, JOSEPH A ED	1973	*	**	**	**	**	**		**	*	*****	**	**	**	**	*	**	*
238	SAFA, HELEN I ET AL EDS	1975	*	**	**	*****	**	**	***		****	***	*	***	*	**	**	**	
239	SAID, ABDUL ET AL EDS	1976	*	**	*	*	*	***			***	***	*	***					
240	SAMORA, JULIAN ED	1966	*	**	**	**	*	**	***		**	**		**					
241	SANDHU, KERNIAL SINGH	1969		**	**	*	*				****	*		***	**	**	**	**	*
242	SAUNDERS, JOHN	1972		**	**		*				****	*		*			*	*	
243	SAVARD, J G ET AL EDS	1975	*	*	**	***					*	****	**	**	***	**	**	***	
244	SCHERMERHORN, ROBERT A	1970		**	**	*	**	**	**		**	****	***	***	***	**	**	**	
245	SCHERMERHORN, ROBERT A	1978		**	*	**	*	*	**	*	**	***	**	**					
246	SCHWARTZ, NORMAN B	1971		*		**	*	*			*		**	**		**			
247	SCHWARTZ, THEODORE	1975		*	**	**	**			*	*		*	**			*		
248	SETON-WATSON, HUGH	1977		**	**		***				*	***		**					*
249	SHEPHERD, G W JR ET AL ED	1970	*	*	*	*	*				*	*******	*	**					**
250	SHIBUTANI, TAMATSU ET AL	1965	*	*	**	**	**			*	**	*	*	*					
251	SILVER, BRIAN	1974	*	*	*	**	*	**					**	**					
252	SIMMONDS, GEORGE W ED	1977		*	**	**	**	***		**		******	*	***	*	*			
253	SINHA, SURAJIT	1965		**	*		**			**	**	**	*	**					
254	SKINNER, G WILLIAM	1958	*	*	*		*	*			***	**	*	**					
255	SKINNER, G WILLIAM	1968		*	*	*	*				*	*	*	**					
256	SMITH, ANTHONY D	1971			*		**			*	**	**	*	**					*
257	SMITH, ANTHONY D	1979		*		*	**				*	*	*	**					
258	SMOCK, DAVID R ET AL	1975		**	**	*	**			*	*	***	**	*					
259	SMOOHA, SAMMY	1978		**	**		*					****	**	***					
260	SNYDER, LOUIS L	1976		*	*		*				*	*	*	*					
261	SRINIVAS, M N	1956	*	*	*		*				*****	***	*	**	*			*	
262	SRINIVAS, M N	1966		*	*	**		*	*		**	***	***	***	**			**	
263	STEIN, HOWARD F ET AL	1977	*	*	**		*	**				**	***	**	**	**	**	**	
264	SUE, STANLEY ET AL EDS	1973	*	***	*	**	*	****			***	****	**	***	**	*		*	
265	SUGAR, PETER F ET AL EDS	1969		*	*	*	**		*	*	***	****	*	**		**			
266	SUHRKE, ASTRI ET AL EDS	1977	*	**	*	*	*	*	*			***	**	**					
267	SVENSSON, FRANCES	1973	*	*	*		**					*	****	*		*			
268	SZWED, JOHN F	1975		*	*		*				**	*	***	**					
269	TAYLOR, RONALD L	1979		*	*		*					**	****	**					
270	TRUSPER, RONALD L	1976	*	**	*	*	*	*				**	*	*					
271	TUMIN, MELVIN M ET AL	1969	*	**	**	**	**				**		****	**	*				
272	TUMIN, MELVIN ET AL EDS	1977		**	**	***	***				**		****	**					
273	TURNER, JONATHAN H ET AL	1978	*									**	****	**					
274	UCHENDU, VICTOR C	1975		*	*	*	*				****	***	*	**					
275	VAN DEN BERGHE, PIERRE L	1970			*	**	**					**	*	***			*		
276	VAN DEN BERGHE, PIERRE L	1970	*	*	*	*	**				****	****	*	*					

NUM	AUTHOR	DATE	1 AB	2 ABCDEF	3 ABCDE	4 ABCDEFGHI	5 ABCDEFGHIJK	6 ABC	7 ABCD	8 ABCD	9 ABCD	10 ABCDEFG	11 ABCD	12 ABCDEFGHI	13 AB	14 ABC	15	16 AB	17
277	VAN DEN BERGHE, P L ED	1972	*											* * *	*	*		*	
278	VAN DEN BERGHE, PIERRE L	1976		*	* *	*	* *					* *	* *	* * * *		* *	*	*	*
279	VAN DEN BERGHE, PIERRE L	1978		*	*	*	*												
280	VAN DEN BERGHE, PIERRE L	1977	*				*	* *			* *	* *	*	* * *		* * * *	*	* *	*
281	VAN DEN BERGHE, P L ET AL	1977	*	*	*	*	*	* * *	*		* *	* *	*	* * * * *					
282	VERMA, G K ET AL EDS	1979	*	* *	* * *	* * *	* *			*	*		* *	* * *		* * *			
283	VONFURSTENBERG, G M ET AL	1974				*	* *			* *		* *	* * *	* *	* *	* * *		* *	
284	WAGATSUMA, HIROSHI	1969		*	*		* *			* *	*		* * *			*	* *	*	
285	WAGATSUMA, HIROSHI	1975											* * *						
286	WALKER, DEWARD E JR ED	1972	*	* *	*	*	*	* * *	* *	* * *	*	*	* *	* *	*	* * *	*	*	*
287	WALLERSTEIN, IMMANUEL	1972	*	*	* *	*	*				* *		*	* *	* *				
288	WALLMAN, SANDRA ED	1979	*	* * *	* *	*	* *	* * *	* *	* *	* *	* * *	*	*	* *	* * *	* *	* *	*
289	WATSON, JAMES L ED	1977	*	* *	*	* *	*		*	* *	*		*	* * * * * * *	* *	* *	*		
290	MAX, MURRAY L	1971		* *	* *		* *	* *		* *		* * * *		*				* *	
291	WEINSTEIN, WARREN ET AL	1976	*	* *	*	*	* * * *				*	* * * * * * *		* * * * * * * *					
292	WEINSTOCK, S ALEXANDER	1969					*	* *			*		*	*		* * *	*	* *	
293	WEST, KATHERINE	1972		*	*	* *	*		*	*		* * *	*	*	*				
294	WILKIE, MARY	1977					* *			* *		* * *		*	*	*		* *	*
295	WILLIAMS, ROBIN M JR	1972		*	* *		*	*			* *	* *	*	* * *		* * *	*	*	
296	WILLIAMS, ROBIN M JR	1975			* * * *	*	* *							* * * *					
297	WILSON, WILLIAM J	1973	*	* *	*		*	* *			*	* * *	* *	* *					
298	WOLFF, HANS	1959			*	* *	* *	* *			* *	* *	* *	* *				* *	
299	WOLFF, HANS	1967		*	*		* *	*			* *	* *	* *	*					
300	YANCEY, WILLIAM L ET AL	1976		*	*	*	* *					* *		* * *					
301	YETMAN, N R ET AL EDS	1971	* *	*	*	* * *	* *		* *	* *		*	*	*	*				
302	YOUNG, CRAWFORD	1976	*	*	*		*			*	* *	* * * * * *	*	* *				*	
303		1971	*	* *	*	* *					* * *	* * *	* *	* * *					
304		1971	*	* *	*						* *	* *	* *	* *					
305		1975	*	* *	*						* *	* *	*	*					
306		1976	*		*														
307		1978	*	* *	*									* *	* *			* *	*
308		1979	*	*									*						

NUM	AUTHOR	DATE	1 AB	2 ABCDEF	3 ABCDE	4 ABCDEF	5 ABCDEFGHI	5 ABCDEFGHIJK	6	7	8	9	10	11	12	13	14	15	16	17
309	ABBOTT, SIMON ED	1971	*	**	*			*	*	*	*		*							
310	ABLON, JOAN	1971		*	*	*	*			**				*						
311	ABRAHAMS, R G	1970			*	*				**			* **							
312	ABRAHAMSON, HAROLD J	1975		*		**	**					*								
313	ACUNA, RUDOLFE	1972		*	*							*								
314	ADAM, HERIBERT	1971		*	*	*	*	*				***								
315	ADAM, HERIBERT A	1975		*	*	*	***	*			* *	***								
316	ADAM, HERIBERT	1977		*	*		*					**								
317	ADAMS, BARBARA ET AL	1975		**	**	**		*		*		*		*						
318	ADAMS, R C	1978		**	*															
319	ADEKSON, J BAYE	1978		*	*	*	**	**				***								
320	ADEKSON, J BAYO	1979				**		**												
321	AGARWAL, N N	1969						**				*								
322	AIGNER, DENNIS J ET AL	1977		*	*				*	*		*			*					
323	AKINSOLA, AKIWOWO A	1963		*	*	*	*	*	*	*		*								
324	ALAPURO, RISTO	1979		*	*		*										*			
325	ALBA, RICHARD D	1976		*	**	**	*					***	*	* *		*				
326	ALBA, RICHARD D	1978		*	**	**	***	*				***	*	*			*			
327	ALBA, RICHARD D ET AL	1979		**	*	*	*	**				**	*	*						
328	ALDERMAN, GEOFFREY	1975		*	*	*		*				*		*						
329	ALDRICH, HOWARD E	1973		*	*	*	*	*	*	*		*								
330	ALERS, M H	1973						**												
331	ALEXANDER, JACK	1977		*	*		*	**			**	*					*			
332	ALFORD, HAROLD J	1972		*	*	*		*	* *			*								
333	ALGER, JANET MERRILL	1974		*	*	*	*	*	* *											
334	ALI, AHMED	1978				*	*	*	* *											
335	ALISJABHANA, S TAKDIR	1971		*	*	*						**								
336	ALLEN, IRVING LEWIS	1975		*	*					*		*		*						
337	ALLEN, JAMES P	1977		**	*	*	*			*		*								
338	ALLEN, SHEILA	1970		*	*															*
339	ALLEN, SHEILA	1971		**	**	*	***	**	*	*	***	***								
340	ALLEN, SHEILA	1971		*	*	*	***	**	*		**	***	**							
341	ALLOWAY, DAVID N ET AL	1970	*				*				*									
342	ALLWORTH, EDWARD	1968		*	*	*						*								
343	ALLWORTH, EDWARD	1971						*												
344	ALLWORTH, EDWARD	1973		**	*	*	*	**				**								
345	ALLWORTH, EDWARD	1975		*	*	*	*	**				*								
346	ALLWORTH, EDWARD	1975				*	*	*			*	*	*							
347	ALLWORTH, EDWARD	1977		*	*															
348	ALMIROL, EDWIN B	1978		**	*	*	**	**		*	*	*								
349	ALMQUIST, ELIZABETH M	1979		*	*	*	*	**	*		*	***	*	* *		*			*	
350	ALPERS, EDWARD A	1974																		
351	ALTMAN, JON C ET AL	1979		*	*	*	*	*	*			*	*	*						
352	ALVERSUN, HOYT S	1974										**								
353	AMELUNXEN, CLEMENS	1972		*	*	*	*					*		*						
354	AMERSFOORT, HANS VAN	1978		*		*	*	**				**								

NUM	AUTHOR	DATE	1 AB	2 ABCDEF	3 ABCDE	4 ABCDEFGHI	5 ABCDEFGHIJK	6	7	8	9	10	11	12	13	14	15	16	17
355	AMFITHEATROF, ERIK	1973		*	*	*	*		*			*								*
356	ANDERSON, BARBARA	1978		*	*	*	*					*	*	* *						
357	ANDERSON, CHARLES H	1970		*	*		*											*		
358	ANDERSON, DAVID D ET AL	1971	*	* *	*	*	*	*										*		*
359	ANGEL, MARC D	1974		*	*		*					*								
360	ANIMASHASUN, G K	1963		*	*	*	*	*				* *							*	
361	ANTI-APARTHEID MOVEMENT	1974		* *	*	*	*	*				* *								
362	ARAM, M	1974		*	*		*				*	*			*					
363	ARCHER, DANE ET AL	1971		*	*	*	*													
364	ARFA, HASSAN	1966		*	*		*													
365	ARLES, J P	1971		*	*	*	*		*											
366	ARLES, J P	1971		*	*	*	* *	* *	*	* *	*	*	*	* *	* *					
367	ARMSTRONG, JOHN A	1968		*	*	*		* *												
368	ARMSTRUNG, JOHN A	1978		*	*	*	* *	* *	*			*	* *							
369	ARNEZ, JOHN A	1971	*	*	*	*	*	*	*	*	* * *	* *					*	*		
370	ARTIBISE, ALAN F J	1976		*	*		*	*	*				*							
371	ASHWORTH, GEORGINA	1977		*	*			* *			* *	* *		* *						
372	ASUNCION-LANDE, NOBLEZA	1971		*	*							* * *								
373	ASWAD, BARBARA C ED	1974	*	* *	*		* *	*	*		*									
374	AUSTIN, B WILLIAM	1975			*		* * *	*				*								
375	AVERY, DONALD	1970		*	*		*	*	* *	* *	* *	* * *	*	*						
376	AVNI, HAIM	1971				*	*													
377	AZRAEL, JEREMY R	1978		*	*		*		* *			* *								
378	BADALIAN, I A	1977						* *	* *											
379	BADDELEY, JOSEPHINE	1977		*	*			* *							* *					
380	BAGENAL, PHILIP H	1970		*	*	*	* *		* *			*								
381	BAGLEY, CHRISTOPHER	1696		*	*		* *	*	* *		* *									
382	BAGLEY, CHRISTOPHER	4970		*	*		*	*		*		* *	*							
383	BAGLEY, CHRISTOPHER	1970		*	*	*		*												
384	BAGLEY, CHRISTOPHER	1972			*	*	*	*			*	*		*						
385	BAGLEY, CHRISTOPHER	1973	*	* *	*	*	*	*	*	*	*	*	*					*		
386	BAGLEY, CHRISTOPHER	1973		*	*	*	*													
387	BAILEY, F G	1961			*															
388	BAIRD, CHARLES S	1885						*												
389	BAIRD, FRANK L, ED	1977	*	*																
390	BAKER, DONALD G	1975		*	*	*	*	*	*		*	* *	* *	*						
391	BAKER, DONALD G	1975		*			*		*		*	*								
392	BAKER, DONALD G	1975			*		* *				* *	* * *								
393	BAKER, DONALD G	1972		*	*		* *	*			* *	*								* *
394	BALAKRISHNAN, T R	1976																		
395	BALDWIN, S L	1970		*	*	*	*													
396	BALL, RICHARD E ET AL	1979		*												*				
397	BALLARD, ROGER ET AL	1977		*	* *		*		*			*	*	*	* *		*			
398	BANERJEE, KALYAN KUMAR	1969		* *	* *	*	* *		* *			* *		*	* *					
399	BANKS, DAVID J, ED	1976		* *	*															
400	BANKS, JAMES A	1975	*							*		*			* * *					*

NUM	AUTHOR	DATE	1 AB	2 ABCDEF	3 ABCDE	4 ABCDEFGHI	5 ABCDEFGHIJK	6	7	8	9	10	11	12	13	14	15	16	17
401	BANNICK, CHRISTIAN JOHN	1971		*	*	*	*	*	*											
402	BANTON, MICHAEL	1953		*							*									
403	BANTON, MICHAEL	1960		*	*			*			*		*	*						
404	BANTON, MICHAEL	1966		**	*	*	**	**			*		*		*				*	
405	BANTON, MICHAEL	1969		**	*		**	*			*		*							
406	BANTON, MICHAEL	1970	*		*	*	*	*			*									
407	BANTON, MICHAEL	1972		*	**	*	*	*			*			*						
408	BANTON, MICHAEL	1979					*						*							
409	BANTON, MICHAEL	1979		*	*	*	***	*					*							
410	BANTON, MICHAEL ET AL	1975		*	*	**	*						*							
411	BARANY, GEORGE	1969		*	*	*	*	*				**								
412	BARANY, GEORGE	1974		*	*	**		*				**	*	***					*	
413	BARGHOORN, FREDERICK C	1974		*	*		*	*				*		*						
414	BARKOW, JEROME H	1976		**	**		*	*					*	*	*	*	*	*		*
415	BARNETT, MARGUERITE ROSS	1974		**	*	*	**	*	*		*	*	*	*						
416	BARNETT, MARGUERITE ROSS	1976		*	*	*	**	**			*	*	*							*
417	BARNDUM, VICTOR	1966					*	*												
418	BARON, HAROLD M	1975		*		*	*	*	*		**	**	*	**	*	**				
419	BARON, SALO WITTMAYER	1971		*		**	**	*		**	**	**	*							
420	BARRON, MILTON L ED	1958	**	*	*	*														
421	BARRON, MILTON L ED	1967	*	***	*	**	**	*	*		**	**							*	
422	BARRON, MILTON L ED	1972	*	*		*	**				*	**								
423	BARRY, BRIAN	1975		*	**		*	*				*		*					*	
424	BARRY, BRIAN	1975					*					*								
425	BARTH, FREDRIK	1964		*	*	*	**	*	*			*	*	*		**				
426	BARTLETT, VERNON	1969		*	**	*	*	*			*									
427	BARTON, JOSEF J	1978					**	*					*	*			*			
428	BASSAND, MICHEL	1975		*	*	*		*												
429	BASTIDE, ROGER	1961					*						*							
430	BATES, ROBERT H	1970		*	*		*						*							
431	BATES, ROBERT H	1974	*	**	*	*	**	*	*		*		*	**	**	*			*	*
432	BATES, TIMOTHY MASON	1973		*	**		*	*	**			**								
433	BAUGHMAN, E EARL	1971		*	*	*	**						*							
434	BAUREISS, GUNTER	1971										*				*				
435	BAYTON, J A ET AL	1956		*			*	*					*							
436	BEAGLEHOLE, J H	1967		*	*	*	**	*	**		**	*	*	*	**	*	*	*	*	*
437	BEALE, CALVIN L	1973		*	**			*	**		*									
438	BEAN, FRANK D ET AL	1978		*	*		*	**	**				*							
439	BEARDSLEY, THEODORE S JR	1976		*		*	**	*			**	*							**	
440	BEATTIE C ET AL	1972						**												
441	BECKER, TAMAR	1973		*	*	*	*	*			**	**	*	*						
442	BECKETT, J C	1971		*	**	**	**	*				**	*	*					**	
443	BEE, ROBERT ET AL	1977		*							*	*								
444	BEEMAN, RICHARD R	1971		*	**	**	*	*			*									*
445	BEER, WILLIAM R	1976		*			*	*				*		*						
446	BEER, WILLIAM R	1977					*	*			*	*	*							

NUM	AUTHOR	DATE
447	BEGG, H M ET AL	1971
448	BEIJBOM, ULF	1971
449	BELL, DANIEL	1975
450	BELL, WENDELL	1973
451	BELL, WENDELL	1974
452	BELLINI, JAMES	1975
453	BELTRAN, GONZALO AGUIRRE	1970
454	BENDER, EUGENE I ET AL	1968
455	BENEDICT, BURTON	1961
456	BENEDICT, BURTON	1962
457	BENEDICT, BURTON	1962
458	BENEDICT, BURTON	1965
459	BENEDICT, RUTH	1972
460	BENITEZ, JOSEPH S	1977
461	BENKIN, RICHARD L	1978
462	BENNETT, GEORGE	1969
463	BENNINGSEN, ALEXANDRE	1971
464	BENNOUNE, MAHFOUD	1975
465	BENSIMON-DONATH, DORIS	1971
466	BERBIEL, GUSTAV	1975
467	BERGER, SUZANNE	1972
468	BERGER, SUZANNE	1977
469	BERKHOFER, ROBERT F JR	1978
470	BERNHEIMER, CHARLES S ED	1971
471	BERREMAN, GERALD D	1960
472	BERREMAN, GERALD D	1966
473	BERREMAN, GERALD D	1966
474	BERRY, BREWTON	1960
475	BERRY, BREWTON	1972
476	BERTSCH, GARY K	1973
477	BERTSCH, GARY K	1974
478	BESSAC, FRANK	1968
479	BETTELHEIM, BRUNO ET AL	1964
480	BHAR, SUPRIYA	1972
481	BHATTACHARYA, D K	1968
482	BIDDISS, MICHAEL D	1966
483	BIENAN, HENRY	1974
484	BIESANZ, JOHN	1950
485	BILINSKY, YAROSLAV	1968
486	BILINSKY, YAROSLAV	1978
487	BILLE JOHN H	1971
488	BILLIGMEIER, ROBERT H	1974
489	BINGHAM, JOHN ET AL	1972
490	BIRCH, ANTHONY H	1978
491	BIRMINGHAM, STEPHEN	1973
492	BISKUP, R	1968

NUM	AUTHOR	DATE
493	BJORK, KENNETH O	1976
494	BLACK, MERLE	1978
495	BLACK, NAOMI	1977
496	BLAIR, PHILIP M	1972
497	BLAIR, WILLIAM C	1952
498	BLASCO, PEDRO GONZALEZ	1974
499	BLAU, JOSEPH	1976
500	BLAUNER, ROBERT	1972
501	BLEDA, SHARON ESTEE	1978
502	BLEDA, SHARON ESTEE	1979
503	BLEGEN, THEODORE C	1931
504	BLOOD, HILARY	1957
505	BLOOM, LEONARD	1948
506	BLOOM, LEONARD	1967
507	BLU, KAREN I	1979
508	BOCOCK, ROBERT J	1971
509	BODNAR, JOHN E ED	1973
510	BOGINA, SH	1968
511	BOISSEVAIN, JEREMY	1971
512	BUNACICH, EDNA	1975
513	BONACICH, EDNA	1976
514	BORALE, P T	1968
515	BORHEK, J T	1970
516	BOROWIEC, WALTER A	1674
517	BOSWELL, DAVID M	1974
518	BOTTOMLEY, GILL	1976
519	BOTTOMS, A E	1967
520	BOURAIN, ANNE MARIE	1976
521	BOURHIS, RICHARD Y ET AL	1973
522	BOURRICAUD, FRANCOIS	1975
523	BOYD, MONICA	1974
524	BRACEY, JOHN H ET AL	1971
525	BRAIN, JAMES L	1973
526	BRAITHWAITE, LLOYD	1953
527	BRAITHWAITE, LLOYD	1960
528	BRAND, JACK	1978
529	BRAROE, NIELS WINTHER	1965
530	BRAROE, NIELS WINTHER	1975
531	BRASS, PAUL R ET AL	1976
532	BRAZEAU, JACQUES ET AL	1977
533	BRETON, RAYMOND	1978
534	BRETON, RAYMOND ET AL	1966
535	BRETELL, CAROLINE B	1977
536	BREUGELMANS, R	1970
537	BREWER, MARILYN ET AL	1976
538	BRIDGE, SUSAN	1977

NUM	AUTHOR	DATE	1 AB	2 ABCDE	3 ABCDEF	4 ABCDEFGHI	5 ABCDEFGHIJK	6	7	8	9	10	11	12	13	14	15	16	17
539	BRIER, ALAN ET AL	1975		*	*	*	*	*	*			*	*						
540	BRIER, ALAN ET AL	1974				*	**	*	*			*	*	*		*	*		
541	BRIGGS, JOHN W	1978		*	*		*					*	*	*	**				
542	BRIGHAM, JOHN C ET AL	1972	*	**	*	*	*							*				
543	BRINTNALL, DOUGLAS E	1979		**			*											
544	BROADBENT, ELIZABETH	1972		*	*	*	*	*		**	**	*						
545	BROCK, PETER	1969		*														
546	BROOKS, DENNIS ET AL	1979		*	*	*	*					*	*					*	
547	BROWN, CAROLYN HENNING	1978		**	*	**				*		*						
548	BROWN, F J ET AL	1937	**	*	*	**												
549	BROWN, THOMAS N	1966		*	*		*	*										
550	BROWNE, WILLIAM P ET AL	1976		*		*	*	**					*					
551	BRUNCKER, ERNEST	1970		*				*										
552	BRUNER, EDWARD M	1961		*		**	**											
553	BRUNER, EDWARD M	1972		*	*	**	*					*	*	**		**	**		
554	BRUNEK, EDWARD M	1974		*				*										
555	BUECHLER, HANS C ET AL	1975		*		*		**		*								
556	BUENKER, JOHN D ET AL	1977				*****	**	*	**	*								
557	BULLOCK, CHARLES ET AL	1975		*	**		*	**	**									
558	BURG, STEVEN L	1978		*		*	**	*										
559	BURGER, HENRY G	1970		*	*	*		*	*						*			
560	BURGESS, THOMAS	1970		**	**	**	*	*	*	*	*	*	**	**	*	**	*	**	*
561	BURLING, ROBBINS	1967		*		*	**	**					*	*				
562	BURMA, JOHN M ED	1970	*	**	**	**	**	**					*	*	***	**	**		
563	BURTON, FRANK	1978		*	*	*	**	**	*				*					
564	BUSCH, PETER A	1974		***	*			**										
565	BUSHNELL, J H	1968		*	*		**					*	*	*				
566	BUSTIN, EDOUARD	1975		*	*	*		*			*	*	*	*				
567	BUTLER, JEFFREY E	1974		*		*		*					*					
568	BUTLER, JOHN S ET AL	1978		*	**								*					
569	BUTTERWORTH, ERIC	1964		*	*	**	*	*	**	**	*		*	*				
570	BUTTERWORTH, ERICK	4967			**	*	**	*	**									
571	CABRERA, YSIDRO A	1972		*	*	*												
572	CAFFERTY, PASTORA S J	1975	*		*		*	**					*					*
573	CAHN, EDGAR S ED	1969	*	*		*	*											
574	CAMEJO, ACTON	1971		*	*		*											
575	CAMERON, DAVID	1974			**													
576	CAMPBELL, ANGUS	1971		*	*	*	*	*	*		*	**	****					
577	CANADA, ROYAL COMMISSION	1978			*	*	**	**	**	**	*	*	*	*				
578	CANADA, ROYAL COMMISSION	1978		**			*	*	*									
579	CANFIELD, ROBERT L	1973		*	*	*												
580	CARDONA, LUIS A	1974		**	**		*			**		*	**	*				
581	CAREY, ISKANDAR	1976		**	*	*												
582	CARLISLE, DONALD S	1975		*	*	**	*	**			*	*	**	*				
583	CARLISLE, RODNEY	1975		*		*	**											
584	CARLSON, LEWIS H ET AL	1972		*	*		*				*	***		*			*	

NUM	AUTHOR	DATE
585	CARRERE D ENCAUSSE, H	1978
586	CARRERE D ENCAUSSE, H	1978
587	CARROLL, TERENCE G	1977
588	CARTER, LEWIS F	1968
589	CASELLI, RON	1974
590	CASHMAN, MARC ET AL EDS	1976
591	CASTELLS, MANUEL	1975
592	CASTLES, GODULA ET AL	1971
593	CASTLES, STEPHEN ET AL	1973
594	CATELLAN, GEORGES	1971
595	CATER, JOHN ET AL	1979
596	CHADNEY, JAMES G	1977
597	CHADWICK, BRUCE ET AL	1975
598	CHADWICK-JONES, J K	1965
599	CHAN, CHAI-HON	1978
600	CHANDRA, KANANUR V	1973
601	CHANDRAS, KANANUR V ED	1978
602	CHARSLEY, S R	1974
603	CHASE, ALLAN	1977
604	CHAUBE, SHIBANI K	1975
605	CHAUHAN, I S	1965
606	CHEBUKSAROV, N N	1970
607	CHIMBOS, PETER D	1974
608	CHIN, AI-LI	1978
609	CHIN, ROCKY	1971
610	CHING, FRANK	1976
611	CHISWICK, BARRY R	1973
612	CHISWICK, BARRY	1978
613	CHITEPO, HERBERT	1970
614	CHOY, BONG-YOUN	1979
615	CHRISTIAN, JOHN ET AL	1976
616	CHRISTIANSEN, JOHN B	1979
617	CHURCH, AVERY G	1978
618	CHURCHILL, CHARLES W	1975
619	CLARK, DAVID	1979
620	CLARK, KENNETH B	1967
621	CLARK, MARGARET, ET AL	1976
622	CLARKE, JOHN H	1976
623	CLAUDE, INIS L	1955
624	CLEM, RALPH S	1973
625	CLEM, RALPH S ED	1975
626	CLISSOLD, STEPHEN	1965
627	CLOSE, M E ET AL	1971
628	COBLENTZ, HARRY S	1974
629	COETZEE, J H	1978
630	COHEN, ABNER	1974

NUM	AUTHOR	DATE	1 AB	2 ABCDEF	3 ABCDE	4 ABCDEFGHI	5 ABCDEFGHIJK	6	7	8	9	10	11	12	13	14	15	16	17
631	COHEN, DAVID S	1974	*							*	*		*			*			*
632	COHEN, DAVID W ET AL EDS	1972		*	*	*	*	*			*		*						
633	COHEN, ERIK	1972		*	*						*								
634	COHEN, ERIK	1977		*	*	*			*				*			*			
635	COHEN, ERIK	1977		*	*	*	******* **							*					
636	COHEN, HAYYIM	1971					*				*								*
637	COHEN, PERCY	1968		*	*		*	*											
638	COHEN, STEVEN M	1974		*	*		***							*		*			
639	COHEN, STEVEN M	1977					*												
640	COHEN, STEVEN M ET AL	1978			*			*									*		
641	COHEN, STEVEN M ET AL	1977		*	*		*												*
642	COLBY, BENJAMIN N	1966			*						*								
643	COLBY, BENJAMIN N	1966		*	*	*	**	*			**		*						
644	COLBY, BENJAMIN N ET AL	1961		*	*		***												
645	COLBY, BENJAMIN N ET AL	1969			*	*	*	*											
646	COLE, LEONARD A	1977		*	*			*					*	*		*		*
647	COLEMAN, ANDREW M	1972		*	*	*	*	**	*	*	*	*		*	**				*
648	COLEMAN, TERRY	1972		*	*	*		***	*	*	*	*	*			**			*
649	COLLINS, SYDNEY	1955																	
650	COLSON, ELIZABETH	1970				*													
651	COMEAU, LARRY R ET AL	1978		*	*	*	*	*		*	*	*	*	*	*	*	*	*	*
652	COMISSAO DE RECENSEAMENTO	1964																	
653	COMMUNITY RELATIONS COMM	1975																	
654	COMPARATIVE POLITICS SEM	1976		**		*													
655	CONNOR, JOHN W	1977	*		*	**	*												
656	CONNOR, WALKER	1967	*	*	*	*		*					*						
657	CONNOR, WALKER	1969		*	*	*													
658	CONNOR, WALKER	1976			*	*		*			*		*	*					
659	CONNOR, WALKER	1977				*	*												
660	CONNOR, WALKER	1978	*				*						*						
661	CONQUEST, ROBERT ED	1967	*	*	*	*	*	*	*	**	**	***	*	*	*	*	*		*
662	CONSTANTINIDES, PAMELA	1977		*	*			*					*						
663	COOK, RAMSAY ED	1969	*	*	*	*		*											
664	COOMBS, H C	1972																	
665	COOPER, MARK N	1974	*	*	*	**													
666	COOPER, MARK N	1974		*	*	*						*							**
667	COOPER, PAULETTE ED	1972	*	**	*	*	**	*			*	*		*					
668	COPPA, FRANK J	1976		**	*	*	**			***	*	*		**			*	*	
669	COPPA, FRANK J ET AL	1976		*	*	*	*			***	*	***	*	*			*		
670	COPPA, FRANK J ET AL	1976	*	*	*	*				***	*	*		*					*
671	CORDASCO, FRANCESCO ED	1975	*	**	*		**			*				*		*			*
672	CORDASCO, FRANCESCO ET AL	1974	*	**	*	*	**			*				**	*	**	*	*	**
673	CORDASCO, FRANCESCO ET AL	1970		*	*	*	*				*			**	*	*	*	*	
674	CORNELIUS, WAYNE A	1978	*	*	*	*		*					*						
675	CORNELL, JOHN B	1964			*		*												
676	CORRADO, RAYMOND B	1975	*	*	*	*		*			*	*	*	*			*	*	*

NUM	AUTHOR	DATE
677	CORTES, CARLOS E ET AL	1976
678	CORWIN, ARTHUR F ED	1978
679	COTRAN, EUGENE	1969
680	COVELLO, LEONARD	1967
681	COX, OLIVER C	1948
682	COX, OLIVER C	1971
683	COX, OLIVER C	1974
684	CRAIN, ROBERT L ET AL	1972
685	CREWE, IVOR ED	1975
686	CROSS, MALCOLM	1971
687	CROSS, MALCOLM	1978
688	CROSS, ROBERT D	1978
689	CROWLEY, DANIEL J	1957
690	CUEVA-JARAMILLO, JUAN	1978
691	CULIN, STEWART	1970
692	CUMMINGS, SCOTT	1977
693	CUKAN, THOMAS J	1976
694	CURTHOYS, ANN ET AL EDS	1978
695	CURTIS, LYNN A	1975
696	CZENANOWSKI, JAN	1961
697	DAALDER, HANS	1971
698	DAALDER, HANS	1973
699	DADRIAN, VAHAKN N	1969
700	DADRIAN, VAHAKN N	1975
701	DAHYA, BADR U D	1965
702	DAHYA, BADR U D	1973
703	DAHYA, BADR U D	1974
704	DAHYA, ZAYNAB	1965
705	DAMROSZ, JERZY	1978
706	DANE, J K ET AL	1972
707	DANIELS, ROGER	1977
708	DANIELS, ROGER	1978
709	DARROCH, A GORDON	1979
710	DARROCH, A G ET AL	1972
711	DAS GUPTA, JYOTIRINDRA	1970
712	DAS GUPTA, JYOTIRINDRA	1974
713	DAS GUPTA, JYOTIRINDRA	1975
714	DASHEVSKY, A ET AL	1972
715	DASHEFSKY, A ET AL	1974
716	DA SILVA, MILTON M	1977
717	DAVID, WILFRED L	1972
718	DAVIDSON, BASIL	1969
719	DAVIDSON, CHANDLER	1972
720	DAVIES, E HUDSON	1968
721	DAVIES, HOWARD B	1978
722	DAVIS, JEROME	1969

NUM	AUTHOR	DATE	1 AB	2 ABCDE	3 ABCDE	4 ABCDEFGHI	5 ABCDEFGHIJK	6	7	8	9	10	11	12	13	14	15	16	17
723	DAVIS, KINGSLEY	1969		*							*		*	*		*			
724	DAVIS, LENWOOD G	1978																	
725	DAVISON, R B	1963		*	*	*	*				*	*	*	*	*			*	*
726	DAWSON, BETTY	1968		*	*	*	*	*	*		*		*	*	*				
727	DAWSON, JOHN	1964			*	*	*						*						
728	DAWSON, JOHN	1965		*	*	*	*	*	*		*	*	*	*					
729	DEAKIN, NICHOLAS	1964			*	*	*	*			*	*	*						
730	DEAKIN, NICHOLAS	1970				*	*	*			*	*	*	*					
731	DEATH, COLIN E ET AL	1977			*		*	*											
732	DEGLER, CARL N	1959		*	*	*		*				*	*						
733	DEGLER, CARL N	1971		*	*	*	*	*			*	*							*
734	DEJONG, GERALD F	1975		*	*	*	*						*					*	*
735	DEKMEJIAN, RICHARD H	1978		*	*	*	*	*			*	*	*						
736	DELF, GEORGE	1963		*		*							*						
737	DELORIA, VINE JR	1970			*	*	*		*			*							
738	DEMEDTS, ANDRÉ	1972		*	*	*	*	*			*	*							
739	DENCH, GEOFF	1975			*	*	*	*	*		*		*	*	*	*	*	*	*
740	DENTAN, R K	1976		*									*						
741	DENTON, TREVOR	1975			*	*	*						*						
742	DE REUCK, ANTHONY ET AL	1966	*	*	*	***	*				*	*	*	*	*	*	*		*
743	DESAI, RASHMI	1963		**	*	*	*	*	*	*									
744	DESBARATZ, JAZQUELINE	1979		**	*	*	*	*											
745	DESHEN, SHLOMO A	1970		**	*	*		*											
746	DESHEN, SHLOMO A	1972		*	*	*		**											
747	DESHEN, SHLOMO A	1974			*	*	*	**											*
748	DESHEN, SHLOMO A	1975		*	*	*	*	**											
749	DESHEN, SHLOMO A	1976		*	*	*	*	**				*						*	
750	DESPRES, LEO A	1964				*	*	*				*	*						
751	DESPRES, LEO A	1968				*		*			*	*							
752	DESPRES, LEO A	1969		**		*		*				*	*		*		*		
753	DESPRES, LEO A	1975		*	*	*	*	**	*	*	*	*		**	*				*
754	DESPRES, LEO A	1975			*	*	*	**		**	*	*		**					
755	DESPRES, LEO A	1975			*	*	*	**	*		**			*			*		
756	DEUTSCH, KARL W ET AL	1970			*	*		*						*					
757	DE VOS, GEORGE	1966		*	*	*	*	*	*										
758	DE VOS, GEORGE	1966		**	*			**	*										
759	DE VOS, GEORGE	1972				*	*	*											
760	DE VOS, GEORGE ET AL	1966		*		*	**	*											
761	DE VOS, GEORGE ET AL	1966		**	*	*	*	*	*										*
762	DE VOS, GEORGE ET AL	1974			*	*	*												
763	DEW, EDWARD	1972		*	*	*				*	*	*	*						
764	DEW, EDWARD	1974		*	*	*	*		**		*	*							
765	DEW, EDWARD	1978		**	*	*	*	*	**		*	*		*					
766	DEY, MUKUL K	1962		*	*			*			*	*							
767	DIAMOND, STANLEY	1970		*				*			*	*	*	*					
768	DICKIE-CLARK, H F	1972		*			*	*	*		*	*	*					*	

NUM	AUTHOR	DATE	1 AB	2 ABCDEF	3 ABCDE	4 ABCDEFGHI	5 ABCDEFGHIJK	6	7	8	9	10	11	12	13	14	15	16	17
769	DICKSON, R J	1966		*	*		*												
770	DINER, HASIA R	1977		*	*		*						* *						
771	DINNERSTEIN, LEONARD ETAL	1977	*	* *	*	* *	*	*			* *	* * *							
772	DISHMAN, ROBERT	1978		*	*			*											
773	DOBBY, E H G	1952		*	*		*	*	*										
774	DOBSON, RICHARD B	1975		*	*	*	*	*	*		*	* *	*	*	*		* *	* *	*
775	DOERSAM, CHRISTOPHER	1977		*	*	*	*												
776	DOLCE, PHILIP C	1976		*	*	*	*	*				* * *	* * *	*					
777	DOLGIN, JANET L	1977		* *	*		*									*			
778	DOLLARD, JOHN	1937	*	* *	*	*	*	*		*	*	*	* * *	*					
779	DONOGHUE, JOHN	1966		*	*	*	*												
780	DOORNBOS, MARTIN R	1976		*	*	*	* *												
781	DOROSHKIN, MILTON	1969		*	*		* *										*		
782	DOROTICH, DANIEL A	1978		*	*	*	*	*					*	*	*		*	* *	*
783	DOSTAL, WALTER ED	1972	*	* * *	*	*	* *	* *	*		*	* *	*						*
784	DOTSON, FLOYD ET AL	1963		*	*	*	*	*											
785	DRAKE, ST CLAIR	1966		*	* *		* *												
786	DREYER, JUNE TEUFEL	1971		*	*	*	*												
787	DREYER, JUNE TEUFEL	1975		* *	*		* *												
788	DREYER, JUNE TEUFEL	1977		*	*		*												
789	DRIEDGER, LEO	1976	*	*	*	* *	*	* * *	*	*	*	* * *	* * * *	* * * * *			* *	* *	*
790	DRIEDGER, LEO	1977		*	* *	* *	* * *	* * * *	*	*	*	*	* * * *	*	*	*		*	*
791	DRIEDGER, LEO	1978	*	* *	*	*	* * *	*				*							
792	DRIEDGER, LEO	1978		*	*	*	*	*											
793	DRIEDGER, LEO	1979		*	*	*	*	*											
794	DRIEDGER, LEO ET AL	1974		*	*	*	*					* * *	* *						
795	DRIEDGER, LEO ET AL	1977		*	* *	*	*				*	* *	*	*			*	*	
796	DRUCKER, HENRY	1978		*	*		*	*											
797	DRUMMOND, ROBERT	1977	*	*	*	* * *	*												*
798	DSYUBA, IVAN	1974		*	*	*	*	*					* *			* *		*	*
799	DUNN, ETHEL ET AL	1973		*	*	*	*												
800	DUNN, JAMES A JR	1972		* *	*	*	*				*	* *	* *	* *	*	*			
801	DUNN, JAMES A JR	1974		*	*	*	* *					*	*	* * *	*	*			
802	DUNN, L C ET AL	1975	*	*	*	* *	* *	*	*	*	*	* *		* *	*	*	*		
803	DUNN, STEPHEN P ET AL	1967		*	*		*												
804	DUNNING, ERIC	1972		*	*	*	*		*	*	*		*						
805	DURRENBERGER, PAUL	1974		* *	* *	* *	*				* *							* *	
806	DU TOIT, BRIAN M	1978		* *	*	* *	* *		*	*	* *	* *	* *						
807	DUTTER, LEE E	1977		*	*		*					*	*						
808	DWORKIN, ANTHONY G	1972		*	*			*											
809	EAMES, EDWIN ET AL	1978		*	*	*	* * *		*	*	*			* * * *	*	*		* *	*
810	EASTMAN, CAROL	1971		* *	*	*	* *							* *					
811	EASTMAN, CAROL	1975		* *	*		*	*											
812	EDEL, M M	1965																	
813	EDELSTEIN, JOEL C	1974		*	*		*	* *		*	* *								
814	EDLEFSON, JOHN B ET AL	1960		*	*		*	*		*	* *								

NUM	AUTHOR	DATE	1 AB	2 ABCDEF	3 ABCDE	4 ABCDEFGHI	5 ABCDEFGHIJK	6	7	8	9	10	11	12	13	14	15	16	17
815	EDMONDS, C J	1971		*	*	*	*					*		*		*				*
816	EDMONDS, JULIET	1968		*							*	*						*	
817	EDMUNDSON, LUCKSLEY	1974		*			F *											*
818	EDWARDS, J R	1976		*	* *	H *	G *											
819	EDWARDS, REGINALD	1978	*	*	*	I *	I *											
820	EGERTON, JOHN	1969		*	*	*	*		*	*	*	*		*		*		*	*
821	EISINGER, PETER K	1978		*	* *	*	*					* *	*					
822	EITZEN, D STANLEY	1968		*			*											
823	ELKHULY, ABDO A	1966		*	* *	*	* *											*	*
824	ELLIOTT, JEAN LEONARD ED	1971	*	* *	*	* *	* *				*	* *				*			*
825	ELLIOTT, JEAN LEONARD ED	1971	*	* *	* *	* *	*					*						
826	ELLMAN, YISRAEL	1970		*			F *					*						
827	EMERSON, RUPERT	1960		*	* *	E *	H *		*		*	* * * *	*	*		*	* *		*
828	ENLOE, CYNTHIA H	1973		*														
829	ENLOE, CYNTHIA H	1974		* *	*	*	H *											
830	ENLOE, CYNTHIA H	1975		*	*	*	F * *		*	*	*	* * *						
831	ENLOE, CYNTHIA H	1976		*	* *	*	E *		*	*		*						
832	ENLOE, CYNTHIA H	1978					F *					*						
833	ENLOE, CYNTHIA H	1978		* *	*	*	G *		*	*	*	* * * *	*					
834	ENLOE, CYNTHIA H	1979		*	*	*	K *		*	*		*	*					
835	EPSTEIN, A L	1958			*				*	*	*	*						
836	EPSTEIN, A L	1969			*				*	*	*							
837	EPSTEIN, A L	1970			*					*								
838	EPSTEIN, A L	1978			*				* *								
839	ERICKSON, CHARLOTTE	1972			*	*	*		*	*	*	* * * *		* *	*		* *	* *
840	ESMAN, MILTON J	1972		* *	*	* *	G *		*	*	*	* * *						
841	ESMAN, MILTON J	1975				* *	H *					* * *						
842	ESMAN, MILTON J	1977					G *											
843	ESMAN, MILTON J	1977		*						*	*	*						
844	ETEROVICH, ADAM S	1966			*													
845	ETEROVICH, ADAM S	1971		*	*	* *	*		*			* *						
846	ETEROVICH, ADAM S	1971				*	*		* *			* *					*	
847	ETHIOPIAWI	1977	*	* *	*		E *											
848	FALLERS, LLOYD A	1974			*	*	F *		*		*				*	*		
849	FARBER, BERNARD ET AL	1979		* *	*		I *		*			*						
850	FARLEY, REYNOLDS	1970		*	*	H *	F *											*
851	FARLEY, REYNOLDS	1978			*	H *	G *				* *	* *	*	*	*	*		
852	FEAGIN, JOE R ET AL	1972		*	*	H *	* *											
853	FEATHERMAN, DAVID L	1971		*	*	H *	E * *											
854	FEATHERMAN, DAVID L ET AL	1976																
855	FEINGOLD, DAVID A	1976		*	* *	*	*		*		* *	* *		* *	*			
856	FEINGOLD, HENRY L	1974		*	*	*	F * *					* *	*	*		*		
857	FEINSTEIN, OTTO ED	1971	*	* *	*	*	I * * *					* *	* *					
858	FEIT, E	1967		*	*	*	F *			*					*			
859	FELDSTEIN, STANLEY ED	1971		*	*	*	*											
860	FELLOWS, DONALD KEITH	1972	*	*	*	*	K *	*	*		* *	* *	* *	*	*			

NUM	AUTHOR	DATE
861	FENNELL, VALERIE	1977
862	FENTON, MIKE	1976
863	FERMI, LAURA	1971
864	FERNANDES, FLORESTAN	1970
865	FERNANDO, TISSA	1972
866	FILIPINAS FOUNDATION INC	1975
867	FINKELSTEIN, LOUIS ED	1971
868	FISCHER-GALATI, STEPHEN	1969
869	FISCHER-GALATI, STEPHEN	1975
870	FISHER, MAXINE P	1978
871	FISHER, WESLEY A	1977
872	FISHMAN, JOSHUA A ET AL	1968
873	FISKE, SHIRLEY	1977
874	FITZGERALD, STEPHEN	1973
875	FLANAGAN, ROBERT J	1973
876	FLANAGAN, ROBERT J	1973
877	FLEMING, JUDITH	1977
878	FLETT, HAZEL	1979
879	FOGEL, WALTER	1978
880	FOLTZ, WILLIAM J	1973
881	FOLTZ, WILLIAM J	1974
882	FONER, NANCY	1977
883	FONER, NANCY	1978
884	FONER, PHILIP S	1974
885	FONER, PHILIP S	1978
886	FONG, STANLEY L M	1973
887	FONSECA, A	1971
888	FOON, CHEW SOCK	1977
889	FORBES, JACK D	1973
890	FORD, HENRY JONES	1915
891	FORD, W SCOTT	1972
892	FOREMAN, SCOTT	1976
893	FORSTER, JOHN	1975
894	FORSYTHE, DAVID P ET AL	1974
895	FORTES, MEYER	1970
896	FOX, RICHARD G ET AL	1978
897	FRANCIS, E K	1951
898	FRANCIS, E K	1968
899	FRANCK, THOMAS M	1960
900	FRANDA, MARCUS F	1971
901	FRAZIER, E FRANKLIN	1957
902	FRAZIER, E FRANKLIN	1957
903	FRAZIER, E FRANKLIN	1968
904	FREEDMAN, MAURICE	1960
905	FREEMAN, GARY P	1978
906	FREEMAN, GARY P	1979

NUM	AUTHOR	DATE	1 AB	2 ABCDEF	3 ABCDE	4 ABCDEFGH	5 ABCDEFGHIJK	6	7	8	9	10	11	12	13	14	15	16	17
907	FREEMAN, RICHARD B	1976		**	*	*	**		*	*	*	**	*		*					
908	FREEMAN, WALTER E	1974		**	*		*					**	*						*	
909	FRENCH, LAURENCE	1978		*	*		*				*	**	**	**						
910	FRENDO, HENRY J	1975		*	*	*	*					*	**	**						
911	FREUND, W M	1976		*		*	*													
912	FREY, WILLIAM H	1978		*	*	*	*	*	*		*	*	*			*				
913	FRIDERES, JAMES S	1971			*						*	*	*							
914	FRIDERES, JAMES S	1978			*		**				*	*	***							
915	FRIED, MORTON H	1975		*	*	*	*	*				*								
916	FRIEDLANDER, DOV ET AL	1979			*	*	*	*			*	*								
917	FRIEDLANDER, EVA	1977		**	*	*	*				*	*	*		*					
918	FRIESAN, JOHN W	1971		*	*	*	*					*		**	*					
919	FRISBIE, W PARKER ET AL	1978				**	*	*						**	*					
920	FRISBIE, W PARKER ET AL	1978		*	*		**	**				*								
921	FUCHS, LAWRENCE W ED	1968	*		*		*					*			*			*		
922	FUGITA, STEVEN S ET AL	1977		*	*	*	*	*			*	**	*		*					*
923	FURNIVALL, JOSEPH S	1942		**	**	**	**				**	**	**	**						
924	FURNIVALL, JOSEPH S	1945		*	*	**	**													
925	FURNIVALL, JOSEPH S	1956		*	*	*	**													
926	GABRIEL, JOHN ET AL	1979		*	*		*	*			**	*								
927	GABRIEL, RICHARD A	1973		*	*		*	*				*								
928	GAGALA, KEN	1973				**					**									
929	GAGALA, KEN	1973		*	*			*	*	*	*	*								
930	GAIGE, FREDERICK H	1975		*	*			*			*								*	
931	GALUSH, WILLIAM	1974		*	*							*								
932	GAMBINO, RICHARD	1974		**	*		**	*	*	**	**	***	***	*	*	**	*			*
933	GAMINO, MANUEL	1969		**	*	*	*	*			**	**	*	**	*					
934	GANN, L H	1958		*	*							*								
935	GANS, HERBERT J	1962		*	*		*									*				
936	GARBARINO, MERWYN S	1971		*	**			*		*	**	**	**	**	*	*				
937	GARCIA, F CHRIS ED	1973	*	*	*	*	*	*	**	*	**	*	**	**	*	*		**	**	*
938	GARCIA, F CHRIS	1973		*	*				*											
939	GARZA, CATARINO ED	1977	*		**		*	*			*	*	*				*		**	
940	GARZA, EDWARD D	1972		*	*	*	*													
941	GELLAR, SHELDON	1973		*	*			*				*								
942	GELLNER, ERNEST	1964		*	*	*	*	*	*		**	*	*	*	*	*	**		**	*
943	GELLNER, ERNEST	1977		*	*		*		*		*					*	**			
944	GELLNER, JOHN ET AL	1968		*	**			*				*								
945	GEORGE, VIC ET AL	1967		*	*	*	*				*	**	*						*	
946	GERHART, GAIL M	1978					*													*
947	GERSON, LOUIS L	1964		*	**	*	**	**	*		**	*		*						
948	GERTEINY, ALFRED G	1966		*	*			*	*			*		*	*					
949	GILBERG, TROND	1974		*	*			*												
950	GILES, HOWARD ET AL	1976		*	*	*	*	*			*	*	*						*	
951	GILLIN, JOHN	1948		*	*			*												
952	GINGRAS, FRANCIUS-PIERRE	1975					*				*	*			*	*				*

NUM	AUTHOR	DATE
953	GINSBERG, PHILIP	1970
954	GINSBERG, YONA	1975
955	GIST, NOEL P	1967
956	GITTLER, JOSEPH D ED	1964
957	GLANZ, RUDOLPH	1966
958	GLANZ, RUDOLPH	1970
959	GLANZ, RUDOLPH	1970
960	GLASER, DANIEL	1958
961	GLASER, RICHARD	1976
962	GLASGOW, ROY ARTHUR	1970
963	GLAZER, NATHAN	1978
964	GLENN, NORVAL D ET AL	1969
965	GLICK, CLARENCE E	1970
966	GLICK, PAUL C	1970
967	GLOCK, CHARLES Y ET AL	1969
968	GLUCKMAN, MAX	1958
969	GLUCKMAN, MAX	1962
970	GLUCKMAN, MAX	1965
971	GLUCKMAN, MAX	1969
972	GMELCH, SHARON B ET AL	1976
973	GOERING, JOHN M	1971
974	GOLDBERG, HARVEY	1977
975	GOLDEN, HILDA H ET AL	1977
976	GOLDSTEIN, MELVYN C	1975
977	GOLDSTEIN, MICHAEL	1971
978	GOLDSTEIN, SIDNEY ET AL	1968
979	GOMEZ, DAVID F	1973
980	GONZALES, ALEX S	1974
981	GONZALEZ, NANCIE L	1969
982	GONZALEZ, NANCIE L	1975
983	GOODY, ESTHER N ET AL	1977
984	GOODY, JACK	1970
985	GOODY, JACK	1973
986	GORDON, ALBERT I	1964
987	GORDON, DAVID M	1972
988	GORDON, LEONARD A	1978
989	GORDON, MILTON M	1975
990	GORDON, MILTON M	1978
991	GORDON, ROBERT	1978
992	GORER, GEOFFREY	1975
993	GOUVEIA, DENNIS HILARY	1972
994	GRAVES, THEODORE D	1967
995	GRAY, RICHARD	1971
996	GREELEY, ANDREW M	1971
997	GREELEY, ANDREW M	1972
998	GREELEY, ANDREW M	1974

NUM	AUTHOR	DATE	1 AB	2 ABCDEF	3 ABCDE	4 ABCDEFGH	5 ABCDEFGHIJK	6 ABCDEFGHIJK	7	8	9	10	11	12	13	14	15	16	17
999	GREELEY, ANDREW M	1976																		
1000	GREELEY, ANDREW M	1976																		*
1001	GREELEY, ANDREW M	1977																		*
1002	GREELEY, ANDREW M ET AL	1975																		
1003	GREEN, ALAN G	1976																		
1004	GREEN, SAMUEL SWETT	1970																		
1005	GREENE, VERA	1975																		
1006	GREENE, VICTOR	1975																		
1007	GREENSTONE, J DAVID	1975																		
1008	GREENWOOD, DAVYDD J	1977																		
1009	GREER, COLIN ED	1974																		*
1010	GREGERSON, MARILYN J	1972																*	*	
1011	GREGOROVICH, ANDREW	1972																		
1012	GREGORY, JAMES R	1976																		
1013	GREIF, STUART W	1975																		
1014	GRIESSMAN, C EUGENE ET AL	1975																		
1015	GRIFFIN, JAMES	1975																		
1016	GRILLO, R D	1969																		
1017	GRILLO, R D	1974																		
1018	GRIMSHAW, ALLEN D	1962																		
1019	GRIMSHAW, ALLEN D ED	1969																		
1020	GROH, GEORGE W	1972																		*
1021	GROVE, D JOHN	1974																		
1022	GROVE, D JOHN	1977																		
1023	GROVE, D JOHN	1978																		
1024	GRUNDY, KENNETH W	1973																		
1025	GUEST, AVERY M ET AL	1976																		*
1026	GUILLEMIN, JEANNE	1975																		
1027	GUILLOTTE, JOSEPH V	1978																		
1028	GUILLOTTE, JOSEPH V	1978																		
1029	GUINDON, HUBERT	1978																*	*	
1030	GULLIVER, P H	1969																		
1031	GULLIVER, P H ED	1969																*	*	
1032	GUMPERZ, JOHN J	1961																*	*	
1033	GUMPERZ, JOHN J	1966																		
1034	GUMPERZ, JOHN J	1978																*	*	
1035	GUMPERZ, JOHN J ET AL EDS	1972																		
1036	GURAK, DOUGLAS T	1978																		
1037	GURIAN, JAY P	1975																		
1038	GUTHIER, STEVEN L	1977																		
1039	GUTHIER, STEVEN L	1977																		
1040	GUTKIND, PETER C W	1957																		
1041	GUTTENTAG, MARCIA	1970																		
1042	GUZMAN, RALPH C	1976																		
1043	GWARTNEY, JAMES D ET AL	1971																		
1044	HABERFELD, STEVEN	1973																		

NUM	AUTHOR	DATE
1045	HAGOPIAN, ELAINE C ET AL	1969
1046	HAIMAN, MIECISLAUS	1939
1047	HALLEY, ROBERT M ET AL	1976
1048	HALLIBURTON, R JR	1975
1049	HAMILTON, HOWARD D	1975
1050	HAMMOND, HAILEY ROSS	1963
1051	HAMMOND-TOOKE, DAVID	1970
1052	HANBY, VICTOR J	1977
1053	HANDLEMAN, DON	1977
1054	HANDLIN, OSCAR	1952
1055	HANDLIN, OSCAR	1957
1056	HANDLIN, OSCAR	1959
1057	HANDLIN, OSCAR	1959
1058	HANDLIN, OSCAR	1971
1059	HANDLIN, OSCAR, ET AL	1955
1060	HANHAM, J H	1969
1061	HANHARDT, ARTHUR M ET AL	1976
1062	HANNERZ, ULF	1969
1063	HANNERZ, ULF	1974
1064	HANSEN, MARCUS LEE	1961
1065	HAREWOOD, JACK	1971
1066	HARNED, FREDERIC T	1975
1067	HARNED, FREDERIC T	1975
1068	HARRE, JOHN	1963
1069	HARRE, JOHN	1966
1070	HARRE, JOHN	1966
1071	HARRIS, GEORGE S	1977
1072	HARRIS, MARVIN	1970
1073	HARRIS, ROSEMARY	1972
1074	HARRISON, BARBARA	1971
1075	HARRISON, BENNETT	1972
1076	HARRISON, JOSEPH	1977
1077	HARRISSON, TOM	1967
1078	HARTMANN, EDWARD GEORGE	1967
1079	HARTMANN, PAUL ET AL	1974
1080	HARVIE, CHRISTOPHER	1977
1081	HASSAN, RIAZ	1970
1082	HASSAN, RIAZ	1971
1083	HASSAN, RIAZ	1978
1084	HASSAN, RIAZ ET AL	1976
1085	HATT, PAUL	1948
1086	HAUG, MARIE R	1967
1087	HAUGEN, EINAR	1967
1088	HAWKINS, BRETT W ET AL ED	1970
1089	HAWKINS, JOHN	1978
1090	HAWS, ROBERT ED	1978

NUM	AUTHOR	DATE	1 AB	2 ABCDEF	3 ABCDE	4 ABCDEFGHI	5 ABCDEFGHIJK	6	7	8	9	10	11	12	13	14	15	16	17
1091	HAYS, WILLIAM C ET AL	1977		*									*			*			*
1092	HAZAREESINGH, K	1966				*					*				*				
1093	HEARD, KENNETH A	1961		*	*								*	*						
1094	HEATON, WILLIAM R JR	1977		*	*		*													
1095	HECHTER, MICHAEL	1973		*				*												
1096	HECHTER, MICHAEL	1976			*		*													
1097	HEILMAN, SAMUEL C	1977																		
1098	HEINEMAN, BENJAMIN W JR	1972		*	*			*												
1099	HELLER, CELIA S	1971		*			*													
1100	HELLER, CELIA S	1975		*	*		*	*				*								
1101	HELM, JUNE ED	1968	*	*			*	*	*			*	*	*			*			
1102	HENDERSON, THOMAS MCLEAN	1976		**	*			**	*											*
1103	HENDRICKS, GLENN	1974		**	*	*		*												
1104	HENG-CHEE, CHAN ET AL	1973		**	*		*	*												
1105	HENRIQUES, FERNANDO	1975			*	*	*	*				*								
1106	HENRY, FRANCES	1973	*	**	**	*		*	*	*	**		**						*	
1107	HEPBURN, A C ED	1979	*	**	**							*								
1108	HEPPLE, BOB	1968		**							**									
1109	HEPPLE, BOB	1968		**				*			**		**							
1110	HERCULES, FRANK	1972		*	*						*									
1111	HERMAN, HARRY V	1979	*	*	*															
1112	HERMASSI, ELBAKI	1972		**	*		*	*												
1113	HERSKOVITZ, MELVILLE J	1966		**			*					*		*						
1114	HERTZBERG, HAZEL W	1971		**						*										
1115	HESS, FJERIL	1970		*	*		*				*									
1116	HESS, GARY R	1974							*											
1117	HETMANEK, ALLEN	1975			*		*	*	*		*		*	*						
1118	HICKS, GEORGE L	1975						***		*	*	**	**	***		*				
1119	HICKS, GEORGE L	1977		**			**	***				*								
1120	HICKS, GEORGE L	1977			*		**	*												
1121	HIGGS, ROBERT	1977		*	*		*	*	*		*		*							
1122	HIGHAM, JOHN	1955		*				*												
1123	HIGHAM, JOHN ED	1978	*	*	*		**	**	*			**	*	*						
1124	HILL, CAROLE	1975			*		*	**												
1125	HILLER, HARRY H	1977		*			*				*									
1126	HIMES, JOSEPH S	1973		*	*			*		*		**	*							
1127	HIMMELSTRAND, ULF	1969		*			**	***	*			**								**
1128	HIMMELSTRAND, ULF	1973		**			**	*				*								
1129	HIRATA, LUCIE C	1975		*	*		*	*				**	*							
1130	HIRSCH, HERBERT	1973		***	*		*													
1131	HODDER-WILLIAMS, RICHARD	1974																		
1132	HODGE, ROBERT W	1973	*	*	*		**	*				*	*				*	*		
1133	HODGE, WILLIAM H	1975			*		**	**				**	**							
1134	HOETINK, HERMANNUS	1967		**	**	*	**	**				**		*						
1135	HOETINK, HERMANNUS	1971					**	**				*								
1136	HOETINK, HERMANNUS	1973		*	*		**	**	**		*	**								

NUM	AUTHOR	DATE	1 AB	2 ABCDEF	3 ABCDE	4 ABCDEFGHI	5 ABCDEFGHIJK	6	7	8	9	10	11	12	13	14	15	16	17
1137	HOETINK, HERMANNUS	1974											*	*					
1138	HOETINK, HERMANNUS	1975		*			*	*	*	*	*	*	*						
1139	HOFFMAN, ABRAHAM	1974		*	*						*	*							
1140	HOFFMAN, GEORGE W	1973		*	*	*		*		*	*								
1141	HOFFMAN, JOAN	1975		*	*	*		*		*									
1142	HOGAN, DENNIS P ET AL	1977			*	*				*	*	*			*				
1143	HOLLOMAN, REGINA E	1975	*	**	*	*	*			*	*	*							
1144	HOLMES, COLIN ED	1978		**	*	**		*		*	*	*	**						
1145	HOLUBNYCHY, VSEVOLOD	1968		*				*		*	*						*		
1146	HOLZBERG, CAROL S	1977	*		*						*	*							
1147	HOLZBERG, CAROL S	1977		*	*		**	*											
1148	HONDIUS, FRITS W	1968		*	*	*	**	*			*	**			*				*
1149	HORMANN, BERNHARD L	1972		*	*	*	**	*	*	*	*	*	*	**	**	*	**	**	*
1150	HOROWITZ, DONALD L	1971		*	*	*		*	*		*	*							
1151	HOROWITZ, DONALD L	1973		**	*	*		*	*			*							
1152	HOROWITZ, DONALD L	1975			*		**	*											
1153	HOROWITZ, IRVING LOUIS	1976					*						*						
1154	HOROWITZ, MICHAEL M	1974											**			*		*	
1155	HOSOKAWA, BILL	1969																	
1156	HOSOKAWA, BILL	1971						*											
1157	HOSOKAWA, FUMIKO	1978		*	*	*	*	*	**			*							*
1158	HOUCHINS, LEE ET AL	1974		*	*	*			**	*	*	*	*	**	**	*	**	**	
1159	HOURANI, ALBERT	1969		*	*	*		*											
1160	HOVANNISIAN, RICHARD G	1974		*	*	*		*				*							
1161	HOWARD, JOHN R ED	1970	*	**	*	*	*	*	*	*	*	*	*	*					
1162	HUBLER, WILLIAM HENRY	1978		*	*	*	*	*											
1163	HUDDLE, FRANK JR	1975							*					*		**			
1164	HUGGINS, NATHAN IRVIN	1978		*				**	**	*		**							
1165	HUGHES, EVERETT C	1964		*	*														
1166	HUNDLEY, NORRIS JR ED	1976	*	*				*	**										
1167	HUNT, LARRY L ET AL	1975		*	*	*		*											
1168	HUNT, LARRY L ET AL	1977		*	*	*	**	*											
1169	HUNTER, A A	1977			*	*						*							
1170	HUNTER, GUY ED	1965	*	*	*	*			**		*			*			*		
1171	HURH, WON MOO	1977		*	*		*	*						*					
1172	HURH, WON MOO	1977										*	*						
1173	HURSTFIELD, JENNIFER	1978		*	*		*			*	*		**	*	*				
1174	HUSBANDS, CHRISTOPHER T	1979		*	*	*		*			*								
1175	HVIDT, KRISTIAN	1975		*	*			*				*				*			
1176	HYLON-SMITH, K	1968			*						*								
1177	IANNI, OCTAVIO	1972		*	*	*		*	*	*	*								
1178	ICHIKAWA, KENJIRO	1976		*	**		*	*	*	**									
1179	INAYATULLAH	1976		*	*	*				*	*								
1180	INBAR, MICHAEL ET AL	1977		*	*						*	*	*						
1181	INDRA, DOREEN	1979		**	*			**	**	*	*								
1182	INGLIS, CHRISTINE	1972		*	*		*	*	*		*		**					*	

NUM	AUTHOR	DATE	1	2	3	4	5	6	7	8	9	10	11	12	13	14	15	16	17
1183	IORIZZO, LUCIANO J ET AL	1971																	*
1184	IRBY, CHARLES C	1978										*	*						
1185	IRELAND, RALPH R	1975											*		*				
1186	IRISH, DONALD P	1952																	
1187	IRVINE, WILLIAM P	1972									*	*	*				*		
1188	ISAACS, HAROLD P	1964																	
1189	ITO, HIROSHI	1966							*	*		*	*	*		*			
1190	IZRAELI, DAFNA NUNDI	1979								*		*	*	*		*			
1191	JACEK, HENRY ET AL	1975															*		
1192	JACKSON, JOHN ARTHUR	1963						*				*	*						
1193	JACKSON, JOHN D	1975																	
1194	JACO, DANIEL E ET AL	1975																	
1195	JACOB, JAMES E	1975								*			*						
1196	JACOBS, PAUL ET AL	1971																	
1197	JACOBS, WILBUR R	1972						*			*	*	*						
1198	JAENSCH, DEAN	1976									*								
1199	JAKLE, JOHN A	1973																	
1200	JALKANEN, RALPH J ED	1969									*	*	*	*	*	*			*
1201	JAMAL, VALI	1976								*		*	*	*	*				
1202	JANICS, KALMAN	1975																	
1203	JAYWARDENA, CHANDRA	1959								*		*							
1204	JAYWARDENA, CHANDRA	1963							*	*	*	*				*		*	*
1205	JEFFREY, PATRICIA	1976										*							
1206	JEFFRIES, VINCENT	1971								*	*				*				
1207	JEROME, DOROTHY	1978																	
1208	JIOBU, ROBERT M	1976													*				
1209	JIRYIS, SABRI	1976																	
1210	JOCANO, F LANDA	1970								*		*		*		*			
1211	JOHNSON, COLLEEN LEAHY	1976							*	*									
1212	JOHNSON, KENNETH F ET AL	1978						*											
1213	JONES, MALDWYN A	1960	*																
1214	JONES, PETER ET AL EDS	1978															*		
1215	JORGENSEN, JOSEPH G	1971																	
1216	JORGENSEN, JOSEPH G	1977							*	*	*	*	*	*		*		*	
1217	JORGENSEN-DAHL, ARNFINN	1975																	
1218	JUPP, JAMES	1969																	
1219	JUSTUS, JOYCE BENNETT	1978							*	*	*	*	*				*		
1220	JUTIKKALA, EINO	1976							*										
1221	KALBACH, WARREN E	1970																	
1222	KALISH, RICHARD A ET AL	1973						*	*	*	*		*	*		*		*	
1223	KALLEN, HORACE M	1956	*																
1224	KAMENETSKY, IHOR ED	1977									*	*	*	*	*	*		*	*
1225	KANDRE, PETER	1967																	
1226	KANDRE, PETER K	1976	*																
1227	KANG, T S ED	1979	*																
1228	KANNAN, C T	1972																	

NUM	AUTHOR	DATE
1229	KANTROWITZ, EDWARD R	1975
1230	KANTROWITZ, NATHAN	1969
1231	KANTROWITZ, NATHAN	1973
1232	KAPLAN, BERNICE A ET AL	1953
1233	KAPLAN, H ROY	1977
1234	KARNI, MICHAEL G ET AL	1975
1235	KATZ, ZEV	1975
1236	KATZ, ZEV	1975
1237	KATZENSTEIN, MARY FAINSOD	1977
1238	KATZENSTEIN, MARY FAINSOD	1979
1239	KATZENSTEIN, PETER J	1977
1240	KATZMAN, MARTIN T	1969
1241	KATZMAN, MARTIN T	1971
1242	KATZNELSON, IRA	1973
1243	KAUFERT, JOSEPH M	1977
1244	KAYAL, PHILIP M	1973
1245	KAZLAS, JUOZAS A	1977
1246	KEECH, WILLIAM R	1972
1247	KEEFE, SUSAN EMLEY	1979
1248	KELLSTEDT, LYMAN A	1974
1249	KELLY, GEORGE ARMSTRONG	1969
1250	KELNER, MERRIJOY	1970
1251	KENDIS, KADRU OGURI ET AL	1976
1252	KENNEDY, STETSON	1959
1253	KENNEY, BRADFORD P ET AL	1977
1254	KENT, DONALD P	1953
1255	KERTZER, DAVID I	1977
1256	KERTZER, MORRIS N	1967
1257	KEYES, CHARLES F	1966
1258	KEYES, CHARLES F	1971
1259	KEYES, CHARLES F ED	1979
1260	KHAN, VERITY S	1976
1261	KHAN, VERITY S	1977
1262	KHAN, VERITY S	1979
1263	KHATENA, JOE	1970
1264	KIBBE, PAULINE R	1946
1265	KIKUMURA, AKEMI ET AL	1973
1266	KILSON, MARTIN	1975
1267	KIM, HYUNG-CHAN ED	1977
1268	KIM, WARREN Y	1971
1269	KIMURA, YUKIKO	1968
1270	KING, ROGER ET AL	1975
1271	KINLOCH, GRAHAM C	1973
1272	KITANO, HARRY H L	1974
1273	KITANO, HARRY H L ET AL	1973
1274	KITROMILIDES, P ET AL	1976

NUM	AUTHOR	DATE
1275	KLAFF, VIVAN Z	1977
1276	KLEIN, GEORGE	1975
1277	KLEWAN, HELGE	1970
1278	KLEWAN, INGE	1970
1279	KLOBUS-EDWARDS, P ET AL	1978
1280	KLOSS, HEINZ	1967
1281	KNOKE, DAVID ET AL	1974
1282	KNOWLES, LOUIS L	1969
1283	KOHLER, DAVID F	1975
1284	KOHN, HANS	1944
1285	KOLEHMAINEN, JOHN I	1968
1286	KOLM, RICHARD	1973
1287	KOOP, JOHN CLEMENT	1960
1288	KOREY, WILLIAM	1968
1289	KOSLOV, V I	1978
1290	KOSMIN, BARRY	1979
1291	KOTHARI, RAJNI	1971
1292	KOTOK, VICTOR	1971
1293	KRAMER, JUDITH R	1970
1294	KRANE, RONALD E ED	1979
1295	KRAUSZ, ERNEST	1977
1296	KRESSEL, GODEON M	1977
1297	KRICKUS, RICHARD	1976
1298	KUMAGI, GLORIA L	1978
1299	KUNG, S M	1975
1300	KUNSTADTER, PETER	1967
1301	KUNZ, PHILLIP R	1968
1302	KUO, CHIA-LING	1977
1303	KUO, EDDIE C Y	1974
1304	KUO, EDDIE C Y ET AL	1976
1305	KUPER, HILDA	1947
1306	KUPER, HILDA	1969
1307	KUPER, LEO	1963
1308	KUPER, LEO	1965
1309	KUPER, LEO	1965
1310	KUPER, LEO	1967
1311	KUPER, LEO	1969
1312	KUPER, LEO	1969
1313	KUPER, LEO	1969
1314	KUPER, LEO	1971
1315	KUPER, LEO	1974
1316	KUROKAWA, MINAKO	1971
1317	KUROKAWA, MINAKO	1971
1318	LABOV, WILLIAM	1966
1319	LACZKO, LESLIE	1978
1320	LADBURY, SARAH	1977

NUM	AUTHOR	DATE	1 AB	2 ABCDEF	3 ABCDE	4 ABCDEFGHI	5 ABCDEFGHIJK	6 ABCDEFGHIJK	6	7	8	9	10	11	12	13	14	15	16	17
1321	LA FONTAINE, J S	1969	*	*	*	*	*	*					*	*						
1322	LAGUERRE, JOHN	1976		*	*				*				*	*						
1323	LAGUMINA, SALVATORE ET AL	1974		*	*			*					*						*
1324	LAMBERT, JOHN R	1970						*			*		*	*					
1325	LAMBERT, RONALD D	1975	*		*	*		*	*		*		*	*					*
1326	LAMPE, PHILIP E	1977	*	*	*		*								*				
1327	LAMPE, PHILIP E	1977		*	*	*	*								*				
1328	LAMPE, PHILIP E	1978		*	*	*								*	*				
1329	LANCASTER, C S	1974		**	*	*	*							* *	*				
1330	LANDAU, JACOB M	1969										*						*	
1331	LANDIS, JOSEPH B	1973	*		*		* *	**	*				*	*					
1332	LANDIS, JOSEPH B	1974			*		*	*	*				*						
1333	LANDMAN, RUTH H	1978				*													
1334	LANDON, KENNETH PERRY	1941		*	**	**		**	*		**	*	*	*	* *				
1335	LANDRY, BART	1977		*	**	*	*	*	*		* *				*		*		
1336	LANE, DAVID	1975		*	*	*	*	*	**		* * *	* *	*						*
1337	LANG, NICHOLAS R	1975		*	*			**	*		*		*						
1338	LANG, NORRIS G	1977		**	*		**	*	*		*								
1339	LANPHIER, C M ET AL	1974		*				*	*				*						
1340	LA RAW, MARAN	1967		*	*			*	*			*	*						
1341	LARRALDE, CARLOS	1976		*	*	*	*	*						*					
1342	LAVENDER, ABRAHAM D	1975		**	*	*								**					
1343	LAVENDER, ABRAHAM D	1975		*	*	*		* *	* *										
1344	LAVENDER, ABRAHAM D ED	1977			*	*		*	**										
1345	LAVENDER, ABRAHAM D ET AL	1976	*	*	*	*		*	*										
1346	LAVONDES, HENRI	1971		*	*		*												
1347	LAWRENCE, DANIEL	1975		*	*										* *	*		**	*
1348	LEAP, WILLIAM L	1974			*	* *	* *	*	**	* *	**	* *	**	**		*	* *		**	**
1349	LEBAR, FRANK M ED	1972		**	*		* *	* *	**	**	**	**	* *	**	**		*	*		**
1350	LEBAR, FRANK M ET AL	1964		**	*		*	*	*	*	**	**	*				*	*		*
1351	LEDERER, IVO J	1969		*	*	*	*	*	*		**	**	*	**					
1352	LEDERHENDLER, ELI M	1977		*	* *		**		*		**	**	*				*		
1353	LEE, FRANK F	1960		*	*	*	*	*	*		*	*	*	*					
1354	LEE, ROSE HUM	1958		**	*			*				*	*						
1355	LEE, ROSE HUM	1960		*	*								*						
1356	LEGTERS, LYMAN, H	1976		*	* *	*	* *	*	*	*		*	*	* *					*
1357	LEGUM, COLIN	1970		*	*			**					*						
1358	LEHMAN, F K	1967		*			*	*			*	*							
1359	LEIGH, DUANE E	1976			* *									*					
1360	LEIS, PHILIP E	1977		*															
1361	LE LOHE, MICHEL J	1975		**	**			**	* *			*	* * *						**
1362	LE LOHE, MICHEL J	1979		*									* * *						
1363	LEMARCHAND, RENE	1972		*	*			*					* *						
1364	LEMARCHAND, RENE	1974		**	*		* *	*				*	* *						
1365	LENDVAI, PAUL	1969		*								*	*						*
1366	LENDVAI, PAUL	1972		*	*		* *	*	*			*	*						*

NUM	AUTHOR	DATE
1367	LEON, JOSEPH J	1975
1368	LEONARD, HENRY B	1976
1369	LEPAGE, R B	1964
1370	LERNER, RICHARD M ET AL	1975
1371	LERNER, RICHARD M ET AL	1975
1372	LESTER, ANTHONY ET AL	1972
1373	LETHBRIDGE, H J	1971
1374	LEVAK, ALBERT E	1974
1375	LEVINE, DONALD N	1974
1376	LEVINE, ELAINE SUE	1976
1377	LEVINE, ELAINE S ET AL	1978
1378	LEVINE, GENE N ET AL	1973
1379	LEVINE, STUART ET AL	1968
1380	LEVI-STRAUSS, CLAUDE	1971
1381	LEVITAN, SAR A ET AL	1975
1382	LEVY, SYDELLE BROOKS	1975
1383	LEWINS, FRANK	1976
1384	LEWIS, E GLYN	1977
1385	LEWIS, I M	1969
1386	LEWIS, OSCAR	1968
1387	LEWIS, ROBERT A	1971
1388	LEWIS, RUSSELL E	1976
1389	LEY, C H	1967
1390	LEYTON, ELLIOTT	1974
1391	LI, PETER S	1978
1392	LIDDLE, R WILLIAM	1970
1393	LIDDLE, R WILLIAM	1972
1394	LIEBERMAN, VICTOR B	1978
1395	LIEBERSON, STANLEY	1963
1396	LIEBERSON, STANLEY	1970
1397	LIEBERSON, STANLEY	1970
1398	LIEBERSON, STANLEY	1978
1399	LIEBERSON, STANLEY	1978
1400	LIEBERSON, STANLEY ET AL	1975
1401	LIEBERSON, STANLEY ET AL	1974
1402	LIEBMAN, CHARLES S	1973
1403	LIGHT, IVAN H	1972
1404	LIGHTBODY, JAMES	1969
1405	LIJPHART, AREND	1968
1406	LIJPHART, AREND	1977
1407	LIJPHART, AREND	1979
1408	LIND, ANDREW W ED	1973
1409	LINDMARK, STURE	1971
1410	LINZ, JUAN	1973
1411	LITHMAN, YNGVE GEORG	1978
1412	LITT, EDGAR	1970

NUM	AUTHOR	DATE	1 AB	2 ABCDEF	3 ABCDE	4 ABCDEFGHI	5 ABCDEFGHIJK	6	7	8	9	10	11	12	13	14	15	16	17
1413	LITTLE, KENNETH	1954			*	*	*	*		*	*			*						
1414	LITTLE, KENNETH	1965		**	*	*	**	*	*		*			*			**			*
1415	LITTLE, KENNETH	1978		*		*	**	*	*			*								
1416	LLOYD, P C	1974		*		*	*													
1417	LOCKHART, AUDREY	1976	*						*	*										
1418	LOCKWOOD, DAVID	1970	*		*		*	*	*		*	**	*	*		*				*
1419	LOCKWOOD, WILLIAM G	1975		*	*	*	**		*		***	**		*		*				
1420	LOEB, LAWRENCE D	1965			*	**	*	**	*		***	*	**	*						
1421	LOEWAN, JAMES W	1971		*	*	*	*	*	*		***	**		**			**			*
1422	LOFCHIE, MICHAEL	1969			*	*	*	*	*		*	*		**						
1423	LOH, WALLACE D	1975		*	*	*	*	*					*							
1424	LONDON, BRUCE ET AL	1977		*			*				*									
1425	LONG, NORTON E	1975		**		*	**						*		*					
1426	LOPATA, HELEN Z	1976		*		**	*											**		
1427	LOPEZ, DAVID E	1978		*		*	*	*	**		*	*		*	*		*			
1428	LOPEZ Y RIVAS, GILBERTO	1973		*	*	*	*	**	*	*	*	*		**	*				*	*
1429	LOVOLL, ODD SVERRE	1975		**	**		**	***			*		*				***			
1430	LUCAS, HENRY S	1955		**	*	**	*				***						*			
1431	LUEBKE, FREDERICK	1978		**			*				***									
1432	LURIE, NANCY OESTREICH	1972		*		*	*	*	*	*	**									*
1433	LUSTICK, IAN	1979					*	*												
1434	LYMAN, STANFORD M	1968		*	**	**	*	*									*			
1435	LYMAN, STANFORD M	1970				*							*		*					
1436	LYMAN, STANFORD M	1972		*	*	*	*	*						*				**		
1437	LYMAN, STANFORD M	1977		*	**	*	**	*										*		
1438	LYMAN, STANFORD M ET AL	1973	*	*	**	*	***	*			***	*		*				*		
1439	MACCORMICK, NEIL ED	1970	*	*	*	*	**	*												
1440	MACGAFFEY, WYATT	1976					*	*							*					
1441	MACHADO, DEIRDRE A M	1977					*	*	*											
1442	MACISCO, JOHN J JR	1968				*			*		***	**								*
1443	MACK, RAYMOND W	1968		*	*	*	*	*			***	**	*			*		*	*	
1444	MACRAE, JOHN	1979		*							**	**	*				*	*		
1445	MADAN, RAJ	1979			*															
1446	MADAN, T N	1972			**		*	*					*							
1447	MADDOX, H	1960		*		*		*												
1448	MAGUBANE, BERNARD	1969		*	**	**	*	*			*	**							*	
1449	MAGUBANE, BERNARD	1974		*	***		***	***			***	**	*							
1450	MAGUBANE, BERNARD	1979		*	*		*	**			***	*								
1451	MAKIELSKI, S J JR	1973					*													
1452	MAKIELSKI, S J JR	1975		*		*					*									
1453	MALCOLM, M VARTAN	1969		*	*	**	**	*	**	*	**	**	*	*	*			*	*	*
1454	MALDONADO, EDWIN	1979		*	*		*	*			*	*		*				*		
1455	MALIK, YOGENDRA K	1969			*		**	*			*									*
1456	MAMAK, ALEXANDER	1977		*	*		**	*				*								
1457	MANGANE, ANTONIO	1971			**		*	*							*					
1458	MANGAT, J	1969	*	*	**	*	**													

NUM	AUTHOR	DATE
1459	MANNING, FRANK E	1974
1460	MAPP, EDWARD	1974
1461	MAPP, ROBERTA E	1972
1462	MAQUET, JACQUES	1970
1463	MAQUET, JACQUES	1970
1464	MARCUS, JACOB	1970
1465	MARDEN, CHARLES F ET AL	1973
1466	MARGER, MARTIN	1978
1467	MARKOWICZ, HARRY ET AL	1978
1468	MARQUAND, LEO	1957
1469	MARSHALL, RAY ET AL EDS	1978
1470	MARSTON, WILFRED G	1969
1471	MARTIN, ELMER P ET AL	1978
1472	MARTIN, JAMES G ET AL	1973
1473	MARTIN, WALTER T ET AL	1977
1474	MARUNCHAK, MICHAEL H	1970
1475	MASON, PHILIP	1966
1476	MASON, PHILIP	1970
1477	MAST, ROBERT	1973
1478	MAST, ROBERT H	1974
1479	MASUOKA, JITSUICHI ET AL	1961
1480	MATEJKO, ALEXANDER	1976
1481	MATTHIASSON, CAROLYN J	1974
1482	MATOSSIAN, MARY KILBOURNE	1968
1483	MATOSSIAN, MARY KILBOURNE	1975
1484	MAXWELL, NEVILLE	1973
1485	MAXWELL, THOMAS R	1977
1486	MAYER, ADRIAN C	1961
1487	MAYER, ADRIAN C	1966
1488	MAYER, KURT B	1968
1489	MAYER, P	1961
1490	MAYKOVICH, MINAKO K	1971
1491	MAYKOVICH, MINAKO K	1972
1492	MAYKOVICH, MINAKO K	1973
1493	MAYKOVICH, MINAKO K	1975
1494	MAZRUI, ALI A	1969
1495	MAZRUI, ALI A	1970
1496	MAZRUI, ALI A	1970
1497	MAZRUI, ALI A	1973
1498	MAZRUI, ALI A	1975
1499	MAZRUI, ALI A	1976
1500	MAZRUI, ALI A	1978
1501	MCARTHUR, MARILYN	1976
1502	MCBEATH, GERALD A	1978
1503	MCCAFFREY, LAWRENCE J	1976
1504	MCCOMBS, VERNON MONROE	1970

NUM	AUTHOR	DATE	1 AB	2 ABCDEF	3 ABCDE	4 ABCDEFGHI	5 ABCDEFGHIJK	6	7	8	9	10	11	12	13	14	15	16	17
1505	MCEVOY, FREDERICK D	1977	*	*	*	*	*			*			*	*						
1506	MCFEE, M	1968		*	*		*	*												
1507	MCKAY, JAMES ET AL	1978																		
1508	MCKENZIE, H I	1966		*	*	*		* *								*				
1509	MCKOWN, ROBERTA E	1974		*	*		*	* *				*								
1510	MCKOWN, ROBERTA E	1975			*	*	* *	*											* *	
1511	MCLEAN, IAIN	1977		*																
1512	MCNICKLE, DARCY	1973		* *	* *	* *	* *	*							* *	*			*	*
1513	MCRAE, KENNETH D	1973		* *	* *	* *	*	* *						*						
1514	MCRAE, KENNETH D ED	1974	*	* *	* *	* *	*	*			*				*					*
1515	MCROBERTS, KENNETH	1979		*	*		*	* * *				*								
1516	MCWILLIAMS, CAREY	1964		*	*			*	* *	*					*			*		
1517	MCWILLIAMS, CAREY	1968		*	* *	* *		*	* *	*										
1518	MCWILLIAMS, CAREY	1968		*	* *	*		*	* *	*									*	
1519	MEDHURST, KENNETH	1975		*	*	*	*													
1520	MEISEL, JOHN ET AL	1972	*	*	*	*	* *				*									
1521	MEISTER, RICHARD J ED	1974	*	*	*	*	*	*	* *	*	*		*		*					*
1522	MELENDY, H BRENT	1972		*	*				* *	*	*									
1523	MELENDY, H BRENT	1977		*	*		*	*												
1524	MENCARELLI, JAMES ET AL	1975		*	*	*	*													
1525	MENNERICK, LEWIS A	1968			*		*													
1526	MEO, LEILA	1977					*												*	*
1527	MERANI, H V ET AL	1979			*			*	*		*	*			*	*				
1528	METZGER, L PAUL	1971			*	*														
1529	MICAUD, CHARLES A	1974	*	*			*	*						*					*	
1530	MICHELENA, JOSE A SILVA	1971		*			*	*												
1531	MIDDLETON, JOHN	1970		*																
1532	MILES, R ET AL	1977						*		*					*					
1533	MILES, ROBERT ET AL	1979			*															
1534	MILLER, ABRAHAM H	1971		*		*	*													
1535	MILLER, ABRAHAM H	1974			* *		*	*	*	*		*	*	*	*	*	*	*	*	*
1536	MILLER, MICHAEL V	1975						*												
1537	MILLER, STUART C	1969		*			*	* *		*		*		*						
1538	MILLER, WAYNE C	1976																		
1539	MILNE, R S	1977			*	*			*					*	* *		*			
1540	MILNER, HENRY	1978		*	*	* *		*	* *					*			*			
1541	MITCHELL, J CLYDE	1956		*	*	* *	* *	* *	* *											
1542	MITCHELL, J CLYDE	1960			*	*									*			*	*	
1543	MITCHELL, J CLYDE	1970				*	*													
1544	MITCHELL, J CLYDE	1970			*			*												
1545	MITCHELL, J CLYDE ET AL	1959		*	* *	*	*	*	* *	*	* *	* *	* *		* *			*		* *
1546	MITTELMAN, JAMES H ET AL	1974									* *	* *	* *						* *	*
1547	MIYAMOTO, S FRANK	1939		*	*			*			* *	* *								* *
1548	MIYAMOTO, S FRANK	1973		*	*							* *		*	*			*		
1549	MOERMAN, MICHAEL	1968			*		*	*												
1550	MOGULL, ROBERT G	1972		*	*			*		*										

NUM	AUTHOR	DATE
1551	MOLINA, JOSE M	1978
1552	MOLNAR, THOMAS	1970
1553	MOLOHON, KATHRYN T ET AL	1979
1554	MONTELL, LYNWOOD	1972
1555	MONTENEGRO, MARILYN	1976
1556	MUNTIEL, MIGUEL ED	1978
1557	MOORE, JOAN	1970
1558	MOORE, ROBERT	1972
1559	MOQUIN, WAYNE ET AL EDS	1971
1560	MORALES, ARMANDO	1972
1561	MORALES, ROYAL R	1974
1562	MORF, GUSTAV	1976
1563	MORGAN, KENNETH O	1971
1564	MORGAN, TED	1978
1565	MORGAN, W J ED	1973
1566	MORNER, MAGNUS	1970
1567	MORNER, MAGNUS	1978
1568	MORRILL, WARREN T	1977
1569	MORRIS, H S	1956
1570	MORRIS, H S	1957
1571	MORRIS, H S	1960
1572	MORRIS, H S	1967
1573	MORSE, STANLEY J	1976
1574	MORSE, STANLEY J	1977
1575	MORSE, STANLEY J ET AL	1977
1576	MORSE, STANLEY J ET AL	1974
1577	MOWLANA, HAMID ET AL	1976
1578	MOYNIHAN, DANIEL P	1979
1579	MUKHERJEE, R	1973
1580	MULLARD, CHRIS	1975
1581	MUNOZ, ALFRED N	1971
1582	MURADOV, GULAM	1974
1583	MURAT, AMAN BERDI	1975
1584	MURPHEE, MARSHALL W	1975
1585	NACHMIAS, DAVID ET AL	1978
1586	NAG, MONI	1968
1587	NAGATA, JUDITH A	1977
1588	NAGATA, SHUICHI	1971
1589	NAHIRNY, VLADIMIR C ET AL	1965
1590	NASH, GARY B ET AL EDS	1970
1591	NASH, MANNING	1957
1592	NASH, MANNING	1958
1593	NASH, MANNING	1964
1594	NAVARRO, MOISES GONZALEZ	1970
1595	NAYAR, BALDEV RAJ	1966
1596	NEFZIGER, E WAYNE ET AL	1976

NUM	AUTHOR	DATE	1 AB	2 ABCDEF	3 ABCDE	4 ABCDEFGHI	5 ABCDEFGHIJK	6 7	8	9 10	11 12	13	14 15	16 17
1597	NELSON, DONNA	1972	*	*	*	*				*				
1598	NELSON, SARAH	1975		*	*		*				*		*	
1599	NETTLEFORD, REX	1965		*	*	*	*				* *		*	*
1600	NETTLEFORD, REX	1972		*	*	*	*			*	* *		*	
1601	NEUMAN, BRIGITTE ET AL	1973			*		*	*	*	* * *				
1602	NEUMAN, STEPHANIE G	1976			*	*	*	*				*		
1603	NEWBURY, M CATHERINE	1978			*	*	* *	*		* *	*			
1604	NEWMAN, DOROTHY K ET AL	1978		*	*	*	*			* *				
1605	NEWMAN, JAMES L	1978			*		* *	*						
1606	NEWMAN, WILLIAM M	1972		*	*	*	* *		*	*	*			
1607	NG, WING-CHEUNG	1977		* *	*	*	*	*		* *				*
1608	NICHOLLS, DAVID	1974			*	* * *	* *		*	*				
1609	NICHOLS, ROGER L ET AL ED	1971	*	*	*	* *	*	*						
1610	NIE, NORMAN H ET AL	1974		*	*		*	* *			* * *			
1611	NNOLI, OKWUDIBA	1974		*	*	*				*				
1612	NOBLE, LELA GARNER	1975		*	*	*	*		*	* *	*			
1613	NOBLE, LELA GARNER	1976		*	*	*				* *				
1614	NOEL, DONALD T	1968								* *				
1615	NOGALES, LUIS G	1971							*	*				
1616	NORDLINGER, ERIC A	1972		*		*		*	*	*				
1617	NORRIS, KATRIN	1962	*	* *		* *	* *			*			*	
1618	NORTHRUP, HERBERT R. ET AL	1970			*	*	*			*	*			
1619	NOVAK, MICHAEL	1971		*	*	*	*		*	* *				
1620	NOVAK, MICHAEL	1977		*		*	*		*					
1621	NUGENT, NEILL ET AL	1979					*			* *	*			
1622	NURGE, ETHEL ED	1970	*	*	*	*		*		* *				
1623	NUSSEY, WILF	1978					*		* *	* * *			*	*
1624	NYBLOM, GOSTA ED	1948					* *	*		*	*		* *	
1625	OAKS, PRISCILLA	1975		*			*			*				
1626	OBALLANCE, EDGAR	1973		* *	*					*				
1627	OBALLANCE, EDGAR	1977		*	*			*		* * *				
1628	OBATALA, J K	1976		*	*	*				*				
1629	OBRIEN, RITA CRUSE	1975		*	*	*		*		*				
1630	OCHOA, JORGE A FLORES	1974		*	*				*					
1631	OCONNOR, RICHARD	1968		*	*	*	*			*				
1632	OFFICER, JAMES E	1971		*	*	*		*	*	*	*			
1633	OGAWA, DENNIS M	1971		*	*	*								
1634	OGRADY, JOSEPH P	1973		*			*		*					
1635	OJIAKU, MAZI OKORO	1972				*				*	*			
1636	OKANE, JAMES M	1969							*	*	*			
1637	OKANE, JAMES M	1975		*	*	*	* *			*	*			*
1638	OKELY, JUDITH	1979		* *	*	*	*			*	* *			* * *
1639	OKPU, UGBANA	1977		* *	*	*	* *			* *				
1640	OLIVIER, M J	1971		*	*	*	*							* *
1641	OLSTED, R ET AL EDS	1971	*	* *	*	*								
1642	OMALLEY, PATRICK	1973		*						*	* * *	*		

NUM	AUTHOR	DATE	1 AB	2 ABCDEF	3 ABCDE	4 ABCDEFGHI	5 ABCDEFGHIJK	6	7	8	9	10	11	12	13	14	15	16	17
1643	ONWUKU, CHUKWUEMEKA	1975		*	*				*			* *		*						
1644	OPELLO, WALTER JR	1975		*	*	*	*					* *							* *	
1645	UPLER, MARVIN K	1955		*	*	*					*	* *					*		*	
1646	OPPENHEIMER, JONATHAN	1977		*			*													
1647	OREILLY, F D	1977		*	*	*	*		*											
1648	ORNSTEIN, JACOB	1968		*	*	*	*	* *							*					
1649	ORNSTEIN, JACOB	1978		*											*					
1650	ORNSTEIN, MICHAEL D ET AL	1978		*				*												
1651	OSTERMAN, PAUL	1975		*		*														
1652	OTITE, ONIGU	1975	*		*	*		*						*	*	*				
1653	OWEN, NANCY H	1975		*	*	*	* *					* *								
1654	PACHAI, BRIDGLAL	1978		*	*	*														
1655	PADILLA, ELENA	1977		*				*					*							
1656	PAINE, ROBERT ED	1977		* *	*		*	*	*			* * *	*	*	*	*				
1657	PALLONI, ALBERTO	1979	*	*		*	* *	* *				* *								
1658	PALMER, RANSFORD W	1974		*	*	*				*										
1659	PALMER, ROBIN	1977		*	*		*	*				* *								
1660	PAREDES, AMERICO	1963		* *																
1661	PAREDES, J ANTHONY	1974		* *	*	*	* *				*	* *								
1662	PARENTI, MICHAEL JOHN	1975		*	*	* *	*	*												
1663	PARKIN, ANDREW	1977			*	*	* *			*									*	
1664	PARKIN, DAVID	1974		*	*							*								
1665	PARMING, TONU	1977		*	*	*	*	*					*					*		
1666	PARSONS, TALCOTT	1975							*					* * *				*		
1667	PASIC, NAJDAN	1971			*	*	* *					*								
1668	PASIC, NAJDAN	1973		*	*	*	* *	*	*	*		* *								
1669	PASIC, NAJDAN	1973		*	*		*	* *					* *							
1670	PATAI, RAPHAEL	1953		*	*			*												
1671	PATEL, HASU H	1973		*	*	*	*	*		*	* *	* * *								
1672	PATEL, NARSI	1974		*	*			*		*	*	*								
1673	PATTERSON, E PALMER II	1975		*	*	*	*	*	*			*								*
1674	PATTERSON, ORLANDO	1968		* *		*		*	*			* * *								
1675	PATTERSON, ORLANDO	1975		*	*		*	*	*											
1676	PATTERSON, SHEILA	1977		*			*													
1677	PAVLAK, THOMAS J	1976		*				* *	*			*								*
1678	PAVLAK, THOMAS J	1977		*	*				*	*	*	*	*	*	*	*	*	*		
1679	PAYNE, STANLEY	1971			*	*			*											
1680	PAYNE, STANLEY G	1975		*	*	*	* *			*		* *	*	*						
1681	PEACH, CERI	1965		*	*															
1682	PEACH, CERI	1968																		
1683	PEARSON, DAVID G	1978		*	*			* *	* *			* *		*		* *			*	
1684	PEELE, STANTON ET AL	1974		*	*	* *		* *	*	*		* *								
1685	PEHOTSKY, BESSIE OLGA	1970																		
1686	PEIL, MARGARET	1974		*			* *	*												
1687	PEIL, MARGARET	1975		*	*						*							*		
1688	PELISI, BARTOLEMES J	1966		*																

NUM	AUTHOR	DATE
1689	PENDLETON, WADE C	1978
1690	PENG, FRED C C ET AL	1974
1691	PENNAR, JAAN	1968
1692	PERES, YOCHANAN	1971
1693	PERES, YOCHANAN ET AL	1969
1694	PERES, YOCHANAN ET AL	1978
1695	PERLO, VICTOR	1975
1696	PETERSEN, WILLIAM	1971
1697	PETERSEN, WILLIAM	1975
1698	PETERSEN, WILLIAM	1976
1699	PHILIP, ALAN BUTT	1975
1700	PHILPOTT, STUART B	1977
1701	PHIZACKLEA, ANNE-MARIE	1975
1702	PHIZACKLEA, ANNIE ET AL	1979
1703	PIENKOS, DONALD E	1974
1704	PIENKOS, DONALD E	1977
1705	PIERSON, JAMES C	1977
1706	PILL,KOISIN	1974
1707	PINCO, PETER C	1977
1708	PINKNEY, ALPHONSO	1976
1709	PIORE, MICHAEL J	1975
1710	PIPES, RICHARD	1975
1711	PISANI, ANDRE DU	1977
1712	PITTOCK, A BARRIE	1975
1713	PITI-RIVERS, JULIAN	1969
1714	PITTS, JAMES P	1974
1715	PLAX, MARTIN	1972
1716	PLAX, MARTIN	1976
1717	PLOTNICOV, LEONARD	1967
1718	PLOTNICOV, LEONARD	1970
1719	PLOTNICOV, LEONARD	1972
1720	PLOTNICOV, LEONARD ET AL	1978
1721	POLLIS, ADAMANTIA	1976
1722	POOL, JONATHAN	1972
1723	POOL, JONATHAN	1978
1724	PORTER, JOHN	1966
1725	PORTER, JOHN	1975
1726	PORTER, JUDITH D R	1971
1727	PORTERFIELD, ERNEST	1978
1728	POSPIELOVSKY, D	1974
1729	POSSONY, STEFAN T	1971
1730	POSSONY, STEFAN T	1975
1731	POSSONY, STEFAN T	1976
1732	POTTER, GEORGE	1960
1733	POTTER, HAROLD H	1961
1734	POWER, PAUL F	1974

NUM	AUTHOR	DATE	1 AB	2 ABCDEF	3 ABCUE	4 ABCDEFGHI	5 ABCDEFGHI	ABCDEFGHIJK	6	7	8	9	10	11	12	13	14	15	16	17
1735	PRANDY, KENNETH	1979		*	*			* *			*	*	* * *		*					*
1736	PRATT, HENRY J	1970		*	*		*	*			*		* * *		*					
1737	PREMDAS, RALPH R	1972		* *	*		*	*					* * *							
1738	PREMDAS, RALPH R	1973		*	*		*	*						*						
1739	PREMDAS, RALPH R	1977		*	*	*	*	*												
1740	PRICE, CHARLES A	1963		*	*		*		*		*	*	*				*			
1741	PRICE, DANIEL O	1969			*		*		*		*	*								
1742	PRICE, JOHN	1966			*											*				
1743	PRICE, JOHN A	1975			*	*		*	*									* *		
1744	PRICE, JOHN A	1976		*	*	*		*										* *		
1745	PRIMOV, GEORGE	1974		*	*					* *	*			* *	*				*	* *
1746	PRINS, JAN	1973		*	*			* *	* *				* *	*						
1747	PRINS, JAN	1977		*	*		* *	*	*					*						
1748	PROCYK, ANNA	1973		*	*		* *	*	*											
1749	PRPIC, GEORGE J	1978		*	*		* *	*	*	*			*	*			*			
1750	PUNDEFF, MARIN V	1969		*	*		*	*	*					* *						
1751	PURANIK, S N	1975		*	*				*											
1752	PURCELL, THEODORE V ET AL	1972		*	* *		*	*	*					* *						* *
1753	PURCELL, VICTOR	1948		* *	*		*	*	*					* *						
1754	PURCELL, VICTOR	1962		*	*		*		*	*				*						
1755	PYE, LUCIAN W	1975		*	*															
1756	QUALEY, CARLTON C	1938			*		* *	*	*											
1757	QUO, F Q	1971		* *	*		* *		* *											
1758	RABUSHKA, ALVIN	1969		*	*									*	* *					
1759	RABUSHKA, ALVIN	1970			*			*	*		*				*					
1760	RABUSHKA, ALVIN	1971		*	*	*					*	* *	* *			* *				
1761	RADECKI, HENRY	1976						*	*		*	*	* *	*		* *				
1762	RADIN, BERYL	1966		*	*			* *	*			* *	* *							*
1763	RADIN, PAUL	1935			*	*														
1764	RADLIAZOWSKI, THADDEUS	1974			*							*	*	* *		*				*
1765	KAGIN, CHARLES	1977		*	*				*	*	*	* *	*	*	*	*		* *		*
1766	RAITZ, KARL B	1974			*	*	* *			*							* *			*
1767	RAITZ, KARL B	1979		*	*		* *		*	* *	*	* *		*			* *			
1768	RAKOWSKA-HARMSTONE, T	1974		*	*			*					*	* *	*					
1769	RAKOWSKA-HARMSTONE, T	1975		*	*			*	*			* *	*	*						
1770	RAKOWSKA-HARMSTONE, T	1976		*	*				*		*			* *						
1771	RAMA, CARLOS M	1970		*	*			*	* *			* *	*							
1772	RANSFORD, H EDWARD	1977	*	*				*					*							
1773	RAO, V VENKATA	1970		*	*			*	*				*	*						
1774	RAO, V VENKATA	1976		*	*		*						*							
1775	RATNAM, K J	1961		*	*		* *								*					
1776	RAVEAU, F H M	1975		*	*			*					*					*		
1777	RAWKINS, PHILLIP M	1978		*	*							*	*						*	
1778	RAYFIELD, J R	1976		*	*															
1779	RAYSIDE, DAVID M	1978		*	*															
1780	REAY, MARIE	1963		*	*	*		*								*				

NUM	AUTHOR	DATE
1781	REAY, MARIE ED	1964
1782	REDFIELD, ROBERT	1956
1783	REECE, JACK E	1977
1784	REECE, JACK E	1979
1785	REISLER, MARK	1976
1786	REITZES, DIETRICH C	1959
1787	RENNER, H	1976
1788	REX, JOHN	1950
1789	REX, JOHN	1970
1790	REX, JOHN	1971
1791	REX, JOHN	1973
1792	REX, JOHN	1979
1793	REX, JOHN ET AL	1967
1794	RHEE, SONG NAI	1973
1795	RICHMOND, ANTHONY H	1967
1796	RICHMOND, ANTHONY H ED	1972
1797	RICHMOND, ANTHONY H	1973
1798	RICHMOND, ANTHONY H	1974
1799	RICHMOND, ANTHONY H	1978
1800	RICHMOND, ANTHONY H ET AL	1976
1801	RICHMOND, ANTHONY H ET AL	1978
1802	RIESDESEL, PAUL L ET AL	1978
1803	RIN, HSIEN	1975
1804	RINDFUSS, RONALD R ET AL	1978
1805	RINGER, BENJAMIN	1967
1806	RIOUX, MARCEL	1978
1807	RITT, LEONARD G	1979
1808	RITTER, KATHLEEN V	1979
1809	RUBERTS, MICHAEL	1978
1810	ROBINSON, GERTRUDE JACK	1974
1811	ROBINSON, IRA E ET AL	1972
1812	RODRIGUEZ, CLARA	1975
1813	RODRIGUEZ, OLGA ED	1977
1814	ROFF, MARGARET	1969
1815	ROGG, ELEANOR MEYER	1974
1816	ROGLER, LLOYD H	1972
1817	ROMANUCCI-ROSS, LOLA	1975
1818	ROMERO, FRED E	1979
1819	RONEN, DOV	1976
1820	ROOF, WADE CLARK	1972
1821	ROOF, WADE CLARK	1978
1822	ROOF, WADE CLARK, ED	1979
1823	ROSALDO, RENATO ET AL EDS	1973
1824	ROSE, ARNOLD M ED	1951
1825	ROSE, ARNOLD M	1969
1826	ROSE, ARNOLD M	1972

The remaining columns (1 AB, 2 ABCUEF, 3 ABCDE, 4 ABCDEFGHI, 5 ABCDEFGHIJK, ABCDEFGHIJK, 6, 7, 8, 9, 10, 11, 12, 13, 14, 15, 16, 17) form a matrix of asterisk markers indicating classification codes for each entry.

NUM	AUTHOR	DATE	1 AB	2 ABCDEF	3 ABCDE	4 ABCDEFGHI	5 ABCDEFGHI	6	7	8	9	10	11	12	13	14	15	16	17
1827	ROSE, HAROLD M	1976		*			*	*								*			
1828	ROSE, PETER I	1968															*		
1829	ROSE, PETER I ED	1969	*	*	*	*	*	*						*					
1830	ROSE, PETER I	1970					*												
1831	ROSE, PETER I ED	1972	*	*	*	*	**												
1832	ROSE, PETER I	1974	*		*	*	**						**						
1833	ROSE, PETER I	1977		**		*	*							*					
1834	ROSE, PETER I ET AL EDS	1973	*	**	*	**	**				**		**	*					
1835	ROSE, PHILIP M	1922					*						*						
1836	ROSEN, BARRY M	1973		*	*	*	*												
1837	ROSEN, BERNARD	1959					*	*						*					
1838	ROSEN, GERALD	1974		*	*	*							**	**					
1839	ROSENSTOCK, MORTON	1976		*		**	*						*	***					
1840	ROSENTHAL, GILBERT S ED	1970	*	*	*	*						**	*						
1841	ROSENWAIKE, IRA	1973		*	*	*	*	**				*							
1842	ROSMAN, ABRAHAM ET AL	1976		*			*				*		**			*			
1843	ROSS, AILEEN D	1954		*	*	*	**				**			*					
1844	ROSS, ARTHUR M ET AL EDS	1967	*	*	*	***	*	**			**								
1845	ROSS, CARL	1977		*		*													
1846	ROSS, E LAMAR	1978		**	*														
1847	ROSS, JACK C ET AL	1971		*	*	*													
1848	ROSS, MARC HOWARD	1975			*		*		*		*	*				*			
1849	ROTBERG, ROBERT I	1965					**		*		*	*	*						
1850	ROTBERG, ROBERT I ED	1978	*	**	*	***	*		**		**	*	*	*					
1851	ROTHCHILD, DONALD	1968		**		*	*	**				**	*						
1852	ROTHCHILD, DONALD	1969		**	*	*	**	*				*	*						
1853	ROTHCHILD, DONALD	1973			*	*		**		*	*	*	*						
1854	ROUCEK, JOSEPH S	1961		*	*		*				*	*	*						
1855	ROUT, LESLIE B JR	1976		*		*	**					**	*			*			
1856	ROWE, JOHN	1974					*					**							*
1857	RUBEL, PAULA G	1971		*	*								*						
1858	RUBIN, ISRAEL	1975																	
1859	RUBIN, JOAN	1968					**	*		*				*		*			
1860	RUBIN, VERA ED	1960	*	**	***	**	**	*				*						*	
1861	RUBIN, VERA	1960					*				*	*							
1862	RUBIN, VERA ED	1960	*	**	***	*	**	*											
1863	RUBIN, VERA	1962		*	*	*	*	*				**							
1864	RUBIN, VERA ET AL	1962		*	*	*	*												
1865	RUDOLPH, JOSEPH R JR	1977											*	**					
1866	RUNCIMAN, W G	1972	*	*		*						*	*						
1867	RUSSELL, MARGO ET AL	1979		*	*	*		*			*	*	*						
1868	RUSSELL-WOOD, A J R	1967		**	*		*												
1869	RUYLE, EUGENE E	1979		*	*	*	*				*	*					*		*
1870	RYAN, SELWYN D	1972		**	*														
1871	SACKS, STEPHEN R	1976	*	*	*	*					**		*						
1872	SAID, ABDUL AZIZ ED	1977	*		*		*	*			**	*							

NUM	AUTHOR	DATE	1 AB	2 ABCDEF	3 ABCDE	4 ABCDEFGHI	5 ABCDEFGHIJK	6	7	8	9	10	11	12	13	14	15	16	17
1873	SAID, ABDUL A ET AL	1976			*		*	*				*							
1874	SALA, GARY CLARK	1975		**	*	*	*				*	*		*					
1875	SALAMONE, FRANK	1975				*	**							*					
1876	SALAMONE, FRANK	1975			*	*	*			*		*		*					
1877	SALIBI, KAMAL S	1971		*	*		*		*		*			*					
1878	SALLET, RICHARD	1974		*	*	*	*	*	*	*				*	*				
1879	SALO, MATT T	1979		*	*	*	**							*					
1880	SALOUTOS, THEODORE	1967							*		*						*		
1881	SALT, JOHN ET AL EDS	1976	*	**	*		**	**	**		*	*	*	*	*	*			
1882	SALZMAN, PHILIP C	1971		*	*	*	*		*		*	*							
1883	SAMKANGE, STANLAKE	1972		*	*	*	*				*								
1884	SAMORA, JULIAN	1971			*		*					*							
1885	SAMORA, JULIAN ET AL	1967				*	*				*	*	**	*					
1886	SAMUELS, FREDERICK	1969		**			**												
1887	SAMUELS, FREDERICK	1970		**	*	*	**				*		*						
1888	SAMUELS, FREDERICK	1970		**	*		**												
1889	SANDBERG, NEIL C	1974		*	*	*	*		**	*	*	*	*	**			*		
1890	SANJEK, ROGER	1977		**	*	*	**	*	**	*	*	*	*	**					
1891	SANTOS, MILTON	1979				*	*					*							
1892	SARHARDI, AJIT SINGH	1974		*	*	*		*											
1893	SARNA, JONATHAN D	1978			*	*	**	*	*			*		*					
1894	SASAKI, YUZURU ET AL	1966					**					*	*	**					
1895	SAXTON, ALEXANDER	1971		*	*		*			*	*	*	*						
1896	SAYIGH, ROSEMARY	1977		*	*	*	***					*	*						
1897	SAYIGH, ROSEMARY	1977			*		*												
1898	SAYWELL, JOHN	1977		**	*														
1899	SCARRIFF, JAMES B ET AL	1970		**	*	*	**		*	*	**	**							
1900	SCHAEFER, RICHARD T	1974		*	*	*	**	*			*	*		**					
1901	SCHAEFER, RICHARD T	1975		*	*	*	*					*		*					
1902	SCHAEFER, RICHARD T	1976			*		*				*	*	*						
1903	SCHEIN, MURIEL D	1975																	
1904	SCHEINMAN, LAWRENCE	1977			*	*	*	*		*	**	**							
1905	SCHERMERHORN, R A	1959			*		*	*			*	*							
1906	SCHERMERHORN, R A	1964			*		*												
1907	SCHERMERHORN, R A	1967			*		*				*	*							
1908	SCHERMERHORN, R A	1974		*		*	*	*			*		*						
1909	SCHIAVO, GIOVANNI E	1928		*	*	*	**	***	**	*		**	**	**			*		
1910	SCHIAVO, GIOVANNI E	1947		*	*	*	**	*	**		*	*	*	*					
1911	SCHIAVO, GIOVANNI E	1952		*	*														
1912	SCHILDKROUT, ENID	1974		*	*	*	*				*								
1913	SCHILLER, BRADLEY R	1971		*		*	*	*											
1914	SCHILLER, NINA GLICK	1977			*		*	*		*	*			*			*		
1915	SCHLACHTER, GAIL ANN	1977						*											
1916	SCHMELZ, U O	1974		*	*	*	*					*							
1917	SCHMITT, DAVID L	1977			*						**	**							
1918	SCHMITT, ROBERT C	1971		*	*	*	*				*	*			*				

NUM	AUTHOR	DATE	1 AB	2 ABCDE	3 ABCDE	4 ABCDEFGHI	5 ABCDEFGHIJK	6	7	8	9	10	11	12	13	14	15	16	17
1919	SCHNALL, DAVID J	1975		*	*		*					*	*	* *					*	
1920	SCHNEIDER, DAVID M	1969		*	*	*	*													*
1921	SCHNEIDER, MARK	1976		*	*				*			* *								
1922	SCHNEIDER, WILLIAM ET AL	1974		*	*	*	*						* *			*				
1923	SCHOEN, ROBERT	1978			*	*	*	*				*		*	*	*	*			
1924	SCHOENFELD, STUART	1978		*	*	*	*											*		
1925	SCHONEWEG, EGON	1977		*	*	*	*				*									
1926	SCHOOLER, CARMI	1976		*							*	*								
1927	SCHUMAN, HOWARD ET AL	1974		*	*	*	*	*			*	*								
1928	SCHUTZ, BARRY ET AL	1975		*		*		*				* *								
1929	SCHWARTZMAN, SIMON	1973		*	*	*	*	*	*				*	*	*	*				
1930	SCHWARZ, HENRY G	1971		*	*		*	*				*							*	
1931	SCHWARZ, JOHN E	1970		*	*	*	*					*								
1932	SCUBIE, EDWARD	1972				*		*			*	*								
1933	SCOTT, DUNCAN	1975		*	*	*		* *	*			*								
1934	SCOTT, FRANKLIN D ED	1968	*	*	*	*				*										
1935	SCOTT, NULVERT P JR	1975		*	*		*	*		*	*	*	* *		* *					
1936	SEGAL, BERNARD A ED	1972	* *	* *	* *	*	*	*****		* *	*									
1937	SEGAL, BERNARD A	1976		*				*												
1938	SEGAL, RONALD	1968			*	*	*					*								
1939	SELLER, MAXINE	1977		*	*	*	*		*			*					*		*	
1940	SELZER, MICHAEL	1968		*	*															
1941	SENGSTOCK, MARY C	1975		*	*	*	*							*						
1942	SENGSTOCK, MARY C	1977		* *	* *		* *			* *	*		* *	* *						
1943	SENIOR, CLARENCE	1965		*	*		*			*					*					
1944	SETON-WATSON, HUGH	1971		*	*															
1945	SHAFER, BOYD C	1972		* *	* *	*											*			
1946	SHAMA, AVRAHAM ET AL	1977				*	*	*												
1947	SHANNON, LYLE W	1979					*													
1948	SHARF, ANDREW	1963		*	*	*		*												
1949	SHARMA, AJIT KUMAR	1976		*	*	*	*	*					* * *	* * *					*	
1950	SHARMA, B S	1973		*	*		*				*	* *	* *	* *		*			*	
1951	SHAROT, STEPHEN	1974		*	*	*	*		* *							*				
1952	SHARP, SAMUEL L	1975		*	. *	*		*												
1953	SHAW, DOUGLAS V	1976			*		*													
1954	SHEPHERD, GEORGE W ET AL	1970		*																
1955	SHERMAN, C BEZALEL	1965		*	*	*	*	*					* * *	* *	* *	*	*			
1956	SHILS, EDWARD	1957																		
1957	SHINKIN, DEMITRI B ET AL	1978	*	* *	* *	* *	* *						* *	* *						
1958	SHOKEID, MOSHE	1971		* *	* *	*	*	*	* *		* *		*	*	*	*				
1959	SHOUP, PAUL	1968																		
1960	SHUVAL, JUDITH T	1962																		
1961	SHYROCK, RICHARD	1977																		
1962	SIBAYAN, BONIFACIO P	1971																		
1963	SIDER, GERALD M	1976																		
1964	SIDORSKY, DAVID ED	1973	*																	

NUM	AUTHOR	DATE	1 AB	2 ABCDEF	3 ABCDE	4 ABCDEFGHI	5 ABCDEFGHIJK	6	7	8	9	10	11	12	13	14	15	16	17
1965	SIGEL, IRVING E ET AL	1977														*			
1966	SIH, PAUL K T ET AL EDS	1976																*	
1967	SILCOCK, T H	1969																	
1968	SILVER, BRIAN	1974																	
1969	SILVER, BRIAN	1974																	
1970	SILVER, BRIAN	1978																	*
1971	SILVER, BRIAN D	1976	*												*		*		
1972	SIMEON, RICHARD ED	1977																	
1973	SIMMER, EDWARD ED	1972																	
1974	SIMMONS, OZZIE G	1974																	
1975	SIMMONS, R D G TH	1961																	
1976	SIMPSON, GEORGE E	1962																	
1977	SIMPSON, GEORGE E ET AL	1972	*														*	*	
1978	SIMS, HAROLD D	1972																	
1979	SINGLETON, JOHN	1977													*			*	
1980	SINHA, M R ED	1971	*																*
1981	SIVANANDAN, A	1973																	
1982	SIVANANDAN, A	1976																	
1983	SIVERTS, HENNING	1969																	
1984	SKINNER, ELLIOTT P	1968														*			
1985	SKINNER, ELLIOTT P	1970																	
1986	SKINNER, ELLIOTT P	1975																	
1987	SKINNER, ELLIOTT P	1978																	
1988	SKINNER, G WILLIAM	1957																	
1989	SKINNER, G WILLIAM ED	1959	*																
1990	SKLARE, MARSHALL ED	1974	*					*											
1991	SKLARE, MARSHALL	1974																	*
1992	SKLARE, MARSHALL	1974	*																
1993	SKLARE, MARSHALL ET AL	1967																	
1994	SLANN, MARTIN	1973																	
1995	SLATER, MARIAM K	1976																	
1996	SLOBODIN, RICHARD	1972																	
1997	SMALL, SYLVIA	1976															*		
1998	SMILEY, DONALD V	1977																	
1999	SMITH, ANTHONY D	1976																	
2000	SMITH, ANTHONY D ED	1976	*																
2001	SMITH, ANTHONY D	1978																	
2002	SMITH, BURTON	1978																	
2003	SMITH, DAVID G	1977																	
2004	SMITH, M ESTELLIE	1974																	
2005	SMITH, M ESTELLIE	1978																	
2006	SMITH, MICHAEL GORDON	1961																	
2007	SMITH, MICHAEL GORDON	1965																	
2008	SMITH, MICHAEL GORDON	1965																	
2009	SMITH, MICHAEL GORDON	1969																	
2010	SMITH, MICHAEL GORDON	1969																	

NUM	AUTHOR	DATE
2011	SMITH, MICHAEL GORDON	1969
2012	SMITH, RAYMOND T	1961
2013	SMITH, RAYMOND T	1962
2014	SMITH, RAYMOND T	1976
2015	SMITH, TIMOTHY L	1978
2016	SMITH, WALDEMAR R	1975
2017	SMOCK, AUDREY C	1971
2018	SMOOHA, SAMMY	1975
2019	SMYTHE, HUGH ET AL	1953
2020	SNYDER, PETER Z	1971
2021	SOEN, DAN	1977
2022	SOLAUN, MAURICIO ET AL	1973
2023	SOLINGER, DOROTHY J	1977
2024	SOON, ALICE TAY EHR	1962
2025	SOPER, EDMUND DAVISON	1947
2026	SORKIN, ALAN L	1976
2027	SORKIN, ALAN L	1978
2028	SOTOMAYOR, MARTA	1977
2029	SOUTHALL, AIDAN	1970
2030	SOUTHALL, AIDAN W	1970
2031	SOUTHALL, AIDAN	1976
2032	SOWELL, THOMAS	1975
2033	SOWELL, THOMAS	1978
2034	SOZON, MICHAEL ET AL	1979
2035	SPAULDING, E WILDER	1968
2036	SPECHLER, DINA ROME	1975
2037	SPECKMAN, J D	1963
2038	SPENCE, J E	1962
2039	SPENCER, JOHN	1971
2040	SPICER, EDWARD	1971
2041	SPICER, EDWARD M ET AL	1972
2042	SPIELERMAN, SEYMOUR ET AL	1976
2043	SPREITZER, ALMER ET AL	1975
2044	SPKY, GRAHAM	1971
2045	SRINIVAS, M N	1952
2046	SRINIVAS, M N	1962
2047	STAHL, KATHLEEN	1969
2048	STANBURY, W T	1975
2049	STANLEY, SAM ED	1978
2050	STARR, PAUL D	1978
2051	STAUSS, JOSEPH H ET AL	1973
2052	STAVROU, NIKOLAOS A	1976
2053	STEIN, BARRY N	1979
2054	STEIN, HOWARD F	1975
2055	STEINER, JURG ET AL	1977
2056	STEINFIELD, MELVIN ED	1973

NUM	AUTHOR	DATE	1 AB	2 ABCDEF	3 ABCDE	4 ABCDEFGHI	5 ABCDEFGHIJK	ABCDEFGHIJK	6	7	8	9	10	11	12	13	14	15	16	17
2057	STENDEL, ORI	1973		* *	*			*	*		* *		*	*		*	*	*	*	*	*
2058	STEPHENSON, GLENN V	1972		*	*	*					*		*		*						*
2059	STEWART, JAMES B ET AL	1979		*			*		*												
2060	STONE, LINDA	1977		*	*	*		*	*				*					*			*
2061	STOUT, HARRY S	1975		*									* *								
2062	STREIB, GORDON F	1974	*	* * * *	* *	* *		* *			*		*	*	*						*
2063	STUART, IRVING R ET AL ED	1973		* * * *	* *	* *	* *	* *	*		*	*	*		*	*	*	*		*	*
2064	STUDLAR, DONLEY T	1978		* *		* *	* *	* *	*												
2065	STUDLAR, DONLEY T	1979		*		*	* *														
2066	STYMEIST, DAVID	1979	*	*	*		*	*													
2067	SUBBA RAO, KOKA	1970		*	*		*														
2068	SUE, STANLEY ET AL	1973		*	*	*	* *	* *	*												
2069	SUE, STANLEY ET AL EDS	1973		*	*		* *	*		*		* * *	*	*		*					
2070	SUGAR, PETER F	1963		*	*			* *	*	*			*								
2071	SUGAR, PETER F	1969		*	*			*	*				*								
2072	SUHRKE, ASTRI	1971		*	*	*		*			*		* * *		*	*				*	
2073	SUHRKE, ASTRI	1975		* *		* *	* *	*			* *		*		*						
2074	SUHRKE, ASTRI ET AL	1977			*		* *	*	*					*		* *				*	
2075	SUHRKE, ASTRI ET AL	1977					* *	*	*												
2076	SULLIVAN, TERESA A	1978		*	*		*		*				*								
2077	SULTAN, GARIP	1968		*	*		*	*					*		*						*
2078	SUNDBERG-WEITMAN, BRITA	1977		* * *	* *	*	* *	* *	*	* *	* *	*	*	* *	*	*		*			*
2079	SUNG, BETTY LEE	1975		*	*	*	* *	*	*		*				* *	*				*	
2080	SUPELL, ROBERT ET AL	1965						*						*							
2081	SURYADINATA, LEO	1976		*	* *		*	*					*								
2082	SUSOKOLOV, A A	1976		*	* *	* *	*	*			*		*		*	*				*	
2083	SUTTLES, GERALD D	1968		*	* *	* *		*													
2084	SUTTON, CONSTANCE R ET AL	1975		* *	*		*	*			*		*	*	* *	* *				*	
2085	SUZUKI, BOB H	1977		*	*		*	*	*	*	*	*	*	*							
2086	SUZUKI, TEIITI	1969		*	* *								*								
2087	SVENSSON, TOM G	1976		*	*		* *	*		*											
2088	SWARTZ, MARC J	1979		*				*		* *											
2089	SWAY, MARLENE	1975		*	*			* *	* *		*							*			
2090	SWEET, JAMES A	1978		*						*											
2091	SWIDERSKI, RICHARD W	1977		*	*		* *						*								
2092	SWIFT, MICHAEL	1962		* *	*	* *	* *	*	*		* *		* *		*		*		*		
2093	SWOBODA, VICTOR ET AL	1972		*	*		* *	*					*	*	* *	* *				*	
2094	SZPORLUK, ROMAN	1975						*													
2095	SZYMANSKI, ALBERT	1975		*	*	*	*	* *			*	*	*								
2096	SZYMANSKI, ALBERT	1976		*	*			*													
2097	TAAGEPERA, REIN	1971		*	*		*	*	*		* *		* *			*			*	*	*
2098	TAAGEPERA, REIN	1975		*	* *			* *			* *	*	* *		*						
2099	TABB, WILLIAM K	1970		*				* *	* * *		* *		* *		*						
2100	TABB, WILLIAM K	1971						* *	*		*		* *		*						
2101	TABB, WILLIAM K	1971		*	*	* *		* *	*		* *		* *		*	*				*	
2102	TACHIKI, AMY ET AL EDS	1971	*	* *	*			* *		*	*		*	*		*				*	*

NUM	AUTHOR	DATE	1 AB	2 ABCDEF	3 ABCDE	4 ABCDEFGHI	5 ABCDEFGHIJK	6	7	8	9	10	11	12	13	14	15	16	17
2103	TAN, ALLEN L ET AL	1969		*	*	*	*	*	*	*	*			*						*
2104	TAPIA, CLAUDE	1974		*	*	*	**	**	**	*	**		*	*	*					
2105	TASHJIAN, JAMES H	1970		*	*	*			*											
2106	TATSUNO, SHERIDAN	1971		*			*													
2107	TATZ, COLIN M	1972		*	*	*		*	*											*
2108	TAX, SOL	1942		*		*	*	*	*		*	*	*							
2109	TAYLOR, PHILIP	1971		*		*	*													
2110	TAYLOR, STAN	1979		*		*		*												
2111	TESKE, RAYMOND H C ET AL	1976		*				*		*							*			
2112	TESSLER, MARK A	1975		*		*	*													
2113	TESSLER, MARK A	1978		*	*	**	*	**					*	**	*					
2114	TESSLER, MARK A ET AL	1973		**		**	**	*					*						*	
2115	THOMAS, COLIN J ET AL	1978		*		*		*												
2116	THOMAS, LADD	1974		*		*							*							
2117	THOMAS, W I ET AL	1918		**		*	*	*	*	*	*		*	*						
2118	THOMPSON, BOBBY ET AL	1975		**	*	*														
2119	THOMPSON, EDGAR T ET AL	1958	**	*		*	*	**				*		**						
2120	THOMPSON, LEONARD	1969		*		*								*						
2121	THOMPSON, RICHARD	1961		*		*	*					**	*	**						
2122	THOMPSON, RICHARD	1969		*		*	*	*				*								
2123	THOMPSON, STEPHEN	1974		*		*		*		*				*						
2124	THOMPSON, STEPHEN I	1977		*		*	**			**	*	*	*	**					*	
2125	THOMPSON, VIRGINIA ET AL	1955		*		*	*	*		**	*			*						
2126	THONG, LEE BOON	1977		*	*	*	**	*	*	*										
2127	THORBURN, H G	1971		*	*	*	**	*				*	**	**						
2128	THORNDIKE, ROBERT L	1977		*		*	*		*				**	*						
2129	TICE, ROBERT D	1974		*		*	*					*								
2130	TILLETT, LOWELL	1977		*		*	*													
2131	TINKER, HUGH	1977		*		*	*	*								*				
2132	TINKER, JOHN N	1973		*		*						*				*			*	*
2133	TJWAN, GO GIEN	1971		*		*	*	*			*	*								
2134	TOBIAS, STEPHEN F	1977		*		*	**	*	**	**	**	**								
2135	TODD, D ET AL	1977		*		*	***	*	**	*	*		**							
2136	TOLL, WILLIAM	1977		*		*											*			
2137	TOLL, WILLIAM	1978		*			*	*												
2138	TOMASI, LYDIO F	1972		*		*	*	*				*								
2139	TOMASI, LYDIO F	1977		*	*	*	***		*	*	**	*	**	*	*	*	*	*	*	**
2140	TOMASI, S M ED	1977	*	*		*		*	**	**	**	**								
2141	TOMASI, SILVANO M ET AL	1970	*	*			*	**	*	*	*	*					*	*		**
2142	TOPLIN, ROBERT BRENT	1971		*		*	*					*		*						
2143	TORNEY, JUDITH V ET AL	1977		*		*	**	*	*											
2144	TOTTEN, GEORGE O ET AL	1966		*		*	*	*					*	*						
2145	TOWNSEND, L T	1970		*				*												
2146	TREJO, ARNULFO D	1975		*		*	*				*									
2147	TRENT, JOHN	1974									*		*							
2148	TRUEBLOOD, MARILYN A	1977		*		*	*	*							*					

NUM	AUTHOR	DATE
2149	TRYGGVASON, GUSTAV	1971
2150	TUDEN, ARTHUR ET AL EDS	1970
2151	TUMIN, MELVIN	1949
2152	TUMIN, MELVIN ED	1969
2153	TURK, AUSTIN T	1972
2154	TWADDLE, MICHAEL	1969
2155	TYLER, GUS ED	1975
2156	UCHENDU, VICTOR C	1970
2157	ULLMAN, ALBERT D	1960
2158	ULRICH-ATENA, ELA	1976
2159	UNITED NAT COMM ON HUM RG	1950
2160	UNITED NAT ECON COMM AFRI	1963
2161	UNITED NAT EDUC SCIE CUL	1961
2162	UNITED NAT EDUC SCIE CUL	1974
2163	UNITED STATES BUR OF CENS	1975
2164	UNITED STATES BUR OF CENS	1979
2165	UNIVER LEAG FOR SOC REFOR	1966
2166	USSACH, STEVEN SAMUEL	1975
2167	VAKAR, NICHOLAS P	1968
2168	VALENTINE, C A	1975
2169	VAN DEN BERGHE, PIERRE L	1960
2170	VAN DEN BERGHE, PIERRE L	1962
2171	VAN DEN BERGHE, PIERRE L	1963
2172	VAN DEN BERGHE, PIERRE L	1964
2173	VAN DEN BERGHE, PIERRE L	1964
2174	VAN DEN BERGHE, PIERRE L	1965
2175	VAN DEN BERGHE, PIERRE L	1967
2176	VAN DEN BERGHE, PIERRE L	1969
2177	VAN DEN BERGHE, PIERRE L	1970
2178	VAN DEN BERGHE, PIERRE L	1970
2179	VAN DEN BERGHE, PIERRE L	1971
2180	VAN DEN BERGHE, PIERRE L	1971
2181	VAN DEN BERGHE, PIERRE L	1973
2182	VAN DEN BERGHE, PIERRE L	1974
2183	VAN DEN BERGHE, PIERRE L	1974
2184	VAN DEN BERGHE, PIERRE L	1975
2185	VAN DEN BERGHE, PIERRE L	1976
2186	VAN DER KROEF, JUSTUS M	1976
2187	VAN DER MERWE, H W ET AL	1975
2188	VAN DER PLANK, P H	1975
2189	VANDERZANDEN, JAMES W	1972
2190	VAN DYKE, VERNON	1977
2191	VAN LIER, R A J	1950
2192	VAN LIER, R A J	1971
2193	VANNEMAN, REEVE D ET AL	1972
2194	VARDYS, V STANLEY	1975

NUM	AUTHOR	DATE	1 AB	2 ABCDEF	3 ABCDE	4 ABCDEFGHI	5 ABCDEFGHIJK	6	7	8	9	10	11	12	13	14	15	16	17
2195	VASQUEZ, MARIO C	1970		*	*	*	*	*												
2196	VAUGHAN, JAMES H JR	1970		*	*							*							*	
2197	VECOLI, RUDOLPH J	1972		*	*					*	*			*	*					
2198	VELTMAN, CALVIN J	1977		* *	*	*		*				*	*							
2199	VERDERY, KATHERINE	1979		*		*	*	*		*	*	*	*							
2200	VILLACORTA, W V ET AL EDS	1976	*	* * *	* *	*	*	*		*	*	*	*							
2201	VILLAMEZ, WAYNE J ET AL	1977			*	*	*	*				*								*
2202	VINCENT, JOAN	1974		*		* *	*													
2203	VINOGRADOV, AMAL	1974					*			*	*	*								
2204	VINYARD, JU ELLEN M	1976		*				*												
2205	VIRGIL, MAURILIO	1978		*				*				*							*	*
2206	VON HAGEN, VICTOR W	1976			*	*		*		*	*							*		*
2207	VREELAND, H H	1958			*								*							
2208	VKGA, DJUKO J ET AL	1969		*	*							*		* * * *						
2209	WADDELL, J D ET AL EDS	1971	*	*	*	*	* *	*		*	*	*			*					*
2210	WAGATSUMA, HIROSHI	1966		*	*		*						*			* *				
2211	WAGATSUMA, HIROSHI	1966			* *								*	*						
2212	WAGATSUMA, HIROSHI	1978			*	*	*					*								
2213	WAGATSUMA, HIROSHI ET AL	1966						*												
2214	WAGENHEIM, KAL	1975		*	*	*	*				* *	*		*	*					
2215	WAGLEY, CHARLES	1960																		
2216	WAGLEY, CHARLES	1969		*	*	*	*	*	*									*		*
2217	WAGLEY, CHARLES ED	1972	*	*	* *	*	*	*	* *	*	* *	* *	*	* *	*	*				*
2218	WAGLEY, CHARLES ET AL	1958		*	*	*	*	*	*		*	*	*	*				*		*
2219	WAGNER, NATHANIEL N ET AL	1971	*	* * *	*	*	* *	*		*	*	*	*	*	*					*
2220	WAI, DUNSTON M	1978			*	*	*	*												
2221	WALD, BENJI	1974		*	*															
2222	WALLERSTEIN, IMMANUEL ED	1966	*		* *	* *	*	*					*						*	*
2223	WALLERSTEIN, IMMANUEL ED	1973		*	* *	*	*	*												
2224	WALLERSTEIN, IMMANUEL ED	1973				*	* *	*												
2225	WALLIMAN, ISIDOR	1974	*	*	*	*	*				*	* *	* *							
2226	WALSH, JAMES P ED	1976	*	*	*		*			*	*	*	*			*				
2227	WARGELIN, JOHN	1972		* *	*		*	*			*				*					
2228	WARNER, W LLOYD ET AL	1945		*				*					*							
2229	WARREN, JIM	1978																		
2230	WARREN, MAX	1964		*	*	*					*	*		*	*				*	*
2231	WASHBURN, WILCOMB E	1975						*	*	*				*	*			*		*
2232	WASSERMAN, PAUL ET AL EDS	1976					*	*	*	*	* *			*	*					
2233	WATANUKI, JOJI	1971		*	* *	* *														
2234	WATSON, G LLEWELLYN	1973					*													
2235	WATSON, G LLEWELLYN	1974		*	*	* *	*	*			*				*		*	*		*
2236	WATSON, JAMES L	1977		*	*					*	*	* *	*		*					
2237	WATSON, JAMES L	1977		* *	*		*	*		* *				*				*		
2238	WATSON, PETER	1974		* *	*															
2239	WATTS, BETTY H	1972		* *	*						* *	*	* * *		*					
2240	WATTS, RONALD L	1970		*			*			*		*				*				

NUM	AUTHOR	DATE
2241	WAX, ROSALIE H ET AL	1961
2242	WEBB, KEITH	1977
2243	WEBER, DAVID J ED	1973
2244	WEBSTER, STATEN W	1972
2245	WEED, PERRY L	1972
2246	WEED, PERRY L	1973
2247	WEIL, SHALVA	1977
2248	WEINER, MYRON	1978
2249	THE WEINER LIBRARY LONDON	1971
2250	WEINSTEIN, WARREN ET AL	1975
2251	WEISBROD, ROBERT G	1975
2252	WEISER, MARJORIE P K ED	1978
2253	WEISS, MELFORD S	1974
2254	WELCH, MICHAEL R	1977
2255	WELLMAN, BARRY	1971
2256	WENZEL, LAWRENCE A	1968
2257	WEPPNER, ROBERT S	1971
2258	WERLING, JOAN	1968
2259	WESTON, J S	1969
2260	WHITAKER, BEN ED	1973
2261	WHITE, NAOMI ROSH	1978
2262	WHITLEY, W H	1969
2263	WHITTEN, NORMAN E JR	1975
2264	WHITTEN, NORMAN E ET AL	1970
2265	WILCOX, JERRY ET AL	1978
2266	WILD, R ET AL	1970
2267	WILEY, NORBERT F	1967
2268	WILLIAMS, COLIN H	1976
2269	WILLIAMS, J ALLEN ET AL	1977
2270	WILLIAMS, JOHN E ET AL	1976
2271	WILLIAMS, LEA E	1966
2272	WILLIAMS, LORETTA J	1975
2273	WILLIAMS, ROBIN M JR	1947
2274	WILLIAMS, ROBIN M JR	1964
2275	WILLIE, CHARLES V	1972
2276	WILLIS, R	1968
2277	WILLMOTT, DONALD EARL	1960
2278	WILLMOTT, W E	1969
2279	WILSON, FRANKLIN D ET AL	1978
2280	WILSON, GODFREY	1942
2281	WIMBUSH, S ENDERS	1976
2282	WINSTON, HENRY	1977
2283	WIRT, FREDERICK M	1979
2284	WISE, JENNINGS C	1971
2285	WITTERMANS, ELIZABETH	1964
2286	WITTERMANS, ELIZABETH P	1972

NUM	AUTHOR	DATE
2287	WITTKE, CARL	1956
2288	WITTKE, CARL	1967
2289	WITTKE, CARL	1967
2290	WITTKE, CARL	1968
2291	WIXMAN, RONALD	1973
2292	WOLLHEIM, U D	1963
2293	WOLPE, HAROLD	1970
2294	WOLPE, HAROLD	1975
2295	WONG, BERNARD	1977
2296	WONG, BERNARD	1978
2297	WOYCHENKO, OLHA	1967
2298	WRIGHT, DAVIE E ET AL	1973
2299	WRIGHT, ERIK OLIN	1978
2300	WRIGHT, FRANKLIN W	1974
2301	WURM, STEPHEN A	1971
2302	WYSZOMIRSKI, MARGARET J	1975
2303	XYDIS, STEPHEN G	1969
2304	YAFFE, SAM	1968
2305	YANAGISAKO, SYLVIA J	1975
2306	YANCEY, WILLIAM L ET AL	1972
2307	YEE, ALBERT H	1973
2308	YIN, ROBERT K ED	1973
2309	YINGER, J MILTON ET AL ED	1978
2310	YOUNG, JARED J	1977
2311	YOUNG, WARREN L	1973
2312	YOUSEF, FATHI S	1978
2313	YUAN, D Y	1966
2314	ZABLE, ARNOLD	1973
2315	ZACEK, JOSEPH F	1969
2316	ZALENY, CAROLYN	1974
2317	ZAPRUDNIK, JAN	1975
2318	ZAVALANI, T	1969
2319	ZENNER, WALTER P ET AL	1972
2320	ZGHAL, ABDELKADER	1973
2321	ZINMAN, ROSALIND	1978
2322	ZOLBERG, ARISTIDE R	1977
2323	ZUBAIDA, SAMI ED	1970
2324	ZUREIK, ELIA T	1976
2325	ZUREIK, ELIA T	1979
2326	ZWICK, PETER	1976
2327		1968
2328		1969
2329		1970
2330		1970
2331		1970
2332		1971

NUM	AUTHOR	DATE	1 AB	2 ABCDEF	3 ABCDE	4 ABCDEFGHI	5 ABCDEFGHIJK	6	7	8	9	10	11	12	13	14	15	16	17
2333		1973	*		*	*	*				*	*							
2334		1973	*	*	*	*	*					*	*	*					
2335		1974		*			*			*		*							
2336		1975	*	*	* *	*	* *				*	*		*	*			*	
2337		1975	*	*	*	*	*				*	*		*				*	*
2338		1976	*				*												

SCHOOL OF INTERNATIONAL STUDIES
PUBLICATIONS ON
ETHNICITY AND NATIONALITY

1. M. Nazif Mohib Shahrani. *The Kirghiz and Wakhi of Afghanistan: Adaptation to Closed Frontiers.* 264 pp., biblio., index, maps, illus. 1979.
2. Charles F. Keyes, ed. *Ethnic Change.* 334 pp. 1981.
3. G. Carter Bentley. *Ethnicity and Nationality: A Bibliographic Guide.* 455 pp., indexes. 1981.